Slavery

Stanley L. Engerman is John H. Munro Prof
Professor of History at the University of Roch
Time on the Cross (1974) and co-editor of *A His*
Slavery (1998).

Seymour Drescher is University Professor of History and Professor
of Sociology at the University of Pittsburgh. He is the author of several
books on slavery and abolition, most recently *From Slavery to Freedom*
(1999).

Robert L. Paquette is Publius Virgilius Rogers Professor of American
History at Hamilton College. His publications include *Sugar is Made*
with Blood (1988).

OXFORD **READERS**

The Oxford Readers series represents a unique resource which brings together extracts of texts from a wide variety of sources, primary and secondary, on a wide range of interdisciplinary topics.

OXFORD **READERS**

Slavery

Edited by Stanley Engerman,
Seymour Drescher, and Robert Paquette

OXFORD
UNIVERSITY PRESS

This book has been printed digitally and produced in a standard specification in order to ensure its continuing availability

OXFORD
UNIVERSITY PRESS

Great Clarendon Street, Oxford OX2 6DP
Oxford University Press is a department of the University of Oxford.
It furthers the University's objective of excellence in research, scholarship,
and education by publishing worldwide in
Oxford New York

Auckland Cape Town Dar es Salaam Hong Kong Karachi
Kuala Lumpur Madrid Melbourne Mexico City Nairobi
New Delhi Shanghai Taipei Toronto
With offices in
Argentina Austria Brazil Chile Czech Republic France Greece
Guatemala Hungary Italy Japan South Korea Poland Portugal
Singapore Switzerland Thailand Turkey Ukraine Vietnam

Published in the United States
by Oxford University Press Inc., New York

Editorial matter and selection © Stanley Engerman, Seymour Drescher
and Robert Pacquette 2001

Reprinted 2009

ISBN 978-0-19-289302-4

Contents

III. Slave Laws

IV. The Slave Trade

V. The Experience of Slavery

VI. Resistance

VII. Economics and Demography

VIII. Abolition and Emancipation

Introduction

By the end of the twentieth century, slavery was no longer legally or morally acceptable anywhere in the world. Only two centuries ago, slavery was still among the most ubiquitous institutions in human societies, and had existed in most times and places throughout history. The five major slave societies described by the noted classical scholar, Sir Moses Finley, include two in the ancient European world (Greece and Rome) and three in the Americas after the start of the sixteenth century (the US South, Brazil, and the Caribbean), although there have been other societies in Africa, Asia, and the Americas where slaves exceeded one-quarter of the total population. In all of these slave societies, slaves performed many different functions. Slavery was also a form of control and organization in many other societies, even where slave occupations were more limited and their numbers relatively smaller. Nevertheless, in many cases the laws and behavior patterns of masters and slaves, and the effects on enslavement upon the slaves, were similar to those in areas where slavery was more demographically important. Slavery had ended in many places before European expansion into the Americas, Africa, and Asia, generally due to social and economic, rather than legal, changes. It was only with the end of the eighteenth century, however, that slavery's legal status was systematically attacked, the slavery system ended, and large numbers of slaves began to be granted their freedom. The modern ending of slavery came first in the nineteenth-century Americas and then in twentieth-century Africa and Asia, often with pressure from the European metropolis and colonizers. Even today, however, controversies persist about the continued existence of slavery and related forms of bondage in some areas of North Africa and in other parts of the former third world.

Slaves were property. They could be bought and sold by members of the slaveowning society, the movements and behavior of slaves were legally controlled by owners, and slave offspring inherited this legal status. While some constraints were imposed on owner behavior, these were considerably less than with other human institutions. Slaves were frequently the result of military capture, but many came from kidnapping, failure to pay debt, or even, when incomes were low, by the voluntary action of those enslaved or by their family members. Historically, however, most slaves were born to that status. The psychological burden of slavery was often enhanced by the fact that in most societies the enslaved consisted only of those who were considered as outsiders, members of a different race, religion, nationality, or ethnicity. Such membership then permitted the dominant society to make the slaves 'rightless.' The slaves were also designated by masters as ignorant, backward, lazy, and untrustworthy, among many other negative characteristics. This combination of economic exploitation, psychological distancing, and cultural degradation was the lot of most slaves.

Few favorable connotations have been ascribed to the institution of slavery and its economic, political, and moral mechanisms. Slavery was generally regarded as undesirable, if at times a necessary evil, even when applied to outsiders. Yet, given the long persistence of slavery, some rationale was necessary to allow societies to justify its existence. One important justification, derived from Aristotle's concept of the 'natural slave,' was that those enslaved merited that status because it was appropriate to their innate characteristics. Selective manumission was regarded as a positive good. It was, however, only in the last two centuries that there emerged a significant attack on slavery as a system, and the belief in emancipation was applied to large numbers of slaves and, ultimately and more generally, to humanity. The abolitionist movement developed primarily in the nations of Western Europe and their overseas offshoots, often without the immediate presence of legal slavery. Even without the presence of legal slavery, slavery's continued negative implications were expanded to attack many other situations of labor control and exploitation, including sexual exploitation.

Until relatively recently, slavery was not a subject at the center of historical scholarship. To slaveowning societies, particularly those with twentieth-century sensibilities, it was regarded as an embarrassing historical phase, inconsistent with current morality. For those who had previously been enslaved, or for their descendants, it was often difficult to confront the continuing cultural and psychological results of the unbalanced master–slave relationship. Thus, slavery was a marginally studied part of the historical record everywhere.

In the past several decades there has been a great increase in the attention given to the economic, cultural, and political role of slavery in different societies. Works now consider slavery as a central aspect of a society, not as a marginal or isolated institution. Historians have reinterpreted existing records and writings, and have also discovered many new sources of information, using these to reinterpret the past. There are now ongoing discussions of slaves and slavery in many different societies. Slavery is seen less as an isolated occurrence, separated from the more palatable aspects of society, than as an institution that often played a central societal role, interacting with and influencing other aspects of social relations. It is now clearer that the non-slaves of the past, whether slaveowners or not, considered slavery to be a normal part of their world, and a more-or-less given institution, not one deserving of unequivocal categorical moral censure. Indeed, it is often the almost matter-of-fact attitudes towards slaves and slavery in the past that we now find most incomprehensible. Yet, if we wish to understand the behavior of those formerly enslaved as well as those who owned or could own slaves, it is necessary to study such day-to-day beliefs and actions of the slaves, slave-owners, and other non-slaves in their historical context. This is not to suggest that our hard-won moral attitudes against slavery be set aside. Rather, we must have an accurate understanding of the importance of seeing what people in the past believed and how they behaved in order to better understand our future as well as our past and present.

In this Reader, we have aimed at providing documents that cover the considerable time and space over which slavery existed. Writings by members of slaveowning societies, free and enslaved, are supplemented by those of contemporary and present-day historians and economists. The selected historical documents derive from a wide range of sources: writings debating slavery and describing its operations; official documents which publicized slave laws, as well as rules for conducting the international slave trades; the records of planters and other slaveowners describing the nature of slavery and their business operations; legal and other discussions generated by slave activities and uprisings; legislative debates concerning the terms and mechanics of the emancipation of slaves; and reflections by slaves and ex-slaves on their lives and perceptions of their condition. In making our selections, we draw upon a wide variety of materials, covering a number of different societies. We do this both in order to offer the reader a broad range of information about the slave experience and to indicate the widespread historical breadth of slavery. These documents illustrate the fundamental similarities of slave societies in dealing with certain questions. They also reveal significant differences that inevitably appeared among different societies. We have tried to limit our selections to those dealing with what was considered by contemporaries (and by ourselves) to be chattel slavery. We have omitted most materials relating to other forms of coerced labor such as serfdom, indentured labor, debt peonage, convict labor, prostitution, and the many variants of such institutions.

The readings are divided into eight sections. At times, our placement into one section rather than another may seem arbitrary. This, of course, befits writings that were never intended to fit into the specific thematic boundaries that historians inevitably impose. Nevertheless, we believe that our categories logically arrange items offering related sets of issues. The edited selections necessarily vary by length, since we wish to emphasize the central aspect of each of the selected writings for the study of slavery. In order to minimize forcing our interpretations of these materials upon the readers, and to maximize the number of selections, we have limited our editorial comments to brief introductions to each section.

Seymour Drescher
Stanley Engerman
Robert Paquette

Section I

....

Meaning

....

INTRODUCTION

Slavery has been one of the most ubiquitous of all human institutions, existing in many times and most places, and persisting in some variants even at the start of the twenty-first century. While there may be precise definitions of slavery, the term is often used to present an unfavorable portrayal of any number of economic and political conditions. Even the legal definitions have been questioned. In general, however, slavery refers to a condition in which individuals are owned by others, who control where they live, at what they work, with how much subsistence they are provided, and where sexual exploitation is permissible. Property rights in slaves and their labor can be bought and sold via market transactions. So onerous is the status of the slave that it is a condition generally reserved for 'outsiders' (however defined), not to members of one's own group. The legal aspects do not reveal all about the treatment and living conditions of slaves, since these have varied with economic, ethno-racial, and political conditions in different societies. There has been a wide range of latitudes granted to slaves. Some scholars outline a spectrum of forms of labor coercion, with different properties, which distinguish them from two polar extremes—slavery and freedom. These forms typically include serfdom, indentured labor, debt peonage, convict labor, 'wage slavery,' and forms of elite slavery, in addition to plantation slavery. Similarly, those who are legally free may suffer from legal, political, and economic constraints that mean they obtain fewer goods and have in actuality fewer controls over working and living conditions than do slaves. One person's vulnerability to political power or to hunger, however legally free that person is, therefore, can be as harsh as another's condition as a legal slave.

In this section, the readings have been selected to draw out the great spatial and temporal extent of slavery and related forms of coerced labor. Ranging from biblical writings to the nineteenth century, they include writings by major philosophers, as well as by historians writing about the past. The importance of slavery in earlier times is seen in the frequency of concern with defining, and either defending or attacking, the slave system. Some defended slavery by arguing that there were 'natural slaves'—i.e. individuals whose slave status was determined by their characteristics—or that they were prisoners of war who might otherwise have been killed, and thus could legitimately be enslaved. Others argued that even while slavery was an evil, it was a necessary one, either to maintain control over other groups or to produce wealth for society. These were all frequently debated issues.

The defense of slavery often meant regarding the enslaved as non-human, and thus not to be treated in the same manner as free individuals. Slaves have been described as animals, who, while lacking perceptions, were not to be treated so harshly as to threaten their life or their productivity. Recognizing the role of the labor of the slave, he (or she) could be described as a 'living tool,' whose function was to be used productively. Owners were admonished not to be more cruel to slaves than was necessary. They were to treat them well and give them opportunities ultimately to achieve freedom. For most of the time, until the late eighteenth and early nineteenth century, however, to advocate such care and kindness was not to challenge the continuation of slavery as a system.

Correspondingly, the nature of the master–slave relation has been the analogy for other types of interpersonal relations in which the distribution of power has been argued to be highly asymmetrical: parent-child, male-female, employer-employee, among others. Those arguing for the emancipation of the slave created precedents for the emancipation of other groups in society. Many slaves were captives—as prisoners of war, convicts, or kidnapped—entering involuntarily into the status of slavery. They were often transported considerable distances from their homelands, with little or no opportunity to return home even after the end of enslavement in those few cases in which freedom was allowed. While the contemporary expectation is that the slave status was generally so bad that no one would voluntarily become one, such a claim overlooks the difficulties facing individuals in many societies where incomes were low, and where famine and starvation were real threats. Under such conditions, the prospects of obtaining a more certain sustenance for individuals and their family members, particularly children, may be seen as an acceptable option. Voluntary slavery would not occur in societies with higher levels of income, or with greater security of property rights, where involuntary slavery resulting from war, kidnapping, and criminal activities formed the major basis of enslavement.

Those who were moved the longest distances were often acquired for productive purposes, producing a surplus over their costs of transfer, subsistence, and care. They were generally used in the cultivation of staple crops for purposes of long-distance trade. Slaves in such societies, as well as in societies without large-scale agriculture, performed a great variety of other economic and social functions. They filled both skilled and unskilled jobs in rural and urban areas; they served states as well as private owners, and within military units. In some societies, they even became members or consorts of the ruling class. In many societies, slaves formed a large majority of the population, in others only a small fraction. Thus, while the institution of slavery was very widespread, the range of variation in treatment and behavior was so diverse that it is difficult to make broad generalizations about the relationship of slaves to non-slaves across the full spectrum of such societies.

1   Excerpts from the Bible

Exodus 21: 2–11

2 If thou buy an Hebrew servant, six years he shall serve: and in the seventh he shall go out free for nothing.

3 If he came in by himself, he shall go out by himself: if he were married, then his wife shall go out with him.

4 If his master have given him a wife, and she have born him sons or daughters; the wife and her children shall be her master's, and he shall go out by himself.

5 And if the servant shall plainly say, I love my master, my wife, and my children; I will not go out free:

6 Then his master shall bring him unto the judges; he shall also bring him to the door, or unto the door post; and his master shall bore his ear through with an aul; and he shall serve him for ever.

7 And if a man sell his daughter to be a maidservant, she shall not go out as the menservants do.

8 If she please not her master, who hath betrothed her to himself, then shall he let her be redeemed: to sell her unto a strange nation he shall have no power, seeing he hath dealt deceitfully with her.

9 And if he have betrothed her unto his son, he shall deal with her after the manner of daughters.

10 If he take him another *wife*; her food, her raiment, and her duty of marriage, shall he not diminish.

11 And if he do not these three unto her, then shall she go out free without money.

Deuteronomy 15: 12–18

12 And if thy brother, an Hebrew man, or an Hebrew woman, be sold unto thee, and serve thee six years; then in the seventh year thou shalt let him go free from thee.

13 And when thou sendest him out free from thee, thou shalt not let him go away empty:

14 Thou shalt furnish him liberally out of thy flock, and out of thy floor, and out of thy winepress: *of* that wherewith the LORD thy God hath blessed thee thou shalt give unto him.

15 And thou shalt remember that thou wast a bondman in the land of Egypt, and the LORD thy God redeemed thee: therefore I command thee this thing to day.

16 And it shall be, if he say unto thee, I will not go away from thee; because he loveth thee and thine house, because he is well with thee;

17 Then thou shalt take an aul, and thrust *it* through his ear unto the door, and he shall be thy servant for ever. And also unto thy maidservant thou shalt do likewise.

18 It shall not seem hard unto thee, when thou sendest him away free from thee; for he hath been worth a double hired servant to thee, in serving thee six years: and the LORD thy God shall bless thee in all that thou doest.

Leviticus 25: 47–54

47 And if a sojourner or stranger wax rich by thee, and thy brother that dwelleth by him wax poor, and sell himself unto the stranger or sojourner by thee, or to the stock of the stranger's family:

48 After that he is sold he may be redeemed again; one of his brethren may redeem him:

49 Either his uncle, or his uncle's son may redeem him, or any that is nigh of kin unto him of his family may redeem him; or if he be able, he may redeem himself.

50 And he shall reckon with him that bought him from the year that he was sold to him unto the year of jubile and the price of his sale shall be according unto the number of years, according to the time of an hired servant shall it be with him.

51 If there be yet many years behind, according unto them he shall give again the price of his redemption out of the money that he was bought for.

52 And if there remain but few years unto the year of jubile, then he shall count with him, and according unto his years shall he give him again the price of his redemption.

53 And as a yearly hired servant shall he be with him: and the other shall not rule with rigour over him in thy sight.

54 And if he be not redeemed in these years, then he shall go out in the year of jubile, both he and his children with him.

Now nature has distinguished between the female and the slave. For she is not niggardly, like the smith who fashions the Delphian knife for many uses; she makes each thing for a single use, and every instrument is best made when intended for one and not for many uses. But among barbarians no distinction is made between women and slaves, because there is no natural ruler among them: they are a community of slaves, male and female. That is why the poets say,—

It is meet that Hellenes should rule over barbarians;

as if they thought that the barbarian and the slave were by nature one.

Out of these two relationships the first thing to arise is the family, and Hesiod is right when he says,—

First house and wife and an ox for the plough,

for the ox is the poor man's slave.

[. . .]

3. Seeing then that the state is made up of households, before speaking of the state we must speak of the management of the household. The parts of household management correspond to the persons who compose the household, and a complete household consists of slaves and freemen. Now we should begin by examining everything in its fewest possible elements; and the first and fewest possible parts of a family are master and slave, husband and wife, father and children. We have therefore to consider what each of these three relations is and ought to be:—I mean the relation of master and servant, the marriage relation (the conjunction of man and wife has no name of its own), and thirdly, the paternal relation (this also has no proper name). And there is another element of a household, the so-called art of getting wealth, which, according to some, is identical with household management, according to others, a principal part of it; the nature of this art will also have to be considered by us.

Let us first speak of master and slave, looking to the needs of practical life and also seeking to attain some better theory of their relation than exists at present. For some are of the opinion that the rule of a master is a science, and that the management of a household, and the mastership of slaves, and the political and royal rule, as I was saying at the outset, are all the same. Others affirm that the rule of a master over slaves is contrary to nature, and that the distinction between slave and freeman exists by convention only, and not by nature; and being an interference with nature is therefore unjust.

4. Property is a part of the household, and the art of acquiring property is

a part of the art of managing the household; for no man can live well, or indeed live at all, unless he is provided with necessaries. And as in the arts which have a definite sphere the workers must have their own proper instruments for the accomplishment of their work, so it is in the management of a household. Now instruments are of various sorts; some are living, others lifeless; in the rudder, the pilot of a ship has a lifeless, in the look-out man, a living instrument; for in the arts the servant is a kind of instrument. Thus, too, a possession is an instrument for maintaining life. And so, in the arrangement of the family, a slave is a living possession, and property a number of such instruments; and the servant is himself an instrument for instruments. For if every instrument could accomplish its own work, obeying or anticipating the will of others, like the statues of Daedalus, or the tripods of Hephaestus, which, says the poet,

of their own accord entered the assembly of the Gods;

if, in like manner, the shuttle would weave and the plectrum touch the lyre, chief workmen would not want servants, nor masters slaves. Now the instruments commonly so called are instruments of production, whilst a possession is an instrument of action. From a shuttle we get something else besides the use of it, whereas of a garment or of a bed there is only the use. Further, as production and action are different in kind, and both require instruments, the instruments which they employ must likewise differ in kind. But life is action and not production, and therefore the slave is the minister of action. Again, a possession is spoken of as a part is spoken of; for the part is not only a part of something else, but wholly belongs to it; and this is also true of a possession. The master is only the master of the slave; he does not belong to him, whereas the slave is not only the slave of his master, but wholly belongs to him. Hence we see what is the nature and office of a slave; he who is by nature not his own but another's man, is by nature a slave; and he may be said to be another's man who, being a slave, is also a possession. And a possession may be defined as an instrument of action, separable from the possessor.

5. But is there any one thus intended by nature to be a slave, and for whom such a condition is expedient and right, or rather is not all slavery a violation of nature?

There is no difficulty in answering this question, on grounds both of reason and of fact. For that some should rule and others be ruled is a thing not only necessary, but expedient; from the hour of their birth, some are marked out for subjection, others for rule.

And there are many kinds both of rulers and subjects (and that rule is the better which is exercised over better subjects—for example, to rule over men is better than to rule over wild beasts; for the work is better which is executed by better workmen, and where one man rules and another is ruled, they may be said to have a work); for in all things which form a composite whole and which are made up of parts, whether continuous or discrete, a distinction between the ruling and the subject element comes to light. Such a duality exists in living creatures, originating from nature as a whole; even in things which have no life there is a ruling principle, as in a musical mode. But perhaps this is matter for a more popular investigation. A living creature consists in the first place of soul and body, and of these two, the one is by nature the ruler and the other the subject. But then we must look for the intentions of nature in things which retain their nature, and not in things which are corrupted. And therefore we must study the man who is in the most perfect state both of body and soul, for in him we shall see the true relation of the two; although in bad or corrupted natures the body will often appear to rule over the soul, because they are in an evil and unnatural condition. At all events we may firstly observe in living creatures both a despotical and a constitutional rule; for the soul rules the body with a des-potical rule, whereas the intellect rules the appetites with a constitutional and royal rule. And it is clear that the rule of the soul over the body, and of the mind and the rational element over the passionate, is natural and expedient; whereas the equality of the two or the rule of the inferior is always hurtful. The same holds good of animals in relation to men; for tame animals have a better nature than wild and all tame animals are better off when they are ruled by man; for then they are preserved. Again, the male is by nature superior, and the female inferior; and the one rules, and the other is ruled; this principle, of necessity, extends to all mankind. Where then there is such a difference as that between soul and body, or between men and animals (as in the case of those whose business is to use their body, and who can do nothing better), the lower sort are by nature slaves, and it is better for them as for all inferiors that they should be under the rule of a master. For he who can be, and therefore is, another's, and he who participates in reason enough to apprehend, but not to have, is a slave by nature. Whereas the lower animals cannot even apprehend reason; they obey their passions. And indeed the use made of slaves and of tame animals is not very different; for both with their bodies minister to the needs of life. Nature would like to distinguish between the bodies of freemen and slaves, making the one strong for servile labour, the other upright, and although useless for such services, useful for political life in the arts both of war and peace. But the opposite often happens—that some have the souls and others have the bodies of freemen. And doubtless if men differed from one another in the mere forms of their bodies as much as the statues of the Gods do from men, all would acknowledge that the inferior class should be slaves of the superior. And if this is true of the body, how much more just that a similar distinc-tion should exist in the soul? But the beauty of the body is seen, whereas the beauty of the soul is not seen. It is clear, then, that some men are by nature free, and others slaves, and that for these latter slavery is both expedient and right.

6. But that those who take the opposite view have in a certain way right on their side, may be easily seen. For the words slavery and slave are used in two senses. There is a slave or slavery by convention as well as by nature. The convention is a sort of agreement—the convention by which whatever is taken in war is supposed to belong to the victors. But this right many jurists impeach, as they would an orator who brought forward an unconstitutional measure: they detest the notion that, because one man has the power of doing violence and is superior in brute strength, another shall be his slave and subject. Even among philosophers there is a difference of opinion. The origin of the dispute, and what makes the views invade each other's territory, is as follows: in some sense excellence, when furnished with means, has actually the greatest power of exercising force: and as superior power is only found where there is superior excellence of some kind, power seems to imply excellence, and the dispute to be simply one about justice (for it is due to one party identifying justice with goodwill, while the other identifies it with the mere rule of the stronger). If these views are thus set out separately, the other views have no force or plausibility against the view that the superior in excellence ought to rule, or be master. Others, clinging, as they think, simply to a principle of justice (for convention is a sort of justice), assume that slavery in accordance with the custom of war is just, but at the same moment they deny this. For what if the cause of the war be unjust? And again, no one would ever say that he is a slave who is unworthy to be a slave. Were this the case, men of the highest rank would be slaves and the children of slaves if they or their parents chanced to have been taken captive and sold. That is why people do not like to call themselves slaves, but confine the term to foreigners. Yet, in using this language, they really mean the natural slave of whom we spoke at first; for it must be admitted that some are slaves every-where, others nowhere. The same principle applies to nobility. People regard themselves as noble everywhere and not only in their own country, but they deem foreigners noble only when at home, thereby implying that there are two sorts of nobility and freedom, the one absolute, the other relative. The Helen of Theodectes says:

Who would presume to call me servant who am on both sides sprung from the stem of the Gods?

What does this mean but that they distinguish freedom and slavery, noble and humble birth, by the two principles of good and evil? They think that as men and animals beget men and animals, so from good men a good man springs. Nature intends to do this often but cannot.

We see then that there is some foundation for this difference of opinion, and that all are not either slaves by nature or freemen by nature, and also that there is in some cases a marked distinction between the two classes, rendering it expedient and right for the one to be slaves and the others to be masters: the one practising obedience, the others exercising the authority and lordship which nature intended them to have. The abuse of this authority is injurious to both; for the interests of part and whole, of body and soul, are the same, and the slave is a part of the master, a living but separated part of his bodily frame. Hence, where the relation of master and slave between them is natural they are friends and have a common interest, but where it rests merely on convention and force the reverse is true.

7. The previous remarks are quite enough to show that the rule of a master is not a constitutional rule, and that all the different kinds of rule are not, as some affirm, the same as each other. For there is one rule exercised over subjects who are by nature free, another over subjects who are by nature slaves. The rule of a household is a monarchy, for every house is under one head: whereas constitutional rule is a government of freemen and equals. The master is not called a master because he has science, but because he is of a certain character, and the same remark applies to the slave and the freeman. Still there may be a science for the master and a science for the slave. The science of the slave would be such as the man of Syracuse taught, who made money by instructing slaves in their ordinary duties. And such a knowledge may be carried further, so as to include cookery and similar menial arts. For some duties are of the more necessary, others of the more honourable sort; as the proverb says, 'slave before slave, master before master'. But all such branches of knowledge are servile. There is likewise a science of the master which teaches the use of slaves; for the master as such is concerned, not with the acquisition, but with the use of them. Yet this science is not anything great or wonderful; for the master need only know how to order that which the slave must know how to execute. Hence those who are in a position which places them above toil have stewards who attend to their households while they occupy themselves with philosophy or with politics. But the art of acquiring slaves, I mean of justly acquiring them, differs both from the art of the master and the art of slave, being a species of hunting or war. Enough of the distinction between master and slave.

[. . .]

13. Thus it is clear that household management attends more to men than to the acquisition of inanimate things, and to human excellence more than to the excellence of property which we call wealth, and to the excellence of freemen more than to the excellence of slaves. A question may indeed be raised, whether there is any excellence at all in a slave beyond those of an instrument and of a servant—whether he can have the excellences of temperance, courage, justice, and the like; or whether slaves possess only bodily services. And, whichever way we answer the question, a difficulty arises; for, if they have excellence, in what will they differ from freemen? On the other

hand, since they are men and share in rational principle, it seems absurd to say that they have no excellence. A similar question may be raised about women and children, whether they too have excellences; ought a woman to be temperate and brave and just, and is a child to be called temperate, and intemperate, or not? So in general we may ask about the natural ruler, and the natural subject, whether they have the same or different excellences. For if a noble nature is equally required in both, why should one of them always rule, and the other always be ruled? Nor can we say that this is a question of degree, for the difference between ruler and subject is a difference of kind, which the difference of more and less never is. Yet how strange is the supposition that the one ought, and that the other ought not, to have excellence! For if the ruler is intemperate and unjust, how can he rule well? if the subject, how can he obey well? If he is licentious and cowardly, he will certainly not do what is fitting. It is evident, therefore, that both of them must have a share of excellence, but varying as natural subjects also vary among themselves. Here the very constitution of the soul has shown us the way; in it one part naturally rules, and the other is subject, and the excellence of the ruler we maintain to be different from that of the subject—the one being the excellence of the rational, and the other of the irrational part. Now, it is obvious that the same principle applies generally, and therefore almost all things rule and are ruled according to nature. But the kind of rule differs—the freeman rules over the slave after another manner from that in which the male rules over the female, or the man over the child; although the parts of the soul are present in all of them, they are present in different degrees. For the slave has no deliberative faculty at all; the woman has, but it is without authority, and the child has, but it is immature. So it must necessarily be supposed to be with the excellences of character also; all should partake of them, but only in such manner and degree as is required by each for the fulfilment of his function.

[From 'Politics' [c.330 BC], in *The Complete Works of Aristotle*, ed. Jonathan Barnes
(Princeton: Princeton University Press, 1984), Vol. II: 1987–92, 1999.]

ARISTOTLE

3   Nicomachean Ethics

But in the deviation-forms, as justice hardly exists, so too does friendship. It exists least in the worst form; in tyranny there is little or no friendship. For where there is nothing common to ruler and ruled, there is not friendship either, since there is not justice; e.g. between craftsman and tool, soul and body, master and slave; the latter in each case is benefited by that which uses it, but there is no friendship nor justice towards lifeless things. But neither is there friendship towards a horse or an ox, nor to a slave *qua* slave. For there is nothing common to the two parties; the slave is a living tool and the tool a lifeless slave. *Qua* slave then, one cannot be friends with him. But *qua* man one can; for there seems to be some justice between any man and any other who can share in a system of law or be a party to an agreement; therefore there can also be friendship with him in so far as he is a man. Therefore while in tyrannies friendship and justice hardly exist, in democracies they exist more fully; for where the citizens are equal they have much in common.

[From *The Nicomachean Ethics of Aristotle* [c.340 BC], trs. David Ross (London: Oxford University Press, 1980), 212.]

CICERO

4   De Officiis

But let us remember that we must have regard for justice even towards the humblest. Now the humblest station and the poorest fortune are those of slaves: and they give us no bad rule who bid us treat our slaves as we should our employees: they must be required to work; they must be given their dues.

[. . .]

XLII. Now in regard to trades and other means of livelihood, which ones are to be considered becoming to a gentleman and which ones are vulgar, we have been taught, in general, as follows. First, those means of livelihood are rejected as undesirable which incur people's ill-will, as those of tax-gatherers and usurers. Unbecoming to a gentleman, too, and vulgar are the means of livelihood of all hired workmen whom we pay for mere manual labour, not for artistic skill; for in their case the very wage they receive is a pledge of their slavery. Vulgar we must consider those also who buy from wholesale merchants to retail immediately; for they would get no profits without a great deal of downright lying; and verily, there is no action that is meaner than misrepresentation. And all mechanics are engaged in vulgar trades; for no workshop can have anything liberal about it. Least respectable of all are those trades which cater for sensual pleasures.

[From *De Officiis* [c.44 BC], trs. Walter Miller (Cambridge, MA: Harvard University Press, 1990), 45, 153.]

JEAN BODIN

5   Six Books of the Commonwealth

The third type of government in the household is that of the lord over his slaves and the master over his servants . . . And seeing that there are slaves all over the world except in that quarter which is Europe, we must necessarily consider the power of masters over their slaves, and the advantages and disadvantages of the institution. It is a matter of moment both to families and to commonwealths everywhere.

Slaves are either naturally so, being born of slave women, or slaves by right of conquest, or in punishment for some crime, or because they have sold or gambled away their liberty to another . . . Household servants are in no sense slaves but free men, and both before the law, and in fact, have an equal liberty of action. All the same they are not simply paid employees or day labourers over whom those who have hired their services have no such authority or right of punishment as the master has over his servants. For so long as they are members of their master's household they owe him service, respect, and obedience, and he can correct and punish them, though with discretion and moderation. Such briefly is the power of masters over their servants, for we do not want here to enter into any discussion of the rules which should govern the conduct proper on each side.

But the institution of slavery raises difficulties which have never been satisfactorily resolved. First of all, is slavery natural and useful, or contrary to nature? And second, what power should the master have over the slave? Aristotle was of opinion that servitude was natural, and alleged as proof that it is obvious that some are born fit only to serve and obey, others to govern and command. On the other hand jurists, who are less concerned with philosophical arguments than with commonly received opinions, hold that servitude is directly contrary to nature, and have always done what they could to defend personal liberty, despite the obscurity of laws, testaments, legal decisions, and contracts. . . .

Let us consider which of these two opinions is the better founded. There is a certain plausibility in the argument that slavery is natural and useful to the commonwealth. That which is contrary to nature cannot endure, and despite any force and violence that one can use, the natural order will always reestablish itself, as is clear from the behaviour of all natural agents. Slavery appeared suddenly in the world after the flood, and at the very same time that the first commonwealths began to take shape, and has persisted from that day to this. Although in the last three or four hundred years it has been abolished in many places, one continually sees it reappearing in some form. For instance in the West Indies, which are three times as extensive as the whole of Europe, people who have no knowledge of divine and positive laws to the contrary, have always had great numbers of slaves. There is not a commonwealth to be found anywhere that has never known the institution, and wise and good men in all ages have owned and employed slaves. What is more, in all commonwealths the master is always recognized as having absolute power to dispose of the lives and belongings of his slaves as he thinks fit, save in a few cases where princes and lawgivers have restricted this power. It cannot be that so many rulers and legislators have upheld an institution which was unnatural, or so many wise and virtuous men approved of them for doing so, or so many peoples for so many centuries maintained the practice of slavery, and even restricted the right of manumission, and still prospered in peace and war, if it had been against nature.

Again, who would deny that it is laudible and charitable to spare the life of a prisoner taken in legitimate warfare who cannot find a ransom, instead of killing him in cold blood, for this was generally the origin of enslavement. Moreover a man is required by divine and positive law to submit to corporal punishment if he cannot pay the forfeit for any act he has committed. No one doubts that those who make violent assaults upon the goods and lives of others are brigands and robbers, deserving of death. It cannot be against nature in such a case to exact services from the malefactor instead of killing him. If it were against nature to have power of life and death over another, all kingdoms and lordships in the world would be against nature, seeing that kings and princes have the like power over their subjects, noble and simple, if they are proved guilty of a capital crime.

All these arguments tend to prove that slavery is natural, useful, and right. I think however that strong objections can be urged against them all. I agree that servitude is natural where the strong, brutal, rich, and ignorant obey the wise, prudent, and humble, poor though they may be. But no one would deny that to subject wise men to fools, the well-informed to the ignorant, saints to sinners is against nature . . . One sees in fact how often quiet and peaceable men are the prey of evildoers. When princes attempt to settle their differences by war, it is always claimed that the victor had right on his side, and the vanquished were in the wrong. If the vanquished did indeed make war without just cause, as do brigands, ought one not rather to make an example of them and put them to death, than to show them mercy? As for the argument that slavery could not have been so enduring if it had been contrary to nature, I would answer that the principle holds good for natural agents whose property it is to obey of necessity the unchanging laws of God. But man, being given the choice between good and evil, inclines for the most part to that which is forbidden, and chooses the evil, defying the laws of God and of nature. So much is such a one under the domination of his corrupt imagination, that he takes his own will for the law. There is no sort of impiety or wickedness which in this way has not come to be accounted virtuous and good. I will be content with one instance. It is sufficiently obvious that there can be no more cruel and detestable practice than human sacrifice. Yet there is hardly a people which has not practised it, and each and all have done so for centuries under the cover of piety. In our own times it was common throughout the Western Isles . . . Such things show how little the laws of nature can be deduced from the practices of men, however inveterate, and one cannot on these grounds accept slavery as natural. Again, what charity is there in sparing captives in order to derive some profit or advantage from them as if they were cattle? For where is the man who would spare the lives of the vanquished if he saw more profit in killing than in sparing them? . . .

I will refrain from setting down in words the base humiliations that slaves have been made to suffer. But the cruelties one reads about are unbelievable, and yet only the thousandth part has been told. For writers only refer to the subject incidentally, and such accounts as we have, come from the most civilized races in the world. Slaves were made to work in the fields chained, as they still do in Barbary, and sleep in the open when work was done, as they still do everywhere in the East, for fear that they would abscond, or fire the house, or murder their masters . . . So much have cities and commonwealths always feared their slaves that they have never dared to permit them the use of arms, or to be enrolled for service. It was forbidden on pain of death . . . Yet they never succeeded so well but that some desperate man, by promising liberty to the slaves, threw the whole state into confusion, as did Viriat the pirate who made himself King of Portugal, Cinna, Spartacus, and others down to Simon Gerson the Jew. All these raised themselves from humble origins to be powerful rulers simply by enfranchising the slaves who joined them. . . .

Since the Christian religion was established however the number of slaves has diminished. The process was hastened by the publication of the law of Mahomet, which enfranchised all who professed that faith. By the year 1200 slavery had been abolished nearly everywhere save in the West Indies, where great numbers were found at the time of their discovery . . . It may be objected that if the Mohammedans really enfranchised their co-religionists, who cover the whole of Asia, the greater part of Africa and even a considerable area of Europe, and the Christians have done the same, how come there to be still so many slaves in the world? For the Jews by the terms of their law may not make slaves of their own people either, nor yet of Christians if they live in a Christian country, still less of Mohammedans among whom they are chiefly settled. The answer is that those who profess all these three religions only partially observe the law of God with regard to slaves, for by the law of God it is forbidden to make any man a slave except with his own entire good will and consent . . . Seeing that the experience of four thousand years has shown us the insurrections, the civil commotions, the disasters and revolutions that commonwealths have suffered at the hands of slaves, and the homicides, the cruelties and barbarities inflicted on slaves by their masters, it was an unmitigated catastrophe that the institution was ever introduced, and then, that once it had been declared abolished, it should ever have been allowed to persist.

[From *Six Books of the Commonwealth* [1576], trs. M. J. Tooley
(Oxford: Blackwell, 1955), 14–18.]

THOMAS HOBBES
....

6   Leviathan

Dominion acquired by Conquest, or Victory in war, is that which some Writers call DESPOTICALL, from Δεσπότης which signifieth a *Lord*, or *Master*; and is the Dominion of the Master over his Servant. And this Dominion is then acquired to the Victor, when the Vanquished, to avoyd the present stroke of death, covenanteth either in expresse words, or by other sufficient signes of the Will, that so long as his life, and the liberty of his body is allowed him, the Victor shall have the use thereof, at his pleasure. And after such Covenant made, the Vanquished is a SERVANT, and not before: for by the word *Servant* (whether it be derived from *Servire*, to Serve, or from *Servare*, to Save, which I leave to Grammarians to dispute) is not meant a Captive, which is kept in prison, or bonds, till the owner of him that took him, or bought him of one that did, shall consider what to do with him: (for such men, (commonly called Slaves,) have no obligation at all; but may break their bonds, or the prison; and kill, or carry away captive their Master, justly:) but one, that being taken, hath corporall liberty allowed him; and upon promise not to run away, nor to do violence to his Master, is trusted by him.

It is not therefore the Victory, that giveth the right of Dominion over the Vanquished, but his own Covenant. Nor is he obliged because he is Conquered; that is to say, beaten, and taken, or put to flight; but because he commeth in, and Submitteth to the Victor; Nor is the Victor obliged by an enemies rendring himselfe, (without promise of life,) to spare him for this his yeelding to discretion; which obliges not the Victor longer, than in his own discretion hee shall think fit.

And that which men do, when they demand (as it is now called) *Quarter*, (which the Greeks called Ζωγρία, *taking alive*,) is to evade the present fury of the Victor, by Submission, and to compound for their life, with Ransome, or Service: and therefore he that hath Quarter hath not his life given, but deferred till farther deliberation; For it is not an yeelding on condition of life, but to discretion. And then onely is his life in security, and his service due, when the Victor hath trusted him with his corporall liberty. For Slaves that work in Prisons, or Fetters, do it not of duty, but to avoyd the cruelty of their task-masters.

The Master of the Servant, is Master also of all he hath; and may exact the use thereof; that is to say, of his goods, of his labour, of his servants, and of his children, as often as he shall think fit. For he holdeth his life of his Master, by the covenant of obedience; that is, of owning, and authorising whatsoever the Master shall do. And in case the Master, if he refuse, kill him, or cast him into bonds, or otherwise punish him for his disobedience, he is himselfe the author of the same; and cannot accuse him of injury.

[From *Leviathan* [1651] (Oxford: Clarendon Press, 1909), 155–6.]

Chapter 1
On civil slavery

Slavery in its proper sense is the establishment of a right which makes one man so much the owner of another man that he is the absolute master of his life and of his goods. It is not good by its nature; it is useful neither to the master nor to the slave: not to the slave, because he can do nothing from virtue; not to the master, because he contracts all sorts of bad habits from his slaves, because he imperceptibly grows accustomed to failing in all the moral virtues, because he grows proud, curt, harsh, angry, voluptuous, and cruel.

In despotic countries, where one is already in political slavery, civil slavery is more bearable than elsewhere. Each one there should be satisfied to have his sustenance and his life. Thus, the condition of the slave is scarcely more burdensome than the condition of the subject.

But in monarchical government, where it is sovereignly important neither to beat down nor to debase human nature, there must be no slaves. In democracy, where everyone is equal, and in aristocracy, where the laws should put their effort into making everyone as equal as the nature of the government can permit, slaves are contrary to the spirit of the constitution; they serve only to give citizens a power and a luxury they should not have.

Chapter 2
The origin of the right of slavery according to the Roman jurists

One would never believe that pity established slavery and that in order to do so it went about it in three ways.

The right of nations wanted prisoners to become slaves so that they would not be killed. The civil right of the Romans permitted debtors whose creditors might have mistreated them to sell themselves; and natural right wanted the children of an enslaved father who was no longer able to feed them to be enslaved like their father.

These reasons of the jurists are not sensible. It is false that killing in war is permissible except in the case of necessity; but, when a man has made another man his slave, it cannot be said that he had of necessity to kill him, since he did not do so. The only right that war can give over captives is that they may be imprisoned so that they can no longer do harm. Murdering in cold blood by soldiers after the heat of the action is condemned by all the nations of the world.

It is not true that a freeman can sell himself. A sale assumes a price; if the slave sold himself, all his goods would become the property of the master; therefore, the master would give nothing and the slave would receive nothing. He would have some *savings*, one will say, but the savings are attached to the person. If it is not permitted to kill oneself because one will be lost to one's homeland, no more is it permitted to sell oneself. The liberty of each citizen is a part of the public liberty. This status in the popular state is also a part of sovereignty. To sell one's status as a citizen is an act of such extravagance that one cannot suppose a man would do it. If liberty has a price for the one who buys it, it is priceless for the one who sells it. Civil law, which has permitted the division of goods among men, could not have put among those goods some of the men who were to take part in the division. Civil law, which makes restitution in contracts that contain some injury, cannot keep from making restitution for an agreement that contains the most enormous of all injuries.

The third way is birth. This falls along with the other two. For, if a man cannot sell himself, even less can he sell a man who has not been born; if a prisoner of war cannot be reduced to servitude, still less can his children.

What makes the death of a criminal lawful is that the law punishing him was made in his favor. A murderer, for example, has enjoyed the law that condemns him; it has preserved his life at every moment; therefore, he cannot make a claim against it. It is not the same with the slave; the law of slavery has never been useful to him; it is against him in every case, without ever being for him, which is contrary to the fundamental principle of all societies.

One will say that the law has been useful to the slave because the master has nourished him. Therefore, those persons incapable of earning their living must be reduced to servitude. But one does not want such slaves as these. As for children, nature, which has given milk to mothers, has provided for their nourishment, and the remainder of their childhood is so nearly at the age when they have the greatest ability to make themselves useful, that one could not say that he who had nourished them, even though he was their master, had given them anything.

Moreover, slavery is as opposed to civil right as to natural right. What civil law could keep a slave from flight, since he is not in society and, consequently, civil laws are not his concern? He can be restrained only by a family law, that is, by the law of the master.

Chapter 3
Another origin of the right of slavery

I would as soon say that the right of slavery comes from the scorn that one nation conceives for another, founded on the difference in customs.

Lopez de Gomara says that 'the Spanish found, close to Sainte-Marie, baskets in which the inhabitants had put produce; there were crabs, snails, crickets, and grasshoppers. The victors treated this as a crime in the vanquished.' The author claims that the right that made the Americans slaves of the Spanish was founded on this, not to mention the fact that they smoked tobacco and that they did not cut their beards in the Spanish fashion.

Knowledge makes men gentle, and reason inclines toward humanity; only prejudices cause these to be renounced.

Chapter 5
On the slavery of Negroes

If I had to defend the right we had of making Negroes slaves, here is what I would say:

The peoples of Europe, having exterminated those of America, had to make slaves of those of Africa in order to use them to clear so much land.

Sugar would be too expensive if the plant producing it were not cultivated by slaves.

Those concerned are black from head to toe, and they have such flat noses that it is almost impossible to feel sorry for them.

One cannot get into one's mind that god, who is a very wise being, should have put a soul, above all a good soul, in a body that was entirely black.

It is so natural to think that color constitutes the essence of humanity that the peoples of Asia who make eunuchs continue to deprive blacks of their likeness to us in a more distinctive way.

One can judge the color of the skin by the color of the hair, which, among the Egyptians, who are the best philosophers in the world, was of such great consequence that they had all the red-haired men who fell into their hands put to death.

A proof that Negroes do not have common sense is that they make more of a glass necklace than of one of gold, which is of such great consequence among nations having a police.

It is impossible for us to assume that these people are men because if we assumed they were men one would begin to believe that we ourselves were not Christians.

Petty spirits exaggerate too much the injustice done the Africans. For, if it were as they say, would it not have occurred to the princes of Europe, who make so many useless agreements with one another, to make a general one in favor of mercy and pity?

Chapter 6
The true origin of the right of slavery

It is time to seek the true origin of the right of slavery. It should be founded on the nature of things; let us see if there are cases where it does derive from it.

In every despotic government, it is very easy to sell oneself; there political slavery more or less annihilates civil liberty.

Mr. Perry says that the Muscovites sell themselves easily: I know the reason well; it is because their liberty is worth nothing.

In Achim everyone seeks to sell himself. Some of the principal lords have no fewer than a thousand slaves, who are the principal merchants, who also have many slaves under them, and these latter many others; they are inherited and there is a traffic in them. In these states, the freemen, who are too weak to oppose the government, seek to become the slaves of those who tyrannize the government.

Here lies the just origin, the one conforming to reason, of the very gentle right of slavery that one sees in some countries, and it has to be gentle because it is founded on the free choice of a master, a choice a man makes for his own utility and which forms a reciprocal agreement between the two parties.

Chapter 7
Another origin of the right of slavery

Here is another origin of the right of slavery and even of that cruel slavery seen among men.

There are countries where the heat enervates the body and weakens the courage so much that men come to perform an arduous duty only from fear of chastisement; slavery there runs less counter to reason, and as the master is as cowardly before his prince as his slave is before him, civil slavery there is again accompanied by political slavery.

Aristotle wants to prove that there are slaves by nature, and what he says scarcely proves it. I believe that, if there are any such, they are those whom I have just mentioned.

But, as all men are born equal, one must say that slavery is against nature, although in certain countries it may be founded on a natural reason, and these countries must be distinguished from those in which even natural reasons reject it, as in the countries of Europe where it has so fortunately been abolished.

Plutarch tells us in the life of Numa that there was neither master nor slave in the age of Saturn. In our climates, Christianity has brought back that age.

[From *The Spirit of the Laws* [1748], trs. and ed. Anne M. Cohler *et al.* (Cambridge: Cambridge University Press, 1989), 246–52.]

Slavery is also as ancient as war, and war as human nature. Society was so accustomed to this degradation of the species that Epictetus, who was assuredly worth more than his master, never expresses any surprise at his being a slave.

No legislator of antiquity ever attempted to abrogate slavery; on the contrary, the people most enthusiastic for liberty—the Athenians, the Lacedæmonians, the Romans, and the Carthaginians—were those who enacted the most severe laws against their serfs. The right of life and death over them was one of the principles of society. It must be confessed that, of all wars, that of Spartacus was the most just, and possibly the only one that was ever absolutely so.

Who would believe that the Jews, created as it might appear to serve all nations in turn, should also appear to possess slaves of their own? It is observed in their laws, that they may purchase their brethren for six years, and strangers forever. It was said, that the children of Esau would become bondsmen to the children of Jacob; but since, under a different dispensation, the Arabs, who call themselves descendants of Esau, have enslaved the posterity of Jacob.

The Evangelists put not a single word into the mouth of Jesus Christ which recalls mankind to the primitive liberty to which they appear to be born. There is nothing said in the New Testament on this state of degradation and suffering, to which one-half of the human race was condemned. Not a word appears in the writings of the apostles and the fathers of the Church, tending to change beasts of burden into citizens, as began to be done among ourselves in the thirteenth century. If slavery be spoken of, it is the slavery of sin.

It is difficult to comprehend how, in St. John, the Jews can say to Jesus: 'We have never been slaves to any one'—they who were at that time subjected to the Romans; they who had been sold in the market after the taking of Jerusalem; they of whom ten tribes, led away as slaves by Shalmaneser, had disappeared from the face of the earth, and of whom two other tribes were held in chains by the Babylonians for seventy years; they who had been seven times reduced to slavery in their promised land, according to their own avowal; they who in all their writings speak of their bondage in that Egypt which they abhorred, but to which they ran in crowds to gain money, as soon as Alexander condescended to allow them to settle there. The reverend Dom Calmet says, that we must understand in this passage, 'intrinsic servitude,' an explanation which by no means renders it more comprehensible.

Italy, the Gauls, Spain, and a part of Germany, were inhabited by strangers, by foreigners become masters, and natives reduced to serfs. When the bishop of Seville, Opas, and Count Julian called over the Mahometan Moors against the Christian kings of the Visigoths, who reigned in the Pyrenees, the Mahometans, according to their custom, proposed to the natives, either to receive circumcision, give battle, or pay tribute in money and girls. King Roderick was vanquished, and slaves were made of those who were taken captive.

The conquered preserved their wealth and their religion by paying; and it is thus that the Turks have since treated Greece, except that they imposed upon the latter a tribute of children of both sexes, the boys of which they circumcise and transform into pages and janissaries, while the girls are devoted to the harems. This tribute has since been compromised for money. The Turks have only a few slaves for the interior service of their houses, and these they purchase from the Circassians, Mingrelians, and nations of Lesser Tartary.

Between the African Mahometans and the European Christians, the custom of piracy, and of making slaves of all who could be seized on the high seas. has always existed. They are birds of prey who feed upon one another; the Algerines, natives of Morocco, and Tunisians, all live by piracy. The Knights of Malta, successors to those of Rhodes, formally swear to rob and enslave all the Mahometans whom they meet; and the galleys of the pope cruise for Algerines on the northern coasts of Africa. Those who call themselves whites and Christians proceed to purchase negroes at a good market, in order to sell them dear in America. The Pennsylvanians alone have renounced this traffic, which they account flagitious.

[. . .]

Section III

Puffendorff says, that slavery has been established 'by the free consent of the opposing parties'. I will believe Puffendorff, when he shows me the original contract.

Grotius inquires, whether a man who is taken captive in war has a right to escape; and it is to be remarked, that he speaks not of a prisoner on his parole of honor. He decides, that he has no such right; which is about as much as to say that a wounded man has no right to get cured. Nature decides against Grotius.

Attend to the following observations of the author of the 'Spirit of Laws,' after painting negro slavery with the pencil of Molière:

'Mr. Perry says that the Moscovites sell themselves readily; I can guess the reason—their liberty is worth nothing.'

[From 'A Philosophical Dictionary' [1764], in The Works of Voltaire, ed. Lord Morley (New York: Dingwall-Rock, 1901), Vol. VII: 213–16, 218–19.]

Slavery (*article by M. le Chevalier de Jaucourt*)

Slavery is the establishment of a right founded on force, making a man belong so completely to another that the latter is the absolute master of the other's life, goods and liberties . . . All men are born free; in the beginning they had but one name, one condition; . . . there were neither master nor slaves, says Plutarch: nature had made all equal. But this natural equality was of short duration. It was slowly discarded and servitude replaced it by degrees. . . .

As a necessary consequence of the proliferation of the human species men began to depart from the simplicity of the earlier times; they sought for new means to increase the amenities of life and to acquire a superfluity of goods. The richer contracted with the poorer to work for them, in exchange for a fixed return. This strategy, seeming to be mutually beneficial, tempted some to make their condition more secure and to attach themselves permanently to the families of others, with the understanding that they would be supplied with food and all the other necessities of life. This servitude was first constituted by voluntary consent and by mutual contract. That relationship was conditional, only for certain things, in accord with the laws of each country, and with the customs of those so engaged. In other words, in such a case 'slaves' were, properly speaking, only servants and mercenaries, rather like our own domestics. But this situation did not last; some found it more advantageous to have others do what they would have been obliged to do for themselves. Insofar as anyone could arrange it by force of arms, they created the custom of offering war prisoners their lives and bodies on condition of perpetual service as slaves. . . .

The law of the strongest, the rights of war, the thirst for conquest, the love of domination and of indolence, introduced *slavery*, which, to humanity's shame, has been accepted by almost all peoples in the world. . . .

There are two sorts of *slavery* or servitude, field and domestic. Field slaves are reserved for cultivation; domestics serve the household. The most extreme forms entail both at the same time. It was only towards the fifteenth century that *slavery* was abolished in most of Europe. However, it still endures, in part, in Poland, Hungary, Bohemia, and in several parts of Germany . . . In any event, almost within a century of the abolition of *slavery* in Western Europe, the Christian powers made conquests in lands where they believed that it was advantageous to have slaves. They allowed slaves to be bought and sold. They forgot the principles of Nature and Christianity, which make all men equal. . . .

Having traced the history of slavery, we are going to prove that it is an affront to the liberty of man; that it is contrary to natural and civil law; that it is offensive to the best forms of government; and that it is useless.

All men have an equal right to freedom; one cannot despoil them of it, unless as punishment for criminal acts. Certainly, in the state of nature, if a man has merited death from someone into whose hands he has fallen, the latter may deal with him and make use of him, without doing him any wrong. In reality, when the criminal deems his *slavery* more unbearable and hideous than the loss of his free existence, he can obtain the death he seeks by resisting and disobeying his master.

Property rights in men and in objects are two very different things. Regardless whether any lord says about someone in his power, *'this person is mine,'* his property in such a man is not the same as when he says, *'this thing is mine'.* Property in a thing implies a complete right to use it, to consume it, and to destroy it, be it for profit or pure whim. However one disposes of it, no wrong is done. But the same formula, applied to a person, signifies an exclusive right to govern the person or prescribe laws for him; the lord is simultaneously under obligations to this subordinate person, and his power, moreover, over the other is very limited.

[. . .]

Not only can there be no property rights, properly speaking, in persons, it is an offense against reason to think that a man, who has no power over his life, can give anyone else, either by consent or by convention, a right that is not his. It is false to say that a free man can sell himself. Sale presupposes a price. In selling himself all the slave's goods become the property of the master. Thus the master would have given nothing and the slave gotten nothing. . . . Every citizen's liberty is a part of public freedom; this quality, in its collective condition, is even a part of sovereignty. If liberty has a price to the purchaser, it is beyond price to the seller.

[. . .]

Moreover, in any government and in any country, however arduous are the prescribed tasks set by society they can all be undertaken by free men: by offering rewards and privileges; by proportioning tasks to capabilities; or by using appropriate technology. (See the proofs of M. de Montesquieu). We can add to the argument of that illustrious author by observing that *slavery* is not useful to the master because the latter contracts all kinds of vices and habits contrary to the laws of society. The master insensibly accustoms himself to the absence of all moral virtue, he becomes proud, impatient, impetuous, hard, sensual, and barbarous.

[. . .]

The laws of war, it was said centuries ago, authorize *slavery* by sparing prisoners of war. . . . We now understand that this presumed charity is nothing but that of a brigand. . . . The only right over captives that war allows is to be able to secure oneself by rendering prisoners harmless. Obtaining slaves by purchase is an even less appropriate way to legitimize *slavery*, because money, or anything that it represents, can't give one the right to deprive someone of his liberty. Besides, dealing with slaves for profit, as though for dumb brutes, is repugnant to our religion—a religion that came to us for the purpose of wiping out all traces of tyranny. *Slavery* is certainly no better grounded in birth. This supposed 'right' disappears as a consequence of the prior discussion. If a man cannot be bought or sold, still less may his unborn infant be bought. If a prisoner of war cannot be enslaved, still less so may his children.

[. . .]

It was arrogant pretension of the ancient Greeks to imagine that barbarians were slaves by nature. On this Greek premise, it would be just to treat all peoples whose manners and dress differ from ours as barbarians, and (without further ado) to attack them in order to put them under our rule. Only prejudices of pride and ignorance make one renounce humanity in others. It goes directly against the rights of peoples and nature, to believe that the Christian religion gives, to those who profess it, a right to reduce to servitude those who do not do so in order to facilitate their conversion. It was just this way of thinking that encouraged the crimes of the destroyers of America. It is not the first time that religion has been invoked against its own maxims, maxims which teach us that behavior towards one's neighbor applies to the whole universe.

[. . .]

Are there, however, no cases or places where *slavery* is indeed implicit in the nature of things? To this question, I answer that, in one sense, there are no such cases. In another sense, I answer, with M. de Montesquieu, that if there are countries in which *slavery* seems to be founded on natural reason, they are ones where heat enervates the body and so enfeebles men's courage that they will fulfill painful duties only in fear of punishment. In such countries, the master acts as basely towards his prince as his slave does towards himself—*civil slavery* is linked to *political slavery*. Note that, in despotic states, where men are already living under *political slavery*, *civil slavery* is more tolerable than elsewhere. Each one is content with his own subsistence and life; and the condition of the slave is hardly more burdensome than the condition of any royal subject. Both conditions merge. Nevertheless, although *slavery* in such countries is, so to speak, based on natural reason, it is no less true that *slavery* is against human nature.

Our conclusion is that *slavery*, instituted by force, by violence and, in certain climates, by excessive servitude, can be perpetuated in the universe only by the same means.

[From *Encyclopédie*, trs. Seymour Drescher from 1755 edn, Vol. 5: 934–43.]

There must doubtless be an unhappy influence on the manners of our people produced by the existence of slavery among us. The whole commerce between master and slave is a perpetual exercise of the most boisterous passions, the most unremitting despotism on the one part, and degrading submissions on the other. Our children see this, and learn to imitate it; for man is an imitative animal. This quality is the germ of all education in him. From his cradle to his grave he is learning to do what he sees others do. If a parent could find no motive either in his philanthropy or his self-love, for restraining the intemperance of passion towards his slave, it should always be a sufficient one that his child is present. But generally it is not sufficient. The parent storms, the child looks on, catches the lineaments of wrath, puts on the same airs in the circle of smaller slaves, gives a loose to his worst of passions, and thus nursed, educated, and daily exercised in tyranny, cannot but be stamped by it with odious peculiarities. The man must be a prodigy who can retain his manners and morals undepraved by such circumstances. And with what execration should the statesman be loaded, who permitting one half the citizens thus to trample on the rights of the other, transforms those into despots, and these into enemies, destroys the morals of the one part, and the amor patriæ of the other. For if a slave can have a country in this world, it must be any other in preference to that in which he is born to live and labour for another: in which he must lock up the faculties of his nature, contribute as far as depends on his individual endeavours to the evanishment of the human race, or entail his own miserable condition on the endless generations proceeding from him. With the morals of the people, their industry also is destroyed. For in a warm climate, no man will labour for himself who can make another labour for him. This is so true, that of the proprietors of slaves a very small proportion indeed are ever seen to labour. And can the liberties of a nation be thought secure when we have removed their only firm basis, a conviction in the minds of the people that these liberties are of the gift of God? That they are not to be violated but with his wrath? Indeed I tremble for my country when I reflect that God is just: that his justice cannot sleep for ever: that considering numbers, nature and natural means only, a revolution of the wheel of fortune, an exchange of situation, is among possible events: that it may become probable by supernatural inter-ference! The Almighty has no attribute which can take side with us in such a contest.—But it is impossible to be temperate and to pursue this subject through the various considerations of policy, of morals, of history natural and civil. We must be contented to hope they will force their way into every one's mind. I think a change already perceptible, since the origin of the present revolution. The spirit of the master is abating, that of the slave rising from the dust, his condition mollifying, the way I hope preparing, under the auspices of heaven, for a total emancipation, and that this is disposed, in the order of events, to be with the consent of the masters, rather than by their extirpation.

[From *Notes on the State of Virginia* [1787], ed. W. Peden (Chapel Hill: University of North Carolina Press, 1954), 162–3.]

IMMANUEL KANT

11 The Science of Right

No individual in the state can indeed be entirely without dignity; for he has at least that of being a citizen, except when he has lost his civil status by a crime. As a criminal he is still maintained in life, but he is made the mere instrument of the will of another, whether it be the state or a particular citizen. In the latter position, in which he could only be placed by a juridical judgement, he would practically become a *slave*, and would belong as property (*dominium*) to another, who would be not merely his master (*herus*) but his owner (*dominus*). Such an owner would be entitled to exchange or alienate him as a thing, to use him at will except for shameful purposes, and to *dispose of his powers*, but not of his life and members. No one can bind himself to such a condition of dependence, as he would thereby cease to be a person, and it is only as a person that he can make a contract. It may, however, appear that one man may bind himself to another by a contract of hire, to discharge a certain service that is permissible in its kind, but is left entirely *undetermined* as regards its measure or amount; and that as receiving wages or board or protection in return, he thus becomes only a servant subject to the will of a master (*subditus*) and not a slave (*servus*). But this is an illusion. For if masters are entitled to use the powers of such subjects at will, they may exhaust these powers—as has been done in the case of Negroes in the Sugar Island—and they may thus reduce their servants to despair and death. But this would imply that they had actually given themselves away to their masters as property; which, in the case of persons, is impossible. A person can, therefore, only contract to perform work that is defined both in quality and quantity, either as a day-labourer or as a domiciled subject. In the latter case he may enter into a contract of lease for the use of the land of a superior, giving a definite rent or annual return for its utilization by himself, or he may contract for his service as a labourer upon the land. but he does not thereby make himself a slave, or a bondsman, or a serf attached to the soil (*glebae adscriptus*), as he would thus divest himself of his personality; he can only enter into a temporary or at most a heritable lease. And even if by committing a crime he has *personally* become subjected to another, this subject-condition does not become *hereditary*; for he has only brought it upon himself by his own wrongdoing. Neither can one who has been begotten by a slave be claimed as property on the ground of the cost of his rearing, because such rearing is an absolute duty naturally incumbent upon parents; and in case the parents be slaves, it devolves upon their masters or owners, who, in undertaking the possession of such subjects, have also made themselves responsible for the performance of their duties.

[From 'The Science of Right,' in *The Critique of Pure Reason* [1781] (Chicago: Encyclopedia Britannica, 1952), 445–6.]

FRIEDRICH NIETZSCHE

12   Beyond Good and Evil

In a tour through the many finer and coarser moralities which have hitherto prevailed or still prevail on the earth, I found certain traits recurring regularly together, and connected with one another, until finally two primary types revealed themselves to me, and a radical distinction was brought to light. There is *master-morality* and *slave-morality*;—I would at once add, however, that in all higher and mixed civilisations, there are also attempts at the reconciliation of the two moralities; but one finds still oftener the confusion and mutual misunderstanding of them, indeed, sometimes their close juxtaposition—even in the same man, within one soul. The distinctions of moral values have either originated in a ruling caste, pleasantly conscious of being different from the ruled—or among the ruled class, the slaves and dependents of all sorts. In the first case, when it is the rulers who determine the conception 'good,' it is the exalted, proud disposition which is regarded as the distinguishing feature, and that which determines the order of rank. The noble type of man separates from himself the beings in whom the opposite of this exalted, proud disposition displays itself: he despises them. Let it at once be noted that in this first kind of morality the antithesis 'good' and 'bad' means practically the same as 'noble' and 'despicable';—the antithesis 'good' and '*evil*' is of a different origin. The cowardly, the timid, the insignificant, and those thinking merely of narrow utility are despised; moreover, also, the distrustful, with their constrained glances, the self-abasing, the dog-like kind of men who let themselves be abused, the mendicant flatterers, and above all the liars:—it is a fundamental belief of all aristocrats that the common people are untruthful. 'We truthful ones'—the nobility in ancient Greece called themselves. It is obvious that everywhere the designations of moral value were at first applied to *men*, and were only derivatively and at a later period applied to *actions*; it is a gross mistake, therefore, when historians of morals start with questions like, 'Why have sympathetic actions been praised?' The noble type of man regards *himself* as a determiner of values; he does not require to be approved of; he passes the judgment: 'What is injurious to me is injurious in itself'; he knows that it is he himself only who confers honour on things; he is a *creator of values*. He honours whatever he recognises in himself: such morality is self-glorification. In the foreground there is the feeling of plenitude, of power, which seeks to overflow, the happiness of high tension, the consciousness of a wealth which would fain give and bestow:—the noble man also helps the unfortunate, but not—or scarcely—out of pity, but rather from an impulse generated by the super-abundance of power. The noble man honours in himself the powerful one, him also who has power over himself, who knows how to speak and how to keep silence, who takes pleasure in subjecting himself to severity and hardness, and has reverence for all that is severe and hard. 'Wotan placed a hard heart in my breast,' says an old Scandinavian Saga: it is thus rightly expressed from the soul of a proud Viking. Such a type of man is even proud of *not* being made for sympathy; the hero of the Saga therefore adds warningly: 'He who has not a hard heart when young, will never have one.' The noble and brave who think thus are the furthest removed from the morality which sees precisely in sympathy, or in acting for the good of others, or in *désintéressement*, the characteristic of the moral; faith in oneself, pride in oneself, a radical enmity and irony towards 'selflessness,' belong as definitely to noble morality, as do a careless scorn and precaution in presence of sympathy and the 'warm heart'.—It is the powerful who *know* how to honour, it is their art, their domain for invention. The profound reverence for age and for tradition—all law rests on this double reverence,—the belief and prejudice in favour of ancestors and unfavourable to newcomers, is typical in the morality of the powerful; and if, reversely, men of 'modern ideas' believe almost instinctively in 'progress' and the 'future,' and are more and more lacking in respect for old age, the ignoble origin of these 'ideas' has complacently betrayed itself thereby.

[. . .]

It is otherwise with the second type of morality, *slave-morality*. Supposing that the abused, the oppressed, the suffering, the unemancipated, the weary, and those uncertain of themselves, should moralise, what will be the common element in their moral estimates? Probably a pessimistic suspicion with regard to the entire situation of man will find expression, perhaps a condemnation of man, together with his situation. The slave has an unfavourable eye for the virtues of the powerful; he has a scepticism and distrust, a *refinement* of distrust of everything 'good' that is there honoured—he would fain persuade himself that the very happiness there is not genuine. On the other hand, *those* qualities which serve to alleviate the existence of sufferers are brought into prominence and flooded with light; it is here that sympathy, the kind, helping hand, the warm heart, patience, diligence, humility, and friendliness attain to honour; for here these are the most useful qualities, and almost the only means of supporting the burden of existence. Slave-morality is essentially the morality of utility. Here is the seat of the origin of the famous antithesis 'good' and 'evil':—power and dangerousness are assumed to reside in the evil, a certain dreadfulness, subtlety, and strength, which do not admit of being despised. According to slave-morality, therefore, the 'evil' man arouses fear; according to master-morality, it is precisely the 'good' man who arouses fear and seeks to arouse it, while the bad man is regarded as the despicable being. The contrast attains its maximum when, in accordance with the logical consequences of slave-morality, a shade of depreciation—it may be slight and well-intentioned—at last attaches itself to the 'good' man of this morality; because, according to the servile mode of thought, the good man must in any case be the *safe* man: he is good-natured, easily deceived, perhaps a little stupid, *un bonhomme*. Everywhere that slave-morality gains the ascendancy, language shows a tendency to approximate the significations of the words 'good' and 'stupid'.—A last fundamental difference: the desire for *freedom*, the instinct for happiness and the refinements of the feeling of liberty belong as necessarily to slave-morals and morality, as artifice and enthusiasm in reverence and devotion are the regular symptoms of an aristocratic mode of thinking and estimating.—Hence we can understand without further detail why love *as a passion*—it is our European specialty—must absolutely be of noble origin; as is well known, its invention is due to the Provençal poet-cavaliers, those brilliant, ingenious men of the '*gai saber*,' to whom Europe owes so much, and almost owes itself.

[From *Beyond Good and Evil* [1886], trs. R. J. Hollingdale
(Harmondsworth: Penguin, 1973), 175–9.]

JEROME BLUM

13   Lord and Peasant in Russia

[T]he personal status of the serf deteriorated in the eighteenth century, and the most that can be said for the nineteenth century is that this deterioration was arrested. Reduced to a chattel who was bought and sold in the market place, the serf was scarcely distinguishable from a slave. The only essential differences between the Russian serf and the American Negro slave that a contemporary apologist for serfdom could think of were that the serf had the privilege of taking the oath of allegiance to the tsar, paying a personal tax, and serving in the army. The throne itself recognized the true status of the serf. Catherine II in her instructions to the Legislative Commission of 1767 referred to the seignorial peasantry not as serfs but as slaves (*raby*). Several decades later Alexander I in a private letter wrote that 'For the largest part the peasants of Russia are slaves; I do not need to dilate on the degradation and the misfortunes of such a position.'

Possibly the only people who saw a clear distinction between serfdom and slavery were the serfs. They did not think of themselves as slaves of their masters, but rather as the true owners of the land they tilled. Such at least is the meaning that has been put upon the phrase that reportedly was often on their lips: 'We are yours,' they told their owners, 'but the land is ours.'

[From *Lord and Peasant in Russia* (Princeton: Princeton University Press, 1961), 468–9.]

DAVID BRION DAVIS

14 **Slavery in the Age of Revolution**

Suppose that Napoleon and Toussaint L'Ouverture are alone in the world, and that each man is convinced he is the emperor of the universe. They are both solipsists, incapable of distinguishing an objective world independent of their own states of consciousness. And since they cannot detect an autonomous object outside themselves, they cannot find an autonomous subject within themselves.

When they first encounter each other, each man perceives the other as an undifferentiated extension of himself—much as young babies, we are told, perceive their parents. The illusion is shattered, however, when both Napoleon and Toussaint begin to discover that the other is an independent consciousness: 'They recognize themselves as mutually recognizing one another.' This discovery could be negated by murder, but then the murderer would be alone as before, having simply confirmed that the specter of another consciousness was part of the 'natural' world. Insofar as each man is 'human,' his greatest desire is to be recognized as a being of transcendent and unique value—as distinct from a temporary system of repetitive biological functions. When the two men do in fact risk death in an elemental struggle, it is to test the truth of their own self-images of omnipotence and indeterminate existence. But Toussaint finally submits—as he did in history—because he prefers Napoleon's vision of truth to his own death. Napoleon accepts the submission—as he did in history—because it validates his own sense of omnipotence. Indeed, that conviction is no longer purely subjective. Toussaint's bondage is an objective proof that Napoleon's freedom is no illusion.

But the paradigm now becomes more complicated. Aristotle defined the slave as a tool or instrument, the mere extension of his master's physical nature. For Aristotle the slave also possessed the rudiments of a soul, allowing him a lower form of virtue if he performed his functions well. The early Christians, drawing on the Cynics, Sophists, and Stoics, also told slaves to be submissive and obedient, but recognized an essential inner freedom that transcended external condition. The world of the flesh did not matter. What mattered was the Christian promise to spare the life of the meanest slave, through all eternity, if he would submit to the greatest Master. Hegel synthesized both the Aristotelean and Christian notions of slavery, and lifted them to a new level.

The master, Hegel argued, sees the slave as an instrument of his own will and demands absolute obedience. Yet every day he must contradict this Aristotelean definition, since he is now dependent on another human life (having spared the life), and since he has found that the 'slavish consciousness' is the object 'which embodies the truth of his certainty of himself'. The act of enslavement has created two opposed forms or modes of consciousness:

The master is the consciousness that exists for *itself*; but no longer merely the general notion of existence for self. Rather, it is a consciousness existing on its own account which is mediated with itself through an other consciousness, i.e. through an other whose very nature implies that it is bound up with an independent being or with thinghood in general.

Hegel developed an intricate dialectic of dependence and independence, of losing and finding one's identity in another consciousness, but his central point is that the master is caught in an 'existential impasse,' to use Alexander Kojève's phrase, because the master's identity depends on being recognized by a slavish and supposedly unessential consciousness. Even to outsiders, his identity consists of being a master who consumes the produce of his slave's work. Accordingly, the master is incapable of transcending his own position, for which he risked his life and for which he could lose his life, should the slave decide on a second match of strength. The master is trapped by his own power, which he can only seek to maintain. He cannot achieve the true autonomy that can come only from the recognition by another consciousness that he regards as worthy of such recognition. The condition of omnipotent lordship, then, becomes the reverse of what it wants to be: dependent, static, and unessential.

At first the slave is dominated by fear and by the desire for self-preservation. Insofar as he assimilates the master's definition of his slavishness, he has denied his capacity for autonomous consciousness. His life becomes immersed in nature and in his work. Yet the slave's fear and desire for self-preservation necessarily counteract the master's image of a negative and unessential 'thing'. And the slave's labor, by transforming elements in the natural world, creates an objective reality that confirms and shapes his own consciousness of self:

Thus precisely in labour where there seemed to be merely some outsider's mind and ideas involved, the bondsman becomes aware, through this re-discovery of himself by himself, of having and being a 'mind' of his own.

As Kojève has suggested, the product of work becomes for the slave the counterpart of the slave himself for the master. But unlike the master, the slave is not a consumer who looks upon 'things' as merely the means of satisfying desires. The products he creates become an objective reality that validates the emerging consciousness of his subjective human reality. Through coerced labor, the slave alone acquires the qualities of fortitude, patience, and endurance. The slave alone has an interest in changing his condition, and thus looks to a future beyond himself. Only the slave, therefore, has the potentiality for escaping an imbalanced reciprocity and for becoming truly free.

It is not fanciful to see in Toussaint's actual deeds a message for later masters and wielders of power, or to see in Hegel's thoughts a message to slaves and the powerless. In their own ways, both men were saying that situations of dominance and submission are not so simple as they seem, and that dominators can never be sure of the future. For a time Hegel perceived the Age of Revolution as the final drama of history, which would terminate the seemingly endless struggle between lords and bondsmen and make the ideal of freedom—which the Stoics had imprisoned within man's subjective soul, and which Christianity had projected to a spiritual afterlife—a worldly reality. What was truly new to the world, however, was not simply revolution, but a nation of former slaves who had achieved independence from a master race.

[From *The Problem of Slavery in the Age of Revolution 1770–1823*
(Oxford: Oxford University Press, 1999), 560–3.]

EUGENE D. GENOVESE

15 Roll, Jordan, Roll

Cruel, unjust, exploitative, oppressive, slavery bound two peoples together in bitter antagonism while creating an organic relationship so complex and ambivalent that neither could express the simplest human feelings without reference to the other. Slavery rested on the principle of property in man—of one man's appropriation of another's person as well as of the fruits of his labor. By definition and in essence it was a system of class rule, in which some people lived off the labor of others. American slavery subordinated one race to another and thereby rendered its fundamental class relationships more complex and ambiguous; but they remained class relationships. The racism that developed from racial subordination influenced every aspect of American life and remains powerful. But slavery as a system of class rule predated racism and racial subordination in world history and once existed without them. Racial subordination, as postbellum American developments and the history of modern colonialism demonstrate, need not rest on slavery. Wherever racial subordination exists, racism exists; therefore, southern slave society and its racist ideology had much in common with other systems and societies. But southern slave society was not merely one more manifestation of some abstraction called racist society. Its history was essentially determined by particular relationships of class power in racial form.

The Old South, black and white, created a historically unique kind of paternalist society. To insist upon the centrality of class relations as manifested in paternalism is not to slight the inherent racism or to deny the intolerable contradictions at the heart of paternalism itself. Imamu Amiri Baraka captures the tragic irony of paternalist social relations when he writes that slavery 'was, most of all, a paternal institution' and yet refers to 'the filthy paternalism and cruelty of slavery'. Southern paternalism, like every other paternalism, had little to do with Ole Massa's ostensible benevolence, kindness, and good cheer. It grew out of the necessity to discipline and morally justify a system of exploitation. It did encourage kindness and affection, but it simultaneously encouraged cruelty and hatred. The racial distinction between master and slave heightened the tension inherent in an unjust social order.

Southern slave society grew out of the same general historical conditions that produced the other slave regimes of the modern world. The rise of a world market—the development of new tastes and of manufactures dependent upon non-European sources of raw materials—encouraged the rationalization of colonial agriculture under the ferocious domination of a few Europeans. African labor provided the human power to fuel the new system of production in all the New World slave societies, which, however, had roots in different European experiences and emerged in different geographical, economic, and cultural conditions. They had much in common, but each was unique.

Theoretically, modern slavery rested, as had ancient slavery, on the idea of a slave as *instrumentum vocale*—a chattel, a possession, a thing, a mere extension of his master's will. But the vacuousness of such pretensions had been exposed long before the growth of New World slave societies. The closing of the ancient slave trade, the political crisis of ancient civilization, and the subtle moral pressure of an ascendant Christianity had converged in the early centuries of the new era to shape a seigneurial world in which lords and serfs (not slaves) faced each other with reciprocal demands and expectations. This land-oriented world of medieval Europe slowly forged the traditional paternalist ideology to which the southern slaveholders fell heir.

The slaveholders of the South, unlike those of the Caribbean, increasingly resided on their plantations and by the end of the eighteenth century had become an entrenched regional ruling class. The paternalism encouraged by the close living of masters and slaves was enormously reinforced by the closing of the African slave trade, which compelled masters to pay greater attention to the reproduction of their labor force. Of all the slave societies in the New World, that of the Old South alone maintained a slave force that reproduced itself. Less than 400,000 imported Africans had, by 1860, become an American black population of more than 4,000,000.

A paternalism accepted by both masters and slaves—but with radically different interpretations—afforded a fragile bridge across the intolerable contradictions inherent in a society based on racism, slavery, and class exploitation that had to depend on the willing reproduction and productivity of its victims. For the slaveholders paternalism represented an attempt to overcome the fundamental contradiction in slavery: the impossibility of the slaves' ever becoming the things they were supposed to be. Paternalism defined the involuntary labor of the slaves as a legitimate return to their masters for protection and direction. But, the masters' need to see their slaves as acquiescent human beings constituted a moral victory for the slaves themselves. Paternalism's insistence upon mutual obligations—duties, responsibilities, and ultimately even rights—implicitly recognized the slaves' humanity.

Wherever paternalism exists, it undermines solidarity among the oppressed by linking them as individuals to their oppressors. A lord (master, padrone, patron, padrón, patrão) functions as a direct provider and protector to each individual or family, as well as to the community as a whole. The slaves of the Old South displayed impressive solidarity and collective resistance to their masters, but in a web of paternalistic relationships their action tended to become defensive and to aim at protecting the individuals against aggression and abuse; it could not readily pass into an effective weapon for liberation. Black leaders, especially the preachers, won loyalty and respect and fought heroically to defend their people. But despite their will and considerable ability, they could not lead their people over to the attack against the paternalist ideology itself.

In the Old South the tendencies inherent in all paternalistic class systems intersected with and acquired enormous reinforcement from the tendencies inherent in an analytically distinct system of racial subordination. The two appeared to be a single system. Paternalism created a tendency for the slaves to identify with a particular community through identification with its master; it reduced the possibilities for their identification with each other as a class. Racism undermined the slaves' sense of worth as black people and reinforced their dependence on white masters. But these were tendencies, not absolute laws, and the slaves forged weapons of defense, the most important of which was a religion that taught them to love and value each other, to take a critical view of their masters, and to reject the ideological rationales for their own enslavement.

The slaveholders had to establish a stable regime with which their slaves could live. Slaves remained slaves. They could be bought and sold like any other property and were subject to despotic personal power. And blacks remained rigidly subordinated to whites. But masters and slaves, whites and blacks, lived as well as worked together. The existence of the community required that all find some measure of self-interest and self-respect. Southern paternalism developed as a way of mediating irreconcilable class and racial conflicts; it was an anomaly even at the moment of its greatest apparent strength. But, for about a century, it protected both masters and slaves from the worst tendencies inherent in their respective conditions. It mediated, however unfairly and even cruelly, between masters and slaves, and it disguised, however imperfectly, the appropriation of one man's labor power by another. Paternalism in any historical setting defines relations of superordination and subordination. Its strength as a prevailing ethos increases as the members of the community accept—or feel compelled to accept—these relations as legitimate. Brutality lies inherent in this acceptance of patronage and dependence, no matter how organic the paternalistic order. But southern paternalism necessarily recognized the slaves' humanity—not only their free will but the very talent and ability without which their acceptance of a doctrine of reciprocal obligations would have made no sense. Thus, the slaves found an opportunity to translate paternalism itself into a doctrine different from that understood by their masters and to forge it into a weapon of resistance to assertions that slavery was a natural condition for blacks, that blacks were racially inferior, and that black slaves had no rights or legitimate claims of their own.

Thus, the slaves, by accepting a paternalistic ethos and legitimizing class rule, developed their most powerful defense against the dehumanization implicit in slavery. Southern paternalism may have reinforced racism as well as class exploitation, but it also unwittingly invited its victims to fashion their own interpretation of the social order it was intended to justify. And the slaves, drawing on a religion that was supposed to assure their compliance and docility, rejected the essence of slavery by projecting their own rights and value as human beings.

[From *Roll, Jordan, Roll: The World the Slaves Made* (New York: Pantheon, 1974), 3–7.]

16 Ancient Slavery and Modern Ideology

The need to mobilize labour-power for tasks that are beyond the capacity of the individual or the family reaches back into prehistory. Such a need was present whenever a society attained a stage of sufficient accumulation of resources and power in some hands (whether king, temple, ruling tribe or aristocracy). And the requisite labour force was obtained by compulsion—by force of arms or by force of law and custom, usually by both together—for all purposes (or interests) not amenable to straightforward cooperation: in agriculture or mining or public works or arms manufacture. Compulsory labour takes a considerable variety of forms, today as in the past—debt bondage, clientship, peonage, helotage, serfdom, chattel slavery, and so on. But whatever the form, the compulsion is fundamentally different from that lying behind hired labour, which implies the conceptual abstraction of a man's labour power from the man himself. The wage-labourer also surrenders some of his independence when he accepts employment, but such loss cannot be classed with that suffered by slaves or serfs.

In early societies, free hired labour (though widely documented) was spasmodic, casual, marginal. Significantly, in neither Greek nor Latin was there a word with which to express the general notion of 'labour' or the concept of labour 'as a general social function'. Only with the development of capitalism did wage labour emerge as the characteristic form of labour for others. *Labour power* then became one of the main commodities in the market-place. With slavery, in contrast, the *labourer himself* is the commodity. The slave is in that respect unique among types of labour despite overlapping with, for example, the most oppressive kinds of serfdom or with convict labour. The slave and the free wage-labourer thus stand at the extreme poles of labour for others, but historically the important contrast is rather between slaves and other types of compulsory labour. As institutionalized systems of organizing labour, other kinds of involuntary labour preceded chattel slavery, and both preceded (and then coexisted with) free hired labour. In order to understand ancient slavery, therefore, some preliminary consideration is required of the labour systems within which it arose and which it largely displaced in key areas of the classical world, though by no means in all.

It must be acknowledged at the outset that in current historical and sociological writing the classification of types of labour is in a bad state. Behind faulty classification there is of course faulty theory, or at least inadequate conceptualization.

[. . .]

At the other extreme there is the tendency to create a 'supra-historical mélange' that 'defies all scientific principles'. One variant, common among Anglo-American anthropologists, goes like this (and it is by no means restricted to slavery). First, a host of, let us say, African statuses and status-terms are translated as 'slaves'; second, it is observed that at essential points these so-called slaves are extremely unlike the slaves of classical antiquity or of the Americas; third, instead of reconsidering their appellation 'slaves' to their own subjects, these anthropologists angrily protest the 'ethnocentrism' of 'western' historians and sociologists and demand that the latter redefine and reclassify slaves in order to provide a place for their own pseudo-slaves.

An even worse situation prevails with regard to the other forms of compulsory labour that have appeared throughout history. It is a sign of our grave difficulty in comprehension that we are unable even to translate the labels into modern western languages: 'helot' is not a translation but an adoption; 'debt-bondsman' is an artificial coinage; *pelatai, laoi, clientes, coloni* have not even been adopted but merely transliterated.

When I say that we cannot translate these terms I do not imply that historians do not translate them all the time, writing about the Graeco-Roman world and even more about the ancient Near East. The magnetism of the traditional tripartite division of labour into slave-serf-free appears to be irresistible. Procedures vary. The most common is to label everyone who is not obviously a slave or a free man a serf.

[From *Ancient Slavery and Modern Ideology* (New York: Viking Press, 1980), 68–70.]

RICHARD HELLIE
17   Slavery in Russia

Voluntary slavery

'Voluntary' slavery was perhaps the most bizarre form (or subform) of human bondage in Muscovy. It is mentioned in a law of 1555 in a rather elliptical fashion. As we shall see later, it has been customary in many societies for servants to be slaves, and Muscovy was no exception. However, it was possible for a person in most of the sixteenth century to serve a lord without formulating a strictly owner–slave legal relationship. Initially, the 'voluntary slave' seems to have been such an individual, one person serving another without having formulated a contractual slavery relationship.

[. . .]

Debt slavery

Another secondary form of servitude in Muscovy was debt slavery, perhaps the form of bondage known to the greatest number of societies. Debt slavery has often been linked with various forms of penal slavery, for default on payment of obligations is regarded as a form of theft. It was known in primitive societies, such as that of the Yurok Indians of northern California, a fishing and food-gathering people. In litigation a plaintiff who was found in the right could collect damages from the defendant. Should the defendant default, he had the option of becoming the plaintiff's debt slave, or of being executed by the plaintiff. This example also reveals one of the original causes for slavery, the deferment of capital punishment, a subject that will be discussed in greater detail later. Debt slavery also was known in Babylonia, Assyria, Palestine, Greece, Egypt, Rome, China, India, Germanic societies, the Philippines, the Christian Assizes of Jerusalem at the beginning of the twelfth century, and was made illegal only in 1874 in Siam where default on gambling debts was the chief cause of persons' selling themselves for debt. Thomas Jefferson's passionate aversion to debt was based on the fact that it could lead to bondage, of which outright enslavement was the most graphic form. His sentiments were only a modern expression of those held by the Greeks and Romans, that any service obligation, such as working off a debt, was 'slave-like'. Usually debt slavery was for a term, during which the principal was worked off, and little or no account was taken of interest on the debt.

[. . .]

Indenture

What is here referred to as 'indenture' was an old form of temporary bondage well known in the *Russkaia Pravda*, and the inclusion of some but not all of the old provisions in the Abridged Version indicates that this form was surviving only feebly (if at all) at the end of the fifteenth century. Its survival was stronger in West Russian law, and then indenture was reborn in the seventeenth century as the older Muscovite forms of bondage became inflexible. In the *Russkaia Pravda* the indentured laborer (*zakup*) was a semifree man, as elsewhere. During the time of his servitude, he was in some cases the agent of his master, and at other times his own man. The master could not sue his indentured laborer for theft. On the other hand (articles 57 and 58), indentured laborers were responsible to their masters for negligence. Reciprocally, indentured laborers had rights vis-à-vis their owners. The lord could not seize the laborer's property, sell the indenture to a third party, or sell the laborer into slavery (articles 59–61). Moreover, the lord could reasonably chastise his indentured laborer, but if he did it without cause the laborer could collect damages from the master (article 62). Most important, the *Pravda* specified sanctions for violations by the master, and also insisted that the indentured laborer had the right to complain to the prince or other officials in case of violations by the master. Again, reciprocally, if the indentured servant ran away, his master could convert him into a slave (article 56).

A sign of the waning of the indenture as an institution by 1500 was the omission of article 56 from the Abridged Version of the *Pravda*. However, the sanctions of articles 59 through 62 were still present.

Legal definitions of slaves

The question of who could be enslaved is inherent in the law governing every slave system. The major point to be made here is that in almost every system the slave is an outsider, and the law is limited to defining and refining that concept. Thus the Spanish could not enslave Spaniards, and Arabs could not enslave Arabs. With the definition of religious ecumenae, it became illegitimate for Muslims and Christians of Europe to enslave their coreligionists. One of the most bizarre aspects of Russian history is the fact that the prohibition against enslaving one's own kind has been ignored there, and thus the problem of who could be enslaved is discussed in terms almost completely different from those found in any other system.

One of the major changes instituted by law in the institution of slavery concerned who could be a slave. At the outset of the period, there was no limitation on who could be a slave. Even a peasant, whose mobility was otherwise limited to the period of St. George's Day by the end of the fifteenth century, had the right to sell himself into slavery at any time, for the obvious reason that, when he was in need of relief such as slavery provided, he could not wait for St. George's Day.

The first restrictions on who could be a slave, however, did not begin with the peasantry. Rather, as was the case in so many Muscovite instances, such restrictions were first applied to members of what might be termed 'the upper classes'. The problem of enslaving members of the armed forces became significant during and after the reign of Ivan IV. The issue had two parts, enslavement for debt and selling oneself into full or limited service contract slavery.

[. . .]

As the Muscovite caste society developed, other social groups were bound to their stations and forbidden to become slaves. Peasants were forbidden to leave their lands, regardless of circumstances, at the time of the Forbidden Years, which began in 1581 and were made universal about 1592, and lords were forbidden to convert their peasants into slaves. Should a lord have done so, and the peasant-slave later fled and sold himself to another master, by 1649 the law explicitly stated that the fugitive was to be returned to his former lord as a peasant, and that all of the slavery documents that might be presented in the case were irrelevant and void. The Slavery Chancellery was supposed to send lists of fugitive peasants throughout the empire to inhibit their selling themselves into slavery. By 1681 a peasant could get only a two-year loan, nothing that juridically might be confused with a limited service slavery contract.

Townsmen were bound to the *posad* beginning in the 1590s, and this became universal in 1637. Thus they could no longer sell themselves into any form of slavery, although they too still could become temporary debt-slaves. Those who were slaves were to be removed from that station and returned to their lawful urban taxpaying status. Those who tried to become slaves in the future were to be beaten with the knout in the marketplace and exiled to Siberia to live on the remote Lena River.

[. . .]

Parents had the legal right to sell their children, apart from themselves. This is hardly surprising in a society that allowed parents to kill their offspring with no sanctions whatsoever, until in 1649 penance was required. As noted, parents who sold their children had to guarantee that their children would serve.

[. . .]

Parents could sell their own children with themselves into slavery with no limitations if the children were under fifteen years of age. Children over fifteen years of age could not be sold in absentia but had to be still in their parents' household. Children who had attained their majority could not be claimed by those to whom their parents sold themselves if the children earlier had sold themselves to someone else or had established their own households.

[From *Slavery in Russia 1450–1725* (Chicago: University of Chicago Press, 1982), 39, 41–2, 44, 77–9, 81.]

PIERRE BONNASSIE

18   From Slavery to Feudalism

But are these creatures who continue to be called *mancipia*, *servi* and *ancillae* truly slaves? Was their lot not changed as compared with that of their predecessors in Antiquity? Here lies the nub of the problem. Let us start from the ultra-classical definition of Aristotle: that of the 'tool with a voice', making simply the correction—accepted, in any case, by both Aristotle and Plato—that this tool might also be regarded as an animal. This is a useful correction given that, since the economy of the early Middle Ages was almost exclusively agricultural, the principal tools of labour were domestic animals employed in the fields.

From this perspective, there can be no doubt that the slaves of the sixth to eighth centuries were ranked with livestock. The clauses in the barbarian laws relating to the sale and theft of cattle apply equally, quite unequivocally, to the *mancipia*. Let us look, for example, at what the law of the Bavarians says about sales:

A sale once completed should not be altered, unless a defect is found which the vendor has concealed, in the slave or the horse or any other livestock sold . . . : for animals have defects which a vendor can sometimes conceal.

This is confirmed by the rare tariffs of tolls which survive for such an early period: that of Arras, for example, deals with slaves under the rubric *De bestiis*.

In cases of theft, the laws generally make no distinction between slaves and cattle. Having stated that the theft of a horse was sanctioned by a reparation of three times the value of the stolen animal, the law of the Thuringians added: 'it is the same for slaves, oxen, cows, sheep and pigs'. Only the price of composition differed; the law of the Burgundians was in this regard the most generous to slaves, estimating their value at twice that of a horse. The Salic law, in its first edition, gave the same tariff (35 sous) for the *servus*, the *ancilla*, the *caballus* and the *iumentum*. In its later versions, it established a scale of values for animals in general (see Table 1).

Table 1 *The scale of values for animals and slaves according to Salic law*

	PACTUS LEGIS SALICAE	LEX SALICA (PEPIN THE SHORT)
pig (two-year old)	15 sous	15 sous
boar	17 sous	17 sous
ancilla	30 sous	35 sous
ox, cow, *servus*	35 sous	35 sous
horse	35 sous	45 sous
bull	45 sous	45 sous

The Gallic laws (the fact that we are moving into the Celtic domain makes no difference in the way of thinking) went even further, if possible, in the process of assimilation; both slaves and cattle served indifferently as units of account in the payment of indemnities for murder and injury:

article 1. If someone voluntarily commits a homicide, let him give in reparation three female and three male slaves.
article 7. If someone injures a man to the extent of cutting off a hand or a foot, let him give in reparation one female or one male slave.

But, equally:

article 35. If someone strikes a man to the extent of breaking only one bone, let him give in reparation three cows.

Such texts speak for themselves. If even more convincing testimony to the sub-humanity of the slave is required, two simple criteria can be employed:

that of punishments and that of sexual relations between free and non-free (or rather, of their prohibition).

The history of punishments has never been written; this is unfortunate. Attempts to define liberty in the Middle Ages have been made in all sorts of ways without realising that, first and foremost, only the man who was not beaten felt himself to be free. Slaves were beaten, and worse. Three types of punishment could be inflicted on them: blows, mutilation and death.

The number of blows that a slave might receive, as revealed by the barbarian laws, was appalling: dozens, hundreds of blows, as many as, and often many more than, for an ox or a dog. What with? Here, too, there is silence on the part of historians fascinated by the most esoteric institutional problems, but lacking any interest, it appears, in the manner in which their ancestors were beaten. Lashing with a whip was probably the normal practice; it was customary at any rate, in Visigothic Spain. Burgundian masters preferred a stick. Salic law was more explicit; slaves were tied to a ladder with their backs bare and struck with rods whose thickness was normally that of a little finger. And it should not be thought that these corporal punishments existed only in the minds of the jurists who compiled the Germanic codes; referring to the great Spanish landlords, King Ervig commented: 'anxious to get their fields worked, they thrashed their multitudes of slaves'.

Mutilation was the practice everywhere, and is frequently attested. A slave might have his hands cut off or his eyes put out (amongst the Bavarians, for example), but brutality of this sort was generally avoided since it diminished, or even destroyed, the victim's capacity for work. Facial mutilation was preferred (cutting off the nose, the ears, the lips or scalping (*decalvatio*), since, whilst being spectacular, it did not take the worker from his work. Castration was not uncommon, either in Spain or Frankish Gaul; certainly it was not without risk (it was quite common for the victim to die), but it presented the double advantage of severely punishing the slave and softening his character. Both Salic and Visigothic law obligingly tell us what was the equivalent for women: 142 blows with rods north of the Pyrenees, cutting off the nose to the south.

Lastly, death. The master retained, of course, the power of life and death over his slaves. There was one exception to this rule: in Spain, around 650, a law of Chindaswinth abolished this right. But, even in this case, ancient practices survived. The law was not observed, or, more accurately, it was got round, as we learn from a text of twenty years later (a law of Recceswinth on the same subject). Prohibited from killing recalcitrant slaves, masters, we are told, 'cut off a hand or the nose or the lips or the tongue or an ear or even a foot, or even put out an eye or severed some part of their body, or gave orders for them to be cut off, put out or severed'.

How are these savage punishments to be explained? They did not spring simply from the sadism of masters, even though this was, in some instances, apparent. They primarily served as examples, and by their terrifying character (the facial mutilations), were intended to discourage any spirit of insubordination amongst the slave population.

[From From Slavery to Feudalism in South-Western Europe, trs. Jean Birrell
(Cambridge: Cambridge University Press, 1991), 17–21.]

PAUL FREEDMAN

19   Peasant Servitude in Medieval Catalonia

At one time it was thought that the immense majority of European peasants of the Middle Ages were legally unfree. Although definitions of serfdom might vary, all serfs were in some measure the property of their lord (associated with their tenements or attached personally to their lords), unable at their own will to leave this hereditarily transmitted dependence. Medieval writers, especially lawyers, often assumed, or tried to assume, that all those falling below a certain level were more or less assimilable into the common designation of serfs. In a celebrated passage the thirteenth-century French jurist Beaumanoir attributed servile status to anyone below the category of privileged townsman. An even more radical maxim from late medieval Germany held that only a wall (i.e. of a town) separated the burgher from the peasant: that both were essentially subordinate.

[. . .]

Contemporary scholars of land tenure and social change define peasants as cultivators of land who pay rent, work as a family, are identified with a property held on long-term lease or by inheritance, and whose liberty is in some measure constrained by the state or a dominant *rentier* class. Peasants do not usually own their land outright, but they have effective possession (*dominium utile*) over a particular parcel; they are not just casually associated with it as short-term lessees. They turn over to a landlord a substantial rent in kind or in money (or in a combination of the two). Peasants are not completely independent of the wider economic market—they are not exclusively subsistence farmers—but produce both to feed themselves and to fulfill the obligations of rent by means of commodities, labor or money for landlords. The social condition of this population is ambiguous but they are tied to the masters of the land by something more than a free contractual relationship. Whether through debt, taxation or privation of legal standing, landlords impose (directly or indirectly) an extra-economic power over peasants that limits their autonomy as purely economic actors.

Medieval agriculture was undertaken by peasants who of course constituted the overwhelming majority of the total population. In various privileged areas (on the frontiers or in strategic isolated regions such as certain

Swiss cantons) there were independent farmers who owed nothing to anyone in return for their land, but most medieval agriculture was undertaken both to feed the producers and to support those who held lordship over them. Medieval social theory at least occasionally acknowledged that the labor of peasants made possible the activities of the military and spiritual elite.

As has been remarked above, it was at one time common to describe the social condition of medieval agriculturalists by simply considering them all more or less as homogeneous 'serfs'. Serfs are understood as in some sense unfree but not slaves. Serfs contracted legally valid marriages and were settled permanently on holdings rather than being bought or sold apart from them. They labored these holdings as a family, not as part of a gang dispatched to various parts of a great estate. They might perform labor service on a lord's own land but this was part of their rent and not the entire sum of their labor. Serfs could not easily depart from their land and its obligations. They tended to belong to their lords as a form of property and transmitted this subordination to their descendants. Within the rural community, however, this unfreedom was mediated through local institutions administered by the serfs themselves.

The ambiguous social position of the serf, between slavery and liberty, made it sometimes difficult to determine what constituted servile condition. This was especially true when attempting to distinguish serfs from a free rural population. According to medieval jurists, followed by an earlier generation of historians, there were tests, indices such as fines paid for marriage or inheritance, that proved servitude and marked those affected off from privileged cultivators.

Serfs were peasants: family farmers on individual holdings providing for themselves and furnishing rent (in labor, kind or money) to a landlord who held a species of jurisdictional power. Not all medieval peasants were serfs, however. It is concerning how widespread serfdom was, and whether legal niceties of status really mattered, that historians of recent decades have altered how rural society in the Middle Ages is imagined.

Marc Bloch in his seminal analysis of feudal society freed agrarian history from its tutelage (if not servitude) to legal history. Bloch cast a much wider net to bring in more elements besides laws that might permit an accurate reconstruction of medieval production and social cohesion. Pointing to the significance of geography, patterns of human habitation, tools, unwritten custom, and private transactions, Bloch depicted a more intricate organization of agriculture and lordship.

Bloch is well-known as the historian of continuity, of the *longue-durée*, for whom the landscape transcended in significance all but the most massive political events. It is important to recognize, however, that in the context of a legal historical tradition that connected serfdom to Roman slavery or the late-imperial colonate, Bloch stressed the specificity of medieval society. Serfdom was not an adaptation of earlier slavery so much as a function of a feudal economy and a society founded on protection and dependence. Bloch described a seigneurial regime, a system of lordship by which nobles exercised formerly public powers of a military, political and fiscal nature. This regime comprised substantially more than a collection of legal customs. It was an organization of productive activity, distinct from earlier economies of slavery and later economies of money, commerce, and state power.

In the seigneurial regime as described by Bloch and his successors lords could obtain revenues from their dependents by means of their military entourage and in the context of immediate local institutions without relying on the more complex administrative and repressive apparatus required by slavery. Serfs acquired physical autonomy, a certain security of property, and the ability to create permanent and identifiable families. They produced more than slaves, their population increased more rapidly, and lords profited from the end of ancient slavery by maintaining a regime of economic exploitation and of semi-liberty.

The seigneurial system was thought to have merged a previously slave population and a previously independent peasantry who could no longer maintain their holdings in the face of the collapse of public authority and the climate of violence. There was thus a simultaneous amelioration of slave conditions and debasement in the status of allodialists. 'Serf' might be a convenient term to describe medieval peasants whose social condition hovered between what Romans (and moderns) regarded as fixed levels of free and slave. The ambiguity of moderate dependence or semi-liberty creates immense obstacles to understanding essential aspects of medieval society. There is the problem of geographical diversity of tenurial forms and of terminology. There is also the question of the relationship between legal categories and economic position once the free/unfree distinction no longer conferred a dramatic difference on how the land was occupied. Blurring the distinction between slave and free makes more complicated and problematic the nature of legal status.

[From *The Origins of Peasant Servitude in Medieval Catalonia* (Cambridge: Cambridge University Press, 1991), 1–2, 4–7.]

DAVID A. E. PELTERET

20 Slavery in Early Mediaeval England

As Finley's work has shown the decision as to which group in a society can be called 'slaves' must be dependent on the terminology of status employed by that society. The Anglo-Saxons had a very large vocabulary of status terms. Fortunately, in that society one group stands out unambiguously as being viewed as chattels and as having both the fewest rights and the heaviest obligations. The general term for a male member of this group was *þeow*, and, significantly, the Anglo-Saxon translators equated him with the Roman *seruus*, the Latin word most widely used to denote a slave.

The Modern English word 'slave' which is employed to describe this group should not be used interchangeably with the word 'serf'. Though the two terms have been used in the past by some writers as virtual synonyms, a clear distinction can be made between them. Whereas slaves were usually in some way regarded as the property of another person or institution, serfs were not personally owned but instead owed obligations to a person or institution in virtue of their occupancy of land. Both groups were to be found in late Anglo-Saxon England. Unfortunately English uses a single epithet 'servile' for the adjectival form of both 'slave' and 'serf'.

[. . .]

How necessary were slaves to the maintenance of the Anglo-Saxon economy? Provided there was interest on the part of an estate owner and adequate supervision, they could increase productivity and, because they must have lived close to a subsistence level, they may frequently have permitted their owners to acquire luxury items or leisure through their labours. In general, however, one may suspect that slaves were not essential to the economy and never had been. Certainly their numbers in Domesday Book suggest that they did not have the importance they had in the Classical world. Yet that same source indicates that they were very useful on major estates, where they performed necessary daily tasks like ploughing and milking. These were not roles that had to be filled by persons of slave status, however. Thus, by the close of the eleventh century the rights and obligations of those performing these tasks had changed sufficiently for the old status terminology to have virtually died out.

[. . .]

[T]he introduction of Roman concepts of land-law into England brought about fundamental changes in Anglo-Saxon society. Slavery did not escape its effects. Through the permanent alienation of land from the tribal domain by means of the legal device of the land-charter the old multiple-estates could be broken up into more compact units divided between the lord's demesne and areas worked by resident peasants. On these estates customs arose that covered many areas of life not regulated by tribal law. These included the rent and services due to a landlord in return for use of the land, matters which were more relevant in day-to-day living than the penalties imposed by tribal law for such crimes as rape, theft, or physical injury. Subjection to the new obligations led to an alternative conception of freedom from that recognised by tribal law. Whereas the latter kind of law had considered the possessor of freedom, that is, a freeman, to be one who held the right to be granted the protection of the law, manorial custom came to recognise someone as free if he or she had the power to leave an estate. Embryo manors may have been coming into existence as early as the seventh century, when the land-charter was introduced into England, and changes in the concept of freedom may have started at that time. But the earliest evidence of this change is in Alfred's translation of Orosius at the end of the ninth century.

This long delay is not surprising, however, since the movement towards the acquisition of bookland—that is, land alienated from the tribe by use of the land-charter—was not a steady one. Inter-tribal warfare up till the ninth century, and then the Scandinavian incursions and settlements during that century, meant that landed estates were likely to have a chequered history. Only with the stability brought by Alfred's successors could there be the continuity of tenure necessary for the growth of manorial custom (and even that was disrupted by the renewed Scandinavian attacks in the late tenth century).

During this period of slow movement towards the subjection of the 'free' peasantry to manorial customs such as the obligation to perform week-work, slaves were acquiring rights and obligations characteristic of freemen. Among the rights they gained was the power to sell what they had been given or what they had made and to keep the fruits for themselves, a right first conceded them in law by Alfred. Manorial custom also decreed that they were entitled to a certain amount of food every day. As for obligations, the slave had long been subject to ecclesiastical regulations governing sabbath labour and fasting (both of which were enforced by tribal law). With the growing influence of penitential discipline under Wulfstan at the end of the tenth century, rules on fasting appear to have been more rigorously enforced, and it seems likely that slaves were also required to observe other penitential regulations.

There was thus a gradual merging of the peasantry of both free and slave origin in the tenth and eleventh centuries into a spectrum of unfree statuses. Yet slaves continued to be manumitted throughout the Anglo-Saxon period, which shows that the slave's status still remained distinct from other groups in the society.

There are grounds for believing that the number of slaves was substantially reduced in the century and a half preceding the Conquest, even though comparative figures cannot be given. To begin with one must note the decline in the wars of conquest after the first quarter of the tenth century. Once the Celtic South-west had been fully tamed, newly enslaved persons had to be brought from distant border regions or else they were local people enslaved for debt or crime. To be sure, the disruptions in the reign of Æthelred led to the enslavement of many, but it is likely that large numbers of those captured by Viking raiders were exported from England. At any rate, the movement towards the unification of Anglo-Saxon England made it more difficult for Anglo-Saxons themselves to enslave their fellow countrymen, even if they did come from another tribe.

[From *Slavery in Early Mediaeval England* (Woodbridge: Boydell Press, 1995), 3, 250–2.]

21 Slavery in Africa

At the heart of any discussion of 'slavery' in Africa—and indeed anywhere—lie the rights that one person or group exercises over another—what anthropologists call 'rights-in-persons'. Such rights, usually mutual but seldom equal, exist in almost all social relationships. Thus, children have the right to support and protection from their parents, who have the right to demand obedience from them; a husband in many Western societies could until recently expect domestic services from his wife in return for material support from him, and they had exclusive rights to each other's sexual activity, adultery on either side being grounds for divorce. Such rights need not be reciprocal: in many other societies, including most African ones, the husband is legally injured by his wife's adultery but she does not have exclusive sexual rights over him. Such rights-in-persons may cover not just a person's services but his entire person—thus, the father in ancient Rome could kill or sell his children.

When the question of rights-in-persons is considered in relation to African cultures, it becomes clear, first, that such rights tend to be explicitly recognized and precisely defined in law; second, that they are the subject of complex transactions; and, finally, that the position of the so-called 'slave' can only be understood in the general cultural context of these rights. It is therefore necessary at this point to discuss them in some detail.

Transactions in rights-in-persons are an integral part of African systems of kinship and marriage. Through the payment of bridewealth, the husband, and behind him his corporate kin group, acquire certain rights in his wife from her kin group; these usually include some rights in the children in addition to domestic services and sexual rights. In a matrilineal society, the right to claim the children as members of one's kin group is not transferred to the husband and they therefore belong to their mother's kin group. On the other hand, in a patrilineal society the husband acquires this right, and the children therefore belong to his group. Hence, in a patrilineal society, 'brideprice,' here called bride-wealth, in fact includes a 'childprice'. There can be variations in these transactions even in the same society. For example, among the Goba of Zambia children belong to their father's group only if the bridewealth is paid in cattle; otherwise they belong to their mother's lineage. Here, no kin group is consistently patrilineal or matrilineal; rather, it consists of members belonging to it sometimes through their fathers and sometimes through their mothers, depending on the marriage contract. Similarly, among the Ijo (Ijaw) of the Niger Delta, a man acquires control over his children if he pays a 'big dowry,' whereas payment of a 'little dowry' enables his wife's lineage to retain her children. Significantly, however, the husband in the latter case may later acquire control over his children by additional payments for each child.

It must be stressed that these transactions are made, and the rights are held, by kin groups acting as corporate bodies and transcending the individuals who belong to them, just as Western corporations transcend their owners and management. Thus, when the husband dies, his various rights are inherited by his lineage. In many parts of Africa, such rights-in-people may belong to political offices. When a chief dies, his successor usually becomes the legal husband, father, and uncle to the surviving wives, children, nephews, and nieces of all previous incumbents of his office, inheriting all their rights. Equally, other forms of corporations may hold rights-in-persons. An unusual instance is found among the Lele of Zaïre; here, all the men of an age-set of a village could jointly acquire a woman who then became the honored and pampered 'village wife,' producing children whose 'father' was deemed to be the village as a whole. It was also possible in some societies, such as the Fon kingdom of Dahomey or the Igbo, for a woman to acquire the rights of a husband over another woman. By this device, a childless wealthy woman could found a lineage of her own, since the children of her 'wife,' sired by an approved mate, belonged to the lineage of their female 'father'.

It is clear from these examples that rights-in-persons and intricate transactions in these rights occur between individuals and offices and also, and indeed more commonly, between corporate groups. Furthermore, these rights can be manipulated to increase the number of people in one's kin group, to gather dependents and supporters, and to build up wealth and power. Westerners tend to regard these transactions with some ambivalence. Although few today would go as far as the League of Nations in 1926 and define bridewealth and transfers of children of the type just described as 'slavery,' nevertheless there are logical extensions of this system that seem to the Westerner highly suspect, and these were in fact outlawed by colonial governments.

[. . .]

Crucial to an understanding of rights-in-persons in Africa is an appreciation of the position of the individual in his kin group. Members of such corporate groups may be said to 'belong' to them in the double sense of the word in English—that is, they are members of the group and also part of its wealth, to be disposed of in its best interests. In order to distinguish between these two concepts, henceforward 'belonging to' will be used to denote that the individual is part of the wealth of his corporate group, while 'belonging in' will refer to his position as a member of the group. In theory, the best interests of the group as a whole override the personal interests of each of its members, whatever the member's age. Elders, however, have a higher position in the lineage hierarchy and a greater participation in its administration than the younger members. The children and younger adults are the most easily disposed of in times of crisis, and are also the most likely to find a buyer, but older people may also be sacrificed in the best interests of the group—thus old men convicted of witchcraft may be executed to eliminate a danger in its midst.

Several points may now be stressed. Concepts of rights-in-persons, various and complex, and transactions in them are widespread in Africa and constitute some of the basic elements of which kinship systems are constructed. While all social systems in the world can be analyzed in terms of such rights, Africa stands out *par excellence* in the legal precision, the multiplicity of detail and variation, and the degree of cultural explicitness in the handling of such rights. They are a formal part of African concepts of kinship relations—and not merely an analytical artifact created by outside observers examining these relations. The transactability of such rights as discrete and separate items is also remarkable. Moreover, transfers of such rights are normally made in exchange for goods and money, and the transfers may cover total rights-in-a-person. Therefore, such phenomena as kinship, adoption, the acquisition of wives and children are all inextricably bound up with exchanges that involve precise equivalences in goods and money.

[From 'Introduction: African "Slavery" as as Institution of Marginality,' in Miers and Kopytoff (eds), *Slavery in Africa: Historical and Anthropological Perspectives* (Madison: University of Wisconsin Press, 1977), 7–11.

JOHN THORNTON

22 Africa and the Africans

We have good reason to believe that Africa did not have small property, that is, plots of land owned by cultivators or let out to rent by petty landlords, just as it did not have great property. Of course, this must be conditioned by saying that African legal systems did ensure security of tenure for petty cultivators. What little we know about peasant land tenure in sixteenth- and seventeenth-century Africa suggests that those who cultivated land had fairly secure rights to farm but probably not to sell, alienate, or rent this land. However, we have every reason to believe that Africans owned *products* of the land (but not the land itself), for they clearly could alienate any agricultural or manufactured product by sale, and therefore it is clear that African law recognized a law of property in general. Presumably this right also protected crops under cultivation and perhaps even fallow land, thus providing secure land tenure that protected cultivated crops and the immediate agronomic rights of producers but did not extend to land as income-producing property.

Dapper, in describing land tenure in Loango, wrote that land was held in common (hence, no private property), and to secure the right to cultivate land, one had to do no more than begin farming in vacant land, although the rights would be surrendered once the peasant ceased cultivation. Peasants in the Gold Coast, according to de Marees, had to seek royal permission to cultivate uncultivated land and agree to pay tax as a condition (hence very close to rent), but they were not bound to the land so cleared or vulnerable to expulsion. The peasants might have individual tenure of the land, or they might work it in common. Dionigio Carli da Piacenza, an Italian Capuchin who lived in Kongo in 1667–8, gave a good description of communal tenure in which the whole village worked land together and divided the product by household 'according to the number of people in each'.

At first glance, this corporatist social structure seems to allow no one to acquire sources of income beyond what they could produce by their own labor or trade if they were not granted a revenue assignment by the state. Modern commentators on Africa have occasionally noted this, and precolonial African societies have sometimes been characterized as unprogressive because the overdeveloped role of the state inhibited private initiative by limiting secure wealth. In particular, these commentators believed that the absence of any form of private wealth other than through the state greatly inhibited the growth of capitalism and, ultimately, progress in Africa.

It is precisely here, however, that slavery is so important in Africa, and why it played such a large role there. If Africans did not have private ownership of one factor of production (land), they could still own another, labor (the third factor, capital, was relatively unimportant before the Industrial Revolution). Private ownership of labor therefore provided the African entrepreneur with secure and reproducing wealth. This ownership or control over labor might be developed through the lineage, where junior members were subordinate to the senior members, though this is less visible in older documentation.

Another important institution of dependency was marriage, where wives were generally subordinate to their husbands. Sometimes women might be used on a large scale as a labor force. For example, in Warri, Bonaventura da Firenze noted in 1656 that the ruler had a substantial harem of wives who produced cloth for sale. Similarly, the king of Whydah's wives, reputed to number over a thousand, were employed constantly in making a special cloth that was exported. Such examples give weight to the often-repeated assertion that African wealth was measured in wives, in the sense both that polygamy was indicative of prestige and that such wives were often labor forces.

Of course, the concept of ownership of labor also constituted slavery, and slavery was possibly the most important avenue for private, reproducing wealth available to Africans. Therefore, it is hardly surprising that it should be so widespread and, moreover, be a good indicator of the most dynamic segments of African society, where private initiative was operating most freely.

[. . .]

From what we know of slave labor in Europe in this period, it would appear that they were employed in work for which no hired worker or tenant could be found or at least was willing to undertake the work under the conditions that the landowner wished. As we shall see, this lay behind most of the employment of slaves in the New World as well. Consequently, slaves typically had difficult, demanding, and degrading work, and they were often mistreated by exploitative masters who were anxious to maximize profits. Even in the case of slaves with apparently good jobs, such as domestic servants, often the institution allowed highly talented or unusual persons to be retained at a lower cost than free people of similar qualifications.

This was not necessarily the case in Africa, however. People wishing to invest wealth in reproducing form could not buy land, for there was no landed property. Hence, their only recourse was to purchase slaves, which as their personal property could be inherited and could generate wealth for them. They would have no trouble in obtaining land to put these slaves into agricultural production, for African law made land available to whoever would cultivate it, free or slave, as long as no previous cultivator was actively using it.

[From *Africa and the Africans in the Making of the Atlantic World, 1400–1680* (Cambridge: Cambridge University Press, 1992), 84–7.]

Section II

The Origins and Methods of Enslavement

INTRODUCTION

No one knows for sure when or where slavery began or whether the prototypical slave was male or female. Slavery has proven to be such an ancient, durable, and ubiquitous institution that it not only appears in a wide variety of societies on all the habitable continents, but in some places it was an antecedent or foundation of civilization. With few critics before the nineteenth century, slavery must have seemed to most of the world's peoples as simply a fact of life, something that had always existed and always would exist. Those who sought a deeper understanding of this and other of life's contradictions would have typically turned to religion for answers. All the world's great religions, however much they restricted who could be enslaved and defined how masters should treat their slaves, provided authoritative approval for human bondage, usually by rooting its existence in the human condition itself. Enslavement served as a way to order and punish human beings, who if not by nature sinful in the Christian sense of the word, manifested a disturbing propensity for wrongdoing. Buddhist theology, for example, with its doctrine of karma and rebirth, could justify enslavement as punishment for a person's wickedness in a previous life. Most Confucians accommodated slavery within a cosmology that stressed natural hierarchy and the dependence of social harmony on unequal statuses. The Christian Church during the early and later Middle Ages—represented in this section by St Augustine and Bishop Ratherius of Verona, respectively—placed the origins of slavery and other forms of servitude in the fall of Man. Men might be free in an Edenic state of nature, but the God-given law of nature permitted the sanction of servitude for sin. Muslims actually preceded Christians in extrapolating a justification for racial slavery from the passages in Genesis (reproduced below) in which Noah pronounces a curse on Canaan, the son of Ham. Centuries later, slaveholders of the antebellum southern United States, rulers of perhaps the world's most modern slave society, continued to see slavery as a divinely ordained institution and went to war defending it to their death with frequent references to Scripture.

Ancient and modern thinkers also rooted the existence of war in human nature. War followed close behind the most common method of obtaining slaves—births to slave parents—producing many of history's most conspicuous mass enslavements and decisively shaping the meaning of slavery as a kind of social death, in which enslaved individuals have been violently uprooted from their societies. Indeed, cuneiform, the world's oldest written language, suggests the intimate connection between war and enslavement by combining the signs of man or woman with that for foreignness to form the ideograph for slave. In a similar vein, the Justinian Code (see Section III) recalled that slaves were called *servi* because Roman generals had long been accustomed to selling their war captives rather putting them death.

West central Africa supplied more slaves for the Americas than any other region of the continent. Well into the twentieth century many rulers still would have agreed with Alfonso I, King of the Congo during the first half of the sixteenth century, that 'one man may be the property of another and may be forced to submit to this state by birth, poverty, punishment for a crime, or the laws of war . . . A slave, like any other property may be passed on by the habitual methods of transmission: sale, trade, gift, or inheritance.' A few decades after the death of King Alfonso, the French political philosopher Jean Bodin, who delved into an ongoing debate on whether slavery was a natural condition (see Section I), also drew heavily on biblical and Roman history in compiling a similarly concise, albeit incomplete, list of the methods of enslavement. Bodin distinguished between war and other forms of organized violence such as raiding and brigandage. Many of the world's peoples, he observed, including the Romans, practiced penal slavery. The global reality of poverty, famine, and starvation forced at least some people in many slaveholding countries to sell family members into slavery, to enslave themselves, or to suffer enslavement because of debt. Bodin called natural slaves those who had inherited the status by birth. In this section, H. J. Nieboer, author in 1900 of the first global study of slavery, extends the list by adding more obscure methods of enslavement, such as tribute collection and child abandonment.

Most of the world's slaveholding cultures relied on several methods of obtaining slaves, whose proportional contribution to the total slave population could fluctuate markedly over time. Republican Rome built a mighty slaveholding empire with a remarkable string of military victories that yielded thousands and sometimes hundreds of thousands of slaves for distribution to markets and households throughout the Mediterranean. During the Empire, however, births to the existing slave population certainly superseded war as the primary means of obtaining slaves. Peoples as diverse as the Visigoths, Chinese, and Ibos at one time or another derived a significant proportion of their slaves from criminal punishments. The Ottoman Empire stands out for the proportion of slaves it acquired as tribute. War and other forms of violence predominated among the original methods of enslavement for the more than eleven million Africans who endured the 'Middle Passage' (see Section IV), although birth eventually replaced war and trade as the primary method of obtaining slaves in every slave society in the Americas. The world's cultures, as Orlando Patterson has documented in a global study of slavery (excerpted in this section), developed multiple, often complex rules to govern the inheritance of status. A child with one enslaved parent might follow the status of the mother, the father, the inferior parent, the superior parent, or none of the above. American slave societies, with few exceptions, adopted the Roman principle of *partus sequitur ventrem* (the status of the child follows that of the mother) in cases of mixed descent.

Portuguese maritime explorations of Africa beginning in the fifteenth century initiated more that four centuries of the Atlantic slave trade by cutting into Muslim sources that for generations had been funneling black slaves to the East. A lively debate has emerged among specialists in African history about the impact of the European presence in coastal Africa during the precolonial period on the processes of enslavement within Africa that fed the Atlantic slave trade. To be sure, the burgeoning European appetite for slaves to populate New World plantations stimulated African suppliers to catch more slaves by war, banditry, punishment, and other means. But in some regions at certain times Europeans had little or no control over the supply of slaves to coastal markets, which were filled by methods stimulated by political causes intrinsic to Africans. West Africa had substantial slave populations long before Columbus, because the collective encumbrances on land, as John Thornton contends, made slaves a particularly valuable form of private property. Every society had defined property in its own way as some particular bundle of rights, claims, duties, and responsibilities. Yet the highly individualized and personalized nature of the domination in slavery allowed African masters and other slaveholders a freedom of usage, a boundary-crossing capacity, that they did not have with land and other forms of property under collective claims.

Because of the dramatic resurgence of slavery that attended European colonization of the Americas, the almost exclusive association of slavery in the Americas with Africans and persons of African descent, and the painful legacy of racism in post-emancipation countries, modern scholarship has focused on the dynamic interplay of race and class, ideas and economics, in explaining the rise and fall of the transatlantic slave system. Although most specialists have come to reject narrow racial or economic explanations of African enslavement for a more systematic, interactive approach, work by Winthrop D. Jordan and others has demonstrated how a loose and inconsistent body of European prejudice against blackness and Africans hardened in the American plantation economies into racial slavery. In contrast, a number of nineteenth-century European thinkers linked the expansion of slavery in the Americas to the ready availability there of abundant 'fresh' soil that could grow cash crops. Where the ratio of land to labor was high, enslavement offered a cost-effective option, at least in the short run, to profit-minded planters faced with labor scarcity. In the long-term, however, slavery might end where it was once established, as soil fertility declined and increasing population density lowered the cost of wages to the point that it made allegedly more productive free labor more attractive than slaves. In 1970, the economist Evsey Domar (see Section VIII), building on the work of Nieboer and others, located the causes of slavery or serfdom in land–labor ratios, asserting that 'free land, free peasants, and non-working landowners' cannot exist together simultaneously. While the Domar model explains the desire to coerce labor, it fails to explain the preference for slavery over other forms of dependent labor, nor does it account for all cases in which slave societies have existed. Economic historians have also discussed the effects of declining transatlantic shipping costs from Africa in the seventeenth century. More recently, David Eltis, also an economic historian, has forcefully argued that declining transatlantic shipping costs cannot fully explain why Englishmen, for example, singled out West Africans for enslavement, since transshipping enslaved criminal or indebted countrymen or similarly vulnerable inhabitants of European rivals would have produced an even cheaper labor option. In short, ideas about the other—religious, ethnocentric and racial—had decisive consequences in the lines that cultures drew in deciding who was suitable for enslavement.

23 Excerpts from the Bible

Genesis 9: 18–27

18 And the sons of Noah, that went forth of the ark, were Shem, and Ham, and Japheth and Ham is the father of Canaan.

19 These are the three sons of Noah: and of them was the whole earth overspread.

20 And Noah began to be an husbandman, and he planted a vineyard:

21 And he drank of the wine, and was drunken; and he was uncovered within his tent.

22 And Ham, the father of Canaan, saw the nakedness of his father, and told his two brethren without.

23 And Shem and Japheth took a garment, and laid it upon both their shoulders, and went backward, and covered the nakedness of their father; and their faces were backward, and they saw not their father's nakedness.

24 And Noah awoke from his wine, and knew what his younger son had done unto him.

25 And he said, Cursed be Canaan; a servant of servants shall he be unto his brethren.

26 And he said, Blessed be the LORD God of Shem; and Canaan shall be his servant.

27 God shall enlarge Japheth, and he shall dwell in the tents of Shem; and Canaan shall be his servant.

ST AUGUSTINE

24   The City of God

Of the liberty proper to man's nature, and the servitude introduced by sin,—a servitude in which the man whose will is wicked is the slave of his own lust, though he is free so far as regards other men

This is prescribed by the order of nature: it is thus that God has created man. For 'let them,' He says, 'have dominion over the fish of the sea, and over the fowl of the air, and over every creeping thing which creepeth on the earth.' He did not intend that His rational creature, who was made in His image, should have dominion over anything but the irrational creation—not man over man, but man over the beasts. And hence the righteous men in primitive times were made shepherds of cattle rather than kings of men, God intending thus to teach us what the relative position of the creatures is, and what the desert of sin; for it is with justice, we believe, that the condition of slavery is the result of sin. And this is why we do not find the word 'slave' in any part of Scripture until righteous Noah branded the sin of his son with this name. It is a name, therefore, introduced by sin and not by nature. The origin of the Latin word for slave is supposed to be found in the circumstance that those who by the law of war were liable to be killed were sometimes preserved by their victors, and were hence called servants. And these circumstances could never have arisen save through sin. For even when we wage a just war, our adversaries must be sinning; and every victory, even though gained by wicked men, is a result of the first judgment of God, who humbles the vanquished either for the sake of removing or of punishing their sins. Witness that man of God, Daniel, who, when he was in captivity, confessed to God his own sins and the sins of his people, and declares with pious grief that these were the cause of the captivity. The prime cause, then, of slavery is sin, which brings man under the dominion of his fellow—that which does not happen save by the judgment of God, with whom is no unrighteousness, and who knows how to award fit punishments to every variety of offence. But our Master in heaven says, 'Every one who doeth sin is the servant of sin.' And thus there are many wicked masters who have religious men as their slaves, and who are yet themselves in bondage; 'for of whom a man is overcome, of the same is he brought in bondage.' And beyond question it is a happier thing to be the slave of a man than of a lust; for even this very lust of ruling, to mention no others, lays waste men's hearts with the most ruthless dominion. Moreover, when men are subjected to one another in a peaceful order, the lowly position does as much good to the servant as the proud position does harm to the master. But by nature, as God first created us, no one is the slave either of man or of sin. This servitude is, however, penal, and is appointed by that law which enjoins the preservation of the natural order and forbids its disturbance; for if nothing had been done in violation of that law, there would have been nothing to restrain by penal servitude. And therefore the apostle admonishes slaves to be subject to their masters, and to serve them heartily and with good-will, so that, if they cannot be freed by their masters, they may themselves make their slavery in some sort free, by serving not in crafty fear, but in faithful love, until all unrighteousness pass away, and all principality and every human power be brought to nothing, and God be all in all.

[From *The City of God* [413–26], trs. Marcus Dods (New York: The Modern Library, 1950), 693–4.]

BISHOP RATHERIUS OF VERONA

25   Praeloquia

XIV.29. Are you a servant? Do not fret; if you serve your lord faithfully, you will be the freedman of the Lord of all; for we are all brothers in Christ. And so listen to the Apostle saying: 'Servants, be submissive to your masters with all fear' [1 Pet. 2.18]. What *fear*? and what does he mean by *all*? First, the fear of God, then that of his earthly lord; then that servile *fear* which perfect love casts out [1 Jn. 4.18]; that is, fear that you will be beaten or whipped, or that you will be imprisoned, and ultimately that you will be put into eternal fire for your contempt. For 'whoever resists power, resists God's ordinance; for there is no power but from God' [Rom. 13.1–2]. Also the psalmist says: 'You have placed men over our heads' [Ps. 65.12]; and according to the opinion of someone: 'He who tries to resist God must necessarily lack great good and incur great evil, because he has gone against the highest Good and become an adherent to the worst evil'. And finally that chaste *fear* which remains for ever and ever, namely that if you are lazy or indolent, you will lose the glory promised in the future for those who do strong work. Therefore, any hours you steal from your lord, give to your creator. And lest you think that it is fortuitous, that is, without God's providence, that you have been subjected to service in whatever rank it happens, listen to Isidore:

Because of the sin of the first man, God's punishment of servitude has been imposed on the human race, in such a way that those whom he sees as not suitable for freedom, of these in his mercy he demands servitude; and though this happened through the original sin, yet the just God differentiated the life of men, making some slaves and some lords, in such a way that the licence of slaves to do ill should be controlled by the power of their lords. For if all were without fear, who would there be to restrain anyone from evil? For that reason also kings and princes were chosen over the nations, that they might restrain their peoples from evil by their terror and coerce them with laws to live aright. For as far as rationality is concerned, God 'has no partiality [Rom. 2.11]; God chose what is low and despised in the world, and even things that are not, to bring to nothing things that are, so that no flesh'—that is, fleshly power—'might boast in the presence of God' [1 Cor. 1.28–29]. For the one Lord gives counsel to lords and servants alike: subjection and servitude are better than pride and liberty; for there are found many who freely serve God, appointed under shameful lords, who, although subject to them in body, are yet superior to them in mind.

Comforted then by this testimony of so great a man, as true as it is eloquent, be a faithful and good servant, ever keeping in your heart the counsel which the angel Agar gave to the handmaiden Sarah: 'Return to your mistress and be humble under her hand' [Gen. 16.9].

> [From 'Praeloquia' [935–7], in *The Complete Works of Bishop Ratherius of Verona*, trs. Peter Reid (New York: Medieval and Renaissance Texts and Studies, 1991), 47–8.]

JAMES BOSWELL

26   Life of Johnson

The argument dictated by Dr. Johnson was as follows:

It must be agreed that in most ages many countries have had part of their inhabitants in a state of slavery; yet it may be doubted whether slavery can ever be supposed the natural condition of man. It is impossible not to conceive that men in their original state were equal; and very difficult to imagine how one would be subjected to another but by violent compulsion. An individual may, indeed, forfeit his liberty by a crime; but he cannot by that crime forfeit the liberty of his children. What is true of a criminal seems true likewise of a captive. A man may accept life from a conquering enemy on condition of perpetual servitude; but it is very doubtful whether he can entail that servitude on his descendants; for no man can stipulate without commission for another. The condition which he himself accepts, his son or grandson perhaps would have rejected. If we should admit, what perhaps may with more reason be denied, that there are certain relations between man and man which may make slavery necessary and just, yet it can never be proved that he who is now suing for his freedom ever stood in any of those relations. He is certainly subject by no law, but that of violence, to his present master; who pretends no claim to his obedience, but that he bought him from a merchant of slaves, whose right to sell him never was examined. It is said that, according to the constitutions of Jamaica, he was legally enslaved; these constitutions are merely positive; and apparently injurious to the rights of mankind, because whoever is exposed to sale is condemned to slavery without appeal; by whatever fraud or violence he might have been originally brought into the merchant's power. In our own time Princes have been sold, by wretches to whose care they were entrusted, that they might have an European education; but when once they were brought to a market in the plantations, little would avail either their dignity or their wrongs. The laws of Jamaica afford a Negro no redress. His colour is considered as a sufficient testimony against him. It is to be lamented that moral right should ever give way to political convenience. But if temptations of interest are sometimes too strong for human virtue, let us at least retain a virtue where there is no temptation to quit it. In the present case there is apparent right on one side, and no convenience on the other. Inhabitants of this island can neither gain riches nor power by taking away the liberty of any part of the human species. The sum of the argument is this:—No man is by nature the property of another: The defendant is, therefore, by nature free: The rights of nature must be some way forfeited before they can be justly taken away: That the defendant has by any act forfeited the rights of nature we require to be proved; and if no proof of such forfeiture can be given, we doubt not but the justice of the court will declare him free.

I record Dr. Johnson's argument fairly upon this particular case; where, perhaps, he was in the right. But I beg leave to enter my most solemn protest against his general doctrine with respect to the *Slave Trade*. For I will resolutely say—that his unfavourable notion of it was owing to prejudice, and imperfect or false information. The wild and dangerous attempt which has for some time been persisted in to obtain an act of our Legislature, to abolish so very important and necessary a branch of commercial interest, must have been crushed at once, had not the insignificance of the zealots who vainly took the lead in it, made the vast body of Planters, Merchants, and others, whose immense properties are involved in that trade, reasonably enough suppose that there could be no danger. The encouragement which the attempt has received excites my wonder and indignation; and though some men of superiour abilities have supported it; whether from a love of temporary popularity, when prosperous; or a love of general mischief, when desperate, my opinion is unshaken. To abolish a *status*, which in all ages God has sanctioned, and man has continued, would not only be *robbery* to an innumerable class of our fellow-subjects; but it would be extreme cruelty to the African Savages, a portion of whom it saves from massacre, or intolerable bondage in their own country, and introduces into a much happier state of life; especially now when their passage to the West-Indies and their treatment there is humanely regulated. To abolish that trade would be to

——shut the gates of mercy on mankind.

[From *Life of Johnson* [1791], ed. George Birkbeck Hill (Oxford: Clarendon Press, 1934), Vol. III: 202–4.]

H. J. NIEBOER

27   Slavery as an Industrial System

Open and closed resources

We have said that among agricultural peoples slavery, as an industrial system, only exists where there is still free land; it disappears as soon as all land has been appropriated. We have also seen that slavery does not prevail to any considerable extent where subsistence is dependent on capital. We may now combine these two conclusions into this general rule: *slavery, as an industrial system, is not likely to exist where subsistence depends on material resources which are present in limited quantity.*

A tribe or nation cannot subsist without labour (though the amount of labour required is sometimes small); but, besides this, material resources are always necessary. The resources which man uses to procure his subsistence are of two kinds: gifts of nature, and products of human labour. The latter are commonly termed capital; their supply is always limited. Most of the former (air, water, the heat of the sun, etc.) exist in unlimited quantity, *i.e.* there is so much of them that nobody wants to appropriate them. Land is also a gift of nature, and in some very thinly peopled countries, where there is much more fertile ground than can be cultivated, it has not any more value than air and water. But as all land has not the same properties, it soon comes to pass that the most fertile and most favourably situated land is appropriated by some men to the exclusion of others. This is the origin of rent. Finally, when the less valuable grounds have also been appropriated, free land no longer exists; there is no piece of land but has its definite owner. This last state of things has social consequences very similar to those which exist where subsistence depends on capital. In both cases indispensable means of production are in the hands of definite persons; therefore a man destitute either of land or of capital (according as subsistence depends on the former or the latter), cannot subsist independently of the owners, but has to apply to them for employment. Moreover, in both cases more than a limited quantity of labour cannot be profitably employed: the owner of capital, or of a limited space of land, cannot derive any profit from employing more than a certain number of labourers. Therefore in either case slavery, as an industrial system, is not likely to exist.

These considerations lead us to an important conclusion. All the peoples of the earth, whether they subsist by hunting, fishing, cattle-breeding, agriculture, trade or manufactures, may be divided into two categories. Among the peoples of the first category the means of subsistence are open to all; every one who is able-bodied and not defective in mind can provide for himself independently of any capitalist or landlord. Among some of these peoples capital is of some use, and some valuable lands are already held as property; but those who are destitute of such advantages can perfectly well do without them, for there are still abundant natural supplies open to them. Among the peoples of the other category subsistence depends on resources of which the supply is limited, and therefore people destitute of these resources are dependent on the owners. It may be convenient to suggest technical names for these two categories. We shall speak of *peoples with open resources* and *peoples with closed resources*. We think the meaning of these terms is clear, and they may be convenient for use. The distinction is an important one. We suppose we have sufficiently proved that the relations between the social classes differ largely, according as resources are open or closed: only among peoples with open resources can slavery and serfdom exist, whereas free labourers dependent on wages are only found among peoples with closed resources. Our distinction may prove valuable in other respects also, *e.g.* over-population and lack of employment are unknown among peoples with open resources; war, which, when resources are open, has sometimes rather the character of a sport, becomes more serious when resources have become closed, for then its object is to extend the supply of land or capital at the cost of the enemy; pessimism is more likely to prevail among peoples with closed than among peoples with open resources, etc.

[. . .]

The different ways in which people become slaves

There are:
    1. Slaves by birth;
    2. Free-born people who become slaves.

In connection with the former point it may be inquired what is in each case the status of children born of two slaves, of a male slave and a free woman, of a female slave and a free man, and especially of a female slave and her master. This inquiry will enable us to find, whether and to what extent slaves are merged in the general population.

The manners in which free-born people become slaves may be distinguished according as slaves are acquired from without or within the limits of the tribe. This reminds us of the distinction we have made between extratribal and intratribal slavery. We may inquire then which of these two forms of slavery appears first. If we should find that extratribal is older than intratribal slavery (which does not seem unlikely), we might examine the economic and social conditions under which intratribal slavery can exist.

Extratribal slaves become such by:

1. Capture in war or kidnapping. Here a wide field of research opens itself. Captives, when they are not enslaved, are killed (eaten, sacrificed), or exchanged after peace has been concluded, or ransomed by their country-men, or adopted into the tribe of the captors. It may be inquired whether any of these modes of treatment can have gradually led to enslavement of the captives (*e.g.* captives are first adopted, and gradually differentiated from the born members of the tribe; or they are first eaten, then preserved to be eaten later on and in the meantime set to work, and finally employed as slaves and no longer eaten). Several of these modes of treatment coexist with slavery (*e.g.* some captives are sacrificed and the rest kept as slaves; or slaves are occasionally sacrificed); does this only occur in the early stages of slavery, and indicate that slavery has not yet fully developed? When is slavery an object, and when is it only an incident of warfare? A remarkable phenomenon, worth a close investigation, is the occurrence of extratribal slavery or adop-tion of aliens together with a preventive check on population (infanticide, abortion). When captives are enslaved, it is worth inquiring in what manner they are distributed among the captors; this will have a strong influence on the division of wealth.

2. Purchase. The prices paid for different classes of slaves show what slaves are most desired (men or women, people of different ages or nationalities). The slaves sold have often been captured by the sellers; but it also occurs that people are sold by their countrymen, especially criminals. Here we may notice the influence of the slave-trade on penal law; people are probably often sold abroad, who otherwise would have been killed or expelled from the community.

Intratribal slaves become such (so far as we know) in the following ways:

1. For non-payment of a debt. Here the general treatment of debtors and the extent to which the rights of creditors are acknowledged by the com-munity are worth examining. Debtor-slaves have often, but not always, a right to become free by paying off the debt. In some cases the creditor does not keep the debtor as a slave, but recovers his money by selling him abroad.

2. As a punishment, either directly, or when the *wergild* is not paid. This subject might be treated in connection with Professor Steinmetz's investiga-tions of early penal law. Criminals often become slaves of the chief or king; a study of this matter would lead to an inquiry into political institutions at large.

3. By marrying a male or female slave. Here we may inquire where and to what extent *connubium* between free people and slaves exists.

4. By offering themselves as slaves, or selling themselves. In the former case it has always carefully to be inquired whether such persons become slaves or voluntary servants; the latter is quite possible, and the terminology of our informants not always reliable, as we have seen when speaking of Oceania. When they really become slaves, there are probably open resources. It is then worth inquiring what can be the reason why, while resources are open and so everybody is able to provide for himself, there are people who throw themselves upon the mercy of men of power.

5. Finally, orphans and other helpless persons are sometimes enslaved.

The different ways in which people cease to be slaves

1. Redemption. Here the question presents itself, where slaves, or certain categories of slaves, have a right to be redeemed.

2. Emancipation. Where, and under what social conditions does this custom prevail, and where is it of frequent occurrence? What are the motives that induce the master to set his slave free? Emancipation as a substitute for sacrifice.

3. Adoption. Connected with this is the fact that in some countries slaves sometimes succeed to their masters' goods. Here we may ask whether or not such adoption and right on inheritance are only found in early stages and have to be regarded as survivals of adoption of aliens.

4. Marriage of a slave with a free person, especially of a female slave with her master.

5. Dedication to a god. Slaves can sometimes become free by devoting themselves to some deity. Further details; power of the priesthood; compare the influence of the church in the Middle Ages.

In whatever way slaves become free, the position of the *liberti* deserves a separate consideration. Are they on a level with free-born men, or do they form a separate class? Do their descendants gradually become merged in the general population?

[From *Slavery as an Industrial System* [1900] (New York: Burt Franklin, 1971), 383–6, 428–31.]

WINTHROP D. JORDAN

28   **White over Black**

Thinking about freedom and bondage in Tudor England was confused and self-contradictory. In a period of social dislocation there was considerable disagreement among contemporary observers as to what actually was going on and even as to what ought to be. Ideas about personal freedom tended to run both ahead of and behind actual social conditions. Both statute and common law were sometimes considerably more than a century out of phase with actual practice and with commonly held notions about servitude.

[. . .]

3. The concept of slavery

At first glance, one is likely to see merely a fog of inconsistency and vagueness enveloping the terms *servant* and *slave* as they were used both in England and in seventeenth-century America. When Hamlet declaims 'O what a rogue and peasant slave am I,' the term seems to have a certain elasticity. When Peter Heylyn defines it in 1627 as 'that ignominious word, *Slave*; whereby we use to call ignoble fellowes, and the more base sort of people,' the term seems useless as a key to a specific social status. And when we find in the American colonies a reference in 1665 to 'Jacob a negro slave and servant to Nathaniel Utye,' it is tempting to regard slavery as having been in the first half of the seventeenth century merely a not very elevated sort of servitude.

In one sense it was, since the concept embodied in the terms *servitude*, *service*, and *servant* was widely embrocive. *Servant* was more a generic term than *slave*. Slaves could be 'servants'—as they were eventually and ironically to become in the ante-bellum South—but servants *should not* be 'slaves'. This injunction, which was common in England, suggests a measure of precision in the concept of slavery. In fact there was a large measure which merits closer inspection.

First of all, the 'slave's' loss of freedom was complete. 'Of all men which be destitute of libertie or freedome,' explained Henry Swinburne in his *Briefe Treatise of Testaments and Last Willes* (1590), 'the slave is in greatest subjection, for a slave is that person which is in servitude or bondage to an other, even against nature.' 'Even his children,' moreover, '. . . are infected with the Leprosie of his father's bondage.' Swinburne was at pains to distinguish this condition from that of the villein, whom he likened to the *Ascriptitius Glebæ* of the civil law, 'one that is ascrited or assigned to a ground or farme, for the perpetuall tilling or manuring thereof'. 'A villeine,' he insisted, 'howsoever he may seeme like unto a slave, yet his bondage is not so great.' Swinburne's was the prevailing view of bond slavery; only the preciseness of emphasis was unusual. At law, much more clearly than in literary usage, 'bond slavery' implied utter deprivation of liberty.

Slavery was also thought of as a perpetual condition. While it had not yet come invariably to mean lifetime labor, it was frequently thought of in those terms. Except sometimes in instances of punishment for crime, slavery was open ended; in contrast to servitude, it did not involve a definite term of years. Slavery was perpetual also in the sense that it was often thought of as hereditary. It was these dual aspects of perpetuity which were to assume such importance in America.

So much was slavery a complete loss of liberty that it seemed to English-men somehow akin to loss of humanity. No theme was more persistent than the claim that to treat a man as a slave was to treat him as a beast. Almost half a century after Sir Thomas Smith had made this connection a Puritan divine was condemning masters who used 'their servants as slaves, or rather as beasts' while Captain John Smith was moaning about being captured by the Turks and 'all sold for slaves, like beasts in a market-place'. No analogy could have better demonstrated how strongly Englishmen felt about total loss of personal freedom.

[. . .]

Indians too seemed radically different from Englishmen, far more so than any Europeans. They were enslaved, like Negroes, and so fell on the losing side of a crucial dividing line. It is easy to see why: whether considered in terms of complexion, religion, nationality, savagery, bestiality, or geo-graphical location, Indians were more like Negroes than like Englishmen. Given this resemblance the essential problem becomes why Indian slavery never became an important institution in the colonies. Why did Indian slav-ery remain numerically insignificant and typically incidental in character? Why were Indian slaves valued at much lower prices than Negroes? Why were Indians, as a kind of people, treated like Negroes and yet at the same time very differently?

Certain obvious factors made for important differentiations in the minds of the English colonists. As was the case with first confrontations in America and Africa, the different contexts of confrontation made Englishmen more interested in converting and civilizing Indians than Negroes. That this cam-paign in America too frequently degenerated into military campaigns of extermination did nothing to eradicate the initial distinction. Entirely apart from English intentions, the culture of the American Indians probably meant that they were less readily enslavable than Africans. By comparison, they were less used to settled agriculture, and their own variety of slavery was probably even less similar to the chattel slavery which Englishmen practiced in America than was the domestic and political slavery of the West African cultures. But it was the transformation of English intentions in the wilder-ness which counted most heavily in the long run. The Bible and the treaty so often gave way to the clash of flintlock and tomahawk. The colonists' percep-tions of the Indians came to be organized not only in pulpits and printshops but at the bloody cutting edge of the English thrust into the Indians' lands. Thus the most pressing and mundane circumstances worked to make Indians seem very different from Negroes. In the early years especially, Indians were in a position to mount murderous reprisals upon the English settlers, while the few scattered Negroes were not. When English-Indian relations did not turn upon sheer power they rested on diplomacy. In many instances the colonists took assiduous precautions to prevent abuse of Indians belonging to friendly tribes. Most of the Indians enslaved by the English had their own tribal enemies to thank. It became a common practice to ship Indian slaves to the West Indies where they could be exchanged for slaves who had no compatriots lurking on the outskirts of English settlements. In contrast, Negroes presented much less of a threat—at first.

[. . .]

And [D]ifference, surely, was the indispensable key to the degradation of Negroes in English America. In scanning the problem of *why* Negroes were enslaved in America, certain constant elements in a complex situation can be readily, if roughly, identified. It may be taken as given that there would have been no enslavement without economic need, that is, without persistent demand for labor in underpopulated colonies. Of crucial importance, too, was the fact that for cultural reasons Negroes were relatively helpless in the face of European aggressiveness and technology. In themselves, however, these two elements will not explain the enslavement of Indians and Negroes. The pressing exigency in America was labor, and Irish and English servants were available. Most of them would have been helpless to ward off outright enslavement if their masters had thought themselves privileged and able to enslave them. As a group, though, masters did not think themselves so empowered. Only with Indians and Negroes did Englishmen attempt so radical a deprivation of liberty—which brings the matter abruptly to the most difficult and imponderable question of all: what was it about Indians and Negroes which set them apart, which rendered them *different* from Englishmen, which made them special candidates for degradation?

[. . .] The heathen condition of the Negroes seemed of considerable importance to English settlers in America—more so than to English voyagers upon the coasts of Africa—and that heathenism was associated in some settlers' minds with the condition of slavery.

[. . .]

The importance and persistence of the tradition which attached slavery to heathenism did not become evident in any positive assertions that heathens might be enslaved. It was not until the period of legal establishment of slavery after 1660 that the tradition became manifest at all, and even then there was no effort to place heathenism and slavery on a one-for-one relationship. Virginia's second statutory definition of a slave (1682), for example, awkwardly attempted to rest enslavement on religious difference while excluding from possible enslavement all heathens who were not Indian or Negro. Despite such logical difficulties, the old European equation of slavery and religious difference did not rapidly vanish in America, for it cropped up repeatedly after 1660 in assertions that slaves by becoming Christian did not automatically become free. By about the end of the seventeenth century, Maryland, New York, Virginia, North and South Carolina, and New Jersey had all passed laws reassuring masters that conversion of their slaves did not necessitate manumission.

[From *White over Black: American Attitudes Toward the Negro 1550–1812* [1968] (Baltimore: Penguin, 1971), 48–9, 52–4, 89–92.]

EDMUND S. MORGAN

29 American Slavery, American Freedom

Slavery is a mode of compulsion that has often prevailed where land is abundant, and Virginians had been drifting toward it from the time when they first found something profitable to work at. Servitude in Virginia's tobacco fields approached closer to slavery than anything known at the time in England. Men served longer, were subjected to more rigorous punishments, were traded about as commodities already in the 1620s.

[. . .]

But to establish slavery in Virginia it was not necessary to enslave anyone. Virginians had only to buy men who were already enslaved, after the initial risks of the transformation had been sustained by others elsewhere. They converted to slavery simply by buying slaves instead of servants. The process seems so simple, the advantages of slave labor so obvious, and their system of production and attitude toward workers so receptive that it seems surprising they did not convert sooner. African slaves were present in Virginia, as we have seen, almost from the beginning (probably the first known Negroes to arrive, in 1619, were slaves). The courts clearly recognized property in men and women and their unborn progeny at least as early as the 1640s, and there was no law to prevent any planter from bringing in as many as he wished. Why, then, did Virginians not furnish themselves with slaves as soon as they began to grow tobacco? Why did they wait so long?

The answer lies in the fact that slave labor, in spite of its seeming superiority, was actually not as advantageous as indentured labor during the first half of the century. Because of the high mortality among immigrants to Virginia, there could be no great advantage in owning a man for a lifetime rather than a period of years, especially since a slave cost roughly twice as much as an indentured servant. If the chances of a man's dying during his first five years in Virginia were better than fifty-fifty—and it seems apparent that they were—and if English servants could be made to work as hard as slaves, English servants for a five-year term were the better buy.

[. . .]

With slavery Virginians could exceed all their previous efforts to maximize productivity. In the first half of the century, as they sought to bring stability to their volatile society, they had identified work as wealth, time as money, but there were limits to the amount of both work and time that could be extracted from a servant. There was no limit to the work or time that a master could command from his slaves, beyond his need to allow them enough for eating and sleeping to enable them to keep working.

[. . .]

Demographically, too, the conversion to slavery enhanced Virginia's capacity for maximum productivity. Earlier the heavy concentration in the population of men of working age had been achieved by the small number of women and children among the immigrants and by the heavy mortality. But with women outliving men, the segment of women and their children grew; and as mortality declined the segment of men beyond working age grew. There was, in other words, an increase in the non-productive proportion of the population. Slavery made possible the restoration and maintenance of a highly productive population. Masters had no hesitation about putting slave women to work in the tobacco fields, although servant women were not normally so employed. And they probably made slave children start work earlier than free children did. There was no need to keep them from work for purposes of education. Nor was it necessary to divert productive energy to the support of ministers for spiritual guidance to them and their parents. The slave population could thus be more productive than a free population with the same age and sex structure would have been. It could also be more reproductive than a free population that grew mainly from the importation of servants, because slave traders generally carried about two women for every three men, a larger proportion of women by far than had been the case with servants. Slave women while employed in tobacco could still raise children and thus contribute to the growth of the productive proportion of the population. Moreover, the children became the property of the master. Thus slaves offered the planter a way of disposing his profits that combined the advantages of cattle and of servants, and these had always been the most attractive investments in Virginia.

[. . .]

It has been possible thus far to describe Virginia's conversion to slavery without mentioning race. It has required a little restraint to do so, but only a little, because the actions that produced slavery in Virginia, the individual purchase of slaves instead of servants, and the public protection of masters in their coercion of unwilling labor, had no necessary connection with race. Virginians did not enslave the persons brought there by the Royal African Company or by the private traders. The only decision that Virginians had to make was to keep them as slaves. Keeping them as slaves did require some decisions about what masters could legally do to make them work. But such decisions did not necessarily relate to race.

Or did they? As one reads the record of the Lancaster court authorizing

Robert Carter to chop off the toes of his slaves, one begins to wonder. Would the court, could the court, could the general assembly have authorized such a punishment for an incorrigible English servant? It seems unlikely that the English government would have allowed it. But Virginians could be confident that England would condone their slave laws, even though those laws were contrary to the laws of England.

The English government had considered the problem in 1679, when presented with the laws of Barbados, in which masters were similarly authorized to inflict punishment that would not have been allowed by English law. A legal adviser, upon reviewing the laws for the Lords of Trade, found that he could approve them, because, he said 'although Negroes in that Island are punishable in a different and more severe manner than other Subjects are for Offences of the like nature; yet I humbly conceive that the Laws there concerning Negros are reasonable Laws, for by reason of their numbers they become dangerous, and being a brutish sort of People and reckoned as goods and chattels in that Island, it is of necessity or at least convenient to have Laws for the Government of them different from the Laws of England, to prevent the great mischief that otherwise may happen to the Planters and Inhabitants in that Island'.

It was not necessary to extend the rights of Englishmen to Africans, because Africans were 'a brutish sort of people'. And because they were 'brutish' it was necessary 'or at least convenient' to kill or maim them in order to make them work.

[From *American Slavery, American Freedom: The Ordeal of Colonial Virginia*
(New York: Norton, 1975), 296–8, 309–10, 313–14.]

RICHARD HELLIE

30   Slavery in Russia

[I]n Muscovy, as in Ancient Mesopotamia, a certain portion of the slaves and their descendants were prisoners of war. Unlike Europe in the Middle Ages and the New World, Muscovy got few slaves generated by other peoples and transmitted to it by the slave trade. Rebellion by peoples subjugated by the Muscovites, such as the various Turkic peoples, could very well have had as its consequence the enslavement of those peoples upon their reconquest. [. . .] It was also true elsewhere that rebellion on the part of peoples of a different race was punished with slavery, as in the Middle Ages, for the conquered Moslems in Spain, and for Amerindians who revolted against European subjugation. [. . .] Tatars for much of Muscovite history were a special category of people, who could be 'outsiders' or 'insiders,' depending upon the circumstances. They could be captured and registered as slaves by their captors, or they could be purchased in the Don frontier area and then registered as slave property. [. . .]

The sale into slavery of children that parents did not want or were unable to provide for was not a rare event in the history of mankind, especially in societies that experienced frequent shortfalls of food, as did Muscovy. For centuries the Chinese (often illegally) and Indians sold children when food was short as a result of conditions ranging from widespread natural calamities to individual improvidence. However, instances of the sale by Muscovite parents of their children were very rare, less than ten being recorded. Instead of selling their children, the Muscovites seemed to have preferred to let them die [. . .] The reasons for that preference can only be speculated on. Certainly, there was no legal prohibition against the selling of offspring: it was illegal for people under fifteen to sell themselves, a prohibition known to have been violated only in the depths of the 1601–3 famine, but nothing was ever written forbidding parents to sell their children. It is also possible that the market for children simply was very small.

[. . .]

It should be of considerable comparative interest to discover how the Muscovites managed to violate so flagrantly a fundamental social science law, the law that, in the words of Moses I. Finley, 'no society could withstand the tension inherent in enslaving its own people'. The concept of 'outsider' is sometimes a relative one, as for example, in some African and Hindu situations, and one of the problems in studying Muscovite slavery is to determine how much explanatory power the notion has for the Muscovite situation. The oddity of Russians enslaving their own kind was observed by mid-nineteenth-century foreign commentators on serfdom, but even that anomaly seems to have been ignored by students of Russians history until the recent work of Peter Kolchin. On the other hand, the contrast between Hitler, who fundamentally abused 'outsiders,' and Stalin, whose primary targets were Soviets, has been noted both in the U.S.S.R. and abroad.

As I now perceive this problem of understanding how the Russians were able to enslave their own kin, it is one of determining the social distance between the slaveowner and his chattel. As David Brion Davis has observed, 'slavery ultimately depends on real or simulated ethnic barriers.'

[. . .]

[M]uch of the peculiar quality of Muscovite slavery, the fact that most of the slaves were natives, must be at least partially attributable to a fundamental lack of ethnic identity and cohesion among the inhabitants of Muscovy.

[. . .]

The consequence of this diversity seems to have been that the in-group ethnic bonding ties were minimized, and the in-group–out-group consciousness was simply overwhelmed by diversity. What this meant was that for the Muscovites, ethnically, there was no such thing as an 'outsider,' for any outsider simply by presence or a verbal declaration could immediately be an 'insider'. In the practical world, this was most evident in the absolute freedom natives of both the upper and lower classes felt about establishing marriage ties with any foreigner, whether a Pole, Tatar, or Georgian. This meant that a Russian woman could be purchased by a Tatar with second thoughts by no one. This also meant that the insider-outsider identification process was very localized, as in the 1930s when Belorussians still recognized no common bond with anything outside their native village—a phenomenon that certainly can be projected back to Muscovy.

[From *Slavery in Russia, 1450–1725* (Chicago: University of Chicago Press, 1982), 370–1, 386–90, 392.]

ORLANDO PATTERSON

31 Slavery and Social Death

Enslavement by birth was, naturally, the consequence of earlier forms of enslavement, but in all societies where the institution acquired more than marginal significance and persisted for more than a couple of generations, birth became the single most important source of slaves. Of the great majority of slaveholding societies the stronger claim may be made that birth during *most* periods was the source of *most* slaves.

The discussion of other means of enslavement has implied estimates of the relative significance of birth, which will not be repeated. However, in view of certain common misconceptions concerning the capacity of slaves to reproduce themselves, a few crucial remarks may clear up some popular confusions. First, it is essential to distinguish between the biological and the social reproduction of a slave population. By 'biological' I refer to the capacity of a slave population to produce a number of persons equal to or greater than itself, whatever the status of the succeeding generation. The only issue is whether the total number of deaths is balanced or exceeded by the total number of births. By 'social' reproduction of a slave population I refer to the degree to which it is able to reproduce itself when, in addition to birth and death, nonnatural factors are taken into account, the most important being manumission and the immigration/emigration rates.

[. . .] [M]ost slave populations had high manumission rates. One major consequence was that many slave populations that were biologically self-reproductive were nonetheless socially *non*reproductive, because of the social leakage of persons from slave to 'free' status. This was the case with many (perhaps most) Islamic slave societies and with most of the Spanish-American slave societies during the eighteenth century. The Mexican and Peruvian populations, for example, virtually disappeared by the end of the eighteenth century not because they were not biologically reproductive, but because of the social loss due to manumission.

A second important point is that where there is a large influx of externally acquired slaves, the claim that a slave population is nonreproductive may well be based on a demographic illusion. In such situations the excess of deaths over births may be entirely a function of the abnormal age structure of the population brought about by the large number of adults—especially adult males—in the population. It is not incorrect, but it is certainly misleading, to say that such populations fail to reproduce themselves naturally. Age-specific mortality and fertility rates may be quite normal. This was true, for instance, of the Cuban and English-speaking slave populations during the nineteenth century. The failure to distinguish between age-specific and general rates of birth and death has led to unwarranted generalizations about slave populations' failing to reproduce out of despair with their lot. True, there have been a few such cases but they are rare in the annals of human slavery. The instinct to reproduce usually triumphs over despair, so that the exceptional cases become all the more poignant. Which were these exceptional cases? The one unambiguous instance is Jamaica during the second half of the eighteenth century. Here all the available data suggest that not only was the mortality rate abnormally high but, more extraordinarily, slave women absolutely refused to reproduce—partly out of despair and outrage, as a form of gynecological revolt against the system, and to a lesser extent because of peculiar lactation practices. The other exceptional cases we can only guess at, given the poor quality of the available evidence. From the ancient world the slave population of rural Rome during the last two centuries of the republic seems likely, as from the modern world does the slave population of the coffee region of Brazil during the nineteenth century.

A third point to be stressed is that even if a slave population is biologically nonreproductive, birth may still remain the single most important source of slaves. There is a tendency among historians to leap from the (correct) observation that birth failed to meet the total demand for slaves to the (often incorrect) assertion that other factors were more important. The simple mathematics of reproduction contradict this thesis. The traditional view of historians of ancient Rome that 'most of the need for slaves' was met by birth after the completion of the aggressive wars in the early empire has recently been sharply disputed. I do not have enough information on ancient Rome to argue the issue in meaningful statistical terms, but the experience of Jamaica during the eighteenth century may be instructive. We have already observed that the Jamaican slave population during most of the eighteenth century was unusual for its biological and social nonreproductivity. Between the end of the seventeenth century and the middle of the eighteenth, the enormous growth of the slave population was due to the massive importation of slaves

from Africa. Males outnumbered females to a degree greater than any estimate ever suggested for the slave population of imperial Rome. And yet by
the end of the 1760s Creole slaves outnumbered Africans. In other words, in
spite of a demographic environment significantly worse than that of Rome
during the period of the early empire, birth remained the most important
source of slaves. Thus the comparative data strongly support the traditional
view expressed by historians such as W. W. Buckland and R. H. Barrow that
birth was 'in historic times, by far the most important of the causes of
slavery'.

Let us turn now to the more important factors that influence the social
reproduction of slave populations, specifically the social and legal patterns
affecting the inheritance of slave status. The manner in which birth determined status was exceedingly complex, varying across cultures as well as
within the same society over time. What complicates the issue is the fact that
in all slave societies in which the number of slaves was of any significance,
free persons interbred with slaves, thus making it difficult to determine the
status of the offspring of mixed parentage. Sometimes these were free, sometimes slave: sometimes they occupied an intermediate status, depending on
the sex, status, and power of the free parent as well as the relationship
between father and mother. A consideration of the factors determining slave
status at birth cannot be divorced from those determining free status, since
once slavery was established not all persons born free were necessarily the
children of parents both of whom were free.

There were five ways in which slave status was determined by birth: (1) by
the mother only, regardless of the father's status: (2) by the father only,
regardless of the mother's status; (3) by the mother *or* the father, whoever had
the higher status; (4) by the mother or the father, whoever had the lower
status; and (5) by neither, the child always being free regardless of the status
of either or both parents. The last case, of course, refers to incipient (non-
hereditary) slavery and is not, strictly speaking, genuine slavery as we understand and use the term. Such cases are, however, important in any attempt to
comprehend the origins of slavery. Next we observe that where both parents
were free, there were several possibilities for determining the status of the
child, for a *category* of free persons may be determined by birth through, or
inherited from, the mother only (matrilineal societies); the father only (patrilineal societies); both parents (double unilineal and bilateral): or optionally
from either parent, that of the one with the more favorable status being
stressed.

[. . .]

External trade

External trade always played a major role in the indirect acquisition of slaves. Few would challenge this statement in the case of the advanced premodern and modern slave systems. What may seem surprising, however, is that it holds too for the most primitive of the societies where slavery was important.

Slaves often constituted the earliest article of trade, especially of external and long-distance trade, among primitive peoples. The only commodity simple peoples could usually offer to more advanced peoples for the luxury goods they desired was fellow human beings. This becomes evident in studies of the indigenous West African markets and trade. Summarizing the findings of his own work and that of his colleagues, Claude Meillassoux concludes that the slave was both a commodity and a producer in West Africa. Sometimes the slave was involved with trade purely as a commodity, especially in the destructive trade with the Europeans. In intra-African trade, the slave figured both as commodity and as producer. Slaves were also vital in long-distance overland commerce as porters and in the capture of more slaves. This, however, was true mainly of the more advanced societies. In the simpler lineage-based communities 'goods circulate through a network of kinship, affinity, and clientage, through prestation, redistribution, or gift exchange. Wealth as an instrument of social control is a privilege of rank or of birth'. In such small-scale communities trade was sometimes a threat to the established order and was therefore circumscribed. Hence imported goods 'acquire a social and political content which makes it difficult to transform them into trade commodities'. Slaves were prestige goods and at best a 'means of social reproduction,' rarely a means of production. In the Sudan the use of slaves as producers for external trade was always accompanied by the rise of both a warrior and a merchant class.

[. . .]

It should by now be clear that slavery was intricately tied up with the origins of trade itself, especially long-distance trade, the bartering of slaves for prestige goods often being the sole form of commercial activity. As the demand for slaves grew, slave trading systems expanded in both organizational complexity and distance between areas of recruitment and areas of use.

Throughout recorded history, even to the first half of this century, slave-trading systems have always existed to meet the widespread demand for slaves. Five systems stand out in terms of the volume of trade and the distances involved: the Indian Ocean; the Black Sea and Mediterranean; the medieval European; the trans-Saharan; and the transatlantic.

[. . .]

The interesting thing about slaves is that in many primitive and archaic societies they constituted the closest approximation to modern multifunctional money. In the ancient Near East, slaves were sometimes used instead of metal as a standard of value and a medium of payment for (among other things) brides, houses, and fines. In Burmese society until a century ago slaves 'were the currency in which a husband was compensated for the violation of his wife—two slaves for a poor but free woman, four for the wife of a merchant, eight for that of a rich man, fifteen for that of a lesser mandarin, and so forth'.

[From *Slavery and Social Death: A Comparative Study* (Cambridge, MA: Harvard University Press, 1982), 132–4, 148–9, 168.]

BERNARD LEWIS

32   **Race and Color in Islam**

2. A factor of importance was the wider range of experience which conquest brought to the Arabs. Before Islam, their acquaintance with Africa was substantially limited to Ethiopia, a country with a relatively high level of moral and material civilization. During the life time of the Prophet the good reputation of the Ethiopians was further increased by the kindly welcome afforded to Muslim refugees from Mecca. After the conquests however there were changes. Advancing on the one hand into Africa and on the other into southwest Asia the Arabs encountered fairer-skinned peoples who were more advanced and darker-skinned peoples who were more primitive. No doubt as a result of this they began to equate the two facts.

3. Coupled with this expansion was the third major development of the early Islamic centuries—slavery and the slave trade. The Arab Muslims were not the first to enslave black Africans. Even in Pharaonic times Egyptians had already begun to capture and use black African slaves, and some are indeed depicted on Egyptian monuments. There were black slaves in the Hellenistic and Roman worlds—but they seem to have been few and relatively unimportant. The massive development of the slave trade in black Africa and the large-scale importation of black Africans for use in the Mediterranean and Middle Eastern countries seem to date from the Arab period. Inevitably, it influenced Arab (and therefore Muslim) attitudes to the peoples of darker skin whom most Arabs and Muslims encountered only in this way.

To the Muslims—as to the people of every other civilization known to history—the civilized world meant themselves. They alone possessed enlightenment and the true faith; the outside world was inhabited by barbarians and infidels. However, in this outside world which lay beyond the vast borders of the Islamic oecumene, the Muslims recognized certain distinctions. To the East there were India and China, countries which were pagan but which were nevertheless respected as possessing some civilized attributes. To the West lay Christendom, first Byzantine then European, recognized as a rival faith, a rival culture, and a rival world order. Apart from these there were the northern and the southern barbarians; the white barbarians of the North, Turks, Slavs, and their like, and the dark-skinned barbarians of the South, in Black Africa.

Both were seen primarily as sources of slaves—to be imported into the Islamic world, moulded in Islamic ways, and, since they possessed no religion of their own worth the mention, natural recruits for Islam. For these peoples, enslavement was thus a benefaction, and was indeed often accepted as such. This attitude is exemplified in the story of a black pagan king who is tricked and kidnapped by Muslim guests whom he has befriended, and sold into slavery in Arabia. Meeting them again years later, he shows contempt but no resentment, since they had been the means of bringing him to Islam.

[. . .]

White slaves were rarely used for rough labor, and filled higher positions in domestic and administrative employment. Both blacks and whites were used as eunuchs, but the blacks soon predominated. The Caliph al-Amīn (reg. 809–813), it is said, collected them in large numbers, and formed separate corps of white and black eunuchs, which he called 'the locusts' (jarrādiyya) and 'the ravens' (ghurābiyya). An Arabic description of the court of the caliph in Baghdad at the beginning of the tenth century speaks of 7,000 black and 4,000 white eunuchs. Later, white eunuchs became rare and costly.

The military slave, so prominent a figure in Islamic history, is overwhelmingly white. In the East he is usually of Turkish origin, in the West of Slavic or other European origin.

Black military slaves are not unknown and indeed at certain periods were of importance. Black soldiers appear occasionally in early Abbasid times, and after the slave rebellion in southern Iraq, in which blacks displayed terrifying military prowess, they were recruited in large numbers into the infantry corps of the caliphs in Baghdad. Aḥmad b. Ṭūlūn (d. 884), the first independent ruler of Muslim Egypt, relied very heavily on black slaves, probably Nubians, for his armed forces; at his death he is said to have left, among other possessions, 24,000 white mamlūks and 45,000 blacks.

[From Race and Color in Islam (New York: Harper and Row, 1971), 27–9, 68–9.]

The reason that slavery was widespread in Africa was not, as some have asserted, because Africa was an economically underdeveloped region in which forced labor had not yet been replaced by free labor. Instead, slavery was rooted in deep-seated legal and institutional structures of African societies, and it functioned quite differently from the way it functioned in European societies.

Slavery was widespread in Atlantic Africa because slaves were the only form of private, revenue-producing property recognized in African law. By contrast, in European legal systems, land was the primary form of private, revenue-producing property, and slavery was relatively minor. Indeed, owner-ship of land was usually a precondition in Europe to making productive use of slaves, at least in agriculture. Because of this legal feature, slavery was in many ways the functional equivalent of the landlord-tenant relationship in Europe and was perhaps as widespread.

Thus, it was the absence of landed private property—or, to be more pre-cise, it was the corporate ownership of land—that made slavery so pervasive an aspect of African society. Anthropologists have noted this feature among modern Africans, or those living in the so-called ethnographic present or traditional societies. Anthropologists have regarded the absence of private or personal ownership of landed property as unusual, because it departs from the European pattern and from the home cultural experience of most anthropological observers, and has therefore seemed to require an explanation.

For example, Jack Goody argued that technological backwardness and low population densities made land plentiful, and hence personal property in land had to await technological change. Likewise, he and others, perhaps influ-enced by European socialist thinking or the liberal economic notion of opportunity for all, argued that the absence of private property in land also meant an absence or at least a mitigation of exploitation and inequality.

The evidence, however, does not necessarily support such explanations. For example, African population densities in many areas were surely large enough to warrant division of land, if landed property is somehow the result of competition for land. The average density in seventeenth-century Lower Guinea (roughly the southern half of Ghana, Benin, Togo, and Nigeria) was probably well over thirty people per square kilometer, or well over the aver-age European density of the time. Indeed, the Capuchins who visited the area in 1662 regarded it as so populated it resembled 'a continuous and black anthill' and noted that 'this kingdom of Arda [Allada] and most of this region

[Lower Guinea] exceed in number and density [the population] of all other parts of the world'. Moreover, African societies surely did possess inequalities and exploitation, as we shall see.

One must remember that landownership is ultimately simply a legal fiction. Owning land in the end never amounts to more than owning dirt, and it is ownership of the product of the land that really matters. European land-owning actually established the right of the owner to claim the product or a rent on the product. Landownership was therefore really ownership of one of the factors of production, with a concomitant right to claim the product of the factor. The division of land was more the result of legal claims than simply a reaction to population pressure. In any case, population pressure itself has historically often been more the result of unequal landownership claims than a product of demography.

But there are other ways to establish a claim of social product, such as taxation (through the rights of the state or other corporate group) or slavery and other personal relations of dependency. Thus, just as ownership of land as a factor of production establishes a right to the product of that factor, so, too, ownership or control of labor (people or slaves) can provide the same right. African law established claims on product through taxation and slavery rather than through the fiction of landownership.

The African social system was thus not backward or egalitarian, but only legally divergent. Although the origins and ultimate significance of this divergence are a matter for further research, one important result was that it allowed African political and economic elites to sell large numbers of slaves to whoever would pay and thus fueled the Atlantic slave trade. This legal feature made slavery and slave trading widespread, and its role in producing secure wealth linked it to economic development.

Exploring this legal divergence can help to elucidate this important factor in African participation in the Atlantic economy. Sixteenth- and seventeenth-century European observers were fully aware that African societies were both politically and economically inegalitarian and that these inequalities were represented in social and legal structures. But their understanding of those social and legal structures was usually shaped by European terms and the institutions they represented. Thus, although some recognized the absence of landed private property, many made Africans into landholders in spite of themselves.

European witnesses, after all, came from an area where the concept of landownership and income based on its lease to tenants was the fundamental starting point of law. Church law on landed property placed its origin in ancient times and made it a universal principle of 'Natural Law'. The *Siete partidas*, the Castillian law code that formed the basis for most Iberian law and had a major impact even on modern law codes, argued that all land should have an owner and that if land was not owned by private persons, it ought to be owned by the state. Thus, productive resources would be divided up (the purpose of law being to allow everyone to 'know his own') so that people could derive their support and income from the production of their own part of these resources. Considerable space was devoted to specifying how ownership of land was established, to preventing tenants from claiming ownership of their landlord's land, and the like.

Coming from this background, the idea that land was not private property was inconceivable. One common way to reconcile African law and the concept that landed property was a natural and essential part of civilization was to describe land in Africa as being owned by the king (as a substitute for corporate ownership by the state). Hence, in 1602, the Dutch trader and traveler Pieter de Marees described the rulers of the Gold Coast as owners of the land, their income being a form of ground rent, and the Italian Capuchin missionary Giacinto Brugiotti da Vetralla spoke of royal ownership of all land in Kongo in 1659.

[. . .]

[T]he fact that military enslavement was by far the most significant method is important, for it means that rulers were not, for the most part, selling their own subjects but people whom they, at least, regarded as aliens. The fact that many exported slaves were recent captives means that they were drawn from those captured in the course of warfare who had not yet been given an alternative employment within Africa. In these cases, rulers were deciding to forgo the potential future use of these slaves. Some of the exports were slaves whom local masters wished to dispose of for one reason or another and those who had been captured locally by brigands or judicially enslaved.

[. . .]

The causes and motivations behind these wars are crucial for understanding the slave trade. Philip Curtin has examined the Senegambian slave trade of the eighteenth century and has proposed a schema for viewing African warfare that resulted in slave captures that can be fruitfully applied to the earlier period as well. He proposes that wars be classified as tending toward either an economic or a political model. In the economic model the wars were fought for the express purpose of acquiring slaves and perhaps to meet demands from European merchants; in the political model wars were fought for mostly political reasons, and slaves were simply a by-product that might yield a profit. Both models are seen as 'ideal types,' and individual wars might contain a mixture of motives, of course. On the whole, however, Curtin believes that the eighteenth-century Senegambian data support a political, rather than the economic, model.

Actually, discerning between an economic and a political model is not easy in practice. Consider the case of Portuguese Angola, a state seemingly founded on the premise of exporting slaves. Angola's wars ought to fit the economic model if any state's would. Yet many of Angola's wars, and the majority of the most lucrative ones in terms of acquiring slaves, had more or less clear-cut political motives. Portugal's early wars in Angola, for example, were as much for establishing a foothold in the area as for capturing slaves. In 1579, after all, the Portuguese were nearly driven out by the forces of Ndongo, and the wars between then and about 1595 were defensive as much as offensive.

[From *Africa and the Africans in the Making of the Atlantic World, 1400–1680* (Cambridge: Cambridge University Press, 1992), 74–7, 99–100.]

DAVID ELTIS

34   Europeans and the Rise and Fall of African Slavery

Of the many post-neolithic slave societies, those of the European-dominated Americas appear to have had the most obvious economic foundations. In the words of a recent, widely read survey, 'The Slaves of the New World were economic property, and the main motive for slaveholding was economic exploitation'. Historians are careful to distance themselves from purely economic theories of human behavior, but on this issue the distance is usually rather short. The often bitter debates on the nature and meaning of New World slavery have produced few since Adam Smith who questioned the basic motivation of the early plantation owners. Simply put, people from one continent forced those from a second continent to produce a narrow range of consumer goods in a third—having first found the third's native population inadequate to their purpose. Even those who have wrestled with the relationship between racism and slavery have seen the racial basis of American slavery primarily as an economic phenomenon. Eric Williams, Oscar Handlin, Carl Degler, Winthrop Jordan, William McKee Evans, and others may disagree on the origins of racism but not on the origins of racial slavery in the Americas. Slaves from Africa were used to grow sugar and other plantation crops, it has been argued, because they comprised the least-cost option. Even George Frederickson, the historian who has perhaps looked furthest beyond class and economics for the sources of racism, has written that if white slavery had appeared profitable, it would have been introduced. And, indeed, everything we know about early modern European commercial elites and planters would support such an interpretation. Whatever our definition of capitalism, we would expect such elites to have used the cheapest option possible within the limits of mercantilist policies.

But did this in fact happen? It has become clear in recent years that economic paradigms have limited usefulness in explaining the ending of slavery. The number of slaveholders who voluntarily converted their slaves into wage-earning laborers in order to increase profits was not large, nor were the numbers of non-slaveholders who benefited directly from abolition. The major studies of abolition now draw rather heavily on the cultural and ideological spheres of human activity. Yet the origins of the system are in need of a similar reassessment. What follows is an attempt at a fresh examination of slavery in the Americas that suggests economics, narrowly defined, is no more capable of explaining its origins than its abolition. Put differently, the question is not why slavery per se but rather which groups are considered eligible for enslavement and why this eligibility changes over time.

Slavery until recently was universal in two senses. Most settled societies incorporated the institution into their social structures, and few peoples in the world have not constituted a major source of slaves at one time or another. The African component may dominate interpretations of slavery in the Atlantic world and, from somewhat earlier, in the Islamic world, but the more fundamental question from a longer and wider view is what separates outsiders—those who are eligible for enslavement—from insiders, who are not. Thus Nathan Huggins has answered the often-asked question of how Africans could enslave other Africans and sell them into the slave trade with the astute response that the enslavers did not see themselves or their victims as Africans. Richard Hellie has made the same point differently in writing about the efforts of slaveowners in sixteenth-century Russia to claim spurious foreign origins for themselves so that the enslaved could be held at a distance. The question of why certain groups are deemed more appropriate than others for enslavement and the degree to which their status can be changed are of interest to anthropologists studying non-Western societies more often than historians and economists. However, posing such questions in the European rather than the Asian, African, and indigenous American contexts promises some new insights.

If almost all societies in Europe, Africa, and the Americas, and, indeed, in the rest of the world, accepted slavery at the time of the Columbian contact, they had very different definitions of 'outsider' status.

[. . .]

If we wish to understand the origins of African slavery in the New World, or indeed in the pre-Columbian Old World, we must first explore the labor options of early modern Europeans—both those that were tried and those that were not. Second, we need to assess how close Europeans came to imposing slavery or slave-like conditions on other Europeans, and, finally, what for them set slavery apart as a status for others. These steps will help clarify the cultural and ideological parameters that at once shaped the evolution of African New World slavery and kept Europeans as non-slaves. Various forms of European forced labor were in fact tried. A comparison of these options across national boundaries reveals differences in what major European colonial powers considered feasible as labor regimes. Yet no West

European power after the late Middle Ages crossed the basic divide separating European workers from full chattel slavery. And while serfdom fell and rose in different parts of early modern Europe and shared characteristics with slavery, serfs were not outsiders either before or after enserfment. The phrase 'long-distance serf trade' is an oxymoron. Even in the twentieth century, totalitarian states have used slave labor primarily as a punitive strategy against enemies of the state and have never instituted full chattel slavery as an economic device.

Although there is no evidence that Europeans ever considered instituting full chattel slavery of Europeans in overseas settlements, the striking paradox is that no sound economic reasons spoke against it. By the seventeenth century, the most cursory examination of relative costs suggests that European slaves should have been preferred to either European indentured labor or African slaves. And while American Indians were cheap to enslave, their life expectancy and productivity in post-Columbian plantation conditions hardly compared with that of pre-industrial or, indeed, post-industrial Europeans.

[. . .]

[T]he evidence presented here points to major non-economic factors in the decision to use African slaves. While it certainly became profitable to replace European indentured servants with African slaves, the main issue was not relative profits but rather the inability of colonists to conceive of Europeans as chattel slaves. Such a conception might well have developed given enough time, but the sugar revolution proceeded too quickly to allow Europeans to adjust perceptions of insiders and outsiders. If Europeans had been able to accord Africans the same rights as themselves in the early modern period, they would not have enslaved them and brought them to the plantation Americas. The absence of European slaves, like the dog that did not bark, is perhaps the clue to understanding the slave trade and the system it supported.

A second implication, less obvious but just as important, is that Europeans, and more particularly the English, failed to take advantage of two significant economic opportunities. For the first, if they had emulated the sixteenth-century Russian aristocracy by creating an ideological distance between the common people and themselves and enslaving some members of their own society, they would have enjoyed lower labor costs, a faster development of the Americas, and higher exports and income levels on both sides of the Atlantic. For those who see European, especially English, economic power built on overseas colonies, it might be argued that, for the underpopulated tropical Americas at least, exploitation of the periphery and the transfer of surplus to the core would have been far more rapid with white slave labor. The second failure to maximize an economic advantage occurred when Europeans gradually widened their perception of what constituted an insider by beginning in the late eighteenth century to include transoceanic peoples. This change in perception brought a very profitable institution to an end. The first 'missed opportunity' created the Atlantic slave trade from Africa; the second ended not only the slave trade but slavery in the Americas as well.

A third implication—really an extension of the previous point—consists of the notion that seventeenth-century capitalism, mercantile or not, was hardly as unrestrained and voracious as many students of early modern Europe have portrayed it. Profit-maximizing behavior occurred within agreed-upon limits, limits defined at least as much by shared values as by the resistance of the less-propertied classes. This should not be surprising. There have always been extensive areas of personal life defined as beyond the limits of the market and profit maximization even in the Western world, and the expansion and contraction of such an area is a major field of study, particularly as it pertains to wage labor. By the seventeenth century, enslavement of fellow Europeans was beyond the limits. More interesting, however, is that the peoples with the most advanced capitalist culture, the Dutch and the English, were also the Europeans least likely to subject their own citizens to forced labor.

The fourth implication is the corollary of this last point. The countries least likely to enslave their own had the harshest and most sophisticated system of exploiting enslaved non-Europeans. Overall, the English and Dutch conception of the role of the individual in metropolitan society ensured the accelerated development of African chattel slavery in the Americas (and Asian slavery in the East Indies) because their own subjects could not become chattel slaves or even convicts for life. Further implications touch the English Revolution as well as its American counterpart of nearly a century later. There may be something to be said for expanding a variation of Edmund Morgan's argument to cover the whole of the British Atlantic, in the sense that the celebration of British liberties—more specifically, liberties for Englishmen—depended on African slavery. But if this route leads to an interpretation of history driven purely by whichever interest group was dominant, then we should pause. Capitalists could have made more by selling European convicts for life than African slaves, and more again if the progeny of those convicts, like Africans, had also been bound to a lifetime of service. In the end, the absence of European slavery suggests that narrowly economic interpretations of history often miss the point.

[From 'Europeans and the Rise and Fall of African Slavery,' *American Historical Review* 98 (December 1993), 1399–400, 1403–4, 1422–3.]

35 The Origins Debate

1. In every seventeenth-century English colony, most Africans were enslaved upon their first arrival and most remained slaves throughout their lives: in 1616 and thereafter in Bermuda (as ninety-nine-year indentures), 1619 in Virginia, 1627 in Barbados, 1630 in Providence Island, 1631 (perhaps 1641) in Massachusetts, 1634 in Maryland, and so forth. Although no Virginia law until 1661 mandated slavery for Africans, no law decreed otherwise; the buyer of human chattel had the protection of English common law of property. Moreover, contemporaneous statements by colonial residents and visitors describe Africans in general as permanent slaves in the English colonies. *No* Europeans, on the other hand, were enslaved by the English.

2. Some of the Africans who arrived as slaves became free through manumission by sympathetic owners, or perhaps by a selfish owner who granted freedom rather than support elderly or incapacitated slaves. Other Africans and early Afro-Americans escaped slavery by buying themselves, and perhaps their kin, through long-term purchase agreements with owners. This was not a slave's *right*; it occurred only if the owner was willing, and it was probably to the owner's long-term profit and with money or credit he permitted the slave to accrue. Instances of self-purchase were apparently few, numbering scarcely a dozen men in seventeenth-century Northampton County, where the practice was probably at its most frequent.

3. A few Africans and Afro-West Indians apparently arrived in Virginia with servant indentures and subsequently gained their contractual freedom. A few others may have gained such contracts after their arrival, perhaps on the basis of conversion to Christianity. But the absence in the official records of most Africans' names or ages or dates of arrival would have thwarted an indenture system based on stipulated periods of service, either by contract or by 'custom of the country' laws. Those statutes set terminal dates for servants arriving without written indentures; in any event they seem to have applied only to English servants. The few recorded black servants, moreover, served unusually long terms.

4. Only free blacks, and sometimes Native Americans, were denied full rights of citizenship despite their nominal freedom. For example, free black women after 1668 (and Indian women within the colony's jurisdiction after 1682) were taxed; other free women were not. And when, late in the century, Africans directly from Africa rather than the West Indies began to arrive in greatly increased numbers, free blacks, even those whose families had lived in the colony for three or four generations, were required to leave Virginia. They were ostracized as a separate, inferior branch of humankind—not yet

designated by the word *race* but nonetheless perceived in just that sense—because many people of similar appearance and roughly similar geographic origin had arrived in the colony.

5. From the outset of British colonization, white Americans (at least those whose opinions survive) identified almost all Africans and Afro-Americans by one or more synonymous European color terms—'negro,' 'neger,' or 'black'; such terms appear in the laws, court records, inventories, diaries, and other literary evidence. Rarely was a geographic or ethnic term such as 'African,' 'Yoruban,' or 'Ashanti' used. And color identifiers were applied regardless of the individual's longevity in America or status as slave or free. Very often the records included only the color labels for Africans, and where a name was used, it was usually a first name only (given by white owners or officials) and was often followed, even if a full name, by the color designation. Virginia's seventeenth-century censuses, moreover, commonly distinguished between only two categories of people: black (usually 'negro') and white (usually 'English' or 'Christian'). There was, in sum, a palpable sense within the English community that Africans were distinctly separate and identifiable by pigmentation. In 1652, Rhode Island's legislature epitomized the prevailing English bifurcation of humanity when it referred to 'blacke mankind or white'.

6. Most references to Africans or Afro-Americans in English writings of the time were in some way pejorative. One of the most prevalent signs (as the previous paragraph implies) was anonymity: headright lists, for example, like censuses and wills and property inventories, show full names for almost all Euro-Americans and a partial name for most of those without full names but usually no names for Africans; instead, the lists acknowledge (for example) the issuance of headrights for 'six negroes,' or 'three negro men and one woman'. This pattern of depersonalization begins with the first mention of Africans in Virginia in 1619 and continues unabated through the century. In some censuses most of the cattle but only a few of the Africans are accorded names. And the various documents that list people, for whatever purpose, usually put Africans at the end, thus subtly implying an inferior status. Nothing comparable can be found for any other human group, including Native Americans, although they came increasingly closer to the Africans' anonymity and pejorative references than did any European nationality.

7. Not until the era of the American Revolution did a substantial body of literature emerge in defense of slavery and in derogation of the Negro 'race'—i.e., a racist literature. But unless one assumes that without a substantial body of literature espousing a set of ideas there is no ideology (a trap into which many intellectual historians but few anthropologists fall), there is no need to see the literary outpouring as a sign of racism's arrival. Rather, I believe, it marked a new stage in the ideology's development, as did, in the antebellum era, the emergence of 'scientific' explanations of 'racial'

differences. Racism, after all, need not be full-blown to be viable. As J. R. Pole observed, Edmund Morgan (and I would add Barbara Fields as well as many other historians) 'seems to suppose that if the historical explanation of slavery lay in racism, it could only be because racism was as profound at the beginnings as it later became, but this is not so. It was only necessary that racism should be sufficient, and that visible identification—already a cause of racial repugnance—should make slavery so easily practicable.'

The *idea* of races—imprecisely defined and inconsistently explained—had arrived, I contend, with the first English settlers. That belief in turn determined to a large extent the set of shared perceptions, assumptions, and experiences that after 1619 shaped Euro-American behavior toward Africans and Afro-Americans in Virginia until the end of the century and beyond. The champions of that ideology had no need to proclaim in writing the beliefs that apparently had little opposition, except, of course, from its victims, and in any event the infant colony had neither presses nor sufficient readers. Still, from a variety of brief statements, especially from the writings of a few outspoken opponents of the ideology, the cluster of beliefs is clear, and it constitutes (to use Fields's definition of ideology) 'the descriptive vocabulary of day-to-day existence, through which people make rough sense of the[ir] social reality'.

The cluster of beliefs that helped seventeenth-century white Virginians make sense of their perceived reality is readily apparent, I think, however irrational it may seem to us. In brief, they held that Africans were perhaps not fully human, and if human, surely inferior to whites in mental and spiritual capacity; that their general appearance and especially their pigmentation proclaimed that inferiority, probably because of the 'curse' on Canaan's descendants, perhaps for other reasons, which in any event were God's doing; and that in light of their divinely ordained inferiority, Africans should be held in abject slavery or at least in a subservient status because they merited nothing else, not even the consolations of Christianity. To that last proposition a few clergymen (such as Morgan Godwyn and Richard Baxter) and laymen (such as Thomas Tryon) dissented. Their impassioned testimony documents the majority's virulent ideology.

[From 'The Origins Debate: Slavery and Racism in Seventeenth-Century Virginia,' in *Roots of American Racism: Essays on the Colonial Experience* (New York: Oxford University Press, 1995), 171–4.]

Section III

Slave Laws

As described above, slavery has existed in many times and places; few societies have lacked some form of enslavement, and slavery was accepted by all religions, major and minor. Slaves were used for many purposes, for economic production, personal services, and military ends. Generally, they represented a valuable asset to their owners, so it was important to be able to establish ownership rights as well as provisions for the transfer in ownership. Because of the value of slaves as commercial assets, and also because they were recognized as human in some respects and thus different from animals, considerable attention was given to all aspects of enslavement—including relations among slaveowners, as well as between slaveowners and slaves, and between slaves and other members of society—in laws, codes, and rules. These would cover issues such as who could be enslaved, how the enslaved were to be treated by their owners and how they should behave toward them, and what constraints could be imposed on slaveowners by the society in which they lived.

Given the very broad range of concerns covered by slave laws, and the fact that slavery existed in many societies, each with its own slave codes and laws, no overall uniformity might be expected. In some cases the laws were enacted by the local society, including resident slaveowners; in others it was imposed by the metropolitan government to control slavery in distant colonies. Frank Tannenbaum, in his insightful work on comparative slavery, *Slave and Citizen: The Negro in the Americas* (New York, 1946), pointed to the New World paradox which showed that the more tight the control by the metropolis, the more lenient were the laws regarding slaves, while in the more autonomous areas slaveowning settlers imposed harsher restraints on the slaves.

Nevertheless, despite the variety of states legislating on slavery, there was a surprising degree of similarity not only in the range of questions discussed, but often in the specific nature of their contents. Concerns over who could be enslaved, under what conditions, and whether it was a status that was inherited generally pointed to the legal role of the outsider within a given society. Laws regarding the conditions of manumission, the terms under which it could be granted, of the legal rights granted after manumission, as well as the relationships allowed between slaves and members of free society, were found in almost all slave law codes. Most frequent, perhaps, were laws controlling the treatment of slaves by their masters, which often covered issues such as diet requirements and punishments allowed for slave misbehavior. Since slaves could be bought and sold, it was necessary to establish commercial codes to cover these transactions, similar to those used in other forms of property. The ending of slavery as a system generally entailed legislation describing the conditions under which slaves and/or their offspring would be freed, and the terms of any compensation to be provided to slaveowners.

In answering questions about the effectiveness of laws regulating slavery, it is necessary to distinguish between the specific terms of slave laws and the nature of the enforcement of such laws. Laws could clearly serve as a possible constraint on the actions of masters and slaves, but the willingness of individuals and society to enforce them would determine their actual impact. At times, slaveowners might treat their slaves more arbitrarily than was permitted by the law, knowing that violations might well not be observed or enforced. Alternatively, however, slaveowners might decide not to take full advantage of what the laws permitted in regard to their property, by, for example, feeding slaves more than the legally prescribed diet or by ignoring the punishments allowed by the law. Slaveowners may, at times, have been more lenient than was allowed for by the law, while at others they might have been tougher, but because of the limited willingness of society to punish slaveowners, it is necessary, in order to fully understand the nature of slave societies, to get beyond the law codes and to examine the actual experiences of slaves within the system.

36   Excerpts from the Bible

Leviticus 25: 39–46

39 And if thy brother that dwelleth by thee be waxen poor, and be sold unto thee; thou shalt not compel him to serve as a bondservant:

40 *But* as an hired servant, and as a sojourner, he shall be with thee, and shall serve thee unto the year of jubile:

41 And then shall he depart from thee, both he and his children with him, and shall return unto his own family, and unto the possession of his fathers shall he return.

42 For they are my servants, which I brought forth out of the land of Egypt: they shall not be sold as bondmen.

43 Thou shalt not rule over him with rigour; but shalt fear thy God.

44 Both thy bondmen, and thy bondmaids, which thou shalt have, shall be of the heathen that are round about you; of them shall ye buy bondmen and bondmaids.

45 Moreover of the children of the strangers that do sojourn among you, of them shall ye buy, and of their families that are with you, which they begat in your land: and they shall be your possession.

46 And ye shall take them as an inheritance for your children after you, to inherit them for a possession; they shall be your bondmen for ever: but over your brethren the children of Israel, ye shall not rule one over another with rigour.

Leviticus 27: 1–7

1 And the LORD spake unto Moses, saying,

2 Speak unto the children Israel, and say unto them, When a man shall make a singuler vow, the persons shall be for the LORD by thy estimation.

3 And thy estimation shall be of the male from twenty years old even unto sixty years old, even thy estimation shall be fifty shekels of silver, after the shekel of the sanctuary.

4 And if it be a female, then thy estimation shall be thirty shekels.

5 And if it be from five years old even unto twenty years old, then thy estimation shall be of the male twenty shekels, and for the female ten shekels.

6 And if it be from a month old even unto five years old, then thy estimation shall be of the male five shekels of silver, and for the female thy estimation shall be three shekels of silver.

7 And if it be from sixty years old and above; if it be a male, then thy estimation shall be fifteen shekels, and for the female ten shekels.

Ephesians 6: 5–9

5 Servants, be obedient to them that are *your* masters according to the flesh, with fear and trembling, in singleness of your heart, as unto Christ;

6 Not with eyeservice, as menpleasers; but as the servants of Christ, doing the will of God from the heart;

7 With good will doing service, as to the Lord, and not to men:

8 Knowing that whatsoever good thing any man doeth, the same shall he receive of the Lord, whether *he be* bond or free.

9 And, ye masters, do the same things unto them, forbearing threatening; knowing that your Master also is in heaven; neither is there respect of persons with him.

Colossians 3: 22–5, 4: 1

22 Servants, obey in all things your masters according to the flesh; not with eyeservice, as menpleasers; but in singleness of heart, fearing God:

23 And whatsoever ye do, do *it* heartily, as to the Lord, and not unto men;

24 Knowing that of the Lord ye shall receive the reward of the inheritance: for ye serve the Lord Christ.

25 But he that doeth wrong shall receive for the wrong which he hath done: and there is no respect of persons.

CHAPTER 4

Masters, give unto your servants that which is just and equal; knowing that ye also have a Master in heaven.

I Timothy 6: 1–3

1 Let as many servants as are under the yoke count their own masters worthy of all honour, that the name of God and his doctrine be not blasphemed.

2 And they that have believing masters, let them not despise *them*, because they are brethren; but rather do them service, because they are faithful and beloved, partakers of the benefit. These things teach and exhort.

3 If any man teach otherwise, and consent not to wholesome words, even the words of our Lord Jesus Christ, and to the doctrine which is according to godliness.

Titus 2: 9–10

9 Exhort servants to be obedient unto their own masters, *and* to please them well in all things; not answering again;

10 Not purloining, but shewing all good fidelity; that they may adorn the doctrine of God our Saviour in all things.

I Peter 2: 18

18 Servants, be subject to your masters with all fear; not only to the good and gentle, but also to the froward.

§ 15

If a man has let a slave of a palace or a slave-girl of a palace or the slave of a villein or the slave-girl of a villein escape by the great gate, he shall be put to death.

§ 16

If a man has harboured a lost slave or slave-girl of a palace or of a villein in his house and then has not brought (them) out at the proclamation of the herald, that owner of the house shall be put to death.

§§ 17–20

[§17] If a man has caught either a slave or a slave-girl fugitive in the open country and hales him to his owner, the owner of the slave shall give him 2 shekels of silver.

[§18] If that slave does not then declare (the name of) his owner, he shall hale him to the palace; the facts of his case shall be found, and they shall restore him to his master.

[§19] If he detains that slave in his house (and) afterwards the slave is caught in his possession, that man shall be put to death.

[§20] If the slave escapes from the hand of him who has caught him, that man shall take an oath by the life of a god for (the satisfaction of) the owner of the slave and he then goes free.

§§ 117–19

[§117] If a man has become liable to arrest under a bond and has sold his wife his son or his daughter or gives (them) into servitude, for 3 years they shall do work in the house of him who has bought them or taken them in servitude; in the fourth year their release shall be granted.

[§118] If he gives a slave or a slave-girl into servitude, the merchant shall let (the period of redemption) expire (and) shall sell (him); he or she shall not be (re)claimed.

[§119] If a man has become liable to arrest under a bond and sells his slave-girl who has borne him sons, the owner of the slave-girl shall pay the money which the merchant has given (for her) and shall redeem his slave-girl.

§§ 175–6

[§175] If either a slave of a palace or a slave of a villein has married a lady and she bears sons, the owner of the slave shall make no claim to the sons of the lady for slavery.

[§176 A] Or, if the slave of the palace or the slave of the villein has married a lady and, when he has married her, she has entered the house of the slave of the palace or of the slave of the villein bringing the dowry from her father's house and (if), since they have lived together (and) made a home (and) acquired chattels, thereafter either the slave of the palace or the slave of the villein goes to (his) fate, the lady shall take her dowry; and they shall divide into two parts anything that her husband and she had acquired after they lived together, and the owner of the slave shall take half (and) the lady shall take half for her sons.

[§176 B] If the lady has not a dowry, they shall divide into two parts anything that her husband and she have acquired since they have lived together, and the owner of the slave shall take half (and) the lady shall take half for her sons.

§§ 196–205

[§196] If a man has put out the eye of a free man, they shall put out his eye.

[§197] If he breaks the bone of a (free) man, they shall break his bone.

[§198] If he puts out the eye of a villein or breaks the bone of a villein, he shall pay 1 maneh of silver.

[§199] If he puts out the eye of a (free) man's slave or breaks the bone of a (free) man's slave, he shall pay half his price.

[§200] If a man knocks out the tooth of a (free) man equal (in rank) to him(self), they shall knock out his tooth.

[§201] If he knocks out the tooth of a villein, he shall pay ½ maneh of silver.

[§202] If a man strikes the cheek of a (free) man who is superior (in rank) to him(self), he shall be beaten with sixty stripes with a whip of ox-hide in the assembly.

[§203] If the man strikes the cheek of a free man equal to him(self in rank), he shall pay 1 maneh of silver.

[§204] If a villein strikes the cheek of a villein, he shall pay 10 shekels of silver.

[§205] If the slave of a (free) man strikes the cheek of a free man, they shall cut off his ear.

§§ 209–14

[§209] If a man strikes the daughter of a (free) man (and) causes her to lose the fruit of her womb, he shall pay 10 shekels of silver for the fruit of her womb.

[§210] If that woman dies, they shall put his daughter to death.

[§211] If he causes the daughter of a villein to lose the fruit of her womb by striking her, he shall pay 5 shekels of silver.

[§212] If that woman dies, he shall pay ½ maneh of silver.

[§213] If he has struck the slave-girl of a (free) man and causes her to lose the fruit of her womb, he shall pay 2 shekels of silver.

[§214] If that slave-girl dies, he shall pay ⅓ maneh of silver.

§§ 215–20

[§215] If a surgeon has made a deep incision in (the body of) a (free) man with a lancet(?) of bronze and saves the man's life or has opened the caruncle(?) in (the eye of) a man with a lancet(?) of bronze and saves his eye, he shall take 10 shekels of silver.

[§216] If (the patient is) a villein, he shall take 5 shekels of silver.

[§217] If (the patient is) the slave of a (free) man, the master of the slave shall give 2 shekels of silver to the surgeon.

[§218] If the surgeon has made a deep incision in (the body of) a (free) man with a lancet(?) of bronze and causes the man's death or has opened the caruncle(?) in (the eye of) a man and so destroys the man's eye, they shall cut off his fore-hand.

[§219] If the surgeon has made a deep incision in (the body of) a villein's slave with a lancet(?) of bronze and causes (his) death, he shall replace slave for slave.

[§220] If he has opened his caruncle(?) with a lancet(?) of bronze and destroys his eye, he shall pay half his price in silver.

§§ 226–7

[§226] If a barber has excised a slave's mark without (the knowledge of) his owner so that he cannot be traced, they shall cut off the fore-hand of that barber.

[§227] If a man has constrained the barber and he excises the slave's mark so that he cannot be traced, they shall put that man to death and shall hang him at his (own) door; the barber may swear 'Surely I excised (it) unwittingly', and he then goes free.

[From *The Babylonian Laws* [18th century BC], ed. and trs. G. R. Driver and John C. Miles (Oxford: Clarendon Press, 1955), Vol. II: 19, 47–9, 69, 77–9, 81–3.]

38   The Digest of Justinian

3 GAIUS, *Institutes, book 1*: Certainly, the great divide in the law of persons is this: all men are either free men or slaves.

4 FLORENTINUS, *Institutes, book 9*: Freedom is one's natural power of doing what one pleases, save insofar as it is ruled out either by coercion or by law. 1. Slavery is an institution of the *jus gentium*, whereby someone is against nature made subject to the ownership of another. 2. Slaves (*servi*) are so-called, because generals have a custom of selling their prisoners and thereby *preserving* rather than killing them: and indeed they are said to be *mancipia*, because they are *captives* in the hand (*manus*) of their enemies.

5 MARCIAN, *Institutes, book 1*: Of slaves, to be sure, there is but a single condition; of free men, on the other hand, some are freeborn (*ingenui*) and some are freedmen. 1. People are brought under our power as slaves either by the civil law or by the *jus gentium*. This happens by civil law if someone over twenty years of age allows himself to be sold with a view to sharing in the price. By the *jus gentium*, people become slaves on being captured by enemies or by birth to a female slave. 2. The freeborn are those who are born of a free woman; it suffices that she was free at the time of birth, even though she was a slave at the time of conception. And in the converse case, if a woman conceives as a free person then gives birth as a slave, it has been decided that her child is born free (and it does not matter whether she conceived in lawful wedlock or in simple cohabitation), because the mother's calamity should not redound to the harm of the child within her. 3. Further to this, the following question has been raised: suppose a pregnant slave is manumitted, then later becomes a slave or is expelled from her *civitas* before she gives birth, is her offspring free or slave? The better view, however, is that he or she is born free, and that it is enough for the child in the womb to have had a free mother albeit only for some of the time between conception and birth.

6 GAIUS, *Institutes, book 1*: Freedmen are those who have been manumitted from lawful slavery.

[From *The Digest of Justinian* [529], ed. Theodor Mommsen with the aid of Paul Krueger, trs. Alan Watson (Philadelphia: University of Pennsylvania Press, 1985), Vol. 1: 16.]

39   Excerpts from the Koran

It is not righteousness that ye turn your faces to the East and the West; but righteous is he who believeth in Allah and the Last Day and the angels and the Scripture and the Prophets; and giveth his wealth, for love of Him, to kinsfolk and to orphans and the needy and the wayfarer and to those who ask, and to set slaves free; and observeth proper worship and payeth the poor-due. And those who keep their treaty when they make one, and the patient in tribulation and adversity and time of stress. Such are they who are sincere. Such are the God-fearing.

[. . .]

It is not for a believer to kill a believer unless (it be) by mistake. He who hath killed a believer by mistake must set free a believing slave, and pay the blood-money to the family of the slain, unless they remit it as a charity. If he (the victim) be of a people hostile unto you, and he is a believer, then (the penance is) to set free a believing slave. And if he cometh of a folk between whom and you there is a covenant, then the blood-money must be paid unto his folk and (also) a believing slave must be set free. And whoso hath not the wherewithal must fast two consecutive months. A penance from Allah. Allah is Knower, Wise.

[. . .]

And marry such of you as are solitary and the pious of your slaves and maid-servants. If they be poor, Allah will enrich them of His bounty. Allah is of ample means, Aware.

And let those who cannot find a match keep chaste till Allah give them independence by His grace. And such of your slaves as seek a writing (of emancipation), write it for them if ye are aware of aught of good in them, and bestow upon them of the wealth of Allah which He hath bestowed upon you. Force not your slave-girls to whoredom that ye may seek enjoyment of the life of the world, if they would preserve their chastity. And if one force them, then (unto them), after their compulsion, Lo! Allah will be Forgiving, Merciful.

[From *The Meaning of the Glorious Koran*, trs. Mohammed Marmaduke Pickthall (New York: New American Library, 1953), 48, 88, 255–6.]

RICHARD HELLIE

40 **The Law Code (*Sudebnik*) of 1550**

76. Legal procedure on bondage. [A man becomes] a full bondman [by selling himself] into full bondage. [A man also becomes a bondman,] after filing a report (*z dokladnoyu*), by becoming a steward (*klyuchnik*) in a rural locale with his wife and children who are [registered] with him with one lord in the same document and who were born in bondage. His children who were born prior to the bondage and have begun to live with another lord or are living by themselves are not bondmen. [A man does not become] a bondman by becoming an urban *klyuchnik*. [A man who marries] a bondwoman becomes a bondman; [a woman who marries] a bondman becomes a bondwoman; [A bondman can be given away] in a testament [and he remains] a bondman. [A man who marries] a bondwoman [being given away] in a dowry becomes a bondman; [a woman who marries] a bondman [being given away] in a dowry becomes a bondwoman. [A man who becomes] a boyar's amanuensis (*tiun*) does not become a bondman without the filling out of a full bondage document and a report document. [A man who becomes] a rural *klyuchnik* is not a bondman without a report document. The full and the report bondman shall not sell his free son who was born prior to the bondage, but he himself [the son] may sell himself to whomever he wishes, to the same lord his father serves or to anyone else he desires. A father and mother shall not participate in registering him [their son] in full bondage and they

shall not buy [him] out of bondage because his father and mother themselves are bondmen. Enter in the full bondage and report bondage documents that he has a father and mother and that they did not participate in the registration of the full bondage document because they themselves are bondmen. If his father is a monk or mother a nun, such a father and mother shall not be present at the registering of their son and daughter in full and report bondage documents and they shall not buy him [*sic*] out of servitude. Write in the full and report bondage documents that he has a father and mother, that they were not present at the registration in the full and report bondage documents because they have taken monastic orders. They shall not sell such children of their own. He himself shall sell himself to whomever he wishes.

77. Manumission documents shall be granted with the approval of the boyars. The boyars shall affix their seals to the manumission documents and the government chancellors (*diaki*) shall sign [them]. Boyars and chancellors shall give manumission documents in Moscow, and the heads of the 'feeding' administration (*namestniki*) and government officials (*diaki*) shall give manumission documents in Great Novgorod and Pskov. The boyar or *namestnik* shall collect a fee for his seal on the manumission document of 9 dengi per head, the chancellor an altyn [6 dengi] per head for his signature, and the scribe who writes the manumission document 3 dengi per head. Manumission documents shall be granted in no other towns besides Moscow, Novgorod, and Pskov. If someone presents a manumission document without boyar approval, without the approval of the Novgorod and Pskov *namestniki*, [or] without the signature of a chancellor, even though [it bears] the signature of his lord, the manumission document is invalid.

78. When free people petition princes, boyars, *deti boyarskie*, and various people, and give limited service bondage contracts (*kabaly*) on themselves [in which they agree] to serve for the interest [on the loan], no one shall get a limited service bondage contract for more than fifteen rubles on a debtor. Old limited service bondage contracts were obtained on free people for more than fifteen rubles prior to this degree and they [the bondmen] are serving them [the creditors] for the interest on the money. Those people [the creditors] brought the limited service bondage contracts to the boyars, the boyars affixed their seals to these limited service bondage contracts and the chancellors signed [them]. Henceforth if someone questions the validity of such a limited service bondage contract, [the validity of] that limited service bondage contract shall be decided at a trial. They shall obtain limited service bondage contracts on free people, but they shall not get limited service bondage contracts on full, reported, or hereditary bondmen. If someone, not verifying, gets a limited service bondage contract on a full, reported, or hereditary bondman, or if someone obtains a fugitive warrant (*beglaya gramota*) against him and someone [else] presents a full or report bondage document on him, or proves him to be an hereditary bondman on the basis

of a will or any other document, the person [who obtained the limited service bondage contract] has lost his money. If the person to whom the bondman belongs says that he [the bondman] stole property when he fled, the losses shall be collected from the person who, without verifying, obtained a limited service bondage contract or a fugitive warrant on another [lord's] bondman. The bondman [belongs] to the lord [who presents] the full or report bondage documents, the will, or [evidence proving that the bondman is] an hereditary bondman.

[From 'The Law Code (*Sudebnik*) of 1550,' in *Readings for "Introduction to Russian Civilization"*: *Muscovite Society*, ed. and trs. Richard Hellie (Chicago: University of Chicago Press, 1970), 243–5.]

41   The Massachusetts Code 1641

The liberties of the Massachusetts collonie in New England, 1641

The free fruition of such liberties, Immunities, and priveledges as humanitie, Civilitie, and Christianitie call for as due to every man in his place and proportion, without impeachment, and infringement, hath ever bene and ever will be the tranquillitie and Stabilitie of Churches and Commonwealths. And the deniall or deprivall thereof, the disturbance if not the ruine of both.

We hould it therefore our dutie and safetie whilst we are about the further establishing of this Government to collect and expresse all such freedomes as for present we foresee may concerne us, and our posteritie after us, And to ratify them with our sollemne consent.

Wee doe therefore this day religiously and unanimously decree and confirme these following Rites, liberties, and priveledges concerneing our Churches, and Civill State to be respectively, impartiallie, and inviolably enjoyed and observed throughout our Jurisdiction for ever.

[. . .]

LIBERTIES OF SERVANTS

85. If any servants shall flee from the Tiranny and crueltie of their masters to the howse of any freeman of the same Towne, they shall be there protected and susteyned till due order be taken for their relife. Provided due notice thereof be speedily given to their maisters from whom they fled. And the next Assistant or Constable where the partie flying is harboured.

86. No servant shall be put of for above a yeare to any other neither in the life time of their maister nor after their death by their Executors or Administrators unlesse it be by consent of Authoritie assembled in some Court or two Assistants.

87. If any man smite out the eye or tooth of his manservant, or maid servant, or otherwise mayme or much disfigure him, unlesse it be by meere casualtie, he shall let them goe free from his service. And shall have such further recompense as the Court shall allow him.

88. Servants that have served deligentlie and faithfully to the benefitt of their maisters seaven yearse, shall not be sent away emptie. And if any have bene unfaithfull, negligent or unprofitable in their service, notwithstanding the good usage of their maisters, they shall not be dismissed till they have made satisfaction according to the Judgement of Authoritie.

LIBERTIES OF FORREINERS AND STRANGERS

89. If any people of other Nations professing the true Christian Religion shall flee to us from the Tiranny or oppression of their persecutors, or from famyne, warres, or the like necessary and compulsarie cause, They shall be entertayned and succoured amongst us, according to that power and prudence, god shall give us.

90. If any ships or other vessels, be it freind or enemy, shall suffer shipwrack upon our Coast, there shall be no violence or wrong offerred to their persons or goods. But their persons shall be harboured, and relieved, and their goods preserved in safety till Authoritie may be certified thereof, and shall take further order therein.

91. There shall never be any bond slaverie, villinage or Captivitie amongst us unles it be lawfull Captives taken in just warres, and such strangers as willingly selle themselves or are sold to us. And these shall have all the liberties and Christian usages which the law of god established in Israell concerning such persons doeth morally require. This exempts none from servitude who shall be Judged thereto by Authoritie.

OFF THE BRUITE CREATURE

92. No man shall exercise any Tirranny or Crueltie towards any bruite Creature which are usuallie kept for man's use.

93. If any man shall have occasion to leade or drive Cattel from place to place that is far of, so that they be weary, or hungry, or fall sick, or lambe, It shall be lawful to rest or refresh them, for competant time, in any open place that is not Corne, meadow, or inclosed for some peculiar use.

[From 'The Liberties of the Massachusetts Collonie in New England, 1641,' in
Charles W. Eliot (ed.), *American Historical Documents 1000–1904*
(New York: Collier, 1910), 70, 82–4.]

40. Calculate the value of the slave labor of those slaves in redeeming a plaintiff's suit at the rate of 5.00 rubles per year for males, and one-half that for wives and mature women; 2.00 rubles per year for their children who are with them and over ten years of age. If they have any minors under ten years of age, do not calculate any value for those minors in the redemption of the plaintiff's suit because such minors at those ages do not perform slave labor.

When such people have worked off the suits of their plaintiffs in full: set them free from those plaintiffs.

If their plaintiffs die, and children survive them, and they [the debtors] have not fully worked off the [plaintiffs'] claims at that point: they shall live out that term which they have not worked off at the homes of the children of those deceased plaintiffs. When they have worked off [what they owe] those children of the plaintiffs: set them free accordingly.

41. Concerning people of all ranks who at times of famine, or any other time, not desiring to feed their slaves, evict them from their houses, but do not grant them manumission documents and will not give them back [their original enslavement] documents; and, with the intention of keeping them in the future, they order them to feed themselves; and for that reason no other people will receive those slaves of theirs in [their] house[s], because they have no manumission documents; and if there is a petition in that matter against them from those slaves of theirs: in response to that slave petition the directors of the Slavery Chancellery shall send for their masters who are evicting them from their houses. Interrogate those masters of theirs, whether they really have evicted them from their houses.

If those masters of theirs testify in the interrogation that they have released those slaves of theirs from their houses: henceforth they shall have no claim to those slaves. Order them to affix their signatures to that testimony of theirs. Concerning those who are illiterate: they shall order someone whom they trust to sign that testimony of theirs in their stead.

Concerning those who will not proceed to sign that testimony because of their obstinacy: order them to sign that testimony against their free will.

When they have signed the testimony: having registered those slaves of theirs in the Slavery Chancellery in the books, grant them freedom. Issue them manumission documents from the Slavery Chancellery.

If as free men they petition to be someone's slaves, they are the slaves of that [person].

Without interrogating those people against whom those slaves proceed to petition about those slaves, do not grant them freedom.

42. If their masters, against whom they petition, testify about those slaves that those slaves of theirs are petitioning against them falsely, that they did not evict them from their houses: give back those slaves to those masters of theirs. Order those masters of theirs to feed them in times of famine, not to starve them with hunger. Moreover, they shall not commit any bad deed against them because they petitioned against them.

43. If someone in a time of famine gives himself and his wife, or his son or a daughter, to someone as a slave in exchange for food; and he gives a note on himself to that effect; or he writes down borrowed money in the note on himself and on his children: on the basis of that note they shall live with that person to whom they gave themselves as slaves until that time when they have redeemed themselves or worked off [the debt].

[From Aleksei Mikhailovich, The Muscovite Law Code (Ulozhenie) of 1649: Text and Translation, ed. Richard Hellie (Irvine: C. Schlacks, 1988), 172–4.]

43 Barbados Act 1661

An act for the better ordering and governing of Negroes

Whereas heretofore many good Laws and ordinances have been made for the governing, regulating and ordering the Negroes, Slaves in this Isle, and sundry punishments appointed to many their misdemeanour, crimes, and offences which yet not met the effect hath been desired and might have been reasonably expected had the Master of Families and other the Inhabitants of this Isle been so careful of their obedience and compliance with the said Laws as they ought to have been. And these former Laws being in many clauses imperfect and not fully comprehending the true constitution of this Government in relation of their Slaves their Negroes an heathenish brutish and an uncertain dangerous pride of people to whom if surely in any thing we may extend the legislative power given us of punishionary Laws for the benefit and good of this plantation, not being contradictory to the Laws of England, there being in all the body of that Law no track to guide us where to walk nor any rule set us how to govern such Slaves, yet we well know by the right rule of reason and order, we are not to leave them to the Arbitrary, cruel, and outrageous wills of every evil disposed person, but so far to protect them as we do many other goods and Chattels, and also somewhat further as being created Men though without the knowledge of God in the world, we have therefore upon mature and serious Consideration of the premises thought good to renew and revive whatsoever we have found necessary and useful in the former Laws of this Isle concerning the ordering and governing of Negroes and to add thereunto such further Laws and ordinances as at this time we think absolute needful for the public safety and may prove to the future behoveful to the peace and utility of this Isle by this Act repealing and dissolving all other former Laws made concerning the said Negroes and for the time to come.

CLAUSE 1:

Be it enacted published and declared and it is by the President, Council, and Assembly of this Isle and by authority of the same enacted, ordained, and published that no Master, Mistress, Commander, or Overseer of any family within this Island shall give their Negroes leave on Sabbath days, Holy days or at any other time to go out of their plantations except such Negroes as usually wait upon them at home and abroad, and them with a ticket under his Master, Mistress, Commander, or Overseers' hand, the said Ticket specifying the time of his or her coming from the plantation and the time allowed for his or her return, and no other Negroes except upon necessary business, and then to send a Christian or Negroes' Overseer along with them with a Ticket as aforesaid upon forfeiting for every Negro so limited to go abroad 500 pounds of Muscavado sugar, half the said five to the Informer and the other half to the public Treasury; And if any Master, Mistress, Commander or Overseer of any plantation shall find any Negro or Negroes at any time in their plantation with out a Ticket and business from his said Master and not apprehend them or endeavour so to do, and having apprehended them and shall not punish them by a moderate whipping, shall forfeit 500 pounds of the like sugar to be disposed of as aforesaid, the said penalty to be recovered before some Justice of the Peace of that precinct where such default shall be made, who is hereby authorised upon Complaint made to examine upon oath to hear and determine the same and by Warrant under his hand directed to the Constable to cause such penalty to be levied as in case of servants wages is appointed.

CLAUSE 2:

It is further enacted, ordained, and published that if any Negro man or woman shall offer any Violence to any Christian as by striking or the like, the Negro shall for his and their first offence, by information given to the next Justice of the Peace, be severely whipped by the Constable by order of the said Justice, for the serious offence of that nature by order of the said Justice of Peace he shall be severely whipped, his nose slit and be burned in face and for his third offence he shall receive by order of the Governor and Council such greater Corporal punishment as they shall think meet to inflict, providing always that such striking or conflict be not in the Lawful defence of their Master, Mistress or owner of their families, or of their goods.

CLAUSE 3:

And it is hereby further enacted that the Negroes shall have clothes to cover their nakedness once every year (that is to say) drawers and caps for men and petticoats for women; And whereas the inhabitants of the Isles have much suffered by the running away of the Negroes and by the keeping such Runaways or fugitive Negroes by several persons in their plantations.

CLAUSE 4:

It is hereby enacted, published, and declared by the authority aforesaid that all persons that are now possessed of any fugitive or Runaway Negroes do within six days after publication of this Act in the parish Church bring them in, and to their proper owners or into the custody of the Provost Marshall for the time being or his appointed deputy at the Town of St Michael's upon pain of paying of ten thousand pounds of good merchantable Muscavado sugar for damage unto the owner, to be by the said owner recovered in the Court of Common Pleas for the precinct where such Trespasser liveth by action of debt or information in which no essoin, protection, injunction, or wager of Law shall be permitted and allowed. And if any Christian Servant so possessed of any such Negro or Negroes not acquainting his Master thereof do neglect or fail to bring them before the time limited as is before enjoined, the said Servant shall immediately upon Conviction thereof receive nine and thirty lashes upon his naked back by order of the next Justice of the Peace to some Constable or the Common Executioner and after Execution of his time of service shall serve the owner of the said Negro the full term and space of seven years and a Record thereof by the said justice before such examination, shall be had.

CLAUSE 5:

And further it is enacted by the authority aforesaid that all overseers of plantations do twice every week search their Negro houses for Runaway Negroes and what overseer shall neglect to do the same shall forfeit 100 pounds of sugar for every default, the one half to the informer the other half to the public use.

CLAUSE 6:

And be it further enacted by the authority aforesaid that whosoever hereafter shall take up any Runaway Negro shall [sic] person shall with forty eight hours after bring the said Runaway to his proper owner or to the Provost Marshall or his deputy upon pain of forfeiting for every day they shall keep such Negro or Negroes beyond the said forty-eight hours and thereof be convicted by Confession or Verdict the sum or quantity of one thousand pounds of merchantable Muscavado sugar, to be levied by the Provost

Marshall or his deputy by order of the Governor for the time being, upon the person so neglecting to bring the said Runaway upon his Lands, goods, or Chattels, the one half thereof to the owner of the said Negro, and the other to him or them that shall inform, the same out of which the said Marshall's fee shall be deducted. And if the said person or persons informing be Servant or Servants to the party so delivering the said Negro that the said person or persons so informing shall be from thenceforth absolutely free and clear from his service any Indenture or Contract to the contrary notwithstanding.

CLAUSE 7:

And it is further enacted by the authority aforesaid that all persons which shall hereafter take up any Runaway or fugitive Negro, and shall so bring them to the Provost Marshall or his deputy shall receive one hundred pounds of Muscavado sugar, or a note for so much that the person may dispose of his own sugar immediately upon the delivery of them from the Treasurer for the time being, who is hereby required to pay the same. And in case he shall refuse to make the said payment upon the presentment of the said Negro, and thereof oath be made before any one Justice of the peace the said Justice is hereby authorised and required to direct his Warrant to any Constable to cause the value thereof to be levied out of the goods of the said Treasurer, and the said Goods to be delivered to the said party.

[. . .]

CLAUSE 11:

And it is further enacted and ordained by the authority aforesaid that every overseer of a family in this Isle shall cause all his Negro houses to be searched diligently and effectually once every fourteen days for clubs, wooden swords, or other mischievous weapons and finding any to take them away and cause them to be burned. As also for Clothes, goods, or any other thing or Commodities particularly suspected flesh that is not given them by their Master, Mistress, Commander, or Overseer and honestly come by, in whose custody they find anything of that kind, and suspected or known to be stolen goods, the same for to seize and to take into their custody and within six days after their discover thereof, to send a Certificate to the Clerk of the Parish for the time being, who is hereby required to receive the same and to enter upon it the day of its receipt and the particulars to file and keep to himself, but to set upon the porch of the Church door a short breviate of such lost goods may the better come to the knowledge where it is by future enquiry of the Clerk who is not to show the particulars until the Enquirer of stolen goods shall first declare what he hath lost and the Marks and description thereof and paid twelve pence for the same by which if the said Clerk shall be convinced that any part of the goods Certified unto him to be found applying to the party enquiring he is to direct the said party enquiring to the place and person where the goods be, who is hereby required to make restitution of what is in being to the true owner, upon the penalty of the forfeiture of 2000 pounds of Muscavado sugar for every neglect by the overseer or Clerk aforesaid in any of the particulars to be levied upon the goods or Chattels for the breach of either of those two last Clauses in breach by precept or Warrant from the Judge or Justice before whom such conviction shall be had, the one half of the five aforesaid to go to the public Treasury, the other half to the person shall inform.

And that all Negroes likewise may receive encouragement to take fugitives and Runaway Negroes.

CLAUSE 12:

It is further ordained and enacted by the authority aforesaid that whatsoever Negro shall at any time of his accord take up any Runaway Negro that have been out above twelve Months shall have for his doing five hundred pounds of sugar to be paid by the owner if he will redeem him within one month during which time the Master of the Negro that took up such Runaway hath power to keep for the purpose aforesaid. But if the owner of the said Runaway Negro will not nor doth not receive him within the said time then the Master in whose custody he is hath hereby power to sell the aforesaid fugitive or Runaway Negro and to take five hundred pounds of sugar to himself for his Negro and the rest return to the Master of the Negro so taken up. And whosoever shall deprive or deceive any Negro that hath so taken up any fugitive of the bone [boon] or reward given him by this Law for so doing shall forfeit three thousand pounds of Muscavado sugar one third to the Country one third to the Informer and one third to the Negro wronged which gift and forfeiture shall be justly employed by the Master of the Negro in Clothes for the said Negro to wear with a Badge of a Red cross on his right Arm whereby he may be known and cherished by all good people for his good service to the Country the aforesaid fine to be recovered by him that shall sue for it in any Court of Record by Action of Debt or information in which no essoin, protection, injunction, or wager of Law shall be admitted or allowed.

And whereas diverse evil disposed persons have heretofore attempted to steal away Negroes by spurious pretences of promising them freedom in another Country against which piritous practice no punishment suitable hath been yet provided.

CLAUSE 13:

Be it therefore enacted and ordained by the authority aforesaid that whosoever shall directly or indirectly at any time hereafter publication hereof tempt or persuade any Negro to leave their Master or Mistress' service to whom they are Slaves, out of intent and design to carry away any of them out of the Isle or whosoever do defraud their Master of them and be thereof convicted by their own Confession or the oaths of two credible Witnesses or by the Confession of such Negro or Negroes with reasonable Circumstances concurring shall be by the Governor of this Isle for the time being or by any Judge of Record or any two Justices of the peace adjudged to pay the said Master of the said Negro or Negroes five thousand pounds of Muscavado sugar by precept or Warrant from the aforesaid Governor, Judge, or Justice before whom the Conviction is made to be levied upon the lands, goods or Chattels of the person so offending by such Constable to whom the aforesaid Warrant shall be directed and delivered to the party grieved by way of damage and the Surplusage (if any be) shall be returned to the owner. And in case the party offending shall not be found worth Lands, goods or Chattel to the value aforesaid then shall the Governor, Judge or Justice adjudge him Servant to the party Injured Seven years and so deliver him over to him and make Record thereof. But if any Man shall so tempt and practice any persons Negroes and them so actually tempted convey carry and send off of the Isle and be after apprehended in the Isle for the same he shall by the Governor and Council for the time being condemned to pay the owners of such Negroes three times the value of them in sugar and Execution for the same from the Governor to issue accordingly unto the Provost Marshall or his deputy.

And whereas many heinous and grievous Crimes, Murder and Burglaries and robbing in the highway, burning of houses and canes be many times Committed by Negroes which offenders for danger of escape are not long to be imprisoned and being brutish Slaves deserve not for the baseness of their Conditions to be tried by the legal trial of twelve Men of their appears or Neighbourhood which truly neither can be rightly done as the Subjects of England are nor is Execution to be delayed towards them in case of such horrid Crimes Committed.

[. . .]

CLAUSE 17:

And it is further enacted, ordained and published by the president, Council and Assembly and by authority aforesaid that if any Negro shall make Insurrection or rise in rebellion against the place or people or make preparation of Arms, powder or offensive Weapons or hold any Council or conspiracy for raising Mutinies or rebellion in the Isle as hath been formerly attempted, that then for the speedy remedy thereof the Governor of the Isle or the superior officer for the time being appoint a Colonel and the field officers of the Regiment of the Island or any four of them to meet in Council and proceed by Martial Law against the Actors, Contrivers, raisers, fomenters and

Concealers of such Mutiny or rebellion and them punish by death or other pain as their Crimes shall deserve. And as the aforesaid Colonel or field officers or any four of them shall seem fit.

And that no Master, Mistress or Commander of a family should be frighted by fear of loss to search into and discover their own Negroes so evilly intended.

CLAUSE 18:

It is further enacted and ordained that the loss of Negroes so executed shall be born by the public and when the present Treasury is not sufficient to satisfy the loss, a public Levy to be presently made upon the Inhabitants for reparation of the same.

And whereas diverse Negroes are and long since have been Runaway into Woods and other fastness of the Isle do continually much mischief to several the Inhabitants of this Island hiding themselves sometimes in one place and sometimes in another so that with much difficulty they are to be found unless by some sudden surprise.

CLAUSE 19:

Be it therefore ordained and enacted and it is hereby ordained and enacted that from and after publication hereof it shall, and may be lawful for any Justice of the peace, Constable or Captain of a Company within this Isle that shall have notice of the residence or hiding-place of any Runaway Negro, fugitive and outlaws to raise any Number of Men not exceeding twenty, to apprehend or take them either alive or dead. And for every Negro which they shall take alive being Runaway from the said Master above six Months they shall receive five hundred pounds of sugar. And for every Negro which hath been Runaway above [blank in text] Months one thousand pounds of sugar from the owner, Master, or Commander of the said Negro if killed they shall receive five hundred pounds of Muscavado sugar from the public any Act or Statute heretofore to the contrary in any wise notwithstanding.

CLAUSE 20:

And it is further enacted and ordained by the authority aforesaid that if any Negro under punishment of his Master or his Order for running away or any other Crimes or misdemeanour towards his said Master shall suffer in life or in Member, no person whatsoever shall be accomptable to any Law therefore, But if any Man whatsoever shall of wantonness or only mindedness and cruel intention wilfully kill any Negro of his own, he shall pay unto the public Treasury three thousand of Muscavado sugar, but if he shall kill another man's he shall pay unto the owner of the Negro double the value and into the public Treasure five thousand pounds of Muscavado sugar. And he shall further by the next Justice of the peace be bound to the good behaviour during the pleasure of the Governor and Council and not to be liable to any other punishment or forfeiture for the same, neither is he who kills another man's Negro by accident liable to any other penalty but the owner's Action at Law. But if any poor small freeholder or other person kill a Negro by night out of the Common path and stealing the provision, swine, or other goods he shall not be accomptable for it, any Law, Statute or ordinance to the contrary notwithstanding.

And to the intent it may be certainly known what Negroes are out in rebellion to their Masters to the public peace.

CLAUSE 21:

It is by the authority aforesaid enacted and ordained that all owners of Negroes within this Isle do within ten days after publication hereof send an account to the Secretary for the time being in writing what Negroes he hath fled and Runaway and of the time they have been gone, and so for the time to come within ten days after any Negro shall absent himself from his service under penalty of paying of one thousand pounds of Muscavado sugar whereof the one half to be to the Informer, the other to the public Treasury, to be recovered by him that shall sue for it in any Court of Record by Action of debt of information in which no essoin, protection, Injunction or wager of Law shall be permitted or allowed.

And because the Negroes of this Isle in these late years past are very much increased and grown to such a great number as cannot be safely or easily governed unless we have a considerable number of Christians to balance and equal their Strength and the richest Men in the Island looking for the present profit, stock themselves only with almost all Negroes neglecting Christians Servants and so consequently their own and public safety.

CLAUSE 22:

Be it therefore enacted and ordained by the President, Council and Assembly and it is enacted and ordained by the authority of the same, that within twelve Months after publication hereof every freeholder provide himself of one Christian Servant for every twenty Acres of Land that he enjoys or possesses. And from the said twelve Months forward that every freeholder possessed of thirty Acres of land or more keep no less than one Man Servant for twenty Acres of Land he is Master, owner or occupier of, upon the penalty of forfeiting three thousand pounds of Muscavado sugar, one thousand to be to the Informer, one thousand to the Governor or Superior officer of this Island for the time being, and one thousand pounds to the Church wardens and overseers of the poor for the use of such poor where and in what parish such default is made, to be recovered against the refusing or neglecting obedience therein in any Court of Record by the party which shall sue for it and the fine to be new laid upon every person every three Months that he Continue his contumacy or refuse or neglect to perform obedience hereunto, Provided that in case Christian Servants cannot possibly be gotten that then those that want the proportion of this Act named to supply themselves with the like number of hired Men which are to be hired for six months at least that then they be not liable to the aforesaid forfeiture;

Lastly to the intent of this Act and every Clause and branch thereof may receive full Execution and no person plead Ignorance therein;

CLAUSE 23

It is ordained and enacted by the authority aforesaid that this Act be read and published in all the respective parish Churches in this Isle the first Sunday in February and the first Sunday in August every year ensuing the date and first publication hereof. Given under my hand, September 27th 1661

Signed: Humphrey Walrond

[From 'An Act for the Better Ordering and Governing of Negroes', *Barbados 1661*
(Public Record Office, Kew, CO 30/2/16–26), 25–8, 32–3.]

44   ***Code Noir* (1685) in Louisiana**

[In 1724] Louis [XV], By Grace of God, King of France and Navarre: . . . The Directors of the Company of the Indies having shown us that the Province and Colony of Louisiana is well established by a great number of our subjects who use Negro Slaves for the cultivation of the soil; we have decided . . . to establish law and certain rules to uphold the discipline of the Catholic, Apostolic and Roman Church; and in order to regulate that which relates to the condition of Slaves in the said islands. . . . For these and other causes which prompt us, and on the advice of our Council, and by our knowledge, power and Royal Authority, we have said, decreed and ordained and desire what follows:

First article

... We enjoin the Directors General of the said Company ... to expel from the said country all Jews who may have established residence ... who, as declared enemies of the Christian name, are commanded to leave in three months time ... under penalty forfeiting their bodies and goods.

II

All slaves who will be in our Province will be instructed in the Catholic, Roman and Apostolic Religion, and baptized. We order inhabitants who will buy newly arrived immigrants to have them instructed and baptized within a reasonable time, under penalty of fine ...

III

We forbid the exercise of any other Religion than the Catholic ... We desire those who contravene be punished as rebels, disobedient to our commands. We forbid all [religious] assemblies ... the same penalties will be applied against Masters who allow them. ...

IV

No overseers will be put in charge of Negroes, who do not profess the Catholic Religion ... under penalty of confiscation of said Negroes. ...

V

We enjoin all our Subjects, whatever their quality and condition, to observe Sundays and Holidays; We forbid them to either work or to make their Slaves work, from midnight to midnight, at tilling the soil or any other tasks under penalty ... of the confiscation of the Slaves. ...

VI

We forbid our white Subjects, of either sex, to contract marriage with Blacks, under penalty of punishment and fine ... or any [clergy] to marry them. We also forbid our white Subjects as well as Blacks, whether freed or born free, from living in concubinage with Slaves. We wish those who will have had one or more children from such a union, including Masters who allowed it, to be punished with a fine of 300 livres, ... and if Slave Masters are parents of the said children, we wish that in addition to the fine, they forfeit both Slave and children ... who will be placed in a hospital, never to be freed. (This will not be applicable if the free black man ... will wed the said slave, who will be freed by this means, and the children rendered free and legitimate).

VII
... The prescribed solemnities ... [of marriage] ... will be observed as much as for Slaves as for free persons, except that only the Master's, not the parents', consent will be necessary.

VIII
We forbid *Curés* to marry Slaves without the consent of their Masters; We also forbid Masters to coerce their slaves into marrying against their inclination.

IX
Children born of Slave marriages will be slaves, who will belong to the Masters of the females, and not to their husband's [master] if the Slaves belong to different masters.

X
We desire, if the slave husband has wed a free woman, that the children, males as well as females, follow the condition of their mother, being free like she is, regardless of the servitude of their father; and, similarly, that if the father is free and the mother slave, the children will be slaves.

XI
Masters will be bound to bury their baptized slaves in holy ground within Cemeteries designated for this purpose. Those who die unbaptized will be interred at night in a field near the spot where they died.

XII
We forbid slaves to carry any offensive arms or large batons, under penalty of whipping and confiscation of their arms to whoever will find and seize them, excepting those [slaves] sent hunting by their Masters and who are bearers of passes.

XIII
We similarly forbid Slaves belonging to different masters, to assemble, by day or night, under the pretext of marriage or otherwise, be it in the habitation of their Masters, or elsewhere, still less in main roads or remote places, under penalty of corporal punishment [whipping]. . . . Cases of repeat offenders, or with aggravating circumstances, can be punished by death.

XIV
Masters convicted of having allowed or tolerated such assemblies, composed of others' Slaves, will be condemned to make restitution for all damages to their neighbors occasioned by the said assemblies ... with double fines for recidivists.

XV

Slaves are forbidden to market or carry for sale, any kind of commodities, even fruits, vegetables, wood, greens, forage for beasts, grain, any other merchandise, or old clothes without the express written permission of their masters . . . under penalty of resale of their goods without restitution, and fines against buyers . . . [and in the case of selling old clothes] with extraordinary damages as receivers of stolen goods.

[. . .]

XVII

Any Subject is permitted to seize anything they find on Slaves moving without tickets from their Masters . . .

XVIII

We desire that the officers of our [Colonial] Superior Council send the quantity of provisions and the quality of clothes that they deem suitable for the Masters to furnish their Slaves. The provisions must be furnished weekly and the clothes annually . . . Masters are forbidden to give any kind of distilled spirits to slaves instead of said subsistence and clothing.

XIX

It is similarly forbidden [for Masters] to dispense with the maintenance of their slaves, by allowing them to work certain days of the week on their own account.

XX

Slaves who are not nourished, clothed and provided for by their Masters, can inform the *Procureur General* . . . Masters will be prosecuted at the request of the said prosecutor without payment of costs for Masters' barbaric and inhuman treatment towards their slaves.

XXI

Slaves disabled by age, sickness, incurable or not, will be nourished and provided for by their masters; case of abandonment, the Slaves will be moved to the nearest Hospital, to which Masters will be condemned to pay eight *sols* for each . . . Slave. . . .

XXII

We declare that slaves can have nothing not belonging to their Masters; anything [acquired] by their own industry or the generosity of others, by whatever means, is the complete property of their Masters; including all [slaves'] rights of inheritance. All Slave wills we declare null . . . being made by people incapable of deposing or contracting. . . .

[. . .]

XXIV
Slaves cannot undertake any public office, nor be constituted Agents by their Masters, nor become Arbitrators, or witnesses, unless their testimony be taken in default of white witnesses. In no case may they serve as witnesses for or against their Masters.

[. . .]

XXVII
The Slave who will have struck his Master, his Mistress, the spouse of his Master, or their children, with consequent contusion, or flow of blood, or in the face, will be punished with death.

[. . .]

XXXII
Fugitive Slaves in flight for more than a month . . . will have their ears severed and marked with a *Fleur-de-Lys* [Royal Symbol] branded on a shoulder. For absences of another month, he will have his hamstring severed, and branded on the other shoulder. On the third time he will be punished with death.

[. . .]

XXXVIII
We forbid all Subjects to practice or authorize torture on their Slaves, under any pretext, or to mutilate a Slave's member, under penalty of confiscation of their Slaves . . . except, when their Slaves will have merited it, to have [the slaves] chained and whipped with wooden switches.

XXXIX
Judicial officers . . . are enjoined to undertake criminal prosecutions against Masters and overseers who will have killed their Slaves or mutilated their limbs . . . They [officers] are to punish the murder according to circumstances, and, in case of judicial absolution, to permit both Masters and Overseers to return [to their positions].

[. . .]

XLII
The Formulas prescribed by our Ordinances and by the Custom of Paris for seizures of mobile property, will be observed for seizures of Slaves . . . ; generally, the condition of Slaves will be regulated in all suits in accord with those over other movable property.

XLIII
We desire nevertheless, that the husband, his wife and their pre-pubescent

children can not be seized and sold separately, if they are all under the power of the same Master. . . .

[. . .]

L

Masters aged twenty-five will be able to free their Slaves during their lifetimes or at death. However, as one may encounter Masters mercenary enough to price the freedom of their Slaves so high as to encourage theft and brigandage, we forbid any persons of whatever quality or condition they may be, to [set conditions for] their Slaves, without having obtained consent of our Superior Council.

[. . .]

LII

We declare that [freed persons] manumitted according to prescribed forms . . . have no need of letters of Naturalization, enjoying the advantages of our Natural born Subjects in our Kingdom, lands and countries owing us obedience.

[. . .]

LIV

We transmit to the freed the same rights, privileges and immunities enjoyed by the free born; We desire that the merit of acquired liberty may produce within them . . . the same effects that the happiness of natural liberty causes in our other Subjects, subject to the exceptions noted in Article LII.

[From *Publications of the Louisiana Historical Society,*
Vol. 4 (1908), 75–90. Trs. Seymour Drescher.]

45   Virginia Slave Code 1705

An act concerning Servants and Slaves

I. *Be it enacted, by the governor, council, and burgesses, of this present general assembly, and it is hereby enacted, by the authority of the same,* That all servants brought into this country without indenture, if the said servants be christians, and of christian parentage, and above nineteen years of age, shall serve but five years; and if under nineteen years of age, 'till they shall become twenty-four years of age, and no longer.

II. *Provided always,* That every such servant be carried to the country court, within six months after his or her arrival into this colony, to have his or her age adjudged by the court, otherwise shall be a servant no longer than the accustomary five years, although much under the age of nineteen years; and the age of such servant being adjudged by the court, within the limitation aforesaid, shall be entered upon the records of the said court, and be accounted, deemed, and taken, for the true age of the said servant, in relation to the time of service aforesaid.

III. *And also be it enacted, by the authority aforesaid, and it is hereby enacted,* That when any servant sold for the custom, shall pretend to have indentures, the master or owner of such servant, for discovery of the truth thereof, may bring the said servant before a justice of the peace; and if the said servant cannot produce the indenture then, but shall still pretend to have one, the said justice shall assign two months time for the doing thereof; in which time, if the said servant shall not produce his or her indenture, it shall be taken for granted that there never was one, and shall be a bar to his or her claim of making use of one afterwards, or taking any advantage by one.

IV. *And also be it enacted, by the authority aforesaid, and it is hereby enacted,* That all servants imported and brought into this country, by sea or land, who were not christians in their native country, (except Turks and Moors in amity with her majesty, and others that can make due proof of their being free in England, or any other christian country, before they were shipped, in order to transportation hither) shall be accounted and be slaves, and as such be here bought and sold notwithstanding a conversion to christianity afterwards.

V. *And be it enacted, by the authority aforesaid, and it is hereby enacted,* That if any person or persons shall hereafter import into this colony, and here sell as a slave, any person or persons that shall have been a freeman in any christian country, island, or plantation, such importer and seller as aforesaid, shall forfeit and pay, to the party from whom the said freeman shall recover his freedom, double the sum for which the said freeman was sold. To be recovered, in any court of record within this colony, according to the course of the common law, wherein the defendant shall not be admitted to plead in bar, any act or statute for limitation of actions.

VI. *Provided always,* That a slave's being in England, shall not be sufficient to discharge him of his slavery, without other proof of his being manumitted there.

VII. *And also be it enacted, by the authority aforesaid, and it is hereby enacted,* That all masters and owners of servants, shall find and provide for their servants, wholesome and competent diet, clothing, and lodging, by the discretion of the county court; and shall not, at any time, give immoderate correction; neither shall, at any time, whip a christian white servant naked, without an order from a justice of the peace: And if any, notwithstanding this act, shall presume to whip a christian white servant naked, without such order, the person so offending, shall forfeit and pay for the same, forty shillings sterling, to the party injured: To be recovered, with costs, upon petition, without the formal process of an action, as in and by this act is provided for servants complaints to be heard; provided complaint be made within six months after such whipping.

[. . .]

XI. And for a further christian care and usage of all christian servants, *Be it also enacted, by the authority aforesaid, and it is hereby enacted*, That no negros, mulattos, or Indians, although christians, or Jews, Moors, Mahometans, or other infidels, shall, at any time, purchase any christian servant, nor any other, except of their own complexion, or such as are declared slaves by this act: And if any negro, mulatto, or Indian, Jew, Moor, Mahometan, or other infidel, or such as are declared slaves by this act, shall, notwithstanding, purchase any christian white servant, the said servant shall, *ipso facto*, become free and acquit from any service then due, and shall be so held, deemed, and taken: And if any person, having such christian servant, shall intermarry with any such negro, mulatto, or Indian, Jew, Moor, Mahometan, or other infidel, every christian white servant of every such person so intermarrying, shall, *ipso facto*, become free and acquit from any service then due to such master or mistress so intermarrying, as aforesaid.

[. . .]

XXXV. *And also be it enacted, by the authority aforesaid, and it is hereby enacted*, That no slave go armed with gun, sword, club, staff, or other weapon, nor go from off the plantation and seat of land where such slave shall be appointed to live, without a certificate of leave in writing, for so doing, from his or her master, mistress, or overseer: And if any slave shall be found offending herein, it shall be lawful for any person or persons to apprehend and deliver such slave to the next constable or head-borough, who is hereby enjoined and required, without further order or warrant, to give such slave twenty lashes on his or her bare back, well laid on, and so send him or her home: And all horses, cattle, and hogs, now belonging, or that hereafter shall belong to any slave, or of any slaves mark in this her majesty's colony and dominion, shall be seised and sold by the church-wardens of the parish, wherein such horses, cattle, or hogs shall be, and the profit thereof applied to the use of the poor of the said parish: And also, if any damage shall be hereafter committed by any slave living at a quarter where there is no christian overseer, the master or owner of such slave shall be liable to action for the trespass and damage, as if the same had been done by him or herself.

XXXVI. *And also it is hereby enacted and declared*, That baptism of slaves doth not exempt them from bondage; and that all children shall be bond or free, according to the condition of their mothers, and the particular directions of this act.

XXXVII. And whereas, many times, slaves run away and lie out, hid and lurking in swamps, woods, and other obscure places, killing hogs, and committing other injuries to the inhabitants of this her majesty's colony and dominion, *Be it therefore enacted, by the authority aforesaid, and it is hereby enacted,* That in all such cases, upon intelligence given of any slaves lying out, as aforesaid, any two justices (*Quorum unus*) of the peace of the county wherein such slave is supposed to lurk or do mischief, shall be and are impowered and required to issue proclamation against all such slaves, reciting their names, and owners names, if they are known, and thereby requiring them, and every of them, forthwith to surrender themselves; and also impowering the sheriff of the said county, to take such power with him, as he shall think fit and necessary, for the effectual apprehending such out-lying slave or slaves, and go in search of them: Which proclamation shall be published on a Sabbath day, at the door of every church and chapel, in the said county, by the parish clerk, or reader, of the church, immediately after divine worship: And in case any slave, against whom proclamation hath been thus issued, and once published at any church or chapel, as aforesaid, stay out, and do not immediately return home, it shall be lawful for any person or persons whatsoever, to kill and destroy such slaves by such ways and means as he, she, or they shall think fit, without accusation or impeachment of any crime for the same: And if any slave, that hath run away and lain out as aforesaid, shall be apprehended by the sheriff, or any other person, upon the application of the owner of the said slave, it shall and may be lawful for the county court, to order such punishment to the said slave, either by dismembring, or any other way, not touching his life, as they in their discretion shall think fit, for the reclaiming any such incorrigible slave, and terrifying others from the like practices.

XXXVIII. *Provided always, and it is further enacted,* That for every slave killed, in pursuance of this act, or put to death by law, the master or owner of such slave shall be paid by the public:

XXXIX. And to the end, the true value of every slave killed, or put to death, as aforesaid, may be the better known; and by that means, the assembly the better enabled to make a suitable allowance thereupon, *Be it enacted,* That upon application of the master or owner of any such slave, to the court appointed for proof of public claims, the said court shall value the slave in money, and the clerk of the court shall return a certificate thereof to the assembly, with the rest of the public claims.

[From 'The Virginia Slave Code 1705,' in William Waller Hening, *The Statutes at Large, Being a Collection of All the Laws of Virginia from the First Session of the Legislature in the Year 1619* (Philadelphia: Thomas Desilver, 1823), Vol. III: 447, 460–1.]

Of Master and Servant

Having thus commented on the rights and duties of persons, as standing in the *public* relations of magistrates and people; the method I have marked out now leads me to consider their rights and duties in *private* oeconomical relations.

The three great relations in private life are, 1. That of *master and servant*; which is founded in convenience, whereby a man is directed to call in the assistance of others, where his own skill and labour will not be sufficient to answer the cares incumbent upon him. 2. That of *husband and wife*; which is founded in nature, but modified by civil society: the one directing man to continue and multiply his species, the other prescribing the manner in which that natural impulse must be confined and regulated. 3. That of *parent and child*, which is consequential to that of marriage, being its principal end and design: and it is by virtue of this relation that infants are protected, maintained, and educated. But, since the parents, on whom this care is primarily incumbent, may be snatched away by death or otherwise, before they have completed their duty, the law has therefore provided a fourth relation; 4. That of *guardian and ward*, which is a kind of artificial parentage, in order to supply the deficiency, whenever it happens, of the natural. Of all these relations in their order.

In discussing the relation of *master and servant*, I shall, first, consider the several sorts of servants, and how this relation is created and destroyed: secondly, the effects of this relation with regard to the parties themselves: and, lastly, it's effect with regard to other persons.

I. As to the several sorts of servants: I have formerly observed that pure and proper slavery does not, nay cannot, subsist in England; such I mean, whereby an absolute and unlimited power is given to the master over the life and fortune of the slave. And indeed it is repugnant to reason, and the principles of natural law, that such a state should subsist any where. The three origins of the right of slavery assigned by Justinian, are all of them built upon false foundations. As, first, slavery is held to arise '*jure gentium*,' from a state of captivity in war; whence slaves are called *mancipia, quasi manu capti*. The conqueror, say the civilians, had a right to the life of his captive; and, having spared that, has a right to deal with him as he pleases. But it is an untrue position, when taken generally, that, by the law of nature or nations, a man may kill his enemy: he has only a right to kill him, in particular cases; in cases of absolute necessity, for self-defence; and it is plain this absolute necessity did not subsist, since the victor did not actually kill him, but made him prisoner. War is itself justifiable only on principles of self-preservation; and therefore it gives no other right over prisoners, but merely to disable them from doing harm to us, by confining their persons: much less can it give a right to kill, torture, abuse, plunder, or even to enslave, an enemy, when the war is over. Since therefore the right of *making* slaves by captivity, depends on a supposed right of slaughter, that foundation failing, the consequence drawn from it must fail likewise. But, secondly, it is said that slavery may begin '*jure civili;*' when one man sells himself to another. This, if only meant of contracts to serve or work for another, is very just: but when applied to strict slavery, in the sense of the laws of old Rome or modern Barbary, is also impossible. Every sale implies a price, a *quid pro quo*, an equivalent given to the seller in lieu of what he transfers to the buyer: but what equivalent can be given for life, and liberty, both of which (in absolute slavery) are held to be in the master's disposal? His property also, the very price he seems to receive, devolves *ipso facto* to his master, the instant he becomes his slave. In this case therefore the buyer gives nothing, and the seller receives nothing: of what validity then can a sale be, which destroys the very principles upon which all sales are founded? Lastly, we are told, that besides these two ways by which slaves '*fiunt,*' or are acquired, they may also be hereditary: '*servi nascuntur;*' the children of acquired slaves are, *jure naturae*, by a negative kind of birthright, slaves also. But this being built on the two former rights must fall together with them. If neither captivity, nor the sale of oneself, can by the law of nature and reason, reduce the parent to slavery, much less can it reduce the offspring.

Upon these principles the law of England abhors, and will not endure the existence of, slavery within this nation: so that when an attempt was made to introduce it, by statute 1 Edw. VI. c. 3. which ordained, that all idle vagabonds should be made slaves, and fed upon bread, water, or small drink, and refuse meat; should wear a ring of iron round their necks, arms, or legs; and should be compelled by beating, chaining, or otherwise, to perform the work assigned them, were it never so vile; the spirit of the nation could not brook this condition, even in the most abandoned rogues; and therefore this statute was repealed in two years afterwards. And now it is laid down, that a slave or negro, the instant he lands in England, becomes a freeman; that is, the law will protect him in the enjoyment of his person, his liberty, and his property. Yet, with regard to any right which the master may have acquired, by contract or the like, to the perpetual service of John or Thomas, this will remain exactly in the same state as before: for this is no more than the same state of subjection for life, which every apprentice submits to for the space of seven years, or sometimes for a longer term. Hence too it follows, that the infamous and unchristian practice of withholding baptism from negro servants, lest they should thereby gain their liberty, is totally without foundation, as well as without excuse. The law of England acts upon general and extensive principles: it gives liberty, rightly understood, that is, protection, to a jew, a turk, or a heathen, as well as to those who profess the true religion of Christ; and it will not dissolve a civil contract, either express or implied, between master and servant, on account of the alteration of faith in either of the contracting parties: but the slave is entitled to the same liberty in England before, as after, baptism; and, whatever service the heathen negro owed to his English master, the same is he bound to render when a christian.

[From 'Of the Rights of Persons,' in *Commentaries on the Laws of England: A Facsimile of the First Edition of 1765–1769* (Chicago: University of Chicago Press, 1979), Vol. I: 410–13.]

47   Danish Slave Code 1733

Whatever the truth of the matter, it remains a fact that the Danish treatment of slaves became increasingly harsh and uncompromising in the opening decades of the 18th century, culminating in the Draconian code of September 5, 1733, which we publish below so that the reader may better understand the fear of a slave revolt, the harshness of the treatment of the slaves, the motives behind the slave revolt later that same year and, finally, the ferocity of the rebellion:

1. The leader of runaway slaves shall be pinched three times with red-hot pincers and then hanged.
2. Each other runaway slave shall lose one leg, or if the owner pardons him, shall lose one ear, and receive one hundred and fifty lashes.
3. Any slave knowing of the intention of others to run away, and not giving information, shall be burned on the forehead, and receive one hundred lashes.
4. Informants of runaway plots shall receive $10 for each slave engaged therein.
5. A slave who runs away for eight days, shall receive one hundred and fifty lashes, for twelve weeks, shall lose a leg, and for six months, shall forfeit life, unless the owner pardons him, in which instance he is to lose one leg.
6. Slaves who steal the equivalent of four rixdalers or more, shall be pinched and hanged; less than four rixdalers, they shall be branded, and receive one hundred and fifty lashes.
7. Slaves who receive stolen goods, as such, or protect runaways, shall be branded and receive one hundred and fifty lashes.
8. A slave who lifts his hand to strike a white person, or threatens him with

violence shall be pinched and hanged, should the white person demand it; if pardoned, he shall lose his right hand.

9. One white person shall be sufficient witness against a slave, and if a slave be suspected of a crime, he can be tried by torture.

10. A slave meeting a white person shall step aside, and wait until he passes; if not, he may be flogged.

11. No slave shall be permitted to come to town with clubs or knives, nor fight with each other, under penalty of fifty lashes.

12. Witchcraft shall be punished by flogging.

13. A slave who attempts to poison his master shall be pinched three times with red-hot pincers, and then broken on a wheel.

14. A free Negro who shall harbor a runaway slave or a thief shall lose his freedom or be banished.

15. All dances, feasts, and plays are forbidden unless permission be obtained from the master or overseer.

16. Slaves shall not sell provisions of any kind, without permission from their overseer.

17. No estate slave shall be in town after drum-beat, otherwise he shall be placed in the fort and flogged.

18. The King's advocate is ordered to see that those regulations be rigorously enforced.

> [From 'The Danish Slave Code 1733,' in Aimery Caron and Arnold Highfield, *The French Intervention in the St. John Slave Revolt of 1733–34*, Occasional Paper no. 7 (St. Thomas, V.I.: Bureaus of Libraries, Museums and Archaeological Services of Conservation and Cultural Affairs, 1981), 15–16.]

48 Sommersett's Case 1772

From Mr. Hargrave's Argument

II. In the outset of the argument I made a second question on Mr. Steuart's authority to enforce his right, if he has any, by transporting the negro out of England. Few words will be necessary on this point, which my duty as counsel for the negro requires me to make, in order to give him every possible chance of a discharge from his confinement, and not from any doubt of success on the question of slavery.

If in England the negro continues a slave to Mr. Steuart, he must be content to have the negro subject to those limitations which the laws of villenage imposed on the lord in the enjoyment of his property in the villein; there being no other laws to regulate slavery in this country. But even those laws did not permit that high act of dominion which Mr. Steuart has exercised; for they restrained the lord from forcing the villein out of England. The law, by which the lord's power over his villein was thus limited, has reached the present times. It is a law made *temp.* William I., and the words of it are, *prohibemus ut nullus vendat hominem extra patriam.*

If Mr. Steuart had claimed the negro as a servant by contract, and in his return to the *habeas corpus* had stated a written agreement to leave England as Mr. Steuart should require, signed by the negro, and made after his arrival in England, when he had a capacity of contracting, it might then have been a question, whether such a contract in writing would have warranted Mr. Steuart in compelling the performance of it, by forcibly transporting the negro out of this country? I am myself satisfied, that no contract, however solemnly entered into, would have justified such violence. It is contrary to the genius of the English law to allow any enforcement of agreements or contracts by any other compulsion than that from our courts of justice. The exercise of such a power is not lawful in cases of agreements for property; much less ought it to be so for enforcing agreements against the person. Besides, is it reasonable to suppose, that the law of England would permit that against the servant by contract, which is denied against the slave? Nor are great authorities wanting to acquit the law of England of such an inconsistency, and to show that a contract will not warrant a compulsion by imprisonment, and consequently much less by transporting the party out of this kingdom. Lord Hobart, whose extraordinary learning, judgment, and abilities, have always ranked his opinion amongst the highest authorities of law, expressly says, that 'the body of a freeman cannot be made subject to distress or imprisonment by contract, but only by judgment'. There is, however, one case, in which it is said that the performance of a service to be done abroad may be compelled without the intervention of a court of justice: I mean the case of an infant apprentice, bound by proper indentures to a mariner or other person, where the nature of the service imports that it is to be done out of the kingdom, and the party, by reason of his infancy, is liable to a coercion not justifiable in ordinary cases. The Habeas Corpus Act goes a step further; and persons who, by contract in writing, agree with a merchant or owner of a plantation, or any other person, to be transported beyond sea, and receive earnest on such agreements, are excepted from the benefit of that statute. I must say, that the exception appears very unguarded; and if the law, as it was previous to this statute, did entitle the subject to the *habeas corpus* in the case which the statute excepts, it can only operate in excluding him in that particular case from the additional provisions of the statute, and cannot, I presume, be justly extended to deprive him of the *habeas corpus* as the common law gave it before the making of the statute.

Upon the whole, the return to the *habeas corpus* in the present case, in whatever way it is considered, whether by inquiry into the foundation of Mr. Steuart's right to the person and service of the negro, or by reference to the violent manner in which it has been attempted to enforce that right, will appear equally unworthy of this court's approbation. By condemning the return, the revival of domestic slavery will be rendered as impracticable by introduction from our colonies and from other countries, as it is by commencement here. Such a judgment will be no less conducive to the public advantage, than it will be conformable to natural justice, and to principles and authorities of law; and this court, by effectually obstructing the admission of the new slavery of negroes into England, will in these times reflect as much honour on themselves, as the great judges, their predecessors, for- merly acquired, by contributing so uniformly and successfully to the suppression of the old slavery of villenage.

The judgment of the court was delivered by Lord Mansfield C. J., after some delay, and with evident reluctance, as follows:—'The only question before us is, whether the cause on the return is sufficient? If it is, the negro must be remanded; if it is not, he must be discharged. The return states, that the slave departed and refused to serve; whereupon he was kept, to be sold abroad. So high an act of dominion must be recognized by the law of the country where it is used. The power of a master over his slave has been extremely different, in different countries. The state of slavery is of such a nature, that it is incapable of being introduced on any reasons, moral or political; but only by positive law, which preserves its force long after the reasons, occasion, and time itself from whence it was created, is erased from memory: It's so odious, that nothing can be suffered to support it, but positive law. Whatever inconveniences, therefore, may follow from the decision, I cannot say this case is allowed or approved by the law of England; and therefore the black must be discharged'.

[From 'Sommersett's Case 1772,' in Herbert Broom, *Constitutional Law* (London: William Maxwell, 1866), 102–5.]

49 *Código Negro* 1789

Royal instruction on the education, treatment and occupation of slaves

Aranjuez, 31 May 1789

The King. In the Code of the Laws of Partida [Laws of Castile compiled by Alfonso X *c*.1263] and other bodies of legislation of these Kingdoms, in that of the Compilation of the Indies, general and particular decrees communicated to my dominions in America from their discovery and in the ordinances that, examined by my Council of the Indies, have merited my Royal approval, the system has been established, observed, and constantly followed of making the slaves useful and has provided that which is proper for their education, treatment, and the work their owners should give them in accordance with the principles and rules that religion, humanity and the good of the state dictate, compatible with slavery and public tranquility. However, since it may not be easy for all my vassals in America who possess slaves to instruct themselves sufficiently in all the provisions of the laws included in said collections and even less in the general and particular decrees and municipal ordinances approved for the various provinces, it should be kept in mind that for this very reason, notwithstanding what was mandated by my August Predecessors on the education, treatment and occupation of the slaves, some abuses inconsistent and even opposed to the system of legislation and to other general and particular measures taken on the subject have been introduced by their owners and administrators. With the end of remedying such disorders and considering that with the freedom of commerce in blacks that I granted to my vassals by the first article of the Royal Decree of 28 February last, the number of slaves in both Americas will increase considerably, this class of individuals of the human race, meriting the proper attention, in the interim, while the general code that is being formed for the dominions of the Indies establishes and promulgates the laws corresponding to this important end, I have resolved that for now the following Instruction be observed punctiliously by all the owners and possessors of slaves of those dominions.

Article I
Education

Every possessor of slaves, of whatever class and condition he might be, should instruct them in the principles of the Catholic religion and in the necessary truths so that they may be baptized within the year of their residence in my dominions, taking care that the Christian doctrine be explained on all the religious holidays, during which they will not be obligated nor will they be permitted to work for themselves, nor for their owners, except during harvest time, when it is customary to give permission to work on the holidays. In these and in other estates that adhere to the precept of hearing mass, the estate owners should pay for a priest who says mass to one and all and from the start explains to them Christian doctrine and administers the holy sacraments, both at the time of Church services and at other times that they ask for or need them, taking care as well that every day of the week, after finishing work, that they pray the rosary in their [master's] presence or in that of their administrator with the greatest composure and devotion.

Article II
On food and clothing

Being constant the obligation incumbent upon the owners of slaves to feed them and clothe them and their women and children, whether these be in the same condition or already free, until they can earn for themselves their maintenance, which they are presumed to be able to do on reaching twelve years of age in women and fourteen in men; and not being able to give a fixed rule on the quantity and the quality of the food and the type of clothing that they should provide, due to the diversity of provinces, climate, temperaments, and other individual causes, it is anticipated that with regard to these points the justices of the district of the estates, in accordance with the town council and the hearing of the syndic in his capacity as protector of the slaves, will indicate and determine the quantity and quality of the foods and clothing that owners should provide daily to the slaves, proportionate to their ages and sexes, in accord with the customs of the country and to those [standards] commonly given to free day-laborers, whose regulation, after being approved by the district Tribunal, will be posted monthly on the doors of the town council and of the Churches of every town and in the oratories and hermitages of the estates, in order that it comes to the notice of everyone and no one can claim ignorance.

Article III
Occupation of slaves

The first and principal occupation of the slaves should be agriculture and other rural labor and not the employments of the sedentary life; and in this way so that the owners and the State obtain the proper use of their labors and that the slave discharges them as is fit, the justices of the cities and towns, in the same way as in the preceding article, will arrange the daily tasks of work of the slave proportionate to their age, strength, and robustness, in such a manner that from the beginning and ending of work, from sun to sun, two hours are left during this time of the day so that they [the slaves] may use the time in manufactures or occupations that accrue to their personal benefit and utility, without the owners or administrators being able to require to work at tasks those over seventy years, nor those younger than seventeen, nor either slave women, nor using them in work inappropriate for their sex, nor in work that has them mixing with men, nor assigning them as day-laborers, and for those who apply for domestic service, [the owners] will contribute the two pesos annually provided for in chapter eight of the Royal decree of 28 February last that has been cited.

Article IV
Diversions

During those religious holidays. when the owners cannot obligate or permit the slaves to work, after these slaves have heard mass and attended to the explication of the Christian doctrine, the owners or in their stead the administrators will see to it that the slaves of their estates, without their assembling with those from the other estates and with the separation of the two sexes, occupy themselves in simple and plain diversions that these same owners and overseers should witness, avoiding excessive drinking and making sure that these diversions are concluded before the ringing of the prayer bell.

Article V
Of the dwellings and infirmary

All the owners of slaves should give them separate dwellings for the two sexes, not being married, and they should be comfortable and sufficient so that [the slaves] may be sheltered from bad weather, with raised beds, the necessary blankets and clothing, and with separation one from the other and at most, two in a room, and another separate space or dwelling, warm and comfortable will be assigned sick slaves and be attended as necessary by their owners; and in case they, by not having room on the estates or because their estates are near populated areas, might want to send them to the hospital, the owner should contribute for their stay a daily quota fixed by justice in the way and form provided in the second article, being likewise the obligation of the owner to pay the cost of interment if death occurs.

Article VI
Of the old and the chronically ill

The slaves who by their advanced age or infirmity are in no condition to work and similarly children and minors of both sexes shall be fed by the owners, without these owners granting them their liberty to unburden themselves from these slaves, unless providing them with a sufficient peculium to the satisfaction of justice at a hearing by the chief magistrate, so that they could maintain themselves without the need of other help.

Article VII
Marriage of slaves

The owners of slaves should avoid illicit conduct of the two sexes, encouraging marriages, without impeding he who marries those slaves of other owners; in which case, if the estates are far apart so that they [the slaves] might not fulfill the conditions of marriage, the wife will follow the husband, his owner buying her at a just valuation made by appraisers named by the parties and by a third party who in case of disagreement will name the judge; and if the owner of the husband does not agree to the sale, then the same action may be taken by the owner of the woman.

Article VIII
Obligations of slaves and corrective punishments

Because the owners of slaves have to sustain them, educate them and employ them in productive labor proportionate to their strength, age, and sex, without forsaking the minors, the old, and the sick, it follows for that very reason that the slaves are also obligated to obey and respect their owners and administrators, to discharge the tasks and work that they are assigned in accordance with their strength and to honor them like a father, and thus he that might fail any of these obligations could and should be punished correctively for the excesses he commits, whether by the owner of the estate or by the administrator, according to the nature of the defect or excess, with imprisonment, shackle, chain, weighted shackle, or stocks, so long as he is not put into it by the head, or receive more than twenty-five lashes and only with a soft instrument that does not cause them serious contusion or flow of blood, which corrective punishment shall not be imposed on slaves by persons other than their owners or administrators.

Article IX
On the imposition of major punishments

When the slaves have failings or commit excesses or transgressions against their owners, or any other person and the corrective penalties dealt with in the preceding article might not be sufficient for punishment or chastisement, the injured party or a person representing him, after the offender has been secured by the owner or administrator of the estate or by whomever finds himself present at the commission of the crime, should inform the magistrate in order to have a hearing with the slave's owner, if he has not relinquished him before answering the summons and is not concerned in the accusation, and in all cases involving the syndic, he, in his capacity as protector of the slaves, shall proceed in conformity with the laws from the beginning of the process to the final decision and at the imposition of the appropriate punishment, according to the gravity and circumstances of the crime, observing in everything what those same laws establish for the trials of offenders of free status. And when the owner does not relinquish the slave and he is condemned to the satisfaction of damages and injuries in favor of a third party, the owner shall be responsible for them, short of corporal punishment, which according to the gravity of the crime, the offending slave will suffer, after having been approved by the district court, if it were to be death or mutilation of a body part.

Article X
Failings and excesses of owners and administrators

The owner of slaves or administrator of an estate who does not fulfill that which is provided for in the articles of this instruction on the education of the slaves, food, clothing, moderation of work and tasks, attendance at wholesome diversions, assignation of dwellings and infirmary or who abandons minors, the old or disabled, will for the first time incur a fine of fifty pesos, the second time, one hundred, and the third time, two hundred, which fines the owner will satisfy even in the case that only his administrator is culpable, if the latter cannot pay, distributing the amount in three parts, to accuser, judge, and collector of fines, who will be handling it. And in case the preceding fines do not produce the desired result and backsliding is verified, the guilty party will be proceeded against with even greater punishments as disobedient to my Royal orders, and I will be informed with evidence so that I can take the appropriate measures.

When the failings of the owners and administrators are due to excesses of corrective punishments, causing the slaves serious contusions, flow of blood or mutilation of a body part, besides suffering the same monetary fines cited, the owner or administrator will be proceeded against criminally at the instigation of the syndic, substantiating the case according to law, and the penalty corresponding to the crime committed will be imposed on him, as if the injured party were free, in addition to having the slave removed to be sold to another owner, if he remains able to work, applying his sale price to the office of fines, and when the slave is unable to be sold, without returning him to the owner or to the administrator who committed the excessive punishment, the owner shall contribute to the daily maintenance that justice requires and clothing for the entire life of the slave, to be paid in advance to third parties.

Article XI
Of those who injure slaves

Since only the owners and administrators can correctively punish slaves with the moderation that has been provided for, any other person who is not their owner or administrator cannot injure, punish, wound, or kill them, without incurring the penalties established by law for those who commit similar excesses or transgressions against free persons, the case to be followed, substantiated and determined at the instigation of the owner of the slave who had been injured, punished, or killed; in his default, at the instigation of the syndic, who in his official capacity as protector of the slaves, will also have the right of intervention in the first case, even though there may be an accuser.

Article XII
List of slaves

The owners of slaves must present annually a list, signed and sworn to by the justice of the city or town in whose jurisdiction their estates are located, of the slaves who are there, distinguished by sex and age, so that it can be registered with the notary of the town council in a specific book that will be formed for this purpose, and it will be kept in the said town council with the list presented by the slaveowner, and he, whenever a slave dies or is missing from the estate, will inform the justice so that with the citation of the syndic it can be noted in the book in order to avoid all suspicion of his [the slave] having met a violent death; and whenever the owner does not fulfill this requirement, it will be his obligation to justify fully the death of the slave or his natural death, since if the contrary occurs the syndic will initiate a corresponding proceeding.

Article XIII
Means to verify the excesses of the owners and administrators

The distances between the estates and the towns, the difficulties that will result if with the pretext of making a complaint, slaves were permitted to depart from the former without identity papers from the owner or administrator that expressed the end point of their departure, and the just disposition of the laws against helping, protecting, and hiding fugitive slaves makes it necessary to advance the most proportionate measures to all these circumstances, so that information may be acquired on how they [the slaves] are treated on the estates. One of these ways is for the clergy who may go there to explain doctrine to them [the slaves] and to say mass to them, so they can learn for themselves and from the slaves themselves the manner of conduct of the owners and administrators and whether the provisions of this instruction are being observed, in order that the syndic of the respective city or town, given secret and confidential information, can proceed to investigate whether the owners or administrators are failing in all or part of their respective obligations without, by insufficient grounds or a confidential denunciation given by the clergyman as a result of his ministry or by complaint of the slaves, remaining responsible for anything, since the information ought only to serve as a basis by which the syndic may initiate and request before the justice that there be named an individual from the town council or another person of good conduct who proceeds to the investigation, forming the appropriate legal summary and delivering it to the same justice, who substantiates and decides the case according to law, hearing the syndic and reporting on the cases provided by the laws and this instruction to the district Tribunal and admitting the petitions of appeal for which there may be a cause in law.

Besides this measure it will be fitting that the judges, with the agreement of the town council and the attendance of the syndics, name a person or persons of character and good conduct who three times a year might visit and closely examine the estates and find out if what is prescribed in this instruction is being observed, reporting on what they find, so that moved by sufficient grounds, a remedy can be placed in a hearing of the syndic, declaring also by public action, that of denouncing the failings or lack of compliance with all or any one of the preceding articles and with the understanding that the name of the denouncer will always be confidential and the designated part of the fine be given him without any responsibility in any case other than the case of very fully and openly establishing that the denunciation or accusation was slanderous.

And finally it is also declared that in the judgments of the *residencia* [judicial review of public officials] the magistrates and syndics will take charge of the failings of omission or commission that might have been incurred by not having been put into effect the necessary measures so that my Royal intentions explained in this instruction may have the desired effect.

[From 'Código Negro' (1789), in Richard Konetzke, *Colecciùn de Documentos para la Historia de la Formaciùn Social de Hispanoamérica 1493–1810* (Madrid: Consejo Superior de Investiguciones Cientificas, 1989), Vol. 3: 643–52. Trs. Robert L. Paquette.]

50 Cuban Slave Code 1842

1. Every slaveholder shall instruct his slaves in the principles of the Holy Roman Catholic Apostolic Religion so that those who have not been baptized may be baptized, and in case of the danger of death, he shall baptize them, since it is known that in such cases anyone is authorized to do so.

2. The aforesaid instruction shall be given at night at the end of work, and immediately afterwards the slave shall recite the rosary or some other devout prayers.

3. On Sundays and feast days of obligation after fulfilling their religious obligations, slaveholders or those in charge of the estates shall employ the slaves for two hours to clean the houses and workshops, but no longer, nor

occupy them in the labors of the landed property, except in harvest time when delay is impossible. In such cases they shall work the same as on week days.

[. . .]

6. Masters shall necessarily give their slaves in the country two or three meals a day as they may think best, provided that they may be sufficient to maintain them and restore them from their fatigues, keeping in mind that six or eight plantains or its equivalent in sweet potatoes, yams, yuccas, and other edible roots, eight ounces of meat or salt fish, four ounces of rice or other pottage or meal is standardized as daily food and of absolute necessity for each individual.

7. [Masters] shall give them two suits of clothes a year in the months of December and May, each consisting of a shirt and pants of nankin or linen, a cap or hat, and handkerchief; in December shall be added alternatively a flannel shirt one year and a blanket for protection during the winter the next.

8. Newly-born or small slave children, whose mothers are sent to work in the field, shall be fed very light food such as soups, *atoles* [a pap made from corn flour], milk, and similar substances until they are weaned entirely and have finished teething.

9. While the mothers are at work, all children shall remain in a house or room that all sugar estates and coffee estates should have, which shall be under the care of one or more female slaves, as the master or administrator may deem necessary, according to the number of children.

10. If [slave children] shall become sick during the lactation period, they shall be nursed by the breasts of their own mothers, who shall be exempted from fieldwork and applied to domestic duties.

11. Until they reach the age of three years, [slave children] shall have shirts of striped gingham; from age three to six they may be of nankin. The girls of six to ten shall be given skirts or long dresses, and the boys of six to fourteen shall be provided with trousers. After these ages the dress shall be like the adults.

12. In ordinary times slaves shall work nine or ten hours daily, the master arranging these hours as best he can. On sugar plantations during harvest time, the hours shall be sixteen, arranged in such a way that the slave shall have two hours in the day to rest and six at night to sleep.

13. On Sundays and on feast days of obligation and in the hours of rest during the week days, slaves shall be permitted to employ themselves within the estate in mechanical labors or occupations, the product of which shall be for their own benefit in order to be able to acquire the means to purchase their freedom.

14. Male and female slaves older than sixty years or less than seventeen shall not be obliged to do strenuous work, nor shall any of these classes

be employed in work not appropriate to their age, sex, strength, and constitution.

15. Those slaves who because of their age or because of sickness are not fit for work shall be maintained by their owners, who shall not be permitted to give them their freedom in order to get rid of them, unless they provide them with sufficient means, according to the dictates of justice and the determination of the *procurador síndico*, so that they may be able to support themselves without need of other assistance.

[. . .]

19. Slaves of one estate shall not be able to visit those of another without the express consent of the masters or overseers of both. When they have to go to another estate or leave their own, they shall take a written pass from the owner or overseer with the description of the slave, the date of the day, month, and year, the declaration of his destination, and the time he must return.

20. Any individual of whatever class, color, and condition he may be is authorized to arrest any slave if he is met outside of the house or lands of his master; if he does not present the written license he is obliged to carry; or if, on the presentation, it shows that the bearer has manifestly changed the route or direction described or the leave of absence has expired. The individual shall conduct said slave to the nearest estate, whose owner shall receive him and secure him and notify the slave's master, should he be from the same district, or the *pedaneo* [district magistrate], so that he may give notice to the interested party in order that the fugitive slave may be recovered by the person to whom he belongs.

[. . .]

27. On each plantation there shall be a room well-closed and secured for each sex and two others besides for contagious diseases where slaves who may fall sick shall be attended in severe cases by physicians and in slight cases, where household remedies are sufficient, by male or female nurses, but always with good medicine, proper food, and with the greatest cleanliness.

28. The sick shall be placed, where it is possible, in separate beds that consist of a straw mattress, mat, or *petate* [a mat made of palm leaves], pillow, blanket, and sheet, or on boards sufficiently convenient for the healing of individuals that lie on them, but in all cases raised from the floor.

29. Masters of slaves shall avoid the illicit contact of both sexes and encourage marriages. They shall not prevent marriages made with slaves of other owners, and they shall give to married couples the means of living under the same roof.

30. To accomplish this end and so that the consorts may fulfill the ends of matrimony, the wife shall follow the husband whose master shall buy her at a price that may be suitable to both sides or else by arbiters appointed by both sides or by a third party in case of disagreement. If the master of the

husband does not want to buy the wife, then her owner shall have the power to buy the husband. In the event that neither of the owners want to make the purchase, then the married slaves shall be sold together to a third party.

31. When the master of the married male slave buys the wife, he shall also buy all her children under three years old, since according to law the mothers are obliged to suckle and nurse them until they attain that age.

32. Masters shall be obliged by the magistrates to sell their slaves when they have injured them, badly treated them, or committed other excesses contrary to humanity and the rational way with which they should be treated. The sale shall be made in these cases at the price fixed by the arbiters of both sides, or by a magistrate in case one of these should refuse to name a price, or by a third person in case of disagreement, when it may be necessary. But if there is a buyer who wants to purchase them without arbitration at the price fixed by the master, then the sale shall be made in his favor.

33. When masters sell their slaves for their own convenience or at their own determination, they shall be at liberty to fix any price that pleases them, according to the greater or lesser estimation of them.

34. No master shall oppose the *coartación* of his slaves if they present at least fifty pesos of their price on account.

35. Slaves *coartados* shall not be sold for a higher price than that fixed in the last *coartación*, and this condition shall pass from buyer to buyer. However, if the slave desires to be sold against the will of his master without just cause or by his bad conduct gives cause to be sold, the master may add to the price the amount of the sales tax and the cost of the deed of sale.

36. As the benefit of *coartación* is very personal, the children of the mothers *coartadas* cannot be participants in it, and they can be sold like any other slave.

37. Masters shall free their slaves as soon as they put together the amount of their evaluation as legitimately fixed. The price, in case the interested parties do not agree, shall be named by an arbiter appointed by the owner of the slave or in his absence by a magistrate, another by the *procurador síndico* representing the slave, and a third chosen by said magistrate in case of disagreement.

[From 'The Cuban Slave Code, 1842,' in Robert L. Paquette, *Sugar is Made with Blood: The Conspiracy of La Escalera and the Conflict Between Empires Over Slavery in Cuba* (Middletown: Wesleyan University Press, 1988), 267–72.]

The Princess Imperial, Regent, in the name of His Majesty the Emperor Senhor D. Pedro II, makes known to all the subjects of the Empire, that the General Assembly has decreed, and that she has sanctioned, the following Law:

ART. I. The children of women slaves that may be born in the Empire from the date of this Law shall be considered to be free.

§ 1. The said minors shall remain with and be under the dominion of the owners of the mother, who shall be obliged to rear and take care of them until such children have completed the age of 8 years.

On the child of the slave attaining this age, the owner of its mother shall have the option either of receiving from the State the indemnification of 600 dollars (milréis) or of making use of the services of the minor until he shall have completed the age of 21 years.

In the former event the Government will receive the minor, and will dispose of him in conformity with the provisions of the present Law.

The pecuniary indemnification above fixed shall be paid in Government bonds, bearing interest at 6 percent per annum, which will be considered extinct at the end of 30 years.

The declaration of the owner must be made within 30 days, counting from the day on which the minor shall complete the age of 8 years; and should he not do so within that time it will be understood that he embraces the option of making use of the service of the minor.

§ 2. Any one of those minors may ransom himself from the *onus* of servitude, by means of a previous pecuniary indemnification, offered by himself, or by any other person, to the owner of his mother, calculating the value of his services for the time which shall still remain unexpired to complete the period, should there be no agreement on the *quantum* of the said indemnification.

§ 3. It is also incumbent on owners to rear and bring up the children which the daughters of their female slaves may have while they are serving the same owners.

Such obligation, however, will cease as soon as the service of the mother ceases. Should the latter die within the term of servitude the children may be placed at the disposal of the Government.

§ 4. Should the female slave obtain her freedom, her children under 8 years of age who may be under the dominion of her owners shall, by virtue of § 1, be delivered up, unless she shall prefer leaving them with him, and he consents to their remaining.

§ 5. In case of the female slave being made over to another owner, her free children under 12 years of age shall accompany her, the new owner of the said slave being invested with the rights and obligations of his predecessor.

§ 6. The services of the children of female slaves shall cease to be rendered before the term marked in § 1, if by decision of the Criminal Judge it be known that the owner of the mothers ill-treat the children, inflicting on them severe punishments.

§ 7. The right conferred on owners by § 1 shall be transferred in cases of direct succession; the child of a slave must render his services to the person to whose share in the division of property the said slave shall belong.

ART. II. The Government may deliver over to associations which they shall have authorised, the children of the slaves that may be born from the date of this Law forward, and given up or abandoned by the owners of said slaves, or taken away from them by virtue of Article I, § 6.

§ 1. The said associations shall have a right to the gratuitous services of the minors, until they shall have completed the age of 21 years, and may hire out their services, but shall be bound—

1st. To rear and take care of the said minors.

2ndly. To save a sum for each of them, out of the amount of wages, which for this purpose is reserved in the respective statutes.

3rdly. To seek to place them in a proper situation when their term of service shall be ended.

§ 2. The associations referred to in the previous paragraph shall be subject to the inspection of Judges of the Orphans' Court, in as far as affects minors.

§ 3. The disposition of this Article is applicable to foundling asylums, and to the persons whom the Judges of the Orphans' Court charge with the education of the said minors, in default of associations or houses established for that purpose.

§ 4. The Government has the free right of ordering the said minors to be taken into the public establishments, the obligations imposed by § 1 on the authorised associations being in this case transferred to the State.

ART. III. As many slaves as correspond in value to the annual disposable sum from the emancipation fund shall be freed in each province of the Empire.

§ 1. The emancipation fund arises from—

1st. The tax on slaves.

2ndly. General tax on transfer of the slaves as property.

3rdly. The proceeds of 6 lotteries per annum, free of tax, and the tenth part of those which may be granted from this time forth, to be drawn in the capital of the Empire.

4thly. The fines imposed by virtue of this Law.

5thly. The sums which may be marked in the general budget, and in those of the provinces and municipalities.

6thly. Subscriptions, endowments, and legacies for that purpose.

§ 2. The sums marked in the provincial and municipal budgets, as also the subscriptions, endowments, and legacies for the local purpose, shall be applied for the manumission of slaves in the provinces, districts, municipalities, and parishes designated.

ART. IV. The slave is permitted to form a saving fund from what may come to him through gifts, legacies, and inheritances, and from what, by consent of his owner, he may obtain by his labour and economy. The Government will see to the regulations as to the placing and security of said savings.

§ 1. By the death of the slave half of his savings shall belong to his surviving widow, if there be such, and the other half shall be transmitted to his heirs in conformity with civil law.

In default of heirs the savings shall be adjudged to the emancipation fund of which Article III treats.

§ 2. The slave who, through his savings, may obtain means to pay his value has a right to freedom.

If the indemnification be not fixed by agreement it shall be settled by arbitration. In judicial sales or inventories the price of manumission shall be that of the valuation.

§ 3. It is further permitted the slave, in furtherance of his liberty, to contract with a third party the hire of his future services, for a term not exceeding 7 years, by obtaining the consent of his master, and approval of the Judge of the Orphans' Court.

§ 4. The slave that belongs to joint proprietors, and is freed by one of them, shall have a right to his freedom by indemnifying the other owners with the share of the amount which belongs to them. This indemnification may be paid by services rendered for a term not exceeding 7 years, in conformity with the preceding paragraph.

§ 5. The manumission, with the clause of services during a certain time, shall not become annulled by want of fulfilling the said clause, but the freed man shall be compelled to fulfil, by means of labour in the public establishments, or by contracting for his services with private persons.

§ 6. Manumissions, whether gratuitous or by means of *onus*, shall be exempted from all duties, emoluments, or expenses.

§ 7. In any case of alienation or transfer of slaves, the separation of husband and wife, and children under 12 years of age from father or mother, is prohibited under penalty of annulment.

§ 8. If the division of property among heirs or partners does not permit the union of a family, and none of them prefers remaining with the family by replacing the amount of the share belonging to the other interested parties, the said family shall be sold and the proceeds shall be divided among the heirs.

§ 9. The ordination, Book 4th, title 63, in the part which revokes freedom, on account of ingratitude, is set aside.

ART. V. The Emancipation Societies which are formed, and those which may for the future be formed, shall be subject to the inspection of the Judges of the Orphans' Court.

Sole paragraph. The said societies shall have the privilege of commanding the services of the slaves whom they may have liberated, to indemnify themselves for the sum spent in their purchase.

ART. VI. The following shall be declared free:

§ 1. The slaves belonging to the State, the Government giving them such employment as they may deem fit.

§ 2. The slave given in *usufruct* to the Crown.

§ 3. The slaves of unclaimed inheritances.

§ 4. The slaves who have been abandoned by their owners.

Should these have abandoned the slaves from the latter being invalids they shall be obliged to maintain them, except in case of their own penury, the maintenance being charged by the Judge of the Orphans' Court.

§ 5. In general the slaves liberated by virtue of this Law shall be under the inspection of Government during 5 years. They will be obliged to hire themselves under pain of compulsion; if they lead an idle life they shall be made to work in the public establishments.

The compulsory labour, however, shall cease so soon as the freed man shall exhibit an engagement of hire.

ART. VII. In trials in favour of freedom—

§ 1. The process shall be summary.

§ 2. There shall be appeal *ex officio* when the decisions shall be against the freedom.

ART. VIII. The Government will order the special registration of all the slaves existing in the Empire to be proceeded with, containing a declaration of name, sex, age, state, aptitude for work, and filiation of each, if such should be known.

§ 1. The date on which the registry ought to commence closing shall be announced beforehand, the longest time possible being given for preparation by means of edicts repeated, in which shall be inserted the dispositions of the following paragraph.

§ 2. The slaves who, through the fault or omission of the parties interested, shall not have been registered up to one year after the closing of the register, shall, *de facto*, be considered as free.

§ 3. For registering each slave the owner shall pay, once only, the emolument of 500 rs., if done within the term marked, and 1 milréis should that be exceeded. The produce of those emoluments shall go towards the expenses of registering, and the surplus to the emancipation fund.

§ 4. The children of a slave mother, who by this Law became free, shall also be registered in a separate book.

Those persons who have become remiss shall incur a fine of 100 to 200 milréis, repeated as many times as there may be individuals omitted: and for fraud, in the penalties of Article CLXXIX of the Criminal Code.

§ 5. The parish priests shall be obliged to have special books for the registry of births and deaths of the children of slaves born from and after the date of this Law. Each omission will subject the parish priest to a fine of 100 milréis.

ART. IX. The Government, in its regulations, can impose fines of as much as 100 milréis, and the penalty of imprisonment up to 1 month.

ART. X. All contrary dispositions are revoked.

Therefore, order all authorities to whom, &c. Given at the Palace of Rio de Janeiro, on the 28th September, 1871. 50th of the Independence and of the Empire.

PRINCESS IMPERIAL, REGENT.

THEODORO MACHADO FREIRE PEREIRA DA SILVA.

[From 'Rio Branco Law, 1871,' in Robert Conrad, The Destruction of Brazilian Slavery
1850–1888 (Berkeley: University of California Press, 1973), 305–9.]

T. R. R. COBB

52   The Law of Negro Slavery

§ 1. *Absolute or Pure Slavery* is the condition of that individual, over whose life, liberty, and property another has the unlimited control. The former is termed a slave; the latter is termed the master. Slavery, in its more usual and limited signification, is applied to all involuntary servitude, which is not inflicted as a punishment for crime. The former exists at this day in none of the civilized nations of the world; the latter has, at some time, been incorporated into the social system of every nation whose history has been deemed worthy of record. In the former condition the slave loses all *personality*, and is viewed merely as *property*; in the latter, while treated under the general class of *things*, he posseses various rights as a person, and is treated as such by the law.

§ 2. A preliminary inquiry presents itself, and demands our first consideration, viz.: By what law or authority does this dominion of one man over another exist? by the law of nature, or by municipal law? And a satisfactory reply to this inquiry is absolutely necessary to the true resolution of many of the perplexing questions which arise from that relation. In the laws of Henry I, we find the declaration, 'servi alii naturâ, alii facto, alii empcione, alii redempcione, alii suâ vel alterius dacione servi'. The Institutes, on the contrary, declared all slavery to be 'contra naturam,' and this declaration, which might be true of a system which ignored entirely the existence of the slave as a person, has been almost universally adopted by courts and jurists. Upon the investigation of the truth of this proposition we propose to enter.

§ 3. That slavery is contrary to the law of nature, has been so confidently and so often asserted, that slaveholders themselves have most generally permitted their own minds to acknowledge its truth unquestioned. Hence, even learned judges in slaveholding States, adopting the language of Lord Mansfield, in Somerset's case, have announced gravely, that slavery being contrary to the law of nature, can exist only by force of positive law. The course of reasoning, by which this conclusion is attained, is very much this: That in a state of nature all men are free. That one man is at birth entitled by nature to no higher rights or privileges than another, nor does nature specify any particular time or circumstances under which the one shall begin to rule and the other to obey. Hence, by the law of nature, no man is the slave of another, and hence all slavery is contrary to the law of nature.

[. . .]

§ 7. The expression 'law of nature' is sometimes, though unphilosophically, used to express those deductions which may be drawn from a careful examination of the operations of the natural world. Hence, it is said that slavery is contrary to the law of nature, because we find no counterpart or analogous operation in the natural world. To this we may say, in the first place, that by such a definition of the law of nature, cannibalism and every other horrid crime of savage or natural man would be justified. Among lower animals, the destruction of their own species is of frequent occurrence. In the second place, that the fact does not exist as stated, for not only is slavery found to coexist with the human race, but even among the lower animals and insects, servitude, in every respect the counterpart of negro slavery, is found to exist. It is a fact, well known to entomologists, and too well established to admit of contradiction, that the red ant will issue in regular battle array, to conquer and subjugate the black or negro ant, as he is called by entomologists. And, that these negro slaves perform all the labor of the communities into which they are thus brought, with a patience and an aptitude almost incredible. These facts, originally noticed and published by Huber, have subsequently been verified by many observers; and M. Latreille has demonstrated, that the rufescent ants, on account of the form of their jaws and the accessory parts of their mouth, have not the physical ability either to prepare habitations for their family, to procure food, or to feed them. Upon this definition, therefore, of the law of nature, negro slavery would seem to be perfectly consistent with that law.

[. . .]

§ 16. On the contrary, the slaves of Europe during the middle ages, and of Britain prior to the Norman invasion, were many of the same race with their masters, their equals in intelligence and in strength, and nothing but the accidents of their birth distinguished them apart. It is not strange, therefore, that their philosophers and jurists should see in such slavery palpable violations of the law of nature, and should have proclaimed that nature made them all free and equal. Montesquieu perceived this distinction and the different conclusions to which these different states of fact gave rise, and hence, whilst he says all slavery must be accounted unnatural, yet he admits, that 'in some countries it is founded on natural reason,' viz., 'countries where the excess of heat enervates the body, and renders men so slothful and dispirited, that nothing but the fear of chastisement can oblige them to perform any laborious duty'. Hence, he says, that 'natural slavery must be limited to some particular parts of the world'. So Puffendorf says: 'It is most evident that some men are endued with such a happiness of wit and parts, as enables them not only to provide for themselves and their own affairs, but to direct and govern others. And that some again are so extremely stupid and heavy, as to be unfit to govern themselves, so that they either do mischief or do nothing, unless others guide and compel them. And farther, that these last being commonly furnished by nature with strong and hardy bodies, are capable of bringing many notable advantages to others by their labor and service. Now, when these have the fortune to live in subjection to a wise director, they are without doubt fixed in such a state of life as is most agreeable to their genius and capacity.'

[From *An Inquiry into the Law of Negro Slavery in the United States of America: To Which Is Attached a Historical Sketch of Slavery* (Savannah: W. T. Williams, 1858), 3–6, 8–9, 18–19.]

JOAQUIM NABUCO

53 **Abolitionism**

To recapitulate, I will sketch in broad strokes what slavery is *legally* in Brazil in 1883:

1. The present bondsmen, born before September 28, 1871, and today at least eleven and a half years old, are slaves until they die, *exactly* like those of earlier generations. The number of these, as will be seen, is more than a million.

2. Whoever is subject to slavery is compelled to obey without question every order received, to do whatever he is told, without the right to demand a thing: neither pay nor clothing, improved food nor rest, medicine nor change of duties.

3. The man so enslaved has no duties—to God, to his mother and father, to his wife or children, or even to himself—which the master *must* respect and allow him to perform.

4. The law does not fix maximum hours of labor, a minimum wage, rules of hygiene, food, medical treatment, conditions of morality, protection of women. In a word, it interferes as much in the organization of the plantation as it does in the supervision of draft animals.

5. There is no law whatever which regulates the obligations and prerogatives of the master; whatever the number of slaves he may possess, he exercises an authority over them which is limited only by his own judgment.

6. The master can inflict moderate punishment upon slaves, says the *Criminal Code*, which compares his authority to the power of a father; but in fact he punishes at will, because justice does not penetrate the feudal domain. A slave's complaint against his master would be fatal, as it has been in practice, and in fact the master is all-powerful. The attitudes of today are what they were in 1852. It is as dangerous now, and just as useless, for a slave to complain to the authorities as it was then. To accuse his master, the slave requires the same will power and determination that he needs to run away or to commit suicide, particularly if he hopes for some security in his servitude.

7. The slave lives in total uncertainty regarding his future; if he thinks he is about to be sold, mortgaged, or pawned, he has no right to question his master.

8. Any person released from the House of Correction or even confined within it, however perverse he may be, whether he be a Brazilian or foreigner, can own or buy a family of respectable and honest slaves and expose them to his whims.

9. Masters can employ female slaves as prostitutes, receiving the profits from this business with no danger of losing their property as a result, just as a father can be the owner of his son.

10. The state does not protect the slaves in any way whatsoever. It does not inspire them with confidence in public justice but instead surrenders them *without hope* to the implacable power which weighs heavily upon them, morally imprisons or constrains them, arrests their movement, and in short destroys them.

11. The slaves are governed by exceptional laws. The use of the lash against them is allowed, despite its prohibition by the Constitution. Their crimes are punished by a barbaric law, that of June 10, 1835, the sole penalty of which is execution.

12. The belief has been spread throughout the nation that slaves often

commit crimes in order to become convicts, in this way escaping from slavery, since they prefer the chain gang to the plantation, as Roman slaves preferred to fight wild beasts, in the hope of achieving freedom if they survived. For this reason a jury of the interior has absolved criminal slaves to be restored later to their masters, and lynch law has been carried out in more than one case. Here we have slavery as it really is! Death by suicide is looked upon by the bondsman as the *cessation of the evils of slavery*, imprisonment with hard labor such *an improvement in his condition* that it can be *an incentive to crime!* Meanwhile we, a humane and civilized nation, condemn more than a million persons, as so many others were condemned before them, to a condition alongside which imprisonment or the gallows seems better!

13. Not all the powers of the master, which, as we have seen, are practically without limit, are exercised directly by him, absent as he often is from his lands and out of contact with his slaves. Instead, these powers are delegated to individuals without intellectual or moral education, who know how to command men only by means of violence and the whip.

[From *Abolitionism: the Brazilian Antislavery Struggle* [1883], trs. and ed. Robert Conrad (Urbana: University of Illinois Press, 1977), 92–4.]

THOMAS D. MORRIS

54   Southern Slavery and the Law

Most slaves in North America were Africans or persons who had African ancestors. That led to a significant principle of American slave law. As Cobb put it, 'the black color of the race raises the presumption of slavery'. With one notable exception the general presumption based on 'blackness' was a commonplace of Southern law by the nineteenth century. The exception was Delaware. *State v. Dillahunt* (1840) involved a black witness in a murder trial who was objected to because it had not been proved that she was free. The court ruled her competent. It admitted that earlier in Delaware 'the fact of the existence of the negro race in a state of bondage to the whites, and a large majority of that color being slaves, was considered sufficiently strong . . . to introduce a legal presumption that a colored person is *prima facie* a slave'. That had changed. Of the 20,000 'persons of color' in Delaware in 1840, fully 17,000 were free and 3,000 were slaves. There was no longer any reason to 'presume slavery from color'.

Despite this exception Cobb was correct. However, he added that the presumption is 'extended, in most of the States, to mulattoes or persons of mixed blood, casting upon them the onus of proving a free *maternal* ancestor'. His textual support for this was that 'in Virginia and Kentucky, one-fourth negro blood presumes slavery, less than that, freedom'. This one-fourth rule, he claimed, was adopted in other states as well. Cobb was careless. What he did was to extend a rebuttable legal presumption of slavery that arose from 'blackness' to a larger category of people and link it to a statutory rule that defined a mulatto. They were not the same. They did involve the problem of legal categorization, and this, perhaps, was the reason for the mistake.

Exactly how did Southern whites categorize people at law and for what purposes? It may seem odd but the only effort to define a 'negro' in statutory law was in the Virginia code of 1849. The whole section was this: 'Every person who has one-fourth part or more of negro blood shall be deemed a mulatto, and the word 'negro' in any other section of this, or in any future statute, shall be construed to mean mulatto as well as negro.' There were other efforts to provide descriptions of a 'negro' in legal sources, but not in statutes. Cobb, for instance, wrote that 'the black color alone does not constitute the negro, nor does the fact of a residence and origin in Africa . . . : the negro race is marked by a black complexion, crisped or woolly hair, compressed cranium, and a flat nose. The projection of the lower parts of the face and the thick lips evidently approximate it to the monkey tribe.' O'Neall observed that the 'term negro is confined to slave Africans, (the ancient Berbers) and their descendants. It does not embrace the free inhabitants of Africa, such as the Egyptians, Moors, or the negro Asiatics, such as the Lascars.'

Some Southern legislators did try to define 'mulattoes'. The Spanish word *mulatto* came into English usage about 1600, but there was no *legal* definition in Virginia until 1705. For over half a century Virginians dealt with miscegenation without any formal legal definition to categorize the offspring.

Mulatto (derived from the Spanish word for a mule) was used to refer to a person with one white parent and one black. When colonial Virginians finally defined a mulatto in a legal text, they departed from the original idea. The Virginians' effort appeared in 1705 at the end of 'An act declaring who shall not bear office in this country'. This law did not create a legal presumption of slavery based on race; rather, it was an attempt to define who would enjoy all the rights and powers of free men and women and who would not. It was blatantly racist, of course, but it had nothing to do with slavery. The definition itself was odd: 'the child of an Indian and the child, grand child, or great grand child, of a negro shall be deemed, accounted, held and taken to be a mulatto.' The law defined as a mulatto a person born to a white and an Indian, an Indian and a black, a white and a black, or several other combinations covered outside the English slave societies by words such as quadroon or octoroon. Virginia's law, in other words, defined as a mulatto the offspring of any racially mixed couple no matter what the racial types.

Virginians, of course, had dealt with interracial sexual relationships before the adoption of this curious definition. Hugh Davis's case is but the earliest recorded example. In 1630 he was 'soundly whipt' before a number of blacks and whites for 'defiling his body in lying with a negro'. The first statute on interracial sexual relationships, however, was not adopted for another thirty-two years. The law of 1662 was introduced because 'doubts have arrisen whether children got by any Englishman upon a negro woman should be slave or ffree'. The principle applied was that the status of the child derived from its mother. By using this rule the legislators closed off the possibility of an innovative racial solution. They could have adopted the Chinese rule that all children born to mixed couples would take the status of the most degraded parent. Race could have been a reasonably firm 'ordering' principle of Southern slave law. But the Virginians left a large gap. What about the status of a child born to a white woman by a black father, especially a slave father? In 1679 Susanna Barnes was ordered to serve an additional two years in Charles City County because she had had a 'Bastard child being a Mulatto'. Nothing was recorded about the child. The void was filled by a law of 1691. It provided that any free Englishwoman who had a bastard by 'any negro or mulatto' would be fined. If she could not pay the fine, she was to serve five years as an indentured servant. Her child would be bound out as a servant until age thirty. In 1705 the age was raised to thirty-one; this law included an explanation: it was because the child was an 'abominable mixture and spurious issue'. The burgesses added another layer in 1723. Any child born to a 'female mullatto, or indian' who was bound to serve for the thirty or thirty-one years would also serve that woman's master. The time of service would be the same as the mother's. By 1765 the ages of service were dropped to twenty-one for males and eighteen for females because it was considered 'an unreasonable severity' to make them serve until the age of thirty-one. By the nineteenth century enforced servitude of children born to a free white woman by a slave father dropped out of the records. During the colonial period it was different. In Charles City County, for instance, Joseph Barham, a bastard 'begot by a negro on the body of a white woman,' was bound out in 1744 according to the law.

Virginia's final effort to define a mulatto was an influential statute copied in other jurisdictions. The 1785 law provided that 'every person who shall have one-fourth part or more of negro blood, shall . . . be deemed a mulatto'. Outside of colonial Virginia, Maryland and North Carolina also tried to define a mulatto. North Carolina developed a couple of definitions but, according to Jordan, 'pushed the taint of Negro ancestry from one-eighth to one-sixteenth'. South Carolina, Georgia, and Delaware did not produce statutory definitions: it was a matter of observation in those jurisdictions. In 1715 Maryland initiated the thirty-one-year servitude rule for mulattoes born to white women, and North Carolina adopted it in 1741.

[From *Southern Slavery and the Law, 1619–1860* (Chapel Hill: University of North Carolina Press, 1996), 21–4.]

Section IV

The Slave Trade

INTRODUCTION

The recruitment of human beings for coercive use, whether productive or reproductive, has varied over the course of human history. It occurred through violent confrontation, including capture in warfare or the kidnapping of outsiders; through a natural process (birth); or through judicial procedures within a community, as a punishment for crimes, including default on debt or taxes. Enslavement could also occur as part of a contractual process, the sale of one's self or one's children for survival or debt, and for limited or indefinite periods of time.

Among all of these possibilities, the use of the market for long-distance exchanges played a major role in the acquisition of servile populations in both premodern and modern times. Long before the development of the transatlantic network enslaved persons were shipped by land and sea from the East Africa coast to India, and further East, to the island networks of Southeast Asia and the Pacific. Slave trading was endemic within the Mediterranean basin and Western Asia for thousands of years. Medieval Europe, from Ireland to Russia, was one site of slave networks, while many others were transported overland within the larger continental land masses of the world, in Africa and the pre-Columbian Americas. Among the most highly developed slave markets, both before and after 1500, was the transcontinental transfer of slaves across the Sahara and the Caucasus. Expansive and dynamic warrior regimes, such as the Aztec empire in the Americas and the Roman and Arabic empires in the Mediterranean, provided suitable political frameworks for large-scale and continuous traffic in slaves. One of the most massive and enduring market systems in human beings flowed in the Islamic orbit from across the Sahara to the South and Eurasia to the North. The trans-Saharan trade alone accounted for the movement of upwards of ten million African slaves during the last millennium.

As indicated by the geographic and temporal extension of this global phenomenon, almost all large human collectives, whether defined by language, culture, or physical traits, were involved in these systems of migration, both as traded and traders. The dominant groups in such exchanges were in a position to set the rules about who was naturally or justifiably enslavable, or otherwise subordinate, and who could be so moved.

Throughout the world, males were the predominant gender among slaves. The most well-documented trade routes, from Africa after 1500, indicate that the ratio of men to women sent into the extra-continental markets varied markedly from one region to another. In part, the overlap between the trans-Saharan and transatlantic markets after 1500 may help to explain local divergences between the relative flow of males to females out of Africa. The trans-Saharan trade absorbed larger proportions of females, who might otherwise have been directed toward the Atlantic. American buyers, usually more concerned with the productive than the reproductive capacities of the enslaved Africans, may have been less emphatic about gender ratios in their purchases than were Arab trans-Saharan purchasers or sub-Saharan sellers. As will be evident from the readings, womens' voices are much more difficult to uncover in the documentary record, even amongst the transatlantic victims. The most famous published autobiographical accounts of the intercontinental trade were predominately male.

Despite many general continuities in the structure of slave trades across time and space, the transatlantic trade between 1500 and the mid-nineteenth century remains exceptional. The dreadful conditions under which the enslaved were transported across the Atlantic—the notorious 'Middle Passage'—probably had parallels only in the trans-Saharan passage or in coerced movements to death and prison camps in twentieth-century Europe. In economic complexity and durability, if not in rates of morality, the Middle Passage probably constitutes an extreme example of a market in human beings. Between 1450 and 1870, Europeans, Euroamericans, Africans, and Americans combined to transport about twelve million Africans northward and westward across the Atlantic. All told, an equal number, or more, may have remained as captives within Africa itself.

At the other end of the Middle Passage lay the regions of destination in the Americas. Even before the first European conquests after 1500, population densities in the Americas were generally lower than in the Old World. This differentiation was dramatically increased over the next two centuries, owing to the decline of the Amerindian populations in the New World, including the circum-Caribbean and Brazil. Sub-Saharan societies were well organized to provide captives for this westward extra-continental trade. Although the enslaved Africans were more successful in resisting fevers of African origin in the tropical Americas, Europe's sources of labor even in the Caribbean Islands consisted initially of Indian slaves or white servants and exiles. The shift of European proprietors from various forms of European labor to African slaves appears to have been the result of cultural constraints and cost considerations as well as demographic realities. By 1800, up to three Africans had been forcibly transported to the Americas for every European who crossed the Atlantic.

A proper understanding of the transatlantic slave trade requires attention to all aspects of the intercontinental exchange complex, including the perspective of rulers and merchants, producers and consumers, religious leaders and warriors, ship captains and caravan guides, and planters and laborers on the four continents bordering the Atlantic. During the first three centuries of its existence, the overseas slave trade generated an unprecedented abundance and variety of documentation. Moreover, as the system came under intensive attack during the last century of its existence, (c.1770–1870), the trade was subjected to close and more continuous scrutiny. The relative documentary wealth of this period is reflected in the range of readings in this section.

55 The Plan of the *Brookes*

During the discussion of the possible regulation of slave vessels, Captain Perry visited Liverpool and examined eighteen vessels, nine of which belonged to James Jones. His report on their measurements is to be found in Add. MSS. 38416, ff. 208–212. The dimensions of the *Brookes*, one of the vessels examined, were: 'Length of the lower deck, gratings and bulkheads included, at A A, 100 feet, breadth of beam on lower deck inside, B B, 25 feet 4 inches, depth of Hold, O O O, from ceiling to ceiling, 10 feet, height between decks, from deck to deck, 5 feet 8 inches, length of the men's room, C C, on the lower deck, 46 feet, breadth of the men's room, C C, on the lower deck, 25 feet 4 inches, length of the platforms, D D, in the men's room, 46 feet, breadth of the platforms in the men's room on each side, 6 feet, length of the boy's room, E E, 13 feet 9 inches, breadth of the boy's room, 25 feet, breadth of platforms, F F, in boy's room, 6 feet, length of women's room, G G, 28 feet 6 inches, breadth of women's room, 23 feet 6 inches, length of platforms, H H, in women's room, 28 feet 6 inches, breadth of platforms in women's room, 6 feet, length of the gun-room, I I, on the lower deck, 10 feet 6 inches, breadth of the gun-room on the lower deck, 12 feet, length of the quarter-deck, K K, 33 feet 6 inches, breadth of the quarter-deck, 19 feet 6 inches, length of the cabin, L L, 14 feet, height of the cabin, 6 feet 2 inches, length of the half-deck, M M, 16 feet 6 inches, height of the half-deck, 6 feet 2 inches, length of the platforms, N N, on the half-deck, 16 feet, 6 inches, breadth of the platforms on the half-deck, 6 feet, upper deck, P P.

'Let it now be supposed that the above are the real dimensions of the ship *Brookes*, and further, that every man slave is to be allowed six feet by one foot four inches for room, every woman five feet ten by one foot four, every boy five feet by one foot two, and every girl four feet six by one foot, it will follow that the annexed plan of a slave vessel will be precisely the representation of

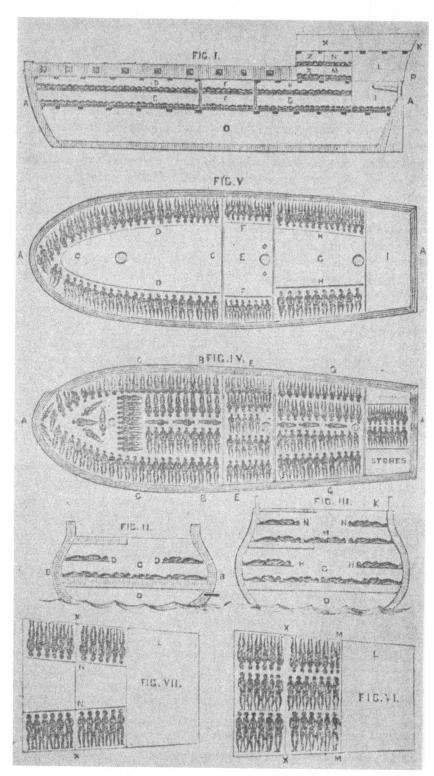

The Plan of the Brookes.

the ship *Brookes*, and of the exact number of persons neither more nor less, that could be stowed in the different rooms of it upon these data. These, if counted, (deducting the women stowed in Z, of figures VI and VII,) will be found to amount to *four hundred and fifty-one*. Now, if it be considered that the ship *Brookes* is of three hundred and twenty tons, and that she is allowed to carry by act of Parliament *four hundred and fifty-four persons*, it is evident that if three more could be wedged among the number represented in the plan, this plan would contain precisely the number which the act directs.

'By the late act of Parliament the space Z, which is half of the half-deck, M Z, is appropriated to the seamen'.

For an account of Captain Perry's results see Clarkson, *Abolition of the Slave Trade*, II. 90–92. Extensive use was made of this diagram in carrying forward the work for abolition. Clarkson took it to Paris with him, where Mirabeau had a small model made from it, which he placed in his dining-room; copies of it were sent to Philadelphia, where 3700 were circulated. It was published in the *Museum* (V. 429–430, May, 1789), with extracts from a descriptive pamphlet published by an abolition society of Plymouth. Here the statement is made that the *Brookes* on one of her voyages carried 609 slaves, double the number shown in this diagram. This was said to have been accomplished by inserting additional shelves between decks.

[From Elizabeth Donnan, *Documents Illustrative of the History of the Slave Trade to America* [1931] (New York: Octagon, 1969), Vol. II: 592 and adjacent page.]

56 Brother Luis Brandaon to Father Sandoval

March 12, 1610

Your Reverence writes me that you would like to know whether the negroes who are sent to your parts have been legally captured. To this I reply that I think your Reverence should have no scruples on this point, because this is a matter which has been questioned by the Board of Conscience in Lisbon, and all its members are learned and conscientious men. Nor did the bishops who were in São Thomé, Cape Verde, and here in Loando—all learned and virtuous men—find fault with it. We have been here ourselves for forty years and there have been [among us] very learned Fathers; in the Province of Brazil as well, where there have always been Fathers of our order eminent in letters, never did they consider this trade as illicit. Therefore we and the fathers of Brazil buy these slaves for our service without any scruple. Furthermore, I declare that if any one could be excused from having scruples it is the inhabitants of those regions, for since the traders who bring those negroes bring them in good faith, those inhabitants can very well buy from such traders without any scruple, and the latter on their part can sell them, for it is a generally accepted opinion that the owner who owns anything in good faith can sell it and that it can be bought. Padre Sánchez thus expresses this point in his Book of Marriage, thus solving this doubt of your Reverence. Therefore, we here are the ones who could have greater scruple, for we buy these negroes from other negroes and from people who perhaps have stolen them; but the traders who take them away from here do not know of this fact, and so buy those negroes with a clear conscience and sell them out there with a clear conscience. Besides I found it true indeed that no negro will ever say he has been captured legally. Therefore your Reverence should not ask them whether they have been legally captured or not, because they will always say that they were stolen and captured illegally, in the hope that they will be given their liberty. I declare, moreover, that in the fairs where these negroes are bought there are always a few who have been captured illegally because they were stolen or because the rulers of the land order them to be sold for offenses so slight that they do not deserve captivity, but these are few in number and to seek among ten or twelve thousand who leave this port every year for a few who have been illegally captured is an impossibility, however careful investigation may be made. And to lose so many souls as sail from here—out of whom many are saved—because some, impossible to recognize, have been captured illegally does not seem to be doing much service to God, for these are few and those who find salvation are many and legally captured.

[From Elizabeth Donnan, *Documents Illustrative of the History of the Slave Trade* [1930] *to America* (New York: Octagon, 1969), Vol. I: 123–4.]

57   Voyage of the *James*, 1675–6

1675. *March.* A journall of my intended voyage for the gold Coast kept by mee Peter Blake Commandr of the Royall Companys Ship *James* in the searvis of the Royall Affrican Company of England. . . .

27. *Saturday.* the Committee came downe consisting of three persons *viz*: Mr. William Roberts Esqr. Capt. Abraham Holditch and Mr. William Stevens. . . .

Aprill, Thursday 1. . . . sent a pylott a shore with my lettr to the company and ordered him to ride through for London. . . . rec'd a packett from Mr. Heron by ordr of the royall company directed to Agent Generall Mellish Esqr. at Cape Corsoe. . . .

An acc'tt of the mortallity of slaves aboard the shipp 'James'.

1675	DAY	MEN	WOMEN	BOYS	GIRLS	
Abbenee [September]	6	1				Departed this Life suddenly.
Temenn October	28			1		Departed this life of Convulsion Fitts
Agga December	20	1				Departed this life of a feavour
Cape Corso January 1675/6	20	1				Rec'd from Wyemba thin and Consumed to Nothing and soe dyed
Ditto	26		1			Rec'd from Wyemba very thin and wasted to Nothing and soe dyed
Suckingdee February 1675/6	8	1				Rec'd from Wyemba very thin and dropsicall and soe departed this life.
Thwort of Butteren	23		1			bought to Windward and departed this life of a Consumption and Wormes.
Ditto	24			1		Received from Wyembah with a dropsy and departed this life of the same disease.
Dirkeys Cove—March	26		1			Rec'd from Wyemba thin and soe Continued Untill Death
Ditto	5		1			Miscarryed and the Child dead within her and Rotten and dyed 2 days after delivery.
Att Sea	13	1				Rec'd from Wyembah very thin and soe Continued untill hee departed this life.
Ditto	15	1				Rec'd from Wyembah very thin and fell into a flux and soe Continued untill his death.

An acc'tt of the mortallity of slaves aboord the shipp 'James'. —*contd*

1676		DAY	MEN	WOMEN	BOYS	GIRLS	
Att Sea	1676	18	1				Rec'd from Wyembah very thin and soe fell into a Consumption and dep'ted this life
Ditto		30	1				Rec'd from Wyembah very thin and soe Continued Wasting untill death.
Ditto		31			1		Very sick and fell overboard in the night and was lost.
Ditto April		6	1				Rec'd from Wyembah thin and Consumed very low and after dyed of a Great Swelling of his face and head.
Ditto		14	1				Rec'd from Wyembah thin and dyed of a flux
Ditto		15		1			Rec'd from Wyembah Sickned and would not eat nor take anything.
Ditto		16	1				bought by mee and dyed of a flux
Ditto		17	2				The one rec'd from Wyembah and dyed of a flux. The other rec'd ditto who Leaped Over boord and drowned himself.
Ditto		20		1			rec'd thin at Wyembah and dyed of a Consumption.
Ditto		21			1		rec'd from Weyembah with a dropsy and soe dyed.
Ditto		26		1			bought by myselfe and being very fond of her Child Carrying her up and downe wore her to nothing by which means fell into a feavour and dyed.

Att Sea	May	1	1	1	Rec'd from Anamabooe departed this life of a flux.
Ditto		2		1	Rec'd from Agga and departed this life of a flux.
Ditto		3	1		Rec'd from Wyembah and dep'ted this life of a dropsy.
Ditto		4	1	1	Rec'd of Mr. Ballwood att Amy Sea and dyed of a feavour by Lying in the Long boat, in the rain in the night which noe man knew of for hee went into her privately.
Ditto		5		1	Rec'd from Wyembah very thin and old and dep'ted this Life of the flux.
Ditto		6	1		Rec'd from Annamabooe and dep'ted this life of a flux.
Ditto		8		1	Rec'd from Wyembah with a Dropsey and departed this life of the same disease.
Ditto		9	1		bought by mee att Anamaboe and departed this life of the flux.
Ditto		12		1	Rec'd from Wyembah thin and Consumed away untill life departed from her.
Ditto		13	1		Rec'd from Wyembah thin and dep'ted of a flux.
			1		Rec'd from Anamaboe and dyed of the Cramp in all his Joynts and all over his body being lately recovered of the flux.
				1	bought by mee dyed of the Cramp.

An acc'tt of the mortallity of slaves aboord the shipp 'James'.—contd

1676		DAY	MEN	WOMEN	BOYS	GIRLS	
Att Sea	May	14		2			the one rec'd from Wyembah very thin departed this life of the flux the other recd from Anamabooe and departed this life of the flux.
	Ditto	16	1				Rec'd from Annamaboe and departed this life of a flux.
	Ditto	20		1			bought by mee and departed this life of Convultions.
Barbados		21	1				Rec'd from Agga and departed this life of a flux.
	ditto	22	1				Rec'd at Wyembah and departed this life of a flux.
	ditto	23	1	1			The woman bought by mee dyed of Convultions the man rec'd att Anamabooe dyed of the flux.
	ditto	29		1			Rec'd from Wyembah and dyed of a Consumption.
	ditto	31		1			Rec'd ditto and dyed of a dropsy.
June 1	ditto	1	1				
		4		1			
		6	2	1			
			23	19	4		

Monday 5. . . . off Cows road . . . sent a letter to bee conveyed to the African howse according to the Direction, and I made saile. . . .

Friday 30th. . . . made the Land of Bonevis

Maie, Saturday 1. . . . eastermost pointe of Saintiaugoo I halled in for Appaia roade . . . went ashoare to the Govern'r whome . . . informed mee that Geo: Parris had ben—but was gone—for Saintiauggoe roade, upon which I retturned aboard and fynding that hee was und'r commaund of the Portingall foarte wee thought it most convenient to saile for Cape Mount and waite his comeing there. . . .

Monday 30. [August]. . . . came in sight of the towne of Assenee . . . sent my pinase with six of my passeng'rs to Cape Corso with all the lett'rs and pap'rs belonging to the Agent. . . .

Tuesday 31st. . . . severall canoes came aboard from this towne to whom I sold severall goods for gold and slaves.

Sept'r 1675, Wednesday 1st. . . . severall canoeoes came . . . to whome I sold severall goods for gold and slaves. . . .

Thursday 2d. . . . severall cannoes aboard of wich I tooke but littell gold and bought 3 slaves. . . .

Friday 3d. . . . I bought two slaves and tooke two ounces of gold. . . .

Monday 6th. . . . a neaggerman dep'ted this life whoe died suddenly. . . .

[From Elizabeth Donnan, *Documents Illustrative of the History of the Slave Trade* [1930] to America (New York: Octagon, 1969), Vol. I: 199, 206–9.]

58 Voyage of the *Hannibal*, 1693–4

[Feb. 27.] The castle of Cabo Corce is the chief of all those our African company have upon this coast, and where their agents or chief factors always reside, to which all the other factories are subordinate. This castle has a handsome prospect from the sea, and is a very regular and well contriv'd fortification, and as strong as it can be well made, considering its situation, being encompass'd with a strong and high brick wall, thro' which you enter by a well-secur'd and large gate facing the town, and come into a fine and spacious square wherein 4 or 500 men may very conveniently be drawn up and exercis'd. It has four flankers which have a cover'd communication with each other, and are mounted with good guns. . . .

In this castle the agents and factors have genteel convenient lodgings; and as to the soldiers, I believe there are not better barracks anywhere than here, each two having a handsome room allow'd them, and receive their pay duly and justly in gold dust once a week for their subsistence. The castle has in all about forty guns mounted, some of them brass, and commonly 100 white men in garrison, with a military land officer to discipline and command them under the agents. . . .

I also carried there on account of the African company, muskets, niconees, tapseals, baysadoes, brass kettles, English carpets, Welsh plains, lead bars, firkins of tallow, powder, etc. None of which did answer expectation, being forc'd to bring back to England a great part of them; and those we sold were at a very low rate. . . .

When we were at the trunk, the king's slaves, if he had any, were the first offer'd to sale, which the cappasheirs would be very urgent with us to buy, and would in a manner force us to it ere they would shew us any other, saying they were the Reys Cosa, and we must not refuse them, tho' as I observ'd they were generally the worst slaves in the trunk, and we paid more for them than any others, which we could not remedy, it being one of his majesty's prerogatives: then the cappasheirs each brought out his slaves according to his degree and quality, the greatest first, etc. and our surgeon examin'd them well in all kinds, to see that they were sound wind and limb, making them jump, stretch out their arms swiftly, looking in their mouths to judge of their age; for the cappasheirs are so cunning, that they shave them all close before we see them, so that let them be never so old we can see no grey hairs in their heads or beards; and then having liquor'd them well and sleek with palm oil, 'tis no easy matter to know an old one from a middle-age one, but by the teeths decay; but our greatest care of all is to buy none that are pox'd, lest they should infect the rest aboard. . . .

When we had selected from the rest such as we liked, we agreed in what goods to pay for them, the prices being already stated before the king, how much of each sort of merchandize we were to give for a man, woman, and child, which gave us much ease, and saved abundance of disputes and wrang-lings, and gave the owner a note, signifying our agreement of the sorts of goods; upon delivery of which the next day he receiv'd them; then we mark'd the slaves we had bought in the breast, or shoulder, with a hot iron, having the letter of the ship's name on it, the place being before anointed with a little palm oil, which caus'd but little pain, the mark being usually well in four or five days, appearing very plain and white after.

[. . .]

The negroes are so wilful and loth to leave their own country, that they have often leap'd out of the canoes, boat and ship, into the sea, and kept under water till they were drowned, to avoid being taken up and saved by our boats, which pursued them; they having a more dreadful apprehension of Barbadoes than we can have of hell, tho' in reality they live much better there than in their own country; but home is home, etc: we have likewise seen divers of them eaten by the sharks, of which a prodigious number kept about the ships in this place, and I have been told will follow her hence to

Barbadoes, for the dead negroes that are thrown over-board in the passage. I am certain in our voyage there we did not want the sight of some every day, but that they were the same I can't affirm.

We had about 12 negroes did wilfully drown themselves, and others starv'd themselves to death; for 'tis their belief that when they die they return home to their own country and friends again.

I have been inform'd that some commanders have cut off the legs and arms of the most wilful, to terrify the rest, for they believe if they lose a member, they cannot return home again: I was advis'd by some of my officers to do the same, but I could not be perswaded to entertain the least thought of it, much less put in practice such barbarity and cruelty to poor creatures, who, excepting their want of christianity and true religion (their misfortune more than fault) are as much the works of God's hands, and no doubt as dear to him as ourselves; nor can I imagine why they should be despis'd for their colour, being what they cannot help, and the effect of the climate it has pleas'd God to appoint them. I can't think there is any intrinsick value in one colour more than another, nor that white is better than black, only we think so because we are so, and are prone to judge favourably in our own case, as well as the blacks, who in odium of the colour, say, the devil is white, and so paint him.

[. . .]

When we come to sea we let them all out of irons, they never attempting then to rebel, considering that should they kill or master us, they could not tell how to manage the ship, or must trust us, who would carry them where we pleas'd; therefore the only danger is while we are in sight of their own country, which they are loth to part with; but once out of sight out of mind: I never heard that they mutiny'd in any ships of consequence, that had a good number of men, and the least care; but in small tools where they had but few men, and those negligent or drunk, then they surpriz'd and butcher'd them, cut the cables, and let the vessel drive ashore, and every one shift for himself. However, we have some 30 or 40 gold coast negroes, which we buy, and are procur'd us there by our factors, to make guardians and over-seers of the Whidaw negroes, and sleep among them to keep them from quarrelling; and in order, as well as to give us notice, if they can discover any caballing or plotting among them, which trust they will discharge with great diligence; they also take care to make the negroes scrape the decks where they lodge every morning very clean, to eschew any distempers that may engender from filth and nastiness; when we constitute a guardian, we give him a cat of nine tails as a badge of his office, which he is not a little proud of, and will exercise with great authority. We often at sea in the evenings would let the slaves come up into the sun to air themselves, and make them jump and dance for an hour or two to our bag-pipes, harp, and fiddle, by which exercise to preserve them in health; but notwithstanding all our endeavour, 'twas my hard fortune to have great sickness and mortality among them.

[From Elizabeth Donnan, *Documents Illustrative of the History of the Slave Trade to America* [1930] (New York: Octagon, 1969), Vol. I: 395–6, 401–3, 407–8.]

JOHN NEWTON

59   Journal of a Slave Trader, 1750–4

The nature and effects of that unhappy and disgraceful branch of commerce, which has long been maintained on the coast of Africa, with the sole and professed design of purchasing our fellow creatures, in order to supply our West India islands and the American colonies, when they were ours, with slaves, is now generally understood. So much light has been thrown upon the subject by many able pens, and so many respectable persons have already engaged to use their utmost influence for the suppression of a traffic which contradicts the feelings of humanity, that it is hoped this stain of our national character will be soon wiped out.

[. . .]

For the sake of method, I could wish to consider the African trade—first, with regard to the effect it has upon our own people; and secondly, as it concerns the blacks, or, as they are more contemptuously styled, the negro slaves, whom we purchase upon the coast. But these two topics are so interwoven together, that it will not be easy to keep them exactly separate.

1. The first point I shall mention is surely of political importance, if the lives of our fellow-subjects be so; and if a rapid loss of seamen deserves the attention of a maritime people. This loss, in the African trade, is truly alarming. I admit, that many of them are cut off in their first voyage, and consequently, before they can properly rank as seamen; though they would have been seamen if they had lived. But the neighbourhood of our seaports is continually drained of men and boys to supply the places of those who die abroad; and if they are not all seamen, they are all our brethren and countrymen, subjects of the British government.

The people who remain on ship-board, upon the open coast, if not accustomed to the climate, are liable to the attack of an inflammatory fever, which is not often fatal, unless the occurrence of unfavorable circumstances makes it so. When this danger is over, I think they might probably be as healthy as in most other voyages, provided they could be kept from sleeping in the dews, from being much exposed to the rain, from the intemperate use of spirits, and especially from women.

[. . .]

But slaves are the staple article of the traffic; and though a considerable number may have been born near the sea, I believe the bulk of them are brought from far. I have reason to think that some travel more than a thousand miles, before they reach the sea-coast. Whether there may be convicts amongst these likewise, or what proportion they may bear to those who are taken prisoners in war, it is impossible to know.

I judge, the principal source of the slave trade, is, the wars which prevail among the natives. Sometimes these wars break out between those who live near the sea. The English, and other Europeans, have been charged with fomenting them; I believe (so far as concerns the Windward coast) unjustly. That some would do it, if they could, I doubt not; but I do not think they can have opportunity. Nor is it needful they should interfere. Thousands, in our own country, wish for war, because they fatten upon its spoils.

Human nature is much the same in every place, and few people will be willing to allow, that the negroes in Africa are better than themselves. Supposing, therefore, they wish for European goods, may not they wish to purchase them from a ship just arrived? Of course, they must wish for slaves to go to market with; and if they have not slaves, and think themselves strong enough to invade their neighbours, they will probably wish for war.—And if once they wish for it, how easy it is to find, or to make, pretexts for breaking an inconvenient peace; or (after the example of greater heroes, of Christian name) to make depredations, without condescending to assign any reasons.

I verily believe, that the far greater part of the wars, in Africa, would cease, if the Europeans would cease to tempt them, by offering goods for slaves. And though they do not bring legions into the field, their wars are bloody. I believe, the captives reserved for sale are fewer than the slain.

[. . .]

With our ships, the great object is, to be full. When the ship is there, it is thought desirable she should take as many as possible. The cargo of a vessel of a hundred tons, or little more, is calculated to purchase from two hundred and twenty to two hundred and fifty slaves. Their lodging-rooms below the deck, which are three (for the men, the boys, and the women), besides a place for the sick, are sometimes more than five feet high, and sometimes less; and this height is divided towards the middle, for the slaves lie in two rows, one above the other, on each side of the ship, close to each other, like books upon a shelf. I have known them so close, that the shelf would not, easily, contain one more. And I have known a white man sent down, among the men, to lay them in these rows to the greatest advantage, so that as little space as possible might be lost.

Let it be observed, that the poor creatures, thus cramped for want of room, are likewise in irons, for the most part both hands and feet, and two together, which makes it difficult for them to turn or move, to attempt either to rise or to lie down, without hurting themselves, or each other. Nor is the motion of the ship, especially her heeling, or stoop on one side, when under sail, to be omitted; for this, as they lie athwart, or cross the ship, adds to the uncomfortableness of their lodging, especially to those who lie on the leeward or leaning side of the vessel.

Dire is the tossing, deep the groans.—

The heat and smell of these rooms, when the weather will not admit of the slaves being brought upon deck, and of having their rooms cleaned every day, would be almost insupportable to a person not accustomed to them. If the slaves and their rooms can be constantly aired, and they are not detained too long on board, perhaps there are not many die; but the contrary is often their lot. They are kept down, by the weather, to breathe a hot and corrupted air, sometimes for a week: this, added to the galling of their irons, and the despondency which seizes their spirits when thus confined, soon becomes fatal. And every morning, perhaps, more instances than one are found, of the living and the dead, like the captives of Mezentius, fastened together.

Epidemical fevers and fluxes, which fill the ship with noisome and noxious effluvia, often break out, and infect the seamen likewise, and thus the oppressors, and the oppressed, fall by the same stroke. I believe, nearly one-half of the slaves on board, have, sometimes, died: and that the loss of a third part, in these circumstances, is not unusual. The ship, in which I was mate, left the coast with two hundred and eighteen slaves on board; and though we were not much affected by epidemical disorders, I find by my journal of that voyage (now before me), that we buried sixty-two on our passage to South Carolina, exclusive of those which died before we left the coast, of which I have no account.

I believe, upon an average between the more healthy, and the more sickly voyages, and including all contingencies, one fourth of the whole purchase may be allotted to the article of mortality: that is, if the English ships purchase *sixty thousand slaves* annually, upon the whole extent of the coast, the annual loss of lives cannot be much less than *fifteen thousand.*

[From *Thoughts upon the African Slave Trade* (London: J. Buckland, 1788), 98, 100–1, 110–11.]

OTTOBAH CUGOANO

60   The Evil of Slavery

Next day we travelled on, and in the evening came to a town, where I saw several white people, which made me afraid that they would eat me, according to our notion as children in the inland parts of the country. This made me rest very uneasy all the night, and next morning I had some victuals brought, desiring me to eat and make haste, as my guide and kid-napper told me that he had to go to the castle with some company that were going there, as he had told me before, to get some goods. After I was ordered out, the horrors I soon saw and felt, cannot be well described; I saw many of my miserable countrymen chained two and two, some hand-cuffed, and some with their hands tied behind. We were conducted along by a guard, and when we arrived at the castle, I asked my guide what I was brought there for, he told me to learn the ways of the *browsow*, that is the white faced people. I saw him take a gun, a piece of cloth, and some lead for me, and then he told me that he must now leave me there, and went off. This made me cry bitterly, but I was soon conducted to a prison, for three days, where I heard the groans and cries of many, and saw some of my fellow-captives. But when a vessel arrived to conduct us away to the ship, it was a most horrible scene; there was nothing to be heard but rattling of chains, smacking of whips, and the groans and cries of our fellow-men. Some would not stir from the ground, when they were lashed and beat in the most horrible manner. I have forgot the name of this infernal fort; but we were taken in the ship that came for us, to another that was ready to sail from Cape Coast. When we were put into the ship, we saw several black merchants coming on board, but we were all drove into our holes, and not suffered to speak to any of them.

[. . .]

These, and all such, I hope thousands, as meet with the knowledge and grace of the Divine clemency, are brought forth quite contrary to the end and intention of all slavery, and, in general, of all slave holders too. And should it please the Divine goodness to visit some of the poor dark Africans, even in the brutal stall of slavery, and from thence to instal them among the princes of his grace, and to invest them with a robe of honor that will hang about their necks for ever; but who can then suppose, that it will be well pleasing unto him to find them subjected there in that defected state? Or can the slave-holders think that the Universal Father and Sovereign of Mankind will be well pleased with them, for the brutal transgression of his law, in bowing down the necks of those to the yoke of their cruel bondage? Sovereign goodness may eventually visit some men even in a state of slavery, but their slavery is not the cause of that event and benignity; and therefore, should some event of good ever happen to some men subjected to slavery, that can plead nothing for men to do evil that good may come; and should it apparently happen from thence, it is neither fought for nor designed by the enslavers of men. But the whole business of slavery is an evil of the first magnitude, and a most horrible iniquity to traffic with slaves and souls of men; and an evil. Sorry I am, that it still subsists, and more astonishing to think that it is an iniquity committed amongst Christians, and contrary to all the genuine principles of Christianity, and yet carried on by men denominated thereby.

[From *Thoughts and Sentiments on the Evil of Slavery*, 1787
(London: Dawsons, 1969), 8–9, 23–4.]

61 Parliamentary Papers, 1795–6

An ACCOUNT of all CARGOES of NEGROES imported into the British West India Islands from the Coast of Africa, in the several Years from 1789 to the latest Period, with the Number that Died from the Time of their being first taken on Board until their Arrival in the West Indies; distinguishing each Year, and the Cargoes brought from that Part of Africa situated between the River Senegal and the River Volta, from those imported from Benin, Bonny, Old and New Calabar, and other Ports South of the Volta, the Southern Boundary of the Gold Coast; as far as the same can be made up.

1789   From the River SENEGAL to the River VOLTA

VESSELS NAMES	TONS	FROM WHAT PART OF THE COAST OF AFRICA	NUMBER TAKEN ON BOARD	NUMBER THAT DIED FROM THE TIME OF THEIR BEING TAKEN ON BOARD	NUMBER THAT ARRIVED IN THE WEST INDIES
Mary	118	Cape Mount	200	3	197
Africa	110	Gambia	160	4	156
Mary	155	Anamaboo	232	1	231
Ann	148	Cape Mount	214	17	197
Alert	162	Anamaboo	276	11	265
Chambers	233	D°	238	4	234
June	242	D°	357	25	332
Lovely Lass	282	D°	408	10	398
Diana	248	D°	357	6	351
Fly	127	D°	239	1	238
Mary	278	Cape Mount	315	44	271
Molly	279	Gold Coast	428	18	410
Hind	126	D°	203	1	202
Edgar	159	Gambia	255	30	225
Ruby	101	Gold Coast	175	5	170
Concord	143	D°	211	3	208
Marian	136	D°	225	4	221
Mentor	136	Gambia	206	16	190
Eliza	109	Cape Mount	73	2	71
			4,772	205	4,567

1789 South of the River VOLTA

VESSELS NAMES	TONS	FROM WHAT PART OF THE COAST OF AFRICA	NUMBER TAKEN ON BOARD	NUMBER THAT DIED FROM THE TIME OF THEIR BEING TAKEN ON BOARD	NUMBER THAT ARRIVED IN THE WEST INDIES
Ned	193	New Calabar	279	25	254
Amachrel	205	D°	340	58	282
Eliza	346	Bonny	483	117	366
Eliza	192	New Calabar	283	73	210
King Pepple	323	Old D°	457	157	300
Wasp	141	New D°	237	79	158
President	254	D°	574	82	492
Brothers	325	D°	455	63	392
Ann	222	D°	358	11	347
Bannister	148	D°	210	46	164
Ally	186	D°	317	51	266
Vulture	314	Bonny	451	7	444
Venus	159	New Calabar	265	12	253
Royal Charlotte	261	Bonny	395	35	360
			5,104	816	4,288
Madam Pookata	110	Angola	183	7	176
Shelburne Castle	130	D°	216	7	209
Christopher	189	D°	315	8	307
Kitty	146	D°	242	1	241
Madam Pookata	114	D°	182	9	173
			1,138	32	1,106

[. . .]

1795   From the River SENEGAL *to the River* VOLTA

VESSELS NAMES	TONS	FROM WHAT PART OF THE COAST OF AFRICA	NUMBER TAKEN ON BOARD	NUMBER THAT DIED FROM THE TIME OF THEIR BEING TAKEN ON BOARD	NUMBER THAT ARRIVED IN THE WEST INDIES
Mary	137	Whydah	227	5	222
Betsey	190	Dº	317	2	315
Mary	316	Anamaboo	453	11	442
Experiment	143	Dº	238	7	231
Commerce	136	Dº	233	—	233
Duke of Buccleugh	239	Bance Island	373	9	364
Queen	387	Anamaboo	523	5	518
Mary	150	Whydah	238	19	219
Gambia	167	Cape Coast	278	5	273
John	120	Africa	200	3	197
Eliza	100	Isle de Los	164	3	161
Fanny	36	Gambia	63	1	62
Bud	169	Anamaboo	281	6	275
			3,588	76	3,512

1795   South of VOLTA

VESSELS NAMES	TONS	FROM WHAT PART OF THE COAST OF AFRICA	NUMBER TAKEN ON BOARD	NUMBER THAT DIED FROM THE TIME OF THEIR BEING TAKEN ON BOARD	NUMBER THAT ARRIVED IN THE WEST INDIES
Mary	293	Bonny	427	19	408
James	203	D°	337	26	311
			764	45	719
Joshua	150	Angola	250	8	242
Eliza	231	D°	372	6	366
Mary	117	D°	195	1	194
Perseverance	334	D°	468	8	460
Mary	41	D°	65	1	64
Louisa	144	D°	230	19	211
Lion	286	D°	420	10	410
Iris	202	D°	284	20	264
Mars	175	D°	292	28	264
Good Intent	135	D°	229	2	227
			2,805	103	2,702

Inspector General's Office,   *Thomas Irving,*
Custom House,   Inspector Gen of the Imports and Exports
London, April 29, 1796.   of Great Britain, and the British Colonies.

Note.—The Accounts required by the 28th of His Majesty, Chap. 54 have been very irregularly transmitted from the West Indies and therefore the preceding Accounts do not apply to all the Cargoes imported into the West Indies, but only to those where the Deaths can be ascertained.

In the Year 1790, the Materials are so defective, that the Inspector Gen can render no Account of that Year.

[From 'An Account of all Cargoes of Negroes Imported into the British West Indies from the Coast of Africa in the Several Years since 1789,' in Parliamentary Accounts and Papers, 1795–6, XLII: 849.]

JEAN-BAPTISTE LABAT
....

62 *Nouveau Voyage*

[Father Jean-Baptiste Labat, in the French colony of Martinique]

It is a very old law that all who take shelter in the lands of the kings of France are free. This is why King Louis XIII, of glorious memory, as pious as he was wise, was so reluctant to agree to let the first inhabitants of the islands have slaves, and agreed only to the pressing demands that were made to him to grant them this permission because it was pointed out to him that it was an infallible means, and the only means, to inspire Africans to the worship of the true God, to remove them from idolatry, and to make them persevere until death in the Christian religion that they had been made to adopt.

The negro slaves that we have in the Islands came to us mostly from the two Companies of Africa and of Sénégal, who alone are authorized by the King for this trade, [which is] restricted to any other. I said for the most part because during times of war, we often have slaves that are taken from enemy vessels that come from other parts of Africa, or that are taken in the raids on their islands and their plantations; and during the peace, we get quite a few more by secret trade with the English and Dutch and the Danish of Saint Thomas.

[. . .]

Some envious [competitors] of this French commerce have spread the rumor among the slaves that we bought them and took them to our colonies in order to eat them. This slander unworthy of people who call themselves Christians caused many slaves to despair during the voyage and try to throw themselves in the sea and drown rather than go to a land where they imagined they would be devoured, as they knew happened in several parts of Africa. I have sometimes seen ships loaded with slaves who, in spite of all that could be done during the voyage to remove this idea from their minds, were not reassured and only believed themselves saved from the slaughterhouse when they saw a large number of their fellows who assured them that they would not be eaten, but only made to work.

[. . .]

When they are purchased and brought to the plantation [in Martinique], it is extremely important to avoid the insatiable greed and horrible harshness of some planters who make them work the moment they arrive, almost without giving them the time to catch their breath. Such actions show no charity nor tact and a lack of understanding of one's own interests. These poor folk are tired from a long voyage during which they were constantly attached two by two with an ankle iron. They are exhausted from hunger and thirst, from which they always suffer greatly during the crossing, to say nothing of their displeasure at being far from their country, with no hope of ever returning. Does it not increase their pain and suffering to push them to work without giving them several days of rest and good food?

After they have arrived at the house, eaten and rested for several hours, it is necessary to have them bathed in the sea, to shave their heads and have their bodies rubbed with palm oil, This loosens their joints, making them more flexible and prevents scurvy, if they were likely to be attacked by it. For two or three days the flour or cassava that is given them must be moistened with olive oil, they should eat sparingly and often, and bathe morning and night. This regime readies them for a little bleeding and a gentle purging that is given them.

This good treatment, together with the clothes they are given and whatever other gentleness is shown them, makes them affectionate and makes them forget their country and the unfortunate situation of their servitude.

After seven or eight days, they can be given some light work to accustom them to it. Most do not wait until one sends them out; they follow the others when the overseer calls.

In order to better train, instruct and integrate them into plantation life, it is good to start the new slaves off in the huts of older slaves. These will take them in willingly, whether they are from their country or not, they take pride that the slave given them is best cared for, best instructed and in better condition than that of their neighbor. They take all possible care of them and treat them as their child, but they have them eat separately and sleep in a different room from them; and when the newcomer notices this separation and asks why they tell him that since he is not Christian he is too beneath them to eat and sleep in their room.

These ways give the new slaves an exalted idea of the position of Christians; and since they are naturally prideful they endlessly beg their masters and priests to baptize them; so that to satisfy them, one takes whole days to teach them the doctrine and prayers.

Beyond the catechism, which is normally done morning and night in the best-ordered households, as are nearly all the plantations of the Lesser Antilles, a well instructed slave is ordinarily set aside to teach the doctrine individually to new slaves, beyond the fact that those with whom they are lodged take marvelous care to teach them, if only to be able to say to the priest or to their master that the slave entrusted to them is ready to be baptized. They usually stand as godparents.

[...]

All the slaves have a great respect for the old. They never call them by their names without adding 'Father'. Although they are not their parents, they obey them and comfort them in all things. They always count the house cook as one of their mothers, and however old she is, they call her mother.

If one treats them a little well, and does so in good humor, they love their master infinitely and will let no danger stop them from saving his life, even at the expense of their own.

[. . .]

They are naturally eloquent, and they use this talent well when they have something to ask of their masters, or to defend themselves against some accusation; to be loved, one must listen to them patiently. They know marvelously well how to skillfully present you their good qualities, their attentiveness to your service, their work, the number of their children and their good education; after that they will list for you all the good that you have done them, for which they will thank you very respectfully, and they finish with the request that they have for you. If the thing is feasible, as it usually is, it should be granted immediately and willingly; if it is not, they should be told the reason and sent away happy by giving them some trinket. It cannot be believed how this will win them over, and provoke their affection.

[. . .]

As a general rule they should never be threatened. They must be punished immediately if they deserve it, or pardoned if appropriate. The fear of punishment often leads them to flee into the woods and become maroon; and once they have tasted this libertine existence, it is enormously difficult to break them of this habit.

Nothing will hold them and prevent them from escaping more than to take measures so that they have something they can profit by, like fowls, pigs, a garden of tobacco, cotton, pasture or something similar. If they leave and don't return within 24 hours by themselves or accompanied by some neighbor or some friend who asks pardon on their behalf, which should never be refused, one has only to confiscate whatever property they might have. For them this is a severe penalty and returns them to their senses far faster than ordinary punishments, no matter how severe. One such example of confiscation is enough to prevent all the slaves of a plantation from perhaps making a similar mistake.

They are very fond of one another and quite willingly help each other in their needs. It often happens that, if one of them makes a mistake, they will all come together to ask his forgiveness, or volunteer to take for him part of the punishment he deserves. They will sometimes go without food to have something to please or comfort those from their country that come to visit them, whom they know needs it.

[From *Nouveau voyage aux isles de l'Amerique* (2 vols, n.p. La Haye, 1724), Vol. 2: 38–54. Trs. John Garrigus.]

[A]n end was put to my happiness in the following manner: Generally, when the grown people in the neighborhood were gone far in the fields to labor, the children assembled together in some of the neighboring premises to play; and commonly some of us used to get up a tree to look out for any assailant, or kidnapper, that might come upon us—for they sometimes took those opportunities of our parents' absence, to attack and carry off as many as they could seize. One day as I was watching at the top of a tree in our yard, I saw one of those people come into the yard of our next neighbor but one, to kidnap, there being many stout young people in it. Immediately on this I gave the alarm of the rogue, and he was surrounded by the stoutest of them, who entangled him with cords, so that he could not escape, till some of the grown people came and secured him. But, alas! ere long it was my fate to be thus attacked, and to be carried off, when none of the grown people were nigh.

One day, when all our people were gone out to their works as usual, and only I and my dear sister were left to mind the house, two men and a woman got over our walls, and in a moment seized us both, and, without giving us time to cry out, or make resistance, they stopped our mouths, and ran off with us into the nearest wood. Here they tied our hands, and continued to carry us as far as they could, till night came on, when we reached a small house, where the robbers halted for refreshment, and spent the night. We were then unbound, but were unable to take any food; and, being quite overpowered by fatigue and grief, our only relief was some sleep, which allayed our misfortune for a short time. The next morning we left the house, and continued travelling all the day. For a long time we had kept the woods, but at last we came into a road which I believed I knew. I had now some hopes of being delivered; for we had advanced but a little way before I discovered some people at a distance, on which I began to cry out for their assistance; but my cries had no other effect than to make them tie me faster and stop my mouth, and then they put me into a large sack. They also stopped my sister's mouth, and tied her hands; and in this manner we proceeded till we were out of sight of these people. When we went to rest the following night, they offered us some victuals, but we refused it; and the only comfort we had was in being in one another's arms all that night, and bathing each other with our tears. But alas! we were soon deprived of even the small comfort of weeping together.

The next day proved a day of greater sorrow than I had yet experienced; for my sister and I were then separated, while we lay clasped in each other's arms. It was in vain that we besought them not to part us; she was torn from me, and immediately carried away, while I was left in a state of distraction not to be described. I cried and grieved continually; and for several days did not eat anything but what they forced into my mouth. At length, after many days' travelling, during which I had often changed masters, I got into the hands of a chieftain, in a very pleasant country. This man had two wives and some children, and they all used me extremely well, and did all they could do to comfort me; particularly the first wife, who was something like my mother. Although I was a great many days' journey from my father's house, yet these people spoke exactly the same language with us. This first master of mine, as I may call him, was a smith, and my principal employment was working his bellows, which were the same kind as I had seen in my vicinity. They were in some respects not unlike the stoves here in gentlemen's kitchens, and were covered over with leather; and in the middle of that leather a stick was fixed, and a person stood up, and worked it in the same manner as is done to pump water out of a cask with a hand pump. I believe it was gold he worked, for it was of a lovely bright yellow color, and was worn by the women on their wrists and ankles.

I was there I suppose about a month, and they at last used to trust me some little distance from the house. This liberty I used in embracing every opportunity to inquire the way to my own home; and I also sometimes, for the same purpose, went with the maidens, in the cool of the evenings, to bring pitchers of water from the springs for the use of the house. I had also remarked where the sun rose in the morning, and set in the evening, as I had travelled along; and I had observed that my father's house was towards the rising of the sun. I therefore determined to seize the first opportunity of making my escape, and to shape my course for that quarter; for I was quite oppressed and weighed down by grief after my mother and friends; and my love of liberty, ever great, was strengthened by the mortifying circumstance of not daring to eat with the free-born children, although I was mostly their companion.

[From *The Interesting Narrative of the Life of Olaudah Equiano Written by Himself* [1789], ed. Robert J. Allison (Boston: Bedford/St. Martin's Press, 1995), 47–8.]

THOMAS FOWELL BUXTON

64 : The African Slave Trade

I am now going to show that, besides the 200,000 annually carried into captivity, there are claims on our compassion for almost countless cruelties and murders growing out of the Slave Trade. I am about to prove that this multitude of our enslaved fellow men is but the remnant of numbers vastly greater, the survivors of a still larger multitude, over whom the Slave Trade spreads its devastating hand, and that for every ten who reach Cuba or Brazil, and become available as slaves, fourteen, at least, are destroyed.

This mortality arises from the following causes:—

1. The original seizure of the slaves.
2. The march to the coast, and detention there.
3. The middle passage.
4. The sufferings after capture and after landing.

And

5. The initiation into slavery, or the 'seasoning,' as it is termed by the planters.

[. . .]

In slave countries, but more especially where the Slave Trade prevails, there is, invariably, a great diminution of human life; the numbers annually born fall greatly below the numbers which perish. It would not be difficult to prove, that in the last fifty years there has been, in this way, a waste of millions of lives; but as this view of the subject would involve the horrors of slavery, as well as of the Slave Trade, I shall abstain from adding anything on this head to the catalogue of mortality which I have already given.

Our calculation may thus be brought into a narrow compass:—

Of 1000 victims to the Slave Trade,
One-half perish in the seizure, march, and detention   500
Of 500 consequently embarked,—
One-fourth, or 25 per cent, perish in the Middle Passage   125
Of the remaining 375 landed, *one-fifth*, or 20 per cent, perish in the
     seasoning   75
                                                   ———

     Total loss   700

So that 300 negroes only, or *three-tenths* of the whole number of victims, remain alive at the end of a year after their deportation; and the number of lives sacrificed by the system, bears to the number of slaves available to the planter, the proportion of *seven* to *three*.

Then applying this calculation to the number annually landed at Brazil, Cuba, &c., which I have rated at   150,000

Of these *one-fifth* die in the seasoning   30,000

Leaving available to the Planter   120,000
The number of lives annually sacrificed, being in the proportion
     of seven to three*   280,000

*This amount may be verified in the following manner:—

Taking the annual victims at	400,000
One-half perish before embarkation	200,000
Embarked	200,000
One-fourth in the Middle Passage	50,000
Landed	150,000
One-fifth in the Seasoning	30,000
Available	120,000

Annual victims of Christian Slave Trade	400,000

Proceeding in like manner with the Mohammedan Slave Trade, we find the numbers to be

Exported by the Imaum of Muscat	30,000
Carried across the Desert	20,000
	50,000
Loss by seizure, march, and detention	50,000
Annual victims of Mohammedan Slave Trade	100,000
,, ,, Christian	400,000
Annual loss to Africa	500,000

[From *The African Slave Trade and its Remedy* [1839] (London: Frank Cass, 1967), 73, 199–201.]

65   China to Cuba Labor Contract 1852

I, Tom Nee, born in the town of Teo Lo province of Canton in China, aged 38 and a labourer, declare that I have agreed with A. E. S. MacKay that I will embark on the English boat, *Sir Thomas Gresham*, in order to be transported to Havana in the island of Cuba, having bound myself upon my arrival there to obey the orders of the Junta de Fomento in pursuing whatever kind of work that it has for me, whether on the sugar plantations or other estates during the customary hours on those estates or off of them according to what may be agreeable to the Junta or to those persons to whom this contract may be passed, and to carry out the said work for the monthly wage of four *pesos fuertes* [Spanish dollars] (which will begin forty-eight hours after landing in Havana) [and] the allowance of eight ounces of good meat, one and a half pounds of plantains, sweet potatoes, and other nutritious roots, medical attention and infirmary, two changes of clothing and one blanket per year and one woolen shirt. It is agreed that in the case of sickness, if it exceeds fifteen days, that my wages will be suspended until I return to work, continuing in the interim to receive attention in the infirmary. Compliance with these obligations will last for the period of eight continuous years as fixed by the terms of this contract, during which time I will not be permitted to leave Cuba nor to deny my services to the aforesaid Junta or to the persons to whom the contract may be passed. My obligations fulfilled, I will be at liberty to work for whom I please. My passage and maintenance aboard the aforesaid boat will be paid by A. E. S. MacKay from whom I swear I have received the amount of nine and a half pesos of silver as my advance on the voyage that I am about to begin, and on reaching land two new changes of clothing, a hat and two pesos. As understood by both parties, 11½ pesos fuertes will be paid in Havana at the order of Snrs. Villoldo, Wardrop and Company with one peso per month deducted from my wages by the afore-said Junta de Fomento or the persons to whom this contract may be passed; it is understood that for no other reason will any be deducted. And con-sequently I will comply punctually with the aforesaid obligations, signed in Hamoa [?] on 31 December 1852.

[From Labor Contract for Transportation from China to Cuba, December 31, 1852. From the collection of Professor Manuel Moreno Fraginals. Trs. Robert L. Paquette.]

IRIS ORIGO

66   The Merchant of Prato

It is after the opening of the Spanish and Genoese branches, too, that we find reference to yet another line—the slave trade, of which the Balearic Islands were then the chief centre in the western Mediterranean. This trade was, of course, nothing new. In the eleventh and twelfth centuries Spain had been the great slave-market of western Europe, and as early as 1128 traders from Barcelona were selling Moslem slaves in the markets of Genoa. But it was the labour shortage after the Black Death of 1348 that suddenly caused a demand for domestic slaves to revive, and brought them to Italy not only from Spain and Africa, but from the Balkans, Constantinople, Cyprus and Crete, and, above all, from the shores of the Black Sea. In Florence a decree of the *Signoria*, issued in 1336, officially authorized their importation—provided only that they were infidels, not Christians, and they were also soon to be found in most prosperous Genoese and Venetian households. Many of them mere children of nine or ten, they belonged to a great variety of different races: yellow-skinned, slanting-eyed Tartars, handsome fair Circassians, Greeks, Russians, Georgians, Alans, and Lesghians. Sold by their parents for a crust of bread, or kidnapped by Tartar raiders and Italian sailors, they were brought from the slave-markets of Tana and Caffa, of Constantinople, Cyprus, and Crete to the Venetian and Genoese quays, where they were bought by dealers and forwarded to customers inland. By the end of the fourteenth century there was hardly a well-to-do household in Tuscany without at least one slave: brides brought them as part of their dowry, doctors accepted them from their patients in lieu of fees—and it was not unusual to find them even in the service of a priest. They were employed, too (as we shall see), in Francesco's own household, and he would sometimes oblige Tuscan friends by selecting one for them through his agents in Genoa or Venice; but the most active part in this trade was taken by his branches in Majorca and Ibiza, where both African slaves bound for Italy and Eastern slaves bound for Spain were collected and sold.

Many letters in these files bear witness to these transactions, though they did not take place on any large scale; the most frequent entries refer rather to a few slaves included in a shipment of other assorted wares. The bill of lading, for instance, of a ship arriving in Genoa from Roumania on May 21, 1396, listed '17 bales of pilgrims' robes, 191 pieces of lead and 80 slaves'. Another ship, sailing from Syracuse to Majorca, carried 1,547 leather hides and 10 slaves, and one sailing from Venice to Ibiza '128 sacks of woad, 55 bales of brass, 15 sacks of raw cotton, 5 sacks of cotton yarn, 4 bales of paper, 3 barrels of gallnuts, and 9 Turkish heads'. The '9 heads' were then forwarded to Valencia to be sold, with a letter stating that one of them was a woman who could 'sew and do everything,' and who was therefore, in the writer's opinion, 'too good for the people of Ibiza'—'for they are like dogs'. 'Your money,' he added, 'will be well placed in her.'

Duty had to be paid on these slaves (as was also the case in Italian cities) both on entering and leaving the Balearics, as well as a sales-tax, and apparently sometimes, if these dues were not met, the owner's other merchandise was confiscated. 'The goods of the Genoese have remained here, because the Flemish ships would not pay the duty on the Moors they took to Alexandria, and it is said that a slave was taken away from them.' Sometimes, too, a trader in Majorca who had sold some slaves to a Spanish buyer would attempt to charge him for their board during the time they had been on the island; but in at least one case the buyer protested. 'You kept our slaves there . . . to load and unload merchandise and to work in your warehouse, and instead of [word missing—'paying'?] for the use of these slaves you add a charge! Think me not so simple, that I cannot see through this!'

Sometimes, too, slaves were procured by the simple method of raiding the coast of Barbary. 'A brig has sailed from here,' says a letter from Ibiza. 'It has gone with a Majorcan ship [*liuto*] and ten men to trade in Barbary, and has brought back 4 heads.'

Very often these 'captives' tried to run away, but generally without success. 'We hear from Ibiza that Ser Antonio Delio has arrived there, with many Moorish captives on his ship, and twelve of them ran away with his rowing-boat . . . But because of the weather, the said Moors came here [Majorca] and for the present have been imprisoned, which has been a great piece of good fortune.' How far indeed a master's hand could reach, and how great the solidarity between the trading-companies was, is shown in a letter in Catalan from Barcelona to Boninsegna di Matteo in Avignon, asking him to catch two runaway slaves who, he thought, might possibly have made their way to Provence. 'One of them is named Dmitri, a big man and very handsome. His flesh is good, fresh and rosy'; the other 'lacks a tooth in front and has rather greenish skin . . . I pray you, *señor*, have them caught, let them be strongly fettered, and send them back by boat to me.'

Apparently, too, slaves sent long distances were sometimes insured, like other goods, against the perils of the voyage, for the Datini papers contain the insurance policy, dated May 9, 1401, of a Tartar slave named Margherita, sent from Porto Pisano to a Catalonian buyer in Barcelona, and insured for the sum of 50 gold florins against 'any risk from the hand of God, the sea, human beings, barter or her master,' but not against any attempt at flight or suicide, 'if she throws herself into the sea of her own accord'. Tragic human merchandise, tossed hither and thither by the seas!

It need hardly be said that no sentimental feelings hampered the dealings of any of the traders. Sick or well, wounded or pregnant, the slaves were merely goods, whose value might increase or deteriorate. Pregnancy, in particular, was regarded as a mishap as inconvenient as it was frequent, since it reduced the mother's market value. The following letter is characteristic in tone:

The slave you sent is sick, or rather full of boils, so that we find none who would have her. We will sell or barter her as best we can, and send you the account. Furthermore, I hear she is with child, two months gone or more, and therefore she will not be worth selling.

A few weeks later the same slave is referred to:

No man will have her. She says she is with child by you, and assuredly seems to be. The pother she makes is so great, she might be the Queen of France.

And here is another brutal letter about a woman who declared her pregnancy to be due to the priest who had been her previous master.

We spake to the chaplain to whom your slave belonged and he says you may throw her into the sea, with what she has in her belly, for it is no creature of his. And we deem he speaks the truth, for had she been pregnant by him, he would not have sent her . . . Methinks you had better send the creature to the hospital.

[From *The Merchant of Prato: Francesco di Marco Datini, 1335–1410* (New York: Alfred Knopf, 1957), 90–3.]

PHILIP D. CURTIN

67   The Atlantic Slave Trade

It is now possible to look at the long-term movement of the Atlantic slave trade over a period of more than four centuries. [. . .] Fig. 26 shows the same data drawn as a graph to semi-logarithmic scale. Together, these data make it abundantly clear that the eighteenth century was a kind of plateau in the history of the trade—the period when the trade reached its height, but also a period of slackening growth and beginning decline. The period 1741–1810 marks the summit of the plateau, when the long-term annual average rates of delivery hung just above 60,000 a year. The edge of the plateau was reached, however, just after the Peace of Utrecht in 1713, when the annual deliveries began regularly to exceed 40,000 a year, and the permanent drop below 40,000 a year did not come again until after the 1840's. Thus about 60 per cent of all slaves delivered to the New World were transported during the century 1721–1820. Eighty per cent of the total were landed during the century and a half, 1701–1850.

[. . .]

For that matter the slave trade—even in its demographic consequences—was merely one aspect of the tightening web of intercommunication which followed the maritime revolution in the Atlantic basin. The new intensity of contact between Africa and Europe began to be felt by the 1480's, with the Americas entering shortly after 1500. The slave trade constituted a movement of people along these new lines of communication, but two other demographically important migrations took place along these same lines—the migration of diseases and the migration of food crops.

It is well known that the Old-World diseases virtually wiped out the American Indian populations of the tropical lowlands and caused a very sharp drop among other New-World populations. Given our present lack of knowledge about the epidemiological history of Africa, it is impossible to say what European (or even American) diseases were new to the tropical African disease environment—and hence what demographic consequences they may have had. For southern Africa, it seems clear that newly imported strains of smallpox and perhaps some other diseases effectively destroyed the integrity of the San or 'Hottentot' community at the Cape. What similar

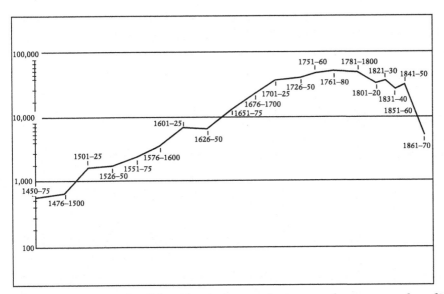

Figure 26: Major trends of the Atlantic slave trade, in annual average number of slaves imported.

events may have taken place in tropical Africa during the sixteenth and seventeenth centuries is not yet known.

As for the migration of food crops, at least two New-World crops were introduced into Africa by the sixteenth century: manioc and maize spread very widely and came to be two of the most important sources of food on that continent. If other factors affecting population size had remained constant, the predictable result would have been population growth wherever these crops replaced less efficient cultigens. Since this process took place over very large areas, it seems possible and even probable that population growth resulting from new food crops exceeded population losses through the slave trade. Whatever population loss may have followed the introduction of new diseases would have been temporary, while more efficient food crops tend to make possible a permanently higher level of population.

[From *The Atlantic Slave Trade: A Census* (Madison: University of Wisconsin Press, 1969), 265–6, 270.]

MARTIN A. KLEIN

68 The Wolof and Sereer of Senegambia

The Senegambian area was the first in Black Africa to enter into relations with Portuguese navigators. It was thus the first to become involved in the Atlantic slave trade and was over the years the base of operations for many

European enterprises. For the historian, one of the results of this extended contact is that we have written accounts in European languages of Senegambian societies and thus can easily trace into the relatively distant past a variety of social and economic institutions.

[. . .]

During the sixteenth century, Senegambia was one of the two or three most important sources of the Atlantic slave trade. It declined in relative importance after that, largely because of the availability of better populated areas farther down the coast and the limitations of a lightly settled hinterland. From 1720 on, there was actually a decline in the number of slaves exported. Nevertheless, the slave trade was a constant, and the Senegambian bases—James Island, Gorée, and St. Louis—provided slaves until the early nineteenth century. No area in Africa was more exposed to the trade over a longer period of time.

The most important question that must be asked about the slave trade is its effect on the participating societies, and in particular, on the development in them of servile institutions. Fifteenth-century Portuguese accounts do not give us many data about social structure, but what they do provide does not sound very different from more recent descriptions. This contrasts with the upper Guinea coast, where Walter Rodney has been able to argue, from the absence of any mention of slavery in early Portuguese accounts, that 'social oppression' was clearly related to participation in the transatlantic slave trade. The only comparable phenomenon in Senegambia was the extension of servitude among the Sereer. Nevertheless, I believe that we can make further remarks about the effects of participation on the Wolof and Sereer.

First, the state controlled the trade and profited from it. The rulers made war, took prisoners, sentenced wrongdoers to enslavement, or sent warriors to attack dissident villages. Similarly, the same rulers and those who served them received most of the benefits of the trade.

Second, the slave trade probably limited the development of other forms of trade and productive activity both because it involved the export of labor and because it created conditions of insecurity not conducive to economic development. This, however, is difficult to measure. Local trade remained important and the export of gum and hides developed parallel to the trade in slaves.

Third, the slave trade contributed to the differentiation of an elite of warriors and nobles from the mass of peasants and led to the emergence of the tyeddo to the point where they controlled crucial political decisions. Boubacar Barry links the development of tyeddo power to the tension between the ruler of Waalo and the more powerful hereditary chiefs. Thus, the creation of slave titles and the expansion of a corps of slave warriors increased the royal power. Barry attributes the expansion of tyeddo power to the period after the *tubenan* rising, a Muslim revolt led by a Mauritanian cleric, which was hostile to the slave trade and briefly dominated northern

Senegal from 1673 to 1677. The tubenans were defeated by an alliance of the traditional elites, the French and the ruler of Saalum.

[From 'Servitude Among the Wolof and Sereer of Senegambia,' in Suzanne Miers and Igor Kopytoff (eds), *Slavery in Africa: Historical and Anthropological Perspectives* (Madison: University of Wisconsin Press, 1977), 335, 341–2.]

HERBERT S. KLEIN

69 The Middle Passage

A rather unusual feature of the Brazilian naval lists, as in those for Portuguese Africa, is the consistent recording of children and infants. In this respect, the findings from Rio de Janeiro are compatible with those found for the mid-18th century Angolan migrations figures. In both the child and infant categories there is a surprisingly low number. In only 27 percent of the total ships arriving were children even listed in the manifests, and they made up less than 1 percent of the total of arriving slaves. This is an even lower proportion than that found for the early 18th-century Atlantic slave migration from Angola. It was not the higher likelihood of death that caused so few children and infants to be taken, since those who crossed the Atlantic suffered approximately the same mortality rates as the adults. Again, one is forced to propose either low American demand and relatively high purchase and transportation costs, or African refusals to permit children to enter the trade. Why the number of children should have declined in the 18th-century Rio de Janeiro trade is even more of a problem to resolve. For, by all the indices, any falsification of records that would have occurred would have encouraged the over-registration of the less taxed children to the very end of Portuguese control over the African slave trade. Either the number of adults was more than sufficient to discourage the turn toward less profitable children, or the constraints on their participation on the part of Africans may have been increasing.

[From *The Middle Passage: Comparative Studies in the Atlantic Slave Trade* (Princeton: Princeton University Press, 1978), 57–8.]

DAVID ELTIS

70 Transatlantic Slave Trade

See Tables 1 to 3.

Table 1: Volume of the transatlantic slave trade from Africa by nationality of carrier (000).

	PORTUGUESE	BRITISH	FRENCH	DUTCH	SPANISH	USA/BR CA	DANISH*	ALL NATIONS
1519–1600	264.1	2.0		0	0	0	0	266.1
1601–1650	439.5	23.0		41.0	0	0	0	503.5
1651–1675	53.7	115.2	5.9	64.8	0	0	0.2	239.8
1676–1700	161.1	243.3	34.1	56.1	0	0	15.4	510.0
1701–1725	378.3	380.8	106.3	65.5	0	11.0	16.7	958.6
1726–1750	405.6	490.5	253.9	109.2	0	44.5	7.6	1,311.3
1751–1775	472.9	859.1	321.5	148.0	1.0	89.1	13.4	1,905.2
1776–1800	626.2	741.3	419.5	40.8	8.6	54.3	30.4	1,921.1
1801–1825	871.6**	257.0	217.9**	2.3	204.8**	81.1	10.5	1,645.1
1826–1850	1,247.7**	0	94.1**	0	279.2**	0	0	1,621.0
1851–1867	154.2**	0	3.2**	0	23.4**	0	0	180.7
All years	5,074.9	3,112.3	1,456.4	527.7	517.0	280.0	94.2	11,062.0
% of Trade	45.9	28.3	13.2	4.8	4.7	2.5	0.9	100

Notes: * Danish includes a few other Scandinavian and German vessels.

** For the 1810–1867 period, shares of slave vessels sailing under Portuguese, French, and Spanish flags are calculated from the dataset and applied to the estimates of slave departures and arrivals (2.7 million departures, 2.4 million arrivals) in Eltis, Economic Growth, pp. 250–54. The amounts are French ships, 301.3 thousand carried from Africa and 262.0 disembarked in the Americas, for Portuguese 1,944.6 thousand departures and 1,692.5 disembarked, and for the Spanish, 493.0 thousand departures and 429.1 arrivals. Recaptive Africans landed at Sierra Leone and elsewhere in Africa have been added to the aggregate arrivals estimated in Economic Growth, and engagés taken by the French 1854–1862 have been excluded from this new figure.

Table 2: *Volume of the transatlantic slave departures by African region (000).*

	SENEGAMBIA	SIERRA LEONE	WINDWARD COAST	GOLD COAST	BIGHT OF BENIN	BIGHT OF BIAFRA	WEST-CENTRAL AFRICA	SOUTH-EAST AFRICA	ALL REGIONS
1519–1600	10.7	2	0	10.7	10.7	10.7	221.2	0	266.0
1601–1650	6.4	0	0	5.2	2.4	25.5	461.9	2.0	503.5
1651–1675	17.7	0.4	0.1	35.4	21.9	58.6	104.3	1.2	239.8
1676–1700	36.5	3.5	0.7	50.3	223.5	51.5	132.6	10.9	509.5
1701–1725	39.9	7.1	4.2	181.5	408.3	45.8	257.2	14.4	958.6
1726–1750	69.9	10.5	14.3	186.3	306.5	166	552.8	5.4	1,311.3
1751–1775	130.4	96.9	105.1	264.1	250.5	340.1	715	3.3	1,905.2
1776–1800	72.4	106.0	19.5	240.7	264.6	360.4	816.2	41.2	1,921.1
1801–1825	91.7	69.7	24.0	69.0	263.3	260.3	700.8	131.8	1,610.6
1826–1850	22.8	100.4	14.4	0	257.3	191.5	770.6	247.5	1,604.5
1851–1867	0	16.1	0.6	0	25.9	7.3	155.0	26.8	231.7
All years	498.5	412.7	182.0	1,043.2	2,034.6	1,517.9	4,887.5	484.5	11,062.0
% of Trade	4.5	3.7	1.6	9.4	18.4	13.7	44.2	4.4	100

Source: The distribution of slaves carried by each nation shown in table 1 is first broken into five year intervals (before 1675, intervals of quarter-century or longer), then distributed by African region. The results of this distribution are then summed by quarter-century for each African region.

Table 3: *Volume of translantic slave arrivals by region of arrival in the Americas and period of years, 1519–1867 (000).*

	BRITISH MAINLAND N. AMERICA	BRITISH LEEWARDS	BRITISH WINDWARDS + TRINIDAD	JAMAICA	BARBADOS	GUIANAS	FRENCH WINDWARDS	ST. DOMINGUE
1519–1600	0	0	0	0	0	0	0	0
1601–1650	1.4	1	0.2	0	25.4	0	2.0	0
1651–1675	0.9	5.6	0	22.3	63.2	8.2	6.5	0
1676–1700	9.8	26.6	0	73.5	82.3	27.8	16.6	4.8
1701–1725	37.4	35.4	0.6	139.1	91.8	24.4	30.1	44.5
1726–1750	96.8	81.7	0.3	186.5	73.6	83.6	66.8	144.9
1751–1775	116.9	123.9	120.0	270.5	120.9	111.9	63.7	247.5
1776–1800	24.4	25.3	197.5	312.6	28.5	71.2	41.2	345.8
1801–1825	73.1	5.3	43.0	70.2	7.6	71.8	58.8	0
1826–1850	0	0	0.5	2.1	0.9	4.8	19.5	0
1851–1867	0.3	0	0	0.4	0	0	0	0
All years	361.1	304.9	362.0	1,077.1	494.2	403.7	305.2	787.4
% of Trade	3.8	3.2	3.8	11.2	5.1	4.2	3.2	8.2

Table 3—contd

	SPANISH N. AND S. AMERICA	SPANISH CARIBBEAN	DUTCH CARIBBEAN	N.E. BRAZIL	BAHIA	S.E. BRAZIL	OTHER AMERICAS	AFRICA	ALL REGIONS
1519–1600	151.6	0	0	35	15.0	0	0	0	201.6
1601–1650	187.7	0	2.0	86.3	60.0	30	0	0	396.0
1651–1675	0	0	38.8	15.6	15.6	15.6	0.6	0	192.8
1676–1700	7.0	0	26.0	30.2	75.9	30.2	11.0	0	421.7
1701–1725	30.0	2.1	30.5	24.3	199.6	122	14.2	0	825.8
1726–1750	12.7	1.6	10.2	51.4	104.6	213.9	8.3	0	1,136.9
1751–1775	5	13	15.3	126.9	94.4	210.4	13.8	0	1,654.0
1776–1800	10.2	56.9	6.9	210.8	112.5	247.2	44.1	0.4	1,735.4
1801–1825	17.5	268.7	0	214.8	182.0	408.7	14.8	22.4	1,458.6
1826–1850	8.7	297.0	0	80.0	146.5	736.4	10.5	91.3	1,398.2
1851–1867	0	152.6	0	0.9	1.9	3.6	1.3	16.8	177.9
All years	430.3	791.9	129.7	876.1	1,008.0	2,017.9	118.7	130.8	9,599.0
% of Trade	4.5	8.2	1.4	9.1	10.5	21.0	1.2	1.4	100

Source: The distribution of the totals of slaves carried by each nation shown in table 1 is first broken into five year intervals (before 1675, intervals of quarter-century or longer are required), then distributed by American region. The results of this distribution are then summed by quarter-century for each American region.

[From 'The Volume of the Transatlantic Slave Trade: A Reassessment,' William and Mary Quarterly 58 (2001).]

71   Chinese Slavery

Until the foundation of the People's Republic in 1949 China had one of the largest and most comprehensive markets for the exchange of human beings in the world. In many parts of China, notably in the south, nearly every peasant household was directly or indirectly affected by the sale of people. A unique feature of the Chinese market was its concentration on children, especially those under the age of ten. Adolescents and younger adults were sometimes bound over to a creditor for a limited time to pay off debts but, in most cases, these people were not exchanged or sold on a permanent basis. The only exceptions were found among the urban elite who bought and sold adult concubines almost as a form of sport. For ordinary peasants the market was directed exclusively at children—male and female—who were sold for cash and were rarely, if ever, returned to their birth parents. In keeping with the highly developed system of commerce and exchange that has character-ised Chinese peasant society for over a thousand years, the sale of a child was legalised by a signed receipt that specified the rights of both buyer and seller down to the minutest detail.

[...]

Prior to the communist victory, the point at which the market in people effectively ended, there were two major sources of saleable children in South China: destitute parents and professional kidnappers. Most children entered the market as a consequence of domestic crises. In the New Territories opium addiction on the part of the father seems to have been a primary cause of family collapse (daughters were sold first, then land, and finally sons). Widows left with young children were another reliable source, especially in non-elite communities where the lineage did not intercede. Except among opium addicts, the decision to sell was not taken lightly. The case of an old woman bursting into tears at the mention of the subject is not unusual; the sale of children is an extremely sensitive issue in the communities I have studied. The guilt and remorse felt by the sellers, notably by mothers, is made all the worse by the callousness of village gossip. Cantonese women are fascinated, one might say possessed, by the topic; they never seem to tire of discussing the marriages of local servant girls and the circumstances under which 'bought sons' were acquired.

Kidnapping was no mere sideline for the bandits that plagued South China during the nineteenth and early twentieth centuries, it was their primary *modus operandi*. The sons of the rich were the main targets of the kidnappers since they could be ransomed for huge sums. Ha Tsuen's wealthiest landlord had to pay an undisclosed amount, rumoured to be in excess of ten thousand silver dollars, in the 1920s for his son who had been taken in a bandit raid. The same gangs occasionally kidnapped the infant sons of ordinary peasants in the absence of anything else worth taking. It is significant that bandits always took male children. I have not discovered a single instance of a girl disappearing in this manner. The reason, of course, is that wealthy fathers were unlikely to pay lavish ransoms for their 'excess baggage'. The genealogies of many elite lineages carry a record of kidnapped sons in case they should return and claim their shares in the ancestral estates. This happened among the *Tang* when, in the 1680s, a local boy was captured by bandits and sold as a domestic slave to a merchant. He was traced ten years later and restored to his rightful position in the lineage. An elder brother accomplished this feat by bribing a former gang member and reimbursing the merchant for his expenses.

Whatever the means by which children entered the market, they were usually sold to an intermediary first. Parents or kidnappers rarely carried out the final transaction themselves, largely because the buyers preferred to have some margin of protection for such a sensitive undertaking. People acquiring a male heir were particularly anxious that the birth parents would never be able to trace the boy at a later date. (In the case cited above, it is doubtful that the kidnapped *Tang* boy would ever have been found if the merchant had acquired him as an heir.) Transactions in girls are less sensitive because there is little at stake; neighbours usually know the origin of most 'bought' women in the village.

[From 'Transactions in People: The Chinese Markets in Slaves, Servants, and Heirs,' in Watson (ed.), *Asian and African Systems of Slavery* (Oxford: Blackwell, 1980), 223, 232–3.]

PHILIP D. CURTIN

72   The Senegambian Slave Trade

But slaves were not a costless export, even though slave raiding can be compared in some ways to the economics of burglary. Most slaves exported from Senegambia (as elsewhere in West Africa) had been kidnapped or captured in warfare. A smaller number had been political prisoners, the product of judicial condemnation, debt pawns sold off by creditors, or the like. Very few were domestic slaves sold by their masters to meet a momentary need for cash. This means that the original enslaver was not concerned with the 'cost of production'—the cost of rearing a child until it was old enough to be sold into the trade. His only concern was the opportunity cost—the value of alternative uses for a captured person who was *not* to be sold into the slave trade. This is a significant fact in trying to understand how the gross sum paid for a slave on the coast, the f.o.b. price, came to be shared among the individuals and groups who were involved in the trade, right back to the ultimate captor, or the judicial authority that condemned a person to be sold into the trade.

The slave trade within Africa involved very high costs for guarding slaves, transporting them, and feeding them until the slavers from Europe turned up at the port. Even in regions immediately adjacent to the ports, holding and transaction costs and the merchants' profit ate up 40 to 50 percent of the f.o.b. price paid for a slave, and this percentage increased with distance from the port or with holding time till the actual date of sale. Such costs were especially high in the case of slaves who came from the far interior, beyond the head of navigation on the Gambia and Senegal rivers; and these slaves were a large proportion of the total exported from Senegambian ports—between about 45 and 85 percent of the total, the overall proportion through the eighteenth century being about two-thirds of the total. For the majority of the Senegambian slave trade, then, whatever payments were made to the original enslavers went to rulers and warriors further east—not to local kings and ceddo.

But that share was also very small. The cost of transportation was so great that the original sellers on the upper Gambia or Senegal rarely received as much as 5 percent of the f.o.b. price paid on the coast. This might have been high enough to encourage the sale of young male enemies—whose opportunity cost must have been very low, if not negative—but it was hardly enough to justify the costs of systematic slave raiding, at least for the sake of the Atlantic trade. The fact that the slaves from the far interior were overwhelmingly male supports this hypothesis. Women had a higher opportunity cost at the point of origin; the margin between the interior price and the coastal price was too small to justify the cost of transportation over this route of more than 400 miles.

But the political authorities along the trade routes profited from the slave trade in quite another way. They collected tolls from passing boats and caravans, usually, in the eighteenth century, at the rate of about 10 to 20 percent for each African jurisdiction. The total payout for a long trip from the upper Niger to the lower Gambia could therefore be considerable, and it was certainly more than the original enslaver might have received. For the Senegal water route from Maxaana to the coast some estimated cost accounts have survived from about 1785; they indicate that 32 percent of the delivered price on the coast went for tolls. As of that time and place, the payoff to the riverine rulers was about ten times the value paid to the original captors.

On this basis, it is possible to make a rough comparison of the income from the slave trade enjoyed by various groups in Senegambian society. The enslavers in the far interior got very little indeed, at least from the Atlantic trade. Enslavers in the coastal and river kingdoms like Waalo, Bawol, Kajor,

Ñomi, Ñaani, or Saalum could have received more, but they supplied only about one-third of the slaves entering overseas trade. Their take per slave was no more than half of the f.o.b. value, so that their maximum total income would have come to about 22 percent of the total value exported. Needless to say, these calculations are very rough, but they illustrate a point that will hold up even with a generous margin for error: historians of the slave trade who have assumed that enslavers received most of the income from the slave trade were wrong. Merchants' costs were certainly the largest share of the total cost, probably followed by tolls paid to political authorities.

[From 'The Abolition of the Slave Trade from Senegambia,' in David Eltis and James Walvin (eds), *The Abolition of the Atlantic Slave Trade: Origins and Effects in Europe, Africa, and the Americas* (Madison: University of Wisconsin Press, 1981), 89–91.]

DAVID MURRAY

73 The Cuban Slave Trade

The year 1861 was an unlikely one for optimistic predictions about a quick end to the Cuban slave trade. In 1859, and again two years later in 1861, more slave-trading expeditions set out for Africa than at any time since 1820 when the African slave trade had been declared illegal within the Spanish empire. British estimates of slave importations into Cuba during the three years 1859–61 were the highest in forty years: a total of 79,332 African slaves had been added to the Cuban slave population, thought to number 370,553 in 1861, and there was every expectation that the Cuban slave trade would carry on at the same high level. The open participation of American ships and capital, combined with improvements in maritime technology, had transformed the African slave trade. Large steamships were supplanting smaller sailing vessels as the main carriers of slaves. The number of slaves who could be transported in a single expedition rose dramatically. Two steamships alone accounted for 3,000, or approximately 10% of the slaves introduced into Cuba in 1859; one steam vessel in 1860 brought a cargo of 1,500 African slaves.

Technological improvements also were transforming the Cuban sugar economy, increasing its productive capacity and aggravating the labour shortage which the planters traditionally had resolved through the slave trade. Cuba's sugar estates had expanded rapidly in both number and size during the middle years of the nineteenth century, an expansion which the adaptation of steam power had accelerated. The construction of railroads enabled planters to overcome Cuba's transportation problems and to open up hitherto inaccessible areas to sugar cultivation, but the building of railroads added to the demand for labour. In part, railroad companies met the demand by initiating a system of contract labour, bringing in indentured Asians and using *emancipados* hired out from the government. But the question of labour in all its complexity, including slavery and the slave trade which fed it, hung as a menacing cloud over Cuba, then entering what one Cuban historian has termed the age of latifundia.

The capital costs of starting a sugar estate were so high by 1860 that only rich capitalists or companies could contemplate such a venture. The most efficient and most profitable plantations were the largest ones, founded or reorganized during Cuba's railway age. High costs were slowly driving out the small sugar cultivators. Just as the other costs of running a plantation rose during this period, so did the price of slaves as the demand for them increased and the supply through the slave trade fluctuated. By 1860, the average price of a slave exceeded 1,000 Spanish dollars, double or triple the average price in the first half of the century. Only the very richest Spaniards or Cubans could afford to outfit a slave-trading expedition, but the enormous profits to be made and the unceasing demand for slaves offered tempting incentives for those with the necessary capital.

The nineteenth-century 'sugar revolution' in Cuba, to use Franklin Knight's phrase, did not imply an immediate cessation of the slave trade even if it laid the groundwork for the ultimate replacement of slave labour. If anything, it stimulated the reverse, an expansion of the trade as the only way to procure the slaves. The figures of slave importations on the eve of the American Civil War bear this out. Not even the influx of thousands of Chinese indentured labourers during the 1850s reduced the demand for African slaves. Yet within six years after 1861, the Cuban slave trade was extinct. Technological change within Cuba was not responsible. The slave trade to Cuba had been crushed by a powerful combination of international forces.

The outbreak of the Civil War in the United States created the conditions in which the Cuban slave trade finally could be extinguished, although the remnants lingered on until after the end of the American struggle. The major powers involved in the suppression—Britain, the United States and Spain—each had to adopt new and stronger measures, and even then it took time for these to be effective. Britain was the first country to initiate a more aggressive policy, a change which arose out of the deep frustrations felt by all members of the British government and Parliament at Britain's continued and humiliating failure to end the Atlantic slave trade.

[From *Odious Commerce: Britain, Spain, and the Abolition of the Cuban Slave Trade* (Cambridge: Cambridge University Press, 1980), 298–9.]

PAUL E. LOVEJOY

74 Transformations in Slavery

In contrast to the disunity reflected in the political fragmentation of the continent, the commercial infrastructure that relayed 10,130,000 slaves to the Americas and the Islamic lands between 1600 and 1800 served to integrate the various parts of Africa with each other and with the external market. This infrastructure did not handle all African slaves by any means, for many slaves never entered the market system. Captives seized in wars and raids were often redistributed among the armies responsible for capturing them. They were occasionally presented as gifts to religious shrines or Muslim scholars; girls and women were parcelled out as concubines and wives; young boys were pressed into military training. Nonetheless, merchants bought and sold the millions of slaves who were exported and millions of others who stayed in Africa.

Slaves were a major item or trade almost everywhere that commerce was well developed, particularly in regions where Muslim merchants operated and where European demand was high. Slaves increased in value as they were moved further from their home country, for the possibility of escape into familiar territory diminished with distance. At the point of capture, slaves were inexpensive, and consequently merchants often lingered around army camps in the hope of buying cheaply and subsequently driving their chattel to distant markets and selling at a better price. The export trade was especially effective in separating slaves from their homes. Captives seized near shipping-points were usually exported for this reason, since these slaves could be the most difficult to manage because of their local origin. Sale to foreign merchants, whether they came from North Africa, Europe, or a distant place within Africa, offered a profitable exchange, even when prices were relatively low. It was better to sell people who knew too much about the area and to replace them with other slaves purchased from the interior.

[From *Transformations in Slavery: A History of Slavery in Africa*
(Cambridge: Cambridge University Press, 1983), 88.]

A. VAN DER KRAAN

75 The Slave Trade in Bali

Pre-colonial Bali had much in common with such traditional Southeast Asian societies as Java, Siam, Cambodia and Vietnam. In Bali, too, wet-rice cultivation, involving complex irrigation systems, was the dominant economic activity. Bali, too, was a densely populated region in which a small aristocratic strata (*triwangsa*) was socially far removed from the peasant masses (*sudra*). And Bali, too, had acquired an elaborate court culture, a rich literary tradition, refined artforms, a calendar, a system of writing—in short, civilization. Yet Bali differed from these societies in supporting an export trade in slaves, not just for a few years or decades, but over a period of at least several centuries.

[. . .]

The structure of the Balinese export trade in slaves was outlined in a remarkably frank 1837 report by the Dutch colonial official Dubois, who was one of the first Europeans to live in Bali for an extended period of time. Dubois wrote his report in response to an inquiry by Batavia as to whether some four hundred women could at short notice be obtained in Bali for the government nutmeg plantations in the Banda islands. He replied that this was indeed possible 'unless changes have occurred in the social system of that island since my return from there in 1831', but warned that 'free' women could not be had for this purpose:

Although ruled in a tyrannical manner, the Balinese people have retained certain privileges which cannot be transgressed upon without danger of rebellion . . . The common Balinese . . . has no other property than his wife and daughters, who have to provide for his sustenance. He is their lord and master. He has bought his wife and shall one day give his daughters in marriage against payment by his sons-in-law . . . A lord would commit the worst offence if he were to arbitrarily seize one of his subordinates' daughters, especially if he were to sell her to foreigners. If he did this he would *at the very least* [Dubois' emphasis] risk losing all his subordinates through flight.

The only way to acquire the women was to purchase them from amongst the ranks of the slaves:

In Bali it is impossible to obtain women other than by buying them from various slaveowning lords . . . In my time, the price of a Balinese woman was 30, 50 even 70 Spanish dollars, according to her physical qualities. But for our purposes it is only necessary to have strong and healthy women, suitable for labour and procreation and between the ages of 18 and 30. This kind of woman costs between 35 and 40 Spanish dollars.

The Rajas and punggawas who agreed to sell some of their slaves had to proceed with the utmost caution because the Balinese people 'consider it one of their privileges not to be *undeservedly* [Dubois' emphasis] shipped outside of Bali':

[The Balinese] regard deportation from their island as the worst possible punishment. This attitude results from their strongly-held conviction that their Gods have no influence outside Bali and that no salvation is to be expected for those who die elsewhere . . . These women cannot be sold to foreigners without a reason. A Lord who did this would be regarded as a great tyrant. However, the slightest mistake, such as breaking a dish or a glass, an errand imperfectly executed, failure to make a *nyembah*—offences of this kind are used to justify deportation.

Dubois continued by advising that Batavia send a high-ranking official to Bali to work out an agreement with the Rajas of Badong in the south and Buleleng in the north, in whose principalities were located the island's only two ports. Kuta (Badong) and Buleleng. It was not necessary to conduct negotiations with any other Raja because, 'not possessing seaports, the other Rajas do not have foreign relations and are in a commercial sense subordinate to Badong and Buleleng, territories through which all their imports and exports must pass'. The envoy should seek to conclude an agreement by which the Rajas permitted Dutch representatives, with their servants and the necessary supplies, to establish themselves in the ports of Kuta and Buleleng. To gain their cooperation it was essential to interest them financially: 'The Rajas of Badong and Buleleng will only allow Government representatives to reside in their territories ... and will only promise protection if they are assured of an export duty on each slave.'

As soon as the Dutch representatives were established in Kuta and Buleleng, a beginning could be made with purchasing the women. This could only be done through the mostly Chinese slave brokers who also resided in these ports. Spanish dollars were to be advanced to these middlemen, who would use part of the money to buy rifles and opium from Buginese merchants trading on Singapore. They would thereupon travel from Kuta into the interior of South Bali and from Buleleng into the interior of the north, visiting the puris of the Rajas and punggawas and buying slaves for Spanish dollars, rifles or opium. After each successful transaction the slave brokers would bring the women back to the Dutch establishments in Kuta and Buleleng where they would be kept until ships arrived to take them to the Banda islands. Dubois concluded by stating his belief that 'to purchase the 400 women is likely to take about 12 months', an observation which gives some idea of the magnitude of the Balinese slave trade. If similar numbers of men and child slaves could be had in any one year, maximum yearly slave export was somewhere in the order of twelve hundred.

In summary, Bali's export trade in slaves was rooted in the nature of the island's social formation. The peculiarities of Balinese society gave rise to various unique circumstances, customs and laws which resulted in the enslavement of large numbers of Balinese men, women and children. In view of the limited opportunities for utilizing slave labour in Bali itself, the supply of slaves tended to outstrip local demand, creating an exportable surplus. The Balinese slaveowners, that is the Rajas and punggawas, sold their surplus slaves to Chinese slave brokers who visited their puris from time to time. These brokers took the slaves to the ports of Kuta or Buleleng where they sold them to foreign slave traders. The latter shipped the slaves to various overseas destinations, which changed over time in accordance with certain shifts in the international economy.

[From 'Bali: Slavery and the Slave Trade,' in Anthony Reid (ed.), *Slavery, Bondage and Dependency in Southeast Asia* (New York: St. Martin's Press, 1983), 315, 327–9.]

DAVID W. GALENSON

76 Traders, Planters, and Slaves

The availability of a steady supply of slaves was critical to the success of the sugar revolution. Initially the planters of Barbados and the Leewards appear to have depended on Dutch traders for their slave cargoes. Although some shipments were brought by private English traders, the transatlantic slave trade was dominated during the 1640s and 1650s by the Dutch West India Company.

English interest in West African trade was growing in this period, and in 1660 Charles II granted a charter to the Company of Royal Adventurers into Africa. This company was ill conceived, for its principal objective was to be the search for gold in West Africa. It was also poorly subscribed and poorly managed, and after several years of desultory trading it surrendered its charter. A new charter was granted in 1663 to a reorganized company, to be known as the Company of Royal Adventurers Trading into Africa. The new charter contained the same provisions concerning gold as that of 1660, but now the investors had added another prospective source of profit: The new charter explicitly mentioned the slave trade, granting the company the exclusive right among English traders to buy slaves on the West African coast.

During the next seven years the Royal Adventurers made some progress in setting up forts and trading outposts on the African coast. The company also established a significant English presence in the transatlantic slave trade: for example, between August 1663 and March 1664, it delivered more than 3,000 slaves to Barbados. By 1665, however, the company had already run into serious financial difficulties, owing chiefly to the failure of colonial planters to pay for the slaves they had purchased on credit. When war broke out between the English and the Dutch on the West African coast in 1665, the company's trade was interrupted, and it could not be renewed until peace was restored by the Treaty of Breda in 1667. The settlement clearly established the right of the English to compete with the Dutch in the slave trade. By this time, however, the outstanding debts of the Company of Royal Adventurers appear to have crippled it, and it never successfully regained a firm position in the slave trade.

[. . .]

A charter was granted to the Royal African Company by Charles II in September 1672. A clause of the charter stated that no English subject other than those thereby incorporated was to visit West Africa except by permission of the company, and empowered the company to seize the ships and goods of all who infringed its monopoly. This charter is the basis from which many historians have concluded that the Royal African Company held an effective economic monopoly of the transatlantic slave trade to the English West Indies from 1672. Yet at least five potential sources of competition existed in part or all of this trade, some legal and others illegal.

[. . .]

The economic threat posed to the Royal African Company by the independent separate traders throughout its career resulted from the interlopers' lower overhead costs. Because they did not bear the cost of maintaining forts and factories in West Africa, the interlopers could prosper on smaller profit margins in the slave trade than the company. As a consequence, convincing complaints were voiced by company agents that interlopers were able both to outbid the company for slaves in Africa and to undersell the company in the West Indies. This advantage of the interlopers was apparently not offset by the risks they ran of seizure. The interlopers were popular among planters in the West Indies, and even when Royal African Company agents were able to seize the ships of interlopers the company was unlikely to receive legal judgments against them in colonial courts dominated by planters who favored free trade in slaves. Indeed interlopers were sometimes awarded damages by colonial courts when they were seized by company agents. The indifference of many colonial governors, and the hostility of others, hampered the defense of the company's monopoly by its agents in the West Indies, for the agents rarely received official assistance in their efforts. The company was somewhat more successful in seizing and prosecuting interlopers in Africa, but the long coastline and many possible trading posts made the task too difficult to produce a high rate of success. Many company employees in Africa themselves served to undermine the company's efforts by trading directly with the interlopers.

[. . .]

The journey from England to West Africa normally took one to three months. The specific African destination might be any one of a large number of ports stretched over 2,000 miles of the West African coast, from the Senegal River at the north to Angola at the south. For commercial purposes, the Royal African Company divided West Africa into six regions; from north to south, these were 'Northern Guinea'—primarily the region around the Gambia River—the Windward Coast, the Gold Coast, Ardra and Whydah, Benin and Calabar, and Angola. Although there were some fluctuations over time in the relative importance of these regions for the company's trade, all remained significant suppliers of slaves throughout the company's principal period of involvement in the slave trade. There were a number of important differences among these regions in the way the Royal African Company conducted its activities, however. The kinds of products the company traded for slaves, and purchased in addition to slaves, varied by region. Even more basically, there were regional differences in the format of the company's trade. The major distinction was between what K. G. Davies has called 'castle-trade' (or 'factory-trade') and 'ship-trade'. Castle-trade was practiced where the company maintained settlements, whether permanent, fortified garrisons, called 'forts,' or small, unfortified, often temporary trading posts with perhaps no more than one or two men, called 'factories'. At any time, the company normally maintained two dozen or more settlements in West Africa, with the largest number on the Gold Coast, where the company's largest permanent fort, Cape Coast Castle, was located. Most of the settlements were small factories with only a few company employees. At its peak level, in 1689, the company's African service numbered about 330 Englishmen, of whom 130 were at Cape Coast; a total of 48 more were at Accra, Ft. Royal, and Anomabu, its next three largest forts on the Gold Coast, leaving about 150 men scattered at more than 20 other settlements, mostly small factories.

In the castle-trade, the ship's captain would be instructed to sail to a specified company fort, or perhaps to one of the larger factories. The captain would deliver his ship's cargo to the company factor who was resident there, and the factor would be responsible for furnishing a designated number of slaves for the ship's cargo. Alternatively, in the ship-trade, which was practiced in regions such as the Windward Coast where the company maintained no settlements, the ship's captain would act as supercargo, and he would personally select the places where he would trade his goods to the natives for slaves. These two types of trade were often both used on a single voyage, as a ship unable to fill its quota of slaves at a fort might travel along the coast looking for opportunities to buy additional slaves directly from native traders. Similarly, many voyages ultimately visited several regions in the course of collecting a cargo of slaves. It was common for the company to instruct captains to go first to Cape Coast and then to proceed elsewhere, often to Whydah, if the Gold Coast failed to provide a full cargo. In recognition of the greater responsibilities of the ship-trade, captains who purchased their own cargoes normally earned commissions of 4 slaves in 100 delivered alive in the West Indies, compared to 2 in 100 on those put on board by company factors.

[From *Traders, Planters, and Slaves: Market Behavior in Early English America* (Cambridge: Cambridge University Press, 1986), 13–14, 18–19, 22–4.]

77   **Economic Growth and the Transatlantic Slave Trade**

Two broadly countervailing forces affected slave exports from Africa after 1790. Economic growth in Europe and the Americas stimulated demand. The St. Domingue rebellion and attempts to suppress the trade reduced demand. The volume figures reflect the struggle between the two. For Africa as a whole, exports declined nearly 8 percent between the 1780s and the 1790s as first the St. Domingue rebellion and then war forced the French to withdraw from the trade. That the decline was not greater is testimony to the speed with which the British and Americans took over the French role as well as to the burgeoning demand for plantation produce. The next decade brought a further and much larger fall of 22 percent, however, as British and U.S. abolition took effect and the difficulties in supplying French and Spanish territories increased during wartime. The fact that prices of most plantation produce rose to record levels in the same period indicates that the underlying demand for slaves remained very high. The ending of the Napoleonic war in the middle of the next decade ensured that the volume of traffic, though declining on a decadal basis, actually recovered strongly after 1814. Thus, although the traffic declined by one third between 1781–90 and 1811–20, more slaves left the Atlantic littoral for the Americas in both the 1820s and the 1830s than in any other decade in the history of the trade prior to 1780.

A clearer impression of the aggregate impact of British and U.S. abolition may be gained from the annual data. Exports averaged forty thousands slaves a year between 1811 and 1814 and, though we have not carried the annual export series back before these years, data for major import regions indicate that annual departures were even lower during 1808–10. The decadal estimate for 1801–10 implies annual exports of close to eighty thousand slaves between 1801 and 1807 and perhaps even higher levels in the two or three years immediately preceding 1808. British and U.S. abolition thus had the temporary effect of halving the trade in the years down to 1814, with much of the remaining traffic being in the South Atlantic. As the latter was largely removed from British scrutiny, it is not difficult to understand the sanguine expectations of the British abolitionists that the trade was about to come to an end. Between 1816 and 1820, however, exports returned to earlier levels of close to eighty thousand slaves per year.

[. . .]

The temporary decline in the volume of the traffic was not distributed equally across major African regions, however. A comparison of the distribution indicates that the relative decline on the nineteenth-century west coast of Africa was accentuated by the advent, for the first time, of significant departures from southeast Africa. Within the west coast area, the Senegambia, Gold Coast and Congo North regions experienced the major declines. The relatively small Senegambian traffic fell off sharply after 1790. Bissau and Cacheu, the most southerly ports of this region, continued to ship slaves until the 1840s, but decadal export volumes for the region as a whole in the nineteenth century probably never approached the levels of the 1790s, much less those of the peak decade after 1780. On the Gold Coast, annual export volumes of five thousand to ten thousand slaves a year in the generation before 1807 fell to a few hundred a year thereafter and continued at this level intermittently down to the late 1830s. The Congo North decline, though much bigger than that of other regions in absolute terms, was only in the order of 50 percent. The decline here was concentrated in the Loango area and can be attributed to the French withdrawal of the early 1790s and, to a lesser extent, British abolition. For both the Gold and Loango coasts, however, it is likely that some redirection of slave departures occurred with Bight of Benin, Congo and Angolan ports shipping slaves that might previously have left the former regions. The Bight of Benin and Angola, with the basis of the demand for their slaves in the Portuguese Americas, were least affected by the events of the generation after 1780. With the exception of the surge in the 1780s, which saw exports at 40 percent above the trend for 1771–1820 (probably due to French activities), export volumes from the Bight of Benin fluctuated only slightly. It is difficult to disaggregate an Angolan export series from the figures for west-central Africa prior to 1810, but it seems that here too fluctuations were much less than elsewhere. Both Upper Guinea and the Bight of Biafra traffics, on the other hand, were dominated by the British before 1807. As a consequence both regions experienced all-time peaks in the 1790s, with probably continued high annual volumes occurring down to 1807. Though the decline thereafter was sharp, the volume during the 1810s was still within 5 percent and 27 percent (in Upper Guinea and the Bight of Biafra, respectively) of the levels of the two decades before 1790: Here Cuban and French slavers who tended to concentrate on regions north of the line quickly filled the gaps left by the British. The Windward coast exported a tiny proportion of aggregate deportees; given problems of disaggregating the eighteenth-century data, it is hard to comment on trends. It is unlikely, however, that the thinly populated hinterland of this region ever made a significant contribution. Finally in southeast Africa we should note that alone of major export zones transatlantic exports probably increased between the 1780s and 1810s, though the numbers remained well below the levels of major west coast regions. In summary, abolition by the British and Americans caused a temporary and fairly sharp drop in west coast exports from north of Portuguese Angola. Within a decade, however, the traffic was once more approaching preabolition levels in the bights and had substantially recovered in Congo North. Only on the Gold Coast, the northern Loango coast and Senegambia (part of the Upper Guinea region) were the effects permanent, and the decline in the latter two regions was already underway well before 1807.

[From *Economic Growth and the Ending of the Transatlantic Slave Trade*
(Oxford: Oxford University Press, 1987), 62–4.]

HERBERT S. KLEIN

78 Economic Aspects of the Eighteenth-Century Atlantic Slave Trade

Though the Atlantic slave trade officially dates its origin from the 1440s and does not end until the 1860s, both the mass of documentation and the period of its greatest importance were in the eighteenth century. Even though over a million and a half Africans had been brought to America before 1700, over six million arrived in the period 1701–1810, or 63 percent of the total who ever landed in the Western Hemisphere. The eighteenth century also marks the definitive shift among all traders from an era of largely monopoly company activities to that of a free trade organization. The trade ends for most Europeans by the last quarter of the eighteenth century and first decades of the nineteenth century, and it officially disappears from the public records of the remaining traders after 1830. For these reasons, the eighteenth century is the best studied of all centuries and the one most representative for almost all trading nations.

Though the slave trade was a concern for scholars, moralists, and politicians from the late eighteenth century and was one of the major areas of activity of British diplomacy and the British navy in the nineteenth century, the systematic study of the trade only dates from the twentieth century. A combination of late nineteenth-century European racism and imperialism and early twentieth-century unease with these concepts led to an era of scholarly neglect in which popular writers dominated the analysis of the trade with their limited and highly emotional accounts based on few observations and a lack of awareness of the realities of African history or society. This rather uncritical literature created a whole set of untested hypotheses about the costs of the trade, the pattern of shipping slaves across the Atlantic, the mortality they suffered, and the ultimate gains and benefits to the Europeans. 'Tight packing' and 'astronomic' mortality rates were tied to the concept of virtually costless slaves. This model of the trade, which still pervades much of the popular literature on the subject, also assumed a totally passive and dependent role of Africans. Research since the beginning decades of this century has shown this model to be badly flawed, and it is this newer research and its implications with which I am concerned in this essay.

By the eighteenth century, the Atlantic slave trade had become one of the most complex international trades developed by European merchants. It involved the direct participation of East Indian textile manufacturers, European ironmongers, African caravan traders, European shippers, and American planters in the purchase, transportation, and sale of the largest transoceanic migration of workers known up to that time in recorded history. At its peak in the last quarter of the nineteenth century, Europeans were moving some 90,000 Africans per annum to America in some 200 to 300 ships under the flag of every major maritime power of western Europe.

[. . .]

Along with the myths about the cheap cost of slaves, the traditional literature stressed the dependent position of the African merchants in the trade. It was thought that prices demanded for slaves were low and invariant, that the trading was all dominated by the Europeans, and that the Africans were passive observers to the whole process. But in fact, all studies show that the mix of goods that went to make up the price in each zone tended to vary over time and reflected changing conditions of demand and supply. Thus African merchants adjusted their demands for goods in response to market conditions. Moreover, two recent studies of the eighteenth- and early nineteenth-century trade have shown that the terms of trade between Africa and Europe were progressively moving in favor of the Africans as the price of slaves rose and the price of European textiles (which by the end of the trade were of equal quality to the East Asian products and were replacing them) steadily fell, along with the price of all European manufactures. Though the two studies differ somewhat on the timing and intensity of the trends, both are in total agreement that the barter terms of England in its trade with Africa dropped by over 50 percent from 1701 to 1800. This same trend was also repeated in the nineteenth century between the 1810s and the 1840s.

Not only was there a trend in favor of the African sellers of slaves throughout the eighteenth and nineteenth centuries, but in all their dealings with Europeans the multiple groups of African traders did everything possible to prevent the Europeans from monopolizing any one source of slaves or any one route. Although Africans could not prevent the Europeans from eliminating each other from a given region—usually through armed conflict—they could prevent the victors from exercising exclusive control on the coast itself. This was a consistent response to European monopoly efforts over all regions of western Africa. The European forts in West Africa and even the Portuguese coastal and interior towns in southwest Africa were ineffective in excluding competing buyers from entering the local market. The forts exercised dominion for only a few miles inland and were more designed to fend off competitors than to threaten suppliers. As for the unique Portuguese settlements, these were unable to prevent the French and English from obtaining Congo and Angolan slaves on a massive scale. Yet these supposedly were domains totally monopolized by the Portuguese.

[From 'Economic aspects of the 18th-century Atlantic Slave Trade,' in James D. Tracy (ed.), *The Rise of Merchant Empires: Long-distance Trade in the Early Modern World, 1350–1750* (Cambridge: Cambridge University Press, 1990), 288–9, 293–4.]

RUTH MAZO KARRAS

79   Slavery in Medieval Scandinavia

Whether or not the Vikings engaged in large-scale slave trading in their day, they certainly have the image of slave traders in the eyes of modern scholars. The extent of this trade is very far from clear. Scandinavians spread through eastern as well as western Europe: to England, Scotland, Ireland, France, the Low Countries, Germany, the Baltic coast, and Russia. The nature of the contacts varied with the different regions; the Vikings, or Varangians as they were called in the east, may have taken captives in all these places, but we do not know whether this amounted to large-scale enslavement, and if so whether they used the slaves in the Scandinavian homeland or as trade goods. Most evidence for slavery in the Viking Age refers to Scandinavians as slave traders but not as slaveholders in their own society.

[. . .]

Slave trading was a major commercial activity of the Viking Age and later. Vikings not only sold slaves to the eastern Islamic countries but possibly traded captives taken in Britain and Ireland to Muslim Spain as well. There were no doubt some slave markets within Scandinavia itself. Irish slaves certainly found their way to the western part of Scandinavia, and since the Danish and Swedish Vikings had traded in slaves it is likely that some of these foreign slaves did find their way to the eastern part of Scandinavia too. It is not possible to conclude from this that Viking Age Scandinavia depended upon a slave economy, but it is possible to see why Scandinavians came to think of all slaves as foreigners or outsiders.

[From *Slavery and Society in Medieval Scandinavia* (New Haven: Yale University Press, 1988), 46, 49–50.]

The original labour patterns [. . .] had already been substantially altered in many parts of the Pacific, often decades before formal colonial incorporation. Colin Newbury has suggested that the partition of the Pacific into colonial entities has obscured unifying patterns in Pacific labour history, which stemmed from the exploitation of the region as a labour reserve. Reconstructing the past through colonial straitjackets has blurred the transnational patterns of capitalist development and the impact of international variables on Pacific labour markets.

Before the late nineteenth century capitalist relations affected many Pacific societies without the presence of colonial states. Integral to capitalist development, however, was the global expansion of European powers since the sixteenth century. This was largely driven by the search for sources of profit, from which capital was accumulated and reinvested to produce more profits. Fundamental to this process were costs of raw materials, production, distribution and consumption. Cheap labour was essential if costs of production were to be kept low. This was particularly significant to the exploitation of resources in the Pacific, as investors frequently argued that if any profits were to be made, then the high costs of transportation necessitated cheap labour input for the extraction of raw materials there. This was often only one stage in the whole process of producing a finished product as further labour input within factories in the industrial nations refined raw materials to produce the finished product for the consumer. Industrialisation in the nineteenth century came to be primarily based on mass production of vast quantities of goods for the consumption of the expanding industrial workforce. Colonies offered potential for off-loading surplus production. Copra provides an example of how labour power and consumption patterns in the Pacific and within industrial Europe were linked to one another through the demand for commodities. By the 1850s, copra, the dried meat of the coconut, could be refined to produce good quality, comparatively cheap sources of vegetable oil for use in the soap and cosmetic industries. The costs of extracting and processing the raw materials were kept down by the low labour costs of Pacific Islanders, while factory workers in Europe then produced the finished products. Mass production was possible through the application of technology to this division of labour. Consumers in Europe purchased the finished goods, such as soap, while a quantity of excess products were exported to the colonies. Through such a process the value of the final product never reflected the true costs and especially the value of labour within the various stages of production.

This stems partly from the patterns of capitalist development, much of which has been based upon the tapping of reserves of labour, both within the metropolitan countries (those at the centre of capitalist development), and those on the fringes, or the periphery. Such reserves were seen as resources to provide labour as required, intermittently or on a more regular basis. Tied in with this was the systematic migration of workers to the site of production, which in the Pacific was usually to plantations or mines. As outlined below, labour reserves of Pacific Islanders, and especially Melanesians, provided the labour for capitalist development both internally, (within the island groups the labour was drawn from), and externally, (to more distant parts of the Pacific and to Queensland). External labour reserves also included a vast pool in Asia from which hundreds of thousands of migratory workers were drawn into the Pacific. Further, as colonial administrations began to regulate labour markets, so capital shifted to drawing upon internal labour reserves to meet periodic demands for labour. Supportive state policies were vital to maintain such reserves, particularly during the twentieth century. After the 1970s, the Pacific again served as a reserve for external markets with the migration of Pacific Islanders to industrial nations on the Pacific rim.

The concept of labour reserves in the Pacific

Labour drawn from a reserve became regulated through systems of migration where migrants were employed on contracts known as indentures. Once state regulation became more enforced after the 1880s, so migrants and employers were, in theory, subjected to increased regulation. . . . [T]he debate on the Pacific labour trade, especially that of migration from the Melanesian reserve, highlights various interpretations on the degree of coercion or voluntarism involved. Overall, migration from labour reserves in the Pacific fits into Michael Burawoy's assessment of such patterns containing elements of economic necessity and coercive regulation. This analysis seeks to demonstrate how labour reserves and regulated migratory labour fitted into colonial economic development. Such contexts created a dual economy in which the worker was doubly dependent upon two separate economies. That is, migratory workers were never fully integrated into a wage economy, but on the other hand, economic necessity (through colonial taxes as well as the desire for material goods) meant that villagers could not exclusively rely upon the subsistence sector. Meillassoux has suggested that traditional societies were preserved by colonial governments to guarantee a regulated labour supply. This is applicable to many parts of the Pacific where colonial governments fostered the maintenance of a subsistence economy through indirect rule, indigenous control of much of the land, restrictions on the mobility of the population and the regulation of the regional distribution of recruitment. Simultaneously, labour regulations ensured that adequate and systematic supplies of cheap labour were available to employers. As outlined in many of the studies in this volume, deferring the bulk of wages, employment at often isolated places far from the workers' home villages, along with the threat of penal sanctions, strengthened control exerted by employers and ensured that contracts would be fulfilled. Workers however did resist and although illegal, employers were not averse to inflicting physical violence.

One of the main features of such a system, based upon the payment of 'bachelor's wages', was that employers and the state did not meet the real costs of the reproduction of labour. Instead this was subsidised through the village economy which also sustained workers between contracts. The workers' links with and dependence upon the village economy were reinforced by colonial labour regulations, which usually insisted that workers be repatriated to their villages of origin upon the expiry of their contracts. Such regulations could be evaded by both workers and employers, but most workers, whether serving an internal or external indenture, did return to their villages. The pattern with *Girmitiyas*, the Indian indentured labourers in Fiji, was different. They were only entitled to a free return passage every ten years and of this, Gillion estimates that only 40 per cent had returned to India by 1957. . . . [W]hen workers' villages were close to the labour site, as for example with stevedores near the port of Suva, so the state tried to ensure that only a small percentage of workers were resident in the city. Peter Fitzpatrick stresses that throughout much of the colonial Pacific, restrictions, such as curfews, vagrancy laws, residential and recreational regulations, were imposed upon Islanders to inhibit mobility and free association in towns.

Economic reasons could be given as the underlying motive behind the colonial fostering of a 'reserve army of labour'. Both employers and the state did not have to meet the real costs of sustaining and renewing a workforce throughout much of the Pacific's colonial period, and took a minimal role in providing educational, health, welfare services, care of the aged and genuine protection of conditions for the workforce. Migrant workers rarely acquired skills which would have permitted them to seek alternative and possibly more remunerative employment. Tied in with economic issues were political ones. As Richard Curtain notes, these included the direct control which the dual economy and the penal regulations of indenture gave employers over migrant workers and to the state through its control of the circulation of labour and as part of the colonial control over Pacific Islander's lives. More generally, the maintenance of a labour system drawing upon reserves and the continued return of workers to the subsistence sector inhibited the formation of a permanent working class. Colonial labour reserves also did not appear to threaten the authority of the indigenous elite and in many instances colonial governments called upon traditional leaders to recruit labour, enforce labour regulations and dissuade workers from engaging in forms of industrial action. Colonial governments sought to inhibit labour unrest and class conflict, in order to promote political stability as this created an environment more conducive to capital investment. However as some of studies in this volume indicate, in spite of such opposition, signs of working class consciousness did develop among migrant workers in the Pacific.

[. . .]

Overall, more than 350,000 Asians supplemented or replaced Pacific workers between 1850 and 1917. Hawaii depended on the largest supplies of Asian labour. Between 1852 and 1899 some 125,000 Chinese and Japanese worked there. Another 100,000 Japanese and a further 4,000 Chinese entered Hawaii during the 17 years after the abolition of the indenture system in 1900 along with a further 30,000 Filipinos and Koreans. Fiji's growing sugar plantation system came to rely almost exclusively upon the almost 61,000 Indians who signed *girmits* (contracts) between 1879 and 1916. [. . .] The French territories tended to draw Asian labour from Indo-China and Java in the Dutch East Indies, along with migration into Tahiti from China. The boom in the nickel industry within New Caledonia was largely responsible for the 22,000 workers brought in from Indo-China, Japan and Java between 1892 and 1915. In German Samoa some 3,800 Chinese labourers came to work on newly established cacao and rubber plantations between 1903 and 1913, while Chinese labour was also of importance in New Guinea, especially during the 1890s.

[From 'An Overview of the Pacific Labour Reserve,' in Clive Moore, Jacqueline Leckie, and Doug Munro (eds), *Labour in the South Pacific* (Townsville: James Cook University of Northern Queensland, 1990), xxvii–xxix, xxxiii–xxxiv.]

STUART B. SCHWARTZ
....

81   The Slave Trade to Brazil

The slaves transported from Africa to Brazil in the sixteenth century came primarily from the area of the Senegambia, what the Portuguese called Guiné. A variety of peoples were caught up in the slavers' trade—Manjacas, Balantas, Bijagos, Mandingas, and Jaloffs, among others. The trade concentrated along the coast at a few spots, although transshipment through the Portuguese outposts at São Tomé and Cape Verde was common. The volume of the trade in this period is unknown, but Mauro's calculation of about 100,000 slaves exported for the whole of the sixteenth century for an average of 1,000 a year seems reasonable if we remember that very few came before 1550 and that the numbers between 1580 and 1600 probably exceeded 2,000 a year. In part, this trade also included slaves shipped from the Congolese port of Mpinda and the area in contact with the kingdom of the Congo, with which the Portuguese also had a long-standing relationship. Increasingly, the Portuguese began to take slaves from the area south of the Dande River in the area that became known as Angola. By the 1620s, the Dutch estimated that Pernambuco alone took 4,000 slaves a year. Bahia, with fewer engenhos, surely had a lower level of importation at that time, so an annual estimate of 2,500 to 3,000 is probably fair for its share.

By the time the Portuguese crown decided to colonize Angola in 1575, a slave trade was already flourishing in the area, and with the foundation of Luanda in that year, the Portuguese slave trade increased in this region. By the last decades of the sixteenth century, between 10,000 and 15,000 slaves from Guiné, the Congo, and Angola disembarked annually in Brazil. Luanda, Benguela, and Cabinda all developed into slaving ports during the seventeenth century as the center of activity shifted to the Angola region. The famous phrase of Padre Antônio Vieira to the effect that 'whoever says sugar says Brazil and whoever says Brazil says Angola' was actually a common expression. The connection between sugar and slavery, Brazil and Angola was obvious.

The period of the Iberian union (1580–1640) provided opportunities that led to intensified Portuguese slaving on the African coast, but it also created supply problems for the planters in Brazil. The connection with Spain not only provided access to iron and other trade goods that allowed the Portuguese to monopolize the slave trade in such areas as the upper Guinea coast; it also led to formalized contracts (asientos) to supply African slaves to Spanish-American ports. The first of these was awarded to a Portuguese merchant in 1587, and between 1595 and 1640 at least 147,779 slaves were carried to Spanish America on vessels registered in Seville. The demand for slave cargoes in Spanish America, where silver was paid for them, caused problems for Brazilian planters who could only offer sugar or other crops in exchange. Slave prices rose in Brazil, and there was a short-lived resuscitation of Indian enslavement in the period.

More serious was the disruption of the slave trade caused by European rivals. The Dutch had attacked São Tomé in 1598–9, but the end of a twelve-year Spanish–Dutch truce in 1621 led to a series of attacks on Portuguese positions in Africa. El Mina fell in 1637, Luanda and Benguela in 1641, and although the latter ports were recaptured within the decade, Portuguese predominance on the African coast had been lost, especially north of the equator, where the Dutch allowed the Portuguese to trade on the Dahomey coast under license and regulations that favored Brazilian traders carrying tobacco from Bahia while limiting the importation of European goods carried by ships from Portugal.

[. . .]

From the slaves' perspective, the constant dependence on the African slave trade meant that cultural forms and traditions were continually reinforced by new arrivals. We cannot know if this process slowed the pace of acculturation to European norms, but undoubtedly African practices and traditions persisted in the colony. The present-day African culture in Bahia, which is heavily Yoruba in origin, dates from the late eighteenth century. Before that, other African traditions existed, of which only a few hints remain in the surviving documentation. Nuno Marques Pereira's work of 1728 mentioned *calundus* or rites of divination and *quinguilla* or taboos, both of which are Angolan in origin. He complained that such 'gentile rites' were condoned by Brazilian planters in order to get along with their slaves. When in the late seventeenth century a large escaped slave community was formed at Palmares, its inhabitants called it *Angola janga* or little Angola. The image of Africa was still vivid for many slaves, and that fact was not lost on the masters. As we shall see, a strong debate developed between two schools of slaveowners and royal officials: those who thought that permitting slaves to maintain their African cultures was a positive way of stimulating differences among them and thus an effective social control, and those who thought that such cultural persistence stimulated rebellion.

[From *Sugar Plantations in the Formation of Brazilian Society: Bahia 1550–1835* (Cambridge: Cambridge University Press, 1985), 339–40, 342.]

ROBERT WILLIAM FOGEL
....

82   **The Origins of the Atlantic Slave Trade**

Over the ages the incidence of slavery has waxed and waned. One high-water mark was reached during the first two centuries of the Roman Empire when, according to some estimates, three out of every four residents of the Italian peninsula—21 million people—lived in bondage. Eventually, Roman slavery was transformed into serfdom, a form of servitude that mitigated some of the harsher features of the older system.

While serfdom was the most characteristic condition of labor in Europe during the Middle Ages, slavery was never fully eradicated. The Italians imported slaves from the area of the Black Sea during the thirteenth century. And the Moors captured during the interminable religious wars were enslaved on the Iberian peninsula along with Slavs and captives from the Levant.

Black slaves were imported into Europe during the Middle Ages through the Moslem countries of North Africa. Until the Portuguese exploration of the west coast of Africa, however, such imports were quite small. About the middle of the fifteenth century, the Portuguese established trading posts along the west coast of Africa below the Sahara and shortly thereafter began to make relatively large purchases of black slaves. Soon the average imports of slaves into the Iberian peninsula and the Iberian-controlled islands off the coast of Africa (the Canaries, the Madeiras, and São Thomé) rose to about 1,000 per year. By the time Columbus set sail on his first expedition across the Atlantic, accumulated imports of black slaves into the Old World were probably in excess of 25,000. Although blacks continued to be imported into the Old World until the beginning of the eighteenth century, it was the New World that became the great market for slaves.

It is customary to date the beginning of the New World traffic in Africans to the year 1502, when the first references to blacks appear in the documents of Spanish colonial administrators. The end of this trade did not come until the 1860s. Over the three and a half centuries between these dates about 9,900,000 Africans were forcibly transported across the Atlantic. Brazil was by far the largest single participant in the traffic, accounting for 41 percent of the total. British- and French-owned colonies in the Caribbean and the far-flung Spanish-American empire were the destination of 47 percent. Dutch, Danish, and Swedish colonies took another 5 percent. The remaining 7 percent represent the share of the United States (or the colonies that eventually became the United States) in the Atlantic slave trade.

To those who identify slavery with cotton and tobacco, the small size of the U.S. share in the slave trade may seem surprising. The temporal pattern of slave imports, however, clearly reveals that the course of the Atlantic slave trade cannot be explained by the demand for these crops. Over 75 percent of all slaves were imported between 1451 and 1810. This fact clearly rules out cotton as a dominant factor in the traffic since the production of cotton was still in its infancy in 1810. There was also an enormous increase in the extent of the Atlantic slave trade during the eighteenth century. This fact rules out the possibility of a major role for tobacco: During the eighteenth century, tobacco imports into Europe increased at an average annual rate of about 350 tons per annum. Since an average slave hand could produce about a ton of tobacco yearly, the total increase in the tobacco trade over the century required an increase of about 70,000 hands, a minuscule fraction of the 5.7 million slaves imported during the same period.

It was Europe's sweet tooth, rather than its addiction to tobacco or its infatuation with cotton cloth, that determined the extent of the Atlantic slave trade. Sugar was the greatest of the slave crops. Between 60 and 70 percent of all the Africans who survived the Atlantic voyages ended up in one or another of Europe's sugar colonies.

The first of these colonies was in the Mediterranean. Sugar was introduced into the Levant in the seventh century by the Arabs. Europeans became familiar with it during the Crusades. Prior to that time honey was the only sweetening agent available to them. After taking over the Arab sugar industry in Palestine, the Normans and Venetians promoted the production of sugar in the Mediterranean islands of Cyprus, Crete, and Sicily. From the twelfth to the fifteenth centuries these colonies shipped sugar to all parts of Europe.

Moreover, the sugar produced there was grown on plantations that utilized slave labor. While the slaves were primarily white, in these islands Europeans developed the institutional apparatus that was eventually applied to blacks.

The rapid growth of European demand for sugar led the Spanish and Portuguese to extend sugar cultivation to the Iberian peninsula and to the Iberian-owned Atlantic islands off the coast of Africa. Here, as in the Mediterranean, slaves on plantations provided the labor for the new industry. While some of these bondsmen were natives of the newly conquered islands, as in the Cape Verde archipelago, most were blacks imported from Africa. For the first century of the Atlantic slave trade, the scope of imports was determined almost exclusively by the needs of the sugar planters in the Canaries, the Madeiras, and São Thomé. Of the 130,000 blacks imported between 1451 and 1559, 90 percent were sent to these islands and only 10 percent to the New World.

During the last half of the sixteenth century, the center of sugar production and of black slavery shifted across the Atlantic to the Western Hemisphere. By 1600 Brazil had emerged as Europe's leading supplier of sugar. Cane was also grown in substantial quantities in Mexico, Peru, Cuba, and Haiti. Although the Old World colonies continued to plant the crop, their absolute and relative shares of the European market declined rapidly. By the close of the seventeenth century sugar production all but disappeared from the Madeiras, the Cape Verde Islands, the Canaries, and São Thomé. The end of sugar production also marked the end of slaves imported into these territories.

The sugar monopoly of the Spanish and Portuguese was broken during the seventeenth century when the British, French, and Dutch became major powers in the Caribbean. The British venture into sugar production began in Barbados during the second quarter of the seventeenth century. In 1655 the British seized Jamaica from the Spanish and shortly thereafter began developing sugar plantations on that island. During the eighteenth century the output of sugar grew rapidly, not only in these colonies but throughout the British West Indies. It has been estimated that the annual export of the sugar crop in the British West Indies in 1787 stood at 106,000 tons, more than five times as much as the exports of Brazil in the same year. The British continued to expand their grip on sugar production, partly by acquiring additional territory during the Napoleonic Wars, so that by 1806 its West Indian colonies accounted for 55 percent of the sugar trade.

The development of the sugar culture in French Caribbean possessions was also spectacular. Haiti (then called Saint Domingue) was the principal sugar colony of the French. The French promoted plantations in that territory from the early seventeenth century until the Haitians revolted against their rule in 1794. By 1787 Haiti was shipping about 86,000 tons and production elsewhere brought the sugar trade of French Caribbean possessions to 125,000 tons. In contrast to Britain and France, Spain had been largely squeezed out of the international sugar trade, ranking a poor fourth in 1787 with slightly over 6 percent of exports. However, its colonies reemerged as a major sugar supplier in the nineteenth century, after the development of extensive plantations in Cuba and Puerto Rico. Sugar was also an important crop in Dutch Guiana (located on the northcentral coast of South America, in terrain that embraces the modern nations of Guyana and Surinam), and in the Danish island of St. Croix. Together they contributed slightly more to the sugar trade in 1787 than the Spanish colonies.

The great majority of the slaves brought into the British, French, and Dutch Caribbean colonies were engaged in sugar production and its ancillary industries. In the 1820s in the British West Indies between two-thirds and three-quarters of the slaves were directly or indirectly engaged in sugar production. In Brazil, perhaps 40 percent of the slaves imported were involved in sugar culture, and in Spanish America the share was probably between 30 and 50 percent. Mining, which probably stood second to sugar in the demand for labor, claimed about 20 percent of the slaves in Brazil. The balance of the blacks brought to the New World were utilized in the production of such diverse crops as coffee, cocoa, tobacco, indigo, hemp, cotton, and rice. Of the relatively small percentage of Africans engaged in urban pursuits, most were usually servants or manual laborers, although some became artisans. However, it is probable that by the mid-eighteenth century most of the urban occupations were held by creoles, slaves born in the New World, rather than by recent arrivals.

[From *Without Consent or Contract: The Rise and Fall of American Slavery* (New York: Norton, 1989), 17–21.]

YEN CHING-HWANG

83 Coolies and Mandarins

The sending of the Cuba Commission was an important event in the history of the overseas Chinese. It marked the beginning of Ch'ing concern for its subjects working overseas, and heralded a new era in the government's sympathetic attitude towards overseas Chinese. As the Commission was sent at the end of 1873 during the height of China's fight against the coolie trade, it must be seen as an integral part of China's effort for the total suppression of the trade.

[. . .] On 17 November 1877, a treaty containing sixteen items was signed between China and Spain over the emigration issue which had dragged on for six years. China had achieved its main objective of protecting the coolies in Cuba and future labourers to that island. The protection was embodied in the following items of the treaty:

Item 3. Both countries agreed that recruited emigrants to Cuba must be on their free will, no Spanish subjects were allowed to use force or tricky methods to recruit emigrants in China. Any Chinese or Spanish who had violated this agreement should be severely punished in accordance with respective laws.

Item 6. China was to send a consul-general to Havana and consuls to other parts of the island where other foreign consuls were stationed; they were to protect Chinese subjects in the island.

Item 7. Chinese subjects in Cuba were allowed to move freely within and outside the island, and were free to take up any occupation.

Item 9. The Chinese consul-general at Havana would be required to work out regulations with the local officials in order to register the coolies in Cuba and future labourers arriving on the island. The consul-general would issue to Chinese subjects, certificates, which would be examined and recorded by the relevant local authorities. At the same time, the local officials would provide the consul-general statistics of Chinese subjects and their names, and facilities would be provided for the consul-general to inspect the work-places where Chinese worked.

Item 11. To return persons with a literary background or holding certain ranks, and the relatives of these people, the Spanish government would pay their passage home. The Spanish government would also provide free passage for aged labourers, widows and women to return to China.

Item 12. The Spanish government would press the employers to return those coolies who had fulfilled the contracts which specified a return passage. Those coolies who had fulfilled the contracts which did not guarantee a return passage would be repatriated to China after appropriate arrangement made between the local officials and the Chinese consul-general.

Item 14. Those coolies who had not fulfilled the contracts must complete the term of labour. The new regulations would apply to them. After the ratification of the treaty, all coolies detained in depots would be released and they would be treated as free persons.

In return for the concessions given by the Spanish, the Chinese government allowed Spaniards to recruit labourers freely in China. Of course, this was a departure from the position taken by China in the Peking Regulations in 1866 which emphasised the protection of prospective emigrants in the recruitment process. But given the fact that the Macao coolie trade was suppressed in early 1874, those protective measures contained in the Peking Regulations appeared to be redundant. From this perspective, the concession given to the Spanish was not a high price to pay. The protection of the Cuban coolies was not put into effect until after the treaty was ratified in December 1878.

[From *Coolies and Mandarins: China's Protection of Overseas Chinese during the Late Ch'ing Period (1851–1911)* (Singapore: Singapore University Press: 1985), 127–8.]

CLAUDE MEILLASSOUX

84   The Anthropology of Slavery

The earliest written accounts of the slave trade in the Sahel refer to Fezzan and date from the seventh century, but from the ninth century onwards the effects of this trade are noted in West Africa. Al-Yakubi (872) refers to the export of *sudan* (black) slaves from Awdaghust and from Zawila, further to the south. 'It has been reported to me', he adds, 'that the kings of the Sudan sell *sudan* [Blacks] in this way, for no reason and not because of war'.

Kawar, a fifteen-day walk from Zawila, had a Muslim population of various origins, mostly Berber, which carried out the trade in Sudan. It seems that this trade was already well organized in the tenth century and centred on Zawila, which the authors of the period situate 'on the frontiers of the Maghreb . . . It is a medium-sized town with a large district bordering on the territory of the Sudan', where the slaves 'sold in the Islamic countries' came from. 'They are a race of a pure black colour' (Al-Istakhri, in the year 951). Most eunuchs, according to Hudud al-Alam (982–3), also came from this Sudan, described as lying between the ocean to the west and the desert to the north: 'Merchants from Egypt come to this region . . . they steal children . . . they castrate them and import them to Europe, where they sell them. Among [the Sudanese] there are people who steal other people's children to sell them to the merchants when they come.' Edrissi (about 1154) repeatedly notes that the populations of the desert and of the Sudanic States (Barisa, Silla, Tekrur, Ghana, Ghiyaro) reduced the Lam-Lam inhabitants to captivity, 'transporting them to their own countries and selling them to merchants who come there and who take them elsewhere'. The Lam-Lam, he explains.

are continually the victims of incursions by the peoples of neighbouring countries who capture them, using various tricks, and carry them off to their own countries to sell them by the dozen to merchants; at the moment a considerable number are being carried off, destined for the western Maghreb.

Elsewhere, al-Idrisi (1154) explains the tactics of the slave-raiders of Ghiyaro: 'These people ride excellent camels; they take a supply of water, travel by night, arrive by day and then, having taken their booty, they return to their country with the number of Lam-Lam slaves which, with the permission of

God, fall to their lot'. He adds that the town of Tekrur was a market where the Moors exchanged wool, glass and copper for slaves and gold.

These exports of slaves are mentioned at various times in the history of the Maghreb: by al-Biruni towards 1050, al-Zuhri towards 1154–61, al-Sharishi towards 1223, Ibn Khaldun towards 1375. In 1416 al-Makrisi further reports that 'a caravan from Takrur arrived for the pilgrimage [to Mecca] with 1,700 head of slaves, men and women and a great quantity of gold' to be sold on arrival. It is possible that these writers merely reiterate what others have written, but they would not do so if events did not also repeat themselves.

These short extracts contain all the features of the history of the slave trade in this region: the formation of military States, the pillage of black populations, apparently particularist and pagan, by these States; the organization of merchant networks stretching from the Sudan to the Maghreb.

How powerful were these States? What, in this context, was the purpose of the wars in which, from all accounts, they were constantly involved?

In the Middle Ages in Africa, these States were first and foremost instruments for the supply of slaves. In the eleventh century, Ghana (a Sahelian State) had large armies and cavalry at its disposal. El-Bekri (1068) claims that the king could put 200,000 warriors into the field, 'of whom more than 40,000 are armed with bows and arrows' as well as his cavalry. 'The people of Ghana', writes al-Zuhri (1154–61), 'fight in the lands of the Barbara, the Amima and seize the inhabitants as others seized them in the past, when they themselves were pagan. . . . The inhabitants of Ghana *raid them every year.*' In other areas war was continuous and was held to be holy: 'The king of Silla [in the valley of the Senegal River] *always* wages war against the Blacks who are infidels.' In this respect he rivals Ghana, just as the king of Ambara, himself once a victim, became a raider. The Beni-Lemtuna waged a holy war against the Blacks. The role of the Almoravids in the eleventh century in supplying the slave markets is not made explicit, but indications are that these holy men did not neglect this activity: Yaya ben Umar, one of Ibn Yacin's warriors, made an alliance with the Lemtuna to attack a non-Muslim Berber tribe. 'The Lemtuna raided them and took captives whom they distributed among themselves, having passed on a fifth of their booty to their emir' (reported by Ibn Idhari, much later, in the fifteenth century). At the sack of Awdaghost (1054–5) the town numbered thousands of slaves and the Almoravids seized every one they found; no mention is made of any emancipation of the captives. Ibn Yacin is also known to have taken a third of the goods owned by those who rallied to his cause: goods which probably included a certain number of slaves.

In the fourteenth century, Al-Omari's description of Mali is similar to that given by El-Bekri of Ghana: the Mali army numbered '100,000 men', including '10,000 horsemen' and its sovereigns '*constantly* wage holy war and are *continually* on expeditions against the pagan Negroes'. According to the *Tarikh es-Sudan*, 'the king of Mali conquered Sonxai, Timbuktu, Zagha, Mima, Baghena and the surrounding country as far as the ocean'. Only the merchant city of Jenne was able to resist his repeated attacks. It is certain that from this time onwards slavetrading was one of the main activities and one of the principal resources of the political and military formations in the Sahelo-Sudanese region: Tekrur, Ghana, Mali, Ghiroy, Silla. During the following centuries, war was a permanent feature of the history of Sonxai. The *chi* (sovereign) Suleyman Dama 'spent *his whole reign* on warlike expeditions'. Soni Ali 'was engaged on warlike expeditions and on the conquest of countries'. He conquered the Baram, the Nunu Sanbadja, Timbuktu, Jenne, the country of the Kunta, Borgu and Gurma as well as tangling with the Mossi. *Askia* Mohammed conquered Bagana, Air, Kingi and Kusata. The sovereign Mohammed Benkan had such an appetite for warlike expeditions that he is said to have exhausted the patience of the people of Sonxai. Thus the chroniclers chant on the interminable list of expeditions and wars, right up to the disappearance of the *askias*.

[From *The Anthropology of Slavery: The Womb of Iron and Gold*, trs. Alide Dasnois [1986] (Chicago: University of Chicago Press, 1991), 44–7.]

THE ECONOMIST

85 The Flourishing Business of Slavery

The trade in child sex has topped the indignation charts in the West this year. But much of it is only the nastiest aspect of a wider evil: slavery. Every country in the world has outlawed this practice, in theory. In fact, millions of people, women and children especially, are still used as slaves.

Child slavery has increased since the 1970s—in part, ironically, because that was when the shah of Iran banned the use of child labour in carpet factories. Many manufacturers promptly moved to Pakistan, Nepal and India, which had fewer qualms. Not only could they hire child labour dirt cheap, they found they could do even better by tapping into traditional systems of 'debt bondage'.

Bonded workers agree to sell their labour in exchange for a lump sum, perhaps to pay a big medical bill. Such deals are common in countries where the poor's only equity is their sweat. But the line is easily crossed into slavery, when low wages, high interest rates and cheating make the debt impossible to repay. South Asia, where many people are illiterate, ignorant of their rights, and thus easily diddled, is the home of this system. The India-based Bonded Labour Liberation Front reckons that, from a small start in the late

1970s, there are now half a million South Asian children thus bonded (sometimes literally, by chains) to their carpet-weaving looms.

In Nepal and Pakistan, millions of bonded labourers work in farming. Here the relationship to slavery is clearest. Bonded debts can be passed on to the next generation. Those who are deemed not to have paid their debt can be sold to another landlord. If a man escapes his place of employment, his family can be held until he comes back, or sold if he does not. Bonded peasants can be sold into marriage.

Bondage-cum-slavery is also common in the brick kilns and mines of South Asia, in some remote areas of Peru and Brazil (with forced prostitution to match), in the servants' quarters and camel race-grounds of the Gulf (Bangladeshi child riders are a speciality), and in the brothels of South-East Asia. In the worst cases, workers are kidnapped, forced to work, assigned a debt, and prevented from escaping by armed guards with shoot-to-kill orders. A Brazilian researcher has estimated there are 60,000 slaves in his country, mostly in the vast Amazon region.

The emergence of AIDS has played a large role in entrapping more and more women and children in sexual slavery. Brothel customers, aware of the risks of infection, want young girls from the countryside, who are presumed less likely to have HIV. And they want brisk turnover. Both desires have led to an increase in the trafficking of Burmese girls and women into Thailand, and of Nepali girls into India; the Nepalis are also highly prized for their fair skin and delicate features.

Thai human-rights organisations reckon there are 20,000 Burmese prostitutes in Thailand at any one time. Some have been kidnapped and literally sold into sexual slavery; a few have left home knowing they will be working as prostitutes. Most are brought under false pretences. The women are routinely forbidden to communicate with their families or even leave the premises.

Nepali prostitutes in India—there are roughly 20,000 in Mumbai (Bombay) alone—have it even worse. The typical pattern is to kidnap or coax a girl away from home with the promise of well-paid work or marriage—some traffickers even go through a marriage ceremony—acculturate her to her work through rape and the lowest kind of prostitution, then sell her on to another brothel or abandon her when she is too old or becomes HIV-infected. Border police put the average age of trafficked girls at 13, but do little to stop the trade.

Slavery in Sudan is also a young and female phenomenon: when armed raiders from the Arab north swoop down on blacks in the south, they take mostly women and children back with them. Girls become concubines, older women become house-servants and younger children tend animals. Some are sold, perhaps even exported: the American embassy in Khartoum has acknowledged as 'credible' reports that Dinka and Nuba children from southern Sudan are being sold on into Libya. The men are either killed or left behind to get together a ransom to reclaim their women and children—if they can find them. According to the London-based Christian Solidarity International, which has ransomed 20 Sudanese slaves, the going rate for a woman is five cows.

The Sudanese government flatly denies that slavery exists there. It is lying: the evidence from human-rights organisations, exiles, traders and former slaves is overwhelming. Louis Farrakhan, the black leader of America's Nation of Islam, and occasional guest of the Libyan and Sudanese governments, has rebuffed assertions of slavery in Sudan as Zionist claptrap. Last March, he challenged journalists to go to Sudan and find it. Two reporters from the *Baltimore Sun* did just that and published their findings in June, sparking off a lively debate among black Americans about how they—and black Muslims in particular—should respond to the plight of enslaved black Africans.

Slavery is as rooted as ever in Mauritania, whose government also denies that it exists. As the government notes, the country has officially abolished slavery three times, most recently in 1980. Yet perhaps 90,000 blacks live as full-time slaves to their Arab masters. Several times that number are only semi-free. Most live in remote rural areas in the east. They have no right to property or marriage; parents have no rights over their children.

Although these are the chief redoubts of modern slavery, the rest of the world is not immune. 'Released' prisoners who are forced to continue working in Chinese labour camps could plausibly be called slaves. So could the several dozen Thai workers who were found locked into their clothing factory in Los Angeles last year. There are reports of women from South Korea, Taiwan and the United States being tricked into forced prostitution in Japan.

Where slavery is systemic and involves the actual buying and selling of human beings, it exists in part because governments are not trying very hard to stop it. Brazil has spoken out strongly against the use of forced labour, but the Amazon region is huge and few policemen and labour inspectors have been assigned to root out abuses. Thailand, Myanmar, India, Pakistan and Nepal all have impressive-sounding laws against slavery, kidnapping and child prostitution, but do little to enforce them. Too often, the police are buddies with the local oligarchs, or esteemed clients at the brothels that they ought to be busting.

The rich world has little leverage to exert against slavery, though there are sporadic efforts. One such comes from Rugmark, an organisation that gives a seal of approval to carpets made without child labour. Another is an agreement by two western sporting-goods makers in Pakistan to send their child workers to school. But such responses can go only so far: most bonded labourers and outright slaves work for industries serving the home market that are immune to outside pressure. And the bosses, who live well off their cheap labour, are much closer to the powers that be than are their wretched workers. Until the penalties for slavery begin to outweigh its rewards, it will not disappear.

[From 'The Flourishing Business of Slavery,' *The Economist*, September 21, 1996, 43–4.]

OLIVIA REMIE CONSTABLE

86 Trade and Traders in Muslim Spain

Slaves

Slaves were the third *major* commodity redistributed through Andalusi markets. As early as the ninth century. Muslim and Jewish merchants brought slaves into al-Andalus from eastern Europe and Christian Spain, and then re-exported them to other regions of the Islamic world. Ibn Khurradādhbih remarked that the Rādhānite merchants sold Andalusi slave girls, and his contemporary, Ibn al-Faqīh, listed slave girls among Andalusi exports to the Maghrib. These women may well have been natives of the northern peninsula, as in a case recorded by the ninth-century jurist Ibn Saʿīd, in which Jewish merchants sold a number of Galician women in Merida. Male slaves, including a Basque musician at the court of ʿAbd al-Rahmān II (822–52), were also brought into al-Andalus from the north of Spain.

Bishop Agobard of Lyons wrote (ca. 826) of two young men abducted from Arles and Lyons by Jewish slavers, with at least one of the pair sent as a slave to Cordoba. Agobard went on to claim that instances of Jewish slaving were common, and insisted that 'it should not be permitted for Jews to sell Christians to Spain,' particularly since the Jews sometimes 'do things [too] horrible to write about'. The context of Agobard's complaint makes it difficult to judge the accuracy of his information. It is significant that he is the only ninth-century writer to object to the taking of Christian captives within Carolingian realms. Other contemporary sources show Jews operating as slave traders in France, but they do not suggest that these merchants enslaved local Christians. Because Agobard was himself a Mozarab, it is likely that he was particularly sensitive to the existence of Christian enslavement in al-Andalus. His complaints may, in fact, reflect an Iberian phenomenon—the enslavement of Basques and Galicians—which he transplanted to France.

Information from the tenth century, however, lends more credibility to Agobard's assertions. Ibn Ḥawqal (writing in the 970s) reported that 'among the most famous exports [from al-Andalus to other Muslim lands] are comely slaves, both male and female, from Frankish (*Ifranja*) and Galician regions'. According to Iṣṭakhrī, likewise, 'white slaves and costly slave girls' came from al-Andalus to other regions of the *dār al-Islām*, but he was surely exaggerating their price when he added that 'slave girls and slaves without skill, depending on their appearance, can be had for one thousand dinars or more'. Liutprand of Cremona described trade in eunuchs between Verdun and Muslim Spain in the same century, confirming the general pattern of traffic through Andalusi emporia.

Ibn Ḥawqal also noted another type of slave, the ṣaqāliba (generally translated as Slavic eunuchs), who came through Andalusi markets for transport abroad. According to this report, 'all Slavic eunuchs on earth come from al-Andalus, because they are castrated in that region and the operation is performed by Jewish merchants'. Muqaddasī, writing at about the same time, provided similar information to the effect that Jews in 'a town behind Pechina' produced ṣaqāliba to be sent from al-Andalus to Egypt. However, not all northern captives were handled by Jews, since an eleventh-century Muslim writer noted that both Jewish and Muslim slavers in the regions along the Andalusi thughūr castrated slaves for foreign export.

Chroniclers mention thousands of Slavic slaves at the Umayyad court in the ninth and tenth centuries, when tensions on the eastern borders of the Carolingian Empire could have fed the supply of ṣaqāliba to Europe and Muslim Spain. The great popularity of the ṣaqāliba in al-Andalus and elsewhere in the Muslim world may have been based on the fact that the distant origins of these slaves tended to promote their loyalty in military and domestic duties. By the eleventh century, in contrast, references to Slavic slaves virtually disappear. Indeed, by this period, many of these former slaves had risen from servitude to join ruling elite in the Taifa states. There are several plausible explanations for this shift. First, the decline of Slavic slavery in the eleventh century may have been owing to the eastward expansion of Europe and the increasing christianization of Slavic lands. Second, perhaps the demise of the centralized Umayyad state, whose rulers had at one time employed thousands of the ṣaqāliba, reduced the demand for a large and loyal corps of Slavic slaves. Meanwhile, Islamic rulers in the Near East began to turn to slave sources on their own eastern and northern borders. Lastly, Brett has put forward the possibility that the arrival of the Almoravids and Almohads created new markets for, and new channels of access to, black slaves in al-Andalus and North Africa, replacing the demand for whites.

Muslim Spanish markets and merchants continued to deal in slaves through the twelfth century, when slaves in Andalusi markets increasingly came from Christian territories in northern Spain, where warfare and border raids provided a steady supply of captives.

[From *Trade and Traders in Muslim Spain: The Commercial Realignment of the Iberian Peninsula, 900–1500* (Cambridge: Cambridge University Press, 1994), 203–7.]

Everything related to the trade in Negroes, in which various European nations have been engaged since the beginning of the sixteenth century on the Guinea Coast, is generally known; but it is astonishing that for all the famous travelers who have visited Egypt none has spoken in their travel accounts of the trade in Negroes conducted in Cairo which, from all appearances, is very old. As this topic seemed interesting to me, and to have some merit for those interested in the history of peoples, I made a special effort to gather together all that pertains to the trade in Negroes in the largest known city in Africa, in which I resided for almost five years.

Travelers have advanced a number of statements, often appalling, on the causes which force Negroes, in their native country, to fall into slavery. I have, for my part, tried to carry out exact researches on this topic. Four different causes appear to be the most frequent.

1. War which, according to all the information that I obtained from the Negroes themselves, arises from the frequent quarrels among their kings or their sultans, that invariably are ended by the force of arms. All then belongs to the victor; the subjects of the vanquished become his captives and they are either kept in his service or are sold or exchanged for commodities such as linen, towels, clothing, cows, camels, horses, etc.

When the Negroes go to war all the family members follow their respective chiefs; even their wives, whether from devotion or from duty, are included. Consequently, the followers of an army are usually far greater in number than the fighting men.

Mr. Browne, in his account of the kingdom of Darfur, relates that when the sultan of Teraub set out to attack Kordofan, he had 500 women in his retinue and he had left an equal number at home. Some had the job of grinding grain, of drawing water, or of preparing the food. Apart from the king's concubines, all of them traveled on foot and carried part of the baggage on their heads.

After the famous battle of the Pyramids, the Negroes and Negresses whom the Mamluks had abandoned with their families in their defeat, admired and praised those Frenchmen who did not exercise the rights of victor over them and sometimes allowed Negresses to dine with them and even to share their beds. Their admiration was even greater since the French had been represented to them as the most inhuman and savage people.

2. The kidnapping of some individuals, which is done even from one hut to another, brings a somewhat smaller number of these unhappy wretches into a state of slavery.

Mischief, audacity, and the habit of stealing from one's fellows sometimes goes so far among them that children have been reported kidnapped while lying at the very side of their mother. A Negro who had been in one of these huts, normally made of cane, took note of the place where the mother usually slept with her daughter aged about three. A few days later this same Negro came during the night, skillfully parted the canes, and took the little Negro girl in her sleep without the unfortunate mother becoming aware of it.

3. Another group of Negro slaves are taken among wandering hordes who have no religion and no form of government. Others, under the rule of some sultan, better educated in the art of destroying their fellow men, armed with muskets and other weapons follow the trails of these hordes which are fairly common and try to blockade them and in particular to deprive them of water. This blockade, or to be more precise, this manhunt, can be fairly long. The besieged, as soon as they realize that they are surrounded, defend themselves with stones; the besiegers on the other hand do no more than fire an occasional musket shot to frighten them. These unfortunate souls, overcome by hunger and thirst, are finally obliged to surrender to their eager oppressors after liberal assurances that nothing will befall them. Each of the besiegers seizes a number of these wretches, binds them with cords and chains, and takes them home, where they are exchanged for other commodities.

4. Mr. Browne mentions a fourth cause of slavery. Whenever a man allows himself even the slightest appearance of trespass on the property of another, his punishment is to have his children or the youngest members of his family reduced to slavery. Worse, if a man sees the footprint of another in his fields, he calls witnesses, lodges a complaint before a magistrate, and once the case is proven, it inevitably costs the offender his son, his nephew, or his niece, whom he is obliged to surrender to the offended party. These incidents which constantly recur cannot fail to produce a great number of slaves. The same punishment is meted out to anyone who, entrusted with making purchases in a distant market, does not exactly carry out the task entrusted to him.

The idea, widespread in Europe, that fathers and mothers or relatives sell their children in the market to the highest bidder is absolutely false. They attach as much value to their children as do the most civilized nations. 'If you white men are capable of believing such absurd stories,' said a Negro to me one day, 'then you should not be astonished if, among ignorant people like us, so many absurd beliefs prevail about the character, manners, and customs of your nation. All animals are grieved when their young ones are taken from them; why would you rank us below all beasts?'

When a father dies and leaves a large family without means and without relatives capable of supporting them, the sultan often takes the children on the pretext of making servants of them and compensates the mother or other persons who would have supported them. Thus he acquires individuals whom he eventually sells to merchants dealing with Egypt. I think that this practice may have given rise to the story that Negroes sell their children in the market like domestic animals.

The *Ghellabis* or slave traders can only go to Egypt in a more or less sizable caravan. The sultan appoints one or two caravan chiefs whom they call *el-Habirri*. They are entrusted not only with maintaining order but further with selling the slaves as well as other products of their country on the sultan's account; and with the proceeds of their sales they buy articles of clothing, weapons etc. in Cairo. The provision of food for the Negroes consists of a type of Turkish wheat or maize which they call *Dourra*. Since the camels of the caravan are burdened with water or with gum-arabic, elephant tusks, tamarind, pots, etc., all the Negroes with the exception of children up to the age of ten or twelve are obliged to follow on foot. If at the moment when the caravan departs, the *Ghellabis* do not take great precautions, many of their Negroes escape. The certainty of never again seeing their native land and the fear of being mistreated by the whites induce them to flee, though the merchants use all their eloquence to persuade them that they will be much better off with foreigners than at home. For the rest, the *Ghellabis* are usually people of a completely inhuman disposition who have more regard for their camels than for their Negroes. If on the way, these do not follow, they make them walk faster by means of a whip or *cortbatche*. Those who wish to cross in greater comfort the desert separating Egypt from the Sudan buy donkeys, which are the best mount, and a parasol made out of oil cloth. The caravan always sets out at daybreak and stops only towards evening. Then some light fires while others grind a portion of *dourra* on a concave stone, which is part of their cooking utensils, and then cook it into a gruel with a very small quantity of salted beef jerky. Lunch likewise consists of a mash of *dourra* but without meat. They are remarkably sparing with water; often the wretched Negroes are only allowed to drink once a day, as a result of which more of them die of thirst than of exhaustion. This way of saving water, in itself so cruel, is dictated by two powerful circumstances. The first is that during a crossing of 36 to 40 days they find water only three or four times, that is to say every ten to twelve days; the second is that often a large number of water-bearers die. Despite all these obstacles, it has been established that the number of Negroes that die on this exhausting journey is infinitely smaller than that sustained in the traffic in Negroes on the Guinea Coast.

Before the arrival of the French, the caravans of Sennar and Darfur stopped at Abu Tig, a little town in Upper Egypt, where it was the practice of the *Ghellabis*, because of their insatiable greed, to have eunuchs made. Curious to know all about this cruel operation, I inquired of the governor of this town. He assured me that they made from one to two hundred eunuchs a year; that the death rate among them was not very significant, and that healing took place relatively quickly. A eunuch normally is sold for double the price of another Negro, and it is this increase in price which prompts the owners, or more appropriately, usurpers to have some of these unfortunate people mutilated. As concerns the procedure of the operation itself, I was unable to obtain very precise or definite information. Nevertheless, the essential is that with one hand the person performing the procedure grasps the scrotum and penis which he extends slightly, then, with a razor in the other hand, he removes everything in a single stroke. This operation, although in itself very simple, requires a certain dexterity and experience: for if the operator stretches the parts too much or cuts them too close, the patient may easily die. If, on the other hand, he does not stretch them enough, a kind of stump will result which leaves the eunuch deformed and which will not fail to alarm a prospective buyer. I do not know the means by which the flow of blood is stopped after the cutting of the parts. Some told me that they applied mule's dung; others that the patient was buried up to the waist in a ditch which was then filled with sand. If in the course of so bizarre a treatment the urethra remains free, the patient has some hope of healing. If, on the other hand, it is blocked, there follows a suppression of the flow of urine which soon leads to death.

In whatever manner this cruel operation is carried out, it is astonishing that the death rate is so low. This evidently results from the strong constitution of the Negroes and the age at which they are subjected to this operation; for they are ordinarily chosen among children of eight to ten and never above. Pietro della Valle reports, however, that in Persia those who are subjected to this operation as a punishment for rape or other crimes of this kind recover very well, even if advanced in age, and that the only treatment is some ashes on the wound.

In the Barbary states, they simply apply liquefied tar to the wound. I have often chatted with eunuchs in Cairo; but none of them was willing to give me accurate information on the operation they had undergone; they constantly avoided the question in an effort to persuade me that they had lost all recollection of it.

The arrival of the French army in Egypt spontaneously stopped the barbaric practice of mutilating Negroes in such an inhuman fashion. By virtue of an order of General Bonaparte, the commanders of the troop corps stationed in Upper Egypt bought, when a caravan stopped there, the Negroes who might be apt for military service. And experience has shown that they are just as capable of becoming good soldiers as are Europeans.

[From 'Memoir on the Traffic in Negroes in Cairo and on the Illnesses to Which They Are Subject upon Arrival There (1802),' trs. Michel Le Gall, in Shaun E. Marmon (ed)., *Slavery in the Islamic Middle East* (Princeton: Markus Wiener, 1999), 70–5.]

The Experience of Slavery

INTRODUCTION

The harsh reality of slavery as a relation of extreme domination and inequality meant that most slaves throughout history were in no position to record their thoughts and feelings about their bondage. Indeed, precisely because masters produced almost all of the documentary evidence, historians have long despaired about the possibility of ever recovering the experience of slavery from the slave's point of view. During the last quarter of the twentieth century, however, a remarkable outpouring of scholarship on slavery has succeeded in amplifying the voice of the slave and thus in narrowing the gap between what happened in slavery and what was said to have happened. In rewriting the history of slavery from the bottom up, modern scholars have imaginatively applied new methods to existing data, mined such unconventional sources as music, folklore, and oral traditions, and sensitized themselves to reading the silences in narratives as well as the narratives themselves.

In virtually all of the slave narratives published during the transatlantic antislavery crusade of the nineteenth century, including those excerpted in this section, the master's violent appropriation of the slave's productive and reproductive capacities stands out as the central experience of slavery. Indeed, Juan Francisco Manzano, author of one of the very few autobiographies ever written by a slave without the aid of an amanuensis, attested to the indelible scars borne by the mind as well as the body after a life of suffering at the hands of a succession of masters and mistresses. In a letter of 1835, published in English translation for the first time in this volume, Manzano apologizes to a white patron for his unworthiness by asking him to remember that the narrator is a slave and, as such, a 'dead being' in the eyes of his master. Yet, the very existence of Manzano's prose attests to another reality: slaves did not cease to be human in their enslavement. Throughout history, slaves have married, raised children, trucked and bartered for themselves, inherited property, formed cults and brotherhoods, celebrated the sacred, buried the profane, and seized their own freedom. By resisting their enslavement they extracted concessions from uncharitable masters, which, in reality, qualified the terms of bondage and limited the master's authority. Certain concessions evolved into rights and privileges, some of which were codified into law by the government. In every slave society slaves challenged the idea of slavery by struggling to redeem themselves from social death. Had the experience of slavery not differed from the theory, had slaves not performed as historical actors, masters would not have had to develop sophisticated methods of discipline and punishment to keep their slaves in line.

At ground level the experience of slavery defies easy generalization, for slaves were acquired and used differently in a wide variety of systems and environments. Historians of plantation slavery in the Americas have richly documented how the master–slave relationship was shaped by the cultural antecedents of Europeans and Africans; by a work regimen; by the operation of markets and technology; by ecology, demography, and biology; and by the location of political power. Clearly, the discrete experience of any given slave in such a highly personalized relation of domination had much to do with the temperament, character, wealth, and status of any given master. Along with exploitation, enslavement also bred intimacy, mutuality, and reciprocal dependency. Strong paternalistic ties to a resident master tended to weaken collective solidarity by binding individual slaves to the master instead of to each other. Nor could slaves in any slaveholding society easily forge a distinctive experience when their numbers were few and their status blurred with other subaltern groups. Although slaves in the Americas are commonly associated with commercialized agriculture, enslavement in some societies on both sides of the Atlantic occurred largely within urban households. Although slavery in the Americas is commonly associated with Africans and persons of African descent, race, from a global perspective, figured as only one of several mutable categories of difference constructed to justify mass enslavements. Plantation slavery has a predominately economic character, and slaves were usually defined by their work, but slaves in many premodern societies consumed more than they produced as status-differentiating adornments in the households of powerful people. In the ancient and modern worlds some slaves succeeded in living apart from their masters and hiring out their own labor. Gender conventions meant that female slaves entered disproportionately into certain kinds of occupation, but at any given moment they could be found performing the same arduous tasks in shops, mines, and fields as did their male counterparts. Some slaves accumulated considerable wealth and even purchased slaves of their own. In some cases literate slaves educated the children of their masters. Indeed, skilled and privileged slaves existed in every slave society. Some, including female slaves, wielded impressive power as surrogates for elite masters. Slave stewards, for example, managed serfs on vast estates in czarist Russia; slave eunuchs held sway in Byzantine, Ottoman, and Chinese courts; slave soldiers in Egypt during the mid-thirteenth century overthrew the Ayubbid Dynasty.

Legal codes from as long ago as the rule of Hammurabi followed the logic of dehumanization inherent in the idea of slavery by enacting property law that grouped slaves with cattle, pigs, and other domesticated animals. In examining the experience of slavery, historians have differentiated between law and practice and paid considerable attention to the question of slave treatment. More recently, social scientists have applied economic and statistical techniques to the existing evidence to come up with more meaningful generalizations. But scholars have not always understood 'treatment' in the same way nor agreed upon the appropriate measure or standard of comparison. Statistical averages may homogenize individual experiences that were anything but homogenous. Some authors have concentrated on the material conditions of life, how slaves were fed, housed, and clothed; others have stressed the relative stability of the slave family, the space for cultural initiatives, and the frequency of manumission. Slaves could be treated relatively well according to one definition, but not according to another. On the one hand, slaves in the antebellum United States, to cite the most thoroughly studied case, partook of material conditions that compared favorably with those of free workers in the early factory systems, typically lived in two-parent households, and reproduced naturally at a rate unmatched by slaves in other plantation societies. They had sufficient space to erect semi-autonomous communities, which practiced a version of Christianity that addressed their particular needs as slaves and fostered aspirations for freedom. On the other hand, slaves in the antebellum South also experienced one of the lowest rates of manumission in the Americas.

Western and non-Western societies tortured their slaves, sometimes as part of a ritualistic judicial proceeding that preceded the spectacle of execution, whether by burning, hanging, or crucifixion. Once again, the theory of slavery had implications for the experience. Torture, derived from the Greek word for touchstone, was designed to extract the truth from dishonored bodies that supposedly lacked a deliberative faculty. Any history of the discipline, management, and punishment of slaves would catalogue a list of practices that could stretch the boundaries of a perverse mind. But, in truth, beings without will do not require deterrence. In every slave society some masters learned that incentives and rewards elicited the desired behavior from slaves more easily than brute force.

In advanced slave systems a self-conscious master class emerged, which sought to translate the power over their slaves into real authority. Scholars continue to debate the results of coercion, the psychological impact of paternalism, and the degree to which slaves internalized their enslavement. The world's slave systems have had varying degrees of rigidity, and comparative research about their closed or open character has led to debates about the general psychology and personality of slaves. Whites in the antebellum southern United States stereotyped their black slaves as indolent, fawning, and irresponsible, and relied on race to explain their behavior. Some modern scholars, by contrast, have rooted the so-called Sambo stereotype in the coerciveness of the institution and suggested that Sambo was a particular example of a more general type of slavish personality, which could be found wherever slavery existed and even in hierarchies without slavery. Whatever the explanation, accommodation to slavery does not equal the acceptance of enslavement. Sambo, it turns out, was frequently feigned. Both rebelliousness and docility existed throughout the slave quarters, alternately surfacing in the personality of individual slaves. The readings in this section suggest that a heightened understanding of the experience of slavery in any country begins with an acknowledgment that the dynamic and malleable relationship between master and slave was, in practice, shaped by both parties, however unequal they were made to be.

88   Life of St Balthild

Here begins the life of the Blessed Queen Balthild

2. The blessed Lord, who 'will have all men to be saved, and to come unto the knowledge of the truth,' works 'all in all' both 'to will and to do'. By the same token, among the merits and virtues of the saints, praise should first be sung of Him Who made the humble great and raised the pauper from the dunghill and seated him among the princes of his people. Such a one is the woman present to our minds, the venerable and great lady Balthild the queen. Divine Providence called her from across the seas. She, who came here as God's most precious and lofty pearl, was sold at a cheap price. Erchinoald, a Frankish magnate and most illustrious man, acquired her and in his service the girl behaved most honorably. And her pious and admirable manners pleased this prince and all his servants. For she was kind-hearted and sober and prudent in all her ways, careful and plotting evil for none. Her speech was not frivolous nor her words presumptuous but in every way she behaved with utmost propriety. And since she was of the Saxon race, she was graceful in form with refined features, a most seemly woman with a smiling face and serious gait. And she so showed herself just as she ought in all things, that she pleased her master and found favor in his eyes. So he determined that she should set out the drinking cup for him in his chamber and, honored above all others as his housekeeper, stand at his side always ready to serve him. She did not allow this dignity to make her proud but rather kept her humility. She was all obedience to her companions and amiable, ministering with fitting honor to her elders, ready to draw the shoes from their feet and wash and dry them. She brought them water to wash themselves and prepared their clothing expeditiously. And she performed all these services with good spirits and no grumbling.

3. And from this noble conduct, the praise and love of her comrades for her increased greatly. She gained such happy fame that, when the said lord Erchinoald's wife died, he hoped to unite himself to Balthild, that faultless virgin, in a matronal bed. But when she heard of this, she fled and most swiftly took herself out of his sight. When she was called to the master's chamber she hid herself secretly in a corner and threw some vile rags over herself so that no one could guess that anyone might be concealed there. Thus for the love of humility, the prudent and astute virgin attempted to flee as best she could from vain honors. She hoped that she might avoid a human marriage bed and thus merit a spiritual and heavenly spouse. But doubtless, Divine Providence brought it about that the prince, unable to find the woman he sought, married another wife. Thereafter it happened, with God's approval, that Balthild, the maid who escaped marriage with a lord, came to be espoused to Clovis, son of the former king Dagobert. Thus by virtue of her humility she was raised to a higher rank. Divine dispensation determined to honor her in this station so that, having scorned the king's servant, she came to be coupled with the king himself and bring forth royal children. And these events are known to all for now her royal progeny rule the realm.

[From 'Life of Saint Balthild,' [c.680] in Jo Ann McNamara and John E. Halborg, eds. and trs., *Sainted Women of the Dark Ages* (Durham: Duke University Press, 1992), 268–70.]

MARY PRINCE

89 A West Indian Slave History

For five years after this I remained in his house [in Bermuda], and almost daily received the same harsh treatment. At length he put me on board a sloop, and to my great joy sent me away [c.1805] to Turk's Island. I was not permitted to see my mother or father, or poor sisters and brothers, to say good bye, though going away to a strange land, and might never see them again. Oh the Buckra people who keep slaves think that black people are like cattle, without natural affection. But my heart tells me it is far otherwise.

We were nearly four weeks on the voyage, which was unusually long. Sometimes we had a light breeze, sometimes a great calm, and the ship made no way; so that our provisions and water ran very low, and we were put upon short allowance. I should almost have been starved had it not been for the kindness of a black man called Anthony, and his wife, who had brought their own victuals, and shared them with me.

When we went ashore at the Grand Quay, the captain sent me to the house of my new master, Mr. D—, to whom Captain I— had sold me. Grand Quay is a small town upon a sandbank; the houses low and built of wood. Such was my new master's. The first person I saw, on my arrival, was Mr. D—, a stout sulky looking man, who carried me through the hall to show me to his wife and children. Next day I was put up by the vendue master to know how much I was worth, and I was valued at one hundred pounds currency.

My new master was one of the owners or holders of the salt ponds, and he received a certain sum for every slave that worked upon his premises, whether they were young or old. This sum was allowed him out of the profits arising from the salt works. I was immediately sent to work in the salt water with the rest of the slaves. This work was perfectly new to me. I was given a half barrel and a shovel, and had to stand up to my knees in the water, from four o'clock in the morning till nine, when we were given some Indian corn boiled in water, which we were obliged to swallow as fast as we could for fear the rain should come on and melt the salt. We were then called again to our tasks, and worked through the heat of the day; the sun flaming upon our heads like fire, and raising salt blisters in those parts which were not completely covered. Our feet and legs, from standing in the salt water for so many hours, soon became full of dreadful boils, which eat down in some cases to the very bone, afflicting the sufferers with great torment. We came home at twelve; ate our corn soup, called *blawly*, as fast as we could, and went back to our employment till dark at night. We then shovelled up the salt in large heaps, and went down to the sea, where we washed the pickle from our limbs, and cleaned the barrows and shovels from the salt. When we returned to the house, our master gave us each our allowance of raw Indian corn, which we pounded in a mortar and boiled in water for our suppers.

We slept in a long shed, divided into narrow slips, like the stalls used for cattle. Boards fixed upon stakes driven into the ground, without mat or covering, were our only beds. On Sundays, after we had washed the salt bags, and done other work required of us, we went into the bush and cut the long soft grass, of which we made trusses for our legs and feet to rest upon, for they were so full of the salt boils that we could get no rest lying upon the bare boards.

Though we worked from morning till night, there was no satisfying Mr. D—. I hoped, when I left Capt. I—, that I should have been better off, but I found it was but going from one butcher to another. There was this difference between them: my former master used to beat me while raging and foaming with passion; Mr. D— was usually quite calm. He would stand by and give orders for a slave to be cruelly whipped, and assist in the punishment, without moving a muscle of his face; walking about and taking snuff with the greatest composure. Nothing could touch his hard heart—neither sighs, nor tears, nor prayers, nor streaming blood; he was deaf to our cries, and careless of our sufferings.—Mr. D— has often stripped me naked, hung me up by the wrists, and beat me with the cow-skin, with his own hand, till my body was raw with gashes. Yet there was nothing very remarkable in this; for it might serve as a sample of the common usage of the slaves on that horrible island.

Owing to the boils in my feet, I was unable to wheel the barrow fast through the sand, which got into the sores, and made me stumble at every step; and my master, having no pity for my sufferings from this cause, rendered them far more intolerable, by chastising me for not being able to move so fast as he wished me. Another of our employments was to row a little way off from the shore in a boat, and dive for large stones to build a wall round our master's house. This was very hard work; and the great waves breaking over us continually, made us often so giddy that we lost our footing, and were in danger of being drowned.

Ah, poor me!—my tasks were never ended. Sick or well, it was work—work—work!—After the diving season was over, we were sent to the South Creek, with large bills, to cut up mangoes to burn lime with. Whilst one party of slaves were thus employed, another were sent to the other side of the island to break up coral out of the sea.

[From *The History of Mary Prince, A West Indian Slave, Related by Herself* [1831], ed. Moira Ferguson (Ann Arbor: University of Michigan Press, 1993), 60–3.]

90   St. Vincent Reports 1824

[An interview of slaves on Fairhall Estate, St. Vincent, 4 August 1824, conducted by John Johnson, London agent of the late James Gordon.]

The [slave] Gang having assembled I required those who had complaints to make to come forward one at a time: the first complainant was

1. Harry Antigua—stated that he and the rest of the Gang [on the sugar plantation] were deprived of their allowance of cloathing and provisions—that instead of six yards of penistons [course woolen cloth] he only received five yards, and that instead of 2 lbs of fish p[er] week he only received 1½ lbs.

2. Joe—(the head Boiler) stated that he received his full allowance of cloathing, but that the statement of the last complainant was otherwise correct—he also complained of not having the usual indulgence and extra allowance on finishing crop.

3. Joshua—stated that some of the Negroes received 6 yards of penistons but most of them got only 5 yards, and that the deficiency in the fish was general. The men particularly complained of ill treatment by punishment.

4th. Christmas—recapitulated the several Statements of the above complainants.

5th. John Taylor—made the same complaint respecting the deficiency of penistons and fish—and also stated that his Sister died leaving 8 children who were not taken care of.

6th. Plato—made the same complaint respecting the cloathing and fish and the want of usual indulgence on finishing Crop. He also stated that the Gang were subject to ill-treatment by Mr. McColl the head Overseer.

7th. Charles—(cattle keeper) repeated the statement of Plato, and complained that Mr. Robertson had flogged him for showing Mr. Johnson some Cattle belonging to him (Mr. R), on the day he (Mr. J) inspected the Stock belonging to the Estate—and that a Cow and Calf of the number had been received by Mr. Robertson in payment of Lent of Store at Ca[l]liaqua [a docking point at the mouth of the Calliaqua River].

8th.   Big Harry ⎫
9th.   Daniel   ⎬ Stated that they received their allowance of penistons,
10th.   William   ⎭ but only 5 yds of Calico & 1½ lbs of fish.

11th. Primus (head Driver) complained of the same deficiency in the penistons and of Mr. McColl's ill-treatment of the Gang.

12th. Will—repeated the statement of the above complainant.

13th. Lucinda—complained of the living in general and the frequent flogging inflicted by Mr. McColl.

14th. Mary Ann—stated that the Negroes were deprived of the Stores sent out for them, and that the Slaves belonging to Eliza were sent by her with Barley, thread candles & other articles belonging to the Estate to Calliaqua for Sale where she has a shop in charge of a woman named Kitty.

15th. Argott—complained of the same deficiencies; and repeats the statement of the above complainant, with the addition of Mr. McColl's ill-treatment, and that the little indulgences they were formerly allowed were suspended when Mr. Robertson came on the property.

16th. Precilla—this woman stated that soap, candles and other things belonging to the Estate were sent to Calliaqua for sale by Eliza, and that they had no indulgence at Christmas—repeated also the statement respecting deficiency of allowance and added that since the Gang came forward to complain to Mr. Johnson, Mr. Robertson had threatened to kill them all as soon as he (Mr. J) quitted the Island.

17th. Ann—stated as the last complainant respecting the sale of Stores belonging to the Estate of Eliza.

18th. Baby—repeated the several statements of Precilla (the 16th complainant).

19th. Clarissa—the complaints of this woman were in recapitulation of the several above recited statements, with the addition that her mother had left 8 children who were not taken care of.

20th. Lead—(the Sick Nurse) this woman acknowledged that she received her proper allowance of cloathing, but that the Gang in general did not—stated that the deficiency originated in the *stretching* of the cloth when being measured.

21. Wilkes (the head Carpenter) stated that the fish was not weight—and that the Negroes had long complained of the deficiency in the cloathing. At Christmas he only received 4 lbs of pork.

22. Primus (the head Driver) stated that the fish and cloathing were deficient and complained of the want of indulgence on finishing crop and the ill-usage of the Gang by Mr. McColl, who would not listen to the good character of a Negro in mitigation of punishment, and frequently checked him (Primus) for speaking in recommendation—stated also that the Negroe's [provision] grounds were not sufficient.

23^d. Lucia—complained of not being allowed Candles and Soap during her confinement.

24th. big Present—stated that she had 5 children to maintain without the least indulgence in consideration thereof.

Primus (the head Driver) again questioned—'Have you any complaints to make against the character of the 1st complainant Harry Antigua.'—'So, So, he good working Negro Massa.' quest: 'What is your opinion of Joshua, of Christmas and Plato?' Ansr. 'No fault—dey good Neger massa.' quest: 'Have you any objections to make towards any of those that have complained?' Ansr. 'No.' quest: 'Were you in the field upon the occasion referred to by Precilla and Baby (the 16th & 18th complainants) when Mr. Robertson threatened (as stated by them) to kill them all as soon as I quitted the Island?' ansr. 'Yes.' quest: 'did you hear Mr. Robertson say so?' ansr. 'No.' quest: 'Do you think you should have heard him if had said so?' ansr. 'Yes.'

[From 'Reports Relating to Mr. Gordon's Estates in the West Indies, 1824,' Beinecke Lesser Antilles Collection, Hamilton College, Clinton, New York.]

JAMES H. HAMMOND

91   Rules Concerning Slaves

Allowances

Allowances are given weekly. No distinction is made among work-hands, whether full hands, or less than full hands, or adjuncts about the yard, stables, etc. A peck of meal apiece is given every Sunday morning. The peck measure is filled and piled up as long as will remain on it, but not packed or shaken. Meat and syrup are given out on Monday night. When meat alone is given, 3 pounds of pickled pork, or bacon, apiece is the allowance. Fresh meat, salted overnight, may be given at any time at rates of $3\frac{1}{2}$ pounds of beef or pork. In summer, but one-half of the allowance may be of fresh meat. As soon as the cold weather sets in fresh pork allowance begins. Of hog offal 4 pounds. With one quart of syrup apiece the meat allowance is reduced to $1\frac{3}{4}$ pounds of pickle pork or bacon, or $2\frac{1}{2}$ of fresh beef or pork, or $2\frac{1}{2}$ of hog offal. No deductions are made for light sickness of a day or so, or for pregnancy. A ditcher who does each task without occasion for annoyance for a week receives on Wednesday night an extra pound of meat. The driver is allowed a small extra of meat and molasses whenever he may apply for it, which is but rarely done. Each ditcher receives every night, when ditching (fall and winter), a dram (jigger), consisting of $\frac{1}{5}$ water and $\frac{4}{5}$ whiskey, with as much asafoetida as it will absorb, and a long string of pepper in the barrel. The dram is a good sized wine glass full. In cotton picking time, when sickness is prevalent, every hand gets a dram before leaving for the field. After soaking rain all exposed to it also get a dram before changing their clothes. Drams are never given as rewards and only as medicinal. From second hoeing, or early in May an occasional allowance of tobacco is given to those that use it—about $\frac{1}{8}$ of a pound, usually after some general operation as a hoeing, ploughing, etc. This is continued until the crops are gathered when each negro can provide for himself. Each man gets in the fall 1 cotton shirt and 1 pr. woolen pants and 1 woolen jacket. In the spring they get 1 shirt and 2 pair of cotton pants. Each woman gets 6 yards of woolen cloth and 3 yards of cotton shirting in the fall, with a needle, skein of thread and $\frac{1}{2}$ dozen buttons. In the spring they got 6 yards of cotton drillings, 3 yards of shirting with needle and buttons. A stout pair of shoes is given to each in the fall and blanket every third year.

Children

There is a separate apartment under the charge of a trusty nurse where the children are kept during the day. Weaned children are brought to it at the last horn blow in the morning—about good day light. The unweaned are brought in at sun rise, after sucking, and left in cradles in charge of the nurse. Allowance is given out daily to the children. 4 quarts of meal, 3 quarts of hominy and 2 pounds of bacon are found sufficient for about 20 children. They have also 1 pint of skimmed milk each a day. Their breakfast consists of hominy and milk. At mid-day their meat is made into soup-pot-liquor generally—with vegetables boiled in it if any are to be had and dumplings or bread. In the afternoon—an hour or so before sun-set—they have hominy and milk again. They are never allowed fresh meat except the bony parts of beef to make soup. $1\frac{1}{2}$ pints of molasses are given among their same number every Wednesday morning. Each child gets a shirt and the girls a frock also; the boys a pair pantaloons reaching the neck and with sleeves every fall and spring, of the same goods as the work hands. A child's blanket is given to each of them every third year. Children born can have a blanket at the time of birth or the fall following according to the necessities of the mother. All children are required to appear in entirely clean clothes twice a week. It is the duty of their mothers to attend to it and of the nurse to see that it is done or immediately to report it. The nurse must also see that no child changes its clothes from thicker to thinner clothes or the reverse at improper times or has on any wet garment at any time.

Plantation hours

The first morning horn is blown one hour before daybreak. Work hands are expected to rise and prepare the cooking, etc. for the day. The second horn is blown at good day light, when it is the duty of the driver to visit every house and see that all have left for the field. The plough hands leave their houses for the stables at the summons of the plough-driver 15 minutes earlier than the gang, the overseer opening the stables. At $11\frac{1}{2}$ A.M. the plough hands stop to feed. At 12 P.M. the gang stop to eat dinner. At 1 P.M. through the greater part of the year all hands return to work. In summer the intermission increases with the heat to the extent of $2\frac{1}{2}$ hours. At 15 minutes before sunset the plows stop for the day and at sunset the rest of the hands. No night work is ever exacted. At night the negroes are allowed to visit among themselves until the horn-blow—at $8\frac{1}{2}$ o'clock in winter and 9 o'clock in summer. After which no negro must be seen out of his house and it is the duty of the driver to go around and see that he is in it.

Sucklers are not required to leave their houses until sun-rise when they leave their infants at the children's house before going to the field. The period of suckling is one year. For six months they return three times a day to suckle their infants—in the middle of the morning, at mid-day and in the middle of the afternoon. Their work lies always within half a mile of the quarter. They are required to be cool before commencing to suckle—to wait 15 minutes at least in summer after reaching the children's house before nursing. It is the duty of the nurse to see that none of them are heated when nursing as well as of the overseer and his wife occasionally to do so. They are allowed 45 minutes at each nursing to be with their children. After 7 months they return to nurse but twice a day missing at mid-day. At 10 months they return at mid-day only. Each woman on weaning her child is required to put it in charge of some woman without a child for two weeks and not to nurse it at all during that time. A suckler does about $\frac{3}{5}$ of a full hand's work, a little increased toward the last. Such hands as can not follow with the prime gang from age or deformity are put with the sucklers. Pregnant women at 5 months are put with the suckler's gang.

The regular plantation midwife shall attend all women in confinement. Some other woman learning the art usually assists her. The confined woman lies up one month, the midwife remaining with her the first 7 days.

There is a hospital adjoining the children's house where all the sick are confined. Every reasonable complaint is promptly attended to and with any marked or general symptom of sickness a negro may lie up a day or so at least. Homeopathy is exclusively as no physician is allowed to practice on the place. There being no homeopathist convenient—each case has to be examined carefully by the master or overseer to ascertain the disease. The remedies next are to be chosen with the utmost discrimination. The vehicles for preparing and administering with are to be thoroughly cleaned. The directions for treatment, diet, etc. most explicitly followed; the effects and changes continuously observed, and finally the medicines securely laid away from accidents and contaminating influences. In case where there is uncertainty the books must be taken to the bedside and a thorough and careful examination of the case and comparisons of medicines made before administering them. The head driver is the most important negro on the plantation. He is to be treated with more respect than any other negro by both master and overseer. He is on no occasion to be treated with any indignity calculated to lose the respect of the other negroes without breaking him. He is required to maintain proper discipline at all times. To see that no negro idles or does bad work in the field, and to punish it with discretion on the spot. The driver is not to be flogged except by the master but in emergencies that will not admit of delay. He is permitted to visit the master at any time without being required to get a card though in general he must inform the overseer when he leaves the place and present himself on returning. He is expected to communicate freely whatever needs attention or he thinks information to the owner.

Marriage is to be encouraged as it adds to the comfort, happiness and health of those entering upon it, besides insuring a greater increase. No negro man can have a wife, nor woman a husband, not belonging to the master. Where sufficient cause can be shown on either side a marriage may be broken but the offending party must be punished. Offenders can not marry again after such divorces for three years. As an encouragement to Marriage the first time any two get married a bounty of $5.00 to be invested in household goods or an equivalent of articles shall be given. If either has ever been married before the bounty shall be $2.50 or equivalent. A third marriage shall not be allowed but in extreme cases and in such cases or where both have been married before no bounty shall be given. No marriage shall take place without the masters expressed consent to it.

Negroes living at one quarter having wives at the other are priveleged to visit them only between Saturday night and Monday morning and must get a pass for each visit. The pass consists of a card with the full name of the place of destination on it and the first letter of the place left below. All visiting with strange negroes is prohibited. All are privileged and encouraged to go to church on preaching days. Not more than six ordinarily can be absent at the same time from one quarter except for church. The pass card must be delivered immediately on reaching the destination and a return card given ready to return. All are subject to the regulation of the place they are at any time upon and it is as much the duty of the overseer and driver to observe them as the others under their ordinary charge.

Each male work-hand shall be allowed to go to town once a year, on a Sunday between crop gathering and christmas. Not more than 10 can go the same day.

Adjoining each negro house is a piece of ground convenient for a garden. They have also patches in various parts of the plantation to cultivate little crops of their own. There is also a small field planted and worked, generally in pinders—the same as the rest of the crop the product of which is divided among them.

At christmas three or four days holyday are given on one of which a barbecue of beef or mutton and pork, bread and coffee are provided. Also a holyday and 'cue in August.

Horses and mules

Every horse and mule when in use is curried in the morning before taken from the stable and at 12 o'clock; also at night when they appear unusually sweaty and fatigued. They feed twice a day; at night as much corn as they can eat, generally nearly a peck and about 8 Hs. of fodder, hay or shucks apiece; and at 12 o'clock 6 ears of corn and about $2\frac{1}{2}$ Hs. of fodder each. When idle they require one third less and curried but once a week on Sunday. Watering is done 3 times a day when idle and 4 times when at work: Always morning and night and before and after 12 o'clock feeding when at work but only before when idle. One gill of salt of best quality is given every other day unless soaked corn is used. When soaked corn is fed it is put in a barrel in the morning and $\frac{2}{3}$ of a gill of salt to each mule sprinkled over it and water enough to cover it. This fed only at night. A gill of dry salt besides is given to each horse twice a week. Horse are haltered in separate stalls. Mules are left loose in another stable. Fresh straw is added daily so as to keep a dry bed always at night.

Hogs in pasture are fed every other day. They are not to be fed constantly at one spot. The amount given at a feeding is about 1 bushel of inferior corn to every 50 little and big. The overseer attends to this in person assisted by such negroes as may be required. A counting of them must be made and entered on the plantation book at least once every month and marking, cutting and speying at least once in every three months. No hogs must be left at large except a few shoats about the lot.

[From 'Rules Concerning Slaves,' in *The Plantation Manual of James H. Hammond of Beach Island, South Carolina, about 1834* (ts. Hammond Papers, South Carolina Historical Society).]

I will give here a very imperfect list of the cruelties inflicted on us by the enlightened Christians of America.—First, no trifling portion of them will beat us nearly to death, if they find us on our knees praying to God,—They hinder us from going to hear the word of God—they keep us sunk in ignorance, and will not let us learn to read the word of God, nor write—If they find us with a book of any description in our hand, they will beat us nearly to death—they are so afraid we will learn to read, and enlighten our dark and benighted minds—They will not suffer us to meet together to worship the God who made us—they brand us with hot iron—they cram bolts of fire down our throats—they cut us as they do horses, bulls, or hogs—they crop our ears and sometimes cut off bits of our tongues—they chain and hand-cuff us, and while in that miserable and wretched condition, beat us with cow-hides and clubs—they keep us half naked and starve us sometimes nearly to death under their infernal whips or lashes (which some of them shall have enough of yet)—They put on us fifty-sixes and chains, and make us work in that cruel situation, and in sickness, under lashes to support them and their families.—They keep us three or four hundred feet under ground working in their mines, night and day to dig up gold and silver to enrich them and their children.—They keep us in the most death-like ignorance by keeping us from all source of information, and call us, who are free men and next to the Angels of God, their property! ! ! ! ! ! They make us fight and murder each other, many of us being ignorant, not knowing any better—They take us, (being ignor-ant,) and put us as drivers one over the other, and make us afflict each other as bad as they themselves afflict us—and to crown the whole of this catalogue of cruelties, they tell us that we the (blacks) are an inferior race of beings! incapable of self government! !—We would be injurious to society and ourselves, if tyrants should loose their unjust hold on us! ! ! That if we were free we would not work, but would live on plunder or theft! ! ! ! that we are the meanest and laziest set of beings in the world ! ! ! ! ! That they are obliged to keep us in bondage to do us good! ! ! ! ! !—That we are satisfied to rest in slavery to them and their children! ! ! ! ! !—That we ought not to be set free in America, but ought to be sent away to Africa! ! ! ! ! ! ! !—That if we were set free in America, we would involve the country in a civil war, which assertion is altogether at variance with our feeling or design, for we ask them for nothing but the rights of man, viz. for them to set us free, and treat us like men, and there will be no danger, for we will love and respect them, and protect our country—but cannot conscientiously do these things until they treat us like men.

[From *David Walker's Appeal, in Four Articles; Together with a Preamble, to the Coloured Citizens of the World, but in Particular, and Very Expressly, to those of the United States of America* [1829], ed. Peter Hinks (University Park: Pennsylvania State University Press, 2000), 68–9.]

JUAN FRANCISCO MANZANO

93 | Letter to Domingo Del Monte, 1835

Havana, 25 June 1835

My Dear Sir Don Domingo [Del Monte]:

I received your esteemed letter of the 15th of this month, and I was surprised that in it you say that you asked me three or four months ago for the story of my life. I cannot help telling you that I have not received so far in advance such notice since on the very day that I received your letter of the 22nd, I began to run through my mind the events of my life, and when I could, I began to write believing that all I would need was a *real*'s worth of paper. But having written somewhat more, even though at times skipping over four and even five years. I still have not reached 1820. But I hope to finish soon, restricting myself only to the most interesting events. On four occasions I almost quit. A sketch of so many calamities does not seem but a massive record of impostures, and even from such a tender age the cruel lashings made me aware of my humble condition. I feel mortified in telling it, and I do not know how to really show the facts leaving the most terrible part in the inkwell. I wish I had other facts with which to fill the history of my life without having to remember the excessive severity with which my former mistress [the Marquesa de Prado-Ameno] treated me, obliging me or pleasing me out of dire necessity to appeal to perilous flight in order to spare my poor body the constant mortification, which I could suffer no more. Thus being prepared to see a debilitated creature, wallowing in the most grave sufferings, delivered to various overseers, being without the least exaggeration the target of misfortune, I fear to be totally undeserving in your eyes. But remember, sir, when you read this that I am a slave and that a slave is a dead being before his master. I hope not to lose in your eyes the worth that I have gained. Consider me a martyr, and you will find that the endless lashes that have mutilated my flesh even before my maturity never debased your most affectionate servant, who trusting in your characteristic prudence, dares to open his mouth on this subject, especially when the one who has caused my suffering still lives.

My wife [María del Rosario Díaz] and I join you in your happiness, and I only regret that she is not your wet-nurse. In that case fate would be smiling on me, but things being as they are, patience and tolerance. The house where I live today is saddened by the imprisonment of Don Francisco Semaná [Francisco de Sentmanat]. No one knows why. I have carried messages to the house of Senora Maria Ynasia de Zayas [Sentmanat's mother, María Ignacia de Zayas-Bazan y Chacón], and she is in bed in consequence of this painful event. The senorita who received the message from me returned it crying, and I was not capable of containing my tears.

I hope that you will remain in good health and bid always to be your very humble and obedient servant.

Juan Francisco Manzano

[From letter, Juan Francisco Manzano to Domingo Del Monte, June 25, 1835, in
José L. Franco (ed.), Autobiografía, cartas y versos de Juan Fco. Manzano (Havana:
Municipio de la Habana, 1937), 84–5. Trs. Robert L. Paquette.]

FREDERICK DOUGLASS

94   My Bondage and My Freedom

Col. Lloyd's plantation [. . .] is a little nation of its own, having its own language, its own rules, regulations and customs. The laws and institutions of the state [Maryland], apparently touch it nowhere. The troubles arising here, are not settled by the civil power of the state. The overseer is generally accuser, judge, jury, advocate and executioner. The criminal is always dumb. The overseer attends to all sides of a case.

There are no conflicting rights of property, for all the people are owned by one man; and they can themselves own no property. Religion and politics are alike excluded. One class of the population is too high to be reached by the preacher; and the other class is too low to be cared for by the preacher. The poor have the gospel preached to them, in this neighborhood, only when they are able to pay for it. The slaves, having no money, get no gospel. The politician keeps away, because the people have no votes, and the preacher keeps away, because the people have no money. The rich planter can afford to learn politics in the parlor, and to dispense with religion altogether.

In its isolation, seclusion, and self-reliant independence, Col. Lloyd's plantation resembles what the baronial domains were, during the middle ages in Europe. Grim, cold, and unapproachable by all genial influences from communities without, *there it stands*; full three hundred years behind the age, in all that relates to humanity and morals.

This, however, is not the only view that the place presents. Civilization is shut out, but nature cannot be. Though separated from the rest of the world; though public opinion, as I have said, seldom gets a chance to penetrate its dark domain; though the whole place is stamped with its own peculiar, iron-like individuality; and though crimes, high-handed and atrocious, may there be committed, with almost as much impunity as upon the deck of a pirate ship,—it is, nevertheless, altogether, to outward seeming, a most strikingly interesting place, full of life, activity, and spirit.

[. . .]

Then here were a great many houses; human habitations, full of the mysteries of life at every stage of it. There was the little red house, up the road, occupied by Mr. Sevier, the overseer. A little nearer to my old master's, stood a very long, rough, low building, literally alive with slaves, of all ages, conditions and sizes. This was called 'the Long Quarter'. Perched upon a hill, across the Long Green, was a very tall, dilapidated, old brick building—the architectural dimensions of which proclaimed its erection for a different purpose—now occupied by slaves, in a similar manner to the Long Quarter. Besides these, there were numerous other slave houses and huts, scattered around in the neighborhood, every nook and corner of which was completely occupied. Old master's house, a long, brick building, plain, but substantial, stood in the center of the plantation life, and constituted one independent establishment on the premises of Col. Lloyd.

Besides these dwellings, there were barns, stables, store-houses, and tobacco-houses; blacksmiths' shops, wheelwrights' shops, coopers' shops—all objects of interest; but, above all, there stood the grandest building my eyes had then ever beheld, called, by every one on the plantation, the 'Great House'. This was occupied by Col. Lloyd and his family. They occupied it; *I* enjoyed it. The great house was surrounded by numerous and variously shaped out-buildings. There were kitchens, wash-houses, dairies, summer-house, green-houses, hen-houses, turkey-houses, pigeon-houses, and arbors, of many sizes and devices, all neatly painted, and altogether interspersed with grand old trees, ornamental and primitive, which afforded delightful shade in summer, and imparted to the scene a high degree of stately beauty. The great house itself was a large, white, wooden building, with wings on three sides of it. In front, a large portico, extending the entire length of the building, and supported by a long range of columns, gave to the whole establishment an air of solemn grandeur. It was a treat to my young and gradually opening mind, to behold this elaborate exhibition of wealth, power, and vanity. The carriage entrance to the house was a large gate, more than a quarter of a mile distant from it; the intermediate space was a beautiful lawn, very neatly trimmed, and watched with the greatest care. It was dotted thickly over with delightful trees, shrubbery, and flowers. The road, or lane, from the gate to the great house, was richly paved with white pebbles from the beach, and, in its course, formed a complete circle around the beautiful lawn. Carriages going in and retiring from the great house, made the circuit of the lawn, and their passengers were permitted to behold a scene of almost Eden-like beauty. Outside this select inclosure, were parks, where—as about the residences of the English nobility—rabbits, deer, and other wild game, might be seen, peering and playing about, with none to molest them or make them afraid. The tops of the stately poplars were often covered with the red-winged black-birds, making all nature vocal with the joyous life and beauty of their wild, warbling notes. These all belonged to me, as well as to Col. Edward Lloyd, and for a time I greatly enjoyed them.

A short distance from the great house, were the stately mansions of the dead, a place of somber aspect. Vast tombs, embowered beneath the weeping willow and the fir tree, told of the antiquities of the Lloyd family, as well as of their wealth. Superstition was rife among the slaves about this family burying ground. Strange sights had been seen there by some of the older slaves. Shrouded ghosts, riding on great black horses, had been seen to enter; balls of fire had been seen to fly there at midnight, and horrid sounds had been repeatedly heard. Slaves know enough of the rudiments of theology to believe that those go to hell who die slaveholders; and they often fancy such persons wishing themselves back again, to wield the lash. Tales of sights and sounds, strange and terrible, connected with the huge black tombs, were a very great security to the grounds about them, for few of the slaves felt like approaching them even in the day time. It was a dark, gloomy and forbidding place, and it was difficult to feel that the spirits of the sleeping dust there deposited, reigned with the blest in the realms of eternal peace.

[From *My Bondage and My Freedom* [1855] (New York: Dover Publications, 1969), 64–8.]

THOMAS AFFLECK

95   Duties of Overseers

It is here supposed that the Overseer is not immediately under his employer's eye, but is left for days or weeks, perhaps months, to the exercise of his own judgment in the management of the plantation. To him we would say—

Bear in mind, that you have engaged, for a stated sum of money, to devote your time and energies, for an entire year, *to one object*—to carry out the orders of your employer, strictly, cheerfully, and to the best of your ability; and, in all things to study his interests. This requires something more than your mere presence on the plantation, and that, at such times as suits your own pleasure and convenience.

On entering upon your duties, inform yourself thoroughly of the condition of the plantation, negroes, stock, implements, etc. Learn the views of your employer as to the general course of management he wishes pursued, and make up your mind to carry out these views fully, as far as in your power. If any objections occur to you, state them distinctly, that they may either be yielded to or overcome.

Where full and particular directions are not given to you, but you are left in a great measure to the exercise of your own judgment, you will find the following hints of service. They are compiled from excellent sources, from able articles in the agricultural journals of the day, from, WASHINGTON's directions to his Overseers, and from personal experience.

'I do, in explicit terms, enjoin it upon you to remain constantly at home, (unless called off by unavoidable business, or to attend divine worship,) and to be constantly with your people when there. There is no other sure way of getting work well done, and quietly, by negroes; for when an overlooker's back is turned, the most of them will slight their work, or be idle altogether; in which case, correction cannot retrieve either, but often produces evils which are worse than the disease. Nor is there any other mode than this to prevent thieving and other disorders, the consequences of opportunities. You will recollect that your time is paid for by me, and if I am deprived of it, it is worse even than robbing my purse, because it is also a breach of trust, which every honest man ought to hold most sacred. You have found me, and you will continue to find me, faithful to my part of the agreement which was made with you, whilst you are attentive to your part; but it is to be remembered, that a breach on one side releases the obligation on the other.'— *Washington's Instructions to his Overseers.*

[. . .]

The health of the negroes under your charge is an important matter. Much of the usual sickness among them is the result of carelessness and mismanagement. Overwork, or unnecessary exposure to rain, insufficient clothing, improper or badly cooked food, and night rambles, are all fruitful causes of disease. A great majority of the cases you should be yourself competent to manage, or you are unfit for the place you hold; but whenever you find that the case is one you do not understand, send for a physician, if such is the general order of your employer. By exerting yourself to have their clothing ready in good season; to arrange profitable in-door employment in wet weather; to see that an abundant supply of wholesome, *well-cooked* food, including plenty of vegetables, be supplied to them *at regular hours*; that the sick be cheered and encouraged, and some extra comforts allowed them, and the convalescent not exposed to the chances of a relapse; that pregnant women be particularly cared for, and in a great measure exempted from labor, and certainly from exposure and undue exertion, for some time before confinement; and that whilst nursing they be kept as near

244 THE EXPERIENCE OF SLAVERY

to the nursery as possible, but at no time allowed to suckle their children when overheated; that the infant be nursed three times during the day, in addition to the morning and evening, until eight months old, when twice a day may suffice; that no whiskey be allowed upon the place at any time, or under any circumstances; but that they have whilst heated and at work, plenty of pure, *cool* water; that care be taken to prevent the hands from carrying their baskets full of cotton on their heads—a most injurious practice; and, in short, by using such means for their comfort as every judicious, humane man will readily think of, you will find the amount of sickness greatly lessened.

[. . .]

It is indispensable that you exercise judgment and consideration in the management of the Negroes under your charge. Be *firm*, and at the same time *gentle* in your control. Never display yourself before them in a passion; and even if inflicting the severest punishment, do so in a mild, cool manner, and it will produce a tenfold effect. When you find it necessary to use the whip—and desirable as it would be to dispense with it entirely, it *is* necessary at times—apply it slowly and deliberately, and to the extent you are determined, in your own mind, to be needful before you began. The indiscriminate, constant and excessive use of the whip, is altogether unnecessary and inexcusable. When it can be done without a too great loss of time, the stocks offer a means of punishment greatly to be preferred.—So secured, in a lonely, quiet place, where no communication can be held with any one, nothing but bread and water allowed, and the confinement extending from Saturday, when they drop work, until Sabbath evening, will prove much more effectual in preventing a repetition of the offence, than any amount of whipping.— Never threaten a negro, but if you have occasion to punish, do it at once, or say nothing until ready to do so. A violent and passionate threat, will often scare the best disposed negro to the woods. Always keep your word with them, in punishments as well as in rewards. If you have named the penalty for any certain offence, inflict it without listening to a word of excuse. Never forgive that in one, that you would punish in another, but treat all alike, showing no favoritism. By pursuing such a course, you convince them that you act from principle and not from impulse, and that you will certainly enforce your rules. Whenever an opportunity is afforded you for rewarding continued good behavior, do not let it pass—occasional rewards have a much better effect than frequent punishments.

Never be induced by a course of good behavior on the part of the negroes, to relax the strictness of your discipline; but, when you have by judicious management, brought them to that state, keep them so by the same means. By taking frequent strolls about the premises, including of course the quarter and stock yards, during the evening and at least twice a week during the night, you will put a more effectual stop to any irregularities than by the most severe punishments. The only way to keep a negro honest, is not to trust him. This seems a harsh assertion; but it is, unfortunately, too true.

You will find that an hour devoted every Sabbath morning to their moral and religious instruction, would prove a great aid to you in bringing about a better state of things amongst the negroes. It has been thoroughly tried, and with the most satisfactory results, in many parts of the south. As a mere matter of interest, it has proved to be advisable—to say nothing of it as a point of duty. The effect upon their general good behavior, their cleanliness and good conduct on the Sabbath, is such as alone to recommend it to the Planter and Overseer.

[From 'Duties of Overseers,' *Cotton Plantation Record and Account Book No. 3 Suitable for a Force of 120 Hands, or under* (New Orleans: B. M. Norman, 7th edn, 1857).]

GABRIEL DEBIEN

96 Night-time Slave Meetings

Charges against the said Jean, negro, suspect. The charges against Jean are found in the depositions:

1. of Sieur Henry Estève, first witness in the continuation of the investigation
2. of his negro valet named Jasmin, 2nd witness
3. of Sieur Jacquin, managing the plantation of M. Estève in the Souffrière district, 2nd witness
4. of Sieur Lagarde, surgeon of the Fouquet plantation, 11th witness
5. of Sr. Molliers, owner of the said negro suspect, 17th witness
6. in the Marmelade district, of the so-called Scipion, negro slave of the LaLanne plantation, 6th witness
7. Philippe, negro slave of Sieur Desplas in the Souffrière district, 9th witness
8. Dimanche, negro slave of Monsieur Estève in the Souffrière district, 21st witness

All these witnesses, after having reviewed their depositions, were confronted with the said negro Jasmin as well, except for M. Molliers, 17th witness, unable due to illness.

Let us analyze a little the text of their depositions. Last August 29 Sieur Henry Estève and his negro valet Jasmin stopped the negro Jean on the plantation of Monsieur the Chevalier de la Rivière in the Ennery canton. The said negro was armed with a hunting knife and a stick at the end of which was a little iron in the form of a bayonet. Moreover, he had around his neck a little sack in which was a case with a passport signed Brûlé carrying the inscription: to the so-called Simon Lafleur. The said Jean believed that he was free.

Monsieur Estève adds that the said negro, once in the stocks, admitted that he was the one who held the gatherings on the plantation of Monsieur Estève his brother and at the place of Monsieur de Saint-Martin in Marmelade, and his negro Jasmin adds that the said Jean came on the plantation of Monsieur de la Rivière where he was arrested to hold other such gatherings, that he had even already sent his emissaries for this purpose to find branches of avocado bushes and others.

M. Jacquin, overseer of Monsieur Estève, says that in the course of the month of last July, he saw clearly through the cracks in the hut of the negro Jean Lodot, the negro Jean in the middle of a considerable gathering, the said negro on his knees before a table covered with a cloth and lit by two candles, raising to different heights a fetish, and that he was not able to clearly identify the negroes silent on their knees during this ceremony, he adds that he found two 'manchettes' crossed on the ground at the spot where the negro Jean had been.

The said Dimanche, negro slave of the plantation of M. Estève, says that he was several times at the gatherings held by the negro Jean on the plantation of M. Estève, his master; that these gatherings were called 'mayombe' or 'bila'. He adds details of the ceremonies practiced there, such as putting strawberry, orange or avocado leaves in their hands, having them kneel and in this posture having them drink cane liquor into which pepper, garlic, and 'blanc d'Espagne' had been mixed and that when this drink made them fall, the said negro would raise them up with a blow from a machete. He adds that the negro Jean carried with him in a bandolier a little sack in which was a crucifix, some pepper, some garlic, some gunpowder, pebbles, nails and a case. Furthermore he adds that he took money from the negroes to spare them from these ceremonies, and telling them that that would save them from any punishment.

The so-called Scipion, negro slave of the LaLanne plantation in the Marmelade district, says that he knows the negro Jean very well from having seen him often come to the plantation of his master in the company of the mulatto Jerome to hold gatherings there. The details that he gives of what happened at these gatherings are the same as those already given, except he adds some new aspects, like saying that they put powder in their hands and lit it and that they drenched them with cane liquor. He adds, like the other witness, that they took money from them for these ceremonies and for the cases that they sold them.

The so-called Philippe, negro slave of Sieur Desplas, planter in Souffrière, says he had often seen the negro Jean at the house of the mulatto Jerome, that he also witnessed several times the gatherings held there and the details that they [sic] give of them are very close to the same as those preceding.

Sieur Lagarde, surgeon, 14th witness, says only that he had hunted the negro Jean at different times during his escape; that the said negro was armed with a machete and a stick.

Sieur Molliers, owner of the suspect negro Jean, says only that the negro was missing from his plantation several times, that among other instances, during one of these escapes he stayed on the lands of Sieur Bélier, master of the mulatto Jerome.

These, My Lords, are the charges brought against the negro Jean, which contain the proof that this negro was joined with the mulatto Jerome and like him held gatherings that are the subject of this trial.

[From 'Assemblées nocturnes d'esclaves à Saint-Domingue (La Marmelade, 1786),' *Annales historiques de la revolution française* 208 (April–June 1972), 278–80. Trs. John Garrigus.]

M. L. E. MOREAU DE SAINT-MÉRY
....
97 **Description of Saint Domingue**

The slaves

Although slaves are not the class of population immediately under that of the whites, it seems appropriate to speak of them before saying anything of the freedmen, since that group shows the outcome of the slavery of some and the freedom of others.

The observation that the white population is not entirely composed of Creoles must be repeated for the Slaves, since two-thirds of those (who are nearly all blacks), come from Africa, while the rest is born in the colony. These two classes must be described separately, since in some respects they have more-or-less distinct characteristics.

Slaves from Africa

Saint-Domingue is the first place in the Americas to have had African slaves, and everyone knows that they were brought there for agriculture, according to Barthelemy Las Casas, who saw several brought to Saint-Domingue by chance after 1505. He suggested substituting them for the natives of the island, who were sorely tried by work in the mines and threatened to disappear completely from their native land. The idea of Las Casas, who was distracted by his very humaneness, was adopted because it presented more resources; for the unfortunate Indians were sacrificed to greed.

From their origins, all the French colonies in the Antilles had African slaves. But Saint-Domingue had them earlier, since its earliest conquerors had them more than a century and a half earlier. It seems that in the early attempts of the Adventurers there were only several blacks that they had kidnapped either from the land or the ships of their enemies and it was only in devoting themselves to agriculture that the French colonists realized their genuine need for Africans. For a fairly long period they even farmed with their own hands, together with a sort of white slave called an indentured servant or '36 months,' names expressing their servile status and its length.

Driven by the desire to go tempt fate in the colonies, a variety of individuals sold themselves in France for 3 years to a ship captain who, for the price of their passage, sold them in turn to a colonist for a prearranged sum. But this custom, remarkably inspired by the English in the North American colonies where it still exists, despite independence, could not be sustained in the French islands. It was up to the period in which tobacco was the main and even sole object of the colonial trade that the indentured servants were considered appropriate for the same work as the blacks. But the planting of indigo and especially that of sugar cane urgently demanded individuals more resistant to the continuous effects of a burning sun; and as those crops offered in turn through their profits, the ability to pay for blacks that merchants took in Africa, the number of slaves has continually grown until the number I have already given, which now has risen to 452 thousand.

[. . .]

Physical characteristics vary widely among the blacks because of the different ports of Africa where they were born. The most reliable method of noting these characteristics is to observe their relations with these places themselves; all the more because this will illustrate how from many peoples the black population of the colony is taken. [over the next 12 pages, Moreau describes the homelands and the physical and cultural characteristics of the *Sénégalais*, the *Yoloffes*, the *Foules*, the *Bambaras*, the *Quiambas*, the *Mandigues*, the *Bissagots*, the *Bouriquis*, the *Misérables*, the *Mesurades*, the *Aradas*, the *Caplaous*, the *Mines*, the *Agouas*, the *Socos*, the *Fantins*, the *Cotocolis*, the *Popos*, the *Fidas*, the *Fonds*, the *Maïs*, the *Aoussas*, the *Ibos*, the *Nagos*, the *Judas*, the *Congos*, the *Mayombés*, the *Mosombés*, the *Mondongues*, the *Malimbes*, the *Franc-Congos*, the *Mozambiques*, the *Quiloi*, the *Qiiriam*, and the *Montfiat*]

[. . .]

Of Creole slaves

Creole slaves are born with physical and moral qualities which give them a real superiority over those brought from Africa, and the fact that domestication has improved the species, while supporting a conclusion of the sublime natural historian, may also belie the abuses for which despotic masters are criticized.

It is nevertheless clear that the qualities of the Creole black have within themselves degrees of comparison, because the product of two Creole blacks, for example, is superior to that of two Bambara blacks, and so on with other combinations and mixings of different peoples; and this last reason is perhaps one of the most influential. In addition to intelligence, the Creole black possesses a graceful figure, lithe movements, a pleasing face and a gentle language unburdened with any of the accents added by Africans. Accustomed from their birth to the products of human genius, their minds are less obtuse than those of Africans who sometimes cannot grasp the difference between pocket change; in a way that he sometimes insists on having the exact coin he was told to ask for or he will not sell. There is no task for which Creole blacks are not preferred, and their value is always at least a quarter above that of Africans, all else being equal. Creole blacks are generally preferred for domestic work and for different trades. It is obvious that, having been raised with whites or near them, the latter grow more attached to them and destine them for less difficult tasks and a more pleasant life, notably one with better food.

The development of black children is commonly faster among Creoles than among those who are brought from Africa at a young age, undoubtedly because nature is set back by the process of acclimation. The young Creole negresses are mature earlier than young Africans. It seems to me that this last difference can be attributed to precocious sexual pleasure which upsets the physical order and perverts the moral order, and which the young Creole black has more opportunity to explore. Especially in the towns, examples of this moral corruption have frequently been seen in women who were not children long enough. It is further distressing, though no less true, that this grievous acceleration is sometimes the result of a calculation designed to benefit their mothers, who should be revolted by the very idea of such a commerce; for they know that a negresse, wherever she is born, will spend her whole life in a kind of dependence on the man who plucks that most precious of all flowers, even if she no longer loves him, and, more strangely, even if she never loved him. It has not been sufficiently realized that one of the obstacles to the reproduction of blacks is this early motherhood, or the abuses that delay motherhood.

[. . .]

I will restrict myself for now to what I have said about the class of blacks, which includes in some manner all the slaves in Saint-Domingue. Among these are those descended from Caribe Indians, from Indians of Guyana, from Fox savages of Canada, from the Natchez of Louisiana, that the government or men violating the Rights of Peoples found necessary or profitable to enslave.

I forgot to say what most sets the Creole black apart from the African, which is that following the example of the English colonists, the planters of the French colony brand their names or initials on the chests of the Africans;

while the others are only [branded] in the extremely rare case where their masters want to humiliate them, precisely because custom usually exempts them. The size of the colony, the fact it is neighbored by a foreign colony, all brought about the adoption of this precaution which is not at all painful. It is nevertheless an obstacle for an African who leaves slavery and becomes a freeman, for by prolonging the memory of his earlier status, it can sometimes raise doubts about his freedom.

But let's see who these freedmen are; I will have ample opportunity in describing this immense colony to round off the character and the ways of the slaves and I will find more occasions to depict the most striking things in the proper context.

[. . .]

There are, therefore, thirteen distinct classes of skin color among the individuals who constitute the population of French Saint-Domingue.

I have already spoken of those who must be considered the elements and bases of all the others, that is the white and the black about which the colonial prejudice has adopted as a maxim that no matter how close to white a non-white woman is, a white can never come from their union; in the same way no matter how close to black a woman of color may be, they can never produce a new person who goes down to the level of black. In more simple terms, therefore, only whites mixed among themselves can make whites and blacks can only be produced by two blacks of the two sexes.

The third shade is that of mulatto which can almost always be divided into two, since mulattoes, when compared, have two very distinct colors which are red-copper and yellow-bronze. They all have kinky hair.

The mulatto is produced in twelve different ways; because in this case as in all the others, take as one sole combination that of a mulatto man with a white woman and that of a white man with a mulatto woman, since only the sex has changed.

1. The mulatto coming from a white man and a black woman and who is truly the average proportionately, of the two.
2. The mulatto coming from a mixed blood man with a black woman.
3.   ,,   ,,   ,,   ,,   ,,   ,,   quadroon man with a Sacatra.
3.   ,,   ,,   ,,   ,,   ,,   ,,   ,,   ,,   ,, black woman.
5. The mulatto coming from a mamelouc with a Sacatra.
6.   ,,   ,,   ,,   ,,   ,,   ,,   ,,   ,, black woman.
6.   ,,   ,,   ,,   ,,   ,, Metíf with a Sacatra.
6.   ,,   ,,   ,,   ,,   ,,   ,,   ,, black woman.
9.   ,,   darker, coming from a quadroon with a griffe woman.
10.   ,,   ,,   ,,   ,, ,,   ,,   ,, ,, Sacatra.
11.   ,,   coming from a mulatto and a Marbou and which is an even darker copper.

12. Finally the mulatto produced by a mulatto with a mulatto. This is called a 'free mulatto' or 'casque'

Of all the combination of white and black it is the mulatto who brings together all of the physical advantages; of all of these crossings of race he is the one who has the strongest constitution, the most appropriate to Saint-Domingue's climate. To the sobriety and the strength of the black he joins the physical grace and the intelligence of the white. He lives to an advanced age if his skin becomes spotted as he ages, he has only the ugliness of age, but not its lapses. Beardless like the black, like him he has a certain woolly character to his hair, but his body hair is longer. Lazy, he is nevertheless passionate about physical exercise and especially riding and that which brings one sex towards the other.

[From *Description topographique, physique, civile, politique et historique de la partie française de l'isle Saint-Domingue* (Philadelphia, 1797), Vol. 1: 44, 47, 59, 83, 89. Trs. John Garrigus.]

C. L. R. JAMES

98   The Black Jacobins

The stranger in San Domingo was awakened by the cracks of the whip, the stifled cries, and the heavy groans of the Negroes who saw the sun rise only to curse it for its renewal of their labours and their pains. Their work began at day-break: at eight they stopped for a short breakfast and worked again till midday. They began again at two o'clock and worked until evening, sometimes till ten or eleven. A Swiss traveller has left a famous description of a gang of slaves at work. 'They were about a hundred men and women of different ages, all occupied in digging ditches in a cane-field, the majority of them naked or covered with rags. The sun shone down with full force on their heads. Sweat rolled from all parts of their bodies. Their limbs, weighed down by the heat, fatigued with the weight of their picks and by the resistance of the clayey soil baked hard enough to break their implements, strained themselves to overcome every obstacle. A mournful silence reigned. Exhaustion was stamped on every face, but the hour of rest had not yet come. The pitiless eye of the Manager patrolled the gang and several foremen armed with long whips moved periodically between them, giving stinging blows to all who, worn out by fatigue, were compelled to take a rest—men or women, young or old.' This was no isolated picture. The sugar plantations demanded an exacting and ceaseless labour. The tropical earth is baked hard by the sun. Round every 'carry' of land intended for cane it was necessary to dig a large ditch to ensure circulation of air. Young canes required attention for the first three or four months and grew to maturity in 14 or 18 months. Cane could be planted and would grow at any time of the year, and the reaping of one crop was the signal for the immediate digging of ditches and the planting of another. Once cut they had to be rushed to the mill lest the juice became acid by fermentation. The extraction of the juice and manufacture of the raw sugar went on for three weeks a month, 16 or 18 hours a day, for seven or eight months in the year.

Worked like animals, the slaves were housed like animals, in huts built around a square planted with provisions and fruits. These huts were about 20 to 25 feet long, 12 feet wide and about 15 feet in height, divided by partitions into two or three rooms. They were windowless and light entered only by the door. The floor was beaten earth; the bed was of straw, hides or a rude contrivance of cords tied on posts. On these slept indiscriminately mother, father and children. Defenceless against their masters, they struggled with overwork and its usual complement—underfeeding. The Negro Code, Louis XIV's attempt to ensure them humane treatment, ordered that they should be given, every week, two pots and a half of manioc, three cassavas, two pounds of salt beef or three pounds of salted fish—about food enough to last a healthy man for three days. Instead their masters gave them half-a-dozen pints of coarse flour, rice, or pease, and half-a-dozen herrings. Worn out by their labours all through the day and far into the night, many neglected to cook and ate the food raw. The ration was so small and given to them so irregularly that often the last half of the week found them with nothing.

Even the two hours they were given in the middle of the day, and the holidays on Sundays and feast-days, were not for rest, but in order that they might cultivate a small piece of land to supplement their regular rations. Hardworking slaves cultivated vegetables and raised chickens to sell in the towns to make a little in order to buy rum and tobacco; and here and there a Napoleon of finance, by luck and industry, could make enough to purchase his freedom. Their masters encouraged them in this practice of cultivation, for in years of scarcity the Negroes died in thousands, epidemics broke out, the slaves fled into the woods and plantations were ruined.

[. . .]

The slaves received the whip with more certainty and regularity than they received their food. It was the incentive to work and the guardian of discipline. But there was no ingenuity that fear or a depraved imagination could devise which was not employed to break their spirit and satisfy the lusts and resentment of their owners and guardians—irons on the hands and feet, blocks of wood that the slaves had to drag behind them wherever they went, the tin-plate mask designed to prevent the slaves eating the sugar-cane, the iron collar. Whipping was interrupted in order to pass a piece of hot wood on the buttocks of the victim; salt, pepper, citron, cinders, aloes, and hot ashes were poured on the bleeding wounds. Mutilations were common, limbs, ears, and sometimes the private parts, to deprive them of the pleasures which they could indulge in without expense. Their masters poured burning wax on their arms and hands and shoulders, emptied the boiling cane sugar over their heads, burned them alive, roasted them on slow fires, filled them with gunpowder and blew them up with a match; buried them up to the neck and smeared their heads with sugar that the flies might devour them; fastened them near to nests of ants or wasps; made them eat their excrement, drink their urine, and lick the saliva of other slaves. One colonist was known in moments of anger to throw himself on his slaves and stick his teeth into their flesh.

Were these tortures, so well authenticated, habitual or were they merely isolated incidents, the extravagances of a few half-crazed colonists? Impossible as it is to substantiate hundreds of cases, yet all the evidence shows that these bestial practices were normal features of slave life. The torture of the whip, for instance, had 'a thousand refinements,' but there were regular varieties that had special names, so common were they. When the hands and arms were tied to four posts on the ground, the slave was said to undergo 'the four post'. If the slave was tied to a ladder it was 'the torture of the ladder'; if he was suspended by four limbs it was 'the hammock,' etc. The pregnant woman was not spared her 'four-post'. A hole was dug in the earth to accommodate the unborn child. The torture of the collar was specially reserved for women who were suspected of abortion, and the collar never left their necks until they had produced a child.

[From *The Black Jacobins: Toussaint L'Ouverture and the San Domingo Revolution* [1938]
(New York: Vintage, 2nd edn, 1963), 9–13.]

GILBERTO FREYRE
··
99   **The Masters and the Slaves**

The pleasing figure of the Negro nurse who, in patriarchal times, brought the child up, who suckled him, rocked his hammock or cradle, taught him his first words of broken Portuguese, his first 'Our Father' and 'Hail Mary,' along with his first mistakes in pronunciation and grammar, and who gave him his first taste of '*pirão com carne*,' or manihot paste with meat, and '*molho de ferrugem*,' or 'rusty gravy' (a thick gravy made with meat juice) as she mashed his food for him with her own hands—the Negro nurse's countenance was followed by those of other Negroes in the life of the Brazilian of yesterday. That of the Negro lad, companion of games. That of the aged Negro, the teller of tales. That of the housegirl or *mucama*. That of the Negro cook. A whole series of varied contacts bringing new relations to the environment, to life, to the world. Experiences that were realized through the slave or under his influence as guide, accomplice, empiric healer, or corrupter.

I have already referred to the young Negro playmate of the white lad—a playmate and a whipping-boy. His functions were those of an obliging puppet, manipulated at will by the infant son of the family; he was squeezed, mistreated, tormented just as if he had been made of sawdust on the inside—of cloth and sawdust, like those Judases on Easter Saturday, rather than of flesh and blood like white children. 'As soon as a child begins to crawl,' writes Koster, who was so astute an observer of the life of the colonial Big Houses, 'a slave of about his own age, and of the same sex, is given to it as a playfellow, or rather as a plaything. They grow up together, and the slave is made the stock upon which the young owner gives vent to passion. The slave is sent upon all errands, and receives the blame for all unfortunate accidents; in fact, the white child is thus encouraged to be overbearing, owing to the false fondness of its parents.' 'There was not a house where there was not one or more *muleques*, one or more *curumins*, who were the victims specially devoted to the young master's whims.' So writes José Verissimo in recalling the days of slavery. 'They were horse, whipping-boy, friends, companions, and slaves.' And Júlio Bello reminds us of the favorite sport of the plantation lads of a former day: that of mounting horseback on sheep—and lacking sheep, it was the *muleque* who served. Their games were often brutal ones, and the Negro boys served every purpose; they were cart-oxen, saddle-horses, beasts for turning the millstone, and burros for carrying litters and heavy burdens. But especially carthorses. To this day, in those rural regions that have been less invaded by the automobile, and where the plantation cabriolet still rolls along over the fertile topsoil, between the fields of sugar-cane, there may be seen small white lads playing horse-and-buggy, 'with Negro boys and even little Negro girls, the daughters of their nurses,' between the shafts. A bit of packing-twine serves as the reins and a shoot of the guava tree as a whip.

It is to be presumed that the psychic repercussion upon adults of such a type of childish relationship should be favorable to the development of sadistic and masochistic tendencies. It was chiefly the child of feminine sex that displayed a sadistic bent, owing to the greater fixity and monotony in the relations of mistress and slave girl. It was even to be wondered at, as Koster wrote at the beginning of the nineteenth century, 'that so many excellent women should be found among them,' and it was 'by no means strange that the disposition of some of them should be injured by this unfortunate direction of their infant years'. Without contacts with the world that would modify in them, as in boys, the perverted sense of human relationships; with no other perspective than that of the slave hut as seen from the veranda of the Big House, these ladies still preserved, often, the same evil dominion over their housemaids as they had exercised over the little Negro girls who had been their playmates as children 'They are born, bred, and continue surrounded by slaves without receiving any check, with high notions of superiority, without any thought that what they do is wrong.' It is again Koster speaking of the Brazilian senhoras. What was more, they frequently flew into fits of rage, shouting and screaming from time to time. Fletcher and Kidder, who were in Brazil in the middle of the nineteenth century, attributed the strident, disagreeable voices of the women of our country to this habit of always shouting out their orders to slaves. For that matter, they might have observed the same thing in the South of the United States, which underwent social and economic influences so similar to those that acted upon Brazil under the regime of slave labor. Even today, owing to the effect of generations of slave-holding ancestors, the young ladies of the Carolinas, of Mississippi and Alabama, are in the habit of shouting just as the daughters and granddaughters of plantation-owners do in northeastern Brazil.

As to the mistresses' being more cruel than the masters in their treatment of the slaves, that is a fact generally to be observed in slave-owning societies, and is one that is confirmed by our chroniclers, by foreign travelers, by folklore, and by tradition. There are not two or three but many instances of the cruelty of the ladies of the Big House toward their helpless blacks. There are tales of *sinhámoças* who had the eyes of pretty *mucamas* gouged out and then had them served to their husbands for dessert, in a jelly-dish, floating in blood that was still fresh. Tales of young baronesses of adult age who out of jealousy or spite had fifteen-year-old mulatto girls sold off to old libertines. There were others who kicked out the teeth of their women slaves with their boots, or who had their breasts cut off, their nails drawn, or their faces and ears burned. A whole series of tortures.

And the motive, almost always, was jealousy of the husband. Sexual rancor. The rivalry of woman with woman.

[From *The Masters and the Slaves: A Study in the Development of Brazilian Civilization*, [1933] trs. S. Putnam (New York: Alfred Knopf, 1946), 349–51.]

SIDNEY MINTZ AND RICHARD PRICE

100 The Birth of African-American Culture

Before any aggregate of plantation slaves could begin to create viable institutions, they would have had to deal with the traumata of capture, enslavement, and transport. Hence the beginnings of what would later develop into 'African-American cultures' must date from the very earliest interactions of the newly enslaved men and women on the African continent itself. They were shackled together in the coffles, packed into dank 'factory' dungeons, squeezed together between the decks of stinking ships, separated often from their kinsmen, tribesmen, or even speakers of the same language, left bewildered about their present and their future, stripped of all prerogatives of status or rank (at least, so far as the masters were concerned), and homogenized by a dehumanizing system that viewed them as faceless and largely interchangeable. Yet we know that even in such utterly abject circumstances, these people were not simply passive victims. In the present context, we are thinking less of the many individual acts of heroism and resistance which occurred during this period than of certain simple but significant *cooperative* efforts which, in retrospect, may be viewed as the true beginnings of African-American culture and society.

Various shreds of evidence suggest that some of the earliest social bonds to develop in the coffles, in the factories and, especially, during the long Middle Passage were of a dyadic (two-person) nature. Partly, perhaps, because of the general policy of keeping men and women separate, they were usually between members of the same sex. The bond between shipmates, those who shared passage on the same slaver, is the most striking example. In widely scattered parts of Afro-America, the 'shipmate' relationship became a major principle of social organization and continued for decades or even centuries to shape ongoing social relations.

In Jamaica, for example, we know that the term 'shipmate' was 'synonymous in their [the slaves'] view with "brother" or "sister"'. It was 'the dearest word and bond of affectionate sympathy amongst the Africans,' and 'so strong were the bonds between shipmates that sexual intercourse between them, in the view of one observer, was considered incestuous'. We know also that the bond could extend beyond the original shipmates themselves and interpenetrate with biological kin ties; shipmates were said to 'look upon each other's children mutually as their own,' and 'it was customary for children to call their parents' shipmates "uncle" and "aunt"'.

[. . .]

We have been suggesting that distinctive, 'mature' African-American cultures and societies probably developed more rapidly than has often been assumed. The early forging of 'shipmate' ties or ritual complexes, as we have phrased them, are intended as arbitrary (though central) examples of much more general processes. Even in the realm of the arts, to choose a less likely example, it could be shown that new cultural subsystems were worked out through the interaction of slaves who had not yet set foot in the Americas. Not only was drumming, dancing, and singing encouraged for 'exercise' on many of the slavers, but Stedman tells us how, at the end of the nightmare of the Middle Passage, off the shores of Suriname: 'All the Slaves are led upon deck . . . their hair shaved in different figures of Stars, half-moons, &c, / which they generally do the one to the other (having no Razors) by the help of a broken bottle and without Soap/.' It is hard to imagine a more impressive example of irrepressible cultural vitality than this image of slaves decorating one another's hair in the midst of one of the most dehumanizing experiences in all of history.

To document our assertions that fully formed African-American cultures developed within the earliest years of settlement in many New World colonies involves genuine difficulties. These stem from the general shortage of descriptive materials on slave life during the initial period, as well as from the lack of research regarding this problem. However, in at least one colony—Suriname—certain fortuitous historical events allow us to pinpoint in time the development of several major cultural subsystems, and we are able to find support for our broader argument.

Language provides one relevant case. Within the first twenty years of settlement, almost all of the English planters who had established the colony of Suriname left for other parts of the Caribbean, taking their slaves with them. During the several years when the newly imported, Dutch-owned slaves overlapped with the soon to depart English-owned slaves the language developed by the English-owned slaves must have been passed on to these new arrivals. This, at least, is our conclusion, because ever since that time, three hundred years ago, an English-based creole (called Sranan, Negro-English, Surinaams, or Taki-Taki) has been the national language of Suriname. This language, a new African-American creation, can reliably be said to have been 'firmly established' within the colony's first two decades.

[From *The Birth of African-American Culture: An Anthropological Perspective* [1976]
(Boston: Beacon Press, 1992), 42–3, 48–9.]

LIEN-SHENG YANG

101   Public Works in Imperial China

Closely connected with convict labor is the problem of slave labor. Slaves, male and female, were known as *nu* and *pi* in Chinese history. As pointed out by Wilbur in his *Slavery in China during the Former Han Dynasty*:

There seem to have been differences as well as similarities between *t'u* and government *nu* or *nu-pi*. There is no evidence that *t'u* were sold, or given away, which is a useful pragmatic test of slave-ownership. An affirmative conclusion cannot be drawn from absence of evidence. Therefore, while it cannot be asseverated that *t'u* were not sold, it cannot be proved that they were. There is plenty of documentary proof, on the other hand, that slaves, including government ones, were sold and given away. Many special pardons of *t'u* were recorded, but very few manumissions of government slaves during the Former Han period. *T'u* were often recruited to fight in China's frontier wars, but government slaves are not reported to have been. There were a number of revolts of *t'u*, but none reported for government slaves, which strongly suggests a fundamental difference in treatment.

There are still other points of differences, including (1) that slaves tended to serve for life whereas convicts were required to serve for only five years or less in Han times and (2) that the position of a slave tended to be hereditary while that of a convict was not. On the first point, one should add that the term ch'ang-t'u 'long-term or permanent convicts,' is found in historical texts of the Six Dynasties, but the number of such convicts does not seem to have been very large. In general, convict labor became less and less important from T'ang and Sung times on. Under the Ming and Ch'ing dynasties, it was common for the government to commute penal servitude into a fine. This was in line with the general trend in recent times of employing more and more hired labor.

In the history of imperial China one can find only a small number of cases in which slave labor was used for the construction or maintenance of public works. For the Han period, Wilbur has suggested certain 'hypothetical spheres of government slave work'. According to his reasoning, 'it seems likely that government slaves would have been employed primarily in service capacities and in skilled work, though certainly a portion of them, being unskilled or untrustworthy, worked in labor gangs'.

In periods after Han, an interesting case of using private slaves for public construction was one in A.D. 371, when the Ch'in ruler Fu Chien drafted slave-bondsmen (t'ung-li) owned by kings, marquises, and powerful and rich families to dig a canal through a mountainous region in central Shensi. This incident, however, should be understood in light of the fact that in the fourth century the government of the Chin dynasty several times drafted privately owned slaves and retainers to serve as soldiers in times of emergency.

Under the Sui dynasty, Emperor Yang-ti ordered government slaves to guard a dam (yen) on the Lo river. Presumably the number of slaves used for the purpose was not large. Under the T'ang dynasty, the T'ang liu-tien provides the rule that in figuring units of work, the labor of three adult male slaves should be counted as equivalent to only that of two free people. This regulation obviously does not speak very highly for the efficiency of slave labor. Altogether, government and private slaves did not play any significant role in public works, even in these relatively early periods of Chinese history when slaves are supposed to have been fairly numerous.

[. . .]

Generally speaking, women were used in public works only during the first thousand years of imperial China, and even in this earlier period the tendency seems to have been toward a sparing use of female labor. In the beginning of this discussion, we mentioned the employment of men and women for the construction of the city of Ch'ang-an in Former Han times and for the digging of canals under Sui Yang-ti. But in the latter case, it was reported that women were used because of the insufficient supply of male adults. With several gigantic projects going on continuously under Yang-ti, the people must have been exhausted. It is no wonder that they said the reign title Ta-yeh should be made to read Ta-k'u-lai, 'great sufferings come,' by breaking the character *yeh* into two characters.

The trend toward reduction of female labor was unmistakable. Liang Wu-ti in 541 issued an imperial decree to stop the employment of female adults (*nü-ting*) all over the country. Under the T'ang dynasty, government regulations made the provision that only males should be registered as *ting* or adults, thus freeing all women from labor service. Local governments under the T'ang, however, still occasionally used female labor for road repair. And females might be drafted to do miscellaneous tasks like cooking for soldiers, as indicated in the famous poem 'Shih-hao li' by Tu Fu. On the whole, the use of female labor seems to have stopped from Sung times on. Perhaps one of the reasons was that the steady increase of population made it unnecessary.

Another factor was the traditional attitude toward a division of labor between male and female. According to the Han penal code, female convicts were not made to render labor service but only to husk grain for the government. When they were condemned to gather firewood from hills, their punishment could be commuted to a payment of 300 coins per month. In contrast with the regular commutation charge of 2,000 coins per month for a male laborer, this also indicates the assumption of a difference between male and female labor. According to the T'ang code, female convicts were to do needlework or to husk grain for the government. Female slaves also were recognized as less useful than male slaves: an adult female slave in performing tasks was considered the equivalent of a secondary adult male slave or half an adult freeman; a secondary adult female slave was equivalent to only one third of an adult freeman.

[From 'Economic Aspects of Public Works in Imperial China,' in Yang, *Excursions in Sinology* (Cambridge, MA: Harvard University Press, 1969), 208–10, 213–14.]

KENNETH KIPLE AND VIRGINIA HIMMELSTEIB KING

102   Another Dimension to the Black Diaspora

The full impact of malaria and epidemic yellow fever on slavery, on the black, and on the South generally can only be speculated upon, for the evidence is skimpy, the variables many, and the questions—those of the relationship of disease to culture, society, and human behavior—enormously complex.

Yet having already taken a tentative step in a speculative direction, it is difficult to resist a few more. First, the manner in which yellow fever and malaria dealt differently with the two races in the South should prove of interest to those who are concerned with differential black and white mortality statistics for the antebellum period. Their collective wisdom at this point would have the life expectancy of slaves only slightly below that of white southerners, which has been interpreted as suggestive of a relatively full life for slaves in a material sense. It has been estimated, however, that yellow fever killed 500,000 North Americans alone, with most of these deaths occurring in the nineteenth-century South. And while malaria's toll will never be known, it was unquestionably the single most important cause of death in the region; its endemic harvest in lives exceeding in gargantuan proportions that of sporadically epidemic yellow fever.

The point here is quite simply that blacks were resistant to both tropical killers that regularly winnowed the white population, yet their life expectancy was nonetheless *below* that of whites. Thus, if the counterfactual is entertained for the moment—had there been no malaria and yellow fever stalking the whites of the South—then their life expectancy might well have been *substantially* above that of their slaves instead of just slightly. If true, this may imply that the material conditions of slave life were somewhat worse than they have been portrayed by many; at least those material conditions that affected life expectancy. On the other side of the demographic coin, researchers have found slave fertility somewhat higher than that of white Southerners; a phenomenon which has also lent itself to interpretations of good material treatment while enhancing the image of the paternalistic (no pun intended) planter.

But some part of the explanation for higher black fertility may be a result of malaria's pervasiveness in the South and in the physiologic changes that a malaria attack can produce. It has been discovered that possessors of the sickling trait have a significantly higher rate of fertility than nonsicklers in malarial regions ranging from the Congo to the Caribbean. Yet the most sensible hypothesis to account for this does not have the trait encouraging fertility but rather its nonpossession discouraging fertility. Put succinctly, malaria attacks elevate male scrotal temperature, and the higher temperature destroys sperm; for some two months following a bout with malaria, a male's sperm count, although gradually increasing, is nonetheless considerably reduced. Thus because two malarial attacks yearly were not unusual, individuals with little or no resistance to the disease might well have been infertile for up to one-third of that year, and to this infertile period must also be added the time actually spent under attack when presumably sexual activity would have been close to the bottom on one's list of priorities.

Sicklers, however, even when attacked have a much shorter duration of fever and consequently less reduction in sperm count. Yet if this hypothesis contains some truth, then it should not apply to just male possessors of the sickle cell trait but to all males endowed with some form of malaria protection as against those without protection, and it should apply not just to falciparum malaria but to all forms of malaria. Because whites were the chief malaria sufferers in the South, then clearly their fertility *should have been lower* than that of blacks.

Malaria and yellow fever have probably shaped the history of the South in many other ways that we have been slow to recognize. For example, traditional historiography holds that the presence of unfree labor in the South was an important factor in disuading free laborers from immigrating to the region. The impact of little immigration was to further enhance the value of slave labor and retard the South's economic and industrial growth vis-à-vis a slave-free North.

Doubtless this is all true, but should not pathogenic barricades share some of the blame for discouraging immigration? It was certainly no secret that the North enjoyed much more salubrity than the South, and given the number of the immigrants who did head southward only, as we have observed, to falter in the yellow fever/malaria gauntlet awaiting them, surely word must have gotten about to avoid the region. In fact, Darrett Rutman believes that the 'word' was first circulated by William Penn who began introducing anti-Virginia material in his pamphlets of the 1680s. Certainly later complaints by individuals such as Hume, who lamented that outsiders were afraid to settle in Charleston, suggest that the word was out.

An argument against this, however, is that following the Civil War the South did experience considerable migration from the North despite its reputation for insalubrity. In part, one suspects this was a function of anticipated profits being worth the risk. But also the risk was somewhat minimized. As previously noted, the federal blockade had kept the South virtually yellow fever-free during the war, while the use of quinine was becoming widespread and its effectiveness against malaria well-known.

But to return to the antebellum period, bad as southern fevers were, the climate at least offered more seasonal relief to the inhabitants than West Indian residents received from the fevers which infected them. This may explain also the differing patterns of slave treatment in the Caribbean as opposed to North America. Despite the crossfire of debate that occasionally erupts on the subject, most contributors to the historiography of slavery today are in agreement that West Indian slaves, regardless of the nationality of their masters, did not live as long or as well as their North American fellows. Interpretations to account for the differential range from the cultural to the economic, with the latter clearly the front runner.

One 'social' difference between the American and West Indian peculiar institutions that receives repeated comment, however, is the factor of absentee ownership in much of the latter region, particularly in the British and French islands. Another difference is the careless attitude of West Indian planters toward life itself. They 'lived fast, spent recklessly, played desperately, and died young'.

But, might not disease (yellow fever and malaria) have been an important determinant in both the absenteeism and in a frenetic fatalistic West Indian life style? For although blacks were mostly immune to these diseases, their masters were frequently not. Surely then those who could afford to absent themselves from the islands for extended periods of time would have done so for health reasons alone, while those who could not may well have sought refuge in dissipation.

Either way the slaves were the losers. If their owners fled the islands, they fell under the supervision of an overseer often more interested in a good crop than the welfare of his charges. Yet, even if the owner remained on the plantation, an individual who 'lived fast' and expected to 'die young' would hardly have been overly solicitous of the lives of his slaves.

[From *Another Dimension to the Black Diaspora: Diet, Disease and Racism* (Cambridge: Cambridge University Press, 1981), 64–8.]

G. A. AKINOLA

103 Slavery in Zanzibar

As early as the medieval period, when the East African coastal city-states attained their apogee before the Portuguese conquest of the early sixteenth century, slaves had featured in the life of the communities on the East African littoral. Apart from those who were exported across the Indian Ocean to the Middle East in exchange for cloths, beads and other oriental products, slaves were used as domestic servants and ship hands. Some were also engaged in cultivating food crops, while an account of the sack of Kilwa by the Portuguese in 1505 speaks of 500 Kilwa archers all of whom were negro slaves of the upper-class merchants and rulers of mixed Arab and negro blood. By the fifth decade of the nineteenth century, the slave population within the East African coastal towns, particularly on the islands of Zanzibar and Pemba, had increased considerably. This was as a result of the creation of the Omani Arab Sultanate of Zanzibar, the immigration of Arab colonists and the development of plantation agriculture which created a rising demand for slave labour.

[. . .]

The social position of the slaves within the East African coastal society was determined by three basic factors. First most of them were imported from among the interior peoples, untouched by the Swahili culture, peoples contemptuously referred to as *shenzi* or uncivilized barbarians by the coastal peoples. Secondly, with the exception of those who had been manumitted or those who worked in the household, the slaves often did not belong to Islam, the official religion of the sultanate to which all the free Swahili adhered.

Thirdly they were the property of their masters and as such enjoyed only such rights as were guaranteed to slaves by the Koran. These three factors made the slaves an exclusive class or caste within the society, albeit a caste whose functions and duties often brought them into contact at all levels with all the other classes in the community.

The slaves may be classified under two broad groups—the *watumwa wajinga* or raw slaves, that is those recently imported from the interior and had not yet been assimilated into the island or coastal slave population; and the *wakulia* who were imported as children and had grown up within the confines of the Zanzibar state. Along with this latter group may be ranked the *wazalia* who were born into slavery. For practical purposes, however, the slaves are best categorized according to the work they performed either in the household of their masters, in the urban areas, or in the plantations.

The domestic slaves differed markedly from the other two classes of slaves in the Sultanate of Zanzibar in social status as well as the number of privileges they enjoyed. By and large they were regarded as members of the families of their masters with whom they often lived especially when young. In fact the relationship between a domestic slave and his master approximated more to that of patron and client rather than that of master and bondsman. For example a domestic slave was addressed as *udugu yangu*—my brother, while many female slaves were *suria* or concubines of their masters. This relationship explains why domestic slaves, even after they had been manumitted, invariably remained with their master at whose death they often bound themselves to his heir or sought the protection of another master.

[. . .]

The extent to which Islamic law in actual practice tended to mitigate the hardships of slavery in the sultanate is a moot point. There is no denying the fact that Islam sought to liberalize the institution of slavery by restricting those who might be enslaved, by spelling out the legal rights of slaves and by recommending manumission in certain instances. Among the slave's legal rights is the freedom to marry, once the consent of his master had been received and the necessary marriage fees paid. In addition a slave's criminal responsibilities under the Muslim code were less rigorous than those of a freeman. For example he might not be stoned to death as in the case of a freeman for unlawful intercourse, while he could only be punished by half the number of lashes to which a freeman was subject for lapses like drinking. Under Islamic law, minor slaves were not to be separated from their parents in sale.

Apart from the above laws, Islam imposed a number of religious duties on all believers, duties which ideally ought to have improved the conditions of slaves. For example slaves were not to be over-worked, and a persistent offender against this injunction might have his slaves compulsorily sold.

Another religious duty was the conversion of slaves to Islam, a practice that seems widespread (at least as far as the domestic slaves were concerned) in the Sultanate of Zanzibar in the nineteenth century.

[. . .]

In sum, the status of the slave in the Sultanate of Zanzibar was one of considerable degradation. He must comport himself, and must be distinguished in his attire, as a slave, 'because one of his station wears no cap . . . nor does he wear shoes nor a long robe to cover his legs'. Where conditions were not intolerable the slave was still a property whose security depended on the changing fortunes as well as the whims of his master. He might be sold or given as pledge for loan or a debt. Moreover, many of the slaves were simply abandoned to fend for themselves, when they were ill or too old to work. They derived little or no material benefit from the prosperity which their labour made possible. And in a society where labour was cheap and could be easily replenished by fresh importation from the interior of the East African territories, very little premium appears to have been placed on human life. This explains in part why slaves were often brutalized by the callous administration of cruel punishments. Discipline was maintained by a free application of whips, fetters, stocks, manacles, chains and the *kongo*, an iron collar with a long beam. Flagellation was a regular punishment for minor misdemeanours, as many as ten to a hundred strokes of the *kiboko* made from hippopotamus hide being inflicted with the culprit kneeling down or tied to a post if he could not keep still. It is therefore not surprising that many of the slaves became hardened and wild. Life offered little solace from the endless toil and drudgery, although the periodic 'gang warfares' on the estates, and the *ng'omas* or dances performed on moonlight nights, might provide an outlet for pent-up feelings. But few had any prospects to look forward to; hence some sought an escape in flight, while others in desperation rebelled against their masters.

[From 'Slavery and Slave Revolts in the Sultanate of Zanzibar in the Nineteenth Century,' *Journal of the Historical Society of Nigeria* 6 (1972), 215–17, 221–3.]

MARY KARASCH

104   Slave Life in Rio de Janeiro

Craftsmen and artisans

The most skilled slaves of Rio, often the highest paid, were the craftsmen. Rented by municipal authorities who needed their skills, they were among the elite slaves of the city and labored at most, if not all, the skilled trades in Rio. Many worked for their owners who were also skilled craftsmen, who had taught them their trades, or on their own account as blacks for hire. Although poor whites initially protested against training slaves as skilled craftsmen in the early nineteenth century, they failed to stop the trend to apprentice slaves to all the skilled crafts in the city. Petitions by whites who could no longer compete with slave apprentices and craftsmen reveal that slaves did so well in the crafts that their owners were able to live off their wages. Even master craftsmen gave up the practice of their craft in preference to training their slaves to perform the work they themselves had once done. In part Ewbank explains why owners used skilled slaves in Rio. He reported that the Carmelite monks of the Lapa Church in Rio preferred to apprentice their slave boys in the city rather than to put them to work on their estate near Rio, because they would realize twice the profit they would have made in agriculture.

Newspaper advertisements reveal how skilled many slaves became. In general, owners described their slaves as *aprendiz* (apprentice), *meio-official* (semiskilled worker), *official* (skilled worker), and *mestre* (master). The most common were *official*, 'good skilled worker,' apprentice, or some other indication that the slave was still learning his trade. For example, an Angolan boy was described as a 'semiskilled shoemaker,' who knew how to cut and make a pair of shoes, for which he received three *patacas* a week in wages. Also evident in the advertisements is that owners trained slaves in one or more skilled occupations, such as the African boy who was learning cooking while training as a bricklayer's apprentice. Slaves like this boy were especially valuable to small slaveowners, since they could use the slave in domestic service in their homes, and live off the wages he earned at an outside employment.

As slaves learned their trades and improved their skills, they were known as 'very good skilled workers' (*muito bom official*) and occasionally as master craftsmen with the title of *mestre*. Many worked for wages, a portion of which they had to return to their owners. According to Maria Graham, there was such a demand for skilled freedmen and slaves that they found full employment and good pay. In fact, Spix and Martius believed that slaves in Rio had more opportunities to enter the skilled crafts than European workers, who were excluded because of guild restrictions in Europe. Their observation appears to hold true in newspaper advertisements until the 1840s, when slaves began to lose their prominent place in the crafts to white competitors.

One of the most common occupations of skilled slaves and freedmen was that of carpentry, or more generally any of the construction crafts, including masonry. As Horner observed, most of the builders were blacks, either free or enslaved. They did everything: splitting logs and sawing wood, laying bricks and tiles, carving wood decorations and balconies, and making furniture and carriages. However, Horner found them slow and inefficient, and in his opinion, one house could be built by them as fast as one block of buildings in the United States. They also repaired, refitted, and caulked ships in the harbor, laboring for a $1.00 a day (in 1842) for their master.

Slaves worked in all the metal crafts—iron, tin, copper, gold, and silver. Skilled slave blacksmiths frequently commanded some of the highest prices and earned good wages. Of less stature were the tinsmiths, who made lanterns, bugles, trumpets, military ornaments, and *funils* (funnels) widely used during carnival. Coppersmiths were essential to the manufacture of the pans, kettles, and other objects used in the homes and sugar mills. When Ewbank visited two copper shops, he observed one in which all fourteen workers were slaves who labored under the supervision of a slave foreman and the Portuguese owner. In another, twenty blacks did all the work themselves. Only the salesclerks were white.

One of the most distasteful types of metalwork that slaves did was manufacture the iron shackles, collars, chains, iron masks, and other torture instruments used on slaves. Both Ewbank and Debret described shops in which slaves performed this form of labor. In fact, Ewbank was waited on by a black man who tried to sell him some chains. Other ironworkers wrought more beautiful objects of iron: ornaments, balconies, grills, grates, lamps, household implements, and ritual objects used by African religious leaders.

Slaves also handled valuable metals, such as silver and gold, turning them into admirable dinner services and items of jewelry. Even the highly critical traveler, Ida Pfeiffer, admired their gold and silver work. Other slaves cut and shaped the amethysts, topazes, emeralds, and diamonds that often filled the gold and silver settings. Since slaves, as well as their owners, wore jewelry of every type of metal, the demand for these symbols of status gave employment to many skilled craftsmen.

Slaves were also important in the skilled trades connected with clothing and personal ornamentation. They made every item of clothing from hats to shoes, including simple sunhats woven of natural fibers, as well as the elegant imperial styles affected by their owners; wooden platform shoes called *tamancos*, leather shoes and belts, gloves, and suits. Because of the clothing demands of an imperial court city, slave tailors and seamstresses found much employment. In the early nineteenth century, European tailors had monopolized the craft, and they had merely used their slaves to carry their equipment when they visited their clients; but as demand for their services increased, more and more tailors employed their slaves to do much of the expert work involved in making suits. On the street of the tailors, black and mulatto slaves sat on benches in front of every door working with the needle. The work must have been intensive, since it deformed the fingers to the point where an escaped slave who had worked as a tailor was easily identifiable, and many tailors' slaves appeared in fugitive advertisements. On the other hand, skilled tailors who earned wages had opportunities to buy their freedom. An African, who had been imported as a slave about 1820, was working as a tailor thirty years later. He had bought his freedom 'with wages earned for work in extra hours'. In 1851 he applied to the British consulate for protection to transport himself and a 'large number of his countrymen to Ambriz [Angola], declaring that there were upwards of 500 similarly situated free Africans desirous to return to Africa'.

While males worked as tailors of men's clothing, female slaves and freedwomen sewed dresses and made lace in the households and dressmaking establishments of the period. Quite often they worked in a clothing store of a French dressmaker. Slave women were also used for making the ornamental flowers and insect jewelry worn by women in Rio. At least one slave made tortoise-shell combs.

[From *Slave Life in Rio de Janeiro 1808–1850* (Princeton: Princeton University Press, 1987), 199–201.]

B. W. HIGMAN

105   Slave Populations of the British Caribbean

Food

West Indian slaveowners followed three quite distinct methods in providing nutrition for their slaves. Some purchased food and distributed it in regular rations. These planters devoted all of their arable land to the production of export staples. The second method also involved the distribution of rations, but most of the food was produced on the plantations and cultivated under the same system of gang labor as used for export staples. The third group of slaveowners simply provided the slaves with land, generally known as provision grounds, on which to produce their own food, though they did distribute rations to a limited extent. All rural slaveowners possessing land permitted their slaves to cultivate garden plots around their houses and to raise small livestock.

The first of these three methods of provisioning was rarely practiced after 1807. Subsistence crises, resulting chiefly from the interruption to trade consequent on the American Revolution, caused the death of thousands of slaves in the British islands and led the planters to avoid dependence on external sources. The Napoleonic Wars had a similar effect. Where almost all land was potential cane land, as in Barbados and some of the Leeward Islands, the planters kept control of the system of production but allocated part of their resources of land and labor to the cultivation of food crops. Where land types were more varied, planters were reluctant to devote potential export crop land to food crops and merely provided lands on which the slaves were expected to produce what they could when they could. This system was seen by the planters as far less costly than purchasing imported food or taking land out of profitable export crops. In some cases the provision grounds fell within the boundaries of the plantation; in others the planters purchased separate areas for that purpose, requiring the slaves to travel distances of up to 15 miles to tend their crops. In some cases the provision grounds comprised marginal, unproductive land; in others the soil was ideal for food crops. These physical and economic factors led to the emergence of the provision ground system in Jamaica long before 1776, but there is no doubt that the subsistence crises of the late eighteenth century gave it an added impetus. The system also became firmly established in the Windward Islands and Trinidad. The situation in the marginal colonies is less certain. The slaves of Barbuda had extensive grounds, but those in British Honduras, Anguilla, the Bahamas, and the Cayman Islands seem to have had only limited access and generally cultivated food crops while under the direct supervision of their masters. Indeed, they often produced little else after the failure of export crops in these islands.

Recent attempts to establish the caloric intake of slaves in the British Caribbean carried out by Robert Dirks and the Kiples, have been based largely on the rationed allowances prescribed by colonial slave laws. Neither of these studies produces systematic estimates for all of the colonies, but it is obvious that precision is impossible because of the variable importance of rations in the slave diet. The slave laws provide a poor guide to actual practice, and Dirks notes major anomalies. Further, there is little hard evidence available on the output of provision grounds and gardens, and much of this produce was in any case retailed by the slaves in public markets and not necessarily consumed or exchanged for food items. Thus, it is difficult to know what to make of Dirks's finding that the 'average estate ration' in the late eighteenth century was between 1,500 and 2,000 calories per day, whereas 'the average energy demand placed on a young man in a first gang must have been in excess of 3,500 calories per day, perhaps 150 calories per day less for a woman'. There are two problems here. The first is that it is uncertain how many calories were obtained from sources other than rations, though it is certain that these supplementary sources became increasingly important after 1807. The second problem is that Dirks's estimate of energy demands derives from an underestimate of slave stature and an admitted understatement of the hours worked by slaves (which he estimated as a daily average of eight hours). There seems no way of resolving these problems with real precision. The approach of the Kiples, who appear simply to assume that adult slaves must have received an average 3,000 calories per day, is even less fruitful. The analysis that follows makes no claim to greater quantitative precision, and for the moment this aspect of the question remains insoluble. Rather, it attempts to establish a firmer comparative foundation, emphasizing differences in food supply between colonies, differences between slaves within the hierarchy of occupational statuses, and differences between seasons.

[. . .]

PROVISION GROUNDS

The system of rationed allowances prevailed throughout Barbados, St. Kitts, Nevis, Antigua, Demerara-Essequibo, and Berbice, with only minor variations in the relative significance of supplements obtained from provision grounds. In the remaining sugar colonies of the British Caribbean the provision ground was everywhere more important than the master's store in the early nineteenth century. It is a revealing fact that the Jamaican abolition act of 1834 made no mention of food. The Montserrat act stated only that the planters were to provide food if the provision grounds failed, and the Tobago act merely stipulated that apprentices over 12 years were to have half an acre of provision grounds within a mile of their houses and children under 12 were to have a quarter acre. The St. Vincent abolition act was unique in specifying quantities: slaves over 10 years were to receive 4 qt of wheat flour or farina or the flour of Indian or Guinea corn or 20 lb of yams or potatoes, and children were to have half-rations. Earlier laws were generally equally vague. The Jamaican slave law of 1816, for example, was careful to specify that the slaves should have sufficient time to cultivate their grounds, but beyond this merely called for a monthly inspection 'in order to see that the same are cultivated and kept up in a proper manner,' and required that where no suitable land was available or where grounds had been made unproductive by drought the planters should 'make good and ample provision' equivalent to 3s. 4d. per week per slave. In Grenada all slaves over 14 years, except domestics, were to be allotted provision grounds as well as one-fortieth of an acre for gardens, but if land suited to provision grounds was unavailable the planter could provide 'a weekly allowance of provisions, completely adequate to their maintenance'. The Tobago slave law of 1794 stated that every plantation should have one acre for every five slaves 'well planted with provisions,' but this seems to have been neglected as provision grounds became increasingly important. In Dominica the slave law of 1821 did stipulate that adults should receive 2 lb of salt provisions weekly, and children half that amount, but the earlier law of 1799 had stated only that masters should provide either 'a sufficient quantity of good and wholesome food' or sufficient land and time to produce it. The masters claimed that slaves with provision grounds got 'not less than half an acre' each.

The Trinidad Ordinance of 1800 was more specific. It required planters to cultivate one quarrée (3.2 acres) per 10 working slaves in provisions, and to give a weekly allowance of 3 lb of salt meat or 4 lb of salt fish to each slave aged 14 years or over. In addition, each of these slaves was to have 'a portion of land allotted to him, adequate to produce, by cultivating it, a sufficiency of ground provisions for himself and his family,' to be cultivated on Saturday afternoons out of crop. Slaves without grounds were to be given 60 plantains or 6 qt of cassava meal weekly, or 3 bits to purchase provisions, in addition to the allowances of salt meat or fish. But Trinidad planters soon began to complain about the high cost of provisions, and sugar estates neglected the cultivation of provision crops. In 1817 it was said that most large estates complied with the ordinance in giving Saturday afternoons, but generally gave only 3 lb of fish. On smaller holdings, however, the slaveowners tended to give no fish but allowed the slaves every Saturday to cultivate their grounds. Thus, there was a rapid shift to heavy dependence on the provision ground system. In 1830 the Protector of Slaves in Trinidad, Henry Gloster, claimed that adult plantation slaves received 3.5 lb of salt cod weekly, as well as three drams of rum per day during crop and a glass a day out of crop. But slaves were given only 4–6 qt of farinaceous food weekly if their provision grounds proved unproductive. Head people got double rations of fish. Children under 14 years had only half-rations but were fed a mess from the owner's kitchen. Special allowances were given at Christmas. For most of the period 1807–34, then, slaves on large plantations in Trinidad received relatively generous allowances of salt fish but little else, and those on small holdings were totally dependent on their provision grounds.

Although the slave laws of the Windward Islands and Jamaica were generally silent on the distribution of rationed allowances, it was customary in most of these colonies for the planters regularly to provide limited quantities of pickled fish and to supply occasional allowances at holidays. In Jamaica, adult slaves got 6–8 pickled herring weekly. The distribution of fish was said by some proslavery observers to have increased after about 1800, but contemporary calculations for Dominica and Jamaica showed that the amount of fish imported was only about half that required to supply the supposed allowances. In Jamaica salt and pickled fish were sometimes termed 'indulgences,' which might be withheld for bad conduct, in contrast to rightful 'allowances'. On sugar estates slaves were allowed to consume cane juice during crop, as in the rationed colonies, and also received rum and molasses out of crop. With the significant exception of the parish of Vere in Jamaica, where the slaves had only limited grounds and depended on allowances of Guinea corn cultivated on the sugar estates as in Barbados, the vast majority of slaves in the Windward Islands and Jamaica relied heavily on the produce of their provision grounds.

In the Virgin Islands slaves had both provision grounds and limited allowances. Around 1830 George Richardson Porter claimed that they received weekly 4–6 pt of corn meal and 6 herring, as well as salt, pork, and flour at Christmas. The slave law of 1798 prohibited the reduction of rations during crop but permitted a reduction of one-fifth out of crop where the grounds were adequate.

The internal organization of the provision grounds was left very largely to the slaves themselves. The planters might subdivide the grounds and allocate them to particular individuals, but beyond this they took little interest, apart from making occasional inspections. In 1814 some planters in Dominica began 'working the gangs on their grounds on the days allotted for that purpose, under the superintendence of the overseers and drivers,' but this was done to prevent the development of a trade between the slaves and maroons, and was very much an exception. Normally the grounds were worked by family groups or individual slaves, with men, women, and children all performing labor. Aged and disabled slaves were allotted grounds, and these were often worked for them by relatives or fellow laborers. Head people, such as drivers and tradesmen, were often allocated larger grounds, and in some cases they actually hired other slaves to work their grounds. The crops cultivated on the grounds varied with locality, but root crops generally predominated, with corn and plantains as subsidiaries. In Dominica it was said that the slaves cultivated 'yams, plantains, bananas, cassada or manioc, eddoes, potatoes, ocoraes [okra], Indian corn, cale, pigeon pease, and several species of beans, and pine apples; and the higher grounds produce many kinds of European garden stuff, such as cabbages, carrots, turnips, beet root, lettuce, asparagus, artichoke, radish, cucumber, cellery, and herbs of all sorts, besides tropical fruits'. Most of these vegetable crops were produced for sale in the public markets, however, and some of the corn and other provisions was fed to pigs and poultry kept in the slaves' garden plots. The slaves of the Windward Islands and Jamaica played an even greater role in supplying the internal markets than those in the rationed colonies, so it is impossible to know how much of the produce of ground and garden entered the slaves' diet directly or was exchanged for other food items and how much was exchanged for nonfood items or accumulated as cash. The provision ground system certainly provided the basis for a more varied diet, but even in the rationed colonies slaves were able to achieve variety by selling produce from their gardens or exchanging their allowances in the market. A simple example of such behavior was the exchange of pickled fish (herring, shad, mackerel) for the salt cod preferred by slaves in most colonies. Without doubt the provision ground system created the framework for relatively independent economic activity, and it was said to be preferred by the slaves themselves, but its ultimate effect on nutrition is less than certain.

[. . .]

DIETARY ADEQUACY

Although West Indian slaves did consume a wide variety of food items from time to time, the basic diet was monotonous even when it was relatively substantial in terms of quantity. Using an 'ideal' diet for the British Caribbean as a whole, and one more varied than that typical for most field slaves, the

Kiples conclude that the basic caloric and protein needs of the slaves were in fact supplied. This general conclusion is probably too optimistic, since it fails to recognize important differences between colonies. But the significant point here is that the Kiples go on to argue that even this 'ideal' diet concealed numerous nutritional deficiencies with epidemiological implications. [. . .] Here it is necessary only to note some of the nutritional deficiencies suggested by the Kiples for their ideal diet. In the first place, this diet was poor in calcium. Milk could have remedied this deficiency but was in short supply, and in any case many of the slaves were lactose intolerant. Some slaves did own cattle in the British Caribbean after 1807, but they were generally kept for their meat and for sale; only in the Virgin Islands was it said that slaves benefited from keeping cattle 'in the use and sale of the milk and butter'. More important than this calcium deficiency was the absence of fats, and this further increased the deficiency of vitamin A in the slaves' diet. But the introduction of the ackee and the mango at the end of the eighteenth century did help to reduce this vitamin A deficiency. The Kiples also argue that the dependence on corn, root crops, and plantains as the major energy source increased requirements for thiamine, since this is necessary for the metabolism of carbohydrates. The availability of thiamine in the slave diet was reduced by the salting and pickling of fish and meat and by the long boiling common in slave cookery. Thus, it may be concluded that even when the slaves' diet was relatively varied it remained deficient in calcium, vitamin A, and thiamine. In periods of seasonal nutritional stress it was also inadequate in calories and, more often, protein. These deficiencies were not evenly spread within the rural slave populations. It must be said, however, that the metabolic pathways of many nutrients remain poorly understood, and that some apparently healthy modern West Indian populations subsist on only 1600–2000 calories per day, significantly less than the level assumed by the Kiples for the slave population.

Slave diets varied between individuals and plantations, but some generalizations can be attempted at the colony level. Among the rural populations, a system of rationed allowances supplied the greater part of the slaves' food in Barbados, St. Kitts, Nevis, Antigua, Demerara-Essequibo, Berbice, and British Honduras. Elsewhere the provision ground system was basic, though supplemented to some extent by rations. Anguilla and the Bahamas fell somewhere between these extremes, and in Trinidad there was a shift from rations to provision grounds within the period. Protein was supplied chiefly by salt fish in the rationed colonies (except that British Honduras depended on salt pork) and by pickled or fresh fish in the other colonies. The staple energy sources were Guinea corn in Barbados and the Bahamas, yams and sweet potatoes in the Leeward Islands, and plantains in Trinidad, Demerara-Essequibo, Berbice, and British Honduras. Elsewhere the staples varied regionally or from plantation to plantation. These local variations make comparative conclusions difficult, but overall the slaves of the marginal colonies probably consumed the least deficient diets in normal times. Of the rationed colonies, the plantain-based diet of Demerara-Essequibo and Berbice probably delivered more calories than that of Barbados, while the smaller allowances of fish given in the Leeward Islands made these colonies further deficient. Of the colonies based on the provision ground system. Trinidad was most generous in its fish rations, but the individual character of the system obscures general tendencies. Although Sidney Mintz asserts that 'it seems quite likely that the provision ground-marketing complex . . . reduced the hunger of the slaves', Dirks is justified in concluding that 'the available evidence seems to indicate that the praedial slaves' efforts to feed themselves were not as successful as many accounts of vigorous gardening, hunting, gathering, and trading activities might lead one to believe'.

Within each of the types of colonies, further variations in diet may have been related to the different crops produced on the plantations, but such variations were minor. To the extent that slave laws affected practice, a certain uniformity at the colony level was imposed from above. It has been noted that poor slaveowners with small holdings were said to give less food than opulent planters, but most of this testimony comes from the latter and may be suspect. Many of the smaller holdings were devoted to provision crops rather than export staples, but the presence of potential food supplies did not necessarily have any effect on the slaves' nutrition. In the same way, the presence of vast stores of energy-rich sugar did not mean adequate food supplies for slaves living on sugar estates.

Differences in diet between individual slaves on particular plantations related chiefly to age and occupational status. The young and the old were often directly dependent on food prepared in their owners' kitchens, but the old were likely to be neglected. Distinctions were not generally made between males and females in the distribution of food, but males occupied most of the supervisory and skilled posts, which were rewarded much more generously in rations or provision grounds than were field laborer positions. Certain occupations provided direct access to food supplies. For example, Richard Price contends that slave fishermen 'undoubtedly dined relatively well, trading surplus fish for vegetables from their neighbors' kitchen gardens'. Domestics had access to great house larders but generally lacked productive provision grounds. Only the sick shared in the variety of food, wholesome and unwholesome, that covered the planters' groaning tables.

[From *Slave Populations of the British Caribbean 1807–1834* (Baltimore: Johns Hopkins University Press, 1984), 204–5, 210–12, 217–18.]

The slaves' Christianity cannot be understood as a façade behind which the countryside practiced pagan rites or wallowed in something called superstition. Nor, alternatively, can the beliefs and practices of the folk be understood as having corrupted the slaves' Christianity. Folk belief, including the belief in magic, constituted a vital element in the making of the slaves' own version of Christianity, and does not appear to have introduced any greater distortion into a supposedly pure Christianity than did those folk beliefs of ancient, medieval, or even modern Europe which steadily helped shape the formation of the high religion.

Even when the churches resolutely fought popular 'superstition,' they had to absorb much of it either by direct appropriation or by bending formal doctrine to provide the spiritual elements that made folk belief attractive. Thus, however harshly the sophisticated urban black ministers waged war on what they considered the pagan residues of their flock, they could not easily convince the conjurers or their supporters of any unchristian doing, nor could they avoid shaping their own doctrine in such a way as to answer the questions that the resort to magic posed.

The folk dynamic in the historical development of Afro-American Christianity saved the slaves from the disaster that some historians erroneously think they suffered—that of being suspended between a lost African culture and a forbidden European one. It enabled them to retain enough of Africa to help them create an appropriate form for the new content they were forging and to contribute to the mainstream of American national culture while shaping an autonomous identity. Their religion simultaneously helped build an 'American' Christianity both directly and as a counterpoint and laid the foundation for a 'black' Christianity of their own. That is, it made possible a universal statement because it made possible a national statement. But, for blacks, the national statement expressed a duality as something both black and American, not in the mechanical sense of being an ethnic component in a pluralistic society, but in the dialectical sense of simultaneously being itself and the other, both separately and together, and of developing as a religion within a religion in a nation within a nation.

Black religion had to be more than slave religion, not only or even mainly because many of its most articulate and sophisticated spokesmen were southern free Negroes and northerners who lived outside slave society, but because the racial basis of slavery laid the foundations for a black identity that crossed class lines and demanded protonational identification. The horror of American racism, as if to prove Hegel right about 'the cunning of Reason,' forced the slaves out of themselves—forced them to glimpse the possibilities of nationality rather than class. Had it not been so, they would have been condemned to the fate of the slaves of the ancient world; they would have remained a pathetic and disorganized mass at the bottom of a single social scale, with no possibility of building an autonomous culture or rising above the role of historical witness to the crime of ultimate class oppression. The Moorish black nationalists of the 1930s knew what they were talking about when they said, 'Before you have a God you must have a nationality'. What they could not see was just how far the slaves had gone toward establishing both.

The origins of black Christian religion in the slave quarters—the roots of an embryonic national religion in the consciousness of the slave class—embodied two contradictions, the transcendence of which has yet to be effected. First, Christianity bound master and slave together in universal communion while it contributed to their separation into antagonistic peoples. Second, it imparted to the slaves, and through them to black America, a collective strength that rested on a politically dangerous kind of individualism.

In entering into Christian fellowship with each other the slaves set themselves apart from the whites by creating a distinctive style, sensibility, and theology. In the hands of militants and revolutionaries, the sense of being a people apart could lead to a belief that whites were the antichrist, but the universality of the Christian religion, embedded in an intimate, paternalistic plantation world, militated against such an interpretation and rendered it an idiosyncratic footnote. For the slaves, whites lived under God and were brothers in Christ. In its positive aspects, this sense of racial brotherhood gave the slaves a measuring rod with which to hold slaveowners to a standard of behavior appropriate to their own professions of Christian faith. By its very nature it forbade slaves to accept the idea that they had no right to judge their masters; it made judgment a duty. In thus being compelled to see some masters as 'good' and some as 'bad,' the slaves had to take conservative ground and admit that a man did not necessarily stop being a Christian by holding slaves, although they did not take this concession to mean that slavery itself could be a proper order for a Christian society. This compromise strengthened their resistance to dehumanization, for it curbed the self-destructive tendency toward hatred. It left them free to hate slavery but not necessarily their individual masters. It left them free to love their masters as fellow sinners before God and yet to judge their relative merits as Christians and human beings. W. E. B. Du Bois could therefore express admiration for their profoundly Christian ability to love their enemies and yet defend them against the notion that in so doing they surrendered their manhood or accepted their masters' world view.

[. . .]

If the contradictory nature of the slaves' religion as part of American Christianity and yet as a faith apart lessened revolutionary inclinations, the contradiction between its individual and its collective aspects proved even more fateful. The religion practiced in the quarters gave the slaves the one thing they absolutely had to have if they were to resist being transformed into the Sambos they had been programmed to become. It fired them with a sense of their own worth before God and man. It enabled them to prove to themselves, and to a world that never ceased to need reminding, that no man's will can become that of another unless he himself wills it—that the ideal of slavery cannot be realized, no matter how badly the body is broken and the spirit tormented.

The spiritual emancipation of the individual therefore constituted the decisive task of religion and the necessary foundation for black collectivity. But communion as a people, under so pressing a demand, reinforced that tendency toward atomization of the quarters which it was combatting. At the very moment that it was helping to create a sense of solidarity through mutual respect and love for each other, it was strengthening an extreme doctrine of the equality of individuals. The slaves desperately needed that doctrine to confront their masters, but they were whole men and women, not a jumble of abstractions; they could not easily assert their claims against the authority of their masters without asserting them against the claims of each other.

[. . .]

These contradictions propelled black religion forward to the creation of collective identity and pride. The black variant of Christianity laid the foundations of protonational consciousness and at the same time stretched a universalist offer of forgiveness and ultimate reconciliation to white America; and it gave the individual slave the wherewithal to hold himself intact and to love his brothers and sisters in the quarters, even as it blocked the emergence of political consciousness and a willingness to create a legitimate black authority. The synthesis that became black Christianity offered profound spiritual strength to a people at bay; but it also imparted a political weakness, which dictated, however necessarily and realistically, acceptance of the hegemony of the oppressor. It enabled the slaves to do battle against the slaveholders' ideology, but defensively within the system it opposed; offensively, it proved a poor instrument. The accomplishment soared heroically to great heights, but so did the price, which even now has not been fully paid.

[From *Roll, Jordan, Roll: The World the Slaves Made* (New York: Pantheon, 1974), 280–4.]

The industrial discipline, so difficult to bring about in the factories of free England and free New England, was achieved on sugar plantations more than a century earlier—partly because sugar production lent itself to a minute division of labor, partly because of the invention of the gang system, which provided a powerful instrument for the supervision and control of labor, and partly because of the extraordinary degree of force that planters were allowed to bring to bear on enslaved black labor. The gang system did not come into being everywhere at the same moment of time. It developed gradually, over many decades, and the process of development began in different places at different times. The rate of growth in the size of plantations was certainly a factor affecting its development, as was the nature of the crop. The gang system developed first on large sugar plantations and later spread to rice, coffee, cotton, and, to a lesser extent, tobacco.

There were, of course, significant differences in the operation of the gang system from sugar plantation to sugar plantation and even greater differences between sugar and cotton plantations. But certain features were common to gang system plantations regardless of location or crop. The most basic of these was the division of the complex activities during each phase of production—planting, cultivating, and harvesting—into a series of relatively simple tasks that could be closely monitored. The gang system thus gave rise to an elaborate division of labor that rested, in the first instance, on a division between those slaves who worked in gangs and those who did not. During the late eighteenth century about half of the adult male slaves (age 16 or over) and five-sixths of the adult female slaves on West Indian sugar plantations labored in gangs. Of the males exempt from field work, about 20 percent held managerial jobs (supervised other slaves) or were craftsmen and the balance worked in semi-skilled jobs or in jobs reserved for the aged and the lame. The division of labor on U.S. cotton plantations was similar, although the proportion of adult males exempt from gang labor was smaller—closer to 25 percent than to 50 percent. On both sugar and cotton plantations field slaves usually worked in gangs of 10 to 20 hands, each of which was headed by a 'driver'—a slave who, with whip in hand, pushed his gang to achieve the assigned task.

Contemporary accounts underscore the importance that U.S. cotton planters attached to the organization of their slaves into highly coordinated and precisely functioning gangs. 'A plantation might be considered as a piece of machinery,' said Bennet H. Barrow in his Highland plantation rules. 'To operate successfully, all its parts should be uniform and exact, and its impelling force regular and steady.' 'Driving,' the establishment of a rigid gang discipline, was considered the crux of a successful operation. Observers, such as Robert Russell, said that the discipline of plantation life was 'almost as strict as that of our military system'. Frederick Law Olmsted described one instance in which he observed two very large hoe gangs 'moving across the field in parallel lines, with a considerable degree of precision'. He reported that he 'repeatedly rode through the lines at a canter, with other horsemen, often coming upon them suddenly, without producing the smallest change or interruption in the dogged action of the labourers'.

Each work gang was based on an internal division of labor that not only assigned every member of the gang to a precise task but simultaneously made his or her performance dependent on the actions of the others. On the McDuffie plantation the planting gang was divided into three classes:

1st, the best hands, embracing those of good judgment and quick motion. 2nd, those of the weakest and most inefficient class. 3rd, the second class of hoe hands. Thus classified, the first class will run ahead and open a small hole about seven to ten inches apart, into which the second class drop from four to five cotton seed, and the third class follow and cover with a rake.

Interdependence and tension were also promoted between gangs, especially during the period of cultivation when the field labor force was divided into plow gangs and hoe gangs. The hoe hands chopped out the weeds that surrounded the cotton plants as well as excessive sprouts. The plow gangs followed behind, stirring the soil near the rows of cotton plants and tossing it back around the plants. Thus, the hoe and plow gangs each put the other under an assembly line type of pressure. The hoeing had to be completed in time to permit the plow hands to carry out their tasks. At the same time the progress of the hoeing, which entailed lighter labor than plowing, set a pace for the plow gang. The drivers or overseers moved back and forth between the two gangs, exhorting and prodding each to keep up with the pace of the other, as well as inspecting the quality of the work. In cotton picking, which did not lend itself as naturally to interdependence as did planting and cultivating, planters sought to promote intensity of effort by dividing hands into competing gangs and offering bonuses on a daily and weekly basis to the gang that picked the most. They also made extensive use of the so-called task methods. These were, literally, time-motion studies on the basis of which a daily quota for each hand was established.

In addition to assembly line methods and time-motion studies to ensure maximum intensity of effort in a particular operation, planters sought to allocate their slaves among jobs in such a manner as to achieve 'full-capacity' utilization of each person. In this connection slaves were given 'hand' ratings—generally ranging from one-eighth to a full hand—according to their age, sex, and physical ability. The strongest hands were put into field work, with the ablest of these given tasks that would set the pace for the others.

Plow gangs were composed primarily of men in their twenties or early thirties. Less sturdy men and boys, as well as prime-aged women, were in the hoe gangs. Older women were occupied in such domestic jobs as house servants and nurses; older men worked as gardeners, servants, and stock minders. Analysis of the records of the Kollock plantation in Georgia in 1860 indicates that the 'hand'-to-slave ratio was 0.9 in field work but only 0.6 in non-field work.

Data on the cotton-picking rates of pregnant women and nursing mothers provide still another illustration of the degree to which planters succeeded in utilizing all those in the labor force. Down to the last week before birth, pregnant women picked three-quarters or more of the amount that was normal for women of corresponding ages who were neither pregnant nor nursing. Only during the month following childbirth was there a sharp reduction in the amount of cotton picked. Some mothers started to return to field work during the second or third week after birth. By the second month after birth, picking rates reached two-thirds of the level for non-nursing mothers. By the third month, the level rose to over 90 percent.

It is sometimes said that the principal function of the gang system was to increase the average number of hours that a slave worked beyond that which was typical of free labor. There is evidence suggesting that the hours of work on slave plantations exceeded those of subsistence farmers in Europe and America before the Industrial Revolution and also of subsistence farmers in the underdeveloped nations of the world today. Nevertheless, it was product per worker and not the number of hours that planters sought to maximize. Many discovered that the way to achieve this objective was not by pushing the number of working hours to the outer limit but by coupling increases in the intensity of labor per hour with a reduction in the total number of hours worked. One planter, for example, experimented with the number and frequency of the rest breaks he should provide during the day, and reached the conclusion that, in addition to the breakfast and lunch breaks, a five-minute rest every half hour increased the productivity of the slaves by 15 percent. Such rest breaks, it was noted, also increased the pace and productivity of the mules. Recent studies of the labor routine on U.S. cotton plantations have revealed that the average workweek during the spring, summer, and fall was about 58 hours, well below the 72 hours thought to have prevailed in English textile mills during the first quarter of the nineteenth century and also below the 60-hour week of northern commercial farmers in the United States during the first quarter of the twentieth century.

[From *Without Consent or Contract: The Rise and Fall of American Slavery* (New York: Norton, 1989), 25–9.]

PETER KOLCHIN
....

108 **Unfree Labour**

Clearly, the cultural break resulting from the forced migration from Africa to America fundamentally differentiated the experiences of American slaves and Russian serfs. The serfs were held on their home turf, where despite their bondage they could continue in many respects to live and act as their ancestors had; the slaves were torn from their homeland and held in a new continent where inevitably, despite strenuous efforts to preserve old ways, a drastic change in life-style and consciousness ensued. Geographic continuity or discontinuity was the most obvious single influence on the degree of cultural continuity among the bondsmen. In this respect the experience of serfs in Russia differed radically not only from that of slaves in the United States but also from that of slaves in other New World societies. The African diaspora was a fundamental fact of black slavery in the Americas, whereby black slaves became outsiders in white, European-derived societies.

There were a number of other significant causes, however, of the contrasting worlds and world views of the Russian and American bondsmen. Most of these have already been touched on and need only to be brought together, but a couple require slightly more elaboration. It is important to note that unlike the African diaspora these other elements did not separate the experience of Russian serfs from that of all New World slaves; concrete historical experiences differentiated the lives of Russian serfs and southern slaves, but the contrast was not one between slaves and serfs per se. Indeed, with respect to culture and community, Russian and American bondsmen stood at two extremes of a broad spectrum or continuum, on which slaves of other countries were fixed in varying more central locations.

Several demographic factors served to facilitate the development of autonomous communal behavior among the Russian serfs while severely restricting its potentiality among American slaves. Most obvious were the differing population mixes in the two countries. Whereas blacks were a minority in the South as a whole and about one-half of the population in the deep South, peasants constituted the overwhelming majority of Russians; similarly, the serfs were typically held in far larger units than the slaves. As a consequence the serfs had far more opportunity to lead autonomous lives than did the slaves. Among slaves held in very small groups the chance to partake of communal activities was often virtually nonexistent, but even among most others simple population ratios meant that they came in contact with whites far more often than most serfs did with noblemen. The internal lives of bondsmen who were widely dispersed among many slaveholders in small units had to be very different from the lives of those who were concentrated among a tiny class of noblemen on large estates.

Even given the southern slaves' numerical disadvantage, an independent black culture could have been reinvigorated by a steady supply of new Africans keeping alive the memory of traditional ways and fostering resistance to European cultural penetration. Precisely this happened in some other New World slave societies. It is therefore significant that the American slave population was largely creole from an early date. In part, this was because alone among major slave societies the United States prohibited the importation of new slaves more than half a century before it abolished slavery, but even more important was the natural population growth that rendered American slaves overwhelmingly creole generations before the end of the slave trade. By the American Revolution only about one-fifth of American slaves were African-born, and during the first half of the nineteenth century the proportion of Africans among southern slaves was insignificant. In contrast to Brazil, Cuba, Haiti, and Jamaica, where traditional African culture was continually buttressed from without, in the United States during the century and a half before emancipation an increasingly creole slave population became more and more divorced from its ancestral roots.

Differences in owner attitudes and behavior strongly reinforced the dichotomy resulting from contrasting demographic patterns in Russia and the United States. The absentee orientation of pomeshchiki allowed most serfs a substantial measure of freedom from direct, day-to-day owner interference; even when serfs had resident owners, those owners usually concerned themselves much less than most American planters with the internal lives of their laborers. The absentee mentality of Russian noblemen thus served to strengthen the autonomy of peasant life. In the United States planter paternalism had the opposite impact: the constant meddling that it engendered in slaves' lives proved destructive of their communal independence. Paternalism not only provided antebellum slaves with one of the world's highest material standards of living; it also subjected them to constant white cultural penetration and thus seriously undermined their cultural autonomy. One might suggest that in a rough sense there was an inverse relationship between the coherence of the masters' civilization and the autonomy of the bondsmen's communal culture: where resident slaveowners took a lively interest in their communities and their property, as southern planters did, that interest tended to have a corrosive impact on the ability of the slaves to maintain their own communal values and customs; where owners tended toward absenteeism, the bondsmen were correspondingly freer to lead their own lives and develop their own separate communal standards. (The process worked the other way as well. Where the bondsmen were in a huge numerical majority and showed strong communal solidarity, their owners found it convenient to put an appropriate distance between themselves and their 'brutish' property.)

There was, finally, an economic basis for the serf community that was largely lacking among American slaves: the existence of a secondary, peasant economy. Except for house servants, serfs grew their own food on their landed allotments and were self-supporting; in addition many—especially those on obrok estates—raised goods for market on 'their' land as well as cultivating their owners' fields. Of course, many southern slaves had garden plots whose produce they used to supplement their diets and even to earn pocket money for luxuries, and on the rice estates of coastal South Carolina and Georgia a real although limited slave economy developed as slaves raised and sold their 'own' provisions on their 'own' time. Nevertheless, the distinction was basic: the slaves received primary sustenance from their masters for whom they worked full-time, and when allowed they supplemented this by cultivating garden plots; the serfs were entirely self-supporting and were increasingly engaged in their own commercial operations. A major function of the commune was to regulate relations inhering in economic independence, from dividing peasant landholdings equitably to adjusting the rent they paid their owners. In short, communal independence rested on economic autonomy. In the slave South, where many planters believed that allowing slave families to cook their own meals promoted excessive independence, the slave community lacked any corresponding economic function.

[From *Unfree Labour: American Slavery and Russian Serfdom* (Cambridge, MA: Harvard University Press, 1987), 233–6.]

ELIZABETH FOX-GENOVESE

109   Within the Plantation Household

Not everyone with a large slave force organized the gangs by gender, but most seem to have done so. Certainly, planters throughout the South, on plantations encompassing a variety of sizes and crops, reserved some tasks for women and others for men. Charles Joyner, in his microcosmic study of the lowcountry, has found that although, on the Rice Coast, both men and women worked in the fields, only the men worked at ditching, embanking, and preparing the fields for the crop. On Robert F. W. Allston's Chicora Wood rice plantation, while the men worked in the pinelands, the women hoed peas; while the men worked on the causeway at the farm, the women carried away the sand from the pits or picked 'volunteer' rice; while the men picked peas, the women hoed the land for rye. In Florida, the overseers at El Destino plantation did not differentiate between men and women when they noted work in the fields, but they did note the special tasks performed by women, notably cooking for the whites, cooking for the hands, tying up fat, and spinning—mostly cooking and spinning. Bennet Barrow, a planter in Louisiana, regularly referred to the women as working at one or another task, frequently spinning. On the Belmead Plantation in Virginia, the women spun, cleaned the water furrows, opened the water furrows, and grubbed the land. Josephine Bacchus, from South Carolina, firmly insisted that women did not attend corn shuckings. 'Dem kind of task was left to de men folks de most of de time cause it been so hot dey was force to strip to do dat sort of a job.'

Division of the field hands' labor by gender prevailed on the sugar as well as the cotton plantations of Louisiana. Franklin Hudson, a sugar planter in Iberville Parish, set the women to digging stubble and the men to working on the road. Once he noted that he allowed his overseer 'to send 6 women in the place of 6 men'. On the LeBlanc family cotton plantation in Iberville, the men rolled logs while the women cleaned up the grounds; the men chopped wood and plowed while the women hoed. Since women on the LeBlanc plantation also sawed wood, it appears that the division between women and men had more to do with the principle of division than with any particular respect for the tasks considered appropriate for women. On H. M. Seale's sugar plantation in Ascension Parish, Louisiana, the women cleaned up the land while the men ditched. On M. W. Philips's cotton plantation in Mississippi—among many throughout the South—the women worked as a group under a male foreman.

Former slave women, recalling their or their mothers' days in the fields, were more likely to emphasize the difficulty and diversity of the tasks than whom they worked with. Gus Feaster, however, explicitly recalled seeing the 'hoe-womens' setting off for the field as a group. Sarah Wilson hoed, chopped sprouts, sheared sheep, carried water, cut firewood, picked cotton, sewed, and was selected to 'work Mistress' little garden where she raised things from seeds they get in Fort Sumter: Green peas and beans and radishes and little things like that'. In the summer and spring, Mary Frances Webb's grandmother plowed and hoed the crops, and in the winter she 'sawed and cut cord wood just like a man. She said it didn't hurt her as she was strong as an ox.' She also spun and wove and sewed. 'She helped make all the cloth for their clothes and in the spring one of the jobs for the women was to weave hats for the men.' For the hats, they 'used oat-straw, grass, and cane which had been split and dried and soaked in hot water until it was pliant, and they wove it into hats'. As a field hand, Callie Donalson's mother also washed, ironed, carded, wove, and was 'a good spinner'. 'She knitted mainly by night. All the stockings and gloves had to be knit.' She taught her daughter to sew 'with our fingers'. But Sally Brown claimed to have had a very hard time. 'I split rails like a man . . . I used a huge glut made out's wood, and a iron wedge drove into the wood with a maul, and this would split the wood.'

Masters commonly assigned slave women to labor that they would have considered inappropriate for white women, but they also had differing expectations for the quantities of work that slave men and women should be expected to perform. James Bertrand, a former slave, recalled that 'out in the field, the man had to pick three hundred pounds of cotton and the woman had to pick two hundred pounds,' but he added that he remembered hearing his mother 'talk about weaving the yarn and making the cloth and making clothes out of the cloth that had been woven'. Because many masters and overseers permitted women to leave the fields before men in order to be able to attend to other matters, it is not clear if the women's lighter loads reflected concern for their physical frailty or simply the desire to free them for other kinds of labor. Yet on a noteworthy, if unmeasurable, number of plantations women matched or overmatched the productivity of the men. Plantation account books usually recorded with special care the amount of cotton picked, and women regularly figured among the top pickers. Some planters made pointed reference to a woman as their best picker or best general field hand.

The overwhelming majority of adult slave women returned from their work in the fields to cook, wash, sew, knit, weave, or do other kinds of work, sometimes for the plantation household, more often for their own families— usually for direct consumption, but sometimes for sale. Occasionally, slave women returned from the fields too tired even to eat, much less cook for their families, but often they used the remainder of the day and much of the night for their second set of tasks. George Washington Browning's mother often returned from a hard day's plowing to card and spin clothes for her family. Fannie Moore's mother worked in the fields all day 'and piece and quilt all night'. She had 'to spin enough thread to make four cuts for de white folks ebber night,' and also had to piece quilts for them. Sometimes Fannie Moore, who 'hab to hold the light for her to see by,' never got to bed. Betty Brown's family 'lived de ole-time way of livin', mammy done de cookin' an' we had plenty good things to eat'. Her mother also 'made all de clothes, spinnin', an' weavin' an' sewin'. Ah learned to spin when ah wuz too little tuh reach de broach, an' ah could hep her thread de loom'. Her mother was also 'a shoe-maker, she'd make moccasins for all o' us'. Hannah Plummer lived with her family in a plank house, 'with three rooms and a shed porch'. Her mother washed their clothes under the porch and at night she made their bed clothes. 'She also made bonnets and dresses' at night and sometimes sold the bonnets. She would give sweets to the child who sat up with her, so Hannah 'sat up with her a lot because I liked to eat'. Billie Smith remembered that some of the spinners would 'sit up at night and card and spin thread. They could sell the thread they spun at night'.

Slave women, whether in the big house or the fields, shared a common female experience that centered particularly around the preparation of food and cloth but also included such forms of basic household production as making candles and soap. Although mistresses sometimes taught their female slaves specific skills, slave women themselves normally transmitted those skills from one generation to the next. Some slave women specialized in household tasks, but, specialists or not, all slave women learned to contribute to general household labor and to provide for their own families. Large plantations had special houses for spinning and weaving; smaller ones might have a shed or a room. Bob Mobley recalled that on his plantation, where his aunt was a weaver, there was a house 'built especially for spinnin' an' weavin''. Two or three of 'the other nigger women made the clothes and they had to make 'em fit'. The mistress kept a close watch on the fit and 'made them be careful so the clothes would look nice'. Other slaves 'even learned to dye the wool so that we could have warm clothes in the winter'. Washing, a central feature of household life, could be done in a wash house or at a creek or stream, normally on the plantation but, in the case of smaller holdings, outside. Soap and candles were made on the place, as were dyes and lye. Slave women sewed in the big house under the direction of their mistresses or a slave seamstress. They sewed in their own cabins with the assistance of their daughters, and they sewed and quilted with the other women of the quarters.

[. . .]

However slave women learned their skills, once they had mastered them they imparted them to the younger women. Many aspects of their crafts exceeded their independent control. The mistress who insisted on cutting the cloth for the slave clothes, as many did, established a mold that the slave sewers had to follow. Their insistence may in part have reflected their concern to establish uniformity in slave clothing, but frequently, if Harriet Martineau's report can be credited, it also reflected their mistrust of their slaves' propensity to cut too generously and, accordingly, to 'waste' cloth. Quilting was another matter. Frequently, slave women quilted together while the men enjoyed corn shuckings. As a man, Ed McCree knew little about the quilting sessions except that they were special occasions. ''Bout dem quiltin's! Now Lady, what would a old Nigger man know 'bout somepin' dat didn't nothin' but 'omans have nothin' to do wid?' Quilting offered slave women the chance to exercise their own imaginations. No white woman dictated their complex patterns, even if the pieces with which they worked were white women's scraps. No outsider interfered with the ceaseless flow of the gossip in which they delighted and through which they wove their own view of the world that usually impinged so heavily on their lives.

Women's work in textiles provides a microcosm of the relations between mistresses and slaves in their shared sphere of women's labor. The white and black sources respectively offer strikingly different perspectives on women's textile production, but they describe the same world. Mistresses did not 'see'—or at least did not bother to write about—most of their slaves' textile work, which accounted for most of the household's textile production. From the mistress's perspective, the 'negro clothes' constituted a burden they frequently shouldered with something less than good grace. From the slaves' perspective, textile labor consisted in the spinning, carding, weaving, and dyeing—the necessary prerequisite to the mistresses' sewing—in which they were specially skilled and in which they passed long hours in the company of other slave women. Had the mistresses considered this labor at all, they would probably have passed over it lightly as one of the many things that almost invisibly got done. Such work did not embody their sense of themselves as women. It did embody the slave women's sense of themselves as women, as did the sewing of the slaves' clothes, which became a labor of love for their people. The textile work of mistresses and slaves met in sewing, on which both prided themselves, yet neither mistresses nor slaves commonly emphasized their having sewed together. Mistresses and slaves shared their respective identifications with the textile labor that made an important contribution to the definition of women's roles within the household. Yet for both, that labor acquired its meaning in their relations to their distinct families and communities.

[From *Within the Plantation Household: Black and White Women of the Old South* (Chapel Hill: University of North Carolina Press, 1988), 175–8, 184–5.]

ALLAN KULIKOFF

110   **Tobacco and Slaves**

By the 1750s, a peculiarly Afro-American life cycle had developed. Afro-Americans lived in a succession of different kinds of households. Children under ten years almost always lived with their mothers, and more than half on large plantations lived with both parents. Between ten and fourteen years of age, large numbers of children left their parents' homes. Some stayed with siblings and their families, others were sold, and the rest lived with other kin or unrelated people. Women married in their late teens, had children, and established households with their own children. More than two-fifths of the women on large plantations and a fifth on small farms lived with husbands as well as children. The same proportion of men as women lived in nuclear households, but because children of separated spouses usually lived with their mothers, large numbers of men, even on big plantations, lived only with other men.

These life-cycle changes can perhaps best be approached through a study of the critical events in the lives of Afro-Americans. Those events probably included the following: infancy, leaving the matricentral cell, beginning to work in the tobacco fields, leaving home, courtship and marriage, child rearing, and old age.

For the first few months of life, a newborn infant stayed in the matricentral cell, that is, received his identity and subsistence from his mother. A mother would take her new infant to the fields with her 'and lay it uncovered on the ground . . . while she hoed her corn-row down and up. She would then suckle it a few minutes, and return to her labor, leaving the child in the same exposure'. Eventually, the child left its mother's lap and explored the world of the hut and quarter. In the evenings, he ate with his family and learned to love his parents, siblings, and other kinfolk. During the day the young child lived in an age-segregated world. While parents, other adults, and older siblings worked, children were 'left, during a great portion of the day, on the ground at the doors of their huts, to their own struggles and efforts'. They played with age-mates or were left at home with other children and perhaps an aged grandparent. Siblings and age-mates commonly lived together or in nearby houses. In Prince George's County in 1776, 86 percent of those from zero to four years of age and 82 percent of those from five to nine years of age lived on plantations with at least one other child near their own age. Many children lived in little communities of five or more children their own age. Children five to nine years old, too young to work full time, may have cared for younger siblings; in Prince George's in 1776, 83 percent of all children under five years of age lived on a plantation with at least one child five to nine years of age.

Black children began to work in the tobacco fields between seven and ten years of age. For the first time they joined fully in the daytime activities of adults. Those still living at home labored beside parents, brothers and sisters, cousins, uncles, aunts, and other kinfolk. (Even on smaller plantations, they worked with their mothers.) Most were trained to be field hands by white masters or overseers and by their parents. Though these young hands were forced to work for the master, they quickly learned from their kinfolk to work at the pace that black adults set and to practice the skills necessary to 'put massa on'.

At about the same age, some privileged boys began to learn a craft from whites or (on the larger plantations) from their skilled kinfolk. Charles Carroll's plantations provide an example of how skills were passed from one generation of Afro-Americans to the next. Six of the eighteen artisans on his plantations under twenty-five years of age in 1773 probably learned their trade from fathers and another four from other kinfolk skilled in that occupation.

For example, Joe, twenty-one, and Jack, nineteen, were both coopers and both sons of Cooper Joe, sixty-three. Joe also learned to be a wheelwright and, in turn, probably helped train his brothers-in-law, Elisha eleven, and Dennis, nine, as wheelwrights.

Beginning to work coincided with the departure of many children from their parents, siblings, and friends. The fact that about 54 percent of all slaves in single-slave households in Prince George's in 1776 were between seven and fifteen years of age suggests that children of those ages were typically forced to leave home. Young blacks were most frequently forced from large plantations to smaller farms. The parents' authority was eliminated, and the child left the only community he had known. Tension and unhappiness often resulted. For example, Hagar, age fourteen, ran away from her master in Baltimore in 1766. 'She is supposed to be harbor'd in some Negro Quarter,' he claimed, 'as her Father and Mother Encourages her in Elopements, under a Pretense she is ill used at home.'

Courtship and marriage (defined here as a stable sexual union) led to substantial but differential changes for slave women and men. The process began earlier for women: men probably married in their middle to late twenties, women in their late teens. Men, who initiated the courtship, typically searched for wives by visiting a number of neighboring plantations and often found a wife near home, though not on the same quarter. Some evidence for this custom, suggestive but hardly conclusive, can be seen in the sex and age of runaway slaves. Only 9 percent of all southern Maryland runaways, 1745–1779, and 12 percent of all Virginia runaways, 1730–1787, were women. Few men (relative to the total population) ran away in their late teens, but numbers rose in the early twenties when the search for wives began and crested between twenty-five and thirty-four, when most men married and began families. Courtship on occasion ended in a marriage ceremony, sometimes performed by a clergyman, sometimes celebrated by the slaves themselves.

Slave men had to search their neighborhood to find a compatible spouse because even the largest quarter contained few eligible women. Some of the potential mates were sisters or cousins, groups blacks refused to marry. When they were excluded, few choices remained on the quarter, and youths looked elsewhere. Charles Carroll united slave couples once they married, but that usually required either bride or groom to move. Only a fifth of the forty-seven identifiable couples on his plantations in 1773 had lived on the same quarter before they married. Either husband or wife, and sometimes both of them, moved in three-fifths of the cases. The other fifth of the couples remained on different quarters in 1773. Yet most planters owned too few slaves, on too few quarters, to permit a wide choice of spouses within their plantations; furthermore, they could not afford to purchase the husband or wife. Inevitably, a majority of slave couples remained separated for much of their married life.

Marriage was far less important for slave women than for white women; slave women, unlike their white counterparts, neither shared property with their husbands nor received subsistence from them. After the relationship was consummated, the woman probably stayed with her family (parents and siblings) until a child was born, unless she could form a household with her new husband. Childbearing, and the child rearing that followed, however, were highly important rites of passage for most slave women. Once she had a child, she moved from her mother's or parents' home to her own hut. The bonding between the slave mother and her child may have been far more important than her relationship with her husband, especially if he lived on another plantation. Motherhood, moreover, gave women a few valued privileges. Masters sometimes treated pregnant women and their newborn children with greater than usual solicitude. For example, Richard Corbin, a Virginia planter, insisted in 1759 that his steward be 'Kind and Indulgent to pregnant women and not force them when with Child upon any service or hardship that will be injurious to them'. Children were 'to be well looked after'.

Marriage and parenthood brought less change in the lives of most men. Many continued to live with other men. Able to visit his family only at night or on holidays, the nonresident husband could play only a small role in child rearing. If husband and wife lived together, however, they established a household. The resident father helped raise his children, taught them skills, and tried to protect them from the master. Landon Carter reacted violently when Manuel tried to help his daughter. 'Manuel's Sarah, who pretended to be sick a week ago, and because I found nothing ailed her and would not let her lie up she run away above a week and was catched the night before last and locked up; but somebody broke open the door for her. It could be none but her father Manuel, and he I had whipped.'

On large plantations, mothers could call upon a wide variety of kin to help them raise their children: husbands, siblings, cousins, uncles, or aunts might be living in nearby huts. Peter Harbard learned from his grandmother, father, and paternal uncles how his grandmother's indentures were burned by Henry Darnall, a large planter in Prince George's County, and how she was forced into bondage. He 'frequently heard his grandmother Ann Joice say that if she had her *just right that she ought to be free and all her children. He hath also heard his Uncles David Jones, John Wood, Thomas Crane,* and also his father Francis Harbard declare as much'. Peter's desire for freedom, learned from his kinfolk, never left him. In 1748, he ran away twice toward Philadelphia and freedom. He was recaptured but later purchased his freedom.

[. . .] As slaves became feeble, some masters refused to maintain them adequately or sold them to unwary buyers. An act passed by the Maryland assembly in 1752 complained that 'sundry Persons in this Province have set disabled and superannuated Slaves free who have either perished through want or otherwise become a Burthen to others'. The legislators uncovered a problem: in 1755, 20 percent of all the free Negroes in Maryland were 'past labour or cripples,' while only 2 percent of white men were in this category. To remedy the abuse, the assembly forbade manumission of slaves by will and insisted that masters feed and clothe their old and ill slaves. If slaveholders failed to comply, they could be fined four pounds for each offense.

As Afro-American slaves moved from plantation to plantation through the life cycle, they left behind many friends and kinfolk and established relations with slaves on other plantations. And when young blacks married off their quarter, they gained kinfolk on other plantations. Both of these patterns can be illustrated from the Carroll plantations. Sam and Sue, who lived on Sam's quarter at Doohoregan Manor, had seven children between 1729 and 1751. In 1774, six of them were spread over four different quarters at Doohoregan: one son lived with his father (his mother had died); a daughter lived with her family in a hut near her father's; a son and daughter lived at Frost's; one son headed Moses' quarter; and a son lived at Riggs. Marriages increased the size and geographic spread of Fanny's relations. A third of the slaves who lived away from Riggs Quarter (the main plantation) were kin to Fanny or her descendants. Two of Kate's children married into Fanny's family; Kate and one son lived at Frost's, and another son lived at Jacob's. Cecilia, the daughter of Carpenter Harry and Sophia, married one of Fanny's grandchildren. Harry and Sophia lived with three of their children at Frost's, and two of their sons lived at Riggs, where they were learning to be wheelwrights with kinsperson Joe, son of Cooper Joe.

Since husbands and wives, fathers and children, and friends and kinfolk were often physically separated, they had to devise ways of maintaining their close ties. At night and on Sundays and holidays, fathers and other kinfolk visited those family members who lived on other plantations. Fathers on occasion had regular visiting rights. Landon Carter's Guy, for instance, visited his wife (who lived on another quarter) every Monday evening. These visits symbolized the solidarity of slave families and permitted kinfolk to renew their friendships but did not allow nonresident fathers to participate in the daily rearing of their children.

Even though this forced separation of husbands from wives and children from parents tore slave families apart, slaves managed to create kinship networks from this destruction. Slave society was characterized by hundreds of connected and interlocking kinship networks that stretched across many plantations. A slave who wanted to run away would find kinfolk, friends of kinfolk, or kinfolk of friends along his route willing to harbor him for a while. As kinship networks among Afro-American slaves grew ever larger, the proportion of runaways who were harbored for significant periods of time on slave quarters seems to have increased in both Maryland and Virginia.

There were three different reasons for slaves to use this underground. Some blacks, like Harry—who left his master in 1779, stayed in the neighborhood for a few weeks, and then took off for Philadelphia—used their friends' and kinfolk's hospitality to reach freedom. Others wanted to visit. About 27 percent of all runaways from southern Maryland mentioned in newspaper advertisements from 1745 to 1779 (and 54 percent of all those whose destinations were described by masters) ran away to visit. For example, Page traveled back and forth between Piscataway and South River in 1749, a distance of about forty miles, and was not caught. He must have received help from many quarters along his route. And in 1756, Kate, thirty years old, ran away from her master, who lived near Georgetown on the Potomac. She went to South River (about thirty miles distant), where she had formerly lived. Friends concealed her there. Her master feared that since 'she had been a great Rambler, and is well known in *Calvert* and *Anne-Arundel* Counties, besides other Parts of the Country,' Kate would 'indulge herself a little in visiting her old Acquaintance,' but spend most of time with her husband at West River.

Indeed, 9 percent of the southern Maryland runaways left masters to join their spouses. Sue and her child Jem, eighteen months old, went from Allen's Freshes to Port Tobacco, Charles County, a distance of about ten miles, 'to go and see her Husband'. Sam, age thirty, lived about thirty miles from his wife in Bryantown, Charles County, when he visited her in 1755. Will had to go more than a hundred miles, from Charles to Frederick County, to visit his wife, because her master had taken her from Will's neighborhood to a distant quarter.

Slave families in the eighteenth-century Chesapeake were often unstable, but Afro-Americans learned to cope with displacement and separation from kindred with some success. Slaves created flexible kinship networks that permitted slaves to adjust to separation. Most slaves were either members of a kin-based household or could call upon kindred on their own or nearby quarters for aid and encouragement. A girl who grew up in a two-parent household on a large plantation, for instance, might be sold in her teens to a small planter, marry a slave from a neighboring farm, and raise her children with minimal help from her husband. She would have learned about alternative child-rearing methods from playmates whose fathers lived elsewhere and would have been familiar with the nocturnal movement of men to visit their families. Her husband's kindred could provide some help and friendship if they lived nearby. If she longed for her old home, she could run away and visit, knowing that kindred and friends would hide her from the whites.

In sum, slave kinship networks provided Afro-Americans with an alternative system of status and authority and thereby set outside limits to exploitation by the master. A slave had not only a place in the plantation work hierarchy, mostly determined by the master, but a position within his kin group. Slave culture and religion developed within this system: blacks participated as kindred at work and in song, dance, celebrations, prayer, and revivals at home.

[From *Tobacco and Slaves: The Development of Southern Cultures in the Chesapeake, 1680–1800* (Chapel Hill: University of North Carolina Press, 1986), 371–80.]

PHILIP D. MORGAN

111   Slave Counterpoint

Play

In words, as in the creation of new figures of speech, African Americans demonstrated the importance of expressiveness, improvisation, and creativity in their lives. Playfulness—in the best sense of the word—was central not just to black verbal art but to black culture in general. Fashioning distinctive sartorial styles, forging a particular sense of humor, even walking in a singular way, slaves demonstrated the importance of play in their lives. Play had a more precise meaning in black culture, too, referring to ceremonies of music and dance, often performed at funerals. African American slaves performed most conspicuously when they sang and danced, two activities that permeated their everyday existence. Such celebrations were dramatic emblems of a more general cultural style.

Just as African languages can be subdivided almost at will and yet grouped into major families, a comparable variety *and* uniformity characterized the continent's music and dance. Thus, according to Richard Waterman, 'Peoples of a large section of Dahomey, for example, manage to do almost entirely without harmony, while the Ashanti, in the neighboring West African territory of the Gold Coast, seem to employ at least two-part and frequently three- and four-part harmony for almost all of their music.' In general terms, however, harmony seems to have played a minor role in almost all West African music. Perhaps the most important shared feature of African music was its centrality to everyday life. Olaudah Equiano put it well when he said, 'We are almost a nation of dancers, musicians, and poets'. More technically, African music is characterized as essentially rhythmic and percussive in its overall effect. As Alan Merriam has pointed out, drumming is important, but 'if a single percussion device were to be singled out as most universally used in Africa, we should certainly have to point to handclapping'.

The great value Africans attached to music and dance, together with their prowess at both activities, was transferred to the New World.

[. . .]

But if the form and occasional content of slave songs owed much to African traditions, their power drew inspiration from a range of sources— from the tragedy of slavery to Christian influences. The bittersweet quality of slave song is captured in a description of a group of slaves, making the great trek from Virginia to the Southwest, 'singing a little wild hymn of sweet and mournful melody'. Even more poignant was the response of slaves to a Methodist preacher who asked a group of slaves why they sang 'Vain tunes'. 'To take away trouble,' they replied. Moravian visitors to the Bryan plantations in South Carolina in 1741 heard 'a slave woman singing a spiritual at the water's edge,' her way of 'jubilating' at attaining 'assurance of the forgiveness of sins and the mercy of God in Christ'. Evangelicals were much taken with slaves' religious singing. John Leland found blacks 'remarkable for learning a tune' and for having 'very melodious voices'. Masters, too, remarked on their slaves' penchant for religious song. Daniel and Dinah, from Piedmont Virginia, were 'much given to singing hymns'; Jack, from South Carolina, enjoyed singing psalms.

Influences from Africa and from the institution of slavery had a significant impact on Africa American music, but so, of course, did the broader Anglo-American culture. Perhaps the best illustration is the use slaves made of Anglophone musical instruments—a development particularly noticeable in the Chesapeake. The most common instrument among Chesapeake slaves was the fiddle or violin. Some black fiddlers gained renown. When William Fearson's slave boy ran away, the master eschewed a description because the fugitive was 'well known in this City [of Williamsburg] by the name of FIDDLER BILLY'; Hannah looked 'a good deal like her father, the well known Fiddler'; and Sy Gilliat, a famous Richmond fiddler, claimed to have played at the governor's palace during Lord Botetourt's tenure. Slave fiddlers earned money. An Eastern Shore fiddler who entertained whites in the 1690s received money and fine cloth for his playing; the owner of mulatto shoemaker Samuel Berry observed, 'As he plays on the fiddle, he has many opportunities of changing his dress'. Fifty Virginia runaways were said to play the fiddle or violin, and a number carried off fiddles when absenting themselves. Most fiddlers were extremely conversant with white culture: they were invariably described as 'smart,' 'artful,' or 'likely'; many were skilled—none more so than Sambo, who made fiddles; most were creoles; and a few could read and write. Fiddlers also seem to have relished the social opportunities that their skills presented: Peter 'delighted in' fiddling 'when he gets any strong drink'; Dick and Daniel played on the fiddle and were good dancers; Bob played the fiddle and was 'fond of singing with it'.

[From *Slave Counterpoint: Black Culture in the Eighteenth-Century Chesapeake and Lowcountry* (Chapel Hill: University of North Carolina Press, 1998), 580–1, 591–2.]

Section VI

Resistance

INTRODUCTION

The institution of slavery, wherever it has existed, represented an extreme form of human dependence and subjugation. No matter how individually privileged, no matter what their religion, sex, color, race, or ethnicity, slaves lived tenuous and dishonored lives, ever vulnerable to a capricious display of their master's arbitrary power. Resistance to such a dehumanizing condition has appeared to be an inevitable, predictable, even a natural response to the fact of enslavement itself. Indeed, no society in human history, from before Plato's Greece to after Hitler's Germany, produced a master class sufficiently powerful to prevent some of its slaves from violently removing their bonds. At one level, as the Marxist historian Herbert Aptheker declared in 1943 in a seminal book on the history of slave revolts in the United States, the answer to the deceptively simple question of why slaves rebelled is no mystery: 'The fundamental factor provoking rebellion against slavery was that social system itself, the degradation, exploitation, oppression, and brutality which it created and with which indeed it was synonymous.'

Yet not all slaves resisted in the same way and for the same reasons. Resistance assumed many forms, passive and violent, individual and collective. Sometimes slave revolt could sweep an entire region; more often it remained confined to a small locality. Some acts of resistance surfaced more or less spontaneously; other cases showed considerable planning with stratified leadership, non-slave recruits, and multiple goals. Some forms of resistance fundamentally challenged the system; much more often, attempts at revolt fell far short of that goal. To say that slaves sought the liberation of themselves or their group is not to say that they necessarily expressed a universalistic abhorrence of slavery as an institution, wrong for all people at all times. History reveals, for example, that some communities of runaway slaves have enslaved others, and that they even returned other runaways for a price or to enhance their own security. In some societies slaves have been known to purchase other slaves, and former slaves have led slave uprisings as well as helped to suppress them. Certain readings in this volume demonstrate that for most of world history, slavery stood as an acceptable form of human servitude, a status given positive sanction by the world's great religions. The antislavery crusade, beginning in England in the second half of the eighteenth century, thus emerges as a singular, epoch-making event. Readings in this section suggest that under the influence of radical political and ideological currents in the transatlantic world during an age of democratic revolution, the patterns of resistance decisively changed, by reflecting ecumenical as well as particularistic motivations. Words such as rights, citizen, liberty, and equality increasingly infiltrated the vocabulary of slaves for use against their masters. In notable cases, such as the great slave revolution in the French colony of St. Domingue, resistance to enslavement combined with resistance to the institution of slavery as a social system. On other occasions, however, slave resistance entailed no fundamental assault on the institution itself, but a violent reaction to violations of local guidelines or boundaries established by negotiation and custom within an evolving system.

Throughout history, slaves have fashioned strategies of resistance that usually reflected a realistic assessment of the daunting forces arrayed against them. Insurrections that lasted more than a month and mobilized thousands of slaves rarely occurred anywhere in the world. This section features readings on three of the largest and longest lasting slave insurrections in history: the Spartacus rebellion (73–71 BCE), the revolt of the Zanj (868–83), and the St. Domingue revolution (1791–1804). In the United States, by contrast, the largest slave revolt, which broke out in the Orleans Territory in 1811, probably involved fewer than 500 slaves. The three most famous acts of collective slave resistance in the history of the United States—Gabriel's conspiracy (1800), Denmark Vesey's plot (1822), and Nat Turner's revolt (1831)—pale into insignificance next to the three largest slave revolts in the history of the nineteenth-century British Caribbean: in Barbados (1816), Demerara (1823), and Jamaica (1831).

Formidable stereotypes that depicted black slaves on antebellum southern plantations as typically docile and contented developed in the United States during the first half of the twentieth century. Much of the work on slavery since World War II effectively refuted this view by, among other things, exposing the white racial bias that informed the previous scholarship. Lively debate continues, however, on the nature and effectiveness of controls and the extent to which they shaped the psychology of the enslaved. To explain the relative frequency and magnitude of slave rebellions, for example, more recent scholarship has focused on the presence of certain structural factors favorable to revolt: divisions within the master class or between groups not enslaved; dense concentrations of slaves within a given region; advantageous terrain; master absenteeism; and openings for the creation of effective leadership. To be sure, masters in every slave society wielded an impressive assortment of blunt and subtle weapons to deter rebelliousness. In theory, the nature of the master-slave relationship was highly personalized and individual. Effective practice of the theory by resident paternalistic masters tended to militate against the collective solidarity of their slaves. For this and other reasons, more slave plots have been betrayed by slaves themselves than ever matured into armed conflict. In explaining why some plots reached the stage of open revolt, scholars have had to pay attention not only to what the rebel slaves did in the process of rising, but also to what their masters failed to do in responding to slave discontent.

The readings in this section reveal a variety of complicating conditions that attended slave resistance. Slaves never formed an undifferentiated mass or uniform class in any slave society. Prospective leaders had to overcome ethnic, status, gender, occupational, and other distinctions (often cultivated consciously by their masters as techniques of divide-and-rule) to organize their fellow slaves into a serious movement. Fully aware that the punishment for failure was horrific, leaders relied on religion, rituals, talismanic objects, and rumors of slaveholder vulnerability to rouse recruits for battle. No clock ever coordinated a slave revolt. In timing rebellion, slaves took advantage of darkness and heightened moments of ruling class distraction—war and holidays, for example—to strike the first blows. On many occasions, privileged slaves showed striking ingratitude to their masters by emerging at the front as charismatic leaders of slave revolts. Slaveholders sometimes learned afterwards how these privileged slaves had used their status and mobility to infuse rebelliousness into other slaves, to recruit followers, and to plan insurrection.

Given the gross imbalance of power in slave societies, historians tend to regard the formation of slave plots and especially slave revolts as remarkable achievements. The search for less dramatic, but more frequent, sustained, and perhaps ultimately more effective examples of slave resistance has uncovered a wide variety of indirect, concealed, and passive behaviors. Such day-to-day resistance, when taken in aggregate, helped to reshape incrementally the experience of slavery in ways more favorable to slaves. Specialists disagree, however, as to what behavior constitutes day-to-day resistance, and the more expansive definitions can look virtually synonymous with slave life itself. As paradoxical as it may seem, resistance of certain kinds, including the day-to-day variety, when kept within manageable limits, could actually serve the cause of maintaining the system even if individual masters rarely appreciated the long-term benefits.

PLATO

112 Laws

Ath. But may we not also say that the soul of the slave is utterly corrupt, and that no man of sense ought to trust them? And the wisest of our poets, speaking of Zeus, says:

'Far-seeing Zeus takes away half the understanding of men whom the day of slavery subdues.'

Different persons have got these two different notions of slaves in their minds—some of them utterly distrust their servants, and, as if they were wild beasts, chastise them with goads and whips, and make their souls three times, or rather many times, as slavish as they were before;—and others do just the opposite.

Meg. True.

Cle. Then what are we to do in our own country, stranger, as regards the right to own and punish slaves seeing that there are such differences in the treatment of them?

Ath. Well, Cleinias, there can be no doubt that man is a troublesome animal, and therefore he is not very manageable, nor likely to become so, when you attempt to introduce the necessary division of slave, and freeman, and master; that is obvious. He is a troublesome piece of goods, as has been often shown by the frequent revolts of the Messenians, and the great mischiefs which happen in states having many slaves who speak the same language, and the numerous robberies and lawless life of the Italian *banditti*, as they are called. A man who considers all this is fairly at a loss. Two remedies alone remain to us,—not to have the slaves of the same country, nor if possible, speaking the same language; in this way they will more easily be held in subjection: secondly, we should tend them carefully, not only out of regard to them, but yet more out of respect to ourselves. And the right treatment of slaves is to behave properly to them, and to do to them, if possible, even more justice than to those who are our equals; for he who naturally and genuinely reverences justice, and hates injustice, is discovered in his dealings with any class of men to whom he can easily be unjust. And he who in regard to the natures and actions of his slaves is undefiled by impiety and injustice, will best sow the seeds of virtue in them; and this may be truly said of every master, and tyrant, and of every other having authority in relation to his inferiors. Slaves ought to be punished as they deserve, and not admonished as if they were freemen, which will only make them conceited. The language used to a servant ought always to be that of a command, and we ought not to jest with them, whether they are males or females—this is a foolish way which many people have of setting up their slaves, and making the life of servitude more disagreeable both for them and for their masters.

[From 'Laws' [*c.*350 BC], in *The Dialogues of Plato*, trs. B. Jowett (Oxford: Clarendon Press, 4th edn, 1953), Vol. IV: 345–6.]

113   Politics

The Thessalian Penestae have often risen against their masters, and the Helots in like manner against the Lacedaemonians, for whose misfortunes they are always lying in wait. Nothing, however, of this kind has as yet happened to the Cretans; the reason probably is that the neighboring cities, even when at war with one another, never form an alliance with rebellious serfs, rebellions not being for their interest, since they themselves have a dependent population. Whereas all the neighbours of the Lacedaemonians, whether Argives, Messenians, or Arcadians, were their enemies. In Thessaly, again, the original revolt of the slaves occurred because the Thessalians were still at war with the neighbouring Achaeans, Perrhaebians and Magnesians. Besides, if there were no other difficulty, the treatment or management of slaves is a troublesome affair; for, if not kept in hand, they are insolent, and think that they are as good as their masters, and, if harshly treated, they hate and conspire against them. Now it is clear that when these are the results the citizens of a state have not found out the secret of managing their subject population.

[From 'Politics' [c.330 BC], in *The Complete Works of Aristotle*, ed. Jonathan Barnes (Princeton: Princeton University Press, 1994), Vol. II: 2014.]

114   The Annals

Soon afterwards one of his own slaves murdered the city-prefect, Pedanius Secundus, either because he had been refused his freedom, for which he had made a bargain, or in the jealousy of a love in which he could not brook his master's rivalry. Ancient custom required that the whole slave-establishment which had dwelt under the same roof should be dragged to execution, when a sudden gathering of the populace, which was for saving so many innocent lives, brought matters to actual insurrection. Even in the Senate there was a strong feeling on the part of those who shrank from extreme rigour, though the majority were opposed to any innovation.

[From 'The Annals' [116], in *The Complete Works of Tacitus*, ed. Moses Hadas, trs. Alfred John Church and William Jackson Brodribb (New York: The Modern Library, 1942), 343.]

The insurrection of the gladiators and the devastation of Italy, commonly called the war of Spartacus, began upon this occasion. One Lentulus Batiates trained up a great many gladiators in Capua, most of them Gauls and Thracians, who, not for any fault by them committed, but simply through the cruelty of their master, were kept in confinement for this object of fighting one with another. Two hundred of these formed a plan to escape, but being discovered, those of them who became aware of it in time to anticipate their master, being seventy-eight, got out of a cook's shop chopping-knives and spits, and made their way through the city, and lighting by the way on several waggons that were carrying gladiators' arms to another city, they seized upon them and armed themselves.

And seizing upon a defensible place, they chose three captains, of whom Spartacus was chief, a Thracian of one of the nomad tribes, and a man not only of high spirit and valiant, but in understanding, also, and in gentleness superior to his condition, and more of a Grecian than the people of his country usually are. When he first came to be sold at Rome, they say a snake coiled itself upon his face as he lay asleep, and his wife, who at this latter time also accompanied him in his flight, his country-woman, a kind of prophetess, and one of those possessed with the bacchanal frenzy, declared that it was a sign portending great and formidable power to him with no happy event.

First, then, routing those that came out of Capua against them, and thus procuring a quantity of proper soldiers' arms, they gladly threw away their own as barbarous and dishonourable. Afterwards Clodius, the prætor, took the command against them with a body of three thousand men from Rome, and besieged them within a mountain, accessible only by one narrow and difficult passage, which Clodius kept guarded, encompassed on all other sides with steep and slippery precipices. Upon the top, however, grew a great many wild vines, and cutting down as many of their boughs as they had need of, they twisted them into strong ladders long enough to reach from thence to the bottom, by which, without any danger, they got down all but one, who stayed there to throw them down their arms, and after this succeeded in saving himself. The Romans were ignorant of all this, and, therefore, coming upon them in the rear, they assaulted them unawares and took their camp. Several, also, of the shepherds and herdsmen that were there, stout and nimble fellows, revolted over to them, to some of whom they gave complete arms, and made use of others as scouts and light-armed soldiers.

Publius Varinus, the prætor, was now sent against them, whose lieutenant, Furius, with two thousand men, they fought and routed. Then Cossinius was sent with considerable forces, to give his assistance and advice, and him Spartacus missed but very little of capturing in person, as he was bathing at Salinæ; for he with great difficulty made his escape, while Spartacus possessed himself of his baggage, and following the chase with a great slaughter, stormed his camp and took it, where Cossinius himself was slain.

After many successful skirmishes with the prætor himself, in one of which he took his lictors and his own horse, he began to be great and terrible; but wisely considering that he was not to expect to match the force of the empire, he marched his army towards the Alps, intending, when he had passed them, that every man should go to his own home, some to Thrace, some to Gaul. But they, grown confident in their numbers, and puffed up with their success, would give no obedience to him, but went about and ravaged Italy; so that now the senate was not only moved at the indignity and baseness, both of the enemy and of the insurrection, but, looking upon it as a matter of alarm and of dangerous consequence, sent out both the consuls to it, as to a great and difficult enterprise.

The consul Gellius, falling suddenly upon a party of Germans, who through contempt and confidence had straggled from Spartacus, cut them all to pieces. But when Lentulus with a large army besieged Spartacus, he sallied out upon him, and, joining battle, defeated his chief officers, and captured all his baggage. As he made toward the Alps, Cassius, who was prætor of that part of Gaul that lies about the Po, met him with ten thousand men, but being overcome in battle, he had much ado to escape himself, with the loss of a great many of his men.

When the senate understood this, they were displeased at the consuls, and ordering them to meddle no further, they appointed Crassus general of the war, and a great many of the nobility went volunteers with him, partly out of friendship, and partly to get honour. He stayed himself on the borders of Picenum, expecting Spartacus would come that way, and sent his lieutenant, Mummius, with two legions, to wheel about and observe the enemy's motions, but upon no account to engage or skirmish. But he, upon the first opportunity, joined battle, and was routed, having a great many of his men slain, and a great many only saving their lives with the loss of their arms.

Crassus rebuked Mummius severely, and arming the soldiers again, he made them find sureties for their arms, that they would part with them no more, and five hundred that were the beginners of the flight he divided into fifty tens, and one of each was to die by lot, thus reviving the ancient Roman punishment of decimation, where ignominy is added to the penalty of death, with a variety of appalling and terrible circumstances, presented before the eyes of the whole army, assembled as spectators.

When he had thus reclaimed his men, he led them against the enemy; but Spartacus retreated through Lucania toward the sea, and in the straights meeting with some Cilician pirate ships, he had thoughts of attempting Sicily, where, by landing two thousand men, he hoped to new kindle the war of the slaves, which was but lately extinguished, and seemed to need but little fuel to set it burning again. But after the pirates had struck a bargain with him, and received his gifts, they deceived him and sailed away. He thereupon retired again from the sea, and established his army in the peninsula of Rhegium; there Crassus came upon him, and considering the nature of the place, which of itself suggested the undertaking, he set to work to build a wall across the isthmus; thus keeping his soldiers at once from idleness and his foes from forage.

This great and difficult work he perfected in a space of time short beyond all expectation, making a ditch from one sea to the other, over the neck of land, three hundred furlongs long, fifteen feet broad, and as much in depth, and above it built a wonderfully high and strong wall. All which Spartacus at first slighted and despised, but when provisions began to fail, and on his proposing to pass further, he found he was walled in, and no more was to be had in the peninsula, taking the opportunity of a snowy, stormy night, he filled up part of the ditch with earth and boughs of trees, and so passed the third part of his army over.

Crassus was afraid lest he should march directly to Rome, but was soon eased of that fear when he saw many of his men break out in a mutiny and quit him, and encamp by themselves upon the Lucanian lake. This lake they say changes at intervals of time, and is sometimes sweet, and sometimes so salt that it cannot be drunk. Crassus falling upon these beat them from the lake, but he could not pursue the slaughter, because of Spartacus suddenly coming up and checking the flight.

Now he began to repent that he had previously written to the senate to call Lucullus out of Thrace, and Pompey out of Spain; so that he did all he could to finish the war before they came, knowing that the honour of the action would redound to him that came to his assistance. Resolving, therefore, first to set upon those that had mutinied and encamped apart, whom Caius Cannicius and Castus commanded, he sent six thousand men before to secure a little eminence, and to do it as privately as possible, which that they might do they covered their helmets, but being discovered by two women that were sacrificing for the enemy, they had been in great hazard, had not Crassus immediately appeared, and engaged in a battle which proved a most bloody one. Of twelve thousand three hundred whom he killed, two only were found wounded in their backs, the rest all having died standing in their ranks and fighting bravely.

Spartacus, after this discomfiture, retired to the mountains of Petelia, but Quintius, one of Crassus's officers, and Scrofa, the quæstor, pursued and overtook him. But when Spartacus rallied and faced them, they were utterly routed and fled, and had much ado to carry off their quæstor, who was wounded. This success, however, ruined Spartacus, because it encouraged the slaves, who now disdained any longer to avoid fighting, or to obey their officers, but as they were upon the march, they came to them with their swords in their hands, and compelled them to lead them back again through Lucania, against the Romans, the very thing which Crassus was eager for.

For news was already brought that Pompey was at hand; and people began to talk openly that the honour of this war was reserved to him, who would come and at once oblige the enemy to fight and put an end to the war. Crassus, therefore, eager to fight a decisive battle, encamped very near the enemy, and began to make lines of circumvallation; but the slaves made a sally and attacked the pioneers. As fresh supplies came in on either side, Spartacus, seeing there was no avoiding it, set all his army in array, and when his horse was brought him, he drew out his sword and killed him, saying, 'if he got the day he should have a great many better horses of the enemies', and if he lost it he should have no need of this. And so making directly towards Crassus himself, through the midst of arms and wounds, he missed him, but slew two centurions that fell upon him together. At last being deserted by those that were about him, he himself stood his ground, and, surrounded by the enemy, bravely defending himself, was cut in pieces.

[From *The Lives of the Noble Grecians and Romans* [c.100–115]
(Chicago: Encyclopedia Britannica, 1952), 442–4.]

JARIR AL-TABARĪ

116   The Revolt of the Zanj

In the early morning of Saturday, the 28th of Ramadān [September 9, 869], ʿAlī set out from [the castle al-Qurashī]. When he had reached the farthest end of the castle precinct, some slaves of one of the Shūrajiyyīn known as al-ʿAṭṭār met him as they were setting about their business. ʿAlī ordered them to be seized, along with their agent, who was placed in fetters. They numbered in all some fifty slaves. ʿAlī next proceeded to a place where al-Sanāʾī worked, and there around five hundred slaves were seized, among them one who was known as Abū Ḥudayd. Their agent was likewise bound with fetters and taken along as well. The place where this occurred was called Nahr al-Mukāthir. ʿAlī proceeded next to a place belonging to al-Sirāfī and captured there another one hundred fifty slaves, among them an individual called Zurayq and another known as Abū al-Khanjar. Then, at a place belonging to Ibn ʿAṭāʾ, Ṭarīq, Ṣubayḥ al-Aʿsar, Rāshid al-Maghribī, and Rāshid al-Qarmaṭī were captured along with eighty more slaves. The next place was that of Ismāʿīl, who was known as a slave of Sahl al-Ṭaḥḥān. ʿAlī continued to operate in this fashion all day until he had amassed a large number of the Shūrajiyyīn slaves.

Assembling them together, 'Alī rose and addressed them, raising their spirits by promising to lead and command them and to give them possession of property. He swore a solemn oath to them that he would neither deceive nor betray them and that they would experience only kind treatment from him. 'Alī then summoned their masters and said to them: 'I wanted to behead you all for the way you have treated these slaves, with arrogance and coercion and, indeed, in ways that Allāh has forbidden, driving them beyond endurance. But my companions have spoken to me about you, and now I have decided to set you free.'

They replied that the slaves were merely habitual runaways, who would flee from 'Alī [at the first opportunity], and then both he and they would be the losers. They said, 'Turn them over to us, and let us pay you compensation for them'. But 'Alī ordered their slaves to bring whips of palm branches and, while their masters and agents were prostrated on the ground, each one was given five hundred lashes. 'Alī extracted a vow from them, on penalty of having to repudiate their wives, that they would neither divulge his whereabouts to anyone nor reveal the size of his following. They were then released and sent on their way to al-Baṣrah.

One of their number, a man named 'Abdallāh and known as Karīkhā, crossed over the Dujayl and warned the Shūrajiyyīn to guard their slaves carefully. There were some fifteen thousand there at the time.

After performing the afternoon prayer 'Alī ventured forth again, and upon reaching the bank of the Dujayl he found there boats laden with compost of dung and ashes (samād) entering port on the rising tide. Together with his partisans he traversed the river in them and then went on to the Nahr Maymūn. He established his quarters in the mosque situated in the middle of the market that stretched along the Nahr Maymūn. He continued efforts to gather blacks (al-sudān) to his camp right up to the time of the prayer breaking the fast of Ramaḍān (salāt al-fitr). On the day of the celebration of the feast he summoned his followers to assemble for prayer. When they had done so, the pole flying his banner was set into the ground. 'Alī prayed with them, and in a sermon (khuṭbah) he recalled the wretched state from which, through him, God had rescued them. 'Alī said that he wanted to improve their condition, giving them slaves (al-'abīd), money, and homes to possess for themselves, and that by them they could achieve the greatest things. He then swore a solemn oath, and when his prayer and sermon were complete he ordered those who had followed his words to instruct those non-Arabic speakers among them who had not understood, in order [also] to raise their spirits. That was done, and 'Alī entered the castle.

A day later he set out for Nahr Būr, where a detachment of his troops encountered a detachment of the [commander] al-Ḥimyarī and drove them off into the desert. The Zanj leader, accompanied by some more troops, joined forces with the others and defeated al-Ḥimyarī and his troops, driving them back as far as the Tigris flats. One of the superintendents of the blacks, called Abū Ṣāliḥ and known as 'the Short,' sought protection for himself and three hundred Zanj. ʿAlī graciously granted this and promised them good fortune. When the numbers of Zanj who had been thus gathered together increased significantly, he appointed leaders for them and said that, for each of them who brought another Zanj, he would be attached to him.

It is also said that ʿAlī did not appoint his commanders until after the battle of slaves (al-khawal) in Bayān and his move to Sabkhat al-Qandal.

[. . .]

Among the momentous encounters that he later had with the forces of the central authorities was one against the Turk Abū Hilāl in Sūq al-Rayyān. One of the Zanj commanders called Rayḥān reported that this Turk had arrived in Sūq al-Rayyān at the head of a force of some four thousand men or more. They were preceded by a group of people wearing bright clothes and sporting flags and drums. The blacks led a ferocious attack against the Turk. One of the blacks fell upon the people's standard-bearer, felling him with blows from the two cudgels he was carrying. The crowd fled, while the blacks pursued their onslaught on Abū Hilāl's troops, slaying nearly one thousand five hundred of them. One of the blacks chased after Abū Hilāl, who managed to save himself by escaping on a horse bareback. Then the darkness of night descended between the blacks and those who had escaped. In the morning the pursuit resumed, and the blacks returned with heads and prisoners, all of whom were then killed.

Following this engagement there occurred another involving the Zanj against the troops of the central authorities, in which ʿAlī b. Muḥammad was also victorious. According to what one of the Zanj leader's commanders reported, the affair commenced as follows. The commander, whose name was Rayḥān, said, 'One night during the course of the year,' (which we have mentioned was one in which his rebellion commenced) ʿAlī b. Muḥammad heard the sound of a dog barking at the gates [of a dwelling owned by] ʿAmr b. Masʿadah. He ordered an inquiry into the source of the barking and sent one of his followers to investigate. He later returned with the news that he had seen nothing at all, and then the barking resumed.'

Rayḥān continued: 'ʿAli then called for me to go to the source of the barking, for it seemed as though the dog barked only at someone it could see. So I set out and suddenly came upon the dog, standing on a breakwater (al-musannah), although I could see nothing else. And then I spied a man sitting on some steps. I spoke to him, and, when he heard me addressing him in Arabic, he replied, introducing himself as Sayrān b. ʿAfwiallāh. He said he had brought letters for ʿAli b. Muhammad from his partisans in al-Baṣrah, he had been one of his associates during ʿAlī's sojourn in al-Baṣrah. So I took him to ʿAlī, who read the correspondence he was carrying. ʿAlī asked Sayrān about al-Zaynabī and the numbers of men he had. He said that al-Zaynabī was mustering a large force of slaves, volunteers, and the factions of the Bilāliyyah and the Saʿdiyyah, which was going to be despatched against ʿAlī at Bayān. ʿAlī told Sayrān to lower his voice lest the slaves be frightened by his news. He then inquired who was to lead this army and was told that one Abū Manṣūr, a Hāshimite *mawlā*, had been selected for the post. Asked whether he had seen this force, Sayrān replied that he had and added that they were also equipped with ropes to bind the hands of any blacks they captured. ʿAlī then told Sayrān to return to the place where he was staying, and he wandered off to ʿAlī b. Abān, Muḥammad b. Salm, and Yaḥyā b. Muḥammad and engaged in discussing matters with them until the dawn broke.'

The Zanj leader then set out to spy upon this new force. When he reached the far side of Tursā, Barsūna, and Sandādān Bayān, a detachment came out to do battle with him. ʿAlī b. Abān was ordered to engage the enemy, and he routed them, capturing from among them one hundred blacks.

Rayḥān resumed: 'I heard ʿAlī b. Muḥammad say to his followers that what they had witnessed was one of the signs of perfection of their mission—that is, the arrival of the detachment with their slaves, who were surrendered into their hands, God increasing thereby the numbers of his own forces. Then the Zanj proceeded until they reached Bayān.'

[. . .]

On Monday, the 14th of Dhū al-Qaʿdah (October 24, 869), the people of al-Baṣrah assembled together and went forth in the wake of what they regarded as a triumph over the Zanj the previous day. The man selected to lead the expedition was a Baṣran by the name of Ḥammād al-Sājī, a sailor experienced in operating and fighting from barges. The force comprised volunteers, archers, people from the main mosque, those from the Bilāliyyah and Saʿdiyyah factions prepared to follow Ḥammād, and onlookers from the Hāshimites, Qurayshites, and other sections of the populace. Three barges were loaded with archers who crowded on board, eager to get to the scene of battle. A mob proceeded on foot, some bearing arms while others were mere spectators without weapons. The barges and boats entered the Umm Ḥabīb canal on the tide after sunset that same day. The procession of foot soldiers and spectators along the canal bank was so dense and numerous that they blocked from view everything in front of them. The Zanj leader had stationed himself on the canal known as al-Shayṭān.

Muḥammad b. al-Ḥasan said the Zanj leader told him that, when his scouts had arrived and he knew of the approaching crowd, he sent off Zurayq and Abū al-Layth al-Iṣbahānī with a detachment of troops along the east bank of the [Shayṭān] canal, and Shibl and Ḥusayn al-Ḥammāmī with another detachment along the western bank. Both parties were to set up ambushes. ʿAlī b. Abān was ordered to take the remainder of his troops to intercept the enemy. They should, however, crouch down facing the enemy, guarding themselves with their shields, allowing no one to attack until the adversaries were close enough to brandish swords at them. When the situation had developed in this way, the Zanj attacked the enemy. The Zanj leader gave orders to the two ambuscades that when the throng [on the banks] were abreast of them and they heard their own troops on the attack, they should emerge on both sides of the canal shouting at the enemy. The Zanj women were ordered to gather bricks and keep the men supplied with them.

Muḥammad b. al-Ḥasan said that after this incident the leader of the Zanj told his followers, 'That day, as I beheld the mob approaching, I was gripped by a terrible fear, such an overwhelming terror that I appealed [to God] for help. I was accompanied by only a few troops, among them Muṣliḥ, and there was not one among us who did not imagine that he was going to meet his doom. Muṣliḥ marveled at the size of the multitude and I motioned to him to contain himself. As the enemy neared, I cried out, "Oh God, this is the hour of trial, so come to my aid!" I had scarcely finished saying this when I saw white birds sweep down upon the enemy, and one of the galleys overturned, and all on board were drowned. The barges met the same fate. My troops then fell upon the enemy they were heading for, shouting at them.' The ambushers emerged from their hiding places on the canal banks behind the boats and the foot soldiers, clubbing those among them and onlookers on shore who tried to flee. A group here was drowned, a group there was killed, while others who fled toward the canal seeking rescue were overtaken by the sword. Those who resisted were slain, while those who ventured into the water were drowned. The foot soldiers on the canal's edge who sought escape in the water were either killed or drowned until most of the enemy forces had been annihilated. None but the odd fugitive was saved. The numbers of Baṣrans missing soared as their wives raised a chorus of lament.

People spoke of this day as the Day of the Barges (yawm al-shadhā). They were horrified by the number killed that day. Among the innumerable host killed were a number of sons of the Hāshimite Ja'far b. Sulaymān and forty famous archers.

The abominable one had the heads [of the slain] collected. He displayed them so that relatives of the deceased who came to him could claim those they recognized. For the rest, which no one claimed, he put aboard a flat-bottomed boat (jarībiyyah), filling it up. The boat was released on the falling tide from the Umm Ḥabīb canal, where it drifted toward al-Baṣrah, stopping at Mashra'ah al-Qayyār. People came and recovered the heads of those they recognized.

After this day the enemy of God became ever more powerful as fear of him gripped the Baṣrans' hearts. They abstained from further battle with him, but the central authorities were informed of his escapades, and Ju'lān al-Turkī was sent with reinforcements to the Baṣrans. Ju'lān ordered Abū al-Aḥwaṣ al-Bāhilī to proceed to al-Ubullah as governor, sending as support a Turk called Jurayḥ.

The abominable one alleged that his followers had boasted to him in the wake of this [recent] battle that they had slaughtered the entire fighting force of al-Baṣrah save for the weak and incapacitated. 'Give us permission to storm the city,' they demanded. 'Alī b. Muḥammad berated them and decried their request. 'On the contrary,' he scolded, 'get as far away from al-Baṣrah as possible, we have instilled fear and terror in them, and now you are safe. The thing to do now is forsake war with them until they come looking for you'. Then he withdrew his forces to a salt flat at the farthest edge of the network of canals and them went on to the al-Hājir canal.

[From 'The Revolt of the Zanj,' in *The History of Al-Tabarī* [c.880–915], trs. David Waines (Albany: State University of New York Press, 1992), Vol. 36: 36–8, 50–2, 64–7.]

GONZALO FERNÁNDEZ DE OVIEDO Y VALDÉS

117   Rebellion in Santo Domingo

The rebellion of the blacks was a surprising occurrence on this island and the beginning of much evil, if God had not stopped it. And there would not be any reason that such a noteworthy thing would fail to be written about because if what happened were kept quiet, then the service that some very honorable men of this city performed would be kept quiet as well. And because this offense could not rest with me, nor could it be thought that because of me the truth of the event remained to be investigated, I will say what in this case I have been able to find out about the persons who had a hand in it; and he who reads this may be certain, that if something is left unsaid, that it will be the fault of those that give information and not of the one who writes. Therefore I will relate the substance of this movement and disturbance of the blacks on the sugar plantation of the admiral Diego Colón: that this rising was initiated by his slaves (and not by all whom he owned), and I will say what I found out about this subject from the admiral himself and other gentlemen and important men, and it is this.

Up to twenty of the admiral's blacks, most of them of the Wolof tongue, by agreement, on the second day of the Nativity of Christ, at the beginning of the year one thousand five hundred twenty two, left the sugar plantation and went to join with such others who were allied with them in a certain place. [The revolt actually broke out on December 25, 1521.] And after they gathered together, up to forty of them killed some unsuspecting Christians in the country and continued along the road to the town of Azua.

The news was heard in this city, by a warning given by the licentiate Cristóbal Lebrón, who was on his own sugar plantation. And with the evil purpose and work of the blacks known, the admiral mounted his horse and pursued them, with a very few on horseback and on foot. But, due to the diligence of the admiral and good support from the Royal Tribunal, all the gentlemen and noblemen, and all those who had a horse in the city and around the district followed him.

And the second day, after it was known here, the admiral went to stop at the edge of the river Nizao, and there found out that the blacks had arrived at a cattle ranch of Melchor Castro, a senior notary of mines and citizen of this city, at nine leagues from here, where they killed a Christian mason, who was working there, and they took from that ranch a black slave and another twelve Indian slaves and robbed the house. And having done all the damage that they could, they moved on, doing the same thing and availing themselves of that which was not offered in order to make things worse.

In the course of their travels after nine Christians had died, they stopped one league from Ocoa, where stands the great sugar plantation of licentiate Zuazo, a judge on the Royal Tribunal, with the result that on the following day, at dawn, the rebellious blacks were planning to strike at that sugar plantation and kill eight or ten Christians who were there and reinforce themselves with more blacks. And they could do it, because there were more than a hundred and twenty blacks on the sugar plantation, with whom, if they were to join forces, they planned to go against the town of Azua and put it to the knife and take possession of the land, joining themselves with many other blacks from other sugar plantations who might be found in the town. Without a doubt they would have joined together in their evil attempt, if Divine Providence did not remedy it in the manner in which it was remedied.

Therefore, the admiral, having arrived at the Nizao riverbank as has been said, and aware of damage that the blacks were doing along the road they were taking, agreed to stop there that night, so that the people with him could rest and those who remained behind could catch up to him, in order to leave from there at the break of dawn in pursuit of the evildoers.

It is known that among those who found themselves there with the admiral was Melchor de Castro, citizen of the city, spoken of above, whose estate and ranch had been damaged. And how his own hardship pained him (above and beyond that common to all who were preparing themselves). He agreed to advance with two others on horseback without saying anything to the admiral (because he thought that if he asked his leave, he would not give it to him nor would he allow him to advance alone), leaving the admiral where it has been stated.

There he joined with another Christian on horseback and he resolved to go forward, and from there he sent word to the admiral that he was going in pursuit of the blacks with three men on horseback who were with him, and that he was requesting that he send him some people, because he was going determined to engage the blacks, inasmuch as the Christians and his lordship were to arrive and since he and those with him were few. This being known by the admiral, he sent him nine men on horseback and seven peons, who reaching him and now joining with Melchor de Castro, amounted to twelve on horseback, and they followed the blacks to where it has been said they were.

Among these people on horseback sent by the admiral to accompany Melchor de Castro to stop the rebelling blacks was the notable Francisco Dávila, citizen of this city, who is now one of its magistrates, and proceeding on their way, at the time that daylight broke over the horizon, they found themselves faced with the blacks who, as these gentlemen perceived, led themselves, and with a great shout, forming into a troop, they engaged those on horseback. The gentlemen, seeing the battle prepared, without waiting for the admiral for the reasons I had said and not waiting for the blacks to join themselves to the blacks of that sugar plantation, they determined to rout them, and gripped their shields and fixed their lances to charge, calling on God and the apostle Santiago, all twelve of them on horseback, made into a small troop of cavalry, but brave men, stirrup to stirrup, reins at the gallop, who went the middle of the battalion against all those blacks, who engaged them with great energy, resisting the sally of the Christians. But the horsemen broke through them and passed to the other side. And from this first encounter some of the slaves fell, but they did not stop forming themselves into groups, throwing rocks and staffs and darts, and with another great cry, they met the second charge of the Christian horsemen, which did not break them, and for that reason notwithstanding their resistance with many tempered staffs that they were throwing, the horsemen turned back upon them, with the same cry to Santiago, and with much courage coursing through them, they turned around to break through them again, passing through the middle of the rebels. These blacks, seeing themselves so unexpectedly separated one from the other and with so much determination and boldness from so few and such brave horsemen, they [the blacks], besieged and defeated, did not dare to wait for the third encounter, which already was being executed. And turning their backs, taking flight through some stones and rocks that were close to where this defeat happened, and the field and the victory remained with the Christians, and there spread out dead, six blacks, and many others of them were wounded. And the said Melchor de Castro, whose left arm they injured with a rod, remained badly wounded.

And the victors remained there on the field until daylight, because as the night was very dark and the terrain was rugged and wooded, they could not see those who were fleeing, nor where they were going. But without withdrawing themselves from the same place where this had happened, Melchor de Castro issued a call, through the voice of one of his cowherds, to his black slave and Indians whom the blacks had stolen from his ranch. And then since the voice was known from he who called them, it gathered them together, and they all came, because being there close by, hidden among the bushes, and from hearing him and recognizing his voice, they reassured themselves, and they went to their lord with great pleasure.

Therefore when it was full daylight, Melchor de Castro and Francisco Dávila and the few on horseback who found themselves in this honorable peril left for the sugar plantation of licentiate Alonso Zuazo to rest, and the admiral and the people who were going with him that day arrived almost at the hour of vespers. And from what was done, all the Christians gave much thanks to Our Lord God for the victory taken. For although these rebelling blacks were not many in number, they were on the way, with their evil intention and work, to where, within fifteen days without being restrained, they would be so many and so difficult to subdue that it would not be possible to do so without expending much time and many Christian lives. God be praised for the good result of this victory, that in its nature was very great.

The admiral ordered Melchor de Castro to come to the city of Santo Domingo in order that he be healed, so he came. And the admiral, remaining in the field, searched for the blacks who had escaped from the battle and who were guilty with such diligence that in five or six days they were all returned, and he ordered them executed and they remained planted at intervals along that road on many gibbets.

But since those who escaped from the battle had hidden themselves in rugged places, it was necessary that people follow them on foot, which was done by captain Pedro Ortíz de Matienzo, who followed them and fought with them and killed some, and captured those to whom he administered the justice that I have said.

And in truth, this gentleman conducted himself very manfully in this, given the difficulty and the ruggedness of the terrain where he reached and defeated the fugitives. In such a manner that the diligence of Melchor de Castro (by virtue of God and his strength and of Francisco Dávila, who went to the aid and support of the captain, as is said, [and] of those eight gentlemen who, joined with Melchor de Castro, were twelve horsemen), the conquest came to such a good end and victory, as has been said. And the punishment was executed to perfection by the brave officer who pursued the blacks and killed some of them and captured the rest, to place them on the gallows and gibbets.

And this punishment being done, the admiral returned to this city, in which he discharged very well his duty to God and their Majesties and to those with whom he lived. And in this manner, the blacks who rose up, were punished in accordance with their audacity and madness, and henceforth all the rest were frightened and assured of what will be done to them, if such a thing were to cross their minds, without any more delay in punishing them than the time it would take for their luck to run out on discovery of their wickedness.

[From 'Rebellion of the slaves of the sugar plantation of Diego Colón (Santo Domingo, 25 December 1521),' *Historia general y natural de las Indies* [1535] (Santo Domingo: Patronato de la Ciudad de Santo Domingo Coleccion Quinto Centenaris, 1994), 219–24. Trs. Evelyn Powell Jennings.]

ROBERT EDGAR CONRAD

118   Children of God's Fire

The great seventeenth-century quilombo *of Palmares: a chronicle of war and peace*

[T]hroughout the history of Brazilian slavery countless slaves sought release from servitude in runaway-slave settlements known as *quilombos* or *mocambos*. Certain features were common to these *quilombos*, whether they were tiny isolated clusters of huts or larger more permanent villages and towns. African culture, evident wherever slaves existed, could flourish freely in such places, although European, Christian, and Indian cultural influences were often strong. Safety from slave hunters was normally more dependent upon favorable geography than upon weapons or tactics, but defense systems, sometimes elaborate and usually African in nature, were characteristic. Leaders were often chosen from among the bravest, wisest persons, some of whom were reputed to have been kings or queens in Africa, and in long-surviving *quilombos* leadership could become hereditary. Domestic animals, notably chickens and pigs, well-tended gardens, stores of food, and fishing and hunting equipment were common adjuncts, supplying fugitives with diets probably far better than those they had known on their masters' plantations. Often located near towns of plantations, *quilombos* at times maintained trade contacts with local merchants and other persons wishing to aid them or to profit from their plight. *Quilombolas* (the inhabitants of *quilombos*) often attacked nearby settlements or plantations to acquire supplies or women. Both to re-enslave them and to eliminate the danger they represented, government forces, bush captains (*capitães-do-mato*), or bands of volunteers often carried out raids against them, resulting in numerous reports of expeditions which are the principal source of information about them.

The following selection is an account of a network of runaway settlements and strongholds which together were known as Palmares, literally 'palm groves'. These settlements were established in the backlands of northeastern

Brazil in the early seventeenth century, and during the long wars against Holland grew and thrived. This narrative is particularly fascinating for the account it gives of a peace treaty entered into in 1678 by one Gangasuma (Ganga-Zumba), the king of Palmares, with the Portuguese governor of Pernambuco. This pact, which recognized the freedom of blacks born in Palmares, was similar to treaties of metropolitan governments made with black fugitives in Mexico, Venezuela, St. Domingue, Jamaica, and elsewhere in the Americas. Unfortunately, peace between the Portuguese and the runaways was not permanent. In 1690 a new campaign was begun against the settlements, the principal stronghold was surrounded and captured in 1694, and resistance ended the following year with the capture of the *zumbi* or war chief, who was later executed.

Published in the *Revista do Instituto Histórico e Geográfico Brasileiro* in 1876, this chronicle of war and peace was written in the late seventeenth century by an unnamed writer. The original manuscript (Codex CXVI-2-13) was found in the Biblioteca Pública in Evora, Portugal.

In a palm forest sixteen leagues northeast of Porto Calvo existed the *mocambo* of the Zambi (a general or god of arms in their language), and five leagues farther north that of Acainene (this was the name of the king's mother, who lived in this fortified *mocambo* about twenty-five leagues northeast of Porto Calvo, and which they called the Acainene Compound, since it was fortified by a wall of earth and sticks).

To the east of these was the *mocambo* of the Wild Canes [Tabocas], and northeast of this one that of Bambiabonga. Eight leagues north of Bambiabonga was the compound called Sucupira; six leagues northward from this the Royal Compound of the Macaco [monkey], and five leagues to the west of this the *mocambo* of Osenga. Nine leagues northwest of the town of Serinhaem was the compound of Amaro, and twenty-five leagues northwest of Alagôas the palm forest of Andolaquituxe, the Zambi's brother.

Among all these places, which were the largest and best-fortified, there were others of less importance and with fewer people. It is widely believed that when blacks were first brought into the captaincies of Brazil they began to live in these Palmares, and it is certain that during the period of Dutch rule their numbers greatly increased.

They called their king Gangasuma (a hybrid term meaning 'great lord' composed of the Angolan or Bunda word 'gang' and the Tupi [Indian] word 'assú'). This king lived in a royal city which they called Macaco. This was the main city among the other towns or *mocambos*, and it was completely surrounded by a wall of earth and sticks.

The second city was that known as Sucupira (later the camp of Good Jesus and the Cross founded by Fernão Carrilho). Here lived the Gangasona, the king's brother. Like the latter, all the cities were under the command of rulers and powerful chiefs, who lived in them and governed them.

Sucupira, the war command center where the confederation's defense forces and sentinels were trained, was also fortified, but with stone and wood. Nearly a league in length, it contained within its boundaries three lofty mountains and a river called Cachingi, meaning 'an abundance of water'.

Before the restoration of Pernambuco from Dutch rule, twenty-five probing expeditions were sent into the area, suffering great losses but failing to uncover the secrets of those brave people. . . . The first was that of Captain Braz da Rocha Cardoso with six hundred men. Little was accomplished by this expedition because of the difficulties of the terrain, the roughness of the trails, and the impossibility of transporting equipment over unknown country. It merely served to show what would have to be overcome in future attempts.

[. . .]

The inhabitants of Alagôas, Porto Calvo, and Penedo were constantly under attack, and their houses and plantations robbed by the blacks of Palmares. The blacks killed their cattle and carried away their slaves to enlarge their *quilombos* and increase the number of their defenders, forcing the inhabitants and natives of those towns to engage in fighting at a distance of forty leagues or more, at great cost to their plantations and risk to their own lives, without which the blacks would have become masters of the captaincy because of their huge and ever-increasing numbers.

[From *Children of God's Fire: A Documentary History of Black Slavery in Brazil* (Princeton: Princeton University Press, 1983), 366–70.]

<hr>

119   Negro Insurrection in South Carolina

Sometime since there was a Proclamation published at Augustine, in which the King of Spain (then at Peace with Great Britain) promised Protection and Freedom to all Negroes Slaves that would resort thither. Certain Negroes belonging to Captain Davis escaped to Augustine, and were received there. They were demanded by General Oglethorpe who sent Lieutenant Demere to Augustine, and the Governour assured the General of his sincere Friendship, but at the same time showed his Orders from the Court of Spain, by which he was to receive all Run away Negroes. Of this other Negroes having notice, as it is believed, from the Spanish Emissaries, four or five who were Cattel-Hunters, and knew the Woods, some of whom belonged to Captain Macpherson, ran away with His Horses, wounded his Son and killed another Man. These marched f [*sic*] for Georgia, and were pursued, but the Rangers being then newly reduced [*sic*] the Countrey people could not overtake them, though they were discovered by the Saltzburghers, as they passed by Ebenezer. They reached Augustine, one only being killed and another wounded by the Indians in their flight. They were received there with great honours, one of them had a Commission given to him, and a Coat faced with Velvet.

Amongst the Negroe Slaves there are a people brought from the Kingdom of Angola in Africa, many of these speak Portugueze [which Language is as near Spanish as Scotch is to English,] by reason that the Portugueze have considerable Settlement, and the Jesuits have a Mission and School in that Kingdom and many Thousands of the Negroes there profess the Roman Catholic Religion. Several Spaniards upon diverse Pretences have for some time past been strolling about Carolina, two of them, who will give no account of themselves have been taken up and committed to Jayl in Georgia. The good reception of the Negroes at Augustine was spread about, Several attempted to escape to the Spaniards, & were taken, one of them was hanged at Charles Town. In the latter end of July last Don Pedro, Colonel of the Spanish Horse, went in a Launch to Charles Town under pretence of a message to General Oglethorpe and the Lieutenant Governour.

On the 9th day of September last [1739] being Sunday which is the day the Planters allow them to work for themselves, Some Angola Negroes assembled, to the number of Twenty; and one who was called Jemmy was their Captain, they suprized a Warehouse belonging to Mr. Hutchenson at a place called Stonehow [sic]; they there killed Mr. Robert Bathurst, and Mr. Gibbs, plundered the House and took a pretty many small Arms and Powder, which were there for Sale. Next they plundered and burnt Mr. Godfrey's house, and killed him, his Daughter and Son. They then turned back and marched Southward along Pons Pons, which is the Road through Georgia to Augustine, they passed Mr. Wallace's Taxern towards day break, and said they would not hurt him, for he was a good Man and kind to his Slaves, but they broke open and plundered Mr. Lemy's House, and killed him, his wife and Child. They marched on towards Mr. Rose's resolving to kill him; but he was saved by a Negroe, who having hid him went out and pacified the others. Several Negroes joyned them, they calling out Liberty, marched on with Colours displayed, and two Drums beating, pursuing all the white people they met with, and killing Man Woman and Child when they could come up to them. Collonel Bull Lieutenant Governour of South Carolina, who was then riding along the Road, discovered them, was pursued, and with much difficulty escaped & raised the Countrey. They burnt Colonel Hext's house and killed his Overseer and his Wife. They then burnt Mr. Sprye's house, then Mr. Sacheverell's, and then Mr. Nash's house, all lying upon the Pons Pons Road, and killed all the white People they found in them. Mr. Bullock got off, but they burnt his House, by this time many of them were drunk with the Rum they had taken in the Houses. They increased every minute by new Negroes coming to them, so that they were above Sixty, some say a hundred, on which they halted in a field, and set to dancing, Singing and beating Drums, to draw more Negroes to them, thinking they were now victorious over the whole Province, having marched ten miles & burnt all before them without Opposition, but the Militia being raised, the Planters with great briskness pursued them and when they came up, dismounting; charged them on foot. The Negroes were soon routed, though they behaved boldly several being killed on the Spot, many ran back to their Plantations thinking they had not been missed, but they were there taken and [sic] Shot, Such as were taken in the field also, were after being examined, shot on the Spot, And this is to be said to the honour of the Carolina Planters, that notwithstanding the Provocation they had received from so many Murders, they did not torture one Negroe, but only put them to an easy death. All that proved to be forced & were not concerned in the Murders & Burnings were pardoned, And this sudden Courage in the field, & the Humanity afterwards hath had so good an Effect that there hath been no farther Attempt, and the very Spirit of Revolt seems over. About 30 escaped from the fight, of which ten marched about 30 miles Southward, and being overtaken by the Planters on horseback, fought stoutly for some time and were all killed on the Spot. The rest are yet untaken. In the whole action about 40 Negroes and 20 whites were killed. The Lieutenant Governour sent an account of this to General Oglethorpe, who met the advices on his return from the Indian Nation He immediately ordered a Troop of Rangers to be ranged, to patrole through Georgia, placed some Men in the Garrison at Palichocolas, which was before abandoned, and near which the Negroes formerly passed, being the only place where Horses can come to swim over the River Savannah for near 100 miles, ordered out the Indians in pursuit, and a Detachment of the Garrison at Port Royal to assist the Planters on any Occasion, and published a Proclamation ordering all the Constables &c. of Georgia to pursue and seize all Negroes, with a Reward for any that should be taken. It is hoped these measures will prevent any Negroes from getting down to the Spaniards.

[From the Georgia State Legislature, 'An Account of the Negroe Insurrection in South Carolina (1739),' *The Colonial Records of the State of Georgia, 1737–40* (New York: AMS Press, 1970), Vol. 22, Part II: 232–6.]

120   The London Magazine

In Holland they have lately had advice from their island of Curassoa [sic] in the West Indies, that about 2 or 300 of the Negroes in that island had entered into a conspiracy to murder most of the white people, in order to make themselves masters of the island. They chose one to whom they gave the name of captain, and charged him with the direction of the undertaking; and they thought themselves so sure of success, that several of them began to behave in the most insolent manner to their masters, which occasioned a suspicion, and then a discovery of the plot. The captain and many of the conspirators were immediately seized, and the rest fled to the woods. The captain had his flesh first pinched with red hot pincers, and then was broke alive upon the wheel; 38 of the others were broke alive upon the wheel, their bodies burnt, and their heads fixed upon stakes, on the 11th, 15th, and 20th of July last [1750]; those that fled to the woods have been since hunted out and killed; and about 13 of the inhabitants who were base enough to conspire with the Negroes, have only been banished the island, and their effects confiscated; tho' they certainly of all others deserved the most severe punishment.

[From *The London Magazine: or, Gentleman's Monthly Intelligencer* 19 (1750), 479.]

DOUGLAS HALL

121   In Miserable Slavery

Of slave unrest there was no word. The usual militia exercises were, as usual, rather infrequently attended; the maroon parties were scarcely seen at Egypt [an estate in Jamaica], having paid only one visit, on the morning of Friday, 1st February when they were entertained with some grog; and the restrictions on the slaves were not always observed.

Friday, 14th March, 1760: Sold Old Sharper the gun I bought from driver Quashe many years ago. He gave me only 10s. for her but paid ready money. He will soon shoot aligators &c. enough at Hill.

On Sunday, 20th May, Thistlewood rode to Paul Island estate and dined with Mr John Parkinson. While there:

About 4 p.m. Mr Roberts come home from his mountain, and brought news of a supposed insurrection tomorrow, when 3,000 Negroe men were to muster in a certain place, from Hanover and this Parish, &c. Told him, by a strange Negro man who came to him in the mountain. In the evening rode home.

There was not, it would appear, much credence given to Mr Roberts' account. It had been a peaceful crop season, just over, and now was the time for relaxation. Perhaps, hopefully, it was just another of those rumours which, from time to time, lent excitement to the conversations of the whites. But was it?

Not so many days before, at about 1 a.m. on Easter Monday morning, Tacky, a Coromantee slave on Frontier Estate in the parish of St Mary, had led a small band of his fellows from Frontier and the adjacent Trinity Estates down into Port Maria. There, they had attacked the fort, killed the sentinel, and captured a large quantity of arms and ammunition. They then moved inland attracting increasing numbers as they went firing through the estates—Trinity, Frontier, Ballards Valley, Esher, and Haywood Hall where they stopped to rest, to celebrate, and to eat. Meanwhile, 'about 130 Whites and trusty Blacks, tolerably armed' had been mustered and were following in pursuit. News had also been sent to the Governor in Spanish Town and two companies of regular troops and a band of Maroons from the central Maroon settlement at Scotts Hall had been dispatched in aid.

Militia, troops, and Maroons attacked Tacky's forces and eventually scattered them into nearby woods where Davy, a Maroon sharp shooter, shot and killed Tacky. His followers were soon defeated.

The revolt was discovered to have been part of an island-wide plan and before all the fighting was over in late September there had been uprisings in St Thomas in the East, St John, Kingston, St James, Hanover, and, on a scale almost equal to that of St Mary, in Westmoreland. By then, over 50 whites had been killed and nearly 400 slaves had lost their lives in battle or in terrible punishments including mutilations, gibbetings, and slow burnings.

The rebel slaves, strengthened by charms provided by obeahmen had fought and died with great courage. Tacky had been killed, but:

... some others of the ringleaders being taken, and a general inclination to revolt appearing among all the Koromantyn Negroes in the island, it was thought necessary to make a few terrible examples of some of the most guilty ... [of three found guilty killing the whites employed on Ballard's Valley] one was condemned to be burnt, and the other two to be hung up alive in irons and left to perish in that dreadful situation. The wretch that was burnt was made to sit on the ground, and his body being chained to an iron stake, the fire was applied to his feet. He uttered not a groan, and saw his legs reduced to ashes with the utmost firmness and composure; after which, one of his arms by some means getting loose, he snatched a brand from the fire that was consuming him, and flung it in the face of the executioner.

By the end of May the revolt had broken out in Westmoreland. Mr Robert's news was accurate. For the next weeks we take Mr Thistlewood's record of events in that parish.

Monday, 26th May 1760: Soon after midnight Messrs Say, Bowen, Walker & Rumbold called me up and told me of Mr Smith at Capt. Forest's being murdered by the Negroes (Mr Smith shot about $\frac{1}{4}$ before ten o'clock); Capt. Hoar sadly chopped, &c. Capt. George Richardson, and Thos. Barnes, &c. running to the Bay on foot, a narrow escape they had. When we reached Col Barclay's I galloped back immediately to Egypt, and secured my keys, writings &c. which had before neglected in my fright, because those who called me were some almost without clothes, and rode bare-back, telling me I should probably be murdered in a short time, &c. &c. Soon returned after I had put my things in order as well as I could, and was down at the Bay about 2 o'clock. Did duty till daylight then was set at liberty by Mr Antrobus to go home and take care of the estate. John Groves, the madman, shot at several Negro boys, wounded Oliver, Mr John Cunningham's waiting-boy. Went to the bay without my orders., &c. but in the evening he returned. The soldiers were soon despatched after the rebellious Negroes. Sailors and militia halted at Egypt, gave them 6 or 8 pails of grog, had a silver spoon stole in the hurry &c. &c. This happened about 9 a.m.

Gave our Negroes today. Strange various reports with torments & confusion.

Mr Walker dined at Egypt. Gave one John Turge, belonging to the [ship] Peter Beckford, Capt. Lovelace, also, dinner. p.m. Mr Walker went away, but John Turge, John Groves, and a sailor who had fallen asleep in the bush and lost his arms, had supper and kept watch by turn all night.

Had 4 Negro men kept watch at the Hothouse door, pen gate, wash house door, and curing house door, & had the words 'all's well' passed.

Vast numbers of people belonging to the Troop, Militia, called, &c. Frequent alarms fired, &c. Vast number of dispatches passing, &c.

[From *In Miserable Slavery: Thomas Thistlewood in Jamaica, 1750–86* (London: Macmillan, 1989), 96–8.]

122 Narrative of a Five Years Expedition

[A]t 10 OClock [August 25, 1775 in Suriname] we met a small Party of the rebels, with each, a Green Hamper on his Back, Who having fired at us Without we Returned it, let drop Down their Bundles And took to their Heels, back towards their Village, And whom we since Learned were Transporting *Rice* to Another Settlement to Subsist *Boneys* people, When they Should be Drove from this Call'd *Gado-Saby* & which they Dayly expected since they had been Discovered by Capt Heyland—The Green Hampers / which were most Curiously Plaited with the Manicole Leafs and which they Call *Warimbo's* / Our men Cut open With their Sabres, from which Actually burst forth the most Beautiful Clean'd Rice, that ever I Saw, Which was Scattered and trampled under Foot, we having no Opportunity to Carry it Along—A Little After this we Saw an empty shade Where an out guard had been kept to give intelligence of the Approach of an Enemy, but Which Deserted theyr Post—We now Vigourously redoubled our Pace till About 12, OClock when two more Musquet Shot were Fired by an Advance Guard of the Enemy as a Signal to *Bony* of our Approach—& A Little again after w^h we Came to a fine field with Rice india Corn &—Viz, Major Medler, and Myself, with the Van Guard, and a Party of the Rangers; We here made a Halt for the *two* Colonels, And to Let up the Long rear some of Whom were at Least 2 Miles Behind us; However in About half an hour we all got together, and we on[c]e more Proceeded by Cutting through a Small Defile of Wood, into Which we no sooner had Entered, than / Ding Dang/ the firing at last Commenced from every Side, the Rebels retiring and we Advancing till finally we Arrived, in the most beautiful Oblong Square field with Rice in full ripeness that ever I saw in my Life, And in Which Appear'd to our View the Rebel Town at a Distance in the form of an Amphitheatre Shelterd by the foliage of a few Ranks of Lofty Trees, Which they had left Standing, the whole Presenting a truly Romantick and Enchanting *Coup Doeuil* to the Unconcerned Spectator—In this field the firing now lasted like one Continued Peal of Thunder for near 40 Minutes, During Which time the Rangers Acted with Wonderful Skill, And Gallantry, While the White Soldiers were too much Animated, the one firing over the other at Random.

[. . .]

The Stratagem of the Enemy in Surrounding and interspearcing the field by the Large Trunks, and the Roots of Fallen Trees we met with made our Advancing verry Different and Dangerous & at the Back of Which Fortifications they lay Lurking, and firing upon us Without themselves Could be Materially hurted, And over Numbers of which Timbers we had to Scramble before we Could Come to the Town; However we keept Advancing, and While I thought this excellent Generalship in them their Superstitious Simplicity Surprised me much of Which I'l only Relate one instance—A poor Fellow trusting in his *Amulet* or *Charm*, by Which he thought himself invulnerable Advanced frequently on one of these trees, till very near us, And having Discharg'd his Piece Walk'd off the Way he Came, to Reload With the Greatest Confidence and Deliberation, till at Last one of my men—/an intrepid Walloon named *Valet*/ With a Ball Broke the bone of his Thigh, And down he Came, now Crawling for Shelter Under the Same Tree which had Suported him but the Soldier Went up to him instantly and Placing the Muzzle of his Musket in his Mouth, blew out his Brains & in Which manner Severals of his Countrymen were Knock'd Down.

[. . .]

In Short being now about to Enter the Town, a Rebel Captain wearing a Tarnish'd Gold Laced hat, & Carrying a Wisp of flaming Straw in his hand Seeing Their Ruin inevitable, frustrated the Storm in our Presence by Setting the town on fire, And which by the Dryness of the Houses instantly Occasion'd One General Conflagration, When the Popping from the Wood immediately Seized [ceased]; And Which *Masterly Manoeuvre* not only Prevented that Carnage to Which the Common Soldier is too Prone in the heat of Victory, but then gave them the opportunity of Retreating With their Wives & Children, and Carrying off their Best Lumber; While our Pursuit, And even our Falling on any of the Spoil, was at once also frustrated by the Ascending flames, And the Unfathomable Marsh Which we soon found to Surround them—Upon the Whole to Draw this Picture Were a fruitless attempt, thus I Shall only say that the incessant Noise of the Firing, Mixed With a Confused Roaring, Hallooing, Damming and Sinking, the Shrill Sound of the Negro Horns, the Crackling of the Burning houses, the Dead & Wounded all Weltering in Blood, the Clowd of Dust in Which we were involved—And flames and Smoak Assending; Were such a Scene of Beautiful Horror /if I may use the Expression/ as would not be unworthy of the Pencil of Hogarth.

[From *Narrative of a Five Years Expedition against the Revolted Negroes of Surinam* (1790), ed. Richard Price and Sally Price (Baltimore: Johns Hopkins University Press, 1988), 404–6.]

GEORGE F. TYSON, JR.

123 Toussaint L'Ouverture

Letter to the Directory, 28 October 1797

Far be it from me to want to excuse the crimes of the revolution in St. Domingue by comparing them to even greater crimes, but citizen Vaublanc, while threatening us in the *Corps Legislatif*, didn't bother to justify the crimes that have afflicted us and which could only be attributed to a small number. . . . However, this former proprietor of slaves couldn't ignore what slavery was like; perhaps he had witnessed the cruelties exercised upon the miserable blacks, victims of their capricious masters, some of whom were kind but the greatest number of whom were true tyrants. And what would Vaublanc say . . . if, having only the same natural rights as us, he was in his turn reduced to slavery? Would he endure without complaint the insults, the miseries, the tortures, the whippings? And if he had the good fortune to recover his liberty, would he listen without shuddering to the howls of those who wished to tear it from him? . . . Certainly not; in the same way he so indecently accuses the black people of the excesses of a few of their members, we would unjustly accuse the entirety of France of the excesses of a small number of partisans of the old system. Less enlightened than citizen Vaublanc, we know, nevertheless, that whatever their color, only one distinction must exist between men, that of good and evil. When blacks, men of color, and whites are under the same laws, they must be equally protected and they must be equally repressed when they deviate from them. Such is my opinion; such are my desires.

Letter to the Minister of Marine, 13 April 1799

The first successes obtained in Europe by the partisans of liberty over the agents of despotism were not slow to ignite the sacred fire of patriotism in the souls of all Frenchmen in St. Domingue. At that time, men's hopes turned to France, whose first steps toward her regeneration promised them a happier future; . . . they wanted to escape from their arbitrary government, but they did not intend the revolution to destroy either the prejudice that debased the men of color or the slavery of the blacks, whom they held in dependency by the strongest law. In their opinion, the benefits of the French regeneration were only for them. They proved it by their obstinate refusal to allow the people of color to enjoy their political rights and the slaves to enjoy the liberty that they claimed. Thus, while the whites were erecting another form of government upon the rubble of despotism, the men of color and the blacks united themselves in order to claim their political existence; the resistance of the former having become stronger, it was necessary for the latter to rise up in order to obtain [political recognition] by force of arms. The whites, fearing that this legitimate resistance would bring general liberty to St. Domingue, sought to separate the men of color from the cause of the blacks in accordance with Machiavelli's principle of divide and rule. Renouncing their claims over the men of color, they accepted the April Decree [1792]. As they had anticipated, the men of color, many of whom were slaveholders, had only been using the blacks to gain their own political demands. Fearing the enfranchisement of the blacks, the men of color deserted their comrades in arms, their companions in misfortune, and aligned themselves with the whites to subdue them.

Treacherously abandoned, the blacks fought for some time against the reunited whites and the men of color; but, pressed on all sides, losing hope, they accepted the offers of the Spanish king, who, having at that time declared war on France, offered freedom to those blacks of St. Domingue who would join his armies. Indeed, the silence of pre-Republican France on the long-standing claims for their natural rights made by the most interested, the noblest, the most useful portion of the population of St. Domingue . . . extinguished all glimmer of hope in the hearts of the black slaves and forced them, in spite of themselves, to throw themselves into the arms of a protective power that offered the only benefit for which they would fight. More unfortunate than guilty, they turned their arms against their fatherland. . . .

Such were the crimes of these blacks, which have earned them to this day the insulting titles of brigands, insurgents, rebels under the orders of Jean François. At that time I was one of the leaders of these auxiliary troops, and I can say without fear of contradiction that I owed my elevation in these circumstances only to the confidence that I had inspired in my brothers by the virtues for which I am still honored today.

Meanwhile, the Spanish, benefiting from the internal divisions to which the French part of St. Domingue had fallen prey and aided by the courage that gave to these same blacks the hope of imminent freedom, seized almost all of the North and a large part of the West. Le Cap, surrounded by them on all sides and besieged by land and sea, was experiencing all the horrors of the cruelest famine. . . . The Republic that had just been proclaimed in St. Domingue was recognized only in the territory from Le Cap to Port-de-Paix, and the guilty excesses of its agents were not calculated to gain it adherents.

But, following their departure for France, they [the Civil Commissioners] left the reins of power in the hands of General Laveaux, who lost no time endearing himself by a wise and paternal administration. It was sometime after this period that, having received the order to attack Le Cap and convinced by my information about the distressing state to which this city was reduced, of its powerlessness to resist the torrent that must engulf it, I went over to the Republic with the blacks under my command.

[. . .]

[From *Toussaint L'Ouverture* (Englewood Cliffs: Prentice-Hall, 1973), 30–1, 43.]

124   A Treaty Proposed by Slaves

My Lord, we want peace and we do not want war; if My Lord also wants our peace it must be in this manner, if he wishes to agree to that which we want.

In each week you must give us the days of Friday and Saturday to work for ourselves not subtracting any of these because they are Saint's days.

To enable us to live you must give us casting nets and canoes.

You are not to oblige us to fish in the tidal pools nor to gather shellfish, and when you wish to gather shellfish send your Mina blacks.

For your sustenance have a fishing launch and decked canoes, and when you wish to eat shellfish send your Mina blacks.

Make a large boat so that when it goes to Bahia we can place our cargoes aboard and not pay freightage.

In the planting of manioc we wish the men to have a daily quota of two and one half hands and the women, two hands.

The daily quota of manioc flour must be of five level *alqueires*, placing enough harvesters so that these can serve to hang up the coverings.

The daily quota of sugarcane must be of five hands rather than six and of ten canes in each bundle.

On the boat you must put four poles, and one for the rudder, and the one at the rudder works hard for us.

The wood that is sawed with a hand saw must have three men below and one above.

The measure of firewood must be as was practiced here, for each measure a woodcutter and a woman as the wood carrier.

The present overseers we do not want, choose others with our approval.

At the milling rollers there must be four women to feed in the cane, two pulleys, and a *carcanha*.

At each cauldron there must be one who tends the fire and in each series of kettles the same, and on Saturday there must be without fail work stoppage in the mill.

The sailors who go in the launch beside the baize shirt that they are given must also have a jacket of baize and all the necessary clothing.

We will go to work the canefield of Jabirú this time and then it must remain as pasture for we cannot cut cane in a swamp.

We shall be able to plant our rice wherever we wish, and in any marsh, without asking permission for this, and each person can cut jacaranda or any other wood without having to account for this.

Accepting all the above articles and allowing us to remain always in possession of the hardware, we are ready to serve you as before because we do not wish to continue the bad customs of the other *engenhos*.

We shall be able to play, relax and sing any time we wish without your hinderance nor will permission be needed.

[From 'Treaty Proposed to Manoel da Silva Ferreira By His Slaves during the Time that They Remained in Revolt [c.1790],' quoted in Stuart Schwartz, 'Resistance and Accommodation in Eighteenth-Century Brazil: The Slaves' View of Slavery,' *Hispanic American Historical Review* 57 (1977), 77–9.]

125 Letter to the *Moniteur de la Louisiane*

Sir,

I request the insertion in the *Moniteur* of the results of the insurrection which broke out last Tuesday evening on the 8th of this month at the residence of Mr. Manuel Andry.

Having arrived from town on horseback at 6:00 a.m. I learned of the event, and immediately went to Mr. [Bouchet] Saint Martin, judge of that parish, in order to receive his orders. I organized twenty men; we immediately began to hunt for the brigands, and to halt the progress of the revolt. But the torrent of rain and the frigid cold prevented us from pursuing them as far as M. Jacques Fortier's where I understood they were encamped. These reasons caused me to return to Judge Saint Martin's, where the militia was gathered. There I found Colonel Andry, badly wounded. Under his orders I assembled 60 men. Then Judge Saint Martin despatched a hasty note to Major Saint-Amand, so that he would send 25 militiamen to our gathering in order to cross the estate of Bernard Bernoudy and move against the enemy.

Early in the morning of the next day, Thursday the 10th, sixty of us left, joined by Colonel Andry, in spite of his wounds. I took the lead in order to accelerate the movement of the militia requested of Mr. Saint Amand, and to reconnoiter the enemy's position. I discovered them moving by forced march towards the high ground. Not yet finding M. Saint Amand's militia in motion, and in view of the urgent situation, I shouted in a loud and intelligible voice: *Let those who are willing follow me, and let's move out!*

Messrs. Derogin, Labranche, Maximilien, Lucien, Victor Brule, Cadet Lambert, Dussuan Jr., and several other brave militiamen joined up. We crossed the Bernard Bermoudy estate. Once there, we saw the enemy at a very short distance, numbering about 200 men, as many mounted as on foot. We vigorously attacked them, and within half an hour, they fled in a complete rout; we pursued them into the woods, leaving 40 to 45 men on the field of battle, among whom were several chiefs.

Following this action I undertook to restore order on all of the estates from the place of combat to Mme. Trepagnier's mother's place. I ordered all the drivers to carry out the accustomed work at the usual hours, which was done. I engaged all the proprietors to return to their properties as soon as possible, so as to maintain good order.

Friday, the eleventh, at 3 a.m., I left with 25 volunteers to beat the bushes, to harass the enemy, and to make contact with those who had fled. We found only the bodies resulting from the previous day's shooting, and we were fortunate to discover and save the unfortunate Madame Clapion, nearly dead of fatigue and cold.

Saturday, the 12th at 4 a.m., I led a new expedition in hopes of recovering the unfortunate Judge Trouard and his two nieces, and in pursuit of the rest of the insurgents. I arrived at Picou's estate, met M. Deslondes, in charge of a picket of cavalry. I informed him of my plan and invited him to enter the woods a league further on in order to put combined pressure on the enemy. Following this, one of my detachments, commanded by Cadet Picou, found two brigand troops, Pierre Griffe, murderer of M. Thomassin, and Hans Wimprenn, murderer of M. Francois Trepagnier, and pressed them closely that they came upon M. Deslonde's picket and were killed. Their heads were then carried to the Andry estate. Our success was incomplete; we had succeeded in finding neither Trouard nor his neices after a whole day's most exacting search. Towards evening I went to the home of Colonel Andry, where a number of rebels were held, among whom were Charles Deslonds, principal chief, Jacques Becknell, Barthelemi Trepagnier, and several others. We tried them and they were executed in succession.

I commend our brave militiamen to the recognition of the public, as well as seven men of color, to wit: Pierre Sauvage, Severe Sabatier, Charles Pain, Georges Jr., Baptiste Langlais, Baptiste Daigle, and Charles Troxler, who in my own presence, helped to defeat the enemy with indefatigable zeal and intrepid courage. These seven names have merited the generosity of the government and a reward from the inhabitants.

Charles Perret

At the moment that we were going to press, we had positive news that M. Achille Trouard has been found with his two nieces. They had withdrawn into the canes alongside the Guillou bayou. We haven't been able to get details on how these unfortunates were saved and subsisted.

[From Charles Perret, *Letter to the 'Moniteur de la Louisiane,'* (January 17, 1811). Trs. Robert Paquette and Seymour Drescher.]

SAMUEL HAMBLETON

126   Letter to David Porter

'The [slave] Insurrection [on the German Coast] is entirely over—four have been hung & one shot in this place [i.e. New Orleans]. They were brung here for the sake of their Heads, which decorate our Levee, all the way up the coast. I am told they look like crows sitting on long poles. The whole number killed in Battle, hung & shot & supposed to have perished in the woods, is about one hundred. The [French] planters have shewed their characteristic barbarity throughout the whole business. Several [slaves] were wrested from the Guards & butchered on the spot. Charles [Deslondes, the alleged rebel leader] had his Hands chopped off then shot in one thigh & then the other, until they were both broken—then shot in the Body and before he had expired was put into a bundle of straw and roasted!'

[From *Letter to David Porter*, (January 25, 1811), Papers of David Porter, Library of Congress.]

127   The Trial of John Smith

Paris's confession; 28th August, 1823

Paris confesses he is guilty of the crimes laid to his charge, and throws himself on the mercy of the court, offering a full disclosure of the whole conspiracy, and of the principals concerned in it.

It is now twelve months since this business began to be first agitated, and the first word I ever heard was from Mr. Smith, the parson, at Le Resouvenir estate, at chapel. One Sunday about that time, after the service was over, there were several of us remained for the evening class meeting; say Quamina, Bristol, Jack, Manuel, Azor (Van Cooten), Joseph (Hopkinson), Telemaque and Prince (Hopkinson), Mars (Van Cooten), and some others whose names I do not recollect at present, when Parson Smith said to us, 'The negroes in this country are fools, for the King had allowed them their freedom, and that the whites in this country had paid (bribed) the Governor not to give it to them; and so if the people did not seek for it themselves, they would not receive it any more.' These were his words, as near as I can recollect them at present. When we left the chapel, Quamina, Jack, Bristol, Manuel, Azor and Mars and I talked over the parson's information, and said it was a very hard thing to have our freedom kept from us; and we agreed to meet often, and talk over the business as to how we were to get our freedom. Nothing more passed at that time. After this time we had private meetings occasionally at our houses. Jack and Quamina engaged to raise the Success people; Bristol and Manuel, the Chateau Margo; Davy, the Bonne Intention; Cudjo, the Goede Verwaghting; Toney and Louis, the Mon Repos and Endraght; William, the Triumph; myself, the Good Hope; Wyore, the Lusignan; Annandale, no head man; New O. Nassau, Providence; Friendship, Luke and Jarvis; Vigilance, Jack, carpenter, who was to be also the leader as far as Mr. Panyea's; Bachelors Adventure, Joseph and Telemachus; Paradise, Hanover; Success, Jack settled every thing from the Success to town; Barre the butcher carried letters from Jack to Sam, the Governor's servant in town, and to the head driver at Herstelling, who was to be the leader of the east side of the river; at Rome, the head driver; at Providence, the head driver and Mr. Blake's cook; at Ruimveld, the head and the second drivers; at La Penitence, the head driver and the manager's cook; but the head driver at Herstelling was to be the head of the whole; on Filleen's estate, the attorney's butler; on Best, the second driver, who was also to be the leader on the west side, and to send over the whole of the negroes from that side to take the town, which was our grand object; Colin, at Mr. Meerten's; head driver at Belle Vue: west coast, Rotterdam first and second drivers, head men of the west coast Wakenam; Good Success, first driver: Essequibo, Annandale, first driver, who was to have passed over to Belle Plaine, with one thousand Bush negroes, and from thence to have found his way to town. Columbia, first driver and butler; Hampton Court, first driver and d^e; Main Stay, first driver and head butler; Tarsus, first driver and head butler; Caledonia, first and second, drivers; Sophienberg, first driver; Hobabo Julius, Mr. Edmonstone's head driver.

The whole colony was to have risen last Monday, and I cannot account for the reasons why only the east coast rose at the time appointed. As soon as we were in possession of the town all the white men were to have been murdered, and the white females taken for our own wives, but not before, as that would only have irritated the whites the more: if we had not succeeded, as has been the case, the ships in the river were to have been burnt. All the doctors that we were fond of we were to have saved, the rest were to be murdered. Doctors Waddell, Robson and Mr. Chambers to be saved in town. Quamina insisted on being the king, Jack the governor; Parson Smith was to have been our emperor, and to have ruled every thing; Mr. Hamilton to be general of our forces, and it was he who told me and Jack and others to bear a hand on Sunday morning, and pull up the bridges, the first thing we did, to prevent the great guns from advancing; and Parson Smith told us to make haste and begin it, or if not the whites would know. Mr. Hamilton had made choice of a lady in town. The parsons were to have been saved.—Sunday 17th, Parson Smith gave us the sacrament, (Mr. Hamilton partook of it also.) He desired us to keep good heart, exhorted us to go on with the business now, or die. Quamina, Jack (Success), Bristol, Manuel, Azor, Mars, Romeo (Resouvenir), Telemachus, Joseph Wyore from Luignan, Providence (N. O. N.) Jack (Vigilance), Luke (Friendship), Louis (Endraght), and plenty more whose names I don't recollect, the Parson Smith and Mr. Hamilton, often, often, in my presence, declared that we were to be free, and that we ought to take our freedom.

[From 'A Copy of the Minutes of the Evidence on the Trial of John Smith, a Missionary, in the Colony of Demerara,' *British Parliamentary Papers: Correspondence and Papers Relating to Slavery and the Abolition of the Slave Trade 1823–24* (Shannon: Irish University Press, 1969), Vol. 66: 172–3.]

128 The Trial of Denmark Vesey

The trial of Denmark Vesey, a free black man—Col. G. W. Cross attending as his counsel.

EVIDENCE

William, the slave of Mr. Paul, testified as follows: Mingo Harth told me that *Denmark Vesey was the chief man, and more concerned than anyone else.* Denmark Vesey is an old man in whose yard my master's Negro woman Sarah cooks. He was her father-in-law, having married her mother Beck, and though they have been parted some time, yet he visited her at her house [in Charleston, South Carolina] near the Intendant's (Major Hamilton), where I have often heard him speak of the rising. *He said he would not like to have a white man in his presence—that he had a great hatred for the whites,* and that if all were like him they would resist the whites. He studied all he could to put it into the heads of the blacks to have a rising against the whites, and tried to induce me to join. He tried to induce all his acquaintances—this has been his chief study and delight for a considerable time. My last conversation with him was in April. He studied the Bible a great deal and tried to prove from it that slavery and bondage is against the Bible. I am persuaded that Denmark Vesey was chiefly concerned in this business.

WITNESS NO. 1, gave the following testimony: I know Denmark Vesey. I was one day on horseback going to market when I met him on foot; he asked me if I was satisfied in my present situation; if I remembered the fable of Hercules and the Waggoner whose waggon was stalled, and he began to pray, and Hercules said, you fool put your shoulder to the wheel, whip up the horses and your waggon will be pulled out; that if we did not put our hand to the work and deliver ourselves, we should never come out of slavery; *that Congress had made us free.* I know that he is intimately acquainted with Rolla—Rolla told me that there had been a sort of disagreement and confusion at their place of meeting, and that they meant to meet at Vesey's. Vesey told me that a large army from Santo Domingo and Africa were coming to help us, and we must not stand with our hands in our pockets; he was bitter towards the whites.

FRANK, Mrs. Ferguson's slave gave the following evidence: I know Denmark Vesey and have been to his house. I have heard him say that the Negro's situation was so bad he did not know how they could endure it, and was astonished they did not rise and fend for themselves, and he advised me to join and rise. He said he was going about to see different people, and mentioned the names of Ned Bennett and Peter Poyas as concerned with him— that he had spoken to Ned and Peter on this subject, and that they were to go about and tell the blacks that they were free, and must rise and *fight for themselves*—that they would take the Magazines and Guard Houses, and the city and be free—that he was going to send *into the country* to inform the people there too. He said he wanted me to join them—I said I could not answer—he said if I would not go into the country for him he could get others. He said himself, Ned Bennett, Peter Poyas, and Monday Gell were the principal men and himself the head man. He said they were the principal men to go about and inform the people and fix them,—that *one party would land on South Bay, one about Wappoo, and about the farms*—that the party which was to land on South Bay was to take the Guard House and get arms and then they would be able to go on—that the attack was to commence about twelve o'clock at night—*that great numbers would come from all about*, and it must succeed as so many were engaged in it—that they would kill all the whites—that they would leave their master's houses and assemble together near the lines, march down and meet the party which would land on South Bay—that he was going to *send a man into the country* on a horse *to bring down the country people* and that he would pay for the horse. He gave $2 to Jesse to get the horse on Saturday week last (15th June), about one o'clock in the day, and myself and No. 3, also put in 25 cents a piece, and he told Jesse, if he could not go he must send someone else. I have seen Ned Bennett at Vesey's. One night, I met at Vesey's a great number of men, and as they came in each handed him some money. Vesey said there was a *little man named Jack* who could not be killed, and who would furnish them with arms, he had a charm and he would lead them—that Charles Drayton had promised to be engaged with them. Vesey said the Negroes were living such an abominable life, they ought to rise. I said I was living well—he said though I was, others were not and that 'twas such fools as I, that were in the way and would not help them, and that after all things were well he would mark me. He said he did not go with *Creighton to Africa, because he had not a will, he wanted to stay and see what he could do* for his fellow creatures. I met Ned, Monday, and others at Denmark Vesey's where they were talking about the business. The first time I spoke with Monday Gell 'twas one night at Denmark Vesey's house, where I heard Vesey tell Monday that he must *send someone into the country to bring the people down.* Monday said *he had sent up Jack* and told him *to tell the people to come down and join in the fight* against the whites and also to ascertain and inform him how many people he could get. A few days after I met Vesey, Monday, and Jack, in the streets under Mr. Duncan's trees at night, where *Jack stated that he had been into the country round by Goose Creek and Dorchester,* and that he had spoken to 6,600 persons who had agreed to join. Monday said to Vesey, that if Jack had so many men they had better wait no longer but begin the business at once, and others would join. The first time I saw Monday at Vesey's, he was going away early, when Vesey asked him to stay, to which Monday replied, he expected that night a meeting at his house to fix upon and mature the plan, and that he could stay no longer. I afterwards conversed with Monday in his shop, where he asked me if I had heard that Bennett's and Poyas' people were taken up, that 'twas a great pity—he said he had joined in the business—I told him to take care he was not taken up. Whenever I talked with Vesey, he always spoke of Monday Gell as being his principal and active man in the business.

ADAM, a Negro man belonging to Mr. Ferguson testified as follows: Denmark Vesey one day asked me to walk to his house, and there asked me for 25 cents to hire a horse to send up into the country. I put down the money on the table and asked what he was going to send into the country for—he said 'twould be for my benefit. As he would tell me no more I took up the money and put it back into my pocket again. I afterwards met the man who was to go into the country, who told me he had set off, but had been brought back by the Patrol; *that he was going up to bring down the black people to take this country from the whites.* I have been at Vesey's house and there it was I met the man who was to go into the country, he was a yellowish man—the witness pointing at Jesse said, that is the man who was to go into the country.

BENJAMIN FORD, a white lad, about 15 or 16 years of age, deposed as follows: Denmark Vesey frequently came into our shop which is near his house, and always complained of the hardships of the blacks. He said the laws were very rigid and strict and that the blacks had not their rights—that everyone had his time, and that his would come round too. *His general conversation was about religion which he would apply to slavery,* as for instance, he would speak of the creation of the world, in which he would say all men had equal rights, blacks as well as whites,—*all his religious remarks were mingled with slavery.*

THE COURT unanimously found Denmark Vesey guilty, and passed upon him the sentence of death. After his conviction, a good deal of testimony was given against him during the succeeding trials. Among others:

WITNESS NO. 9, a Negro man, testified as follows: Denmark Vesey has frequently spoken to me about the intended insurrection, and endeavored to persuade me to join them. He inquired of me *if my master had not arms in his house, and tried to persuade me to get them for him.* The blacks stand in great fear of him, and I so much so, that I always endeavored to avoid him.

EDWIN, a Negro man belonging to Mr. Paul, gave the following evidence: Charles Drayton told me that Denmark Vesey and Monday Gell knew about the insurrection of the blacks, and that my fellow servant *William, in consequence of what he had said, would run great risk of his life if he went out.* I have heard everybody, even the women say, when several were apprehended at first, that they wondered why Denmark Vesey and Monday Gell were not taken up.

[From *The Trial Record of Denmark Vesey* [1822], intro. by John Oliver Killens (Boston: Beacon Press, 1970), 61–5

---

129 Anonymous Report in Cuba

Don Juan de Dios Gómez, alderman of Matanzas, has two sugar plantations in the district of Camarioca. The first plantation called Viejo has a gang of slaves that, from any way you look at it, is demoralized and very disposed to disturb the public peace. These slaves, spoiled by their master to the point that they do not even permit their overseers to give them salutary correction, keep the peaceful and respectable local residents in a state of anguished alarm. Not long ago these slaves, in rebellion against their overseer, placed him in the stocks and gave him so many lashes that they left him for dead. Gómez resolved this outrageous affair and employed the overseer again on another estate. Three years ago these same slaves said that they were waiting for a day during Holy Week to unite with their comrades to finish off the whites. These voices were already so public that the alarmed local residents feared the explosion at any moment of some kind of conspiracy of these slaves. In fact, at the end of 1837, the firebell on Gómez's Viejo sugar plantation was heard one day and later the blaze of a great fire was noticed. As his neighbors went to help, they ran into the overseer of another sugar plantation to whom the blacks themselves had said: *Get on your horse and run and do not return here ever again, if you want to live.* The fact is that after they threw out the overseer they took out all their beds (because all of them had beds) and simultaneously set fire to all of their huts. Given what the overseer said, no one dared help to put out the fire. Captain Fulgencio García was informed and later he arrived with an armed party. They forced their way in from all directions and surrounded the blacks in a way that subdued them without firing a shot. The owner arrived immediately from Matanzas and by his presence, order was reestablished. Don Félix de la Cruz, a respectable head of household, complained and wanted to start summary legal proceedings, but this *was throttled,* and the overseer who was thrown off the Viejo sugar plantation [by the slaves] returned to Gómez's employ at the new sugar plantation. There is not one of Gómez's neighbours who can fail to count a thousand crimes and offences perpetrated by this band of slaves. In particular, Don Nicolás Campos, engineering official and Gómez's next-door neighbour, certainly can. He is certain that the loss of many animals and food crops is caused by these slaves. Besides seeing them all around, passing by his estate with the excuse of going to Gómez's new sugar plantation, it happened last year that the field overseer followed the trail of a calf that was taken from his ranch, and he found the meat and the skin in the hut of one of Gómez's slaves. The deed proved, Gómez paid with another calf, but without further judicial process. Slaves with such a track record that they leave work when they please and if not, they remain in bed, who throw out the Administrator who does not accommodate them, who frequently utter subversive voices, who rob and even insult many of the region's inhabitants always threaten the public peace and endanger the respectable householder who can only maintain his property with arms in hand. For better understanding, a sketch of Gómez's sugar plantations, of those of his most notable neighbours, and of the town of Camarioca is presented here.

[From *Anonymous Report to Captain General Joaquín de Ezpeleta*, Cuba, February 1839, in
Escoto Papers, Box 11, Houghton Library, Harvard University.
Trs. Robert L. Paquette and Joseph Dorsey.]

130   Confession of Nat Turner

Agreeable to his own appointment, on the evening he was committed to prison [in Southampton County, Virginia], with permission of the Jailor, I visited NAT on Tuesday, the 1st November [1831], when, without being questioned at all, he commenced his narrative in the following words:

SIR—You have asked me to give a history of the motives which induced me to undertake the late insurrection, as you call it. To do so I must go back to the days of my infancy, and even before I was born. I was thirty-one years of age the 2d of October last, and born the property of Benj. Turner, of this county. In my childhood a circumstance occurred which made an indelible impression on my mind, and laid the ground-work of that enthusiasm, which has terminated so fatally to many, both white and black, and for which I am about to atone at the gallows. It is here necessary to relate this circumstance—trifling as it may seem, it was the commencement of that belief which has grown with time, and even now, sir, in this dungeon, helpless and forsaken as I am, I cannot divest myself of. Being at play with other children, when three or four years old, I was telling them something, which, my mother overhearing, said it had happened before I was born. I stuck to my story, however, and related some things which went, in her opinion, to confirm it. Others being called on were greatly astonished, knowing that these things had happened, and caused them to say in my hearing, I surely would be a prophet, as the Lord had shown me things that had happened before my birth. And my father and mother strengthened me in this, my first impression, saying in my presence, I was intended for some great purpose, which they had always thought from certain marks on my head and breast— [a parcel of excrescences, which I believe are not at all uncommon, particularly among negroes, as I have seen several with the same. In this case he has either cut them off or they have nearly disappeared.] My grandmother, who was very religious, and to whom I was much attached; my master, who belonged to the church, and other religious persons who visited the house, and whom I often saw at prayers, noticing the singularity of my manners, I suppose, and my uncommon intelligence for a child, remarked I had too much sense to be raised, and if I was, I would never be of any service to any one as a slave. To a mind like mine, restless, inquisitive, and observant of everything that was passing, it is easy to suppose that religion was the subject to which it would be directed, and although this subject principally occupied my thoughts, there was nothing that I saw or heard of to which my attention was not directed. The manner in which I learned to read and write, not only had great influence on my own mind, (as I acquired it with the most perfect ease, so much so, that I have no recollection whatever of learning the alphabet,) but to the astonishment of the family, one day when a book was shown me to keep me from crying, I began spelling the names of the different objects. This was a source of wonder to all in the neighborhood, particularly the blacks, and this learning was constantly improved at all opportunities. When I got large enough to go to work, while employed, I was reflecting on many things that would present themselves to my imagination, and whenever an opportunity occurred of looking at a book, when the school children were getting their lessons, I would find many things that the fertility of my own imagination had depicted to me before. All my time, not devoted to my master's service, was spent either in prayer, or in making experiments in casting different things in moulds made of earth; in attempting to make paper, gunpowder, and many other experiments, that although I could not perfect, yet convinced me of its practicability if I had the means. I was not addicted to stealing in my youth, nor have ever been, yet such was the confidence of the negroes in the neighborhood even at this early period of my life, in my superior judgment, that they would often carry me with them when they were going on any roguery, to plan for them. Growing up among them, with this confidence in my superior judgment, and when this, in their opinions, were perfected by Divine inspiration, from the circumstances already alluded to in my infancy, and which belief was ever afterwards zealously inculcated by the austerity of my life and manners, which became the subject of remark by white and black, having soon discovered to be great, I must appear so, and therefore studiously avoided mixing in society, and wrapped myself in mystery, devoting my time to fasting and prayer. By this time, having arrived to man's estate and hearing the scriptures commented on at meetings, I was struck with that particular passage which says: 'Seek ye the kingdom of heaven and all things shall be added unto you'. I reflected much on this passage, and prayed daily for light on this subject. As I was praying one day at my plough, the Spirit spoke to me, saying: 'Seek ye the kingdom of heaven and all things shall be added unto you'.

[. . .]

Since the commencement of 1830, I had been living with Mr. Joseph Travis, who was to me a kind master and placed the greatest confidence in me; in fact, I had no cause to complain of his treatment to me. On Saturday evening, the 20th of August, it was agreed between Henry, Hark, and myself, to prepare a dinner the next day for the men we expected, and then to concert a plan, as we had not yet determined on any. Hark, on the following morning, brought a pig, and Henry, brandy, and being joined by Sam, Nelson, Will, and Jack, they prepared in the woods a dinner, where, about three o'clock, I joined them.

Question.—Why were you so backward in joining them?

Answer.—The same reason that had caused me not to mix with them for years before.

I saluted them on coming up, and asked Will how came he there. He answered, his life was worth no more than others, and his liberty as dear to him. I asked him if he thought to obtain it. He said he would, or lose his life. This was enough to put him in full confidence. Jack, I knew, was only a tool in the hands of Hark. It was quickly agreed we should commence at home (Mr. J. Travis') on that night, and until we had armed and equipped ourselves, and gathered sufficient force, neither age nor sex was to be spared, (which was invariably adhered to.) We remained at the feast until about two hours in the night, when we went to the house and found Austin; they all went to the cider press and drank except myself. On returning to the house, Hark went to the door with an axe for the purpose of breaking it open, as we knew we were strong enough to murder the family if they were awaked by the noise; but reflecting that it might create an alarm in the neighborhood, we determined to enter the house secretly and murder them whilst sleeping. Hark got a ladder and set it against the chimney, on which I ascended, and hoisting a window, entered and came down stairs, unbarred the door, and removed the guns from their places. It was then observed that I must spill the first blood, on which, armed with a hatchet, and accompanied by Will, I entered my master's chamber. It being dark I could not give a death blow; the hatchet glanced from his head; he sprang from the bed and called his wife; it was his last word; Will laid him dead with a blow of his axe, and Mrs. Travis shared the same fate, as she lay it bed. The murder of this family, five in number, was the work of a moment, not one of them awoke. There was a little infant sleeping in a cradle that was forgotten until we had left the house and gone some distance, when Henry and Will returned and killed it. We got here four guns that would shoot and several old muskets, with a pound or two of powder. We remained some time at the barn, where we paraded. I formed them in line as soldiers, and after carrying them through all the manouvres I was master of, marched them off to Mr. Salathul Francis', about six hundred yards distant. Sam and Will went to the door and knocked. Mr. Francis asked who was there. Sam replied it was him, and he had a letter for him; on which he got up and came to the door. They immediately seized him, and dragging him out a little from the door, he was dispatched by repeated blows on the head. There was no other white person in the family. We started from there for Mrs. Reese's, maintaining the most perfect silence on our march, where, finding the door unlocked, we entered, and murdered Mrs. Reese in her bed while sleeping. Her son awoke, but it was only to sleep the sleep of death; he had only time to say who is that, and he was no more. From Mrs. Reese's we went to Mrs. Turner's, a mile distant, which we reached about sunrise, on Monday morning. Henry, Austin, and Sam, went to the still, where, finding Mr. Peebles, Austin shot him, and the rest of us went to the house. As we approached the family discovered us and shut the door. Vain hope! Will, with one stroke of his axe, opened it, and we entered and found Mrs. Turner and Mrs. Newsome in the middle of the room, almost frightened to death. Will immediately killed Mrs. Turner with one blow of his axe. I took Mrs. Newsome by the hand, and with the sword I had when I was apprehended, I struck her several blows over the head, but not being able to kill her, as the sword was dull, Will turning around and discovering it, dispatched her also. A general destruction of property and search for money and ammunition, always succeeded the murders. By this time my company amounted to fifteen, and nine men mounted, who started for Mrs. Whitehead's (the other six were to go through a by-way to Mr. Bryant's, and rejoin us at Mrs.

Whitehead's.) As we approached the house we discovered Mr. Richard Whitehead standing in the cotton patch, near the lane fence. We called him over into the lane, and Will, the executioner, was near at hand, with his fatal axe, to send him to an untimely grave. As we pushed on to the house I discovered some one run around the garden, and thinking it was some of the white family, I pursued them, but finding it was a servant girl belonging to the house, I returned to commence the work of death, but they whom I left had not been idle. All the family were already murdered but Mrs. Whitehead and her daughter Margaret. As I came round to the door I saw Will pulling Mrs. Whitehead out of the house, and at the step he nearly severed her head from her body with his broad axe. Miss Margaret, when I discovered her, had concealed herself in the corner, formed by the projection of the cellar cap from the house. On my approach she fled, but was soon overtaken, and after repeated blows with the sword, I killed her by a blow on the head with a fence rail.

[. . .]

Charged with making insurrection and plotting to take away the lives of divers free white persons, &c., on the 22d of August, 1831.

The court composed of——, having met for the trial of Nat Turner, the prisoner was brought in and arraigned, and upon his arraignment pleaded *not guilty*: saying to his counsel that he did not feel so.

On the part of the Commonwealth, Levi Waller was introduced, who, being sworn, deposed as follows: (*agreeably to Nat's own Confession.*) Col. Trezvant was then introduced, who, being sworn, numerated Nat's Confession to him, as follows: (*his Confession as given to Mr. Gray.*) The prisoner introduced no evidence, and the case was submitted without argument to the court, who, having found him guilty, Jeremiah Cobb, Esq., Chairman, pronounced the sentence of the Court in the following words: 'Nat Turner, stand up! Have you anything to say why sentence of death should not be pronounced against you?'

Answer.—I have not; I have made a full confession to Mr. Gray and I have nothing more to say

Attend then to the sentence of the Court! You have been arraigned and tried before this Court, and convicted of one of the highest crimes in our Criminal Code. You have been convicted of plotting, in cold blood, the indiscriminate destruction of men, of helpless women, and of infant children. The evidence before us leaves not a shadow of doubt but that your hands were often imbued in the blood of the innocent; and your own confession tells us that they were stained with the blood of a master, in your own language, 'too indulgent'. Could I stop here your crime would be sufficiently aggravated. But the original contriver of a plan, deep and deadly one that can never be effected, you managed so far to put it into execution as to deprive us of many of our most valuable citizens; and this was done when they were asleep and defenseless, under circumstances shocking to humanity. And while upon this part of the subject, I cannot but call your attention to the poor, misguided wretches who have gone before you. They are not few in number—they were your bosom associates—and the blood of all cries aloud and calls upon you as the author of their misfortune. Yes! You forced them unprepared, from time to eternity. Borne down by this load of guilt, your only justification is that you were led away by fanaticism. If this be true, from my soul I pity you; and while you have my sympathies, I am, nevertheless, called upon to pass the sentence of the Court. The time between this and your execution will necessarily be very short, and your only hope must be in another world. The judgment of the Court is, that you be taken hence to the jail from whence you came, thence to the place of execution, and on Friday next, between the hours of 10 A. M. and 2 P. M., be hung by the neck until you are dead! dead! dead! and may the Lord have mercy upon your soul.

[From *The Confession, Trial and Execution of Nat Turner, the Negro Insurrectionist . . . 1831* (Petersburg: John B. Ege, 1881), 7–9, 12–14, 21–2.]

131   Harriet Whitehead Case

To the Honorable, the Judge of the Circuit Superior Court of Law and Chancery of Southampton County [Virginia]. Humbly complaining show to the Court, your complainant Harriet Whitehead.

That she is and ever has been a single woman and unmarried—that sometime about the year 1831, during the insurrection of the negroes in Southampton County, and whilst all near the scene of action were in the greatest *possible* state of excitement, the house of her friend and relative with whom she resided was attacked in the night by the negroes, and in the general and awful alarm consequent thereon, your complainant succeeded in secreting herself between some beds, whilst her sister and the remainder of the inmates of the house were murdered in a few feet of her; that by the aid of some friendly negroes she escaped the general slaughter—that the fright and alarm produced by these causes so operated on the mind of your complainant that both her body and mind became weakened and impaired thereby. That so powerful and overwhelming was the effect thus produced that she became depressed in spirits, weak in body and mind, hysterical and easily excited, and when in such a state of mind has resorted to stimulating medicines, drinks and the like, which have frequently rendered your complainant unfit to enter into any contract of consequence or of importance. That this state of feelings and mind continued until after the year 1843, and even now occasionally afflicts her.

[From 'Harriet Whitehead Case, November 1848', John Richardson Kilby Papers, Correspondence 1840–50, in the Perkins Library, Duke University.]

HENRY BLEBY

132   Death Struggles of Slavery

Edward Hylton, one of the original conspirators, whose life was spared, gave us the following account of the origin of the insurrection:—During the year 1831, (he could not tell the month,) he received a message at Mountain Spring from Sam Sharpe, desiring him to meet him on the following Saturday night at the house of Johnson, at Retrieve estate in St. James [Parish in Jamaica]. This was the Colonel Johnson who led the attack, and was killed, at Montpelier. Hylton neglected to obey the summons; and a few days afterwards was sternly rebuked by Sharpe, when he met with him at Montego Bay, for not going to Retrieve. Sharpe then told him that he had something very particular to communicate, and requested that Hylton would meet him and several other persons the following week at Retrieve. At the time appointed Hylton went to Retrieve, where he met with Sharpe, Johnson, and others whom he named. After they had held a prayer-meeting, most of the people went away, Sharpe, Johnson, Hylton, and a few more, remaining behind: and the party was afterwards enlarged by several others, who stealthily and with extreme caution made their way into the house, and who were evidently expected by those already assembled. After the lapse of some time, Sharpe rose to address the meeting, speaking in a low, soft tone, that his voice might not be heard beyond the walls of the building. He began by expressing his gratification that Hylton had accepted his invitation, as he had something to impart to him which he would be glad to hear. He then proceeded with his address to those around him, speaking for a long time on various topics relating to the great subject he had at heart, and with an eloquence which from Hylton's account, kept all his hearers fascinated and spell-bound from the beginning to the end of his speech.

He referred to the manifold evils and injustice of slavery; asserted the natural equality of man with regard to freedom; and, referring to the holy Scriptures as his authority, denied that the white man had any more right to hold the blacks in bondage than the blacks had to enslave the whites. He told them a great deal of what he had read both in the English and colonial newspapers, showing that both the king and the English people wished the negroes to be emancipated, and expressed his belief that the 'free paper' had already been sent out, and that the only obstacles which they had to overcome, in order to secure their freedom, were the obstinacy and selfishness of the planters. Referring to the threats which the colonists held out, of transferring their allegiance to the United States of America, he argued that it was because the king had determined to put an end to slavery; and that the negroes had, therefore, nothing to fear from the opposition of the British troops, if they determined to take their freedom. He concluded by observing, that because the king had made them free, or was resolved upon doing it, the 'whites and Grignon' were holding secret meetings, with the doors shut close, at the house of Mr. Watt of Montego Bay, and had determined ('were making a studiation,' as Hylton expressed it) to kill all the black men, and save all the women and children, and keep them in slavery; and if the black men did not stand up for themselves and take their freedom, the whites would put them out at the muzzles of their guns, and shoot them like pigeons.

This address, delivered with great fluency, and with all the pathos and earnestness of which Sharpe was eminently capable, told with powerful effect upon his auditors. Hylton, however, felt that it was a momentous undertaking to which Sharpe was persuading them, and highly dangerous; and that they ought not to enter into it without the greatest caution. Without, therefore, directly impugning any of Sharpe's assertions, some of which, he said, he knew to be true, for he had read the same in the newspapers; yet, as they knew that black men could speak false as well as the whites, he thought they could not agree to act upon these statements, unless Sharpe, for the satisfaction of all parties, would 'kiss the Book upon it'. Further discussion ensued, and their deliberations were carried on far into the night; when, all scruples being set at rest, and the plan of operations more fully detailed by Sharpe, the whole party bound themselves by oath not to work after Christmas as slaves, but to assert their claim to freedom, and to be faithful to each other. If 'buckra' would pay them, they would work as before; but if any attempt was made to force them to work as slaves, then they would fight for their freedom. Sharpe first kissed the Book, and then all present followed his example.

From this time the conspiracy was carried on vigorously, though with strict secresy; and its ramifications were widely and rapidly extended. All to whom it was divulged were sworn—'made to kiss the Book'—that they would keep the secret, and be faithful. By the conspirators advantage was often taken of the prayer-meetings of the Baptists, held on the estates, to enlist other slaves in the enterprise; and thus it was that many of the Baptist people were found to be implicated in this unfortunate and disastrous movement.

Hylton also informed us, that on the morning of Christmas-day, 1831, a day or two before the insurrection broke out, he, with several others of the insurgent leaders, breakfasted at the house of a black man named Taylor, at the Long Store in Montego Bay. At this meeting an English newspaper was produced from under the bed, from which Taylor read extracts on the subject

of slavery; the substance of which was that 'the English people were determined no longer to submit to such brutish things;' meaning, as he afterwards
explained, 'such a brutish system as slavery'.

> [From *Death Struggles of Slavery: Being a Narrative of Facts and Incidents which Occurred in a
> British Colony, during the Two Years Immediately Preceding Negro Emancipation* [1853]
> (Coconut Grove: Dewar's, 1972), 122–5.]

FREDERICK DOUGLASS

133   **My Bondage and My Freedom**

The whip is all in all. It is supposed to secure obedience to the slaveholder,
and is held as a sovereign remedy among the slaves themselves, for every
form of disobedience, temporal or spiritual. Slaves, as well as slaveholders,
use it with an unsparing hand. Our devotions at Uncle Isaac's combined too
much of the tragic and comic, to make them very salutary in a spiritual point
of view; and it is due to truth to say, I was often a truant when the time for
attending the praying and flogging of Doctor Isaac Copper came on.
  [. . .]
  Well, my dear reader, this battle with Mr. Covey,—undignified as it was,
and as I fear my narration of it is—was the turning point in my '*life as a slave*'.
It rekindled in my breast the smouldering embers of liberty; it brought up
my Baltimore dreams, and revived a sense of my own manhood. I was a
changed being after that fight. I was *nothing* before; I WAS A MAN NOW. It
recalled to life my crushed self-respect and my self-confidence, and inspired
me with a renewed determination to be A FREEMAN. A man, without force, is
without the essential dignity of humanity. Human nature is so constituted,
that it cannot *honor* a helpless man, although it can *pity* him; and even this it
cannot do long, if the signs of power do not arise.
  He only can understand the effect of this combat on my spirit, who has
himself incurred something, hazarded something, in repelling the unjust and
cruel aggressions of a tyrant. Covey was a tyrant, and a cowardly one, withal.
After resisting him, I felt as I had never felt before. It was a resurrection from
the dark and pestiferous tomb of slavery, to the heaven of comparative freedom. I was no longer a servile coward, trembling under the frown of a brother
worm of the dust, but, my long-cowed spirit was roused to an attitude of
manly independence. I had reached the point, at which I was *not afraid to die*.
This spirit made me a freeman in *fact*, while I remained a slave in *form*. When a
slave cannot be flogged he is more than half free. He has a domain as broad as
his own manly heart to defend, and he is really '*a power on earth*'. While slaves
prefer their lives, with flogging, to instant death, they will always find

christians enough, like unto Covey, to accommodate that preference. From this time, until that of my escape from slavery, I was never fairly whipped. Several attempts were made to whip me, but they were always unsuccessful. Bruises I did get, as I shall hereafter inform the reader; but the case I have been describing, was the end of the brutification to which slavery had subjected me.

[. . .]

The slaveholder, kind or cruel, is a slaveholder still—the every hour violator of the just and inalienable rights of man; and he is, therefore, every hour silently whetting the knife of vengeance for his own throat. He never lisps a syllable in commendation of the fathers of this republic, nor denounces any attempted oppression of himself, without inviting the knife to his own throat, and asserting the rights of rebellion for his own slaves.

[. . .]

To make a contented slave, you must make a thoughtless one. It is necessary to darken his moral and mental vision, and, as far as possible, to annihilate his power of reason. He must be able to detect no inconsistencies in slavery. The man that takes his earnings must be able to convince him that he has a perfect right to do so. It must not depend upon mere force; the slave must know no Higher Law than his master's will. The whole relationship must not only demonstrate, to his mind, its necessity, but its absolute rightfulness. If there be one crevice through which a single drop can fall, it will certainly rust off the slave's chain.

[From *My Bondage and My Freedom* [1855] (New York: Dover
Publications, 1969), 72, 246–7, 269–70, 320.]

ABRAHAM LINCOLN

....

134   Address at Cooper Institute 1860

Much is said by Southern people about the affection of slaves for their masters and mistresses; and a part of it, at least, is true. A plot for an uprising could scarcely be devised and communicated to twenty individuals before some one of them, to save the life of a favorite master or mistress, would divulge it. This is the rule; and the slave revolution in Hayti was not an exception to it, but a case occurring under peculiar circumstances. The gunpowder plot of British history, though not connected with slaves, was more in point. In that case, only about twenty were admitted to the secret; and yet one of them, in his anxiety to save a friend, betrayed the plot to that friend, and, by consequence, averted the calamity. Occasional poisonings from the kitchen, and open or stealthy assassinations in the field, and local revolts extending to a score or so, will continue to occur as the natural results of slavery; but no general insurrection of slaves, as I think, can happen in this country for a long time. Whoever much fears, or much hopes for such an event, will be alike disappointed.

[From 'Address at Cooper Institute, New York City, February 27, 1860,' in R. P. Basler (ed.), *The Collected Works of Abraham Lincoln* (New Brunswick: Rutgers University Press, 1953), Vol. III: 540–1.]

HERBERT APTHEKER

135 American Negro Slave Revolts

There are few phases of ante-bellum Southern life and history that were not in some way influenced by the fear of, or the actual outbreak of, militant concerted slave action. In some cases the influences were of a minor, if not of a merely formal, nature. Such appears to be the case when Southerners appealed for the annexation of Louisiana in order to take it out of the hands of a possibly hostile and apparently revolutionary France, which might use that possession as a means of arousing slave rebellion in the United States. Similar arguments were used to justify other annexations, as those of East and West Florida and Texas, and pronouncements of imperialistic designs, such as the Ostend Manifesto. Another argument, however, used in all the territorial advancements of the slave society, to the effect that the South needed new lands in order to lessen the danger of revolt by checking the concentration of Negroes within a limited area, seems to have been a rather important consideration in the minds of Southern leaders.

Associated with this latter idea was the colonization movement which attempted to attack the problem of Negro concentration either by persuading or by forcing the free Negroes to leave, thus ridding the slave society of a living refutation of its rationalizations. The Governor of North Carolina, for example, was urged to further the cause of the American Colonization Society, because it might 'rid us more expeditiously of our greatest pest and danger—the free people of colour'. It is this that explains the fact that, as has been shown, the discovery of slave conspiracies or the suppression of insurrections, as in 1800, 1816, 1831, brought a resuscitation of this colonization movement. Thus, one of the first proposals of such a plan, that coming from New Jersey in 1772, was put forward by one moved to write because of a recent plot in his own neighborhood. Yet, although most 'respectable' channels of propaganda were friendly to it, and although governments and wealthy individuals liberally provided it with funds, the movement was an utter failure. An essential reason for this was the bitter and well-nigh unanimous opposition of the Negro people themselves to any movement seeking to remove them from their homes.

Another line of approach to the problem of curtailing Negro concentration was through restrictions on slave importations. Measures having this as their inspiration were frequently passed by colonial, state, and federal governments, as has been noted, and such action generally occurred during or immediately following periods of considerable servile unrest. But these efforts were also, in large part, ineffective, undoubtedly because of the powerful economic interests which profited by defying their provisions.

The prime motive, on the part of the slaveholders of the antebellum South, was the maintenance of its type of social order. Internally, the ultimate threat to this stability was disaffection and unrest on the part of the slaves, particularly organized, militant activity threatening the order's security. Thus it came about that a basic consideration in the formulation of the legal, social, and theological aspects of pre-Civil War Southern life was how best to prevent or how most efficiently to suppress mass Negro rebelliousness.

Thus was fostered the colossal myth of the sub-humanity of the Negro, a myth basic to the entire social order, and which demanded the corruption of political science, theology, and anthropology. Acceptance of this idea had to be demonstrated by all, Negro and white, in their daily behavior, their mode of eating and speaking, their demeanor, their occupations and activities, their worshipping and love-making, their every feature and phase of living had to acknowledge the immutability, indeed, the divine origin of the status quo. Failure to abide by this meant—for the white—ostracism, both social and economic, explicit warning, or overt punishment, tar and feathers, lashing, imprisonment, hanging; for the Negro, sale, torture, death.

This was the foundation. Upon this was reared the structure itself. Laws hampered and penalized the free Negro, and finally called for his removal or enslavement. They told the slave where he might go, how, and when. They forbade him to learn to read or write, or to testify against a white man, or to possess weapons, or to resist the demands and commands of his master. The slaveocracy supplied overseers and patrolmen and city guards and militiamen and volunteer armed groups and federal soldiers, but these were not always sufficient to allay the terror that ever underlay that life, like some dark brooding evil spirit, and that became reality at the first intimation—'The slaves are plotting—the Negroes have risen!' Instant action—blood, burning flesh, swaying bodies—was then the cry and nothing else would do, so that vigilance committees and lynchings were so common as to become institutionalized.

An outstanding characteristic of ante-bellum Southern economic life was its predominantly agrarian nature. Undoubtedly the fact that the institution of slavery froze billions of dollars of capital into human beings was of great importance in maintaining this way of life. But the belief that urban, proletarian Negroes were difficult to control was a factor not to be overlooked in explaining the reluctance of the Southern rulers to do more than they did to bring their section's life closer into line with the prevailing trend of the nineteenth century.

Philosophically, too, the effect was considerable. It has been demonstrated that the prevalence of revolutionary sentiments and slogans frequently reached the consciousness of America's slaves and affected their behavior. The irreconcilability of a progressive political ideology with the persistence of a commercialized plantation slavery was well understood by many Southern leaders. The fear that the former would lead to the destruction of the latter did much to hasten the South in its repudiation of Jeffersonian equalitarian doctrines. Back in 1794 a Virginia aristocrat pointed out that the democrats favored the common, poor people and asked, 'Who so poor as our slaves, who therefore so fit to participate in the spoils of the rich and to direct the affairs of the nation?' To the slaveocracy of the nineteenth century the Declaration of Independence became but the mouthings of an irresponsible and dangerous fanatic, a ridiculous, high-sounding concoction of obvious absurdities.

[. . .]

The weakness, from a military standpoint, of the slave area was a prominent consideration in the minds of southern and national leaders. And, in times of stress, as during the Revolution, the War of 1812, and the Civil War, the measures taken in an attempt to insure continued subordination or to suppress evidences of unrest, resulted in serious weakening of the prowess of the South. This, as has been shown, entered prominently into the discussions, pro and con, among the dominant class in the 1850's, and down to the moment of decision, as to the advisability of pursuing the policy of secession. One of the important causes aggravating the already severe strain placed on the acquiescence of the poorer whites in continued domination by the Bourbons were certain of the precautionary measures thought necessary by the Confederacy, particularly that which exempted from military service in the first conscription act one white (owner or overseer) for every twenty slaves, and which was later changed to one for every fifteen slaves.

This study has attempted to meet the need, which has become increasingly evident in recent years, of depicting in realistic terms the response of the American Negro to his bondage. The data herein presented make necessary the revision of the generally accepted notion that his response was one of passivity and docility. The evidence, on the contrary, points to the conclusion that discontent and rebelliousness were not only exceedingly common, but, indeed, characteristic of American Negro slaves.

[From *American Negro Slave Revolts* [1943] (New York: International
Publishers, 1970), 368–72, 374.]

The first such problem is that of slave resistance. Slavery signified, of course, involuntary migration and coerced labor. From Argentina to Canada, slave populations gave ample evidence that New World slavery was intolerable, and they did so by resisting their condition. But the forms and frequencies of such resistance were highly variable in time and in space. There has been a wholly understandable tendency recently to equate resistance with violence, and to seek to pinpoint violent resistance, whenever possible. Such a tendency, however, runs the risk of distorting the very diverse processes by which slave populations actually dealt with the daily realities of slavery. More, to equate resistance with violence is to impose on slave consciousness a rigidity and unresourcefulness that misrepresents both the nature of the institution of slavery and the capacities of the slaves themselves. If one were to generalize about the total span of the slavery experience, it would surely be nearer the truth to contend that the masters were far more dependably violent than the slaves—hardly a daring contention when one remembers that slavery itself was rooted in acts of violence, and that the institution consistently armed itself against even the most trivial show of contrary force. The sharpest evidence of slave resistance, then, is not the historical record of armed revolts, important though these were, so much as the codes that legalized branding, flogging, burning, the amputation of limbs, hamstringing and murder to keep the slaves 'non-violent'. One may thus ask of the historical record how the slaves resisted in the face of the most cruel codes of modern times—and there should be neither surprise nor disappointment in the discovery that considerable resistance involved as its precondition some processes of culture change, of adaptation, on the part of the slaves themselves. This is not an idle issue. The house slave who poisoned her master's family by putting ground glass in the food had first to become the family cook. The runaway slaves who created viable communities in the hinterlands of so many slave societies needed to learn techniques of cultivation in an alien environment. And the slaves who plotted armed revolts in the marketplaces had first to produce for market, and to gain permission to carry their produce there.

[From 'Toward an Afro-American History,' *Journal of World History* 13 (1971), 320–1.]

The slaves of the Old South, unlike those of the Caribbean and Brazil, did not take up arms often enough or in large enough numbers to forge a revolutionary tradition. The southern slaves' role in shaping an organic master-slave relationship unfolded under objectively unfavorable military and political circumstances that compelled a different course. But those slaves who rejected the dialectic of accommodation and resistance at its root bore witness, by their rebellion, not only to their own personal courage but to the limits of their masters' hegemony.

More than any other scholar Herbert Aptheker, in his *American Negro Slave Revolts* and pioneering essays, has argued for a revolutionary tradition among the slaves. He demolished the legend of the contented slave, which Ulrich Bonnell Phillips especially promoted despite his own excellent work showing the opposite. Whatever Aptheker's exaggerations and doubtful evaluations, his careful analysis, sharpened by that passionate commitment to the struggle for black liberation which has informed his life's work, unearthed much evidence of insurrection, maroon activity, and other forms of physical resistance and compelled a new departure in the historiography. Kenneth M. Stampp's *Peculiar Institution*, which in 1956 delivered the *coup de grâce* to Phillips's more tendentious interpretations, could not so easily have swept the field had not Aptheker and a few others already cleared away so much rubbish. But in arguing for a revolutionary tradition from a slim evidential base, Aptheker drew attention away from the slaves' deeper cultural and social resistance and from the organic relationships inherent in the slaveholders' hegemony; he focused instead on forms of overt resistance that, while important in their own right, did not lay bare the essence of the slave experience. By no means unaware of those dimensions, he was among the first to follow W. E. B. Du Bois in pointing out their strength; but his choice of emphasis flowed from an empirical error and led to an incorrect theoretical assessment. Satisfied that he had discovered a revolutionary tradition, he missed the chance to apply his considerable professional talent and critical Marxist perspective to the problem of the weakness and limited extent of the revolts and to move the discussion toward a reconsideration of those preconditions for hemispheric slave revolt which can tell us so much about the general conditions of slave life. That problem remains.

The significance of the slave revolts in the United States lies neither in their frequency nor in their extent, but in their very existence as the ultimate manifestation of class war under the most unfavorable conditions. The resort to insurrection in the United States, especially when more than merely a violent outburst against vicious local conditions, provides a yardstick with which to measure the smoldering resentment of an enslaved people who normally had to find radically different forms of struggle. A Gabriel Prosser or a Nat Turner presents the opposite limiting case to the slavish personality delineated in Stanley Elkins's celebrated model. The slaves as a class cannot be understood apart from the combination of these two images, for every slave, being flesh and blood, necessarily had within him elements of both. The preponderance of the one over the other in their peculiar and innumerable combinations ultimately depended on the totality of social conditions.

Notwithstanding the occurrence of insurrections in the Old South that command attention, they did not compare in size, frequency, intensity, or general historical significance with those of the Caribbean or South America. The largest slave revolt in the United States took place in Louisiana in 1811 and involved between 300 and 500 slaves; it alone was comparable in size to those of the Caribbean—that is, comparable to the modest ones. Nat Turner had about 70 slaves with him. Gabriel Prosser and Denmark Vesey apparently expected to raise many more but never had the chance. Risings such as those of 25 or so in New York City in 1712 or of 50 to 100 at Stono, South Carolina, in 1739, although impressive in themselves, qualify as minor events in the general history of slave revolts in the Americas.

[. . .]

Those slaves whose disaffection turned into violence and hatred—those who resisted the regime physically—included slaves who made stealing almost a way of life, killed their overseers and masters, fought back against patrollers, burned down plantation buildings, and ran away either to freedom or to the woods for a short while in order to effect some specific end, as well as those who took the ultimate measures and rose in revolt. Class oppression, whether or not reinforced and modified by racism, induces servility and feelings of inferiority in the oppressed. Force alone usually has not sufficed to keep the lower classes in subjugation. Slavishness constitutes the extreme form of the psychology of the oppressed, although we may doubt that it ever appears in pure form. It longs for acceptance by the other, perceived as the epitome of such superior qualities as beauty, goodness, virtue, and above all, power. But the inevitable inability of the lower classes, especially but not uniquely slave classes, to attain that acceptance generates disaffection, hatred, and violence.

The slaves' response to paternalism and their imaginative creation of a partially autonomous religion provided a record of simultaneous accommodation and resistance to slavery. Accommodation itself breathed a critical spirit and disguised subversive actions and often embraced its apparent opposite—resistance. In fact, accommodation might best be understood as a way of accepting what could not be helped without falling prey to the pressures for dehumanization, emasculation, and self-hatred. In particular, the slaves' accommodation to paternalism enabled them to assert rights, which by their very nature not only set limits to their surrender of self but actually constituted an implicit rejection of slavery.

Stark physical resistance did not represent a sharp break with the process of accommodation except in its most extreme forms—running away to freedom and insurrection. Strictly speaking, only insurrection represented political action, which some choose to define as the only genuine resistance since it alone directly challenged the power of the regime. From that point of view, those activities which others call 'day-to-day resistance to slavery'—stealing, lying, dissembling, shirking, murder, infanticide, suicide, arson—qualify at best as prepolitical and at worst as apolitical.

These distinctions have only a limited usefulness and quickly lose their force. Such apparently innocuous and apolitical measures as a preacher's sermon on love and dignity or the mutual support offered by husbands and wives played—under the specific conditions of slave life—an indispensable part in providing the groundwork for the most obviously political action, for they contributed to the cohesion and strength of a social class threatened by disintegration and demoralization. But 'day-to-day resistance to slavery' generally implied accommodation and made no sense except on the assumption of an accepted status quo the norms of which, as perceived or defined by the slaves, had been violated.

The definition of resistance as political response nonetheless draws attention to a break—a qualitative leap—in the continuum of resistance in accommodation and accommodation in resistance The slaves who unambiguously chose to fight for or fly to freedom represented a new quality. They remained a small portion of the total, but their significance far transcended their numbers. The maturation of that new quality, so vital to the health and future of the black community, depended upon those less dramatic efforts in the quarters which produced a collective spiritual life.

[From *Roll, Jordan, Roll: The World the Slaves Made*
(New York: Pantheon, 1974), 587–8, 597–8.]

EUGENE D. GENOVESE

138 **From Rebellion to Revolution**

The restorationist vision gave way in Saint-Domingue, where the slaves of the New World wrote their most glorious chapter in the midst of a booming sugar industry that had created the world's richest colony. The slaves, in an uneasy and inconsistent alliance with a large minority of propertied mulattoes, defeated the Spanish, inflicted a defeat of unprecedented proportions on the British, and then made their country the graveyard of Napoleon's magnificent army as well as of his imperial ambitions in the New World. In the end, the Americas had their first black national state.

The story of that magnificent revolution, which C. L. R. James has recounted with literary and analytic power, need here concern us only in its bare outlines. The colony had half a million slaves, brutally driven in the midst of an extraordinary economic boom presided over by a class of slave-holders who, when not absentees, wished they were. Of these slaves, at least half and probably two-thirds had come from Africa. Their religion, Vodûn, although it later merged with Catholicism, remained close to its eclectic African origins during the slave period and became a creed of opposition to the white regime and its official religion. Macendal, who has been described as a Muslim, led the most important early resistance movement, and Bouk-man, a Vodûn priest, led the rising that sparked the great revolution itself.

Many of the leaders who emerged during the revolution came from the privileged slave strata. Toussaint had risen to the position of foreman and could read and write, although not well. Henri Christophe had worked as a hotel waiter and had had some military experience. Those who led the mulatto rising in the south were cultured and sophisticated men of property, not slaves at all. The early leaders of the black revolution in the north, Jean-François and Biassou, had established careers in the military campaigns on the Spanish border. The revolutionaries had behind them knowledge of protracted maroon warfare in the eastern part of the island.

Finally, the ruling class split asunder. The planters and *petits blancs* fought each other and together conspired to keep the mulattoes, many of them rich slaveholders, in racial subordination. The white and mulatto colonials resisted the French bourgeoisie and state, which milked them in the slave trade as well as in an imposed system of unequal trade and tariffs. The metropolitan power crumbled after 1789, and the colonials scampered to choose the win-ning side and to use events in France to advantage against each other. The arrival of revolutionary French troops, with *liberté, égalité, fraternité* on their lips, hardly helped the slaveholders' cause. And then the white powers fell on each other and bid for black and mulatto support. Toussaint and his generals brilliantly played one ruling-class group against the other and, in the end, made themselves masters of all. In short, Saint-Domingue witnessed the conjuncture of ideal preconditions for slave revolt.

[. . .]

The revolutionary army in Saint-Domingue might in fact have succumbed to the heavier French firepower, yellow fever or no, if it had not been sup-ported by an indomitable mass movement that turned defeats into victories. As the French advanced, writes C. L. R. James, the 'people burned San Domingo flat so that at the end of the war it was a charred desert'. And as David Brion Davis pointedly remarks in *The Problem of Slavery in the Age of Revolution*:

No doubt Haitian independence, like that of the United States and the Latin American republics, depended upon a variety of circumstances. But if the black population had been easily subdued, the yellow fever epidemic would have made little difference. Both sides knew that the fever would come, like the tropical rains, but only the blacks used the knowledge to their own advantage.

Haiti's emergence meant much more than a major black victory over whites and the creation of a black state. Both had precedents. The maroons of Jamaica, Surinam, and even Saint-Domingue, among others, had defeated the whites and large, autonomous black communities—if not quite 'states'— had arisen in Palmares and the back country of several countries. Haiti's special significance rested on more than the greater magnitude of its revolution, its victory, and its emergent territorial state. If the British, French, Dutch, Spanish, and Portuguese could come to terms with large maroon colonies and use them to help crush slave revolts, why should they tremble so at an oversized maroon colony in the middle of the Caribbean?

The revolution under Toussaint, a leader of genius, did not aspire to restore some lost African world or build an isolated Afro-American enclave that, whatever its cultural merit, could have played no autonomous role in world affairs and would have had to become a protectorate of one or another European power. Toussaint, and after his death Dessalines and Henri Christophe, tried to forge a modern black state, based on an economy with a vital export sector oriented to the world market. The ultimate failure of their basically Jacobin program ushered in one of history's most grimly ironical counterrevolutions. Pétion's and Boyer's political relaxation and land reform replaced Henri Christophe's iron dictatorship and maintenance of the sugar plantations under rigorous work discipline. Haiti slowly became, in Sidney Mintz's words, 'The Caribbean area's most thoroughgoing peasant country'.

[From *From Rebellion to Revolution: Afro-American Slave Revolts in the Making of the Modern World* (Baton Rouge: Louisiana State University Press, 1979), 85–9.]

JOÃO JOSÉ REIS AND P. F. DE MORAES FARIAS

139   Islam and Slave Rebellion in Bahia, Brazil

The state of Bahia, in northeastern Brazil, was one of the most important areas of sugar production and slavery in the New World. Its slaves were feared for their rebelliousness by slave-masters all over Brazil, who avoided buying captives from the region. More than twenty slave revolts and conspiracies are known to have occurred in Bahia during the nineteenth-century. These rebellions struck both the sugar plantations of the Reconcavo, the area bordering the Bay of All Saints, and the city of Salvador, capital of Bahia and of the Portuguese empire in the Americas until 1763, when it was replaced by Rio de Janeiro

[. . .]

The authors who see the 1835 movement as a *jihâd* hold, with scant support from the evidence, that the assassination of African pagans supposedly planned by the rebels is sufficient proof that the uprising was a holy war. But, in fact, Bastide rightly pointed out that there were pagans within the rebel group. [. . .] [T]he conspirators recruited non-Muslim kinsmen and work partners, and their plan was to incite an insurrection of all the African slaves of Salvador and the Reconcavo.

The Muslim doctrine is not unambiguous about whether pagans may participate in a *jihâd*. There are those who maintain that Muslims should not ask pagans for help but that they should accept such a help when offered. Usuman Dan Fodio seems to have held the opinion that help from pagans, i.e., from non-Muslims who are not followers of Scriptural Religions such as Judaism and Christianity, should neither be asked for nor accepted. But in reality many pagans fought in his *jihâd*. Although pagan participation does not deny the 'holiness' of Muslim wars, the Bahian rebellion differs from the Sokoto *jihâd* and other models in that the 1835 Muslim leaders *sought* help most and probably received it from African pagans.

The 1835 rebellion was definitely not directed against the African *kafirai*. Nor was it, in spite of another of Bastide's suggestions, directed against Christians as such. In their depositions the defendants systematically identified their foes as the whites or, less often, the creoles and mulattos, never the Christians as such. Bastide brought a European model of Christian/Islamic conflict into the 1835 scenario by asserting that Islam is *in principle* fanatical and intolerant, thus neglecting to explain the intense symbolic commerce between African Islam and ethnic religions both in Africa and in Bahia. Goody reaches a similar conclusion through a different route, mainly the ability of Muslim slaves to communicate in written form, which would have facilitated the conspiracy, and the role of a universalistic Religion of the Book in creating a strong ideological bond among its followers and intransigence vis-à-vis non-Muslims. As we already mentioned, Islamic literacy was probably a goal of Bahian Muslims—as it is a goal of Muslims in general—but in Bahia very few of them were able to write fluently and no Arabic paper containing secular messages has yet been discovered. Perhaps because he lacked more detailed information on the 1835 rebellion, Goody underestimates—though he does not deny—the role of the written word as magical protection, a 'reading' of Islam more often found among African slaves in Bahia than any other. It is therefore difficult to accept that a struggle based on the West African jihadic models, mainly the Sokoto *jihâd*, was reproduced in Bahia. Not because the *jihâd* is necessarily a form of state imperialism, as Kent has argued, for this is certainly not always the case. The *jihâd* led by Usuman Dan Fodio, for example, was not an external war meant to expand an existing Islamic state. Rather, it was an internal revolution aimed at creating an Islamic state to replace state institutions of a different nature.

[From 'Islam and Slave Rebellion in Bahia, Brazil,' *Islam et sociétés au sud du Sahara* 3 (1989), 41, 56–7.]

MICHAEL CRATON

140   Testing the Chains

The African contribution to Afro-Caribbean slave resistance was, of course, even more pervasive than, though quite as complex as, that of the Amerindians. Over a subtle range of political and commercial systems in Africa, native rulers and traders generally and quite successfully resisted European takeover, while individuals and groups of slaves universally resisted enslavement. In the African context there was an obvious disjunction between the two types of resistance, since the quest for political and economic independence rested heavily on the enslavement of individuals. Yet both types are relevant in considering the roots of resistance in the American plantations. For besides the parallels between Africa and America in the forms of slave resistance, and an actual bridge in the shipboard risings on the Middle Passage, the leadership in plantation slave rebellions owed much to the example of African rulers seeking to preserve—or even to create—ambits of political and economic autonomy. In addition, white slave traders and planters alike slowly came to recognize certain common features in African responses to enslavement and common elements in those responses in Africa, the Middle Passage, and West Indian plantations, which called for a range of counterresponses on the part of the whites.

The range of examples, spanning 350 years and involving slaves from 5,000 miles of African coastline illustrated in Elizabeth Donnan's magisterial four-volume collection of slave trade documents shows that resistance was general and might erupt into open revolt at any time during the process of enslavement. Early slavers, such as John Hawkins, suffered costly and embarrassing losses from some African tribes. Once the African slave trade became organized, though, the Europeans found it no longer necessary (or indeed possible) to penetrate far inland in Africa or to capture slaves for themselves. They were clearly content to let African kings and traders fight wars and organize raids on their behalf and shared an interest with these assistants in establishing prisonlike barracoons on the coast, euphemistically called forts or factories. However, once the slaves had been sold and transferred to the ships and the ships had set sail, resistance not only redoubled but became a daily nightmare to the European traders.

Revolts that led to the takeover of slave vessels, such as the seizure of the *Thomas* in 1797 or the even more famous *Amistad* case of 1839, were rare enough to make news throughout the Atlantic sphere. Even general uprisings that were bloodily suppressed, such as the *Eagle* and *Ferrers* incidents in the 1720s, which were graphically described by William Snelgrave, were no more than occasional episodes. Perhaps no more than one slave voyage in ten experienced an actual outbreak. But few voyages were ever completed without the discovery or threat of slave conspiracy, and no slaving captain throughout the history of the Atlantic trade ever sailed without a whole armory of guns and chains plus as many white crewmen as he could recruit and keep alive to act as seaborne jailers.

White traders came to expect resistance but were still baffled by the variety of its manifestations and were unable either to prevent uprisings or to predict them with any certainty. These failings were shared by the planters to whom they sold the slaves. Part of the trouble stemmed from the dependence of the planters on the white slavers and of the slavers on the African kings and *caboceers*. But the sheer ignorance of all whites about internal African conditions, the complexity of African cultures, and the general psychology of slave resistance compounded the problem.

West Indian planters had a clear idea of the type of slaves they wanted and developed preferential stereotypes of the ethnic groups they encountered. But by and large they took the slaves they could find and afford, and the stereotypes they invented tell us more about the whites themselves and the needs of the plantations than about Africans and their availability. Slaves were commonly labeled according to their African port of embarkation rather than by true ethnic origin, if they did not bear a quasi-ethnic label based on observed characteristics that ignored true origin altogether. These designations demonstrate the faultiness of European stereotypes, as do the different scales of preference and labels associated with various European trading nations—although different countries were in fact tapping different areas of Africa because of different patterns of trade and access.

[From *Testing the Chains: Resistance to Slavery in the British West Indies*
(Ithaca: Cornell University Press, 1982), 23–5.]

The control of slaves, as Frederick Cooper has observed, 'was not simply a matter of physical repression, but of creating ties of dependency'. Through such bonds slaveowners intended to lead slaves into accepting their moral authority over them, but in reality, dependency for most slaves was never as complete as slaveowners may have wished, since there were areas of the slaves' lives with which masters did not interfere. They simply could not control every facet of the slaves' existence in order to mold abject dependents. Moreover, it was also quite clear to both masters and slaves that masters depended heavily upon their bondmen, without whose cooperation they could not operate their plantations and other businesses. In order to win such cooperation, which many masters perceived sprang from dependency, but which from the slaves' point of view more accurately reflected a shrewd appraisal of the necessary degrees of compliance, masters wielded authority through variable combinations of fear, coercion, and negotiation. These helped determine patterns of master-slave relations and the tone of life in Antigua slave society. Masters were not therefore in control as fully as they would have liked; they were not able to extract slave compliance from a position of complete authority.

One result of this dimension of master-slave relations was that masters failed to stifle the sense of injustice or hostile feelings that slaves could act upon from time to time, in one form or another, in response to specific or more general grievances perpetrated by masters who had thereby broken the unwritten contract of mutual obligations between themselves and their bondmen. Ultimately, whatever techniques of control masters used to establish supremacy over partly dependent slaves did not make slave resistance impossible even among those who may have generally shown marked inclinations to identify with masters' interests. Such identification did not preclude the expression of hostile feelings. Instead of submitting, slaves adapted their responses in most cases to the changing conditions of life around them, struggling to make the best of their situation short of shattering their chains for collective freedom, although under propitious conditions that too would come. Emergent patterns of slave behavior in Antigua, individual and collective, are therefore best studied or illustrated in relation to the changing environment of life and labor as the society and economy developed.

From the early years of emergent slave society in Antigua in the seventeenth century down to emancipation in the nineteenth, slaves engaged in resistance precipitated either by specific grievances or by a generalized disaffection aimed at destroying the system or hampering its effective operation. Most slaves were neither strictly nor unambiguously docile or rebellious. Because of the wide range of responses possible between the poles of abject submission and total resistance that reflected a delicate balance between the slaves' urge to resist and yet at the same time survive, adjustments of most slaves must be seen as infinitely more complex. Slave resistance in this sense was largely accommodative. Accommodation, as an integral part of resistance, allowed slaves to survive, to accept 'what could not be helped without falling prey to the pressures for dehumanization, emasculation, and self-hatred', but at the same time it helped camouflage subversive action. Resistance in accommodation and accommodation in resistance, to use Genovese's phrase, were not beyond most slaves, who shrewdly weighed the costs, personal and collective, of different kinds of resistance. 'Once the complexities of resistance and survival are acknowledged,' writes Mintz, 'it becomes obvious that the struggle of the slaves was a subtle, involved and delicate phenomenon.' The 'house slave who poisoned her master's family by putting ground glass in the food had first to become the family cook,' Mintz has cogently observed. 'And the slaves who plotted armed revolts in the marketplaces had first to produce for the market, and to gain permission to carry their produce there.'

But it has been claimed that what is loosely called slave resistance is not resistance at all, strictly speaking, except perhaps in the case of insurrection, because resistance is a political concept denoting 'organized collective action which aims at affecting the distribution of power in a community'. Moreover, even though there exists an abundance of evidence on slave behavior that cannot be equated with cooperation with the slave system, it is hazardous to translate these into political resistance. Part of the difficulty, of course, lies in the absence of incontrovertible evidence pointing to the internalized processes behind the acts, the slaves' 'subjective disposition' or motivation. Resistance, therefore, may not even be a particularly useful descriptive term for largely undramatic, day-to-day slave activities that harassed the plantation system. Nonetheless, as Genovese has argued, they can with justification still be regarded as a useful foundation from which slaves could develop an edifice of subversion leading to maturation in collective political resistance or insurrection. At the same time it should be understood that there is indeed a big step, a product of slave adaptation, between individual acts of defiance, however frequent, and the emergence of a collective consciousness built around such acts. Along the continuum of resistance, an important qualitative difference does emerge between individual acts of resistance and those that were collective or had collective potential; between small, uncoordinated, yet persistent acts, and collective, organized, unambiguous opposition; between elusive and openly defiant behavior. Slave resistance in Antigua from the seventeenth century to 1763 spanned the continuum.

[From *Bondmen and Rebels: A Study of Master–Slave Relations in Antigua* [1985]
(Durham: Duke University Press, 1993), 171–3.]

Eugene Genovese's *From Rebellion to Revolution* stands as the best general introduction to slave resistance in the Americas. Among other things, it addressed the question of the influence of trans-Atlantic political and ideological currents on the character of slave revolts in the Americas. Genovese argued that the 1791 slave revolution in Saint Domingue marked the integration of slave revolts into the Age of Democratic Revolution, a decisive shift away from restorationist revolts directed at withdrawal from the prevailing social arrangements, to revolts directed at a fundamental liberal-democratic restructuring of society.

The argument has drawn fire. Genovese, according to his critics, has denied the existence of slave revolutionary behavior before 1791. He has located the wellspring of slave revolutionary behavior in Europe. He has ignored the slaves' own libertarian heritage. He has not properly distinguished between the view of rebel leaders and those of the soldiery. He overestimates the influence of the Saint Domingue revolution on slaves and underestimates its influence on free people of color.

On careful reading, it seems to me, Genovese need not seek absolution for these sins. As Barry Gaspar noted in his excellent study of the 1736 slave conspiracy in Antigua, when Genovese 'uses the term *decisively* to describe the shift from 'restorationist' revolt to revolutionary overthrow of the slave system, he takes into account that the transition may have begun earlier . . .' Confusion derives from the failure of some students of slave resistance to distinguish analytically between the resistance to enslavement and the resistance to slavery as a social system. From time immemorial slaves have manifested a desire to escape their bondage if for no other reason than the fact that the struggle of the individual against society, between liberation and order, is itself timeless. At another level, slave revolt often represented the narrow assertion of rights for specific collectivities. Individual slaves, for example, might escape their bondage to enter a maroon community that sanctioned forms of dependency including slavery. Much particularist resistance to enslavement mobilized Saint Domingue's oppressed masses to be sure, but the insurrectionary process became a turning point in the history of slave resistance because it also manifested an ecumenical crusade against the system of slavery and thereby bore witness to the revolutionary politics and ideology of the wider world. Like it or not, the antislavery crusade emanated from Europe, and many of Saint Domingue's rebel leaders, most notably Toussaint L'Ouverture, asserted the rights of their people by looking well beyond the referent of their own insular community. In practice, of course, ecumenical movements against slavery and particularist resistance to enslavement could easily converge and be confounded as slave and free colored leaders dealt with political and tactical exigencies.

Genovese's book has prompted a number of reviewers to call for more detailed examinations of specific slave revolts in specific countries. Despite the outpouring of studies on slavery during the last two decades or so, a good deal of hard digging on slave resistance in archives remains to be done. Herbert Aptheker's exchange on slave revolts with C. Vann Woodward in the 3 March 1988 issue of *The New York Review of Books* suggested clear gaps in knowledge of even the content and magnitude of specific slave revolts in the United States. The largest and one of the bloodiest slave revolts in United States history, broke out in territorial Louisiana in 1811. It has not yet received intensive treatment. And those who underestimate the influence of the Saint Domingue revolution on slaves should recall that this revolt was actually led by a privileged slave from Saint Domingue.

My recent study of Cuba's Conspiracy of La Escalera, one of the largest movements of slave and free-colored resistance to slavery in the history of the Americas, qualified but generally sustained Genovese's argument. Broad support can also be found in the recent studies of collective slave resistance in Bahia, Brazil, by Stuart Schwartz and João José Reis; in Richmond, Virginia, by Douglas Egerton; and in colonial Louisiana by Gwendolyn Midlo Hall. Genovese confessed that the mechanisms of ideological transmission are often obscure. Happily, Julius Scott's forthcoming book on African-American currents of communication during and after the Saint Domingue revolution will shed some needed light.

Michael Craton, in his valuable study of slave resistance in the British Caribbean, concluded that 'Slavery was such an intolerable condition that slaves were ever likely to rebel. All that changed, or varied, were the forms of defiance and the occasions'. He concluded perhaps more than he would allow about the role of ideology in slave resistance. Without getting into heated debates about philosophical realism, ideology as form cannot easily be separated from human reality and should be studied by social historians as a vital mediating link between structure and process on the one hand and behavior on the other hand. To the extent that forms of slave resistance change, does not also the reality of those involved? However difficult it is to establish the means of transmission, ideas do have consequences.

Too many recent studies of slave resistance tend to romanticize all forms of slave resistance, to overlook changing patterns of slave resistance, and to oversimplify insurgent motivation and behavior. In some cases collective slave resistance now appears to spring spontaneously from structure or to bubble up from below with little or no credit given to organization and leadership. The complexities of the Saint Domingue revolution, the Tailors' revolt in Brazil, Gabriel's conspiracy in Richmond, the Pointe Coupée conspiracy in

Louisiana, the conspiracies of Aponte and La Escalera in Cuba, Bussa's rebellion in Barbados, Sharpe's rebellion in Jamaica, and many other prominent acts of collective slave resistance in the Americas should warn against the imposition of ideological uniformity on the insurgents. Persons of color of different origins, colors, and statuses participated in these struggles against slavery. Distinctions between African phases of collective resistance for the pre-nineteenth century Americas and later Creole phases simply will not do. African-born slaves and American-born slaves, privileged slaves and field hands, blacks and mulattoes, slaves and free people of color, slave men and slave women could at a specific historical moment under a common experience of oppression come together to attack a common target. Yet they also brought different experiences which could translate into significantly different or competing visions and aspirations. Analysis of variance within movements could help to account for so many tragic failures. It could also lead to a far more searching discussion of leadership, how it ramified through movements, and how it functioned to mobilize resistance.

Instances of collective slave resistance in the Americas reveal competing notions over such essentials as freedom and property. Orlando Patterson has noted that in almost all non-Western slaveholding societies, the idea of a 'free' person had no sanction in law. Indeed, most non-Western languages had no word for freedom before contact with Western peoples. The antithesis of slavery in most non-Western societies was a notion of belonging or embeddedness. If so, to what extent did people of African descent in the Americas adopt the language of freedom and by their struggles over everything from names to land try to infuse it with the substance of embeddedness? Slaves many generations removed from Africa and free people of color deeply involved in urban trades might well have had a more Eurocentric understanding of freedom. Certainly, for many slave rebels, the meaning of freedom did not entail self-actualization through the marketplace, however much they were able, say, by their cultivation of provision grounds to engage the market when it served their interests. John Stuart Mill's emphasis on self-regarding actions as the proper sphere of liberty would have appeared woefully lacking or unnatural to many American slaves. An African-informed freedom would have placed great emphasis on community, kinship, and social responsibility. The slave's banner of freedom would, paradoxically, bear the colors of social order.

Related attention to slave culture and moral economy has generated renewed, if problematic, interest in the day-to-day resistance of slaves. Under the influence of James Scott, the political scientist who studied the day-to-day resistance of Malaysian peasants, students of slavery have elevated the role of accumulated spontaneous, individual, often selfish acts of resistance in transforming systems. Leadership counts for little; distinctions between political and apolitical resistance blur. 'Just as millions of anthozoan polyps create, willy-nilly, a coral reef,' Scott writes, 'so do thousands upon thousands of individual acts of insubordination and evasion create a political or economic barrier reef of their own'.

The problem is that Scott's barrier reef also takes shape by the action of a larger predatory water world in which the reef is dependent. Few scholars today would deny that conflict and mutual dependence characterize the master-slave relation. But having accepted this fact, some have gone on to make rather extravagant claims about the autonomy of slave culture. A world shaped by conflict and mutual dependence would presumably have produced social norms, however gray, fluid, or contested. Slave resistance in such a world would counter dehumanization and could possibly serve to pre-pare individuals or groups for explicit political action. But certain kinds of resistance, including everyday resistance, could readily fit into patterns of accommodation, regardless of whether masters appreciated the fact.

Take, again, the work of Barry Gaspar. The revolutionary slave conspiracy of 1736 in Antigua occurred when most available land had come under culti-vation. Declining opportunities for maroonage increasingly forced slave accommodation. Yet accommodation created space for hatching the more ambitious resistance of 1736. In light of what the authorities uncovered then, maroon activity appears to have served as a safety valve against the complete overthrow of the planter regime.

In short, properly-managed resistance of the day-to-day variety can further system maintenance and may well be essential to its survival. Slave theft or shirking, for example, may challenge discrete elements of a larger moral code but given mutual dependency, also may entail drawbacks for the slaves' con-struction of a coherent and more just alternative order. In bad hands, the arguments of James Scott could offer chaos as the alternative to the prevailing system of exploitation. To succeed, oppressed peoples, unlike some social historians, can ill afford to misconstrue license as moral economy.

[From 'Slave Resistance and Social History', *Journal of Social History* 24 (Spring 1991), 681–4.]

JONATHON GLASSMAN

143   Feast and Riot

Even on the worst of the Mauya estates, slaves found their bonds defined in the ideological language of *shamba* slavery, a language that allowed them to expect opportunities for autonomous participation in the commercial and community life of the Shirazi towns. Their Arab masters, intent on a radical reduction of those opportunities, were therefore confronted by slaves who invoked what might be described as a moral economy of client slavery. The slaves' rhetoric was made more effective by the fact that the values of this moral economy were still widely shared by the majority of Pangani's free-born population, values enshrined not only in the general language of clientelist social relations but also in the specific language of slavery. Although the plantation sector was gaining in commercial importance, few patricians were involved in it; their preferred economic activities, as we have seen, depended on well-cultivated relations of clientele with their slaves. Mauya plantation slavery was regarded as an aberration; all around them sugar slaves could see other patterns of slavery still in operation, albeit under siege. As they were whipped in the cane fields or prevented from raising cash crops on their *makonde*, gang slaves knew that nearby their counterparts were enjoying the prerogatives of urban *mafundi* or winning prestige as porters and caravan leaders.

Although the tactics of slave resistance often involved an invocation of 'custom,' it would be mistaken to think that slave rebels longed to return to a golden age when masters treated them with paternalistic indulgence. Slaves knew that the client slavery that existed before and outside of the plantation sector had never been without conflict and that slaves who were lucky enough to command their own households or engage in trade had won those privileges only through struggle. Nor did rebellious slaves yearn to turn away from the rapid commodification of coastal society that had given rise to the plantation sector. On the contrary, one of their chief aspirations was active and aggressive participation in urban commerce—not as forced laborers, but on their own terms. Even when their masters' power and intransigence pushed slaves into fleeing from the coast, runaways did not seek escape from urban society so much as they used flight as a strategy for claiming a fuller role in urban institutions of commerce and community.

Thus the most common form of slave rebellion embraced a paradox: fugitive slaves ran away from the Swahili communities in order to intrude more forcefully into them. Despite the fact that many runaways or *watoro* (sing., *mtoro*) had been born upcountry, the settlements they built in the inaccessible margins of the towns' hinterlands constituted outposts of coastal Muslim culture. They prayed in mosques, lived in square, Swahili-style houses, and when possible engaged in commerce and the production of cash crops. Flight did not express a desire to break with urban society, but a desire to become more fully integrated into it. Although the *watoro* and their former masters differed over the particular nature of relations of servitude, they shared an underlying ideological framework in which the ideal community was Muslim, commercial, and—perhaps above all—governed by interlocking networks of patrons and clients. Slave rebels sought community, not 'independence'. The social structures in which they struggled to participate consisted not of free and equal individuals, but of strong men and weak (the strong were almost always men), in which the former protected the latter in return for pledges of personal loyalty. Accordingly, after running away from their masters, *watoro* sought other patrons who could help them participate in the institutions of coastal urban society.

[. . .]

The most dramatic indication of the changing tenor of slave–master conflict was the massive slave revolt of 1873, which led to the founding of the powerful *watoro* community of Makorora. Whereas most previous acts of flight had been performed by individuals or by small knots of slaves, the flight to Makorora, which occurred just as Mauya sugar production was entering its boom phase, can be regarded as a conscious social movement, sparked by the efforts of the planter class to impose a new labor regime. Yet even at this moment, when tensions between masters and slaves sharpened into something that might plausibly be called class conflict, the motivations of the rebels remained highly ambiguous. The rebels did not articulate a clearly delineated class consciousness; they neither demanded 'freedom' nor did they reject the slave-owning society of their masters. Although many, if not most, were born in the southern interior, the *watoro* of Makorora built their community along the lines of their masters' culture and sought the protection of powerful Arab patrons. Their motivating consciousness was a complex web of paternalist ideologies, into which were woven ideals of patriarchy, commerce and tributary submission to an Omani overlord.

The earliest record of the revolt dates from July 1873, when John Kirk, reporting to his superiors on the events of the previous six months, wrote that 'slaves on the Pangani [River] have . . . left their masters in a body'. The consul-general may have learned of the revolt during his visit to Pangani two months earlier, when he explained the contents of the impending slave-trade treaty to the *liwali*. Kirk, a major figure in abolitionist circles, initially attributed the rebellion to news of the treaty he had negotiated, and this would seem to support the argument that slave rebels were motivated by ideals of 'freedom' imparted by Western consuls and catechists. But as we've seen, Kirk's conversation with the *liwali* could have given little indication that emancipation was the purpose of the treaty and in a later dispatch he retreated from his abolitionist idealization of the rebels' motives. 'Although these runaway slaves assert their own independence,' he wrote, 'it would be a great mistake to suppose they have any sympathy for freedom in the abstract, as experience of existing settlements of the kind shows that they hold slaves, and engage in slave trade like any other—it would be indeed strange were it otherwise'. At any rate, neither the British nor any of their treaties are mentioned in oral traditions preserved by the rebel leaders' descendants.

Both written and oral sources suggest that the rebel were defending their status as autonomous clients against attempts by Arab masters to subject them to regimented plantation labor. A contemporary German wrote that many of the rebels were caravan traders resisting enslavement for debts incurred in the ivory trade. This cannot be exactly correct because Swahili customs of debt slavery would have prohibited the enslavement of Muslim caravan personnel. (It is in fact uncertain whether debt slavery was practiced at all.) It is more likely that the caravaners described by this observer had been not free traders enslaved for debt but rather *vibarua* or *fundi* slaves such as those who had always been autonomous participants in Pangani's ivory trade. In the late 1860s and early 1870s, just as the commercial boom was opening opportunities to which such trading slaves were eager to respond, their masters tried to force them into the role of *shamba* slaves on the new sugar estates.

[From *Feast and Riot: Revelry, Rebellion, and Popular Consciousness on the Swahili Coast, 1856–1888* (Portsmouth: Heinemann, 1995), 106–7, 109–10.]

DAVID PATRICK GEGGUS

144   Slavery in the Greater Caribbean

Black resistance to slavery took a variety of forms in this period. Generally, the most massive or protracted conflicts, the ones that most severely challenged colonial rule, were those in which emancipated slaves resisted attempts to reenslave them (Saint Domingue, 1793–1798, 1802–1803; Saint Lucia, 1795–1797; Guadeloupe, 1802; Prospect Bluff, Florida, 1815–1816), or where free coloreds or Black Caribs made common cause with slaves in a joint war of liberation (Grenada and Saint Vincent, 1795–1796). These were usually epic contests, featuring pitched battles, staggering death tolls, and episodes of striking heroism. Also unnerving for colonial regimes were the war against the Boni maroons in Surinam (1789–1793) and the Jamaican Maroon War of 1795–1796, though there slavery was less directly at issue. It is significant that none of these contests strictly speaking was a slave revolt. Each profited greatly from organization, experience, and weaponry available only outside the state of slavery.

The table 'Slave Rebellions and Conspiracies, 1789–1815' at the end of this [extract] is an attempt to identify what may be most properly termed slave revolts and conspiracies, those which proportionately involved slaves more than other groups, whose principal target was the slave regime, and which were organized within slavery rather than outside it. It is still not a well-defined category and far from homogeneous, with events in Saint Domingue dwarfing all the others put together in magnitude, consequences, and duration. No restrictive criteria regarding size were applied, as information on this was often lacking. A few of the cases perhaps do not meet the standard of ten participants used in Herbert Aptheker's pioneering study of slave rebellions in the United States. On the other hand, small numbers of slaves executed, punished, or even arrested indicate planter parsimony and prudence as often as the true dimensions of a conspiracy or revolt.

Further problems of definition are posed by certain borderline cases. The 1802 Dominica mutiny of soldiers in the Second West India Regiment might have been included, since the legal status of black troops in the British Army was then still unsettled, and fear of being sold motivated the mutineers. Another group of uncertain status, persons who successfully asserted their claim to freedom at this time, were the 1,000 Cobreros of eastern Cuba, though theirs was largely a nonviolent rebellion. The hundreds of fugitive slaves armed by the British in the War of 1812 who raided frontier plantations and later held a fort in the Florida panhandle against a U.S. Army force similarly do not fit usual categories; nor do the thousands of bondsmen who joined both sides in the Spanish American War of Independence. The 'Swiss' slaves who joined the free coloreds of west Saint Domingue in their early struggles were omitted from the table because they and their interests remained subordinated to the free coloreds, though they evidently hoped to gain their own liberty. The long resistance of the Dominica maroon bands in 1809–1814 and the 'rebellious runaways' of northern Jamaica in 1798, whose activities fell halfway between insurrection and marronage, provide other cases. So, too, do the one or two hundred slaves who apparently joined the Trelawny Maroons in the war of 1795.

What constituted a conspiracy also can be problematic. Some historians question the existence of several of the plots listed in the table and attribute them to the imagination of nervous colonists or to slaves' discussing fantasies of retribution. The Jamaica 1791 conspiracy and the Puerto Rico conspiracy of 1812 may fall in this category, as might the 1795 Trinidad plots mentioned by V. S. Naipaul. Evidence for some of the revolts is also scanty. I have omitted several cases mentioned in recent historiography that I judged to be spurious. On the other hand, it is possible I have overlooked conspiracies or small rebellions that contemporaries sought to cover up.

With these limitations in mind, we may suggest that slave revolts and conspiracies in the Greater Caribbean averaged at least two per year during the period 1789–1815 and nearly four per year in the 1790s, with revolts more numerous than conspiracies that did not reach fruition. About a dozen of the rebellions involved one hundred or more slaves. Outside of Saint Domingue, the only insurrections to mobilize 1,000 slaves occurred in Guadeloupe (August 1793) and in tiny Curaçao (1795 and 1800), though thousands of slaves joined in the multiclass risings in the British Windward Islands in 1795. Initially slave resistance was most prominent in France's colonies. Then, in the mid-1790s, the Spanish Caribbean saw an upsurge of activity. Another spate occurred in 1811–1812, though in general overt resistance diminished considerably after 1800. This pattern clearly had much to do with the impact of the French Revolution, though some historians have exaggerated its importance. Certainly, two other causal factors need to be taken into account: the variations in military strength experienced by different colonies and the influence of European antislavery and reformism.

Table 1: *Slave rebellions and conspiracies, 1789–1815.*

TIME AND PLACE	REVOLT (R) OR CONSPIRACY (C)	DETAILS
1789		
1. August, Martinique	R	Saint Pierre district 300–400 slaves.
2. Demerara	R	1 plantation. Widespread conspiracy.
1790		
3. January, Cuba	R	1 plantation.
4. April, Guadeloupe	R?	Petit Bourg, etc. 100+ punished.
5. Spring? Venezuela	R	1 plantation. 1 overseer killed.
6. May, Tortola	R	1 plantation. 2 slaves executed.
7. October–December, Martinique	R	West coast. Pillage and killing.
1791		
8. January 1, Saint Lucia	C	Soufrière, 1 plantation.
9. Early January, Dominica	R	Work stoppage / desertion / confrontation.
10. Mid-January, Dominica	R	Free colored leader. 1 white killed.
11. January, Saint Domingue	C	Port Salut. 200 slaves.
12. May, Guadeloupe	C?	Saint Anne. Led by mulatto slave.
13. June–July, Saint Domingue	R	Separate revolts on 3 estates.
14. July, Louisiana	C	Pointe Coupée. 17 slaves arrested.
15. August, Marie-Galante	C	Saint Domingue. Free colored hanged.
16. August–November, Saint Domingue	R	North Province. 100,000+.
17. November–December, Jamaica	C?	North Coast.
1792+		
18. Saint Domingue	R	Revolt spreads beyond North. 1,000s.
1793		
19. March, Santo Domingo	C	Hinche. 19 arrested. No executions.
20. April, Guadeloupe	R	Trois Rivières. 200. 20 whites killed.
21. April, Guadeloupe	C	Baillif. 5 death sentences.
22. April, Guadeloupe	C	Basse-Terre region. 14 punished.

Table 1 – contd.

TIME AND PLACE	REVOLT (R) OR CONSPIRACY (C)	DETAILS
23. August, Guadeloupe	R	Saint Anne. 1,000? slaves and freemen.
24. Saint Lucia	R	
1794		
25. February, Martinique	R	Saint Luce. During British invasion.
1795		
26. Early, Santo Domingo	C	Samaná. 7 blacks, 3 French whites.
27. Trinidad	C?	2 conspiracies in south and north.
28. April, Louisiana	C	Pointe Coupée. 23 slaves executed.
29. May, Bahamas	C	Nassau. Francophone slaves.
30. May, Venezuela	R	Coro. 300 slaves and free blacks.
31. July, Cuba	R	Puerto Principe. 15 slaves.
32. July? Puerto Rico	R?	Aguadilla. A few slaves.
33. August, Curaçao	R	2,000 slaves? 29 slaves executed.
34. Demerara	R	Cooperation with maroon attacks.
1796		
35. February–April, Louisiana	C	Pointe Coupée, German Coast. 3 plots?
36. May, Cuba	C	Puerto Principe. 5 'French' slaves.
37. October, Santo Domingo	R	Boca Nigua. 100 slaves. 7 executed.
1797		
38. August, Bahamas	C	Nassau. 'French' slaves. 5 executed.
1798		
39. January, Venezuela	C	Carúpano/Cumaná. African slaves.
40. June, Cuba	R	Puerto Principe. 20 slaves punished.
41. July, Cuba	C	Trinidad. 5 slaves tried, 2 hanged.
42. October, Cuba	R	Güines. 23 slaves on 1 estate.
1799		
43. April, New Granada	C	Cartagena. French slaves, freemen.
44. May, Venezuela	C	Maracaibo. French and local freemen.
1800		
45. September, Curaçao	R	Large multiclass rising.
1801		
46. December, Tobago	C	7 or 16 estates. 7 slaves executed.
1803		
47. June, Jamaica	C	Kingston. 2 executed.

Table 1 – contd.

TIME AND PLACE	REVOLT (R) OR CONSPIRACY (C)	DETAILS
1805		
48. December, Trinidad	C	4 slaves executed.
1806		
49. Jamaica	C	Saint George's. 1 slave executed.
50. Puerto Rico	R	Humacao. Slaves attack guard-house.
1807		
51. December, Demerara	C	20 slaves arrested. 9 executed.
1809		
52. March, Jamaica	C	Kingston. 2 executed.
1811		
53. January, Louisiana	R	German coast. 400–500 slaves.
54. September, Martinique	R	Saint Pierre. 15 executed.
55. Cuba	C	Widespread, centered on Havana.
1812		
56. January, Puerto Rico	C?	Widespread. 16 punished.
57. January, Cuba	R	Puerto Principe. 8 hanged; 73 whipped.
58. February, Cuba	C	Bayamo. Probably part of Aponte plot.
59. March, Cuba	R	Guanabo. 1 estate.
60. August, Louisiana	C	New Orleans. 1 white executed.
61. August, Santo Domingo	R	Eastern region. 3 executed.
1815		
62. December, Jamaica	C	Saint Elizabeth. 250 Africans. 1 hanged.

[From 'Slavery, War, and Revolution in the Greater Caribbean, 1789–1815,' in David Barry Gaspar and David Patrick Geggus (eds), *A Turbulent Time: The French Revolution and the Greater Caribbean* (Bloomington: Indiana University Press, 1997), 5–7, 46–9.]

JAMES C. SCOTT

145 Domination and the Arts of Resistance

Until quite recently, much of the active political life of subordinate groups has been ignored because it takes place at a level we rarely recognize as political. To emphasize the enormity of what has been, by and large, disregarded, I want to distinguish between the open, declared forms of resistance, which attract most attention, and the disguised, low-profile, undeclared

Table 2: Domination and Resistance.

	MATERIAL DOMINATION	STATUS DOMINATION	IDEOLOGICAL DOMINATION
Practices of domination	appropriation of grain, taxes, labor, etc.	humiliation, disprivilege, insults, assaults on dignity	justification by ruling groups for slavery, serfdom, caste, privilege
Forms of public declared resistant	petitions, demonstrations, boycotts, strikes, land invasions, and open revolts	public assertion of worth by gesture, dress, speech, and/or open desecration of status symbols of the dominant	public counter-ideologies propagating equality, revolution, or negating the ruling ideology
Forms of disguised, low profile, undisclosed resistance, infrapolitics	everyday forms of resistance, e.g. poaching, squatting, desertion, evasion, foot-dragging Direct Resistance by Disguised Resisters, e.g. masked appropriations, threats, anonymous threats	hidden transcript of anger, aggression, and disguised discourses of dignity e.g., rituals of aggression, tales of revenge, use of carnival symbolism, gossip, rumor, creation of autonomous social space for assertion of dignity	development of dissident subcultures e.g., millennial religions, slave 'hush-arbors,' folk religion, myths of social banditry and class heroes, world-upside-down imagery, myths of the 'good' king or the time before the 'Norman Yoke'

resistance that constitutes the domain of infrapolitics (see accompanying table). For contemporary liberal democracies in the West, an exclusive concern for open political action *will* capture much that is significant in political life. The historic achievement of political liberties of speech and association has appreciably lowered the risks and difficulty of open political expression. Not so long ago in the West, however, and, even today, for many of the least privileged minorities and marginalized poor, open political action will hardly capture the bulk of political action. Nor will an exclusive attention to declared resistance help us understand the process by which new political forces and demands germinate before they burst on the scene. How, for example, could we understand the open break represented by the civil rights movement or the black power movement in the 1960s without understanding the offstage discourse among black students, clergymen, and their parishioners?

Taking a long historical view, one sees that the luxury of relatively safe, open political opposition is both rare and recent. The vast majority of people have been and continue to be not citizens, but subjects. So long as we confine our conception of *the political* to activity that is openly declared we are driven to conclude that subordinate groups essentially lack a political life or that what political life they do have is restricted to those exceptional moments of popular explosion. To do so is to miss the immense political terrain that lies between quiescence and revolt and that, for better or worse, is the political environment of subject classes. It is to focus on the visible coastline of politics and miss the continent that lies beyond.

Each of the forms of disguised resistance, of infrapolitics, is the silent partner of a loud form of public resistance. Thus, piecemeal squatting is the infrapolitical equivalent of an open land invasion: both are aimed at resisting the appropriation of land. The former cannot openly avow its goals and is a strategy well suited to subjects who have no political rights. Thus, rumor and folktales of revenge are the infrapolitical equivalent of open gestures of contempt and desecration: both are aimed at resisting the denial of standing or dignity to subordinate groups. The former cannot act directly and affirm its intention and is thus a symbolic strategy also well suited to subjects with no political rights. Finally, millennial imagery and the symbolic reversals of folk religion are the infrapolitical equivalents of public, radical, counter-ideologies: both are aimed at negating the public symbolism of ideological domination. Infrapolitics, then, is essentially the strategic form that the resistance of subjects must assume under conditions of great peril.

The strategic imperatives of infrapolitics make it not simply different in degree from the open politics of modern democracies; they impose a fundamentally different logic of political action. No public claims are made, no open symbolic lines are drawn. All political action takes forms that are designed to obscure their intentions or to take cover behind an apparent meaning. Virtually no one acts in his own name for avowed purposes, for that would be self-defeating. Precisely because such political action is studiously designed to be anonymous or to disclaim its purpose, infrapolitics requires more than a little interpretation. Things are not exactly as they seem.

The logic of disguise followed by infrapolitics extends to its organization as well as to its substance. Again, the form of organization is as much a product of political necessity as of political choice. Because open political activity is all but precluded, resistance is confined to the informal networks of kin, neighbors, friends, and community rather than formal organization. Just as the symbolic resistance found in forms of folk culture has a possibly innocent meaning, so do the elementary organizational units of infrapolitics have an alternative, innocent existence. The informal assemblages of market, neighbors, family, and community thus provide both a structure and a cover for resistance. Since resistance is conducted in small groups, individually, and, if on a larger scale, makes use of the anonymity of folk culture or actual disguises, it is well adapted to thwart surveillance. There are no leaders to round up, no membership lists to investigate, no manifestos to denounce, no public activities to draw attention. These are, one might say, the elementary forms of political life on which more elaborate, open, institutional forms may be built and on which they are likely to depend for their vitality. Such elementary forms also help explain why infrapolitics so often escapes notice. If formal political organization is the realm of elites (for example, lawyers, politicians, revolutionaries, political bosses), of written records (for example, resolutions, declarations, news stories, petitions, lawsuits), and of public action, infrapolitics is, by contrast, the realm of informal leadership and nonelites, of conversation and oral discourse, and of surreptitious resistance. The logic of infrapolitics is to leave few traces in the wake of its passage. By covering its tracks it not only minimizes the risks its practitioners run but it also eliminates much of the documentary evidence that might convince social scientists and historians that real politics was taking place.

Infrapolitics is, to be sure, real politics. In many respects it is conducted in more earnest, for higher stakes, and against greater odds than political life in liberal democracies. Real ground is lost and gained. Armies are undone and revolutions facilitated by the desertions of infrapolitics. De facto property rights are established and challenged. States confront fiscal crises or crises of appropriation when the cumulative petty stratagems of its subjects deny them labor and taxes. Resistant subcultures of dignity and vengeful dreams are created and nurtured. Counterhegemonic discourse is elaborated. Thus infrapolitics is, as emphasized earlier, always pressing, testing, probing the boundaries of the permissible. Any relaxation in surveillance and punishment and foot-dragging threatens to become a declared strike, folktales of oblique aggression threaten to become face-to-face defiant contempt, millennial dreams threaten to become revolutionary politics. From this vantage point infrapolitics may be thought of as the elementary—in the sense of foundational—form of politics. It is the building block for the more elaborate institutionalized political action that could not exist without it. Under the conditions of tyranny and persecution in which most historical subjects live, it *is* political life. And when the rare civilities of open political life are curtailed or destroyed, as they so often are, the elementary forms of infrapolitics remain as a defense in depth of the powerless.

[From *Domination and the Arts of Resistance: Hidden Transcripts* (New Haven: Yale University Press, 1990), 198–201.]

Section VII

Economics and Demography

INTRODUCTION

Discussions of the economics and demography of slavery and slave systems, those based on plantation production as well as on domestic slavery, focus on two issues. First, arguments about economic and demographic issues have been central to the attacks on slavery, as well as its defense. It has long been maintained that slavery was unprofitable to slave-owners, inefficient and unproductive as an economic system. It therefore would have to be replaced by a free labor system if economic growth were to occur. The proslavery defense was that slavery permitted economic growth to occur where it otherwise would not have done so. Even if slavery posed moral problems, it was a necessary evil providing for increased output. The demographic focus of the antislavery movement was on the significant rates of mortality sustained in acquiring, transporting, and employing slaves. The proslavery response stressed the survival of enslaved captives, who would otherwise have been killed, and the high standard of living made available to slaves in the interests of obtaining high productivity levels. Much of the data on slave systems, particularly in the modern era, has been generated as a result of these controversies.

Second, the study of economic and demographic issues offers considerable insight into the actual operation of slave systems and the behavior and beliefs of slaveowners and slaves. There are many contemporary studies on these issues, which give advice on how to keep slavery operating while permitting profits for owners and survival for the slaves. To understand how the slave economy operated and what the demographic outcomes were thus becomes vital to understanding many other aspects of slavery.

Slave labor has been used for many different purposes, and there are few tasks that slaves did not at some time perform. To owners, there were always advantages in redistributing production or in forcing a greater labor input, whatever task was involved and even if the slaves were producing goods and services similar to those for which non-slave labor was also used. Slaves performed skilled tasks, military service, domestic and household labor, and elite management, in addition to unskilled agricultural work and mining. Yet in those societies in which slavery was most significant and most economically productive slaves worked at tasks not performed by free workers, particularly on large-scale units in mines or in agriculture. In the latter case these were generally undertaken on large-scale plantations, with production systems based on gang labor. In the modern era the crops grown on these plantations, such as sugar, coffee, and cotton, generally need a semi-temperate or tropical climate. In the relative absence of sufficient labor, it became necessary to import workers from elsewhere, leading to a long-distance trade in slaves. In European serfdom, however, such movements were not necessary, as the coerced population was already in place.

Attacks on the economic productivity of slave labor were occasionally presented in the Greek and Roman world, but it was only with the eighteenth century, at the time of the debates on the transition from slavery and serfdom to what was considered to be free labor, that these critiques become more widespread. Economists such as Smith and Marx presented widely quoted arguments against slavery, based on the lack of proper incentives to slaves and to slaveowners. Slavery was seen as an unproductive residue of the past, to be replaced, sooner or later, by more efficient systems of labor institutions not entailing the ownership of others. Curiously, some parts of the proslavery defense also pointed to the unprofitability of the system. In this case, how-ever, slavery was regarded as a system to be maintained as a social means of controlling barbaric people and not because the slaveowners desired profits and wealth. There were, of course, positions that pointed to some positive aspects of slavery in contributing to economic growth, either because of its importance for a source of demand for European outputs, particularly indus-trial goods, or because it generated output from an otherwise unproductive people.

Even those who argued for the profitability of slavery in their own time could indicate that it was only for a limited period of time. Presumably it would soon come to an end, to be replaced by free labor. Slavery, it was argued, could be profitable for only a limited period of time and for a limited range of crops. It was created by the need to offset a scarcity of labor that could be made to work on plantations. In this scenario, it was expected that population growth would end the labor scarcity and with it any need to bring in new slave labor. As the population increased, so too did society's prospects for the replacement of slavery by free labor. Even if slavery were profitable to planters, it was argued, it still retarded long-term economic growth. It pre-vented the development of a modern industrialized sector, leaving societies basically agrarian in orientation.

The study of the economic effects of slavery has been expanded beyond issues of profits to the levels of income and rates of growth of income within the slave society itself. Based on its role in transatlantic commerce, slave-grown commodities and the profits of slave labor were deemed to be a central factor in the emergence of Western European economies, and par-ticularly in stimulating the British Industrial Revolution. Conversely, the slave trade, in drawing on the populations of Africa, has been seen as not only playing a part in depopulating Africa, but also in distorting African economies. In this respect, even with proceeds of sales of slaves coming into Africa, the sub-Saharan economies were trapped into a dependency on the European world.

The pervasive and highly commercial nature of slavery in some Atlantic societies has meant that a considerable amount of information on slave prices and trade arrangements persists, reflecting the business concerns of slave-owners and sellers. Such interests developed because slaves were an important source of wealth in many societies. The existence of a market in slaves often meant that estimates of prices were available. Slaves were traded in internal as well as international markets, and at various stages prices of transactions were sometimes recorded. Thus, it is possible to determine price differentials between areas, as well as trends in the prices of slaves over time, reflecting expectations of future developments.

While innumerable functions were performed by slave labor, in most cases the masters' intent was to obtain profits from their production. The problem confronting slaveowners was made most familiar by Adam Smith's critique of the presumed lack of incentives for slave laborers to produce efficiently. This motivational problem was familiar to slaveowners. Some of the earliest, as well as the latest, writings on slavery discussed this problem and the possibility of using positive incentives going beyond the sole use of the whip. While some historians debated whether slaveowners on large units were capitalist or non-capitalist, lacking either an interest in or the ability to organize efficient levels of production, contemporary descriptions of plantation operations indicate both their complexity and the creation of detailed systems of control. For an increasing number of historians, the notion of sugar plantations as 'factories in the fields' emphasizes this modern aspect of slave-based agricultural production.

In the discussions of the abolitionists, the demographic performance of slaves has long been considered to have differed from that of other populations. Rates of fertility were so low and of mortality so high, that the maintenance of slave populations required the continual introduction of replacements, either by trade or by military operations. The standard argument for the low fertility rates was that people, as with animals, would not breed in captivity. Later arguments added in factors of slave promiscuity and venereal disease, master-induced undermining of the family structure, or the economic advantages to masters of buying as opposed to breeding. The higher mortality rate was based on masters' assumed willingness to work slaves to death in the interests of profit-maximization, as long as fresh supplies of slaves were available. While this was seen as the main cause, the location of slaves in unhealthy tropical climates and their hard labor for long periods in the sun could also have led to high mortality rates, even if this was not the deliberate intention of the masters, who often tried to provide better care and easier working conditions than were legally permissible.

The modern debate on demographic performance of slave as opposed to free laborers begins with the 1750s discussion on the population of ancient and modern nations between David Hume and Robert Wallace, which raised many of the issues discussed by subsequent writers. Hume argued that slave populations in the ancient world were incapable of a positive natural rate of increase. Similar arguments were made by classical economists and their contemporaries, along the lines described above. These propositions were intended to account for the general reality, both past and present, that slave populations suffered from a natural decrease because rates of mortality exceeded those of fertility. This required a continuous stream of new imports just to maintain their numbers. The negative rates varied by area and over time. There was only one major slave society, however, in which a positive rate of natural increase occurred: on mainland North America beginning in the early eighteenth century and continuing until the abolition of US slavery after 1860. Surprisingly, American slaves had rates of natural increase and fertility comparable to those of the free population of North America, making it unusual not only for a slave society but, given how high those rates were, most contemporary societies as well. The US reached its position as the society with the largest slave population in the Americas, with far fewer slave imports than Brazil or the Caribbean. Both of the latter areas experienced a natural decrease. The high growth rate in the US occurred well before the closing of the international slave trade in 1808. The slave trade to the British West Indies, which also ended in 1808, did not lead to any marked change in rates of fertility or natural increase.

The high rate of increase of the US slave population, along with its westward movement, led to the raising of a 'slave breeding' argument by US abolitionists. They claimed that slaves were deliberately forced to breed in order to obtain new slaves, yielding financial reproductive benefits to the owners of their mothers. This helped to reconcile the arguments that slaves would not voluntarily wish to bring children into that status with the recorded high fertility rates. More recently, other aspects of slave social patterns and customs have been invoked to explain high US fertility rates. Nevertheless, the antislavery argument could use both high and low fertility rates as a basis for attack, attributing either to different forms of master interference in different circumstances or places. The discussion of slave reproduction was also important for another major aspect of the abolitionist attack on the immortality of the slave society: its effect in destroying family relationships. The instability of the slave family, however possible given the legal impediments, may not always have accorded with actual slave practice.

SOCRATES. What if I also show you something about slaves: in some households they are nearly all chained, but run away again and again, while in others they are unchained and want to stay and work? Wouldn't you think that in this too I'd be demonstrating to you a principle of estate management worth examining?

[. . .]

Slaves need some good thing to look forward to no less, in fact, even more than free men so that they may be willing to stay. The man who said that farming is the mother and nurse of the other arts spoke truly. When farming is successful, all the other arts prosper, but wherever the earth is forced to lie barren, the other arts, both on earth and sea, are virtually extinguished.

[. . .]

ISCHOMACHUS [. . .] For it is difficult to learn to do anything well if the teacher demonstrates it badly. And when the master shows that he lacks concern, it is difficult for a slave to be concerned. In short, I don't think I've ever come across a bad master with good slaves: on the other hand, I've seen bad slaves belonging to a good master; however, they, at least, didn't escape punishment. But the master who wants to make his men be concerned must be in the habit of supervising their work and inspecting it, be prepared to reward any slave who is responsible for work that's well performed, and not hesitant to impose the due punishment on any slave who lacks concern. 'I think', he added, 'that the well-known reply of the foreigner is very relevant: I mean, when the king had acquired a good horse and wanted to fatten him up as quickly as he could, he asked one of those who had a reputation as an expert on horses "What fattens a horse most quickly?" They say that he replied, "his master's eye". This applies to everything, I think, Socrates: the master's eye produces beautiful and good work.'

[. . .]

'And in the case of human beings it is possible to make them more obedient merely by talking to them, pointing out that it is to their advantage to obey. But for slaves the method of training that is accepted for wild animals is very effective in teaching obedience. For if you gratify their desires by filling their bellies, you may get a great deal out of them. Those who are naturally ambitious become even keener with praise; for some natures hunger for praise as much as others do for food and drink. These methods, then, are exactly the ones that I use myself, because I believe that I shall have more obedient people in my employ as a result, and I teach them to those I wish to appoint as foremen. And I also help them in the following ways: I make sure that the clothing and the shoes which I must supply for the workers are not identical, but some are of inferior quality, and others superior, so that I can reward the better workers with superior garments and give the inferior ones to the less deserving. For, Socrates,' he continued, 'I'm convinced that good workers become very discouraged when they see that although they have done all the work, nevertheless those who are unwilling to work or, when necessary, to run risks, earn rewards equal to their own. I, myself, then, by no means think that better workers should receive the same treatment as worthless ones. And when I know that the foremen have distributed the best things to the most deserving workers, I praise them; but when I see someone favoured beyond the rest as a result of flattery or some other worthless service. I am not unconcerned, but I reprimand the foreman, and try to teach him, Socrates, that favouritism is not beneficial, not even to himself.'

'Ischomachus,' I said, 'when he has become capable of ruling, so that he can make them obedient, do you think he is a perfect foreman, or is there anything else that the man who has the qualities you mentioned needs to have?'

'Yes, by Zeus,' responded Ischomachus. 'He must keep his hands off his masters' property and not steal. For if the man who handles the crops dares to abscond with them, so that there is not enough left for the work to create a profit, what benefit would result from running a farm under his care?'

'Then do you undertake to teach this kind of honesty too?', I asked.

'Certainly,' replied Ischomachus. 'However, I don't find that everyone is prepared to learn from my teaching at first. Nevertheless,' he continued, 'by applying some provisions from the laws of Draco and some from the laws of Solon, I try to put my slaves on the path of honesty. Because', he said, 'I believe these men enacted many of their laws in order to teach honesty such as this.

'For it is enacted that offenders should be punished for acts of theft, and that anyone convicted of attempted theft should be imprisoned, and even killed if caught in the act. It is clear', he continued, 'that they enacted these laws because they wanted to make greed unprofitable for the unjust. By applying some of these laws,' he said, 'and by adding other enactments from the laws of the kings of Persia, I attempt to make my slaves honest in their handling of property. For the former laws only contain penalties for wrong-doers, but the laws of the kings not only penalize the dishonest, but also reward the honest. So, because they see that the honest become wealthier than the dishonest, many lovers of profit continue firmly to refrain from dishonesty. However, when I perceive that people attempt to act dishonestly, despite good treatment, I refuse to have anything more to do with them, on the grounds that they are incorrigibly greedy. On the other hand, if I learn of some who are induced to be honest not only because of the advantages they gain through being honest, but because of a desire to be praised by me, I treat them as if they were free men, not only do I make them wealthy, but I even honour them like gentlemen. For, Socrates,' he said, 'I think an ambitious man differs from a greedy one in that, for the sake of praise and honour, he is willing to work hard and to run risks.'

[From *Oeconomicus: A Social and Historical Commentary* [*c*.355 BC], trs. Sarah Pomeroy (Oxford: Clarendon Press, 1995), 117, 133, 175, 177–9.]

ARISTOTLE

147 *Oeconomica*

Of property, the first and most indispensable kind is that which is also best and most amenable to Housecraft; and this is the human chattel. Our first step therefore must be to procure good slaves. Of slaves there are two kinds; those in positions of trust, and the labourers. And since it is matter of experience that the character of the young can be moulded by training, when we require to charge slaves with tasks befitting the free, we have not only to procure the slaves, but to bring them up (for the trust).

In our intercourse with slaves we must neither suffer them to be insolent nor treat them with cruelty. A share of honour should be given to those who are doing more of a freeman's work, and abundance of food to those who are labouring with their hands. And whereas the use of wine renders even free men insolent, so that in many countries they too refrain from it—as, for instance, the Carthaginians do when they are on campaign—it follows that we must either deny wine to slaves altogether, or reserve it for rare occasions.

We may apportion to our slaves (1) work, (2) chastisement, and (3) food. If men are given food, but no chastisement nor any work, they become insolent. If they are made to work, and are chastised, but stinted of their food, such treatment is oppressive, and saps their strength. The remaining alternative, therefore, is to give them work, and a sufficiency of food. Unless we pay men, we cannot control them; and food is a slave's pay.

Slaves, again, are no exception to the rule that men become worse when better conduct is not followed by better treatment, but virtue and vice remain alike unrewarded. Accordingly we must keep watch over our workers, suiting our dispensations and indulgences, to their desert; whether it be food or clothing, leisure or chastisement that we are apportioning. Both in theory and in practice we must take for our model a physician's freedom in prescribing his medicines; observing at the same time that food differs from medicine in that it requires to be constantly administered.

The best labourers will be furnished by those races of mankind which are neither wholly spiritless nor yet overbold. Each extreme has its vice; the spiritless cannot endure hard labour, and the high-spirited will not readily brook control.

Every slave should have before his eyes a definite goal or term of his labour. To set the prize of freedom before him is both just and expedient; since having a prize to work for, and a time defined for its attainment, he will put his heart into his labours. We should, moreover, take hostages (for our slaves' fidelity) by allowing them to beget children; and avoid the practice of purchasing many slaves of the same nationality, as men avoid doing in towns. We should also keep festivals and give treats, more on the slaves' account than on that of the freemen; since the free have a fuller share in those enjoyments for the sake of which these institutions exist.

[From *Oeconomica* [*c.*320 BC], trs. C. Cyril Armstrong (Cambridge, MA: Harvard University Press, 1962), 335–9.]

148   Instructions to the Jesuits

[From a manual of the administration of Jesuit estates in Mexico, probably of the mid-eighteenth century.]

As said in the last chapter, the care and good education of the slaves should be preserved, excluding only some things that pertain to free servants. But because the typical slave gang on the sugar plantations, workshops and mills is a numerous community composed of many and diverse groups, it also requires a special economic and Christian mode of government, on the one and the other hinges the spiritual and temporal well being of the estate, and from its absence follow conspicuous problems, and sometimes also its total ruin. So in order to avoid these injuries, in addition to what was said in the last chapter, the Administrators will observe the following admonitions.

Firstly see that the encampment of the slaves, where the slaves little houses are, be enclosed with a firm and high fence, and that it have only one door that is closed at night and is opened in the morning, such a door has to be in view of the house in order that those who enter and leave may be seen. Over this door a bell has to be hung to call them to work in the morning, and in the evening to the rosary, and throughout the day whenever its operations might be needed.

You [the administrators] will single out as a leader a loyal slave, of good judgment and mature age, that might serve you as an instrument to give orders on all that has to be done on the estate, and he might be the overseer that attends to the operations of the field and the house: that he accompany the Administrator, when he goes to give assignments and to receive them and when the rations of corn and meat are divided up, and on similar occasions. Also the leader has to tell him [the Administrator] about what has been done, and advise him of the most urgent operations that are proper to do, and finally [the leader] should make him aware of any disorder that there might be between people to avoid it and to remedy it later. And in order that he carry out his obligations, every night after the line up of the people, you will call him [the leader] and you will ask for an accounting of the operations of that day, and you will give him orders to execute the next day.

[. . .]

When the case to punish a slave arises, do not do it carried away by anger, even though he may be very guilty; first calm your spirit and afterwards with calm and serenity announce the transgression [and] the judgment of punishment for their correction and as a warning for others. And never join the punishments with scurrilous language, or insults, or injuries or tiresome arguments, because this exasperates the spirits of all, and the guilty instead of being corrected get worse. Do not imitate in this the tyrannies that the secular administrators of sugar plantations usually use, like the length of prison sentences, [like] the excess of lashes, distributed by novenaries at fifty lashes each day. Take note that in this you could sin gravely against charity, and so as not to err, you [the administrators] will take the advise and counsel of the Father Rector and of the Attorney of the School, and also of the Father Chaplain wherever he be found.

[. . .]

For group crimes, never try to punish everyone, because this risks flight or upheavals; in such cases either dissimulate, as though you do not know about it, or punish only a few of the leaders that might be most guilty, and forgiving the rest and giving to all a suitable reprimand.

Never threaten individual delinquents with punishment later, because with that you will give them occasion to flee. What you must do is pretend for the time being, and if this cannot be done, reprimand them gently without threats, and when you have them secure, punish them later, with the guilt satisfied by the punishment, they will not be left with the desire to flee because they no longer are owed it [punishment].

[. . .]

Every week you will provide the slaves with the necessary sustenance, giving them rations of maize, meat, salt, peppers, and tobacco and a bit of honey when there is some, this is for meat days, and for Friday and Saturday, fast days, and Lent, they are to be given in place of meat, fish, or beans or something similar. And take care that in the time when not abstaining from meat, do not give them the meat for Friday along with the meat ration, because they usually eat it beforehand, and hold back the meat for Friday and Saturday; give it on Thursday afternoon and you will remove from them this opportunity.

[. . .]

Do not have young slaves idle, make them work from the age of eight years old on up, occupying them with work proportionate to their powers. To help them, you will designate an old female slave from those unable to do tasks, this slave should take them to mass in the morning, wherever it might be, everyday. But before mass, she has to gather them in the cemetery of the Church, and, the boys seated on one side and the girls on the other, they are to recite the Christian Doctrine, the old woman who cares for them teaching them, or a boy who knows it [the Doctrine] well; if there is a mass they will enter and hear it with devotion kneeling with the same separation; if there is no mass, they will sing the hymn to the Sacrament after the Doctrine and they will leave for breakfast.

[From *Instrucciones a los hermanos Jesuitas administradores de hacienda: Manuscrito del siglo XVIII*, ed. François Chevalier (Mexico: Universidad Nacional Autonoma de Mexico, 1950). Trs. Evelyn Powell Jennings.]

JAMES STEUART

149   **Principles of Political Oeconomy**

For this purpose slavery was calculated: it had two excellent effects with respect to population. The first, that, in unpolished nations, living upon the spontaneous fruits of the earth, and almost continually in war, lives were preserved for the sake of making slaves of the captives. These, sold to private people, or different states, were sure of being fed; whereas, remaining in their own country, they occupied a place only, which, by the force of the generative faculty, as has been observed, was soon to be filled up by propagation: for it must not be forgot, that when numbers are swept off, by any sudden calamity, which does not proportionally diminish subsistence, a new multiplication immediately takes place. Thus we perceive the hurt done by plagues, by war, and by other devastations, either among men, or cattle, repaired in a few years, even in those countries where the standard number of both is seldom found to increase. What immense quantities of cattle are yearly slaughtered! Does any body imagine that if all were allowed to live, numbers would increase in proportion? The same is true of men.

The second advantage of slavery was, that in countries where a good police prevailed, and where the people had fewer wants by far than are felt in modern times, the slaves were forced to labour the soil which fed both them and the idle freemen, as was the case in Sparta; or they filled all the servile places which freemen fill now, and they were likewise employed, as in Greece and in Rome, in supplying with manufactures those whose service was necessary for the state.

Here then was a violent method making mankind laborious in raising food; and provided this be accomplished, (by any means whatever,) numbers will increase.

Trade, industry, and manufactures, tend only to multiply the numbers of men, by encouraging agriculture. If it be therefore supposed, that two states are equally extended, equally fruitful, and equally cultivated, and the produce consumed at home, I believe they will be found equally peopled. But suppose the one laboured by free men, the other by slaves, what difference will be found in making war? In the first, the free hands must, by their industry and labour, purchase their food, and a day lost is in a manner a day of fasting: in the last, the slaves produce the food, they are first fed, and the rest costs nothing to the body of free men, who may be all employed in war, without the smallest prejudice to industry.

From these principles it appears, that slavery in former times had the same effect in peopling the world that trade and industry have now. *Men were then forced to labour because they were slaves to others; men are now forced to labour because they are slaves to their own wants.*

I do not, however, pretend, that in fact slavery in ancient times did every where contribute to population, any more than I can affirm that the spirit of industry in the Dutch is common to all free nations in our days. All that is necessary for my purpose is, to set forth the two principles, and to shew the natural effects of the one and the other, with respect to the multiplication of mankind and advancement of agriculture, the principal objects of our attention throughout this book.

[From *An Inquiry into the Principles of Political Oeconomy* [1770], ed. Andrew Skinner (Edinburgh: Oliver and Boyd, 1966), Vol. I: 50–1.]

ADAM SMITH

150 Wealth of Nations

The wear and tear of a slave, it has been said, is at the expence of his master; but that of a free servant is at his own expence. The 'wear and tear' of the latter, however, is, in reality, as much at the expence of his master as that of the former. The wages paid to journeymen and servants of every kind must be such as may enable them, one with another, to continue the race of journeymen and servants, according as the increasing, diminishing, or stationary demand of the society may happen to require. But though the 'wear and tear' of a free servant be equally at the expence of his master, it generally costs him much less than that of a slave. The fund destined for replacing or repairing, if I may say so, the 'wear and tear' of the slave, is commonly

managed by a negligent master or careless overseer. That destined for performing the same office with regard to the free man, is managed by the free
man himself. The disorders which generally prevail in the œconomy of the
rich, naturally introduce themselves into the management of the former:
The strict frugality and parsimonious attention of the poor as naturally establish themselves in that of the latter. Under such different management, the
same purpose must require very different degrees of expence to execute it. It
appears, accordingly, from the experience of all ages and nations, I believe,
that the work done by freemen comes cheaper in the end than that performed by slaves. It is found to do so even at Boston, New York, and
Philadelphia, where the wages of common labour are so very high.

The liberal reward of labour, therefore, as it is the effect of increasing
wealth, so it is the cause of increasing population. To complain of it is to
lament over the necessary effect and cause of the greatest publick prosperity.

[. . .]

But if great improvements are seldom to be expected from great proprietors, they are least of all to be expected when they employ slaves for their
workmen. The experience of all ages and nations, I believe, demonstrates
that the work done by slaves, though it appears to cost only their maintenance, is in the end the dearest of any. A person who can acquire no property,
can have no other interest but to eat as much, and to labour as little as
possible. Whatever work he does beyond what is sufficient to purchase his
own maintenance, can be squeezed out of him by violence only, and not by
any interest of his own. In antient Italy, how much the cultivation of corn
degenerated, how unprofitable it became to the master when it fell under the
management of slaves, is remarked by both Pliny and Columella. In the time
of Aristotle it had not been much better in antient Greece. Speaking of
the ideal republick described in the laws of Plato, to maintain five thousand
idle men (the number of warriors supposed necessary for its defence)
together with their women and servants, would require, he says, a territory
of boundless extent and fertility, like the plains of Babylon.

The pride of man makes him love to domineer, and nothing mortifies him
so much as to be obliged to condescend to persuade his inferiors. Wherever
the law allows it, and the nature of the work can afford it, therefore, he will
generally prefer the service of slaves to that of freemen. The planting of
sugar and tobacco can afford the expence of slave-cultivation. The raising of
corn, it seems, in the present times, cannot. In the English colonies, of which
the principal produce is corn, the far greater part of the work is done by
freemen. The late resolution of the Quakers in Pennsylvania to set at liberty
all their negro slaves, may satisfy us that their number cannot be very great.
Had they made any considerable part of their property, such a resolution
could never have been agreed to. In our sugar colonies, on the contrary, the
whole work is done by slaves, and in our tobacco colonies a very great part of

it. The profits of a sugar-plantation in any of our West Indian colonies are generally much greater than those of any other cultivation that is known either in Europe or America: And the profits of a tobacco plantation, though inferior to those of sugar, are superior to those of corn, as has already been observed. Both can afford the expence of slave-cultivation, but sugar can afford it still better than tobacco. The number of negroes accordingly is much greater, in proportion to that of whites, in our sugar than in our tobacco colonies.

[From *An Inquiry into the Nature and Causes of the Wealth of Nations* [1776] (Oxford: Oxford University Press, 1976), Vol. I: 98–9, 387–9.]

JOHN STUART MILL

151 Principles of Political Economy

[*Slavery in relation to production*] So long as slave countries are underpeopled in proportion to their cultivable land, the labour of the slaves, under any tolerable management, produces much more than is sufficient for their support; especially as the great amount of superintendence which their labour requires, preventing the dispersion of the population, insures some of the advantages of combined labour. Hence, in a good soil and climate, and with reasonable care of his own interests, the owner of many slaves has the means of being rich. The influence, however, of such a state of society on production, is perfectly well understood. It is a truism to assert, that labour extorted by fear of punishment is inefficient and unproductive. It is true that in some circumstances, human beings can be driven by the lash to attempt, and even to accomplish, things which they would not have undertaken for any payment which it could have been worth while to an employer to offer them. And it is likely that productive operations which require much combination of labour, the production of sugar for example, would not have taken place so soon in the American colonies, if slavery had not existed to keep masses of labour together. There are also savage tribes so averse from regular industry, that industrial life is scarcely able to introduce itself among them until they are either conquered and made slaves of, or become conquerors and make others so. But after allowing the full value of these considerations, it remains certain that slavery is incompatible with any high state of the arts of life, and any great efficiency of labour. For all products which require much skill, slave countries are usually dependent on foreigners. Hopeless slavery effectually brutifies the intellect; and intelligence in the slaves, though often encouraged in the ancient world and in the East, is in a more advanced state of society a source of so much danger and an object of so much dread to the masters, that in some of the States of America it was a highly penal offence to teach a slave to read. All processes carried on by slave labour are conducted in the rudest and most unimproved manner. And even the animal strength of the slave is, on an average, not half exerted. The unproductiveness and wastefulness of the industrial system in the Slave States is instructively displayed in the valuable writings of Mr. Olmsted.

[From *Principles of Political Economy, Books I–II* [1848] (Toronto: University of Toronto Press, 1965), 246–7.]

EDWARD GIBBON WAKEFIELD

152   A View of the Art of Colonization

Slavery is evidently a make-shift for hiring; a proceeding to which recourse is had, only when hiring is impossible or difficult. Slave labour is on the whole much more costly than the labour of hired freemen; and slavery is also full of moral and political evils, from which the method of hired labour is exempt. Slavery, therefore, is not preferred to the method of hiring: the method of hiring would be preferred if there were a choice: but when slavery is adopted, there is no choice: it is adopted because at the time and under the circumstances there is no other way of getting labourers to work with constancy and in combination. What, then, are the circumstances under which this happens?

It happens wherever population is scanty in proportion to land. Slavery, except in some mild form, as the fading continuation of a habit, and with some advantage to the nominal slaves but real dependents, whom at least it sheltered from the evils of competition, has been confined to countries of a scanty population, has never existed in very populous countries, and has gradually ceased in the countries whose population gradually increased to the point of density. And the reason is plain enough. Property in land is the object of one of the strongest and most general of human desires. Excluding the owners of land, in whom the desire is gratified, few indeed are those who do not long to call a piece of the earth their own. Landowners and persons who would be glad to be landowners, comprise the bulk of mankind. In populous countries, the desire to own land is not easily gratified, because the land is scarce and dear: the plentifulness and cheapness of land in thinly-peopled countries enables almost everybody who wishes it to become a landowner. In thinly-peopled countries, accordingly, the great majority of free people are landowners who cultivate their own land; and labour for hire is necessarily scarce: in densely-peopled countries, on the contrary, the great majority of the people cannot obtain land, and there is plenty of labour for hire. Of plentifulness of labour for hire, the cause is dearness of land: cheapness of land is the cause of scarcity of labour for hire.

[. . .]

The operation of superabundance of land in causing a scarcity of free labour and a desire for slaves, is very distinctly seen in a process by which modern colonists always have endeavoured to obtain free labour. Free labour, when it can be got and kept in a colony, is so much more productive than forced, that the colonial capitalist is always ready to pay for it, in the form of wages, more than slave labour would cost, and far more than the usual rate of wages in an old country. It is perfectly worth his while to pay, besides these high wages, the cost of the passage of free labour from the old country to the colony. Innumerable are the cases in which a colonial capitalist has done this, confident of the prudence of the outlay. It was commonly done by the founders of our early colonies in America, and has been done by many capitalists in Canada, South Africa, the Australias, and New Zealand. To do this appears such a natural, suitable, easy way of obtaining labour for hire, that every emigrant capitalist thinks of doing it; and thousands (I speak within compass) have tried the experiment. It is an experiment which always fails: if it always or generally succeeded, scarcity of labour for hire would not be a colonial evil. I have never missed the opportunity of tracing one of these experiments to its results; and I assure you that I have never been able to discover a single case of success. The invariable failure is produced by the impossibility of keeping the labour, for the passage of which to the colony the capitalist has paid: and it happens as follows.

[. . .]

It was cheapness of land that caused Las Casas (the Clarkson or Wilberforce of his time as respects the Red Indians of America) to invent the African slave trade. It was the cheapness of land that brought African slaves to Antigua and Barbadoes; and it is a comparative dearness of land, arising from the increase of population in those small islands, which has made them an exception from the general rule of West-Indian impoverishment in consequence of the abolition of slavery before land was made dear. It was cheapness of land that caused the introduction of negro slaves into Virginia, and produced the various forms of bondage practised by all the old English colonies in America. It is cheapness of land in Brazil, Porto Rico, and Cuba, which causes our African squadron, and not only prevents it from serving its purpose, but causes it to be a means of aggravating the horrors of the African slave trade.

[From *A View of the Art of Colonization in Present Reference to the British Empire in Letters between a Statesman and a Colonist* [1849] (New York: A. M. Kelley, 1969), 324–9.]

153 The Negro Question

For nearly two centuries had negroes, many thousands annually, been seized by force or treachery and carried off to the West Indies to be worked to death, literally to death; for it was the received maxim, the acknowledged dictate of good economy, to wear them out quickly and import more. In this fact every other possible cruelty, tyranny, and wanton oppression was by implication included. And the motive on the part of the slave-owners was the love of gold; or, to speak more truly, of vulgar and puerile ostentation. I have yet to learn that anything more detestable than this has been done by human beings towards human beings in any part of the earth. It is a mockery to talk of comparing it with Ireland. And this went on, not, like Irish beggary, because England had not the skill to prevent it,—not merely by the sufferance, but by the laws of the English nation. At last, however, there were found men, in growing number, who determined not to rest until the iniquity was extirpated; who made the destruction of it as much the business and end of their lives, as ordinary men make their private interests; who would not be content with softening its hideous features, and making it less intolerable to the sight, but would stop at nothing short of its utter and irrevocable extinction. I am so far from seeing anything contemptible in this resolution, that, in my sober opinion, the persons who formed and executed it deserve to be numbered among those, not numerous in any age, who have led noble lives according to their lights, and laid on mankind a debt of permanent gratitude.

After fifty years of toil and sacrifice, the object was accomplished, and the negroes, freed from despotism of their fellow-beings, were left to themselves, and to the chances which the arrangements of existing society provide for those who have no resource but their labour. These chances proved favourable to them, and, for the last ten years, they afford the unusual spectacle of a labouring class whose labour bears so high a price that they can exist in comfort on the wages of a comparatively small quantity of work. This, to the ex-slave-owners, is an inconvenience; but I have not yet heard that any of them has been reduced to beg his bread, or even to dig for it, as the negro, however scandalously he enjoys himself, still must: a carriage or some other luxury the less, is in most cases, I believe, the limit of their privations—no very hard measure of retributive justice; those who have had tyrannical power taken away from them, may think themselves fortunate if they come so well off; at all events, it is an embarrassment out of which the nation is not called on to help them: if they cannot continue to realize their large incomes without more labourers, let them find them, and bring them from where they can best be procured, only not by force. Not so thinks your anti-philanthropic contributor. That negroes should exist, and enjoy existence, on so little work, is a scandal in his eyes, worse than their former slavery. It must be put a stop to at any price. He does not 'wish to see' them slaves again 'if it can be avoided;' but 'decidedly' they 'will have to be servants,' 'servants to the whites,' 'compelled to labour,' and 'not to go idle another minute'. 'Black Quashee,' 'up to the ears in pumpkins,' and 'working about half an hour a day,' is to him the abomination of abominations. I have so serious a quarrel with him about principles, that I have no time to spare for his facts; but let me remark, how easily he takes for granted those which fit his case. Because he reads in some blue-book of a strike for wages in Demerara, such as he may read of any day in Manchester, he draws a picture of negro inactivity, copied from the wildest prophecies of the slavery party before emancipation. If the negroes worked no more than 'half an hour a day,' would the sugar crops, in all except notoriously bad seasons, be so considerable, so little diminished from what they were in the time of slavery, as is proved by the Customhouse returns? But it is not the facts of the question, so much as the moralities of it, that I care to dispute with your contributor.

A black man working no more than your contributor affirms that they work, is, he says, 'an eye-sorrow,' a 'blister on the skin of the state,' and many other things equally disagreeable; to *work* being the grand duty of man. 'To do competent work, to labour honestly according to the ability given them; for that, and for no other purpose, was each one of us sent into this world.' Whoever prevents him from his 'sacred appointment to labour while he lives on earth' is 'his deadliest enemy'. If it be 'his own indolence' that prevents him, 'the first *right* he has' is that all wiser and more industrious persons shall, 'by some wise means, compel him to do the work he is fit for'. Why not at once say that, by 'some wise means,' every thing should be made right in the world? While we are about it, wisdom may as well be suggested as the remedy for all evils, as for one only. Your contributor incessantly prays Heaven that all persons, black and white, may be put in possession of this 'divine right of being compelled, if permitted will not serve, to do what work they are appointed for'. But as this cannot be conveniently managed just yet, he will begin with the blacks, and will make them work *for* certain whites, those whites *not* working at all; that so 'the eternal purpose and supreme will' may be fulfilled, and 'injustice,' which is 'for ever accursed,' may cease.

This pet theory of your contributor about work, we all know well enough, though some persons might not be prepared for so bold an application of it. Let me say a few words on this 'gospel of work'—which, to my mind, as justly deserves the name of a cant as any of those which he has opposed, while the truth it contains is immeasurably farther from being the whole truth than that contained in the words Benevolence, Fraternity, or any other of his catalogue of contemptibilities. To give it a rational meaning, it must first be known what he means by work. Does work mean every thing which people *do*? No; or he would not reproach people with doing no work. Does it mean laborious exertion? No; for many a day spent in killing game, includes more muscular fatigue than a day's ploughing. Does it mean *useful* exertion? But your contributor always scoffs at the idea of utility. Does he mean that all persons ought to earn their living? But some earn their living by doing nothing, and some by doing mischief; and the negroes, whom he despises, still do earn by labour the 'pumpkins' they consume and the finery they wear.

Work, I imagine, is not a good in itself. There is nothing laudable in work for work's sake. To work voluntarily for a worthy object is laudable; but what constitutes a worthy object? On this matter, the oracle of which your contributor is the prophet has never yet been prevailed on to declare itself. He revolves in an eternal circle round the idea of work, as if turning up the earth, or driving a shuttle or a quill, were ends in themselves, and the ends of human existence. Yet, even in the case of the most sublime service to humanity, it is not because it is work that it is worthy; the worth lies in the service itself, and in the will to render it—the noble feelings of which it is the fruit; and if the nobleness of will is proved by other evidence than work, as for instance by danger or sacrifice, there is the same worthiness. While we talk only of work, and not of its object, we are far from the root of the matter; or if it may be called the root, it is a root without flower or fruit.

In the present case, it seems, a noble object means 'spices'. 'The gods wish, besides pumpkins, that spices and valuable products be grown in their West Indies'—the 'noble elements of cinnamon, sugar, coffee, pepper black and grey,' 'things far nobler than pumpkins'. Why so? Is what supports life, inferior in dignity to what merely gratifies the sense of taste? Is it the verdict of the 'immortal gods' that pepper is noble, freedom (even freedom from the lash) contemptible? But spices lead 'towards commerces, arts, politics, and social developments.' Perhaps so; but of what sort? When they must be produced by slaves, the 'politics and social developments' they lead to are such as the world, I hope, will not choose to be cursed with much longer.

[From *The Negro Question* [1850], ed. Eugene August (New York: Appleton-Century-Crofts, 1971), 40–3.]

FREDERIC BASTIAT

154 Economic Sophisms

Slavery furnishes a second and striking example of the impotence of religious and humanitarian sentiments in a conflict with the powerful force of self-interest. This may seem regrettable to certain modern schools of thought that expect self-denial to be the principle that will reform society. Let them begin, then, by reforming the nature of man.

In the Antilles, the masters, from father to son, have been professing the Christian religion ever since slavery was established there. Several times a day they repeat these words: 'All men are brothers: to love thy neighbor is to fulfill the whole of the law.' And yet they have slaves, and nothing seems to them more natural or legitimate. Do the modern reformers expect that their ethical principles will ever be as universally accepted, as well-known, as authoritative, or as often on the lips of everyone, as the Gospel? And if the Gospel has been unable to pass from the lips to the heart, over or through the great barrier of self-interest, how do they expect their ethical principles to perform this miracle?

Is slavery, then, indestructible? No. *Self-interest*, which created it, will destroy it, provided that the special interests that have inflicted the wound are not protected in such a way as to nullify the general interests that tend to heal it.

Another truth demonstrated by political economy is that free labor is essentially progressive, whereas slave labor is necessarily static. Hence, the triumph of the first over the second is inevitable. What has become of the cultivation of indigo by the Negroes?

Free labor employed in the cultivation of sugar will lead to a continual reduction in its price. The slave will become proportionately less profitable to his master. Slavery would have collapsed of its own weight long ago in America if European laws had not kept the price of sugar artificially high. Therefore we see the masters, their creditors, and their legislative representatives making vigorous efforts to keep these laws in force, for they are today the pillars of the whole edifice of slavery.

Unfortunately, these laws still have the support of people among whom slavery has disappeared; from this it is clear that here, too, public opinion is sovereign.

[From *Economic Sophisms* [1854], trs. Arthur Goddard (New York: Foundation for Economic Education, 1964), 135–6.]

HERMAN MERIVALE

155 **Lectures on Colonization and Colonies**

The diminution in the numbers of the native inhabitants of the Spanish colonies in America drove the conquerors, in little more than half a century after its first discovery, to resort to the importation of negro slaves to supply the deficiency. For three centuries, from that time to the present, every year has witnessed the arrival of fresh cargoes of these doomed children of servitude on the shores of the Western continent and its islands; destined in part to replace the waste which excessive toil and unnatural restrictions continually make in their numbers, in part to accelerate the multiplication of the black and coloured races in that hemisphere, which seems likely either to balance or to outweigh the influence of the white and civilized race over great part of its surface. The difficult and intricate character of the questions involved in this fatal subject of slavery—the very wide extent of the interests embraced by it—the feeling of reluctance, and almost abhorrence, with which the mind approaches the mere economical consideration of matters so deeply interesting to every social and moral feeling of our nature,—all these render it extremely difficult for me to enter on it at all, and make it almost a bewildering endeavour to compress the treatment of it within the compass of a lecture.

[. . .]

Of the great multitude of labourers, of coloured race, enslaved and free, inhabiting former or existing dependencies of European states, almost the whole are occupied, directly or indirectly, in raising exportable produce, chiefly for the European market. Nearly all our sugar, and the greater part of our cotton, tobacco, and coffee, not to mention other and less important articles, are raised by negro labour; nine tenths of which is that of slaves. About one third of our export trade is now carried on to slave countries, and the products which we receive in exchange for the goods which we send there are raised by slaves.

[. . .]

After the consideration which we gave in a former lecture to the subject of the scarcity of labour in the new or increasing colonies, it will be easily understood, that the great demand for slaves and the great profitableness of slavery, at the present day, arise altogether from that scarcity. Slave labour, it has almost passed into an axiom, is dearer than free; that is, whenever the demand for labourers is abundantly supplied. When the pressure of population induces the freeman to offer his services, as he does in all old countries, for little more than the natural minimum of wages, those services are very certain to be more productive and less expensive than those of the bondsman, whose support is a charge to the master, and who has nothing to gain by his industry. This is true, without any exception for the effects of climate, which some have set up as a kind of justification or excuse for the enforcement of compulsory labour. Free Indians raised sugar in Mexico before the Revolution; the labour of Portorico has been, up to a recent time, performed almost entirely by free whites and coloured men. In the burning atmosphere of the Malay islands, the free Chinese labourer exerts skill and energies as far superior to those of the enslaved negro as the power of the English peasant is to that of the Russian serf.

This being the case, it is obvious that the limit of the profitable duration of slavery is attained whenever the population has become so dense that it is cheaper to employ the free labourer for hire. Towards this limit every community is approximating, however slowly. And although political institutions and old habits may prolong the existence, either of slavery or of villenage, to a much later period, as they did among the Greeks and Romans, and as they still do among the nations of the east of Europe, still, from that moment, the state of society becomes favourable to its abolition.

But it happens most unfortunately, in some respects, for the interests of society, that this favourable turn of events, as far as regards colonial slavery, is rendered almost incalculably distant by the extent of fertile unappropriated soil in or adjoining to the principal slave countries. As has been already remarked (and it is a truth to be particularly remembered in all discussions on this subject), neither skill, nor capital, nor abundance of labour have ever been found able to compete, in tropical cultivation, with the advantage of a new and fertile soil.

[. . .]

It seems, therefore, but too evident that no economical cause can be assigned on which we may rely for the extinction of slavery, and that those who have persuaded themselves that nations will gradually attain a conviction that its maintenance is unfavourable to their interests are under a delusion. What political or moral reasons may operate against its continuance in those societies in which it prevails, it is not within my province to inquire. It is certain that in most slave-holding communities, in which the population contains any intermediate class between slaves and masters, that class has an interest in its abolition; although prejudices sometimes interfere to prevent its being clearly perceived by them.

[From *Lectures on Colonization and Colonies* [1861] (New York: A. M. Kelley, 1967), 300–1, 304–6, 309–10.]

KARL MARX

156 Capital

The discovery of gold and silver in America, the extirpation, enslavement and entombment in mines of the aboriginal population, the beginning of the conquest and looting of the East Indies, the turning of Africa into a warren for the commercial hunting of black-skins, signalised the rosy dawn of the era of capitalist production. These idyllic proceedings are the chief momenta of primitive accumulation. On their heels treads the commercial war of the European nations, with the globe for a theatre. It begins with the revolt of the Netherlands from Spain, assumes giant dimensions in England's anti-jacobin war, and is still going on in the opium wars against China, &c.

[. . .]

With the development of capitalist production during the manufacturing period, the public opinion of Europe had lost the last remnant of shame and conscience. The nations bragged cynically of every infamy that served them as a means to capitalistic accumulation. Read, *e.g.*, the naïve Annals of Commerce of the worthy A. Anderson. Here it is trumpetted forth as a triumph of English statecraft that at the Peace of Utrecht, England extorted from the Spaniards by the Asiento Treaty the privilege of being allowed to ply the negro-trade, until then only carried on between Africa and the English West Indies, between Africa and Spanish America as well. England thereby acquired the right of supplying Spanish America until 1743 with 4800 negroes yearly. This threw, at the same time, an official cloak over British smuggling. Liverpool waxed fat on the slave-trade. This was its method of primitive accumulation. And, even to the present day, Liverpool 'respectability' is the Pindar of the slave-trade which—compare the work of Aikin [1795]—'has coincided with that spirit of bold adventure which has characterised the trade of Liverpool and rapidly carried it to its present state of prosperity; has occasioned vast employment for shipping and sailors, and greatly augmented the demand for the manufactures of the country'. Liverpool employed in the slave trade, in 1730, 15 ships; in 1751, 53; in 1760, 74; in 1770, 96; and in 1792, 132.

Whilst the cotton industry introduced child-slavery in England, it gave in the United States a stimulus to the transformation of the earlier, more or less patriarchal slavery, into a system of commercial exploitation. In fact, the veiled slavery of the wage-earners in Europe needed, for its pedestal, slavery pure and simple in the new world.

[From *Capital: A Critique of Political Economy* [1867], ed. Frederick Engels (New York: The Modern Library, 1936), 823, 832–3.]

MAX WEBER

157   The Theory of Social and Economic Organization

The use of slaves and serfs, the latter including various types of dependents, as part of a process of budgetary administration and not as workers in a profit-making enterprise, was typical of Antiquity and of the early Middle Ages. There are, for instance, inscriptions which mentioned slaves 'of a Persian prince who were bound out as apprentices on the understanding that they might be used for labour services in the household, but might also be allowed, in return for a payment to the owner, to work independently for customers'. Though by no means without exception, this tended to be the rule for Greek slaves; and in Rome this type of independent economic activity became a legal institution which involved providing the slave with a *peculium* or *merx peculiaris*. He was naturally obligated to make payments to his owner. In the Middle Ages, body serfdom frequently involved merely a right to claim payments. This was usual in western and southern Germany. In Russia, also, an actual limitation to the receipt of these payments (*obrok*) from an otherwise free serf was though not universal, very common. Its legal status was, however, precarious.

[. . .]

With respect to the freedom of labour and of jobs from appropriation, it is true that certain types of unfree labour, particularly full-fledged slavery, have guaranteed what is formally a more complete power of disposal over the worker than is the case with employment for wages. But there are various reasons why this is less favourable to rationality and efficiency than the employment of free labour: (a) The amount of capital which it was necessary to invest in human resources through the purchase and maintenance of slaves has been much greater than that required by the employment of free labour; (b) the capital risk attendant on slave ownership has not only been greater but specifically irrational in that slave labour has been exposed to all manner of non-economic influences, particularly to political influence in a very high degree; (c) the slave market and correspondingly the prices of slaves have been particularly subject to fluctuation, which has made a balancing of profit and loss on a rational basis exceedingly difficult; (d) for similar reasons, particularly involving the political situation, there has been a difficult problem of recruitment of slave labour forces; (e) when slaves have been permitted to enjoy family relationships, this has made the use of slave labour more expensive in that the owner has had to bear the cost of maintaining the women and of rearing children. Very often, he has had no way in which he could make rational economic use of these elements as part of his labour force; (f) hence the most complete exploitation of slave labour has been possible only when they were separated from family relationships and subjected to a ruthless discipline. Where this has happened it has greatly accentuated the difficulties of the problem of recruitment; (g) it has in general been impossible to use slave labour in the operation of tools and apparatus, the efficiency of which required a high level of responsibility and of involvement of the operator's self-interest; (h) perhaps most important of all has been the impossibility of selection, of employment only after trying out in the job, and dismissal in accordance with fluctuations of the business situation or when personal efficiency declined.

Hence the employment of slave labour has only been possible in general under the following conditions: (a) Where it has been possible to maintain slaves very cheaply; (b) where there has been an opportunity for regular recruitment through a well-supplied slave market; (c) in agricultural production on a large scale of the plantation type, or in very simple industrial processes. The most important examples of this type of relatively successful use of slaves are the Carthaginian and Roman plantations, those of colonial areas and of the Southern United States, and the Russian 'factories'. The drying up of the slave market, which resulted from the pacification of the Empire, led to the decay of the plantations of Antiquity. In North America, the same situation led to a continual search for cheap new land, since it was impossible to meet the costs of slaves and pay a land rent at the same time. In Russia, the slave 'factories' were barely able to meet the competition of the Custar type of household industry and were totally unable to compete with free factory labour. Even before the emancipation of the serfs, petitions for permission to dismiss workers were common, but they disappeared with the introduction of shops using free labour.

[From *The Theory of Social and Economic Organization* [1921], trs A. M. Henderson and Talcott Parsons (New York: Oxford University Press, 1947), 234–5, 276–7.]

158 Slave Trader Newsletter 1860

Betts & Gregory,
Auctioneers,
Franklin Street,
Richmond, VA

Richmond, July 20th 1860

Dear Sir:

We beg leave to give you the state of our Negro Market, and quote them as follows:

Extra Men	$1550 to $1625
No. 1 do.	$1450 to $1550
Second rate or Ordinary do.	$1100 to $1200
Extra Girls	$1375 to $1450
No. 1 do.	$1300 to $1350
Second rate or Ordinary do.	$900 to $1100
Goode Boys 4 feet high	$ 575 to $675
,, Boys 4 feet 3 inches high	$ 675 to $775
,, Boys 4 feet 6 inches high	$ 850 to $950

„	Boys 4 feet 9 inches high	$1000 to $1150
„	Boys 5 feet high	$1150 to $1275
„	Girls of same height of boys about the same prices.	
„	Young woman and first child	$1250 to $1450

Goode Negroes are selling readily at the above figures, but inferior ones are rather dull.—Now is the time to buy good ones and bring them in.

Hoping to see you soon with a good lot.
We are very truley

Betts & Gregory

> [*Slave Trader Newsletter*, 20 July 1860. General list from Betts and Gregory, Auctioneers, Richmond, Virginia, showing what certain classes of slaves are selling for and general comments and predictions on the market. South Carolina Historical Society.]

159 **Slave Sale Advertisement 1861**

See page 396.

A GANG OF 20 CHOICE

Plantation Slaves!

ACCLIMATED & ACCUSTOMED TO THE CULTURE OF SUGAR,

FROM ONE PLANTATION IN THE PARISH OF JEFFERSON.

SOLD TO PAY DEBTS.

BY C. E. GIRARDEY & CO.

OFFICE, NO. 37 MAGAZINE STREET.

ON WEDNESDAY, FEBRUARY 20, 1861,

AT 12 O'CLOCK, M., WILL BE SOLD,

AT THE CITY HOTEL, COMMON STREET,

BETWEEN CAMP AND MAGAZINE STREETS,

THE FOLLOWING CHOICE SLAVES·WIT:

1. ELIZA, - black, aged 16 years, sugar-field hand.
2. LIDDY, " 20 " cook, washer and ironer.
3. MILLY, " 15 " sugar-field hand.
4. HANNAH, " 24 " " " cook, washer and ironer.
5. JULIA ANN, " 18 " " "
6. EVE, " 28 " " " and her child
7. LUCY, " 12 " " "
8. JACKSON, " 24 " a first-rate cook, etc,
9. MARSHAL, " 24 " No. 1 field hand, teamster, etc. and his wife
10. JANE, " 22 " No. 1 sugar-field hand. etc.
11. MARY, " 20 " " "
12. DICK, " 30 " A No. 1 carpenter and blacksmith, and his wife
13. SALLY, " 27 " " cook, washer and ironer, and their child
14. OCTAVIE, " 8 "
15. EMANUEL, " 24 " No. 1 field hand, ploughman and axeman, & his brother
16. NELSON, " 22 " engineer, can run sugar engine and saw mill, & his wife
17. MARTHA, " 20 " very stout and likely, sugar-field hand.
18. HARRY, No. 1 molasses barrel cooper ; can make 4 hhds. per day
19. SAM, " 22 " an extra hand. No. 1 ditcher, chopper and field hand—powerful fellow.
20. HENRY, orphan, " 11 " a likely house boy.
21. DAVID, " 24 " ploughman and good carriage driver.
22. JOHN, " 24 " ploughman and teamster.

All one gang, very likely, and fully guaranteed against the vices and maladies prescribed by law.

These negroes are sold only to pay debts. They are acclimated and accustomed to the culture of sugar ; good subjects, and well drilled.

TERMS.

One-half cash ; balance at 12 months' credit, for approved city acceptance, secured by mortgage on the slaves, and bearing interest at the rate of 8 per cent. per annum.

Acts of sale before P. C. Cuvellier, Notary Public, at the expense of the purchasers.

The Slaves will be at the office of the auctioneer, for public inspection the day preceding sale.

[OVER.]

[*Slave Sale Advertisement*, February 20, 1861, New Orleans, Louisiana.]

Capitalism and Slavery

According to Adam Smith, the discovery of America and the Cape route to India are 'the two greatest and most important events recorded in the history of mankind'. The importance of the discovery of America lay not in the precious metals it provided but in the new and inexhaustible market it afforded for European commodities. One of its principal effects was to 'raise the mercantile system to a degree of splendour and glory which it could never otherwise have attained to'. It gave rise to an enormous increase in world trade. The seventeenth and eighteenth centuries were the centuries of trade, as the nineteenth century was the century of production. For Britain that trade was primarily the triangular trade. In 1718 William Wood said that the slave trade was 'the spring and parent whence the others flow'. A few years later Postlethwayt described the slave trade as 'the first principle and foundation of all the rest, the mainspring of the machine which sets every wheel in motion'.

In this triangular trade England—France and Colonial America equally—supplied the exports and the ships; Africa the human merchandise; the plantations the colonial raw matterials. The slave ship sailed from the home country with a cargo of manufactured goods. These were exchanged at a profit on the coast of Africa for Negroes, who were traded on the plantations, at another profit, in exchange for a cargo of colonial produce to be taken back to the home country. As the volume of trade increased, the triangular trade was supplemented, but never supplanted, by a direct trade between home country and the West Indies, exchanging home manufactures directly for colonial produce.

The triangular trade thereby gave a triple stimulus to British industry. The Negroes were purchased with British manufactures; transported to the plantations, they produced sugar, cotton, indigo, molasses and other tropical products, the processing of which created new industries in England; while the maintenance of the Negroes and their owners on the plantations provided another market for British industry, New England agriculture and the Newfoundland fisheries. By 1750 there was hardly a trading or a manufacturing town in England which was not in some way connected with the triangular or direct colonial trade. The profits obtained provided one of the main streams of that accumulation of capital in England which financed the Industrial Revolution.

The West Indian islands became the hub of the British Empire, of immense importance to the grandeur and prosperity of England. It was the Negro slaves who made these sugar colonies the most precious colonies ever recorded in the whole annals of imperialism. To Postlethwayt they were 'the fundamental prop and support' of the colonies, 'valuable people' whose labor supplied Britain with all plantation produce. The British Empire was 'a magnificent superstructure of American commerce and naval power on an African foundation'.

Sir Josiah Child estimated that every Englishman in the West Indies, 'with the ten blacks that work with him, accounting what they eat, use and wear, would make employment for four men in England'. By Davenant's computation one person in the islands, white or Negro, was as profitable as seven in England. Another writer considered that every family in the West Indies gave employment to five seamen and many more artificers, manufacturers and tradesmen, and that every white person in the islands brought in ten pounds annually clear profit to England, twenty times as much as a similar person in the home country. William Wood reckoned that a profit of seven shillings per head per annum was sufficient to enrich a country; each white man in the colonies brought a profit of over seven pounds. Sir Dalby Thomas went further—every person employed on the sugar plantations was 130 times more valuable to England than one at home. Professor Pitman has estimated that in 1775 British West Indian plantations represented a valuation of fifty millions sterling, and the sugar planters themselves put the figure at seventy millions in 1788. In 1798 Pitt assessed the annual income from West Indian plantations at four million pounds as compared with one million from the rest of the world. As Adam Smith wrote: 'The profits of a sugar plantation in any of our West Indian colonies are generally much greater than those of any other cultivation that is known either in Europe or America'.

[. . .]

Mercantilists were enthusiastic. The triangular trade, and the associated trade with the sugar islands, because of the navigation they encouraged, were more valuable to England than her mines of tin or coal. These were ideal colonies. But for them Britain would have no gold or silver, except what she received from illicit commerce with the Spanish colonies, and an unfavorable balance of trade. Their tropical products, unlike those of the northern part of the mainland, did not compete with those of the home country. They showed little sign of that industrial development which was the constant fear where the mainland was concerned. Their large black population was an effective guarantee against aspirations to independence. It all combined to spell one word, sugar. 'The pleasure, glory and grandeur of England,' wrote Sir Dalby Thomas, 'has been advanced more by sugar than by any other commodity, wool not excepted.'

There was one qualification—monopoly. The economic philosophy of the age had no room for the open door, and colonial trade was a rigid monopoly of the home country. The mercantilists were adamant on this point. 'Colonies,' wrote Davenant, 'are a strength to their mother kingdom, while they

are under good discipline, while they are strictly made to observe the fundamental laws of their original country, and while they are kept dependent on
it. But otherwise, they are worse than members lopped from the body politic,
being indeed like offensive arms wrested from a nation to be turned against it
as occasion shall serve.' The colonies, in return for their prosperity, owed the
mother country, in Postlethwayt's view, gratitude and an indispensable
duty—'to be immediately dependent on their original parent and to make
their interest subservient thereunto.'

[From *Capitalism and Slavery* [1944] (New York: Capricorn, 1966), 51–3, 55.]

WALTER RODNEY

161 How Europe Underdeveloped Africa

Europe and the Roots of African Underdevelopment to 1885

To discuss trade between Africans and Europeans in the four centuries before
colonial rule is virtually to discuss slave trade. Strictly speaking, the African
only became a slave when he reached a society where he worked as a slave.
Before that, he was first a free man and then a captive. Nevertheless, it is
acceptable to talk about the trade in slaves to refer to the shipment of captives
from Africa to various other parts of the world where they were to live and
work as the property of Europeans. The title of this section is deliberately
chosen to call attention to the fact that the shipments were all by Europeans
to markets controlled by Europeans, and this was in the interest of European
capitalism and nothing else.

[. . .]

Many things remain uncertain about the slave trade and its consequences
for Africa, but the general picture of destructiveness is clear, and that
destructiveness can be shown to be the logical consequence of the manner of
recruitment of captives in Africa. One of the uncertainties concerns the basic
question of how many Africans were imported. This has long been an object
of speculation, with estimates ranging from a few millions to over one hundred million. A recent study has suggested a figure of about ten million
Africans landed alive in the Americas, the Atlantic islands and Europe.
Because it is a low figure, it is already being used by European scholars who
are apologists for the capitalist system and its long record of brutality in
Europe and abroad. In order to white-wash the European slave trade, they
find it convenient to start by minimising the numbers concerned. The truth is
that any figure of Africans imported into the Americas which is narrowly
based on the surviving records is bound to be low, because there were so
many people at the time who had a vested interest in smuggling slaves (and

withholding data). Nevertheless, if the low figure of ten million was accepted as a basis for evaluating the impact of slaving on Africa as a whole, the conclusions that could legitimately be drawn would confound those who attempt to make light of the experience of the rape of Africans from 1445 to 1870.

On any basic figure of Africans landed alive in the Americas, one would have to make several extensions—starting with a calculation to cover mortality in transhipment. The Atlantic crossing or 'Middle Passage', as it was called by European slavers, was notorious for the number of deaths incurred, averaging in the vicinity of 15 per cent to 20 per cent. There were also numerous deaths in Africa between time of capture and time of embarkation, especially in cases where captives had to travel hundreds of miles to the coast. Most important of all (given that warfare was the principal means of obtaining captives) it is necessary to make some estimate as to the number of people killed and injured so as to extract the millions who were taken alive and sound. The resultant figure would be many times the millions landed alive outside of Africa, and it is that figure which represents the number of Africans directly removed from the population and labour force of Africa because of the establishment of slave production by Europeans.

The massive loss to the African labour force was made more critical because it was composed of able-bodied young men and young women. Slave buyers preferred their victims between the ages of 15 and 35, and preferably in the early twenties; the sex ratio being about two men to one woman. Europeans often accepted younger African children, but rarely any older person. They shipped the most healthy where-ever possible, taking the trouble to get those who had already survived an attack of smallpox, and who were therefore immune from further attacks of that disease, which was then one of the world's great killer diseases.

[. . .]

No one has been able to come up with a figure representing total losses to the African population sustained through the extraction of slave labour from all areas to all destinations over the many centuries that slave trade existed. However, on every other continent from the 15th century onwards, the population showed constant and sometimes spectacular natural increase; while it is striking that the same did not apply to Africa.

[. . .]

The changeover to warlike activities and kidnapping must have affected all branches of economic activity, and agriculture in particular. Occasionally, in certain localities food production was increased to provide supplies for slave ships, but the overall consequence of slaving on agricultural activities in Western, Eastern and Central Africa were negative.

[. . .]

One tactic that is now being employed by certain European (including

American) scholars is to say that the European slave trade was undoubtedly *a moral evil*, but it was *economically good* for Africa. Here attention will be drawn only very briefly to a few of those arguments to indicate how ridiculous they can be. One that receives much emphasis is that African rulers and other persons obtained European commodities in exchange for their captives, and this was how Africans gained 'wealth'. This suggestion fails to take into account the fact that several European imports were competing with and strangling African products; it fails to take into account the fact that none of the long list of European articles were of the type which entered into the productive process, but were rather items to be rapidly consumed or stowed away uselessly; and it incredibly overlooks the fact that the majority of the imports were of the worst quality even as consumer goods—cheap gin, cheap gunpowder, pots and kettles full of holes, beads, and other assorted rubbish.

[. . .]

A few of the arguments about the economic benefits of the European slave trade for Africa amount to nothing more than saying that exporting millions of captives was a way of avoiding starvation in Africa! To attempt to reply to that would be painful and time-wasting. But, perhaps a slightly more subtle version of the same argument requires a reply: namely, the argument that Africa gained because in the process of slave trading new food crops were acquired from the American continent and these became staples in Africa. The crops in question are maize and cassava, which became staples in Africa late in the 19th century and in the present century. But the spread of food crops is one of the most common phenomena in human history. Most crops originated in only one of the continents, and then social contact caused their transfer to other parts of the world. Trading in slaves has no special bearing on whether crops spread—the simplest forms of trade would have achieved the same result.

[From *How Europe Underdeveloped Africa* (London: Bogle-L'Ouverture, 1972), 103–6, 108, 110–12.]

MANUEL MORENO FRAGINALS

162   **The Sugarmill**

The slave as such, and the trade in blacks, were typically capitalist phenomena. The Cuban slave's function was almost exclusively to produce merchandise for the world market. What we had was a slave system with a 'Factory Act,' with specific labor-task regulations that often did more good for the slave than did English laws for the wage-worker. Many mills, for instance, recognized minimal property rights for the slave, who cultivated the ground and traded his products with the master.

[. . .]

To think that our sugar producers were slavers because their mental attitude was opposed to progress would be absurd. We have seen how Havana's sugarocracy awoke to the capitalist world with a profound bourgeois awareness. Production for the world market imposed on them the essential laws of the capitalist system. They were slavers because they lacked wage-workers, because only slavery could make the initial sugar expansion possible. In Cuba, as in all colonies, there was a passionate desire for cheap and submissive labor, of a type to which our nascent capitalists could dictate conditions rather than have to submit to those labor imposed.

[. . .]

The Cuban sugarocracy very soon perceived the disadvantages of slavery and tried to form a class of cheap wage-workers: the so-called colonization projects were nothing more than this. The pluses and minuses of the two labor systems were already being analyzed in the first half of the eighteenth century.

[. . .]

The whole discussion reveals how the economic contradictions of sugar production awoke the consciousness of our producers. The slavers themselves, with their interest in maintaining the anti-economic slavery system, joined in the polemic with rationales for the continued importing of blacks. The barbarous exploitation of wage-workers by the English in the first half of the nineteenth century was a potent argument for slavery. No reader of Engels' pitiful descriptions of the Irish in Great Britain, of the 'white slaves' in England, can hold the Cuban slave traders to have been entirely in the wrong.

[. . .]

We have said that although slave and wage labor always coexisted in the sugarmill, the primary quantitative solution was slavery. In the eighteenth century Wakefield called it the sole natural basis of colonial wealth. Marx quoted him and commented that without workers—that is, without slavery—capital would have perished, or at least been reduced 'to that small amount which each individual could employ with his own hands'. In other words, it would have stopped being capital, for capital only exists where there is a coincidence of the conditions necessary for the means of production to function as means of exploitation and enslavement of the worker. Capitalism had furthermore organized the broad system of trading in Africans with incredible efficiency. Cuban sugarmen initiated large-scale production by using existing channels to fill their mills with slaves, which meant that one objective condition of sugar production did not depend on the Cubans themselves. But the producers quickly realized that they could not depend on foreigners to solve their labor problems. Cuban sugar needed a Cuban slave trade; they had to have their own suppliers of hands, and so was born the Hispano-Cuban organization of the slave trade as a subsidiary business.

[. . .]

From the outset the traffic in Chinese was clearly a more productive and less dangerous business than slaving, and naturally everyone wanted to control it. Slavers fought against it with outcries about the mixed-race threat to Cuba. But the Junta flatly denied the need for any concern about the possible results of introducing a new race. The problem was economic: 'Territorial production and the agricultural industry need hands; those which the introduction of Asiatics promise to supply fill a small part of the need, as results will show'. By now Cuba's bourgeoisie had shed the figleaves hiding its economic pudenda.

Contracts for Chinese bodies sold at first for 60 pesos and were up to 300 by 1860. Chinese became a big business and special regulations became necessary in the mills. Feijóo y Sotomayor proposed the following:

1. They should not be allowed off the farms.
2. They should get the same food as black slaves.
3. Wages should not be paid them when they were ill, sickness being a natural accident under the contract.
4. Masters should have jurisdictional power over them.
5. They should not be allowed to obtain freedom until the end of the contract, or to leave the farm after the contract if still in debt.
6. Marriage with white women should not be allowed.
7. There should be political equality with the free mulatto.
8. There should be fifteen hours' work a day.

These, more or less, were the conditions actually imposed. In 1854 a labor code similar to that for the slaves was promulgated for Chinese and Yucatecans. Poey, who had many Chinese working for him in Las Cañas mill, admitted that the harvest season work day was eighteen hours. One understands why the Matanzas mayor's office began a report with the words: 'Free Asiatics, as everyone is pleased to call them, live on our farms exactly as do slaves'.

Although it seemed the same, it was not. The Chinese colonist was a miserably paid wage-worker—precisely the one our producers wanted, cheaper than the slave and capable of making the mechanized mill a viable proposition and launching the great sugar transformation. Many masters tried to submit him to slave conditions, thereby wiping out the advantages of wage-labor, but the highly mechanized mills avoided that mistake. In one of his letters Sagra wrote: 'I think I am justified in saying that the introduction of Asiatics has been most beneficial: without it, who knows how the advances already made would have been possible?' All the highly mechanized mills filled their boiling rooms with Chinese.

[. . .]

The conditions of life in the sugarmill describe a curve beginning with the semi-patriarchal regime of the early eighteenth-century factories, arching through the super-barbarity of the first half of the nineteenth century, and ending in the 1860s and 1870s with what *hacendados* called 'good treatment of the slave'. Economic determinants were the variables of the slaves' treatment, and these were, primarily, the volume of labor available, the price of slaves, production techniques, and market conditions. In this aspect, as in all that we are studying, there is no unity of time and place: the slave's fate was subject to the period and to the type of mill in which he worked.

[From *The Sugarmill: The Socioeconomic Complex of Sugar in Cuba, 1760–1860* [1964], trs. Cedric Belfrage (New York: Monthly Review Press, 1976), 131–2, 141–2.]

EVSEY D. DOMAR

163   The Causes of Slavery or Serfdom

A simple economic model may sharpen the argument (if any sharpening is needed) and help to develop it further. Assume that labor and land are the only factors of production (no capital or management), and that land of uniform quality and location is ubiquitous. No diminishing returns in the application of labor to land appear; both the average and the marginal productivities of labor are constant and equal, and if competition among employers raises wages to that level (as would be expected), no rent from land can arise, as Ricardo demonstrated some time past. In the absence of specific governmental action to the contrary (see below), the country will consist of family-size farms because hired labor, in any form, will be either unavailable or unprofitable: the wage of a hired man or the income of a tenant will have to be at least equal to what he can make on his own farm; if he receives that much, no surplus (rent) will be left for his employer. A non-working class of servitors or others could be supported by the government out of taxes levied (directly or indirectly) on the peasants, but it could not support itself from land rents.

[. . .]

In a traditional society without technological progress and capital accumulation, the end of slavery is, paradoxically, more certain. As population continues to increase and the society eventually becomes Malthusian, the marginal product of labor descends to the subsistence level. Now the free man costs little more to employ than the slave, while, hopefully, being less bothersome and more productive. The ownership of human beings becomes pointless because of the great multiplication of slaves, and they become free provided they stay poor. It is land that becomes valuable, and rents collected from estates worked by free laborers or tenants without any non-economic compulsion are sufficient to support an army of servitors or idlers. If the Muscovite government could have only waited a few hundred years!

[. . .]

The United States. The American South fits my hypothesis with such embarrassing simplicity as to question the need for it. The presence of vast expanses of empty fertile land in a warm climate, land capable of producing valuable products if only labor could be found seems to me quite sufficient to explain the importation of slaves. What is not clear to me is the failure of the North to use them in large numbers. Besides social and political objections, there must have been economic reasons why Negro slaves had a comparative advantage in the South as contrasted with the North. Perhaps it had something to do with the superior adaptability of the Negro to a hot climate, and/or with his usefulness in the South almost throughout the year rather than for the few months in the North. I have a hard time believing that slaves could not be used in the mixed farming of the North; much food was produced on southern farms as well, most of the slave owners had very few slaves, and many slaves were skilled in crafts. A study of the possible profitability of slavery in the North, along Conrad and Meyer's lines, which could show whether the North could have afforded paying the market price for slaves, would be most welcome.

I have not come across any good evidence that slavery was dying out in the United States on the eve of the Civil War, and I side here with Conrad and Meyer, though, in truth, I am not sure that such a thorough investigation was required to prove the profitability of slavery in the South.

[From 'The Causes of Slavery or Serfdom: A Hypothesis,' *Journal of Economic History* 30 (1970), 19, 23, 30.]

B. W. HIGMAN
....

164   **Slave Populations of the British Caribbean**

Mortality

Analysis of mortality patterns is inhibited by the understatement of infant deaths in the slave registration returns. [. . .] [T]his understatement chiefly pertained to children born and dying within a registration interval and so prevents direct comparisons of infant mortality levels. A solution to this problem has been sought in the use of model life tables as a means of estimating the extent of under-registration. Because of variations in registration practice it is necessary to regard the adjusted mortality rates with caution, though they are undoubtedly a better guide to the reality than are direct calculations from the raw registration data. Age-specific mortality rates can, however, be calculated directly from the registration data for slaves 5 years of age and above.

Mortality differentials at the colony level did not conform closely to the threefold classification of colonies in terms of natural increase. In part, this lack of conformity resulted from the ambiguous correlations between mortality, fertility, and natural increase. It was also affected by the association, in many colonies, between high fertility and high infant mortality rates. Thus, some colonies achieved significant positive natural increase in the face of heavy mortality, through high fertility and a consequently high infant mortality rate. Barbados is the outstanding example of this pattern, experiencing mortality levels very similar to those characteristic of the third-phase sugar colonies. In the marginal colonies, however, infant mortality accounted for a smaller component of total mortality, and so the latter was considerably less.

In the period after 1807 most colonies experienced a decrease in the crude death rate. But exceptions to this general decline came from all of the classes of colonies. The rise in mortality in Jamaica, Demerara-Essequibo, and Grenada after 1807 is not unexpected, but the same trend in Antigua and Montserrat is surprising. Anguilla also probably experienced an increase in the crude death rate toward the end of the 1820s, as a result of the island's subsistence crisis. In order to understand the apparent differences in the colonies' crude death rates, however, it is essential first to take into account the effects of variations in their age and sex structures. Mortality and the slave sex ratio were positively correlated at the colony level, though the correlations were not significant at the 99 percent level. Stronger correlations existed with the age structure. The crude death rate for male slaves was clearly associated with the proportion of males aged 15–44 years ($r = .62$), and to a weaker, though significant, degree for females ($r = .46$). Thus, differences in total mortality at the colony level may reflect contrasts in age structure.

SEX AND AGE

With few exceptions, crude death rates at the colony level were significantly higher for males than for females. This contrast occurs in most populations, of course, but it is important to recall that in the slave populations of the British Caribbean there was a substantial concentration of females in the field gangs of plantations and that females shared the heavy demands on labor. The significance of this relationship will be considered further in the discussion of occupation and mortality, below. Of the exceptions to the general trend, the most important occurred in Trinidad between 1816 and 1822. The reasons for this unusually high female mortality are not clear, but the period was unique in showing a rising sex ratio as the result of the movement of slaves to Trinidad from other Caribbean colonies. This may have created short-run distortions in age structure.

[. . .]

For male infants the death rate ranged from about 580 to 240 per 1,000, and for females from 480 to 200. These rates are only approximations and may not fully take into account the prolonged breast-feeding periods typical of the West Indian slave population, but they do show that there was a wide disparity between the experience of the marginal colonies and the sugar colonies. The ordering of the sugar colonies in terms of infant mortality is more difficult to explain, especially the low rates for Jamaica. But the model life table estimates do suggest that rates in excess of 400 per 1,000 were typical of most eastern Caribbean colonies and that infant mortality levels in the old sugar colonies were not dramatically superior to those in the new sugar colonies.

A comparison of age-specific death rates for slaves 5 years of age and above, calculated directly from the registration data, with rates indicated by the appropriate model life tables shows a very close correspondence in the middle range of mortality levels, with wider disparities at the extremes. For slaves aged 5–69 years there is a close congruence between the two measures in the case of St. Kitts at West 3, for example. But the high level of mortality experienced by adult slaves in Tobago exceeded that predicted by West 1, while in Anguilla registered mortality rates were lower than those expected for West 9. This suggests that there are limitations to the value of the model life tables as indicators of mortality patterns in the slave populations. This is hardly surprising. No doubt a similar range of error applies to the infant mortality estimates, but no independent check is available. In the analysis of mortality at ages 5 years and above, however, rates calculated directly from the registration data provide a superior indication of reality and will be used in preference to the model life table estimates.

The broad contrast between the crude death rates of the sugar colonies and marginal colonies was equally obvious in terms of age-specific mortality levels. It was apparent at all ages and affected males as well as females. But the relative ordering of the colonies is changed to some degree as a result of their differing age structures. Colonies with relatively large proportions of slaves aged over 40 or under 5 years generally showed high crude death rates because of the particularly high mortality affecting those age groups. These effects were complicated, but overall it appears that the adjusted crude death rates do provide a reliable indication of comparative mortality levels. Thus, the slave population of Tobago, with the highest crude death rate of all the colonies, suffered extreme mortality levels in almost all age groups among both males and females. Berbice showed relatively lower mortality among children, but its female slaves matched the Tobago rates after 35 years, and its males after 55 years. St. Lucia, however, came much closer to the Tobago rates among those under 20 years, while dropping below both Tobago and Berbice in the older age groups. The old sugar colony of St. Kitts was distinguished from those new sugar colonies by lower rates of mortality among children and old people. But in the principal working age groups, particularly among male slaves of 25–45, there was little difference between St. Kitts and Berbice or St. Lucia. Nevis and the Virgin Islands followed the same general trends as St. Kitts. The relatively low mortality levels that were reached in Dominica by the end of the 1820s were apparent at most ages but were particularly marked among those under 20 years. Similarly, the considerably lower mortality of the marginal colonies was not confined to any one age group, though it was most marked among those under 50 years of age. To some extent, the contrast between the marginal colonies and the sugar colonies may be explained by change during the 1820s, but there is little reason to doubt that the difference in age-specific mortality was as great in earlier periods.

In general, then, the new sugar colonies experienced heavier mortality than the old sugar colonies and, to a greater degree, the marginal colonies, even when differences in the age and sex composition of the slave populations are taken into account. Thus, the apparent differences in mortality observed in the crude death rates were not mere artefacts but represented real contrasts in mortality experience. These contrasts were apparent at all ages, though they were particularly marked among those under 20 years of age. This suggests that mortality differences were influenced by factors generally affecting the slave populations rather than being determined simply by labor regimes.

[. . .]

In general, the most important causes of slave deaths in the new sugar colonies were ordered roughly as follows: diarrhea and dysentery, dropsy, fevers (malaria and yellow fever), tuberculosis, nervous system diseases, and digestive system diseases. These diseases accounted for 75 percent of all classifiable deaths in Grenada and 59 percent in Berbice, the other colonies falling within this range. Although the sample is relatively small, it is of interest to compare this pattern with that found in the plantation books of Newton and Colleton Plantations, Barbados, for the periods 1811–25 and 1819–34, respectively. Of the classifiable deaths (189), the ordering was as follows: dropsy (14.3 per cent), tuberculosis (12.2), diarrhea (9.0), marasmus (9.0), nervous system diseases (7.9), scarlet fever (6.9), and leprosy (5.8). The most obvious contrast with the pattern in the new sugar colonies is the relative unimportance of diarrhea and dysentery, digestive system diseases, and fevers in Barbados. The island was peculiar in remaining relatively free of malaria throughout its history. Causes accounting for relatively large proportions of deaths in Barbados were scarlet fever, teething, and diphtheria, reflecting the youthfulness of the creole population. The pattern of causes of death in Jamaica during the 1820s seems to have approximated more closely that found in Barbados than in the new sugar colonies.

[From *Slave Populations of the British Caribbean 1807–1834* (Baltimore: Johns Hopkins University Press, 1984), 314–22, 341.]

STUART B. SCHWARTZ

165   Death in the Tropics

It is generally agreed that slavery was bad for the health. The life expectancy of slaves seems invariably to have been lower than that of free persons living in the same environment, and the conditions of sugar plantations throughout the Americas seem to have been worse than on other kinds of slave properties. Although there is no agreement on the rate of mortality, virtually all observers of slavery in colonial Bahia concur in their belief that its slave population suffered an annual rate of decline; a situation in which the number of births was constantly exceeded by the number of deaths so that maintenance of the population was possible only by continually importing new slaves from Africa.

Observations of the high mortality among slaves begin in the seventeenth century. Bernardo Ribeiro, agent for the countess of Linhares wrote in 1601, 'The properties of engenhos in this state are very laborious and costly because they depend on slaves with whom little can be done; the work is great and many die'. In the same decade, Governor Diogo de Meneses wrote of the cost to planters of the many slaves bought on advances from merchants who died leaving the planters with great debts.

By the early nineteenth century, observers began to offer estimates of the rate of decline of the slave population. One author in 1832 placed the rate of decline at 5 percent per year, meaning that the slave force would be reduced to half its size in seven years if no additions were made. Another observer, writing in the mid-nineteenth century, placed the decline at 8 percent a year, with an additional loss of 2.75 percent due to interprovincial sales southward. Although there was a divergence of opinion on the actual rate of decrease, there seems to have been no doubt about the situation of demographic decline. Charles Pennell, the British consul in Salvador and a supporter of the 5 percent a year loss figure, wrote in 1827:

The annual mortality on many sugar plantations is so great that unless their numbers are augmented from abroad the whole slave population would become extinct in the course of about twenty years; the proprietors act on the calculation that it is cheaper to buy male slaves than to raise Negro children.

[. . .]

Robert Slenes has estimated life expectancy at birth (e_o) of between nineteen and twenty-seven years for Brazilian slaves in the late nineteenth century, a figure only slightly under the 27.08 years that has been calculated for the Brazilian population as a whole in 1879. Still, he characterized this situation as one of extremely high mortality, considerably above that of slaves in the U.S. South in the mid-nineteenth century. Using a somewhat different technique, Pedro Carvalho de Mello reached similar conclusions, placing a male slave's life expectancy at birth at 18.3 years, compared to 27.4 for the population as a whole in 1872. The male slave's life expectancy at birth in Brazil was thus 30 percent less than that of the whole population, and it was only half that of a male slave in the United States about 1850 ($e_o = 35.5$), which in turn was only 12 percent less than that of the entire U.S. population.

[. . .]

The disease environment, poor nutrition, and lack of medical care affected a large segment of the free population as well as the slaves in Bahia, but there is little doubt that the slave condition created certain peculiar conditions of mortality. The apparently very high rates of slave neonatal and child mortality may have been due to poor nutrition and the labor demands made on mothers as well as planter calculations that raising a child until the age of labor was a risky business given its chances of dying first. This attitude and the demands made on pregnant slave women may have also resulted in a higher proportion of stillbirths among slaves than among the rest of the population. Data from Maranhão in 1798 reveal a ratio of stillbirths to total births among slaves of 10.3, compared with 5.7 among whites and 6.5 among free pardos.

Although infant mortality seems to have been a major factor in the pathology of Brazilian slave demography, the work regime, especially that demanded of those in sugar agriculture, also had its costs. Past the age of fifty, slaves suffered higher mortality rates than free persons. At least this is suggested by age distributions. About 6 per cent of the slaves listed as sick in inventories of sugar properties suffered from cansaço or exhaustion. Some authors believe that cansaço is a particular disease, but I have never seen a document in which a free person is listed with this ailment in the eighteenth century. I believe that cansaço refers to a condition of slavery, of being worn out or exhausted to the point of incapacity. During the safra, when the work demands were highest, there was little time for rest, especially in the sugar mill itself. Fatigue could have deadly results, as it probably did for Francisco, a slave from Mina, who in 1816 died at an engenho in São Francisco after falling into a kettle of boiling sugar syrup.

Finally, there is the difficult-to-measure but very real psychological effect of slavery on its victims. Plantation accounts hint at infanticide and abortion. Despair in the face of enslavement led to suicides on slave ships and on plantations. Ship captain Felipe Nery reported from Pernambuco in 1812 that he had lost three of his human cargo when on entering the River Zaire three men who had suffered a flogging had 'despairingly thrown themselves into the sea'. Antonil, who visited the Recôncavo in the late seventeenth century, and Benci, who lived in Bahia at the same time, both admonished slaveowners to treat slaves with decency because poor care and mistreatment often led the slaves to take their own lives, a matter with serious implications for these churchmen.

[From *Sugar Plantations in the Formation of Brazilian Society: Bahia, 1550–1835* (Cambridge: Cambridge University Press, 1985), 364–5, 369–71.]

ROBERT WILLIAM FOGEL

166 Without Consent or Contract

Some special aspects of the evolution of slavery in the United States

The United States stood apart from the other slave-importing territories, not only because of its comparatively small share in the Atlantic slave trade, but also because of the minor role played by its sugar industry in the growth of U.S. slavery. The commercial production of sugar in Louisiana did not begin until 1795, barely a decade before the United States withdrew from the international slave trade. At the time of the U.S. annexation of Louisiana, annual sugar production was a mere 5,000 tons. Even at its antebellum peak, sugar was never more than a minor southern crop that utilized less than 10 percent of the slave labor force.

The absence of the sugar culture had a profound effect on the development of slavery in the U.S. colonies. For one thing, it affected the rate at which the slave labor force grew, both in absolute numbers and in relative importance. While African labor was introduced into Virginia earlier than in Barbados, there were six times as many blacks in the British Caribbean in 1700 as there were in all of the North American colonies. Some 80 years after the first group of slaves landed in Virginia, the black population of that colony was just 16,000, while all the other North American colonies contained a mere 11,000 blacks. In the British Caribbean the slave population climbed to 60,000 within 30 years after the beginning of the British presence. It took her North American colonies 110 years to reach the same absolute level, despite the higher rate of natural increase of slaves in North America and the high mortality rate in the Caribbean.

As late as 1680 the relatively few slaves in Britain's North American colonies (under 7,000) were widely distributed in general farming and domestic occupations, but a concentration of slave labor in tobacco had already begun to develop in the Chesapeake. By the middle of the 1730s, the slave population had risen to about 120,000 with tobacco production requiring the concentrated effort of perhaps a third of the hands and rice another tenth. Thus, the majority of slaves were still employed mainly in general farming, in domestic service, in crafts, or in other non-farm occupations. This basic pattern continued for the next three decades, although by the mid-1760s the share of the labor of slave hands claimed by the three principal plantation crops—tobacco, rice, and indigo—had risen to a bit over 50 percent and there were rapidly growing slave populations in the Carolinas and Georgia. Allowing for the slaves engaged in crafts, domestic service, and secondary-market products, plantations specializing in these three crops may have accounted for two-thirds of the slave labor.

Cotton did not emerge as a major southern crop until the beginning of the nineteenth century, after the cotton gin lowered the cost of fiber. At the beginning of the nineteenth century about 11 percent of all slaves lived on cotton plantations. With the swelling demand, production rose so rapidly that by 1850 the proportion engaged on cotton plantations had risen to about 64 percent. The tobacco share had dwindled to 12 percent; sugar was next with 5 percent; rice had about 4 percent; and indigo was no longer commercially produced in the South.

The differences in the U.S. and West Indian patterns of crop specialization led to striking differences in the ratios of blacks to total population. As early as 1650, blacks formed 25 percent of the population in the British Caribbean. In 1770 the ratio stood at 91 percent. The experience in the French Caribbean was similar. By contrast, blacks formed only 4 percent of the population of the North American colonies in 1650 and rose to a pre-Revolutionary peak of 22 percent in 1770. In the southern U.S. colonies the percentages for 1650 and 1770 were 3 and 40, respectively. Thus, while blacks were the overwhelming majority of the population and labor force of the Caribbean during most of the colonial era, they were generally a minority of the population of the U.S. colonies and for most of the colonial period a relatively small minority, even in the South. It was only toward the middle of the eighteenth century, after slaves became geographically concentrated, that they emerged as the majority of the population in certain counties.

The U.S. pattern of crop specialization also affected the size of the units on which slaves lived and had far-reaching effects on the development of slave culture. During the colonial era, the median size of tobacco plantations remained below 20 slaves, and it increased only slightly thereafter. Slaves who labored in tobacco typically worked on plantations consisting of a white family and a few slave families; even large tobacco plantations were usually organized as a series of small units. Cotton plantations were not much larger; the median in 1860 was 35 slaves. The biggest plantations in the United States were in rice and sugar. There were about 100 slaves on the typical Louisiana sugar plantation in 1860. Although this figure exceeds the averages for tobacco, cotton, and even rice, it falls below the averages of sugar estates in the Caribbean or Brazil. And so, U.S. slave plantations were dwarfed by those of the West Indies. Blacks in these islands, particularly in Jamaica, had relatively little contact with the European culture of the white slave owner both because of the small percentage of whites who lived there and because of the enormous size of the typical plantation. But blacks in the U.S. colonies were usually a minority of the population and, even toward the end of the antebellum era, lived on relatively small units (generally fewer than seven or eight families), which brought them into continuous contact with their white masters.

U.S. slaves were not only in closer contact with European culture, they were also more removed from their African origins than were slaves in the Caribbean. Down through the end of the eighteenth century and into the nineteenth century, the majority of the slave populations of the British and French Caribbean islands and of Brazil were born in Africa because Africans were continually imported to offset the high death rates there. Indeed, as late as 1800, one-quarter of the population of Jamaica consisted of Africans who had arrived in the New World within the previous decade. On the other hand, creoles (slaves born in the New World) made up the majority of the slave population in the U.S. colonies as early as 1740. By the time of Washington's presidency, the African-born component of the black population had shrunk to a bit over 20 percent. It hovered close to this share from 1780 to 1810 and then rapidly headed toward zero. By 1850 all but a minute fraction of U.S. slaves were native born, and most of them were third-, fourth-, or fifth-generation Americans. This finding does not contradict the view that African heritage played a large role in shaping the culture of blacks, but it does serve to emphasize the extent to which black culture had, by 1860, been exposed to indigenous American influences.

[From *Without Consent or Contract: The Rise and Fall of American Slavery* (New York: Norton, 1989), 29–32.]

PATRICK MANNING

167 Slavery and African Life

Why did Africans supply slaves for sale, either on domestic or intercontinental markets? [. . .] [T]he prices offered by European merchants were high enough that some Africans could not resist profiting from the sale of slaves. But this reasoning is insufficient to explain why the slave trade should have continued at a high level for over two centuries. How could Africans have continued to export slaves from region after region, even when the total population declined as a result of those exports?

Many Africans saw the consequences of slavery, and some fought bravely against its continuation and expansion. Certain whole societies managed to avoid tainting themselves with slavery. On the whole, however, enough Africans participated actively in the capture, commerce, and exploitation of slaves to prolong these forms of oppression into the twentieth century. Explaining African complicity in slavery is a complex matter, and I can only hope to offer a simplified beginning. The answers I will suggest are gathered under four general headings: (1) Africans were unaware of the damage the slave trade was doing to the continent; (2) they were unable to escape the social pressures to participate in the slave trade; (3) they were unable to escape the economic pressures to participate in the slave trade; and (4) they did not think enough about the consequences of their actions.

[...]

To begin with, few people in the eighteenth and nineteenth centuries knew that the African population was declining, for the statistical data and comparative framework were missing. In England Thomas Malthus, one of the founding figures of the science of demography, began his writings on population in the late eighteenth century, in the midst of a great controversy over whether the English population was growing or declining. We now know it to have been growing rapidly, at a rate of over one percent per year. But if the population growth rate for little England was unknown at the time, despite the many available records, how could anyone have been sure that the population was declining for the immense Western Coast of Africa?

Further, African population decline, while serious, was far less serious than the depopulation of the Americas and of Oceania. In the Americas, the total population fell from scores of millions to under 10 million between 1500 and 1700, and only then did it begin to recover. Most of the New World's demographic devastation, however, was brought by diseases over which there was almost no possible control: smallpox, measles, typhus, pneumonia, and other such diseases, which were introduced from the Old World by European conquerors and merchants. Africa too suffered from new diseases, especially smallpox, though less drastically so than the Americas. The decline in the African population came later (from 1730 to 1850 on the Western Coast, and later on the Eastern Coast), and it was smaller in absolute and relative terms than that of the Americas. The African decline was therefore less striking, though it was perhaps equally tragic, in that it was brought about through conscious human agency (that is, through the slave trade) more than through the biological reflexes of disease.

One further and important reason why it was not possible for Africans to know about the decline in their population was that they did not then accept the notion of a common African identity. It would be unfair for us to project back into the past the Pan-African and racial consciousness which is characteristic of the twentieth century. Africans, while they could recognize racial and cultural groupings as well as anyone else, did not have a consciousness of themselves as a unitary group in the eighteenth century. Quite the contrary, it was the experience of slavery and the attendant racial discrimination which brought Pan-Africanism and black race consciousness into being. And while Pan-Africanism today condemns, of necessity, not only the European demand for and use of slaves but also the African participation in slavery, there existed no possible realistic basis for such a vision of African unity in the early days of the slave trade.

Significant areas of Africa escaped, at least for periods of time, any devastation and depopulation from the slave trade: people of such areas as the interior of modern Cameroon and Gabon were perhaps ignorant of the damage being done elsewhere. At the village level of those areas which suffered more seriously, on the other hand, even without modern statistics, the loss of population through mortality and slave exports was quite evident. Such was the case among the Mahi people of the central Bénin Republic, whose numbers were reduced in the nineteenth century. In response to such losses, villages under attack defended themselves, families ransomed captured relatives, and large African states attempted to prevent the export of their subjects as slaves. Yet even where they were aware of their demographic decline, the only principles on which Africans opposed slavery were the narrow self-interest of a family, ethnic group, or state. With the exception of those peoples whose law did not provide for slave status, there was no principled African opposition to slavery: the ideology of anti-slavery did not even begin to develop until the mid-eighteenth century, and even in that time there was almost nowhere in the world one could go without finding evidence of fundamental social oppression, or cruel and unusual punishment.

[. . .]

Slave prices followed some clear trends from the sixteenth through the nineteenth centuries. We shall have to proceed cautiously, however, so as not to exaggerate the dependability of the data. Slave prices were complex and variable at best, and they are poorly documented. Prices paid by Africans to Africans were only infrequently recorded. Prices paid by Atlantic merchants to African sellers were more frequently recorded, but they remained complex. Even when payment was made (or at least recorded) in cash, the historian must convert these prices by the appropriate exchange rate to a common basis of comparison, such as British pounds at their 1780 value.

Most often, Atlantic merchants purchased slaves in lots, rather than as individuals, and they often paid in wide assortments of goods rather than in cash. On the eighteenth-century Gold Coast, for instance, an assortment of goods was established as an equivalent of a trading 'ounce,' and an ounce was given an equivalent in a number of slaves. At Luanda, the largest and most unique African slave port, Portuguese merchants provided import goods and credit, Luanda-based Luso-African merchants owned the slaves during their transatlantic voyage, and Brazilian shippers provided the transport. In both these cases, the cost of a lot of slaves on the African coast must be calculated as the purchase price (in Europe, usually) of the goods exchanged for the slaves (this is known as *prime cost*), plus the cost of shipping the goods to Africa. (The shipping cost, while roughly as great as the cost of the goods, is itself difficult to document.) The price per slave, then, is this total cost divided by the number of slaves in the lot. Prices are usually reported as prime cost per slave. [. . .] A better measure would be prime cost plus transport cost of import goods per slave: this measure would rise more slowly with time than prime cost per slave, since transport costs declined with time.

Further, the values of slaves varied significantly by sex and especially by age. Young adults fetched the highest prices, while prices of infants and the old fell very low. The 'average price' of a lot of slaves depended in part, therefore, on the age and sex composition of the group. Some estimates of slave prices have attempted to correct for these variations, usually by adjusting prices and reporting them as prices for 'prime males,' that is, young adult males in good health.

Quite aside from these difficulties of measuring slave prices, there was a great variety of influences combining to set the price levels. The level of productivity—the value of the output of an African man or woman—was the most basic determinant of slave prices. But when we note, for instance, that the average price of slaves rose by a factor of from five to six over the course of a century, we can be sure that this does not mean the productivity of African workers increased by a similar factor. That is, we shall have to account for a variety of market factors and institutional factors which caused fluctuations in the prices and quantities of slaves sold.

In short, I have begun this analysis with two cautions. First, African slave prices are known in general, but only imprecisely. (Further research, of course, has the potential of reconstructing slave prices in greater precision.) Second, our analysis of how slave prices were determined must go beyond simple considerations of cost and productivity, and must include a number of other market and institutional factors.

Let us turn to the main trends in prices. [. . .] Prices are presented in terms of the value of an English pound in 1780 (a date chosen because it is roughly halfway through the period of highest Occidental slave exports), and they refer to prices on the African coast, in regions actively involved in slave exports across the Atlantic.

During the sixteenth century, prices for average slaves gradually increased from an average £10 in 1550 to £14 in 1600. Prices remained unchanging until the 1630s and then fell, dipping below £5 in the 1670s. Prices then rose to £25 in the 1730s, and fluctuated about that level into the 1790s. With the Napoleonic wars, prices fell to £15 and remained stable or declined slightly thereafter. By the 1860s prices for the few remaining slaves exported across the Atlantic averaged just over £10.

[. . .]

Further, this same structure of prices can be used to infer the movements of slaves on the African mainland. If a slave merchant some distance from the coast had both male and female captives, he would not necessarily march them all to the coast. For female slaves, he might get a good price on the spot, and sell them without risking the transit. For male slaves, on the other hand, prices in the interior were so low that the only way to get a good price was to send them to the coast.

This factor provides a very neat correlation for the slave exports of the Western Coast. In those areas where slaves were captured near to the coast and exported, the exports included relatively large proportions of women. Thus in such areas as the Bight of Benin and the Bight of Biafra, where slaves came from areas near the coast, the proportion of females among exports was relatively high. From areas such as Angola and Senegambia, where slaves came from the distant interior, the proportion of females and children among exports was relatively low. Hausa slaves, who came to the coast from 500 kilometers inland as a result of the wars at the turn on the nineteenth century, were adult males almost without exception. And while most slave exports from Senegambia were male Bambara from inland areas, slaves captured in the immediate area of Dakar included as many females as males.

The movement of men and women according to prices had its reflection in African marriage patterns. Let us divide the Western Coast into the littoral and the hinterland, thinking especially of Angola and the Ivory Coast. In the hinterland, local demand and prices for male slaves were low, while the local demand for female slaves kept their prices higher than those of males. On the littoral, the export demand for male slaves kept male prices higher than those of females. At the same time, however, the concentration of purchasing power in the hands of slave merchants on the littoral meant that the prices of female slaves were higher there than in the hinterland. Thus prices for both male and female slaves were higher on the littoral than in the hinterland, though the differential was far greater for males.

The hinterland thus exported virtually all its male slaves and perhaps half of its female slaves to the littoral, and developed a high rate of polygyny. Enslavement along the littoral, in contrast, led to the export of a relatively large proportion of women. Thus the littoral was at once buying, raiding, and selling female slaves, but the net result was a lower rate of polygyny than in the hinterland. In sum, most male slaves exported from Angola came from the hinterland, while most female slaves exported from Angola came from the littoral. The drain on the hinterland population took the form of the export of many men and some women. The drain on the littoral population, if dominated by the loss of males, included the export of women in larger proportions than from the hinterland, though this loss was partially mitigated by the import of women from the hinterland.

[From *Slavery and African Life: Occidental, Oriental and African Slave Trades* (Cambridge: Cambridge University Press, 1990), 86–8, 93–4, 98.]

DR LOUIS FRANK

168   Memoir on the Traffic in Negroes in Cairo

Although the Negroes are normally healthy, strong, and robust, they are nevertheless subject to various diseases upon their arrival in Cairo, most of which are a natural outcome of their long and trying journey across the deserts and especially the result of the great climatic differences between Egypt and their land, always more or less part of the torrid zone. The main illness to which they are subject are the following:

1. Colds or afflictions of the respiratory tract. Given that the caravans normally arrive in Cairo in September when the nights are becoming cool and humid and that, in addition to their complete nudity, the Negroes are crammed at night into little rooms where they are constantly exposed alternately to hot and cold conditions, they frequently come down with colds. These by and large never have serious outcomes and always go away of their own.

2. Ophthalmia. Ophthalmia, which is endemic in Egypt, does not affect the Negroes as vehemently as it does the Europeans. It is difficult to determine in a satisfactory fashion the root causes of this disease. I have reviewed this subject in accordance with my findings in an appendix to a work that I propose to publish when circumstances permit.

3. Smallpox. This disease is often disastrous for the Negroes and *Ghellabis*. It seems to be less widespread in the Sudan than in Egypt, but it is always deadly. The *Ghellabis* maintain that smallpox never breaks out in their land except when the germ of infectious disease is brought there. This assertion seems to be borne out by two observations. First, among the Negroes brought to Cairo, often two-thirds are found to have not yet suffered from this disease. Second, Doctor Poncé, who was sent for a century ago by the king of Abyssinia, notes in his travel report that his caravan had been stopped in Nubia to make sure that no one was suffering from smallpox. When it was detected, it was customary to subject the caravan to a quarantine. I have gathered information from numerous persons in order to determine whether this practice still persists. But no one was able to give me satisfactory information in this regard.

Smallpox is generally widespread among the Negroes. The onset of the disease is often accompanied by more complications than among whites, in all likelihood because Negroes have thicker and denser skin. The fever that proceeds the onset of the disease is often very high. Unless one has already observed this disease several times among the Negroes, it is difficult for a European doctor to diagnose it as such, unless concomitant symptoms or a broader epidemic point to the nature of the disease. The little spots which manifest themselves at the time of the outbreak are all the more ambiguous because one cannot detect any nuance of white or red. The color of the skin and the spots is identical. Moreover, since the new arrivals are subject to a skin disease, of which I will speak later, and are often covered with spots, the result of mosquito bites, the doctor finds himself facing doubts about the real nature of the disease. It is likely that the *Ghellabis* would lose fewer Negroes if they attended to them a little, and especially if they were willing to consult a European doctor. But either they cannot grasp this reality or they are not in the least disposed to allow for any such expense.

[. . .]

8. Venereal disease. The Negroes often bring this disease from their country. Diagnosis is sometimes difficult. Consequently, it is wise to warn those who buy a Negresse that having relations with her is not without possible dangerous consequences.

Frambosia or yaws, which kills so many Negroes in America, is completely unknown in Egypt.

[From 'Memoir on the Traffic in Negroes in Cairo and on the Illnesses to Which They Are Subject upon Arrival There (1802),' trs. Michel Le Gall, in Shaun E. Marmon (ed.), *Slavery in the Islamic Middle East* (Princeton: Markus Wiener, 1999), 82–3, 86.]

Section VIII

Abolition and Emancipation

INTRODUCTION

Slavery has expanded and declined in many societies and cultures throughout human history. Occasionally, traditions have emerged in which there was a powerful appeal for kind treatment, for generous manumission policies, or for the full integration of the descendants of slaves into the dominant group. Never, however, did the overwhelming majority of non-slaves in such societies suggest that the institution itself was so immensely evil that it ought to be abolished forever within and beyond those societies to the entire globe. That radical idea had to await a millennium of development in the Western world. Meanwhile, religious leaders, moralists, and jurists propagated a variety of formulas to assure non-slave members of societies that people could be simultaneously objects of ownership, human beings, and assigned to functions fit only for servile outsiders.

On the eve of the age of abolition, even intellectuals who were morally opposed to slavery were far more impressed by its power and durability than by its weaknesses. Adam Smith reminded his students that only a small portion of the earth was being worked by free labor, and that it was unlikely that slavery would ever be totally abandoned. Across the channel, Abbe Raynal could envisage the end of New World slavery only through a fortuitous conjunction of philosopher-kings in Europe or of a heroic Spartacus in the Americas. In such a perspective, no historical trend toward general emancipation could be assumed.

Little more than a century later, the passage of the 'Golden Law' through the Brazilian legislature—to the accompaniment of music, public demonstrations, and street festivities at every stage—was regarded as only a belated provincial rendezvous with human destiny and civilization's progress. From the formation of the first abolitionist societies in the late 1780s, the Brazilian action precisely marked a 'century of progress'. The ending of American slavery set the stage for the 'civilizing' emancipation of Africa and Asia.

For pre-abolitionist periods historians must ask why a slave system would tend to disintegrate in the absence of strong political or cultural forces aligned against the institution. Moses Finley's analysis, typically, describes the decline of one of the world's major slave systems in the millennia before the end of the eighteenth century in the complete absence of any abolitionist sentiment. By the 1840s Alexis de Tocqueville could look back on the long agitation which brought British colonial slavery to an end in the 1830s as an example of the triumph of ideas and modes of activity which would soon 'shatter and destroy servitude throughout the entire world'. Given such a transformation in the expectations of Western culture, the main task confronting Western statesmen was to arrange the transition to societies without slaves. It was easy to explain or rationalize the violence, corruption, or impoverishment of ex-slave societies such as Haiti or parts of Spanish America, where emancipation had come in the wake of violent revolution, civil war, scorched earth warfare, and deep racial conflict. It was more difficult to assess the balance of satisfaction or disappointment with the controlled social 'experiment' in the British Caribbean. Ten years after emancipation, Lord Stanley, author of the British Emancipation Act of 1833, had much to be proud of. However, Stanley recognized that the impact of emancipation on the production and consumption of sugar was producing a new crisis of confidence both within the British metropolis and abroad even as he spoke. Only three years later the parliamentary speech of the son of William Wilberforce shows the depth of that crisis. Samuel Wilberforce, Bishop of Oxford, vigorously insisted that free labor in the British sugar colonies could not contend with colonies continually supplied by African slaves. Such a confession, broadly accepted by 1850, subverted one of the fundamental abolitionist premises about the superiority of free labor. It also threatened to undermine faith in the British naval suppression of the transatlantic slave trade, a policy vigorously pursued by the British after the abolition of their trade in 1808. The policy was partly salvaged by direct British naval assault on the Brazilian slave trade in 1850, and was confirmed by successful Anglo-American pressure on Cuba in the early 1860s.

The inability of the British sugar colonies to sustain their levels of production or their competitive position in the world market also opened the way to a more virulent European discourse on race toward the middle of the nineteenth century. In Britain, Thomas Carlyle was able to use the economic situation of the ex-colonies as ammunition for a twofold attack upon both the abolitionists' free labor ideology and the racial capacity of Africans. In America the ordeal of free labor in the British Caribbean became fuel for pro-slavery propagandists. Eastward, across the Channel, the debate over the combined results of British slave trade suppression and colonial slave emancipation radiated into debates over Continental emancipation. French students of 'racial' science attempted to demonstrate the applicability of their findings to European policy toward Africa on both sides of the Atlantic. On the eve of the French slave emancipation in 1847, the Paris Ethnological Society debated the 'natural' relationship between the white and black races, in terms of the 'potential' of the African race for civilization. One of the most significant aspects of the debate was the acceptance of fundamental differences between races and genders as unquestioned premises. Only a few months before he decisively precipitated colonial slave emancipation, Victor Schoelcher, France's most outspoken abolitionist, found himself engaged in an uphill battle to convince his skeptical colleagues of the inherent ability of Africans to become 'civilized' equals of Europeans.

The same range of topics and preoccupations fueled discussion on the other side of the Atlantic. There, debates over the future of slavery culminated in the most bloody conflicts afflicting the system. The cultural sources and social bases of opposition to slavery were often similar on both sides of the Atlantic. As in Britain, the North American abolitionist impulse was stirred by the political and religious mobilizations of the late eighteenth century. Dissenting groups such as the Wesleyan Methodists began to discuss and to adapt rules to encourage the manumission of slaves by members of the denomination. This emerging trend was quickly challenged in areas where slavery was important. The year after a Virginia Methodist conference condemned slavery, the ruling was suspended following threats of wholesale withdrawal by southern members. Even the rhetoric of the American Revolution was used to legitimize a full-blown proslavery defense.

Half a century later the progressive triumph of antislavery in Britian was paralleled by the formation of abolitionist societies in Continental Europe and North America. In January 1831, William Lloyd Garrison launched an uncompromisingly abolitionist movement in Boston. Abolitionism proved to be less immediately successful than its British counterpart in mobilizing opinion. Nevertheless, by 1860, the expansion of political antislavery America, symbolized by the election of Abraham Lincoln as President, induced the majority of the Southern slave states to withdraw from the Federal Union. A Southern slaveholder brought his peculiar perspective to bear 'upon the negro race and upon negro slavery', although he belatedly conceded that black slaves, like their predecessors of all shades, desired liberty. Southern claims to hold descendants of Africans as chattels remained also grounded, as elsewhere, in legal traditions developed over centuries. African-Americans added their collective voice and traditions to the antislavery crusade.

In contrast to the relatively peaceful emancipations of slavery in the colonies of Great Britain, the provinces of Brazil, and the Northern United States, Southern US emancipation, like that of Haiti and Spanish America, issued from a combination of revolutionary and military exigencies. In the American Civil War, President Abraham Lincoln took the first major step in his capacity as commander-in-chief of the Union army. His Emancipation Proclamation of January 1863 freed all persons held as slaves in areas of the United States still militarily resisting the authority of the Federal government. In the American South, slaves, like their counterparts in Latin America, exploited opportunities to claim their own freedom and to participate in the destruction of the institution. Finally, the Thirteenth Amendment to the

Federal Constitution freed all remaining people held in involuntary servitude in the United States. It was ratified in December 1865, eight months after the surrender of the Confederate armies.

Each ending of slavery was followed by a variety of adjustments and struggles over the terms of labor, as well as of civil and political rights for ex-slaves. The outcomes reflected the disparities in demographic, economic, racial, and political traditions in each area of the Americas. The ending of slavery in the Americas turned world attention to the institution of slavery in the eastern hemisphere. In the wake of European-sponsored gradual emancipations in Africa and Asia following Brazilian emancipation no one anticipated that within one century Europe itself would briefly contain more slave laborers than had ever existed at any one time in the Americas. Other forms of bondage and coerced labor have persisted into the third millennium, more than two centuries after the emergence of the first abolitionist movements, despite the United Nations Universal Declaration of Human Rights and the proliferation of the extra-governmental organizations to agitate for their implementation.

MOSES I. FINLEY

169 Ancient Slavery and Modern Ideology

I shall now argue that the fundamental change in the political-military structure which occurred in the course of Roman imperial history was perhaps the decisive factor in the gradual replacement of slaves by other types of labour. I imply no naive cause-and-effect development but a dialectical one. Nor do I suggest a deliberate, thought-out change in policy with respect to labour in general or slavery in particular. On the contrary, there was only a slow process of shifting practices, locality by locality, in response to the continuing need on a large scale for labour on the land. Changes in the practice were made possible by the new political and juridical developments, and in turn stimulated and reinforced the latter. Only later, centuries later, did it become evident that the labour regime had been undergoing a basic transformation, specifically in those central regions that had long been genuine slave societies.

[. . .]

The pressure on the little men that continued and mounted all through the Empire was already present in the Republic. Debt-bondage in its formal sense may have long since been abolished, but defaulting debtors were always subject to *addictio*, which in effect meant compulsory labour. Strictly speaking, the authority of a magistrate was required, but who is prepared to argue that due process of law had been applied to all the bondsmen involved in the conspiracy of Catiline, to the *obaerati* (or *obaerarii*) of Varro, or to the citizens tied by debt (*nexi*) with whom, Columella reports disapprovingly, some wealthy landowners staffed their holdings? Or that the *coloni* of Ahenobarbus who joined his private fleet along with his slaves and freedmen went along as willing volunteers who shared their landlord's political views? Why, in a different context, did the younger Pliny's tenants stay on after they had failed to pay their rents and had had their possessions sold up? The jurists tell us that a tenant was free to leave at the end of his contract, normally five years. Yet Hadrian found it necessary to condemn the 'inhuman practice (*mos*)' of retaining tenants on public land against their will; a century later, in 244, an emperor ruled that 'neither unwilling tenants nor their heirs are to be retained after the completion of the period of the lease', and added three ominous words, *saepe rescriptum est* (it has often been laid down in rescripts).

This kind of evidence, these hints, if one prefers, convince me that there was a gradual erosion in the capacity of the lower classes to resist working for the benefit of others under conditions of less than full 'freedom of contract'. Significantly, much of the evidence comes from Italy during precisely the centuries when it was the centre, the heart, of the ancient slave society, and it comes from the agricultural sector, the critical sector. The process was not initiated by the state, but it was also not interfered with, and in certain respects it was soon abetted by the state. Once upon a time the peasant had been incorporated into the community as a full member, with all the far-flung consequences we considered earlier. In Rome, to be sure, he never achieved quite the status of his Athenian counterpart, but his citizenship, and especially his indispensable military contribution, counted for much. From the time of Augustus on, everything changed, and changed with some rapidity. Citizenship lost its old meaning: the political rights that it embraced soon disappeared completely, and for some three centuries conscription was replaced by voluntary enlistment, relieving men of military age of a burden but at the same time removing from them an important weapon, indeed for most men the only one they possessed with respect to the state. The change is neatly symbolized by the appearance, early in the second century A.D., of a formal distinction between *honestiores* and *humiliores*, which can be roughly rendered as 'upper classes' and 'lower classes'. Inequality before the law, never eliminated in the realities of life, was now officially introduced into the criminal law, and the *humiliores* were liable to what had heretofore been considered 'slavish' forms of cruel punishment.

[. . .]

The social distribution of these burdens was, as usual, uneven. Land taxes lay most heavily, directly or indirectly, on those who actually worked the land, peasants and tenants. Some also fell on the owners of slave-worked estates, which could not be passed on, but the wealthiest among them were the most adept at tax evasion. The emperor Julian, we are told, refused the traditional remission of tax arrears on the express ground that 'this profited only the wealthy', while the poor had to pay on the dot. For many peasants, the double burden of taxation and war led either to outlawry or to the one available source of protection, a powerful local individual. That was what the institution known as *patrocinium* was about: in return for protection and a measure of relief, the peasant accepted the personal authority of a landlord (or landlord's agent) over himself and his holding, hence the loss of what remained of his independence. The six rulings (dated between 340 and 415) in Book IX, Title 24, *De patrociniis vicorum*, of the *Theodosian Code*, are explicit about this. That was the same period in which Libanius complained, in his 47th oration, that protection of *his* peasants was being taken over by others, and not even the family of the much more influential Quintus Aurelius Symmachus was immune from such interference.

[. . .]

The workers in the imperial factories formed a group apart, a group whose status has resisted attempts at conventional definition. The only collective terms applied to them in the texts, *collegiati*, *corporati*, are not helpful. It has been argued that because the certainly servile labels—*mancipi* or *ex familia*—are attested only for the weavers, dyers and collectors of purple dye, they alone were genuine slaves. But work in the imperial factories had been added to the list of severe punishments, like the older condemnation to the mines, and that makes one pause a bit. We then notice that the mint employees, a more esteemed group, were not only branded but were regarded as slaves under the terms of the *senatus consultum Claudianum*. An edict of 380 forbade any woman of higher rank from cohabiting with a *monetarius* under penalty of losing her freedom under that ancient law. The old Roman juristic categories had lost their validity.

The availability of an 'internal' labour supply, in sum, rendered it unnecessary for the *possessores* to do more than they did in recruiting a complement of slave labour. I am unable to discover any considerations, or consciousness, of relative productivity in the long slow process I have tried to pin down, no searching for an 'increase of production' on the part of 'clear-sighted social groups'. Late antique moralists complained about the idleness and shiftlessness of the city population, both slave and free, in contrast to the hardworking rustic population, but their predecessors grumbled in the same way about slaves and tenants alike: witness Columella or the younger Pliny. Ideologically significant though they may be, such texts are no more revealing of the facts of economic behaviour than the similar grumbles of American slave-owners or of letters to *The Times* about the idleness and indiscipline of English workingmen. None of the grumblers suffered in their purses.

On the 'location' test, the world of late antiquity was no longer a slave society, despite the continued presence of slaves in large numbers. Slaves no longer dominated large-scale production in the countryside; large-scale production in the cities had been reduced to the state factories; slaves no longer provided the bulk of the property revenues of the élites. Only in the domestic sphere did they remain predominant, and the top of that pyramid was now occupied by the court eunuchs. A structural transformation had clearly occurred, in which slaves were gradually replaced in the towns by men who remained juridically free but were no longer the free citizens of the classical world, and in the countryside by men who were neither juridically nor politically free in the old sense. However, the *organization* of the rural economy does not appear to have been transformed. I am unable to fit late antiquity into any neat series of stages. Although rudiments of a manorial (or seigneurial) system have been detected on the imperial estates of North Africa and in one or two other places, that system and its feudal superstructure were not to emerge before the time of Charlemagne, as Marc Bloch correctly insisted. Slave society did not immediately give way to feudal society.

[From *Ancient Slavery and Modern Ideology* (New York: Viking Press, 1980), 141–4, 146, 148–9.]

SEYMOUR DRESCHER

170 Capitalism and Antislavery

Just as economically-oriented historians have been drawn to reflect upon the general correlation between British abolitionism and the industrial revolution, so religiously-oriented historians take as their point of departure the chronological correlation between the British abolitionist take-off and the rise of evangelicalism. Some historians, including Roger Anstey, have identified antislavery as derivative of emergent Protestant nonconformity in theology, ideology, rhetoric and organization. Thus behind the specific problem of British abolition lies the wider question of the relation of organized Christianity to the demise of slavery.

Within this wider framework linking Christianity and abolition presents at least as many anomalies as does the correlation between industrialization and abolition. It is difficult to overlook the coexistence of Christianity with ancient and medieval Mediterranean slavery, with Eastern Christian slavery and with Atlantic slavery. Christianity made its peace with the institution as readily as Judaism or Islam. Europeans transported both African slaves and Christian institutions to the New World.

What was true of Christianity in general for more than a millennium and a half was true of British Christianity in the slave colonies for a century and a half after the settlement of Barbados. In the British, as in every other New

World system, Christian institutions, liturgy and theology were established alongside the institution of slavery. The Established Church of England and the various dissenting groups made adjustments to the new colonial system within and beyond the plantation areas. The Anglican Church functioned much like other Old Régime churches in the sugar, coffee, cotton, rice and tobacco areas. Its clergy made no attempt to mobilize the slave population as a whole for conversion nor were they pressed to do so by their metropolitan superiors. Anglicanism enjoyed its dominant position in the plantation colonies, endowed with glebe lands, housed in parish churches, and staffed with a university-educated clergy. If they were characterized by a general lack of evangelical zeal even among their white parishioners, this was no more than was expected of them in eighteenth-century Britain itself.

[. . .]

However, one must also note the significance of the major religious difference between the metropolis and the islands even before the age of abolition. Whatever the other parallels between squire and planter, West Indian Christianity did not act as an agent of communal reinforcement. If one out of ten English parishes were unattended to by ministers of the Establishment, nine out of ten souls in the islands were not served at all by its clergy. The religious rituals and rites of passage which, in England, were designed to bind local society together from top to bottom in dependent solidarity, bound only the Europeans together and separated them from the mass of the population over which they ruled. Most planters, like the slave traders, never pretended that the massive conversion of slaves was either the norm of the islands or their particular aim. The plantation system was held together not by a paternal religious system but by a tacit acceptance of the slaves' cultural autonomy in religion and social customs as long as it did not threaten the economic system. As the English Establishment had made its tacit peace with the 'half-pagan popular culture' of the metropolis, with its fairs, its sports, its drink and its hedonism, so the planters made an even greater accommodation with their wholly pagan slaves. With relatively little opposition the Afro-Caribbeans developed their own spiritual hierarchy, myths, festivals, musical and dance forms. They created a cultural world of their own as distinctive as their autonomous marketing system beyond the plantation.

However, the same cultural autonomy which mitigated the masters' control also acted to insulate the slaves against new cultural offers from beyond the line. Before abolitionism, most planters clearly found this balance of social control and autonomy much more palatable than mass conversion to Christianity. In addition to the punishments of whips, chains, branding and mutilation, they could capitalize on the inherently divisive ethnic disparities produced by the African slave trade and on the differential opportunities for individual mobility accorded to colour, concubinage and craftsmanship. It seems clear that left to themselves the sugar planters found the presumed risks of conversion far greater than the benefits. The traditional Established Church therefore had little difficulty in effecting a *modus vivendi* between Christianity and New World planters. It endured not only until the end of the eighteenth century, but in many respects until the actual passage of emancipation.

What, then, was the impact of the new evangelical crusade which coincided with the age of abolition and which has led historians like Anstey and Edith Hurwitz to conclude that abolitionism was essentially a product of religious revival? In terms of temporal priorities, the pressure for religious change clearly came from the metropolitan side. The great social shift which was slowly undermining the position of the Established Church in England before 1790 had no parallel in the contemporary Caribbean. In the islands there was no wave of enclosures, no erosion of the remnants of a traditional agrarian economy, no surge of popular evangelical religion from below, and no general demand for a cultural awakening from above.

The most dynamic centre of Protestant expansion in the age of abolition is as easily identified as the most dynamic centre of antislavery. The peak period of mass abolitionism in Britain coincided almost precisely with the foundation of a world-wide Anglo-American missionary network abroad. Between 1790 and 1820 British missionary enterprise overwhelmingly dominated Protestant Christianity. Of the missions founded outside Anglo-America between 1792 and 1820 three-quarters were British, and all but one of the remainder were American. America's own great surge of overseas enterprise caught up with Britain's in the generation after 1820, while its own abolitionist movement entered a new intensive phase.

Just when Britain began its most dramatic era of geographical expansion the Catholic overseas empires were moving in precisely the opposite direction. For more than two generations after the American Revolutionary War, European Catholic enterprise was virtually paralysed. The Catholic monarchist attacks on the Society of Jesus, culminating in its dissolution, entailed the recall or displacement of hundreds of colonial missionaries. This erosion accelerated when the French Revolution caused the Catholic Church to concentrate on rebuilding its shaken European core.

During the first half of the nineteenth century, there was little to tempt either the Papacy or its European hierarchies into an attack on slavery. Little of the church's depleted economic and human resources were directed towards overseas conversion. For the entire age of British popular abolitionism the Catholic Church was geopolitically and socially in a defensive posture. Only on the eve of the Revolutions of 1848 were there signs of a modest missionary revival in France as well as an emerging affiliation between popular Catholicism and abolitionism. In 1847 the most activist lay Catholic newspaper in France, *L'Univers*, looked forward to a popular campaign for emancipation in 1848. Abbé Dupanloup, one of the clerical leaders of liberal

Catholicism, promised to gather 20,000 signatures for the cause. The Archbishop of Paris, after a decade of silence towards the abolitionist movement, gave evidence that he too would support public clerical action. The spark was snuffed out in the wake of the events of 1848 in France and Italy.

Beyond France the Church of the early nineteenth century was dependent upon political and social régimes which still relied heavily upon various forms of bound labour, serfdom in Central Europe, and slavery in the colonies of Spain and Portugal. The general affiliation of the Catholic episcopacy with the *status quo* was similar to that of its Establishment Protestant counterparts. Latin American revolutions which moved to abolish slavery did not rely on the clergy for a Catholic mobilization of antislavery opinion. The pattern of transatlantic migration and social conflict before 1840 did not enhance the growth of popular Catholic overseas abolitionism in the Americas. In the US the oldest Southern Catholics of Maryland and Louisiana, aligned with their sectional economic interest. Only after 1840 did the expansion of immigrant working classes in some Southern cities begin to create even potential seedbeds for Catholic working-class antagonism to planter slave capitalism. In the North ethno-class conflict kept the large mass of Irish immigrants at arm's length from Protestant evangelical abolitionism.

[. . .]

As of 1770 the conscience of the revival had not been clearly sensitized to slavery as an overriding moral issue. John Wesley's own great awakening to the evil of slavery seems to have come in response to the sharpening of public discussion over the Somerset case in 1772 and through the writings of the Quaker Anthony Benezet. In a widely publicized essay of 1774, Wesley declared that liberty came not just when one breathed English air but with the breath of life itself. From the mid-1770s there was an increasingly clear recognition of slavery as an internal moral problem for the Methodist faithful. The 'second generation' of evangelicals also gave notice in America of the emergence, if not the dominance, of a new attitude towards slaves as members of the community of the faithful, and towards slave-owners as embodiments of excessive wealth and arbitrary power.

Since Methodism was the most centralized of all the new revivalist sects, the fate of Wesley's abolitionist impulse may provide us with the best proxy indicator for the general relationship between the Anglo-evangelical religious and antislavery mobilizations. As noted before, he originally had scant hope of effecting any good by an appeal to the popular will on such an issue. Wesley and Clarkson were working the same fertile grounds in Manchester in 1787, Wesley on one of his last great circuits for Methodism, Clarkson on his first in support of abolition. As soon as Manchester demonstrated the full potential of mass political abolitionism Wesley threw his personal influence behind the movement. Although they were never more than a substantial minority of the British abolitionists, the Methodists may also afford us the best means of understanding the social context of mass abolitionism. In our international context their network developed almost simultaneously in Britain and the Americas. In the metropolitan context, as we shall see, they offer us the most complete evidence linking membership and mass abolitionist participation of any social grouping in Britain during the age of abolition.

[. . .]

In the very early years of the revival, the unmobilized planters had tolerated, if they did not encourage, various experiments on Moravian and Methodist plantations. As in Britain there was no fundamental change in attitude before the abolitionist take-off. As late as the 1780s even black Baptists from America were allowed to establish themselves as preachers to black converts, to preach before open-air meetings and to build chapels, as long as they did not attempt to convert slaves without their master's approval. Not every contemporary Southern American community was so amenable. Coke's first service in the West Indies to an integrated audience was interrupted by gentlemen 'inflamed by liquor' but this was no more than standard operating fare for Methodist preachers in England. Coke was genuinely impressed by the courtesy shown him by most whites. Above all, the authorities did not interfere. Coke's reception was far more civil than it had been in Virginia where he faced angry mobs and threats of flogging or lynching. One of the essential differences, of course, was that Coke never mentioned an antislavery requirement as the *sine qua non* for Methodist membership in the islands.

[. . .]

For all this, nonconformity proved to be *more* dangerous and subversive than its counterpart on the American mainland. This was obviously not because conversion was itself inherently subversive of slavery or on account of the symbolism of liberation embedded in evangelical ideology. Christianity did provide slaves with a new sense of individual worth, an alternative hierarchy of status and new opportunities for leadership, but it also divided slaves. It competed with the status hierarchy of the plantation which had its own material and social rewards. It required converts to withdraw from Afro-Creole amenities in the same way that English converts were required to withdraw from the hedonistic culture of their compatriots.

Still, British mobilization for overseas religious activity after 1790 decisively affected the rate of slave conversion in the short run and the pace of emancipation in the longer run. The new missionary movement in Britain produced a decisive shift in the relationship between the metropolis and the colonies. The 'latent' event in the British colonies in the years after 1780, and especially after 1800, was the entrance of a pluralistic missionary enterprise, sanctioned by the metropolitan government and focused primarily on the black population. Faced with the subversion of their African trade by the abolitionists and prevented by the imperial government from retaliating against the missionaries for the actions of their metropolitan patrons, many planters attempted to make the most of the line drawn by Coke between the abolitionist evangelicals in Britain and neutral missionaries in the colonies. As long as the primary focus of metropolitan abolitionism was on the African slave trade this appeared to be a workable compromise. By the time the metropolitan evangelicals began to attack slavery itself in the 1820s the transformation had occurred. It was one of the principal elements in eroding the line between metropolis and colony. In the years between the 1780s and the 1820s the heathen African became a fellow Christian. It was precisely such a change which helped to override the perception of racial and cultural differences.

[. . .]

Artisans could also realistically subscribe to a work discipline quite unlike that demanded by the factory system. They might trade off traditional leisure patterns for social mobility, or at least respectability, in the pre-Victorian sense. Here I think we may relate the life experience which tied together the artisan's distaste for factory labour and his willingness to subscribe to antislavery. Abolitionists were not being distracted from what went on within the factory walls by the image of the plantation or the slave ship. The unrelenting *externality* of both slave and factory discipline would have struck a deep chord of enmity in the artisanry. The institution of slavery affronted their moral economy at its source, depriving its field workers of supplementary gain from any extension of their labour. Thus antislavery appeals made special sense both to those who were succeeding through their own reinvestment of time and resources and to those who aspired to do so. As we shall see, they would have seemed especially true in the booming 1780s. Conversion to the new evangelicalism fortified this moral economy by communal fellowship. It would be misleading to impose a sharp line between artisan workers and small capitalists at this early stage of industrialization. The ranks of nonconformity thrived in an expanding economy of independency where the artisan might still feel closer to the petty capitalist than to the unskilled labourer.

International comparisons seem to confirm the heavily artisanal sources of popular antislavery, even in the absence of Anglo-American nonconformity. The French case presents a striking example. Since there was so little room for mass petitioning in France in the decades before 1848 we have only a few hints about abolitionism's potential social base. We do know that the first mass petition in favour of French abolition was organized among the skilled artisans of Paris in 1844. The petitions were gathered at the workplace, and in most cases were sent to the Chamber of Deputies workshop by workshop. The workers of Lyons joined in, designating themselves as 'Proletarians'. The working-class petitioners explicitly rejected the ideological analogy between themselves and plantation slaves, whether preferred by the spokesmen of slave-owners or by socialists. At that point no major French élite or bourgeois initiatives at mass mobilization had ever been undertaken on behalf of emancipation. A generation later French middle-class organizers of a drive on behalf of American freedmen were still astounded to find that their single greatest tally of contributors turned out to be 10 000 workers of Mulhouse, supported by workers in Paris and Lyons.

[From *Capitalism and Antislavery: British Mobilization in Comparative Perspective* (New York: Oxford University Press, 1987), 111–17, 120–2, 132–3.]

171 **Methodist Resolution of 1784**

Resolution of 1784

'*Question 42.—What methods can we take to extirpate slavery?*'

'*Answer.*—We are deeply conscious of the impropriety of making new terms of communion for a religious society already established, except on the most pressing occasion; and such we esteem the practice of holding our fellow creatures in slavery. We view it as contrary to the golden law of God, on which hang all the law and the prophets; and the unalienable rights of mankind, as well as every principle of the Revolution, to hold in the deepest abasement, in a more abject slavery than is, perhaps, to be found in any part of the world, except America, so many souls that are all capable of the image of God.

'We therefore think it our most bounden duty to take immediately some effectual method to extirpate this abomination from among us; and for that purpose we add the following to the rules of our society, viz.:—

'1. Every member of our society who has slaves in his possession, shall, within twelve months after notice given to him by the Assistant, (which notice the Assistants are required immediately and without delay to give in their respective circuits,) legally execute and record an instrument, whereby he emancipates and sets free, every slave in his possession—those between the ages of 25 and 45 immediately, or in five years; if between 20 and 25, within ten years; if under 20, at the age of 25 at farthest; and every infant born in slavery after the above mentioned rules are complied with, immediately on its birth.

'2. Every Assistant shall keep a journal, in which he shall regularly minute down the names and ages of all the slaves belonging to all the masters in his respective circuit; and also the date of every instrument executed and recorded for the manumission of the slaves, with the name of the court, book and folio in which the said instruments respectively have been recorded; which journal shall be handed down in each circuit to the succeeding Assistants.

'3. In consideration that these rules form a new term of communion, every person concerned, who will not comply with them, shall have liberty quietly to withdraw himself from our society within the twelve months succeeding the notice given as aforesaid, otherwise the Assistant shall exclude him in the society.'

[From the Methodist Resolution of 1784, in Lucius C. Matlock, *The History of American Slavery and Methodism from 1780 to 1849* . . . (New York: Lucius C. Matlock, 1849), 15–16.]

172 Virginia Petition 1785

To the General Assembly of Virginia

The Petition of sundry of the Inhabitants of Brunswick County, humbly sheweth. That Whereas, We are credibly informed, That Petitions are secretly handed about for subscription, by Persons We may reasonably suppose disaffected to our State and Government; who not being satisfied with the Act, already made, 'To authorize the Manumission of Slaves['] make bold to Petition your August Assembly for a general Emancipation of them: pretending to be moved by Religious Principles and taking for their motive universal Charity. But We your Petitioners, who are of opinion, That it was ordained by the Great and wise Disposer of all Things, That some Nations should serve others; and that all Nations have not been equally free: Which may be supported by the following Texts of Scripture. Genesis Chap: 9. Verses 25. 26. and 27th. 'And he said cursed be Canaan; a Servant of Servants shall he be unto his Brethren. And he said, blessed be the Lord God of Shem; and Canaan shall be his Servant. God shall enlarge Jepheth, and he shall dwell in the Tents of Shem; and Canaan shall be his Servant.' Genesis Chap: 21. Verses 9. 10. 11. 12. and 13th. 'And Sarah saw the Son of Hagar the Egyptian, which She had born unto Abraham, mocking. Wherefore She said unto Abraham, Cast out this Bond-Woman, and her Son: for the Son of this Bond-Woman shall not be Heir with my Son, even with Isaac. And the thing was very grievous in Abraham's Sight, because of his Son. And God said unto Abraham, let it not be grievous in thy sight, because of the Lad, and because of thy Bond-Woman; in all that Sarah hath said unto thee, hearken unto her voice: for in Isaac shall thy seed be called. And also of the Son of the Bond-Woman will I make a Nation, because he is thy Seed.['] Genesis Chap: 27th. verse 29th. 'Let People serve thee, and Nations bow down to thee; be Lord over thy Brethren, and let thy Mother's Son bow down to thee: cursed be every one that curseth thee, and blessed be he that blesseth thee.['] And verses 38. 39. and 40th. 'And Esau said unto his Father, hast thou but one blessing my Father? bless me, even me also, O my Father. And Esau lift up his Voice and wept. And Isaac his Father answered, and said unto him, Behold, thy dwelling shall be the fatness of the Earth and of the Dew of Heaven from above, And by thy Sword shalt thou live, and shalt serve thy Brother.['] And as it appears that Abraham the Father of the Faithful, bought and kept Slaves, See Genesis Chap: 19. Verse 27th. 'And all the Men of his House, born in the House, and bought with Money of the Stranger, were Circumcised with him.['] And that God speaking to Moses from Mount Sinai, Licences or Commands his People to buy and keep Slaves; See Leviticus Chap: 25. Verses 44. 45. and 46th. 'Both thy Bond-men, and thy Bond-maids, which thou shalt have, shall be of the Heathen that are round about you; of them shall ye buy Bond-men and Bond-maids. Moreover, of the Children of the Strangers that do sojourn among you, of them shall ye buy; and of their Families that are with you, which they beget in your Land: and they shall be your Possession. And ye shall take them as an Inheritance for your children after you, to inherit them for a Possession; they shall be your Bond-men forever'. And Solomon had Servants born in his House. Ecclesiastes Chap: 2d. Verse 7th.

Seeing then, That according to Scripture and observation, it hath been the practice and custom, for above 3500 Years, down to the present time, for one Nation to buy and keep Slaves of another Nation: That God so particularly (as above recited) Licenced or Commanded his People, to buy of other Nations and to keep them for Slaves: And that Christ and his Apostles hath in the mean time, come into the World, and past out of it again, leaving behind them the New-Testament, full of all instructions necessary to our Salvation; and hath not forbid it: But left that matter as they found it, giving exortations to Masters and Servants how to conduct themselves to each other.

We your Petitioners therefore conclude, that We have a right to retain such Slaves, as We have justly and legally in Possession. And without Pleading the inexpediency, the impolicy, and the impracticability of such a Measure; Pray that no Act may ever pass in this Assembly, for the general Emancipation of Slaves, And that one Act passed May 6th. 1782. entituled, An Act to authorize the Manumission of Slaves; as already productive of a very great and growing evil; be, immediately and totally Repealed. And your Petitioners shall ever pray etc.

[Brunswick County, November 10, 1785, with 266 signatures.]

[From the *Petition from Brunswick County to the General Assembly of Virginia* (November 10, 1785), in Frederika Teute Schmidt and Barbara Ripel Wilhelm, 'Early Proslavery Petitions in Virginia,' *William and Mary Quarterly* 30 (1973), 143–4.]

173   **The Liberator**

To the public

In the month of August, I issued proposals for publishing 'THE LIBERATOR' in Washington city; but the enterprise, though hailed in different sections of the country, was palsied by public indifference. Since that time, the removal of the Genius of Universal Emancipation to the Seat of Government has rendered less imperious the establishment of a similar periodical in that quarter.

During my recent tour for the purpose of exciting the minds of the people by a series of discourses on the subject of slavery, every place that I visited gave fresh evidence of the fact, that a greater revolution in public sentiment was to be effected in the free states—*and particularly in New-England*—than at the south. I found contempt more bitter, opposition mere active, detraction more relentless, prejudice more stubborn, and apathy more frozen than among slave owners themselves. Of course, there were individual exceptions to the contrary. This state of things afflicted, but did not dishearten me. I determined, at every hazard, to lift up the standard of emancipation in the eyes of nation, *within sight of Bunker Hill and in the birth place of liberty.* That standard is now unfurled: and long may it float, unhurt by the spoilations of time or the missiles of a desperate foe—yea, till every chain be broken, and every bondmen set free! Let southern oppressors tremble—let their secret abettors tremble—let their northern apologists tremble—let all the enemies of the persecuted blacks tremble.

I deem the publication of my original Prospectus unnecessary as it has obtained a wide circulation. The principles therein inculcated will be steadily pursued in this paper excepting that I shall not array myself as the political partisan of any man. In defending the great cause of human rights, I wish to derive the assistance of all religions and of all parties.

Assenting to the 'self-evident truth' maintained in the American Declaration of Independence, 'that all men are created equal, and endowed by their Creator with certain inalienable rights—among which are life, liberty and the pursuit of happiness,' I shall strenuously contend for the immediate enfranchisement of our slave population. In Park-street Church, on the Fourth of July, 1829, in an address on slavery, I unreflectingly assented to the popular but pernicious doctrine of *gradual* abolition. I seize this opportunity to make a full and unequivocal recantation, and thus publicly to ask pardon of my God, of my country, and of my brethren the poor slaves, for having uttered a sentiment so full of timidity, injustice and absurdity. A similar recantation, from my pen, was published in the Genius of Universal

Emancipation of Baltimore, in September, 1829. My conscience is now satisfied.

I am aware, that many object to the severity of my language; but is there not cause for severity? I *will be* as harsh as truth, and as uncompromising as justice. On this subject, I do not wish to think, or speak, or write, with moderation. No! no! Tell a man whose house is on fire, to give a moderate alarm; tell him to moderately rescue his wife from the hands of the ravisher: tell the mother to gradually extricate her babe from the fire into which it has fallen—but urge me not to use moderation in a cause like the present. I am in earnest—I will not equivocate—I will not excuse—I will not retreat a single inch—AND I WILL BE HEARD. The apathy of the people is enough to make every statue leap from its pedestal, and to hasten the resurrection of the dead.

It is pretended, that I am retarding the cause of emancipation by the coarseness of my invective, and the precipitancy of my measures. *The charge is not true.* On this question my influence—humble as it is,—is felt at this moment to a considerable extent, and shall be felt in coming years—not perniciously, but beneficially—not as a curse, but as a blessing, and posterity will bear testimony that I was right. I desire to thank God, that he enables me to disregard 'the fear of man which bringeth a snare,' and to speak his truth in its simplicity and power.

[. . .]

[From *The Liberator*, January 1, 1831), 1.]

ALEXIS DE TOCQUEVILLE

174   Emancipation of Slaves

One must be fair even to rivals and adversaries. We have been told that the English nation was driven only by selfish mercenary motives in abolishing slavery; that its only aim was to crush others' colonies, and thereby to gain a monopoly of sugar production for its own establishments in India. This charge will not withstand scrutiny. A reasonable man cannot suppose that England, in order to strike at other nations' sugar colonies, has started out by ruining its own, several of which were in a state of extraordinary prosperity. That would be the most insane Machiavellianism imaginable. At the time that abolition was declared, the English colonies produced 220 million kilos of sugar, that is, four times as much as French colonial production during that period. Among the British colonies were Jamaica, third of the Antilles in beauty, fertility, and size; and, on the mainland, Demerara whose territory was, in a sense, limitless, and whose wealth and production had been growing incredibly for a number of years.

England would have to be supposed to have sacrificed these admirable colonies, indirectly obtaining the destruction of sugar production in all countries where it is cultivated by slave labor, in order to relocate it in India where it can be obtained at low cost without recourse to slavery. This would be easier to believe if, on the one hand, India were already a large-scale producer and, on the other, if sugar were not already cultivated elsewhere, and with greater success, by free labor. But when abolition was declared, India's annual production was still only 4 million kilos of sugar, and the Dutch had already created in Java the fine colony which sent 60 million kilos a year to the European markets.

Thus, after having destroyed the competition of slave labor in one hemisphere, the English would immediately find themselves engaged in competition with free labor in the other. To achieve such a result, this nation, so hard-headed about its own interests, would not only have administered the destruction of its finest possessions, but would furthermore have imposed on itself the obligation of paying its colonists an indemnity of 500 million! The absurdity of such contrivances is too evident to require elaboration.

The truth is that the emancipation of the slaves was a parliamentary reform, the act of the nation and not of its rulers. The English Government struggled as long as it could against the adoption of the measure. It resisted the abolition of the slave trade for fifteen years, and the abolition of slavery for twenty-five years. When it could not prevent its passage it tried to at least delay it, and when it gave up all hope of postponement, it sought to dilute the consequences, but always in vain; the popular torrent prevailed and swept it along.

Of course, once emancipation was resolved upon and accomplished, English statesmen used all their skill so that foreign nations would gain as little as possible from the revolution that they had just brought about in their colonies. It was certainly not pure philanthropy which made them display all that untiring fervor in order to curb the slave trade on the high seas and so halt the development of countries which still maintained slaves. It is clear that the English, while abolishing slavery, were deprived of certain benefits which they did not want nations not following their example to enjoy. Obviously they are using, as they usually do, every means—violence, deceit, hypocrisy, and duplicity—to achieve their ends, but all these acts are subsequent to the abolition of slavery and do not rule out the fact that this great event was produced by a philanthropic and above all a Christian impulse. As soon as the question is approached from a practical point of view, this truth becomes indisputable. It has been obscured, however, by all those who are inconvenienced by the English example. A full and open recapitulation was necessary before going on to the details of English emancipation themselves, which otherwise would have been poorly understood.

[. . .]

Probably no human event has ever been written and spoken about as much as the English emancipation. The English, and foreigners as well, have published a mass of books, pamphlets, articles, sermons, official reports, and investigations in this cause. The subject has recurred a hundred times in ten years of parliamentary discussions. Its documentation alone could fill a large library. Reading the literature, one is at first shocked and almost frightened to see how men can appraise the same fact in such different and even opposite ways, not men who are born long after the event took place, but contemporaries who witnessed it. However, if at the outset we recognize the personal interests and the party passions which motivate most of the testimony, and, above all, the enormity of the revolution which is being explained, we realize that the enactment of such a social transformation in nineteen countries at once was naturally bound to result in very different and often quite contrary outcomes according to the time and place studied, and that those who spoke of them were able to say things at once quite contradictory and quite true.

To force our readers to go through these clashing depositions would mean leading them into a labyrinth. It is quicker and more effective to stick to the facts themselves, choosing for presentation those among them which are incontestable. The colonists asserted that as soon as the Negroes were set free they would give themselves up to the most criminal outrages. They predicted scenes of disorder, of pillage, and of massacre. This is precisely the language of our own colonial planters. Let us look at the facts. Up to this moment the abolition of slavery in the English colonies has not produced *a single* insurrection; it has not cost the life of *a single* man, and yet the Negroes are twelve times as numerous as the whites in the English colonies. As the Report of the Commission on Colonial Affairs accurately observes, calling 800,000 slaves to freedom on the same day and hour has not caused a tenth of the disorder in ten years which ordinarily results from the most minor political question that agitates opinion in the civilized nations of Europe—the latest census in France, for example.

[. . .]

Another indisputable fact: from the moment the Negroes felt the stimulus of liberty, they almost threw themselves into the schools. The unbelievable fervor with which they register can be imagined when one is aware that there is now estimated to be one school for every six hundred souls in the English colonies. One out of nine individuals attends—which is a higher proportion than in France. While the mind is developed, habits become steadier. This is conspicuously revealed by an equally unimpeachable fact. We know what licentious mores, bordering on promiscuity, prevail among our colonial Negroes. The institution of marriage is virtually unknown there, which is not surprising, since one can see that such an institution is incompatible with slavery. Marriages were also extremely uncommon among the English colonial Negroes. They have multiplied enormously since freedom was granted. 1,582 marriages were celebrated as early as 1835; 1,962 in 1836; 3,215 in 1837; and 3,881 in 1838—the last reported year.

[. . .]

To sum up: a complete lack of disorders, rapid progress of the black population toward good mores, education, and comfort, an increase of one-third in exports from the mother country, a decrease of one-quarter in sugar production in the colonies, a considerable rise in the price of this commodity in the mother country's market, an excessive increase in wages with consequent difficulties for the colonists and ruin for some of them—these at present are the good and bad results produced by emancipation, as they emerge from proven facts and official figures.

[. . .]

The English Government should therefore have refused the Negroes the right to acquire land, at least for a time; but it had no clear idea of the danger except when there was no longer time to avert it. At the moment of abolition, the black population would have accepted such a restriction without a murmur; later it would have been imprudent to impose it. However, the English have not lost heart; the very people accused of so much indifference to the fate of the sugar colonies have made and are still making gigantic efforts to make good the unfortunate consequences of their error. It is in the process of searching in Africa, India, Europe, and the Azores for the manpower it lacks. All the slaves captured by its patrol fleets in such large numbers on the high seas are not returned to their place of origin; they are transported as free laborers to the emancipated colonies. It is the English who now benefit most from the slave trade they are repressing, and it is perhaps to this that one must attribute the extraordinary zeal they show in seizing slave-ships and their equally striking apathy when faced with proposals to take effective action to suppress the slave-markets themselves. If Europe allows it, they will soon be buying blacks on the Guinea coast in order to make free workers at Jamaica and at Demerara, thereby aiding the development of slavery in Africa at the very moment they are abolishing it in the New World.

Despite the application of these heroic remedies, it can be foreseen that it will be a long time before the English Government puts right the mistakes produced by its inexperience. The English, in abolishing slavery, have shown other nations what must be done and what must be avoided. They have simultaneously provided us with some important positive and some important negative lessons. In another article we will see what France can do to make the best of both.

[. . .]

Note that between the end of slavery and actual independence, the Commission, like the British Government, saw fit to insert an intermediary stage intended primarily for the education of the Negroes; but it conceived of this intermediate stage differently than the English. The latter had begun by proclaiming that slavery was abolished, but that each slave, converted into an apprentice, would nonetheless continue to remain with his former master and to work for him without wages. This mixed condition, where liberty seemed to be withheld after having been granted, was misunderstood by everyone. It created interminable disputes between the two races. The Negroes were embittered and the whites had not been at all satisfied with it. Enlightened by this experience, the Commission decided that it was necessary to abolish the term 'slavery' only when the principal features which characterize it would really be obliterated. It was thought wiser to give more in reality than seemed to have been promised, instead of advertising, like the English, more than was being given.

At the end of the preparatory period, the compulsory connection between master and servant would be at an end; labor would become remunerative, slavery would cease in fact as well as in name. But this does not mean that colonial society would have to adopt the pattern of the society of mainland France at that instant, nor that the emancipated Negro would immediately obtain the enjoyment of all the rights that the laborer possesses among us. The English example was there to prevent us from making such a mistake. The Commission understood it perfectly; it decided that the greatest danger that the colonies would have to face during the period of emancipation would not stem from the evil inclinations of the blacks, as was believed until now; and that even when, during the final years of slavery, they had achieved all the progress in morality and in civilization which experience has proven them to be capable of, it would still be imprudent suddenly to give them the same independence which the French working classes enjoy. It decided that if some artificial means were not used to draw and confine the Negroes to the sugar refineries and to prevent an excessive rise in wages, the instant that compulsory labor no longer existed, sugar production would receive a swift and serious blow, and the colonies, thus exposed to a sudden dislocation in their chief and almost only industry, would suffer enormously.

[. . .]

The final guarantee which can justly be given to the colonists is an indemnity representing the monetary value of the freed slaves. According to the Commission's system, during the ten years which elapse between the date when the principle of abolition is adopted and when slavery is actually destroyed, the slaves are being prepared for freedom and the indebtedness of colonial property is being liquidated. During this period the colonists are not jeopardized and therefore have no right to indemnification. But on the day that servitude ends, Negro labor is no longer free, and the question of the indemnity is introduced. Is the slave really property? What is the nature of this property? To what extent is the State, which has made it disappear, bound in law and equity? The duc de Broglie has dealt with this very difficult and delicate aspect of his report as an economist, a philosopher, and a statesman. It is the most striking part of this great work; we would like to present it to our readers, but our self-imposed limitation forbids it. So we will confine ourselves to saying that the Commission succeeds in demonstrating that it would be contrary to all concepts of equity and the obvious interests of metropolitan France to seize the colonists' slaves without indemnifying them for their loss.

The Commission, after long and conscientious effort, thought itself obliged to set the indemnity for the Negroes at 1200 francs a head. The English had discharged the indemnity in two ways: at the moment of abolition they had released half the promised sum to the planters, and in addition had assured them of a part of the unpaid labor of the freedmen for seven years. They had estimated the price of this labor as equivalent to the unpaid balance at the end of seven years. The Commission has adopted an analogous, if not identical measure.

[From 'On the Emancipation of Slaves' [1843], in *Tocqueville and Beaumont
On Social Reform*, ed. and trs. S. Drescher (New York: Harper and
Row, 1968), 149–51, 153–6, 160–1, 163–4, 169–70.]

LORD STANLEY
175 Hansard 1843

These statements showed, he thought, this, that as far as the labourers were concerned in Jamaica and Demerara, and though varying in degree, they were a sample of the whole of our colonies, the experiment had been not only successful in placing them in a situation of great physical enjoyment beyond the anticipations of their boldest friends, but they also proved, that they had learned to turn to advantage their newly-acquired gift of freedom in accumulating property, the product of their industry, and cultivating habits worthy of freemen. If he wanted another proof of this, he had it ready to his hand in the amount of exports to the West Indies from this country, during the period of apprenticeship subsequent to complete emancipation. The average value of the exports from this country to the West-India colonies in the six years preceding emancipation was 2,783,000l. The average during the four years of the apprenticeship, 1835 to 1838, was 3,573,000l. The amount, during the first year of freedom, 1839, was 4,002,000l., and during the second year of freedom, the amount was 3,492,734l. He would not trouble the House with further statements with respect to the number of schools and chapels which had been built. He hoped he had said enough to indicate to the House the social condition of the negroes, and if that were the only part of the subject to which he felt it necessary to call their attention, however gratifying the statement might be to him, from the part he had taken in this question, he certainly should not be entitled to call for a select committee to investigate the circumstances connected with the agricultural and rural population of the West Indies. But, notwithstanding this great prosperity and improvement, to which he was not insensible, having been the instrument to ask for that vote by which this great experiment had been put in progress, he could not shut his eyes to the fact, that although the paramount object of emancipation had been fully realized, in the condition and prosperity of the negro population, the West-India planters were now suffering from the very circumstances he had before alluded to, serious loss and injury, and it was with a view to ascertain the causes and the measures which should be resorted to for the mitigation of these evils, that he proposed a select committee. When he looked to the average quantity of sugar imported into the United Kingdom from the West Indies, he found, that during the six years preceding the apprenticeship it was 3,905,034 cwt.; that during the four years of apprenticeship, it fell to 3,486,225 cwt.; that during the first year of freedom, 1839, it fell to 2,824,106 cwt.; and that during the second year of freedom, 1840, it fell to 2,210,226 cwt. If the House would permit him to state this case fully and fairly, they would find, that the deficiency of the quantity had been made up by the increased value of the produce in the different intervals. For instance, the average value of sugar for the six years preceding the apprenticeship was 5,320,021l.; and that for the four years of the apprenticeship it was 6,217,801l. In the first year of freedom the amount was 5,530,000l., and in the next year 5,424,000l.; and although in this year there would be a large reduction, still there would be a fair remuneration for what was lost by the diminution of produce. Consequently, the planters had not sustained any very serious diminution of their income from this cause, but they had suffered a very serious and ruinous expense in the cultivation of their estates from the want and scarcity of labour—from the abstraction of labour in consequence of the industrious application of the labourers to their own farms, and from their having become possessors of property instead of mere cultivators of the soil. The result of this was, that the planters were compelled to pay exorbitant and enormous wages, and from the information he had received, he believed, that in several of the colonies the rate of wages and the expenses of cultivation were so extravagant that unless some remedy could be provided it would be impossible for the owners to continue to cultivate many of the estates. He had some reports on the subject from Trinidad, where a committee of planters had collected evidence as to the result of the enormous expenses incurred in the cultivation of estates. Another committee had been appointed on the same subject in Demerara, and he must say, that from those reports it appeared impossible for cultivation to be carried on if they contained statements at all approximating to truth. He had a report of 62 sugar estates, from the 1st of January to the 31st of October, 1841, in which period the expenditure was $1,091,000, while the return was $217,000, making a gross loss upon the whole estates of $874,000, and to December, the same committee stated the expense to be $1,295,000, and the total revenue $312,000, the loss being $983,000. He did not, of course, pretend to vouch for the entire accuracy of these statements, but he could only say they were founded on the report of a committee which had investigated the subject very carefully, and had directed their inquiries into the estates of those parties who had hitherto carried on their plantations with success and prosperity. Governor Light, whose merits or defects, be they what they might, could not be complained of as being unduly interested in favour of the planters, had forwarded a statement, made, as he described, by a gentleman of moderate opinions, and well disposed to the Government, whose name he deemed proper to withhold, with respect to estates, described as 1, 2, 3, and 4. He said the expense was ruinous, and certainly if all estates were in the same predicament, the condition of the planters must be very critical. This was a statement with respect to four of the best estates in Demerara, and according to the statement of the gentleman whose name he did not know, but who was a gentleman of moderate opinions, the result on one estate was altogether an excess of revenue over the expenditure of $5,891. On the other estates, there had been an actual loss; and the gross profit of the four estates, which formerly produced 1,100 or 1,200 hogsheads of sugar per annum, was $5,060. These were the statements which had been made, and which were well deserving the attention of a committee. These were questions of vast importance, and deserved to be considered dispassionately, calmly, and deliberately, as he trusted they would be by any committee that sat to consider them. The planters were naturally anxious for the application of a remedy, and it appeared quite clear, that there were two, and two only, by which the cultivation of these estates could be profitably carried on. First, by the reduction of the expense of cultivation by means of a better mode of management. This subject he was naturally anxious that a committee should especially inquire into; and the other practicable remedy consisted in increasing the population by a large amount of immigration, and by the effect of competition decreasing the amount of wages.

[From *Hansard*, 3rd series, Vol. 61 (1843), 1099–102.]

SAMUEL WILBERFORCE

176 **Hansard 1846**

The argument which has been brought forward to induce your Lordships to pass this Bill is this—the people of England are now supplied with an insufficient quantity of an article, if not entirely essential to their well-being, essential certainly to their comfort, essential in a high degree even to their well-being; the quantity therefore which is now supplied must be increased; the increase can only come from facilitating the trade in that article with Cuba and Brazil; and therefore you must facilitate the admission of Cuba and Brazil sugar, in order, first, to supply the people at home with a sufficient quantity of this article, which is so necessary; and, secondly, to provide a vent for your manufactures, the production of which is the main livelihood of your home population. This, I think, is the argument put before us. Now, this argument implies this, that a larger quantity of sugar must be exported from Cuba and Brazil, to be imported into this country. And it necessarily implies this, for this reason, that the deficiency of the supply in the English market is not because the English market is not able to command this article in preference to other markets, but because the entire production of sugar, in all sugar-producing countries, is so limited that you cannot increase, as you wish, the supply to the English market, without increasing the production in the sugar-producing countries.

[. . .]

I say, therefore, my Lords, that this argument of the necessity of an increased supply of sugar for the people falls utterly through. But then it has been attempted to be supported, as weak arguments often are, by a second weak one, as if two weak positions joined together would make a strong one; and it is a common fallacy for reasons of this kind to be supported in this way: it is said, though the argument as to the supply of the people may not be maintainable, yet, after all, we believe that in the long run, as a commonly admitted principle, free trade will do away with the Slave Trade and slavery. The proof is attempted in this way—it is stated that slave labour is dearer than free, and that if the countries cultivated by slave labour are brought into competition with those where free labour is used, they will, by the necessity of that competition, be forced to adopt the free system. This argument is produced with something like force, for it has the appearance of a weapon taken from our own camp. You say the emancipationists and abolitionists were always telling us free labour is cheaper than that of slaves: but what is really the argument? It is this, that free labour, *cæteris paribus*, is cheaper than slave labour; that if put together, the lash on the one hand, and the inducements to work furnished by a domestic and family existence on the other, then the free man will do more work than the slave. This is undoubtedly true; but this argument is altogether inapplicable when a new condition is introduced, and is therefore altogether annihilated when it is permitted to the slaveholder to introduce an unlimited number of full-grown slave labourers to replace those who may be killed off by the work, or rendered valueless. It is not true then that free labour is cheaper than that of slaves, in the sense of a more immediate production of wealth. It is altogether untrue. I do not for a moment mean to say that the great Governor of this world has so ordered things that the larger reward will be to the unjust man who uses his fellow being as a slave, above the man who justly uses his hired labourer; but there is a more immediate return of wealth in one case than in the other; because wealth alone is not to be the measure of the blessing given by Providence upon one sort of labour compared with the other. Wealth may be obtained by slavery, but obtained in that evil way it brings a curse, not alone on the individual, but on the nation that so obtains it; and thus we see that slave labour, while it produces more immediate riches, produces also evils which are the sure witness of God against it. It introduces miseries and evils of every kind; every uncertainty as to the rights of property, every uncertainty of the tenure of life, not to the oppressed only, but to the oppressor; while it poisons all the relations of family life with regard to both. The history of all slave communities shows this to be so. It is true, indeed, that men may gain great riches by the system; but with it comes a curse that poisons the wealth, and makes it valueless to its possessors; men tremble in their very houses lest the instruments by which they have amassed the treasure, may at any moment become the avengers of the crimes by which they were made the instruments of obtaining it. As it is, slave labour, with an unlimited supply to replace those killed off, is undoubtedly cheaper than the labour of the free man, than the labour of those free men raised patiently through the years in which they can do no work, and maintained at the end of their lives through the years in which they can do but little. But it is said that in Cuba and Brazil this increase of slave labour, without stint or limit, is acting wholesomely, in checking the importation by creating a fear of the slaves themselves. An abundant answer to this is, that the fear and the love of gain do not possess the same parties. The fear dwells principally upon the wealthy planter; the desire of gain rests upon the indigent, needy, and adventurous planter, and on the unscrupulous and greedy slavetrader who has no stake in the country. Whilst the greatest terror possesses the large capitalist, cupidity inspires the other; and the two elements, instead of checking one another, co-exist together. There may be a perfect dread in one portion of society of the continued importation of slaves; but there is a perfect thirst for gold in the other; and the conflict only serves to produce intestine discord, and to aggravate the condition of the negroes so introduced. What I say is, that with this power of an unlimited supply of slaves to cultivate the virgin soils, slave labour is absolutely cheaper than free; and by this measure you will stimulate the transference of the negro from Africa to these sugar-producing countries in the exact degree to which you introduce their sugar into your own market.

[. . .]

My Lords, when it is said that the abolition of the Slave Trade has been a failure, I certainly feel some sensation approaching to indignation in my mind. It has been, my Lords, no failure at all. To those men, those honoured men, our common ancestors, who fought the battle, and to those still living who have taken part in it, the object to be gained was not the Quixotic idea of putting down slavery at once all over the face of the earth, by putting an end to it in their own country, or in lands subject to its control. It was that which they unflinchingly proclaimed before their fellow countrymen, and that at least has been no failure. Who can say how much, in the inscrutable decrees of Providence, the faithfulness of England to the truth in this point may have been the redeeming part of her character among a multitude of failings, and been the means of drawing down those blessings of Heaven of which all have been partakers, and with which all are at this moment enriched? The arguments used against us now were equally used against our forerunners. They were told, as we are, 'what is the use of abolishing the Slave Trade? It will only be taken up by other nations, by the Dutch, the Spaniards, or the Portuguese'. It was not denied; the answer was, 'We trust in the long run we shall bring them over; but granting we fail—their own iniquity be upon them. Because others commit robbery and murder, shall we commit murder and robbery in a gentler manner, and with less of suffering to our victims?' We are told we do not and cannot stop the Slave Trade by our efforts: I reply, we keep ourselves free from it, and if you pass this Bill, you will no longer do so. I think it is done ignorantly. I shall earnestly repudiate it myself; but I am convinced if Her Majesty's Government believed, as I believe, that this measure will give a direct sanction to the Slave Trade, and a great stimulus to slave labour, they would not propose it. But, at the same time, though done ignorantly, it is done directly. You want cheap sugar, and you are going to say—import abundantly the slave labour that produces the cheap sugar we want. You say we give way upon principle; we have struggled long enough; we have been beaten; we will be untruthful to our principle; we are determined to enjoy the advantages we have lost by adherence to it; we will share them with you. This, my Lords, is the fearful step you are called on to take. I can only say, in conclusion, I have a fervent belief that if you take that step, it will be one more adverse to the opinion, the principles, and the convictions of the mass of this people of England than any step taken within my memory. I believe the history of the whole abolition cause has been this—slavery was shown to be contrary to the will of Providence, the happiness of man, and the revealed word of God, and therefore must be a blot and injury to the country. The announcement of the great truth enlisted on its side the strong religious feeling of the country, and the battle was won by the Christian principle of Christian England. I believe the antislavery cause, from various reasons, has rather fallen to an argument of a different kind, and that it has become something of a political and sectional question. But let there be an announcement that, directly or indirectly, you are going to plunge this country again into the guilt of this great crime, and I believe the people will rise again and pronounce against it with the same feelings of indignation with which they put it down when it before existed. And I would urge it on your notice, that the only respect in which the contest upon this question differs now from that by which it was formerly put down, is, that the advocates of truth and justice fought at a disadvantage in pulling down an existing evil; those who resisted them only maintained things as they were. But, we are called upon, for the first time, to make a direct step on the opposite path. We are for the first time called on to commit an act of retrogression, and to declare that the idea then written on the minds of the English people—the principle which, in spite of all the difficulties and hindrances it met with at a time when every free opinion wore the semblance of Jacobinism, and was thought to threaten the institutions of the land, enthroned itself into the hearts of the English nation—must be abandoned; that we must take a step in the opposite direction; that we must reopen what our predecessors closed; renew what, upon conviction, they abolished, believing that this great political crime can be, in this world of God, nothing but a political error. We are called on to declare that we may improve our revenues, amend our finances, and increase and make abundant the supplies the people need, by doing a wrong, encouraging injustice, and giving occasion to the perpetration of the cruellest wickedness and the darkest evils that this earth ever groaned under. Believing this, feeble as I am, I should think myself unworthy of a place in this House if I did not express that opinion by moving that this Bill be read a second time this day three months.

[From *Hansard*, 3rd series, Vol. 88 (1846), 651, 660–2, 665–7.]

VICTOR SCHOELCHER

177   Paris Ethnological Society Debate 1847

Mr. Schoelcher contended that the first blacks were brought from Africa to the Antilles by the Spanish in order to replace the native race almost entirely destroyed by the barbarism of the conquerors. From the beginning of the 15th century, a rather large number of blacks had been carried off from Africa as slaves, and imported into Spain and Portugal. It was from Spain itself that the Spanish drew the first blacks that they transported to the Antilles. Only later was a direct trade established with the African coast. The celebrated Las Casas initially erred in encouraging this commerce, which he saw as a means of preserving for the unfortunate Indians.

Mr. Schoelcher, claims for France the initiative in the abolition of slavery. This was the result of the great and fruitful ideas that dominated the Revolution. Of course, imperial reaction re-established slavery.

In 1833, England fulfilled an idea that we had conceived. Slave emancipation was a victory of popular sentiment over the reluctance of the colonists, the aristocracy and the government. Today, the colonists, are frustrated at finding themselves somewhat dependent upon the workers due to a shortage of hands relative to the demands of production. They are trying to obtain from the government permission to import more Africans. They are also trying to obtain new regulations to make the labor compulsory. One must hope that the English people, who have a passion for emancipation and who have abolished slavery throughout their empire, will defeat these projects. Nevertheless it is regrettable that these colonialist projects seem to rely on the doctrines expressed in this Society, assuming the need of the white race to force the blacks to work, in order to improve the intertropical regions.

Mr. Schoelcher rejects the notion that the blacks have never had the initiative in civilization. The civilization of Egypt was their work. The monuments of Ethiopia are there to attest to it. Even in beyond these facts, we have no more reason to use the past of the blacks as an argument against their potential future, than the Romans to come to a similar conclusion about the potential the Gauls and the Germans to emerge from the barbarity which they observed among these peoples.

As for the argument presented by Mr. d'Eichthal, on the analogy between the black and the white on the one hand, and women and men on the other, it is too undeveloped to be usefully discussed. Nor does *Mr. Schoelcher* agree that there is a lack of scientific initiative among the blacks. On the contrary, he thinks, that the blacks developed the civilization of Ethiopia and Egypt, hence the civilization of Antiquity. Again, regardless of such evidence, the absence of scientific development among the blacks in the past and in the present does not authorize us to contest the possibility of its development in the future. After all, Aristotle regarded some Europeans, the peoples among whom modern civilization has developed, as barbarians, as a race inferior to the Greeks. And yet, the history of the following centuries has demolished the allegation.

As for the opinions of delegates from the colonies, who have just been invoked, *Mr. Schoelcher* views them as sincere sentiments. Nevertheless, they are opinions tainted by what one would call family prejudices. The idleness for which the blacks are reproached is the consequence of the treatment to which they have been subjected. They would work better if they were paid in anything else than lashings. Climate does have an influence that is very unfavorable for work, and that effects whites as well as blacks. The evidence lies in the Ibaros of Puerto Rico and the *petits blancs* of the Island of Bourbon. Be that as it may, even the testimony of the colonial delegates shows that the black race is improving itself in the Antilles. There, and, not in Africa, we should study his civilizability. The example of the English colonies, in particular, shows how far the freed Negroes can rise.

[As to Africa,] Europe actually owes Africa great and solemn reparations.

She robbed Africa of 30,000,000 inhabitants and made them perish in the cane fields. What a debt! And to repay it we say to the Negroes: 'You are inferior people; we will try to make something of you by cross-breeding!' This will produce mulattoes, but it will not improve the Negro race.

It is civilization that must be cross-bred, not men. Let us cease morally and materially devastating Africa by this murderous dealing in slaves. Let us bring to its shores schools of all types—elementary, scientific, industrial. Let us create real colonies, and from these will flow beneficial and enlightening influence.

[. . .]

Even in slavery, the Negroes in contact with civilization have profited from it. Is this not a powerful reason to recognize their intellectual aptitude? The contact between slave and master is so slight, and servitude itself is so brutalizing that we should well be astonished by such rapid progress. Another of our colleagues, Mr. de Lisboa, a Brazilian, has established this fact of improvement, and has drawn the natural conclusion from it. 'Consider this observation,' he says, 'I believe that we may conclude that intellectual weakness among the African Negroes derives from the imperfections of the social state in which they live, more than from any important difference of organization. This superiority of the Creole Negro [to the African] is the more remarkable in that it is not the fruit of study, because Creoles are, generally, deprived of all instruction. Their superiority results uniquely from their contact with a more civilized social sphere.'

Mr. Schoelcher recalls that in the emancipated British colonies, the directors of elementary schools consulted by him, have affirmed that Negro children showed themselves as studious and as capable as the whites. In these same colonies the mulattoes and also the Negroes have succeeded in all the functions of the magistracy and of administration. The venerable Abb. Gregoire, in his book on the *Literature of the Negroes*, collected the biographies of a certain number of Negroes who, overcoming the obstacles which drag them down, have been able to rise to eminence: [inter alia] . . . Othello, Cugoano, Ottobah, the Negress Phyllis; more recently Manzano, a Negro from Cuba, distinguished himself as a poet. According to the testimony of Clot-Bey, Negresses placed in the Cairo School of Medicine to learn midwifery, have shown great aptitude, for the exercise of their profession or in perfecting of their general instruction.

Mr. Schoelcher deals with the native idleness attributed to the Negroes. He regrets that the declarations of the colonial delegates was cited as reliable information about the unrest of 1839. A document of this nature cannot be considered impartial. The good faith of colonists must be suspected, but the influence of the social sphere in which they live biases the integrity of their judgement even without their being aware of it. This might seem strange at first, but it is true: Morally speaking, the colonists do not know their

Negroes. They see before them only a race degraded by its condition. The man who is free and the man who is a slave are no longer the same.

Mr. Schoelcher, responding to the accusation about the natural indolence of the Negroes, offers, among others, the opinion of Laird, a traveler in Africa: 'One can no longer declare,' says Laird, 'that Negroes, left to their own devices, do not want to work: the facts have reversed this antiquated prejudice. In 1808, the importation of palm oil from Africa did not exceed 100 or 200 barrels per year. Today 14,000 barrels are imported. Twenty years ago, African woods were unavailable markets; today 13 to 15 consignments are imported per year. And if one realizes that this commerce developed in spite of the slave trade, that it was not encouraged by any legal protection, by any policy motive, that despite these obstacles it has grown in a uniform and constant manner, one must be convinced that there are no people more intelligent in business, and of better disposition than the Africans. I can assure European businessmen that they would be well received by the inhabitants of the interior of Africa; They would meet no hostile tendency there. On the banks of the Niger, life and property will be as safe as it is on the banks of the Thames. The only thing that hinders trade between the nations of the interior and the European settlements on the coast is the terror that the reputation of the white man carries—a terror cleverly spread by the people of the coast, and maintained by the disorganization of the country produced by the slave trade.'

On the whole, [Mr. Schoelcher] thinks that if one considers the Negroes an inferior race because they are not yet entirely civilized, we need to pronounce today the same judgement about all races which are not yet raised, or which have fallen below the level of the race of White Europeans. It is necessary to consider as inferior the Indians of America, the Hindus, and the Chinese. We could even find ourselves driven to severely judge certain French populations.

After all, if the race which has produced Phyllis, Toussaint Louverture, Christophe and Manzano is not equal to ours, I no longer know what equality is. If this race has been able to furnish some superior men, although it was scarcely in a position to have any, it is not permitted to say that it is inferior. Otherwise, the supposed superiority of the White race crumbles at its own base, because we cannot deny that it too contains stupid individuals, and some very bad reasoners as well. I hope, gentlemen, that you do not think that I need to prove it here.

[From 'Debates of the Société Ethnologique,' in Mémoires de la Société Ethnologique de Paris (Paris: Dondet-Duprey, 1841–7), Vol. II: 151–74. Trs. Seymour Drescher.]

The West Indies, it appears, are short of labour; as indeed is very conceivable in those circumstances. Where a Black man, by working about half-an-hour a-day (such is the calculation), can supply himself, by aid of sun and soil, with as much pumpkin as will suffice, he is likely to be a little stiff to raise into hard work! Supply and demand, which, science says, should be brought to bear on him, have an uphill task of it with such a man. Strong sun supplies itself gratis, rich soil in those unpeopled or half-peopled regions almost gratis; these are *his* 'supply'; and half-an-hour a-day, directed upon these, will produce pumpkin, which is his 'demand'. The fortunate Black man, very swiftly does he settle *his* account with supply and demand:—not so swiftly the less fortunate White man of those tropical localities. A bad case, his, just now. He himself cannot work; and his black neighbour, rich in pumpkin, is in no haste to help him. Sunk to the ears in pumpkin, imbibing saccharine juices, and much at his ease in the Creation, he can listen to the less fortunate white man's 'demand,' and take his own time in supplying it. Higher wages, massa; higher, for your cane-crop cannot wait; still higher,—till no conceivable opulence of cane-crop will cover such wages. In Demerara, as I read in the Blue-book of last year, the cane-crop, far and wide, stands rotting; the fortunate black gentlemen, strong in their pumpkins, having all struck till the 'demand' rise a little. Sweet blighted lilies, now getting-up their heads again!

Science, however, has a remedy still. Since the demand is so pressing, and the supply so inadequate (equal in fact to *nothing* in some places, as appears), increase the supply; bring more Blacks into the labour-market, then will the rate fall, says science. Not the least surprising part of our West-Indian policy is this recipe of 'immigration'; of keeping-down the labour-market in those islands by importing new Africans to labour and live there. If the Africans that are already there could be made to lay-down their pumpkins, and labour for their living, there are already Africans enough. If the new Africans, after labouring a little, take to pumpkins like the others, what remedy is there? To bring-in new and ever new Africans, say you, till pumpkins themselves grow dear; till the country is crowded with Africans; and black men there, like white men here, are forced by hunger to labour for their living? That will be a consummation. To have 'emancipated' the West Indies into a *Black Ireland*; 'free' indeed, but an Ireland, and Black! The world may yet see prodigies; and reality be stranger than a nightmare dream.

[. . .]

And first, with regard to the West Indies, it may be laid-down as a principle, which no eloquence in Exeter Hall, or Westminster Hall, or elsewhere, can invalidate or hide, except for a short time only, That no Black man who will not work according to what ability the gods have given him for working, has the smallest right to eat pumpkin, or to any fraction of land that will grow pumpkin, however plentiful such land may be; but has an indisputable and perpetual *right* to be compelled, by the real proprietors of said land, to do competent work for his living. This is the everlasting duty of all men, black or white, who are born into this world. To do competent work, to labour honestly according to the ability given them; for that and for no other purpose was each one of us sent into this world; and woe is to every man who, by friend or by foe, is prevented from fulfilling this the end of his being. That is the 'unhappy' lot: lot equally unhappy cannot otherwise be provided for man. Whatsoever prohibits or prevents a man from this his sacred appointment to labour while he lives on earth,—that, I say, is the man's deadliest enemy; and all men are called upon to do what is in their power or opportunity towards delivering him from that. If it be his own indolence that prevents and prohibits him, then his own indolence is the enemy he must be delivered from: and the first 'right' he has,—poor indolent blockhead, black or white,—is, That every *un*prohibited man, whatsoever wiser, more industrious person may be passing that way, shall endeavour to 'emancipate' him from his indolence, and by some wise means, as I said, compel him, since inducing will not serve, to do the work he is fit for. Induce him, if you can: yes, sure enough, by all means try what inducement will do; and indeed every coachman and carman knows that secret, without our preaching, and applies it to his very horses as the true method:—but if your Nigger will not be induced? In that case, it is full certain, he must be compelled; should and must; and the tacit prayer he makes (unconsciously he, poor blockhead), to you, and to me, and to all the world who are wiser than himself, is, 'Compel me!' For indeed he *must*, or else do and suffer worse,—he as well as we. It were better the work did come out of him! It was the meaning of the gods with him and with us, that his gift should turn to use in this Creation, and not lie poisoning the thoroughfares, as a rotten mass of idleness, agreeable to neither heaven nor earth. For idleness does, in all cases, inevitably *rot*, and become putrescent;—and I say deliberately, the very Devil is in *it*.

[. . .]

Fair towards Britain it will be, that Quashee give work for privilege to grow pumpkins. Not a pumpkin, Quashee, not a square yard of soil, till you agree to do the State so many days of service. Annually that soil will grow you pumpkins; but annually also, without fail, shall you, for the owner thereof, do your appointed days of labour. The State has plenty of waste soil; but the State will religiously give you none of it on other terms. The State wants sugar from these Islands, and means to have it; wants virtuous industry in these Islands, and must have it. The State demands of you such service as will bring these results, this latter result which includes all. Not a Black Ireland, by immigration, and boundless black supply for the demand;—not that, may the gods forbid!—but a regulated West Indies, with black working population in adequate numbers.

[From *The Negro Question* [1849], ed. Eugene August (New York: Appleton-Century-Crofts, 1971), 6–7, 9–10, 31.]

EDMUND RUFFIN

179   Diary

Oct. 30. Sunday [1864].—As much as I had thought & written upon the negro race & upon negro slavery, this war has served to develope some features which had not been supposed or suspected to exist before, or to such extent as has recently been shown. I had before believed in the general prevalence of much attachment & affection of negro slaves for the families of their masters, & especially in the more usual circumstances of careful & kind treatment of the slaves. But, though some few cases of great attachment & fidelity have been exhibited, there have been many more of signal ingratitude & treachery of slaves to the most considerate & kind of masters—& the far greater number have merely shown indifference & entire disregard of all such supposed ties of attachment & loyalty. Judging from the almost universal unwillingness, & refusal when at their option, of the slaves, in the war of 1812, to desert to the English invaders, I expected like results as to the invitations of Yankee invaders. (I had not anticipated the resort to the abduction of the slaves by force, which has been used whenever convenient, & where the milder course of invitation, seduction, & deception had failed.) But the results, in the general conduct of the slaves, in these two wars, were completely reversed. Wherever the Yankee land or naval forces have had decided supremacy in any part of our invaded country, &, by their aid, the slaves could *safely* escape to a Yankee camp, or a gunboat, the greater number, soon or late, availed themselves of the opportunity thus to become free. The treatment they had previously received from their masters had very little influence on the fleeing or staying of the slaves. . . . Example seemed more than anything else to direct the course of the slaves. If a few went off early, from any farm, nearly all the others would follow in different detachments, if not prevented by their removal to a distant locality. . . . Every Yankee soldier or camp-follower was a diligent missionary & abolition agent, to persuade (before the more summary course of force was used,) the negroes to assert their freedom. And to back the invitation, the most extravagant falsehoods were uttered & believed. The negro, going to Yankee protection, was to be free from all work, unless at his or her own free choice—to be well fed, if in idleness—& to have very high wages, & always plenty of employment, if choosing to be employed. As to the necessity of laboring continually for support, for the maintenance of helpless members of a family, & for providing for sickness & old age, these newly freed men & women never thought once, before the stern necessity arrived. They had always before had their wants provided for & supplied, & equally, whether at work or idle, in sickness, or entire disability, as in health. In their new state of freedom, they foolishly expected the same provision, added to the supreme happiness of complete idleness.—The causes of difference of conduct of the negro slaves in the two wars may be clearly traced. The war of 1812 began but 31 years after the revolutionary war ended. At the later time, there were slaves still living in every neighborhood who remembered the horrible sufferings, & bad treatment by the British, of the thousands of their fellows (& in many cases of themselves,) who had been seduced to accept the freedom offered & proclaimed by Dunmore, & later more invitingly & substantially held out by Arnold & Cornwallis. The absconding negroes had perished in misery by thousands, or had barely survived, under the inflictions of small-pox or camp & jail fever, and starving in besieged military posts. As many of these fugitives as could escape from their new condition of freedom, & from the freedom-givers, did so, & returned gladly to their masters & to the provision afforded by slavery for their wants—& to teach to the next generation of negroes their sufferings from British friends & freedom-givers. . . . On the other hand, as to Yankees, they, from the ending of the revolutionary war to the beginning of this, had had open to them the perfectly free ingress & passage through every part of the slaveholding states—& there was not a county or village that had not been visited, sojourned in, & thoroughly examined by Yankees, & in many cases by hundreds of Yankees. And for the latter 30 years, in which the abolition fanaticism of the northern states had risen & raged, almost all of these tens of thousands of travelling or sojourning Yankees were more or less active through secret & quiet voluntary agents, & in numerous cases engaged missionaries, operating to indoctrinate & seduce slaves. . . . Under such circumstances of facility for abolition agents . . . it is not to be wondered at that the minds of the slaves were generally affected by such influences, & that many of them were made discontented with their before happy condition, & made to look on their masters & the white class as their enemies, oppressors, & tyrants. It was on a soil so well prepared by previous & long-continued labors, that, with the ample opportunities afforded by this war & the invasion & desolation of our lands by their armies . . . the Yankees came to reap the crop of negro freedom & insurrection which they had before so carefully planted & nursed. . . .

    [. . .]

[June 18, 1865] I here declare my unmitigated hatred to Yankee rule—to all political, social & business connection with Yankees—& to the Yankee race.

Would that I could impress these sentiments, in their full force, on every living southerner, & bequeath them to every one yet to be born! May such sentiments be held universally in the outraged & down-trodden South, though in silence & stillness, until the now far-distant day shall arrive for just retribution for Yankee usurpation, oppression, & atrocious outrages—& for deliverance & vengeance for the now ruined, subjugated, & enslaved Southern States! May the maledictions of every victim to their malignity, press with full weight on the perfidious Yankee people & their perjured rulers—& especially on those of the invading forces who perpetrated, & their leaders & higher authorities who encouraged, directed, or permitted, the unprecedented & generally extended outrages of robbery, rapine & destruction, & house-burning, all committed contrary to the laws of war on non-combatant residents, & still worse on aged men & helpless women!

Edmund Ruffin sen.

[From *The Diary of Edmund Ruffin* (Baton Rouge: Louisiana State University Press, 1989), Vol. III, *A Dream Shattered, June 1863–June 1865*, 624–6, 946.]

180 Mississippi Legislature 1850

Resolutions
of
The Legislature of Mississippi,
on

The subject of slavery and the questions in controversy between the northern and southern States growing out of that institution.
MAY 8, 1850.
Read, and ordered to lie on the table and be printed.

Report of the joint select committee on federal and state relations, adopted by both branches of the legislature of the State of Mississippi.

The joint standing committee on federal and state relations, to whom was referred so much of the governor's message as relates to the subject of slavery and the unhappy agitation of it which at present distracts the councils of the nation, and threatens the dissolution of our Union as a confederacy of States, have had the subject under consideration, and have instructed me to make the following report:

We have arrived at a period in the political existence of our country when the fears of the patriot and philanthropist may well be excited, lest the noblest fabric of constitutional government on earth may, ere long, be laid in ruins by the elements of discord engendered by an unholy lust for power and the fell spirit of fanaticism acting upon the minds of our brethren of the non-slaveholding States, and that beneath its ruins will be forever buried the hopes of an admiring world for the political regeneration of enslaved millions. The fact can no longer be disguised, that our brethren of the free States, so called, disregarding the compromises of the constitution—*compromises without which* it never would have received the sanction of the slaveholding States—are determined to pursue towards those States a course of policy, and to adopt a system of legislation by Congress, destructive of their best rights and most cherished domestic institutions. In vain have the citizens of the slave States appealed to their brethren of the free States, in a spirit of brotherly love and devotion to that constitution framed by our fathers, and cemented by their blood, as a common shield and protection for the rights of all their descendants. In vain have they invoked the guaranties of that sacred instrument as a barrier to the encroachments of their brethren upon their rights. The spirit of forbearance and concession which has been for more than thirty years manifested and acted on by the slaveholding States has but strengthened the determination of their northern brethren to fasten upon them a system of legislation, in regard to their peculiar domestic relations, as fatal in its effects to their prosperity and happiness as members of the confederacy, as it is unjust and contrary to the principles and provisions of the constitution.

Slavery, as it exists in the southern States, recognised and protected by the constitution of the United States, is a domestic relation, subject to be abolished or modified by the sovereign power alone of the States in which it prevails; it is not a moral or political evil, but an element of prosperity and happiness both to the master and slave.

Abolish slavery, and you convert the fair and blooming fields of the South into barren heaths, their high-souled and chivalrous proprietors into abject dependants, and the now happy and contented slaves into squalid and degraded objects of misery and wretchedness!

The southern States have remonstrated and forborne until forbearance is no longer a virtue. The time has arrived when, if they hope to preserve their existence as equal members of the confederacy, and to avert the calamities which their northern brethren, actuated by an insatiate and maddening thirst for power, would entail upon them, they must prepare *to act*—to act with resolution, firmness, and unity of purpose, trusting to the righteousness of their cause and the protection of the Almighty Ruler of the destinies of nations, who ever looks benignantly upon the exertions of those who contend for the prerogatives of freemen. Therefore, be it

Resolved by the legislature of the State of Mississippi, That they cordially approve of the action of the Southern State Convention held at the city of

Jackson on the first Monday of October, 1849, and adopt the following resolutions of said body as declaratory of the opinions of this legislature, and of the people of the State of Mississippi:

1st. *Resolved*, That we continue to entertain a devoted and cherished attachment to the Union; but we desire to have it as it was formed, and not as an engine of oppression.

2d. That the institution of slavery in the southern States is left, by the constitution, exclusively under the control of the States in which it exists, as a part of their domestic policy, which they, and they only, have the right to regulate, abolish, or perpetuate, as they may severally judge expedient; and that all attempts, on the part of Congress or others, to interfere with this subject, either directly or indirectly, are in violation of the constitution, dangerous to the rights and safety of the South, and ought to be promptly resisted.

3d. That Congress has no power to pass any law abolishing slavery in the District of Columbia, or to prohibit the slave trade between the several States, or to prohibit the introduction of slavery into the territories of the United States; and that the passage by Congress of any such law would not only be a dangerous violation of the constitution, but would afford evidence of a fixed and deliberate design, on the part of that body, to interfere with the institution of slavery in the States.

4th. That we would regard the passage by Congress of the 'Wilmot proviso' (which would, in effect, deprive the citizens of the slaveholding States of an equal participation in the territories acquired equally by their blood and treasure) as an unjust and insulting discrimination, to which these States cannot without political degradation submit, and to which this convention, representing the feelings and opinions of the people of Mississippi, solemnly declare they will not submit.

5th. That the passage of the Wilmot proviso, or of any law abolishing slavery in the District of Columbia, by the Congress of the United States, would, of itself, be such a breach of the federal compact as, in that event, will make it the duty, as it is the right, of the slaveholding States, to take care of their own safety, and to treat the non-slaveholding States as enemies to the slaveholding States and their domestic institutions.

6th. That, in view of the frequent and increasing evidence of the determination of the people of the non-slaveholding States to disregard the guaranties of the constitution, and to agitate the subject of slavery, both in and out of Congress, avowedly for the purpose of effecting its abolition in the States; and also in view of the facts set forth in the late 'Address of the southern members of Congress,'—this convention proclaims the deliberate conviction that the time has arrived when the southern States should take counsel together for their common safety; and that a convention of the slaveholding States should be held at Nashville, Tennessee, on the first Monday in June next, to devise and adopt some mode of resistance to these aggressions.

7th. That, in the language of an eminent northern writer and patriot, 'The rights of the South in African service exist not only *under*, but *over*, the constitution. They existed before the government was formed. The constitution was rather sanctioned by them than they by the constitution. Had not that instrument admitted the sovereignty of those rights, it never would have been itself admitted by the South. It bowed in deference to rights older in their date, stronger in their claims, and holier in their nature, than any other which the constitution can boast. Those rights may not be changed, even by a change of the constitution. They are out of the reach of the nation, as a nation. The confederacy may dissolve and the constitution pass away, but those rights will remain unshaken—will exist while the South exists; and when they fall, the South will perish with them.'

[From *Resolutions of the Legislature of Mississippi* (1850), in US Congress, Senate, 31st Congress, 1st Session, Miscellaneous Document 110, 1–3.]

181   Black Abolitionist Papers 1863

Manifesto of the colored citizens of the state of New York, in convention assembled

The war now raging so fiercely over the broad and fertile acres of this, the best heritage ever enjoyed by man, is not a 'fratricidal conflict,' as many deem it, but, on the contrary, by reason of the momentous issues at stake and involved therein, is one of the most justifiable wars that was ever inaugurated beneath the smiling, radiant dome of all the broad heavens. It is one of the most sacred which the earth has ever groaned under or mankind ever witnessed, for the reason that it is a combat for the sacred rights of Man against the myrmidons of Hell itself. It is a battle for the right of self-government, true democracy, just republicanism, and righteous principles, against anarchy, misrule, barbarism, human slavery, despotism, and wrong. On the one side is arrayed the hosts of Belial, backed by willfulness, injustice, usurpation, anger and passion; on the other, in serried ranks, stand honor, human liberty, justice, truth, and honesty. This is not a battle of boys but [a] struggle of giants. Let the North be conquered, and the salt tears of the oppressed will water the ground for many a long decade of years, and many a hecatomb will uprear its head, and many a sod be nurtured by the blood of liberty-loving human beings. The strife now waging is not between North and South—is not only in behalf of the Negro; but the greatest principles the world has ever known constitute the two halves of the *casus belli*—barbarism and freedom—civilization and slavery; it is a death struggle between the feudal ages and the nineteenth century; and every drop of blood shed from Northern veins is a sacrifice on the holy altars of human freedom, and those forever consecrate to the ever-blessed Redeemer of Mankind! The impending issues are such that if the representatives of human liberty yield the battle, and retire ingloriously beaten, the age will recede a century, and the hands upon the clock of Progress will cease to move across the face of Time. Let the cohorts of freedom be beaten and disgraced, and not only all true lovers of the race will suffer, but every lover and true worshipper of the living God will mourn over the desolation.

This contest is one in which every son and daughter of the land is and of necessity must be interested. It is the bounden duty of us all—all who are not craven cowards—all in whom the warm blood leaps, and all who feel what a terrible thing is HUMAN SLAVERY—to up and struggle for God and the Right.

Defeat in this momentous epoch of human history means more than a rout upon the battlefield, inasmuch as such defeat will not only rivet our chains still firmer than of yore, but will forever stand as the synonym of American disgrace and will be the record of our perpetual disfranchisement, and be the bouleversement of human society, civilization and democratic republican institutions, from progress and health to anarchy, decay and final ruin—a ruin utter, total and complete; for the common sense of mankind cannot fail to see that if the cause of freedom fails now, human advancement will be something read about in books, instead of being a living, ever-present fact; and in the reign of tyranny thence ensuing, the human heart must of necessity become chilled and frozen; art, science and religion must go out like oilless lamps; darkness must eclipse the light; the garden of the mind run to waste and weeds; human genius be vagabond, stifled and dumb as of old, and the spirit of misrule will sweep the fair green earth with the besom of destruction, scattering desolation far and wide, and inaugurating such a reign of horror as never yet has been known on earth. Let the cohorts of freedom now yield an inch, and the blood of Jesus will almost have been shed in vain; for in their defeat, Christianity itself must suffer; the sacrifice of Calvary prove a failure, the spontaneity of the human soul be chilled and frozen; human genius be stifled, talent be warped, and eloquence be dumb, as in the dead years of the far off past. Great God! What a spectacle in this nineteenth century! A million of men arraying themselves in arms against liberty! and in favor of their own degradation!

[From C. Peter Ripley (ed.), *The Black Abolitionist Papers (1859–1865)* (Chapel Hill: University of North Carolina Press, 1992), Vol. V, *The United States, 1859–1865*, 224–6.]

We left Beaufort, S. C., on the afternoon of July 9th, 1863. In former narrations I have sufficiently described the charm of a moonlight ascent into a hostile country, upon an unknown stream, the dark and silent banks, the rippling water, the wail of the reed-birds, the anxious watch, the breathless listening, the veiled lights, the whispered orders.

[. . .]

The battery—whether fixed or movable we knew not—met us with a promptness that proved very shortlived. After three shots it was silent, but we could not tell why. The bluff was wooded, and we could see but little. The only course was to land, under cover of the guns. As the firing ceased and the smoke cleared away, I looked across the rice-fields which lay beneath the bluff. The first sunbeams glowed upon their emerald levels, and on the blossoming hedges along the rectangular dikes. What were those black dots which everywhere appeared? Those moist meadows had become alive with human heads, and along each narrow path came a straggling file of men and women, all on a run for the river-side. I went ashore with a boat-load of troops at once. The landing was difficult and marshy. The astonished negroes tugged us up the bank, and gazed on us as if we had been Cortez and Columbus. They kept arriving by land much faster than we could come by water; every moment increased the crowd, the jostling, the mutual clinging, on that miry foothold. What a scene it was! With the wild faces, eager figures, strange garments, it seemed, as one of the poor things reverently suggested, 'like notin' but de judgment day'. Presently they began to come from the houses also, with their little bundles on their heads; then with larger bundles. Old women, trotting on the narrow paths, would kneel to pray a little prayer, still balancing the bundle; and then would suddenly spring up, urged by the accumulating procession behind, and would move on till irresistibly compelled by thankfulness to dip down for another invocation. Reaching us, every human being must grasp our hands, amid exclamations of 'Bress you, mas'r,' and 'Bress de Lord,' at the rate of four of the latter ascriptions to one of the former. Women brought children on their shoulders; small black boys carried on their backs little brothers equally inky, and, gravely depositing them, shook hands. Never had I seen human beings so clad, or rather so unclad, in such amazing squalidness and destitution of garments. I recall one small urchin without a rag of clothing save the basque waist of a lady's dress, bristling with whalebones, and worn wrong side before, beneath which his smooth ebony legs emerged like those of an ostrich from its plumage. How weak is imagination, how cold is memory, that I ever cease, for a day of my life, to see before me the picture of that astounding scene!

[. . .]

I wish that it were possible to present all this scene from the point of view of the slaves themselves. It can be most nearly done, perhaps, by quoting the description given of a similar scene on the Combahee River, by a very aged man, who had been brought down on the previous raid, already mentioned. I wrote it down in tent, long after, while the old man recited the tale, with much gesticulation, at the door; and it is by far the best glimpse I have ever had, through a negro's eyes, at these wonderful birthdays of freedom.

'De people was all a hoein', mas'r,' said the old man. 'Dey was a hoein' in the rice-field, when de gunboats come. Den ebry man drap dem hoe, and leff de rice. De mas'r he stand and call, 'Run to de wood for hide! Yankee come, sell you to Cuba! run for hide!' Ebry man he run, and, my God! run all toder way!

'Mas'r stand in de wood, peep, peep, faid for truss [afraid to trust]. He say, 'Run to de wood!' and ebry man run by him, straight to de boat.

'De brack sojer so presumptious, dey come right ashore, hold up dere head. Fus' ting I know, dere was a barn, ten tousand bushel rough rice, all in a blaze, den mas'r's great house, all cracklin' up de roof. Did n't I keer for see 'em blaze? Lor, mas'r, did n't care notin' at all, *I was gwine to de boat.*'

[. . .]

'De brack sojers so presumptious!' This he repeated three times, slowly shaking his head in an ecstasy of admiration. It flashed upon me that the apparition of a black soldier must amaze those still in bondage, much as a butterfly just from the chrysalis might astound his fellow-grubs. I inwardly vowed that my soldiers, at least, should be as 'presumptious' as I could make them. Then he went on.

'Ole woman and I go down to de boat; den dey say behind us, 'Rebels comin'! Rebels comin'!' Ole woman say, 'Come ahead, come plenty ahead!' I hab notin' on but my shirt and pantaloon; ole woman one single frock he hab on, and one handkerchief on he head; I leff all-two my blanket and run for de Rebel come, and den dey did n't come, did n't truss for come.

'Ise eighty-eight year old, mas'r. My ole Mas'r Lowndes keep all de ages in a big book, and when we come to age ob sense we mark em down ebry year, so I know. Too ole for come? Mas'r joking. Neber too ole for leave de land o' bondage. I old, but great good for chil'en, gib tousand tank ebry day. Young people can go through, *force* [forcibly], mas'r, but de ole folk mus' go slow.'

[From *Army Life in a Black Regiment* [1870] (Boston: Beacon Press, 1962), 170–4.]

By the President of the United States of America: A Proclamation

Whereas on the 22d day of September, A.D. 1862, a proclamation was issued by the President of the United States, containing, among other things the following, to wit:

'That on the 1st day of January, A.D. 1863, all persons held as slaves within any State or designated part of a State the people whereof shall then be in rebellion against the United States shall be then, thenceforward, and forever free; and the executive government of the United States, including the military and naval authority thereof, will recognize and maintain the freedom of such persons and will do no act or acts to repress such persons, or any of them, in any efforts they may make for their actual freedom.

'That the executive will on the 1st day of January aforesaid, by proclamation, designate the States and parts of States, if any, in which the people thereof, respectively, shall then be in rebellion against the United States; and the fact that any State or the people thereof shall on that day be in good faith represented in the Congress of the United States by members chosen thereto at elections wherein a majority of the qualified voters of such States shall have participated shall, in the absence of strong countervailing testimony, be deemed conclusive evidence that such State and the people thereof are not then in rebellion against the United States.'

Now, therefore, I, Abraham Lincoln, President of the United States, by virtue of the power in me vested as Commander-in-Chief of the Army and Navy of the United States in time of actual armed rebellion against the authority and government of the United States, and as a fit and necessary war measure for suppressing said rebellion, do, on this 1st day of January, A.D. 1863, and in accordance with my purpose so to do, publicly proclaimed for the full period of one hundred days from the first day above mentioned, order and designate as the States and parts of States wherein the people thereof, respectively, are this day in rebellion against the United States the following, to wit:

Arkansas, Texas, Louisiana (except the parishes of St. Bernard, Plaquemines, Jefferson, St. John, St. Charles, St. James, Ascension, Assumption, Terrebonne, Lafourche, St. Mary, St. Martin, and Orleans, including the city of New Orleans), Mississippi, Alabama, Florida, Georgia, South Carolina, North Carolina, and Virginia (except the forty-eight counties designated as West Virginia, and also the counties of Berkeley, Accomac, Northhampton,

Elizabeth City, York, Princess Anne, and Norfolk, including the cities of Norfolk and Portsmouth), and which excepted parts are for the present left precisely as if this proclamation were not issued.

And by virtue of the power and for the purpose aforesaid, I do order and declare that all persons held as slaves within said designated States and parts of States are, and henceforward shall be, free; and that the Executive Government of the United States, including the military and naval authorities thereof, will recognize and maintain the freedom of said persons.

And I hereby enjoin upon the people so declared to be free to abstain from all violence, unless in necessary self-defense; and I recommend to them that, in all cases when allowed, they labor faithfully for reasonable wages.

And I further declare and make known that such persons of suitable condition will be received into the armed service of the United States to garrison forts, positions, stations, and other places, and to man vessels of all sorts in said service.

And upon this act, sincerely believed to be an act of justice, warranted by the Constitution upon military necessity, I invoke the considerate judgment of mankind and the gracious favor of Almighty God.

[From 'The Emancipation Proclamation, January 1, 1863,' in Henry Steele Commager (ed.), *Documents of American History* (6th edn, New York: Appleton-Century-Crofts, 1958), 420–1.]

184   The Thirteenth Amendment

Art. XIII—Dec. 18, 1865

Sec. 1. Neither slavery nor involuntary servitude, except as a punishment for crime whereof the party shall have been duly convicted, shall exist within the United States, or any place subject to their jurisdiction.

Sec. 2. Congress shall have power to enforce this article by appropriate legislation.

[From Article XIII, December 18, 1865, in Henry Steele Commager (ed.), *Documents of American History* (6th edn, New York: Appleton-Century-Crofts, 1958), 147.]

Slavery, however complex its internal variation within the Americas, had been at its core a system of labor discipline. Africans had been forcibly transported to the New World in order to labor under compulsion. Once they and their descendants had escaped from that system of coercion, the question of what would—or could—come in its wake took on great urgency.

For those who commanded resources in society, the question had a particular meaning: if staple production was to be maintained, some scheme to secure reliable access to labor had to be put in place. But the range of possibilities was relatively broad: there were precedents in most agrarian societies for wage labor and tenantry, labor rents and share rents, sharecropping and smallholding. Land could be allocated to or withheld from the former slaves; labor could be compensated in money or goods; wages could be paid by the day, the task, the week, or the year. Contracts could be for varying lengths of time and could be written, oral, or customary. As employers sought strategies that would ensure their continued control, policy makers debated the implications of juridical freedom in the sphere of production and pondered the precise meaning of the concept of 'free labor'.

For those who had been slaves and who did not command substantial material resources, the question of the nature of free labor had a special significance and urgency. Not only material well-being but social and cultural life and the possibility of political voice were at stake. Recent research has made it clear that former slaves throughout the Americas sought access to productive resources and deployed whatever power they could to try to shape both the character of their labor and the social relations in which their work was embedded.

One way of discerning patterns within this complex struggle is to examine its unfolding in areas that shared a concentration on the same crop—in this case, the cane regions of Louisiana, Cuba, and Brazil. The perishability of cane put a premium on reliable access to a disciplined seasonal work force, and sugar production increasingly required large-scale units for profitable processing. All sugar producers faced similar uncertainties in markets and instabilities in prices. But the patterns of labor that emerged in these three societies varied. The specific features of cane as a crop and sugar as a commodity seem to have constrained, but not determined, the organization of work and the evolution of labor relations. These variations represent something more than different strategies adopted by planters under different circumstances. Sugar plantation societies had long been a locus not only of coerced production and exceptionally high mortality but also of communities of enslaved workers capable of rebellion and day-to-day negotiation. Moreover, the process of emancipation had in nearly every instance witnessed important initiatives taken by those who were enslaved. In each of the cases examined here, planters' class power was reconstructed—but the work relations on which it rested were shaped by the assertions and challenges of former slaves and other rural workers.

Exploring this contest in comparative perspective reveals the importance of a shared reliance on a crop with specific characteristics but also affords evidence against the 'crop determinism' that sugar sometimes inspires. Such comparison illuminates the ways in which work relations in sugar conditioned the character of collective action in each region. The process was a reciprocal one: individual and collective challenges by former slaves helped to determine the disposition of resources and the patterns of work that emerged, and the composition of the labor force and the organization of work in turn shaped the possibilities for further collective action. Thus the dramatic strikes in the 1870s and 1880s in Louisiana, and the cross-racial anti-colonial insurgency that shook Cuba from 1895 to 1898, reflected the specific ways in which many of their participants earned a livelihood in the world of cane.

[. . .]

Years after emancipation, in Cuba, Brazil, and Louisiana, impoverished workers still headed into the fields at first light to carry out the backbreaking work of cutting, lifting, and hauling sugar cane. But the mechanisms by which their labor was elicited, and the class relations in which their work was embedded, had changed markedly since the time of slavery. Moreover, despite the physical similarity of their situations, those who grew and cut cane in Cuba, Brazil, and Louisiana were differently situated in terms of access to productive and organizational resources. Equally important, the social relations among workers and between workers and employers reflected very different constructions of race and politics.

It seems clear that the production of sugar does impose certain limits on the kinds of labor systems that can be adopted: cutting and processing must be closely coordinated to prevent loss of sucrose in the cane, and the peak demand for labor during harvest must be met reliably in order to get the cane in before the rains (in Cuba) or frost (in Louisiana). As one economist has noted, a given staple crop, while not determining the socio-political environment, 'will imprint certain patterns of its own on whatever environment happens to be around'. The variety of labor relations associated with sugar production in the decades after the end of slavery suggests that the 'imprinting' process is a complex one. Indeed, however great the temptation to personify sugar itself, it is the worker and the planter who remain central to the story.

[. . .]

In each area, the state showed differing degrees of willingness and capacity to intervene, as well as different policies on the question of labor control. In Louisiana, the Union Army reinforced early efforts to impose annual contracts, but the turmoil of occupation and Reconstruction opened up some space for the freed people to gain ground in their struggle with former masters. Later, strikebreaking was endorsed by the state militia, and waves of repression and disenfranchisement completed the task of silencing workers in the cane. In Cuba, the colonial state's reluctance to provoke opposition restrained efforts at direct labor control, and its encouragement of Spanish immigration helped to guarantee a multi-ethnic rural labor force. But the authoritarian conduct of Spanish officials in the island strengthened Cuban nationalism, reinforcing the separatist ideology that brought black, white, and mulatto Cubans together to challenge colonial domination.

In northeastern Brazil, landholders were prepared to undertake the disciplining of labor on their own terms. The demand for labor, at least in Pernambuco, was if anything in decline as modern equipment increased productivity in a period of limited markets for Brazilian sugar. Northeastern workers thus did not have the leverage that periodic labor shortages in an expanding sugar industry afforded their Cuban counterparts. Stagnation in output was matched by relative stability in social relations. In moments of crisis, however, like the mass movement under the leadership of Antônio Conselheiro, military force was made available to restore the class power of landowners and eliminate the challenge to established social relations.

Planters thus made choices in response to evolving markets, available technology, and the possibility of employing resources from the state. At the same time, however, they had to contend with the efforts of the newly freed to achieve security, voice, and a degree of proprietorship. There would be no cane planted, weeded, cut, or ground without some form of compliance from the workers themselves. In Louisiana, the freed people's dream of proprietorship was thwarted, but repeated strikes raised wages above their immediate postwar levels. In Cuba, a series of tenacious cross-racial movements encompassing sugar workers made it imprudent for any imperial power—Spain or the United States—to attempt direct coercion on the sugar plantations. Spanish forces attempting to take over estates in 1896 were often met with gunfire; employers hoping to pay in scrip in 1901 often found themselves bereft of workers. Even in Brazil, where the continuities of control seem so thoroughgoing, rights to land and subsistence were deeply entrenched, and the final dispossession of the labor force in sugar awaited the middle of the twentieth century.

[From 'Defining the Boundaries of Freedom on the World of Cane: Cuba, Brazil, and Louisiana after Emancipation,' *American Historical Review* 99 (1994), 70–2, 98–102.]

Slavery by any other name

If you thought slavery was abolished in eighteen something or other, think again. Countless slaves have been freed since the days of William Wilberforce, the nineteenth-century British abolitionist. Slavery is illegal everywhere. Yet Britain's Anti-Slavery Society (ASS), the United Nations Working Group on Slavery, and national groups such as India's Bonded Liberation Front, say they have hard evidence that slavery is entrenched in Asia, Africa and Latin America.

Really? Well, it depends how you define slavery. For these groups the term covers more than the buying and selling of human beings—the chattel slavery of the past. The 1956 UN Supplementary Convention on Slavery considers anyone to be a slave if he is unable to withdraw his labour voluntarily. Into that category fall:

- bonded labourers who work for nothing to pay off money-lenders;
- serfs who cannot leave the agricultural estates where they work;
- exploited children who are cut off from their families to work long hours for a pittance or (more often) nothing.

Across the globe there are at least 200m such 'slaves', and probably many more. Most live in conditions so abject that there is little to distinguish them from the most wretched chattel slaves of the past.

Chattel slavery persists here and there in the Arabian peninsula, where slavery was not abolished officially until the 1960s and 1970s. From Amazonia come chilling reports of Indians enslaved by ranchers or miners. In Sudan chattel slavery is spreading fast, as a consequence of the civil war between the black Christian and pagan southerners and the Arab, Muslim north.

Arab tribal militias formed and armed by the northern-dominated government are trafficking in slaves from the southern Dinka tribe. Dinka children and women seized in raids are either kept by the militias or sold north. In February 1988 a Dinka child could be bought for $90; so many slaves are available that the price has now fallen to $15. The government has yet to keep a promise, made a year ago, to let the ASS investigate.

Perpetual bondage often follows when someone agrees to work to pay off a loan carrying a usurious interest rate only to find himself forever in debt. Latin America has at least 8m bonded labourers, Africa millions more. But the heart of the problem is in Asia, especially India. The Indian government admits to fewer than 200,000 bonded labourers; the ASS puts the number at more than 5m. They are found in road-building gangs, in quarries and brick-works, on plantations and in sweatshops.

Wives and children are frequently entrapped. Children can inherit the debts and the bondage of their parents: in the stone quarries outside Delhi, three generations of bonded labourers work side by side. Bonded labourers often come from minority groups: 80 per cent of India's bonded labourers are drawn from tribes or 'scheduled castes' ('untouchables') whose psycho-logical subservience helps to perpetuate their enslavement. In Malaysia's palm-oil and rubber plantations the labourers are Tamils, descendants of low-caste workers originally imported from India. The creditors who run the bondage schemes are often the local landowners, magistrates or paymasters of political parties.

The Bonded Liberation Front estimates that there are 25m bonded children in India, Pakistan, Bangladesh, Nepal and Sri Lanka. In India alone more than 50m child labourers work in conditions often indistinguishable from slavery. Throughout the third world—in the Philippines sweatshops, in the Moroccan and Turkish carpet industries, in the Latin American drugs business, in Sri Lanka's male-prostitute trade, in the tea plantations—child workers are cheap, exploitable and expendable.

The child-slaves of India's Uttar Pradesh carpet belt, around the holy city of Varanasi (Benares), are the subject of a detailed ASS study. The region's 55,000 looms employ more than 100,000 boys, many of them only six years old; 15 per cent of them are bonded labourers 'sold' to the loom-owners by their parents. Small boys are said to tie the finest knots, but the real reason they are used is that they are cheap. They work 12 hours a day, six or seven days a week, sleeping at their looms, for the equivalent of 40 cents a week. They suffer malnutrition, poor eyesight, bone deformation and respiratory diseases.

There are hundreds of thousands of child slaves in Thailand, many of them in child prostitution. The pretty girls and boys end up in the sex trade, the not-so-pretty in back-street sweatshops. When they burn out in their late teens, they are thrown out. Some are kidnapped from the countryside or from Bangkok's large population of street children. Many more are 'bought' from their parents in the backward north-east and sold to employers. The going rate for a child in Bangkok is $130.

Debt bondage and child slavery are sometimes viewed as a distasteful but inevitable feature of a developing economy. Apologists argue that the cheap labour provided by children and bonded workers helps economic develop-ment. But child labourers grow up unhealthy and ill educated. The use of child labour also means fewer adults in work.

Putting an end to slavery is more than a matter of passing laws. Abolition means tackling the poverty that forces parents to sell off their children. It also means education, particularly where slavery is entrenched in local cultures and economies sometimes by the psychological subservience of the victims themselves. Those working to end the scourge often face official connivance or participation. The Thai authorities, for example, are less than enthusiastic about stopping the child prostitution that boosts Thailand's tourist industry.

One experimental venture between the Uttar Pradesh state government, a group of voluntary organisations and local carpet maufacturers aims to end child slavery in the carpet belt. Project Mala plans to break the cycle of exploitation by offering local children education, training, medical care and an adequate diet. Schools are being set up, each serving a cluster of villages. Children attending school will be taught a trade, and paid a small wage to replace the pittance they would have earned at the loom. The hope is that Project Mala will serve as a model for similar schemes in India and, perhaps, in other countries as well.

[From 'Slavery by Any Other Name,' *The Economist* (January 6, 1997), 42.]

Bibliography

As befits an institution that has long existed and occurred in most parts of the world, there is an enormous scholarly literature on the subject of slavery. The most recent edition of Joseph Miller's bibliography of twentieth-century writings on slavery worldwide includes entries for more than 14,000 books and articles. For this reason we have generally limited our entries to the last quarter of the twentieth century, and only a limited number of books for that period. Further reference is made to the selections in this volume.

The most complete bibliography on slavery is Joseph C. Miller (ed.), *Slavery and Slaving in World History, A Bibliography* (Millwood, NY: Kraus International Publishers, 1999) updated annually in *Slavery and Abolition*.

In recent years there have been published three encyclopedias dealing with slavery: Seymour Drescher and Stanley Engerman (eds.), *A Historical Guide to World Slavery* (New York: Oxford University Press, 1998); Paul Finkelman and Joseph C. Miller (eds.), *Macmillan Encyclopedia of World Slavery* (New York: Macmillan Reference USA, 1998); and Junius P. Rodriguez (ed.), *The Historical Encyclopedia of World Slavery* (Santa Barbara, CA: ABC-CLIO, 1997).

SLAVERY IN WORLD PERSPECTIVE

David Brion Davis, *Slavery and Human Progress* (New York: Oxford University Press, 1984), Orlando Patterson, *Slavery and Social Death* (Cambridge, MA: Harvard University Press, 1982), and Claude Meillassoux, *The Anthropology of Slavery* (Chicago: University of Chicago Press, 1991).

THE ANCIENT WORLD: GREEK AND ROMAN SLAVERY

Thomas Weidemann, *Greek and Roman Slavery* (Baltimore: Johns Hopkins University Press, 1981), Keith Bradley, *Slaves and Masters in the Roman Empire* (New York: Oxford University Press, 1987), Keith Bradley, *Slavery and Society at Rome* (Cambridge: Cambridge University Press, 1994), Keith Hopkins, *Conquerors and Slaves* (Cambridge: Cambridge University Press, 1978), Moses I. Finley, *Ancient Slavery and Modern Ideology* (New York: Viking Press, 1980), N. R. E. Fisher, *Slavery in Classical Greece* (London, Bristol Classical Press, 1993), and G. E. M. de Ste. Croix, *The Class Struggle in the Ancient Greek World* (Ithaca, NY: Cornell University Press, 1980).

SLAVERY IN EUROPE IN THE MEDIEVAL PERIOD

Pierre Bonnassie, *From Slavery to Feudalism in Southwestern Europe* (Cambridge: Cambridge University Press, 1991), Marc Bloch, *Slavery and Serfdom in the Middle Ages* (Berkeley: University of California Press, 1975), Richard Hellie, *Slavery in Russia*

(Chicago: University of Chicago Press, 1982), Ruth Mazo Karras, *Slavery and Society in Medieval Scandinavia* (New Haven: Yale University Press, 1988), William D. Phillips Jr., *Slavery from Roman Times to the Early Transatlantic Trade* (Minneapolis: University of Minnesota Press, 1985), and David A. E. Pelteret, *Slavery in Early Mediaeval England* (Woodbridge: Boydell Press, 1995).

SLAVERY IN THE MODERN WORLD

David Brion Davis, *The Problem of Slavery in Western Culture* (Ithaca, NY: Cornell University Press, 1966), Robin Blackburn, *The Making of New World Slavery* (London: Verso, 1997), David Eltis, *The Rise of African Slavery in the Americas* (Cambridge: Cambridge University Press, 2000), Robin Blackburn, *The Overthrow of Colonial Slavery, 1776–1848* (London: Verso, 1988), Barbara L. Solow (ed.), *Slavery and the Rise of the Atlantic System* (Cambridge: Cambridge University Press, 1992), David Brion Davis, *The Problem of Slavery in the Age of Revolution, 1770–1823* (Ithaca, NY: Cornell University Press, 1975), Herbert S. Klein, *African Slavery in Latin America and the Caribbean* (New York: Oxford University Press, 1986), Kenneth Kiple, *The Caribbean Slave* (Cambridge: Cambridge University Press, 1984), and Richard Sheridan, *Sugar and Slavery* (Baltimore: Johns Hopkins University Press, 1974).

THE TRADE IN SLAVES

Johannes Postma, *The Dutch in the Atlantic Slave Trade, 1600–1815* (Cambridge: Cambridge University Press, 1990), Herbert S. Klein, *The Atlantic Slave Trade* (Cambridge: Cambridge University Press, 1999), and Philip D. Curtin, *The Atlantic Slave Trade: A Census* (Madison, WI: University of Wisconsin Press, 1969).

SLAVERY AND ABOLITION IN THE AMERICAS

BRITISH: Michael Craton, *Searching for the Invisible Man* (Cambridge MA: Harvard University Press, 1978), Eric Williams, *Capitalism and Slavery* (Chapel Hill: University of North Carolina Press, 1944), Richard S. Dunn, *Sugar and Slaves* (Chapel Hill: University of North Carolina Press, 1974), Seymour Drescher, *Capitalism and Antislavery* (Oxford: Oxford University Press, 1986), Michael Craton, *Testing the Chains* (Ithaca, NY: Cornell University Press, 1982), Howard Temperley, *British Antislavery, 1833–1870* (Columbia: University of South Carolina Press, 1972), William A. Green, *British Slave Emancipation* (Oxford: Clarendon Press, 1976), and B. W. Higman, *Slave Populations of the British Caribbean, 1807–1834* (Baltimore: Johns Hopkins University Press, 1984).

SPANISH: Robert L. Paquette, *Sugar is Made with Blood* (Middletown, CT: Wesleyan University Press, 1988), Rebecca J. Scott, *Slave Emancipation in Cuba* (Princeton, Princeton University Press, 1985), Leslie B. Rout, *The African Experience in Spanish America* (Cambridge: Cambridge University Press, 1976), and Francisco Scarano, *Sugar and Slavery in Puerto Rico* (Madison, WI: University of Wisconsin Press, 1984).

FRENCH: Robert L. Stein, *The French Slave Trade in the Eighteenth Century* (Madison,

WI: University of Wisconsin Press, 1979); C. L. R. James, *The Black Jacobins* (2nd rev. edn, New York: Vintage Books, 1963); and Dale Tomich, *Slavery in the Circuit of Sugar* (Baltimore: Johns Hopkins University Press, 1990).

BRAZIL: Robert Edgar Conrad, *The Destruction of Brazilian Slavery* (Berkeley: University of California Press, 1972), Gilberto Freyre, *The Master and the Slaves* (2nd English edn., New York: Knopf, 1956), Mary Karasch, *Slave Life in Rio de Janeiro, 1800–1850* (Princeton: Princeton University Press, 1987), Katia M. de Queiro Mattoso, *To be a Slave in Brazil* (New Brunswick, NJ: Rutgers University Press, 1986), and Stuart B. Schwartz, *Sugar Plantations in the Formation of Brazilian Society* (Cambridge: Cambridge University Press, 1986).

UNITED STATES: Robert William Fogel, *Without Consent or Contract* (New York: Norton, 1989), Ira Berlin, *Many Thousand Gone* (Cambridge, MA: Harvard University Press, 1999), Herbert G. Guman, *The Black Family in Slavery and Freedom, 1750–1925* (New York: Pantheon, 1976), Brenda E. Stevenson, *Life in Black and White* (New York: Oxford University Press, 1992), Edmund Morgan, *American Slavery, American Freedom* (New York: Norton, 1975), Winthrop D. Jordan, *White Over Black* (Chapel Hill: University of North Carolina Press, 1968), Elizabeth Fox-Genovese, *Within the Plantation Household* (Chapel Hill: University of North Carolina Press, 1988), Eugene D. Genovese, *Roll, Jordan, Roll* (New York: Pantheon, 1974), Robert W. Fogel and Stanley L. Engerman, *Time on the Cross* (Boston: Little, Brown, 1974), Philip Morgan, *Slave Counterpoint* (Chapel Hill: University of North Carolina Press, 1998), Michael Tadman, *Speculators and Slaves* (Madison, WI: University of Wisconsin Press, 1989), Peter Kolchin, *American Slavery, 1619–1877* (New York: Hill and Wang, 1993), and Claudia Goldin, *Urban Slavery in the American South, 1820–1860* (Chicago: University of Chicago Press: 1976).

ASIAN SLAVERY

Bernard Lewis, *Race and Slavery in the Middle East* (New York: Oxford University Press, 1990), Anthony Reid (ed.), *Slavery, Bondage, and Dependency in Southeast Asia* (New York: St. Martin's Press, 1977), and James Watson (ed.), *Asian and African Systems of Slavery* (Oxford: Basil Blackwell, 1980).

AFRICAN SLAVERY

John Thornton, *Africa and Africans in the Making of the Atlantic World, 1400–1680* (2nd edn. Cambridge: Cambridge University Press, 1998), Frederick Cooper, *Plantation Slavery on the East Coast of Africa* (New Haven: Yale University Press, 1977), Paul E. Lovejoy, *Transformations in Slavery* (Cambridge: Cambridge University Press, 1983), Suzanne Miers and Igor Kopytoff (eds.), *Slavery in Africa* (Madison, WI: University of Wisconsin Press, 1977), Robert C. H. Shell, *Children of Bondage* (Hanover, NH: University Press of New England, 1994), Nigel Worden, *Slavery in Dutch South Africa* (Cambridge: Cambridge University Press, 1985), Martin Klein (ed.), *Breaking the Chains* (Madison, WI: University of Wisconsin Press, 1993), and Suzanne Miers and Richard Roberts (eds.), *The End of Slavery in Africa* (Madison, WI: University of Wisconsin Press, 1988).

Biographical Notes

THOMAS AFFLECK (1812–68) migrated from Scotland to the United States in 1832 and became a successful planter in Mississippi and Texas, and a popular publisher of southern agricultural almanacs and account books.

G. A. AKINOLA teaches history at the University of Ibadan in Nigeria. He has published a number of articles on African history and the problems of nation-building in the *Journal of the Historical Society of Nigeria*.

HERBERT APTHEKER, a Marxist intellectual and political activist, has written dozens of books on the African-American experience and has edited a multi-volume collection of the correspondence of W. E. B. Du Bois. His *American Negro Slave Revolts* (1943), was a path-breaking history of slave resistance in the United States.

ARISTOTLE (384–322 BC), Ancient Greek philosopher, student of Plato in Athens, and author of numerous works on all aspects of philosophy, including *Politics*, *Metaphysics*, and the *Nicomachean Ethics*.

ST AUGUSTINE (354–430) was one of Christendom's most influential theologians. Born in North Africa, he charted his spiritual journey in the *Confessions* and subsequently elaborated on doctrinal matters in *The City of God* (413–26), a classic of Western civilization.

ST BALTHILD (d. 680), wife and mother of three Frankish Kings of Saxon birth, was linked with an attempt to put down slavery.

FRÉDÉRIC BASTIAT (1801–50) was a French political economist whose published works were in favor of laissez-faire and free trade.

SIR WILLIAM BLACKSTONE (1723–80) was an English jurist, author of the four-volume *Commentaries on the Laws of England* (1765–69), long the leading English language work on understanding and interpreting the law.

HENRY BLEBY (1830–82) lived more than a decade in Jamaica as an antislavery Methodist missionary, and his conversation with a jailed Samuel Sharpe, one of the leaders of the 1831 rebellion, was recounted in *Death Struggles of Slavery* (1853).

JEROME BLUM (1913–93), formerly Professor of History at Princeton University, was author of several major works on the Russian and European peasantry and serfdom.

JEAN BODIN (c.1530–96) was a French philosopher whose published works dealt mainly with domestic and international political matters.

PIERRE BONNASSIE is Professor of Medieval History at the University of Toulouse and is the author of *From Slavery to Feudalism in South-Western Europe* (1991) and other works on slavery in early medieval Europe.

JAMES BOSWELL (1740–95) was a biographer and author of the *Life of Samuel Johnson* (1791). He was an apologist for the continuation of the slave trade.

SIR THOMAS FOWELL BUXTON (1786–1845) was a leading abolitionist in the British Parliament and author of *The African Slave Trade and its Remedy* (1839).

THOMAS CARLYLE (1795–1881), essayist and historian, was author of 'Occasional Discourse on the Nigger Question,' published in *Fraser's Magazine* in 1849, a racialist attack on philanthropic emancipation.

YEN CHING-HWANG is Associate Professor of History at the University of Adelaide, and author of several books on the overseas Chinese.

CICERO (106–43 BC) was a Roman orator, political figure, and author of several works, including *De Officiis*.

T. R. R. COBB (1823–62) was a Georgian lawyer, secessionist, and Confederate congressman who wrote *An Inquiry into the Law of Negro Slavery* (1858).

ROBERT CONRAD, previously Professor of History at the University of Illinois in Chicago, has written and edited several books on the Brazilian slave trade and slavery.

OLIVIA REMIE CONSTABLE is Associate Professor of History at the University of Notre Dame. Her research interest is medieval Iberia and her major publication is *Trade and Traders in Muslim Spain* (1994).

MICHAEL CRATON is Distinguished Professor of History Emeritus at the University of Waterloo. He has published several books on Caribbean slavery, including *Testing the Chains: Resistance to Slavery in the British West Indies* (1982) and *Empire, Enslavement and Freedom in the Caribbean* (1997).

OTTOBAH CUGOANO (1757–1791) was an Afro-Briton and author of *Thoughts and Sentiments on the Evil and Wicked Traffic of the Slavery and Commerce of the Human Species, Humbly Submitted to the Inhabitants of Great Britain by Ottobah Cugoano, A Native of Africa* (1787).

PHILIP D. CURTIN, Herbert Baxter Adams Professor of History Emeritus at The Johns Hopkins University, is author of *The Image of Africa* (1964), *The Atlantic Slave Trade: A Census* (1969), and numerous other works on the history of Africa and Atlantic history.

DAVID BRION DAVIS is Sterling Professor of History at Yale University and the author of several prizewinning books on modern slavery and abolition.

GABRIEL DEBIEN (1906–90), a French historian, was one of the foremost authorities on the history of plantation slavery in the French Caribbean. He wrote scores of books and articles, including, most notably, *Les esclaves aux Antilles français* (1974).

DENIS DIDEROT (1713–84) was a French intellectual and editor of the rewritten version of the *Encyclopédie*, which was a political tract as well as a collection of knowledge.

EVSEY D. DOMAR (1914–97), formerly Professor of Economics at MIT, was the author of important essays on the theory of economic growth, Russian economics, slavery, and serfdom.

ELIZABETH DONNAN (1883–1955), was editor of *Documents Illustrative of the History of the Slave Trade* (1930–5), and other historical works.

FREDERICK DOUGLASS (1818–95), born into slavery on a Maryland plantation, escaped his bondage in 1838. He became the most prominent black abolitionist in the antebellum United States, publishing two antislavery newspapers and three autobiographies, including, *My Bondage and My Freedom* (1855).

SEYMOUR DRESCHER, University Professor of History and Professor of Sociology at the University of Pittsburgh, is the author of several books on slavery and abolition, most recently *From Slavery to Freedom* (1999).

DAVID ELTIS is Professor of History at Queen's University, Kingston, Ontario. His major publications include *Economic Growth and the Ending of the Transatlantic Slave*

Trade (1987) and *The Rise of African Slavery in the Americas* (2000), and he is a co-preparer of the Du Bois Institute database on the Atlantic Slave Trade.

STANLEY L. ENGERMAN, John H. Munro Professor of Economics and Professor of History at the University of Rochester, is co-author of *Time on the Cross* (1974) and co-editor of *A Historical Guide to World Slavery* (1998).

OLAUDAH EQUIANO [or Gustavus Vassa] (1745–97), Afro-Briton, was author of *The Interesting Narrative of the Life of Olaudah Equiano, or Gustavus Vassa, Written by Himself* (1789).

SIR MOSES I. FINLEY (1912–86) was born in the United States and emigrated to England, where he became Professor of Ancient History at the University of Cambridge. He wrote numerous books on the ancient world, including *The Ancient Economy* (1973) and *Ancient Slavery and Modern Ideology* (1980).

ROBERT WILLIAM FOGEL is Charles Walgreen Distinguished Professor of American Institutions and Director of the Center for Population Economics at the University of Chicago School of Business. He was co-winner of the Nobel Prize in Economic Science in 1993.

ELIZABETH FOX-GENOVESE is the Elenore Raoul Professor of the Humanities at Emory University and founder of its women's studies program. Her many publications include *Within the Plantation Household: Black and White Women of the Old South* (1988).

DR LOUIS FRANK (1761–1825) was a French physician who was in Egypt from 1797 to 1801, where he observed the operations of the slave trade. He was later a physician in Italy, France, Corfu, and Austria.

PAUL FREEDMAN is Professor of History at Yale University and has published several books on peasants in medieval Europe, including *The Origins of Peasant Servitude in Medieval Catalonia* (1991).

GILBERTO FREYRE (1900–87), a Brazilian anthropologist, was the twentieth century's most influential interpreter of the history of Brazilian slavery and race relations. His most famous books are *Casa grande e senzala* (*The Masters and the Slaves*) (1933), and *Sobrados e mucambos* (*The Mansions and the Shanties*) (1936).

DAVID W. GALENSON is Professor of Economics at the University of Chicago and author of *White Servitude in Colonial America: An Economic Analysis* (1981) and *Traders, Planters, and Slaves: Market Behavior in Early English America* (1986).

WILLIAM LLOYD GARRISON (1805–79) was a leading American abolitionist and publisher of an abolitionist newspaper, *The Liberator*, begun in 1831.

DAVID BARRY GASPAR is Professor of History and Director of the African and African-American Studies Program at Duke University. His major publications include *Bondmen & Rebels: A Study of Master-Slave Relations in Antigua* (1985).

DAVID GEGGUS is Professor of History at the University of Florida. The author of numerous books and articles on slavery in the Caribbean, he has, most recently, co-edited (with David Barry Gaspar) *A Turbulent Time: The French Revolution and the Greater Caribbean* (1997).

EUGENE D. GENOVESE, now retired from teaching and living in Atlanta, has written numerous important works on US slavery, including *Roll, Jordan, Roll: The World the Slaves Made* (1974) and, most recently, *A Consuming Fire: The Fall of the Confederacy in the Mind of the White Christian South* (1998).

JONATHON GLASSMAN is Associate Professor of History at Northwestern University.

His book *Feasts and Riot: Revelry, Rebellion, and Popular Consciousness on the Swahili Coast, 1856–1888* (1995) won the Herskovits Award of the African Studies Association.

DOUGLAS HALL was the long-time Professor of History at the University of the West Indies (Jamaica). He is the author of several books and numerous articles on the history of Jamaica and on the British West Indies. After his retirement he authored *In Miserable Slavery* (1989) based on the diaries of Thomas Thistlewood.

SAMUEL HAMBLETON (1777–1851) served as a purser in the United States Navy, and was stationed in New Orleans at the time of the Louisiana slave revolt of 1811.

JAMES HENRY HAMMOND (1807–64) was a prominent South Carolinian planter and politician, noted for writing several tracts in defense of slavery. In 1831 he owned a large cotton plantation along the Savannah River, which at the time of his death had about 300 slaves.

RICHARD HELLIE is Professor of History at the University of Chicago. His major publications include *Slavery in Russia, 1450–1725* (1982) and *The Economy and Material Culture of Russia, 1600–1725* (1999).

THOMAS W. HIGGINSON (1823–1911) was a Massachusetts-born minister, active in the antislavery movement, and, during the Civil War, commanded the first regiment composed of former slaves.

BARRY W. HIGMAN was long-time Professor of History of the University of the West Indies (Jamaica) and is currently Professor in the History Program at the Research School of Social Sciences of the Australia National University. He has written extensively on the history and demography of the British West Indies.

THOMAS HOBBES (1588–1679) was a seminal figure in the development of modern political philosophy. His magnum opus, *Leviathan* (1651), influenced by the English civil wars, attempted to establish a secular, materialist justification for absolute monarchy.

C. L. R. JAMES (1901–89), born in Trinidad, was one of the more prominent Marxist intellectuals and Pan-Africanists of the twentieth century. Among his prolific writings, *The Black Jacobins: Toussaint L'Ouverture and the San Domingo Revolution* (1938) stands as an epic account of the slave insurrection that created Haiti.

THOMAS JEFFERSON (1743–1826), Virginia-born, was the drafter of the Declaration of Independence, third President of the United States, and a founder of the University of Virginia.

JOHN JOHNSON was a British legal agent, hired by James B. Gordon, an absentee Scottish landlord, to investigate the management of his plantations in St. Kitts, Antigua, and St. Vincent. His meticulous reports, beginning in 1824, reside in a bound volume, part of the Beinecke Lesser Antilles Collection at Hamilton College.

SAMUEL JOHNSON (1709–84) was a celebrated English man of letters, immortalized in a biography written by his close friend James Boswell. His many writings, which span almost a half century, include *A Dictionary of the English Language* (1755).

WINTHROP D. JORDAN is William F. Winter Professor of History and Professor of Afro-American Studies at the University of Mississippi. His major publications include two prizewinning books: *White Over Black: American Attitudes Toward the Negro, 1550–1812* (1968) and *Tumult and Silence at Second Creek: An Inquiry into a Civil War Slave Conspiracy* (1993).

JUSTINIAN (c.482–565) was Emperor of Rome and responsible for the publication of works presenting all legal statutes and enactments of his time.

IMMANUEL KANT (1724–1804) was a major German philosopher of the idealist school, whose works include *Critique of Pure Reason* (1781), and *Critique of Practical Reason* (1788).

MARY KARASCH is Professor of History at Oakland University. Her *Slave Life in Rio de Janeiro, 1808–1850* (1987) won the Albert J. Beveridge Award of the American Historical Association.

RUTH MAZO KARRAS, Professor of History at the University of Minnesota, is the author of *Slavery and Society in Medieval Scandinavia* (1988).

VIRGINIA HIMMELSTEIB KING, co-author of *Another Dimension to the African Diaspora*, has used her knowledge as a nutritionist to co-author several articles with Kenneth Kiple on the history of black health and disease.

KENNETH F. KIPLE is Distinguished University Professor of History at Bowling Green State University. A leading authority on the history of disease, medicine, and nutrition, he has edited and written several books, including *The Cambridge World History of Human Disease* (1993), and was the author of *The Caribbean Slave: A Biological History* (1984).

HERBERT S. KLEIN, Professor of History at Columbia University, is author of numerous books and articles, including *Slavery in the Americas* (1967), *The Middle Passage* (1978), and *African Slavery in Latin America and the Caribbean* (1986).

MARTIN KLEIN is Professor of History Emeritus at the University of Toronto. He has written and edited several books on slavery and emancipation in Africa. His most recent book is *Slavery and Colonial Rule in French West Africa* (1998).

PETER KOLCHIN is Henry Clay Reed Professor of History at the University of Delaware. His books include *Unfree Labor: American Slavery and Russian Serfdom* (1987) and *American Slavery: 1619–1877* (1993).

IGOR KOPYTOFF is Professor of Anthropology at the University of Pennsylvania and has written widely on slavery and abolition in Africa.

ALFONS VAN DER KRAAN has taught at Murdoch University and written on the history of Bali.

ALLAN KULIKOFF is Professor of History at Northern Illinois University. His books include *Tobacco and Slaves: The Development of Southern Cultures in the Chesapeake, 1680–1800* (1986) and *The Agrarian Origins of American Capitalism* (1992).

JEAN-BAPTISTE LABAT was a Jesuit traveler in the Caribbean and author of *Voyages aux isles de l'Amerique* (172?).

JACQUELINE LECKIE is professor of anthropology at the University of Otago (New Zealand), co-author of *Labour in the South Pacific* (1990), and author of *To Labour with the State* (1997), on the Fiji Public Service Association.

BERNARD LEWIS is Cleveland E. Dodge Professor of Near Eastern Studies Emeritus at Princeton University and one of the foremost modern interpreters of the relations between Europe and the Muslim world. His many books include *Race and Slavery in the Middle East: A Historical Enquiry* (1990) and *The Middle East: A Brief History of the Last 2,000 Years* (1997).

ABRAHAM LINCOLN (1809–65) rose from relative obscurity as an Illinois lawyer and politician to become the sixteenth President of the United States. His actions in the Civil War led to the abolition of slavery in the United States.

TOUSSAINT L'OUVERTURE (1734?–1803) was born a slave on a sugar plantation in the French colony of Saint Domingue. Years before the outbreak of the slave revolution in 1791, he obtained his freedom and although he did not immediately join the rebel forces, he eventually emerged as their towering military leader and the architect of the Haitian nation.

PAUL E. LOVEJOY, Professor of History at the University of Wisconsin, is author of *Transformations in Slavery: A History of Slavery in Africa* (1983) and co-author of *Slow Death for Slavery: The Course of Abolition in Northern Nigeria 1897–1936* (1993).

PATRICK MANNING is Professor of History and African-American Studies at Northeastern University and author of several books on African economic history, including *Slavery and African Life* (1990).

JUAN FRANCISCO MANZANO (1799–1853), a Cuban poet, taught himself to read and write while serving elite families in Havana as a domestic slave. Intellectual white patrons, attracted by both his character and verse, persuaded him to write his autobiography and eventually raised the money to purchase his freedom in 1836.

KARL MARX (1818–83) was a German scholar whose major work was *Das Kapital*. He is generally regarded as the father of modern Communism.

CLAUDE MEILLASSOUX is Directeur Honoraire de Recherches at the Centre Nationale de la Recherche Scientifique in Paris. He is author of *The Anthropology of Slavery: The Womb of Iron and Gold* (1991).

HERMAN MERIVALE (1806–74) was an English economist who wrote about the nature of colonization, most importantly, *Lectures on Colonization and Colonies* (1861).

SUZANNE MIERS is Professor of History Emeritus at Ohio University and has written and co-edited several books on slavery and abolition in Africa including *Britain and the Ending of the Slave Trade* (1977).

JOHN STUART MILL (1806–73) was an English economist and philosopher whose published works include *Representative Government* (1861) and *Utilitarianism* (1861) as well as *Principles of Political Economy* (1848).

SIDNEY W. MINTZ is William L. Straus, Jr. Professor of Anthropology Emeritus at The Johns Hopkins University. He has written a number of influential works on the Atlantic world, including (with Richard Price) *The Birth of African-American Culture: An Anthropological Perspective* (1976) and *Sweetness and Power: The Place of Sugar in Modern History* (1985).

BARON DE MONTESQUIEU (1698–1755) was a major French philosopher, whose important work *De l'esprit des lois* (1748) provided numerous novel ideas debated by subsequent generations.

MÉDÉRIC LOUIS ÉLIE MOREAU DE SAINT-MÉRY (1750–1819) was a lawyer and early partisan of the French Revolution who served in the Constituent Assembly as a deputy from his native Martinique. He traveled widely in the Caribbean and published two multivolume works on the French colony of Saint Domingue based on years of residence there.

MANUEL MORENO FRAGINALS was born in Cuba and is currently Professor of History at Florida International University. He has written several books on slavery in Cuba, including one translated into English as *The Sugarmill* (1976).

EDMUND S. MORGAN is Sterling Professor of History Emeritus at Yale University. His many distinguished writings on the history of colonial and revolutionary America include the prizewinning books *American Slavery, American Freedom: The Ordeal of*

Colonial Virginia (1975) and *Inventing the People: The Rise of Popular Sovereignty in England and America* (1988).

PHILIP D. MORGAN is Professor of History at The Johns Hopkins University. His most recent book, winner of several prizes, is *Slave Counterpoint: Black Culture in the Eighteenth Century Chesapeake and Low Country* (1998).

THOMAS D. MORRIS is Professor of History at Portland State University and has published several books on the legal aspects of slavery, most recently *Southern Slavery and the Law, 1619–1860* (1996).

DAVID MURRAY is Professor of History at the University of Guelph and the author of *Odious Commerce: Britain, Spain, and the Abolition of the Cuban Slave Trade* (1980).

JOAQUIM NABUCO (1849–1910) was a Brazilian abolitionist and diplomat, part of Pernambuco's planter elite, Member of Parliament, and author of *O Abolicionismo* (1883).

JOHN NEWTON (1725–1807) was an Englishman who, after a career as a captain in the African slave trade, became an evangelist and the vicar of a church in London. He wrote many hymns (including the enduring 'Amazing Grace'), as well as works attacking the slave trade.

H. J. NIEBOER (1873–1920) was a Dutch ethnographer whose publication *Slavery as an Industrial System: Ethnological Researches* (1900) was the first systematic attempt to understand the origin of slavery from a global perspective.

FRIEDRICK WILHELM NIETZSCHE (1844–1900) was a German philosopher and iconoclast, whose writings were anti-Christian and developed the idea of the superman.

MARCHESA IRIS ORIGO (1902–88) was born in England, but spent most of her life in Italy. She published several books and memoirs, including a work about the wealthy fourteenth-century merchant Francesco di Marco Datini, entitled *The Merchant of Prato* (1957).

ROBERT L. PAQUETTE is Publius Virgilius Rogers Professor of American History at Hamilton College. His publications include *Sugar is Made with Blood* (1988).

ORLANDO PATTERSON is John Cowles Professor of Sociology at Harvard University. Born in Jamaica, he has written widely on slavery, race, racism, and the meaning of freedom.

DAVID A. E. PELTERET is on the staff of New College in the University of Toronto and is the author of *Slavery in Early Mediaeval England* (1995).

CHARLES PERRET (1768–1849) owned a sugar plantation in St. Charles Parish, Louisiana, with more than twenty slaves. When a major slave revolt swept the district in 1811, he participated as a militiaman in the revolt's suppression.

PLATO (*c.*427–347 BC) was a philosopher in ancient Greece and author of two major dialogues offering views on slavery, *The Republic* and *The Laws*.

PLUTARCH (*c.*46–*c.*120) was a Greek historian and moral philosopher. His fame derives in large part from *Bioi parallelio* (Parallel Lives), a collection of didactic essays on the lives of fifty notable Greeks and Romans.

RICHARD S. PRICE is Duane A. and Virginia S. Dittman Professor of American Studies, Anthropology, and History at the College of William and Mary. His prizewinning books include *First Time: The Historical Vision of an Afro-American People* (1983) and *Alabi's World* (1990).

MARY PRINCE (1788?–?), was born a slave and served a succession of masters in Bermuda, the Turks Islands, and Antigua. While attending the family of her

Antiguan master on a trip to London, she met Thomas Pringle, secretary of the London Anti-Slavery Society, who elicited her narrative, *The History of Mary Prince, A West Indian Slave Related By Herself*, which was first published in 1831.

RATHERIUS (887?–974), trained by Benedictine monks near his native Liege, was a reformist Catholic theologian who in 931 became Bishop of Verona. Among his collected writings, *Praeloquia* (935–937), stands out for its social and religious commentary.

JOÃO JOSÉ REIS teaches history at the Universidade Federal de Bahia in Brazil. His major publications include *Slave Rebellion in Brazil: The Muslim Uprising of 1835 in Bahia* (1986).

WALTER RODNEY (1942–74) was born in Guyana and was active politically there until killed. He was the author of several books on African slavery and the Guyanese working class.

EDMUND RUFFIN (1794–1865), a Virginian writer and secessionist, committed suicide in June 1865, unwilling to live under the US government. His diaries have been published in three volumes.

VICTOR SCHOELCHER (1804–93) was the principal French abolitionist in the Revolutionary Government of 1848 that decreed French slave emancipation and was later Senator in the Third French Republic.

STUART SCHWARTZ is Professor of History at Yale University. He has written several books on Brazilian and Latin American history, including *Sugar Plantations in the Formation of Brazilian Society: Bahia, 1550–1835* (1985).

JAMES SCOTT is Eugene Meyer Professor of Political Science and Anthropology at Yale University. His major publications include *Weapons of the Weak: Everyday Forms of Peasant Resistance* (1987) and *Domination and the Art of Resistance: The Hidden Transcript of Subordinate Groups* (1990).

REBECCA J. SCOTT is Professor of History at the University of Michigan and author of *Slave Emancipation in Cuba: The Transition to Free Labor* (1985).

ADAM SMITH (1723–90), was a Scottish economist whose book *The Wealth of Nations* has been regarded as the starting point of modern political economy and economic analysis.

EDWARD GEORGE GEOFFREY SMITH STANLEY, fourteenth Earl of Derby (1799–1869) was a Member of Parliament and mover of the Emancipation Bill for the abolition of slavery in the British Colonies in May 1833.

JOHN GABRIEL STEDMAN (1744–97), born in Holland, the son of a military officer, arrived in Surinam in 1773 as a captain in a corps of volunteer soldiers. After returning to Holland in 1777, he began a detailed narrative of his service in the Dutch plantation colony and his life there among the slaves that was first published in 1796.

SIR JAMES STEUART (1712–80) was a political economist, author of *An Inquiry into the Principles of Political Oeconomy, being an Essay on the Science of Domestic Policy of Free Nations . . .* (1770), acknowledged by Malthus as a predecessor of the latter's *Essay on Population*.

JARIR AL-TABARĪ (839–923), an Arab scholar, wrote *Ta'rikh al-rusul wa'l-muluk* (The History of Prophets and Kings), a monumental history of the Islamic world, when working and teaching in Baghdad, the center of Abbasid caliphate, during the Zanj revolt in 869.

TACITUS (56?–118) rose from minor administrative posts in the service of imperial Rome to become one of its most accomplished orators and perhaps its greatest historian. Only parts of his *Historiae* (Histories), which covers the years 69 to 96 from the rule of Galba to Domitian, have survived.

THOMAS THISTLEWOOD (1721–86) left England in 1750 to become an estate overseer in Jamaica and eventually a planter and slaveholder in his own right. He recorded details of his life on the island in numerous diaries, which survive in England in the Lincolnshire County Archives.

JOHN THORNTON, a specialist in the history of precolonial West Africa, is Professor of History at Millersville University of Pennsylvania. His major books include *The Kingdom of Kongo: Civil War and Transition, 1641–1718* (1983) and *Africa and Africans in the Formation of the Atlantic World, 1400–1800* (2nd edn., 1998).

ALEXIS DE TOCQUEVILLE (1805–59), French statesman, abolitionist, and political philosopher, was the author of *Democracy in America* (1835–40) and *The Old Regime and the Revolution* (1856).

NAT TURNER (1800–31), a highly intellectual field slave and Christian prophet from Southampton County, Virginia, led the bloodiest slave revolt in United States history. Turner's band, which, at it peak, numbered little more than sixty rebels, killed more than fifty whites; Turner and more than twenty of his followers were hanged or died during the revolt.

GEORGE F. TYSON, Jr., is a public historian in St. Thomas, US Virgin Islands, who has taught at the University of the Virgin Islands. He has written articles on the history of the Danish West Indies and edited a volume on Toussaint L'Ouverture (1973).

GONZALO FERNÁNDEZ DE OVIEDO Y VALDÉS (1478–1557), a Spanish official and author, participated in several expeditions to the Americas. His *Historia general y natural de las Indias*, the first part published in 1535, ranks as one of the most important chronicles of the first half of the century of Spain's discovery and settlement of the Indies.

ALDEN T. VAUGHAN, an authority on race relations in colonial America, is Professor of History Emeritus at Columbia University. His major books include *New England Frontier: Puritans and Indians, 1620–1675* (1965) and *Roots of American Racism: Essays on the Colonial Experience* (1995).

DENMARK VESEY (1767?–1822) purchased his freedom from bondage in Charleston, South Carolina in 1799 after winning a lottery. A gifted artisan and religious leader, he masterminded the most sophisticated and extensive plot against slavery in the history of the United States.

FRANÇOIS VOLTAIRE (1694–88) was a wide-ranging French writer, and author of *Candide* (1758) and many other political and philosophical works.

DAVID WALKER (1796–1830) a free person of color born in Wilmington, North Carolina, moved to Boston as a young adult and became a small shopkeeper as well as an antislavery activist. His *Appeal . . . to the Coloured Citizens of the World* (1829) is considered one of the founding documents of black nationalist thought in the United States.

EDWARD GIBBON WAKEFIELD (1796–1862) was an English economist whose books *A View of the Art of Colonization* (1849) and *A Letter from Sydney* (1829) helped to frame British colonial policy, particularly regarding Australia, in the nineteenth century.

JAMES L. WATSON, Fairbank Professor of Chinese Society and Professor of

Anthropology at Harvard University is editor of *Asian and African Systems of Slavery* (1980).

MAX WEBER (1864–1920) was a German economist and sociologist whose works include *The Protestant Ethic and the Spirit of Capitalism* (1904–5) and numerous books and essays on historical and sociological topics.

HARRIET WHITEHEAD was one of the daughters of Mrs. Catherine Whitehead, a slaveowner of Southampton County, Virginia. Catherine died during the Nat Turner revolt, along with her son, four daughters, and a grandchild, but Harriet was able to survive the uprising with some help from one of the family's slaves.

SAMUEL WILBERFORCE (1805–73), Bishop of Oxford and son of William Wilberforce, was a parliamentary leader of the British abolitionists.

ERIC WILLIAMS (1911–81) was born in Trinidad and received a Ph.D. at the University of Oxford. A revised version of his dissertation was published as *Capitalism and Slavery* (1944). He wrote several other books on Caribbean history and in 1964 became the first prime minister of the independent nation of Trinidad and Tobago.

XENOPHON (435–354 BC) was a Greek writer and military figure whose writings dealt with historical, political, philosophical, and economic issues.

LIEN-SHENG YANG (1914–90), a native of China, joined the faculty of Harvard University in 1947 and became Harvard-Yenching Professor of Chinese History. His major books include *Money and Credit in China: A Short History* (1952) and *Excursions in Sinology* (1969).

Acknowledgements

Affleck, Thomas, 'Duties of Overseers', in *Cotton Plantation Record and Account Book No. 3 Suitable for a Force of 120 Hands, or under* (New Orleans: B. M. Norman, 7th edn, 1857).

Akinola, G. A., 'Slavery and Slave Revolts in the Sultanate of Zanzibar in the Nineteenth Century', *Journal of the Historical Society of Nigeria 6* (1972).

Aptheker, Herbert, *American Negro Slave Revolts* (New York: International Publishers, 1970).

Aristotle, *The Complete Works of Aristotle*, ed. Jonathan Barnes (Princeton: Princeton University Press, 1994).

Aristotle, *The Nicomachean Ethics of Aristotle*, trs. David Ross (London: Oxford University Press, 1980).

Aristotle, *Oeconomica*, trs. C. Cyril Armstrong (Cambridge, MA: Harvard University Press, 1962).

Augustine, St, *The City of God*, translated by Marcus Dods (New York: The Modern Library, 1950).

Barnes, Jonathan (ed.), *The Complete Works of Aristotle* (Princeton: Princeton University Press, 1984).

Bastiat, Frederic, *Economic Sophisms*, trs. Arthur Goddard (New York: Foundation for Economic Education, 1964).

Beinecke Lesser Antilles Collection, 'Reports Relating to Mr. Gordon's Estates in the West Indies, 1824' (Hamilton College, Clinton, New York).

Blackstone, William, 'Of the Rights of Persons', in *Commentaries on the Laws of England: A Facsimile of the First Edition of 1756–1769* (Chicago: University of Chicago Press, 1979).

Bleby, Henry, *Death Struggles of Slavery: Being a Narrative of Facts and Incidents which Occurred in a British Colony, during Two Years Immediately Preceding Negro Emancipation* (Coconut Grove: Dewar's, 1972).

Blum, Jerome, *Lord and Peasant in Russia* (Princeton: Princeton University Press, 1961).

Bodin, Jean, *Six Books of the Commonwealth*, trs. M. J. Tooley (Oxford: Blackwell, 1955).

Bonnassie, Paul, *From Slavery to Feudalism in South-Western Europe* (Cambridge: Cambridge University Press, 1991).

Boswell, James, *Life of Johnson*, ed. George Birkbeck Hill (Oxford: Clarendon Press, 1934).

British Parliamentary Papers: Correspondence and Papers Relating to Slavery and the Abolition of the Slave Trade 1823–24 (Shannon: Irish University Press, 1969).

Broom, Herbert, 'Sommersett's Case 1772', in *Constitutional Law* (London: William Maxwell, 1866).

Buxton, Thomas Fowell, *The African Slave Trade and its Remedy* (London: Frank Cass, 1967).

Carlyle, Thomas, *The Negro Question*, ed. Eugene August (New York: Appleton-Century-Crofts, 1971).

Caron, Aimery, and Highfield, Arnold, 'The Danish Slave Code', in *The French Intervention in the St. John Slave Revolt of 1733–34*, Occasional Paper no. 7 (St. Thomas, V.I.: Bureaus of Libraries, Museums and Archaeological Services of Conservation and Cultural Affairs, 1981).

Chevalier, François (ed.), *Instrucciones a los hermanos Jesuitas administrados de hacienda: Manuscrito del siglo XVIII* (Mexico: Universidad Nacional Autonoma de Mexico, 1950). Translated by Evelyn Powell Jennings.

Ching-Hwang, Yen, *Coolies and Mandarins: China's Protection of Overseas Chinese during the Late Ch'ing Period (1851–1911)* (Singapore: Singapore University Press, 1985).

Cicero, *De Officiis*, trs. Walter Miller (Cambridge, MA: Harvard University Press, 1990).

Cobb, T. R. R., *An Inquiry into the Law of Negro Slavery in the United States of America: To which Is Attached a Historical Sketch of Slavery* (Savannah: W. T. William, 1858).

Commager, Henry Steele (ed.), *Documents of American History* (New York: Appleton-Century-Crofts, 6th edn, 1958).

Conrad, Robert E., *The Destruction of Brazilian Slavery 1850–1888* (Berkeley: University of California Press). Copyright © 1972.

Conrad, Robert E., *Children of God's Fire: A Documentary History of Black Slavery in Brazil* (Princeton: Princeton University Press, 1983).

Constable, Olivia Remie, *Trade and Traders in Muslim Spain: The Commercial Realignment of the Iberian Peninsula, 900–1500* (Cambridge: Cambridge University Press, 1994).

Craton, Michael, *Testing the Chains: Resistance to Slavery in the British West Indies* (Ithaca: Cornell University Press, 1982). Reprinted by permission of the publisher.

Cugoano, Ottobah, *Thoughts and Sentiments on the Evil of Slavery, 1787* (London: Dawsons, 1969).

Curtin, Philip D., 'The Abolition of the Slave Trade from Senegambia' in David Eltis and James Walvin eds., *The Abolition of the Atlantic Slave Trade* (Madison: University of Wisconsin Press, 1981). Copyright © 1981. Reprinted by permission of The University of Wisconsin Press.

Curtin, Philip D., *The Atlantic Slave Trade*. © 1969. Reprinted by permission of The University of Wisconsin Press.

Davis, David Brion, *The Problem of Slavery in the Age of Revolution 1770–1823* (Oxford: Oxford Universtiy Press, 1999), reprinted by permission of the author.

Debien, Gabriel, 'Assembleés nocturnes d'esclaves à Saint-Domingue (La Marmelade, 1786)', in *Annales historiques de la révolution française* 208 (April–June 1972). Translated by John Garrigus.

Diderot, Denis, *Encyclopédie* (1755 edn). Translated by Seymour Drescher.

Domar, Evsey, D., 'The Causes of Slavery or Serfdom: A Hypothesis', *Journal of Economic History* 30 (1970).

Donnan, Elizabeth, *Documents Illustrative of the Slave Trade to America* (New York: Octagon, 1969).

Douglass, Frederick, *My Bondage and My Freedom* (New York: Dover Publications, 1969).

Drescher, Seymour, *Capitalism and Antislavery: British Mobilization in Comparative Perspective* (New York: Oxford University Press, 1987).

Driver, G. R., and Miles, John C. (eds. and trs.), *The Babylonian Laws* (Oxford: Clarendon Press, 1955).

Eliot, Charles W. (ed.), 'The Liberties of the Massachusetts Collonie in New England, 1641', in *American Historical Documents 1000–1904* (New York: Collier, 1910).

Eltis, David, *Economic Growth and the Ending of the Atlantic Slave Trade*. Copyright © 1989 by Oxford University Press. Used by permission of Oxford University Press, Inc.

Eltis, David, 'Europeans and the Rise and Fall of African Slavery', in the American Historical Review 98 (December 1993). Reprinted by permission of The Trustees of Indiana University.

Eltis, David, 'The Volume of the Transatlantic Slave Trade: A Reassessment', *William and Mary Quarterly* 58 (2000). Reprinted by permission of the author.

Equiano, Olaudah, *The Interesting Narrative of the Life of Olaudah Equiano Written by Himself*, ed. Robert J. Allison (Boston: Bedford/St Martin's Press, 1995).

Escoto Papers, *Anonymous Report to Captain General Joaquín de Ezpeleta* (Escoto Papers, Box II, Houghton Library, Harvard University). Translated by Robert L. Paquette and Joseph Dorsay.

Ferguson, Moira (ed.), *A History of Mary Prince, a West Indian Slave* (Ann Arbor: The University of Michigan Press, 1993). Copyright © 1993 by The University of Michigan Press.

Finley, Moses I., *Ancient Slavery and Modern Ideology* (New York: Viking Press, 1980).

Fogel, Robert William, *Without Consent or Contract: The Rise and Fall of American Slavery*. Copyright © 1989 by Robert William Fogel. Used by permission of W. W. Norton & Company, Inc.

Fox-Genovese, Elizabeth, *Within the Plantation Household: Black and White Women of the Old South*. Copyright © 1988 by the University of North Carolina Press. Used by permission of the publisher.

Frank, Louis, 'Memoir on the Traffic in Negroes in Cairo and on the Illnesses to Which They Are Subject upon Arrival There', trs. Michel le Gall, in Shaun E. Marmon (ed.), *Slavery in the Islamic Middle East* (Princeton: Markus Wiener, 1999).

Freedman, Paul, *Peasant Servitude in Medieval Catalonia* (Cambridge: Cambridge University Press, 1991).

Freyre, Gilberto, *The Masters and the Slaves: A Study in the Development of Brazilian Civilisation*, trs. S. Putnam (New York: Alfred Knopf, 1946).

Galenson, David W., *Traders, Planters and Slaves, Market Behavior in Early English America*. Published by CUP, 1986. Reprinted by permission of Cambridge University Press, and the author.

Gaspar, David Barry, *Bondmen and Rebels: A Study of Master-Slave Relations in Antigua*. Copyright © 1985, Duke University Press. All rights reserved. Reprinted with permission.

Geggus, D. P., 'Slavery, War, and Revolution in the Greater Caribbean, 1789–1815', in Gaspar, D. and Geggus, D. (eds.), *A Turbulent Time: The French Revolution and the Greater Caribbean*. Published by Indiana University Press, 1997.

Genovese, Eugene D., *From Rebellion to Revolution: Afro-American Slave Revolts in the Making of the Modern Word*. Copyright © 1979 by Louisiana State University Press.

Genovese, Eugene D., *Roll, Jordan, Roll: The World the Slaves Made* (New York: Pantheon, 1974).

Georgia State Legislature, 'An Account of the Negroe Insurrection in South Carolina', in *The Colonial Records of the State of Georgia, 1737–40* (New York: AMS Press, 1970).

Glassman, Jonathon, *Feasts and Riot: Revelry, Rebellion, and Popular Consciousness on the Swahili Coast, 1856–1888* (Portsmouth: Heinemann, 1995).

Hambleton, Samuel, *Letter to David Porter, January 25, 1811*, in the Papers of David Porter, Library of Congress.

Hall, Douglas, *In Miserable Slavery: Thomas Thistlewood in Jamaica, 1750–86* (London: Macmillan, 1989).

Hammond, James H., 'Rules Concerning Slaves' in *The Plantation Manual of James H. Hammond of Beach Island, South Carolina, about 1834* (ts. Hammond Papers, South Carolina Historical Society).

Hansard, 3rd series, Vol. 61 (1843) and Vol. 88 (1846). Parliamentary copyright material is reproduced with the permission of the controller of Her Majesty's Stationery Office on behalf of Parliament.

Hellie, Richard (ed. and trs.), 'The Law Code (*Sudebnik*) of 1550', in *Readings for "Introduction to Russian Civilization": Muscovite Society* (Chicago: University of Chicago Press, 1970).

Hellie, Richard, *Slavery in Russia 1450–1725* (Chicago: University of Chicago Press, 1982). Reprinted by permission.

Hening, William Waller, *The Statutes at Large, Being a Collection of All the Laws of Virginia from the First Session of the Legislature in the Year 1619* (Philadelphia: Thomas Desilver, 1823).

Higginson, Thomas Wentworth, *Army Life in a Black Regiment* (Boston: Beacon Press, 1962).

Higman, B. W., *Slave Populations of the British Caribbean 1807–1834* (Baltimore: Johns Hopkins University Press, 1984).

Hobbes, Thomas, *Leviathan* (Oxford: Clarendon Press, 1909).

James, C. L. R., *The Black Jacobins: Toussaint L'Ouverture and the San Domingo Revolution* (New York: Vintage, 2nd edn, 1963).

Jefferson, Thomas, *Notes on the State of Virginia*, ed. W. Peden (Chapel Hill: University of North Carolina Press, 1954).

John Richardson Kilby Papers, 'Harriet Whitehead Case, November 1848' (Correspondence 1840–50) in the Perkins Library, Duke University.

Jordan, Winthrop D., *White over Black: American Attitudes Toward the Negro 1550–1812* (Baltimore: Penguin, 1971).

Kant, Immanuel, 'The Science of Right', in *The Critique of Pure Reason* (Chicago: Encyclopedia Britannica, 1952).

Karasch, Mary, *Slave Life in Rio de Janeiro 1808–1850* (Princeton: Princeton University Press, 1987).

Karras, Ruth Mazo, *Slavery and Society in Medieval Scandinavia* (New Haven: Yale University Press, 1988).

Killens, John Oliver (ed.), *The Trial of Denmark Vesey* (Boston: Beacon Press, 1970).

Kiple, Kenneth, and King, Virginia Himmelsteib, *Another Dimension to the Black Diaspora: Diet, Disease and Racism* (Cambridge: Cambridge University Press, 1981).

Klein, Herbert S., 'Economic aspects of the 18th-century Atlantic Slave Trade', in James D. Tracy (ed.), *The Rise of Merchant Empires: Long-distance Trade in the Early Modern World, 1350–1759* (Cambridge: Cambridge University Press, 1990).

Klein, Herbert S., *The Middle Passage: Comparative Studies in the Atlantic Slave Trade* (Princeton: Princeton University Press, 1978).

Kolchin, Peter, *Unfree Labour: American Slavery and Russian Serfdom* (Cambridge, MA: Harvard University Press, 1987).

Konetzke, Richard, *Colecciùn de Documentos para la Historia de la Formaciùn Social de Hispanoamerica 1493–1810*. Reprinted by permission of the Consejo Superior De Investigaciones Cientificas. Translated by Robert L. Paquette.

van der Kraan, A., 'Bali: Slavery and the Slave Trade', in Anthony Reid (ed.), *Slavery, Bondage and Dependency in Southeast Asia* (New York: St Martin's Press, 1983).

Kulikoff, Allan, *Tobacco and Slaves: The Development of Southern Cultures in the Chesapeake, 1680–1800*. Copyright © 1986 by the University of North Carolina Press.

Labat, Jen-Baptiste, *Nouveau voyage aux isles de l'Amerique* (La Haye, 1724). Translated by John Garrigus.

Leckie, Jacqueline, 'An Overview of the Pacific Labour Reserve', in Clive Moore, Jacqueline Leckie, and Doug Munro (eds), *Labour in the South Pacific* (Townsville: James Cook University of Northern Queensland, 1990).

Lewis, Bernard, *Race and Color in Islam* (New York: Harper and Row, 1971), reprinted by permission of the author.

Lincoln, Abraham, 'Address at the Cooper Institute, New York City, February 27, 1860', in R. P. Basley (ed.), *The Collected Works of Abraham Lincoln* (New Brunswick: Rutgers University Press, 1953).

The London Magazine: or, Gentleman's Monthly Intelligencer 19 (1750).

Lovejoy, Paul E., *Transformations in Slavery: A History of Slavery in Africa* (Cambridge: Cambridge University Press, 1983).

Manzano, Juan Francisco, 'Letter, Juan Francisco Manzano to Domingo Del Monte, June 25, 1835', in *Autobiografia, cartas y versos de Juan Fco, Manzano*, ed. José L. Franco (Havana: Municipio de la Habana, 1937). Translated by Robert L. Paquette.

McNamara, J. and Halborg, J., with E. Gordon Whately (eds. and trans.), 'Queen Balthilde' from *Sainted Women of the Dark Ages*. Copyright © 1992, Duke University Press. Reprinted by permission of the publisher

Manning, Patrick, *Slavery and African Life: Occidental and African Slave Trades* (Cambridge: Cambridge University Press, 1990).

Marx, Karl, *Capital: A Critique of Political Economy*, ed. Frederick Engels (New York: The Modern Library, 1936).

Matlock, Lucius C., *The History of American Slavery and Methodism from 1780 to 1849* (New York: Lucius C. Matlock, 1849).

Meillassoux, Claude, *The Anthropology of Slavery: Womb of Iron and Gold* © The Althone Press and The University of Chicago.

Merivale, Herman, *Lectures on Colonization and Colonies* (New York: A. M. Kelley, 1967).

Miers, Suzanne and Kopytoff, Igor, *Slavery in Africa*. © 1977. Reprinted by permission of The University of Wisconsin Press.

Mikhailovich, Alexei, *The Muscovite Law Code (Ulozhenie) of 1649: Text and Translation*, ed. Richard Hellie (Irvine: C. Schlacks, 1988).

Mill, John Stuart, *The Negro Question*, ed. Eugene August (New York: Appleton-Century-Crofts, 1971).

Mill, John Stuart, *Principles of Political Economy, Books I–II* (Toronto: University of Toronto, 1965).

Mintz, Sidney, 'Toward an Afro-American History', *Journal of World History* 13 (1971).

Mintz, Sidney and Price, Richard, *The Birth of African-American Culture*. Copyright © 1976 by the Institute for the Study of Human Issues. Reprinted by permission of the Beacon Press, Boston.

Mommsen, Theodor and Krueger, Paul (eds.), *The Digest of Justinian*. Translated by Alan Watson. Copyright © 1995 University of Pennsylvania Press. Reprinted with permission.

Montesquieu, Baron de, *The Spirit of the Laws*, trs. and ed. Anne M. Cohler *et al.* (Cambridge: Cambridge University Press, 1989).

Moreau de Saint-Méry, M. L. E., *Description topographique, physique, civile, politique et historique de la partie française de l'isle Saint-Domingue* (Philadelphia, 1797). Translated by John Garrigus.

Moreno Fraginals, Manuel, 'Labor Contract for Transportation from China to Cuba, December 31, 1852', from the collection of Manuel Moreno Fraginals. Translated by Robert L. Paquette.

Moreno Fraginals, Manuel, *The Sugarmill: The Socioeconomic Complex of Sugar in Cuba, 1760–1860*, trs. Cedric Belfrage (New York: Monthly Review Press, 1976).

Morgan, Edmund S., *American Slavery, American Freedom: The Ordeal of Colonial Virginia*. Copyright © 1975 by W. W. Norton & Company, Inc. Used by permission of W. W. Norton & Company, Inc.

Morgan, Philip D., *Slave counterpoint: Black Culture in the Eighteenth-Century Chesapeake and Low Country*. Copyright © 1998 by the University of North Carolina Press. Used by permission of the publisher.

Morris, Thomas D., *Southern Slavery and the Law, 1619–1860*. Copyright © 1996 by the University of North Carolina Press. Used by permission of the publisher.

Murray, *Odious Commerce: Britain, Spain, and the Abolition of the Cuban Slave Trade* (Cambridge: Cambridge University Press, 1980).

Nabuco, Joaquim, *Abolitionism: The Brazilian Antislavery Struggle*, trs. and ed. Robert Conrad (Urbana: University of Illinois Press, 1977).

Newton, John, *Thoughts upon the African Slave Trade* (London: J. Buckland, 1788).

Nieboer, H. J., *Slavery as an Industrial System* (New York: Burt Franklin, 1971).

Nietzsche, Friedrich, *Beyond Good and Evil*, trs. R. J. Hollingdale (Harmondsworth: Penguin, 1973).

Origo, Iris, *The Merchant of Prato: Francesco Di Marco Datini*. Copyright © 1957 by Iris Origo. Used by permission of Alfred A. Knopf, a division of Random House Inc.

Paquette, Robert L., 'Social History Update: Slave Resistance and Social History' from *Journal of Social History*. Reprinted by permission of Carnegie Mellon University.

Paquette, Robert L., 'The Cuban Slave Code, 1842', in *Sugar is made with Blood: The Conspiracy of La Escalera and the Conflict Between Empires Over Slavery in Cuba* (Middletown: Wesleyan University Press, 1988).

'An Account of all Cargoes if Negroes Imported into the British West Indies from the Coast of Africa in the Several Years since 1789'. *Parliamentary Accounts and Papers*, 1795-6. Parliamentary copyright material is reproduced with the permission of the controller of Her Majesty's Stationery Office on behalf of Parliament.

'An Act for the Better Ordering and Governing of the Negroes', *Barbados 1661* (Public Record Office, Kew). Reproduced with the permission of the controller of Her Majesty's Stationery Office on behalf of Parliament.

Patterson, Orlando, *Slavery and Social Death: A Comparative Study* (Cambridge, Mass.: Harvard University Press). Copyright © 1982 by the President and Fellows of Harvard College. Reprinted by permission of the publisher.

Pelteret, David A. E., *Slavery in Early Medieval England* (Woodbridge: Boydell Press, 1995).

Perret, Charles, *Letter to the 'Moniteur de la Louisiance'*. Translated by Robert Paquette and Seymour Drescher.

Plato, 'Laws', in *The Dialogues of Plate*, trs. B. Jowett (Oxford: Clarendon Press, 4th edn, 1953).

Plutarch, *The Lives of the Noble Grecians and Romans* (Chicago: Encyclopedia Britannica, 1952).

Publications of the Louisiana Historical Society (1908). Translated by Seymour Drescher.

Ratherius of Verona, Bishop, *The Complete Works of Bishop Ratherius of Verona*, trs. Peter Reid (New York: Medieval and Renaissance Texts and Studies, 1991).

Reid, Anthony, *Slavery, Bondage and Dependency in Southeast Asia*. Copyright © Anthony Reid. Reprinted with permission of St. Martin's Press, LLC.

Reis, João José, and Moraes Farias, P. F., 'Islam and Slave Rebellion in Bahia, Brazil', in *Islam et sociétés au sud du Sahara 3* (1989).

Ripley, Peter C. (ed.), *The Black Abolitionist Papers (1859–65)* (Chapel Hill: University of North Carolina Press, 1992).

Rodney, Walter, *How Europe Underdeveloped Africa* (London: Bogle-L'Ouverture, 1972).

Ruffin, Edmund, *The Diary of Edmund Ruffin* (Baton Rouge: Louisiana State University Press, 1989).

Schmidt, F. T., and Wilhelm, B. R., 'Early Proslavery Petitions in Virginia', *William and Mary Quarterly 30* (1973).

Schoelcher, Victor, *Mémoires de la Sociétés Ethnologique de Paris* (Paris: Dondet-Duprey, 1841–7). Translated by Seymour Drescher.

Schwartz, Stuart B., *Sugar Plantations in the Formation of Brazilian Society: Bahia 1550–1835* (Cambridge: Cambridge University Press, 1985).

Schwartz, Stuart B., 'Resistance and Accommodation in Eighteenth-Century Brazil: The Slaves' View of Slavery', *Hispanic American Historical Review* 57 (1977).

Scott, James C., *Domination and the Arts of Resistance: Hidden Transcripts* (New Haven: Yale University Press, 1990).

Scott, Rebecca C., 'Defining the Boundaries of Freedom on the World of Cane: Cuba, Brazil, and Louisiana after Emancipation', *American Historical Review* 99 (1994).

Smith, Adam, *An Inquiry into the Nature and Causes of the Wealth of Nations* (Oxford: Oxford University Press, 1976).

Stedman, John Gabriel, *Narrative of a Five Years Expedition against the Revolted Negroes of Surinam*, ed. Richard Price and Sally Price (Baltimore: Johns Hopkins University Press, 1988).

Steuart, James, *An Inquiry into the Principles of Political Oeconomy*, ed. Andrew Skinner (Edinburgh: Oliver and Boyd, 1966).

Al-Tabarī, Jarir, *The History of Al-Tabarī*, trs. David Waines (Albany: State University of New York Press, 1992).

Tacitus, 'The Annals', in *The Complete Works of Tacitus*, ed. Moses Hadas, translated by Alfred John Church and William Jackson Brodribb (New York: The Modern Library, 1942).

Thornton, John, *Africa and the Africans in the Making of the Atlantic World, 1400–1680* (Cambridge: Cambridge University Press, 1992).

Tocqueville, Alexis de, *Tocqueville and Beaumont on Social Reform*, translated and edited by Seymour Drescher. Copyright © 1968 by Seymour Drescher. Reprinted by permission of HarperCollins Publishers, Inc.

Turner, Nat, *The Confession, Trial and Execution of Nat Turner, the Negro Insurrectionist . . . 1831* (Petersburg: John B. Ege, 1881).

Tyson, George F., Jr., *Toussaint L'Ouverture* (Englewood Cliffs: Prentice-Hall, 1973)

US Congress, *Resolutions of the Legislature of Mississippi* (Senate, 31st Congress 1st Session Miscellaneous Document 110, 1850)

Valdés, Gonzalo Fernández de Oviedo y, *Histori general y natural de las Indies* (Santo Domingo: Patronato de la Ciudad de Santo Domingo Coleccion Quinto Centenaris, 1994). Translated by Evelyn Powell Jennings.

Vaughan, Alden T., 'The Origins Debate: Slavery and Racism in Seventeenth-Century Virginia', in *Roots of American Racism: Essays on the Colonial Experience* (New York: Oxford University Press, 1995).

Voltaire, François de, *The Works of Voltaire*, ed. Lord Morley (New York: Dingwall-Rock, 1901).

Wakefield, Edward Gibbon, *A View of the Art of Colonization in Present Reference to the British Empire in Letters between a Statesman and a Colonist* (New York: A. M. Kelly, 1969).

Walker, David, *David Walker's Appeal, in Four Articles; Together with a Preamble, to the Coloured Citizens of the World, but in Particular, and Very Expressly, to those of the United States of America*, ed. Peter Hinks (University Park: Pennsylvania State University Press, 2000).

Watson, James L., 'Transactions in People: The Chinese Markets in Slaves, Servants, and Heirs', in James L. Watson ed., *Asian and African Systems of Slavery* (Oxford: Blackwell, 1980). Reprinted by permission.

Weber, Max, *The Theory of Social and Economic Organization*, trs. A. M. Henderson and Talcott Parsons (New York: Oxford University Press, 1947).

Williams, Eric, *Capitalism and Slavery* (New York: Capricorn, 1966).

Xenophon, *Oeconomicus: A Social and Historical Commentary*, trs. Sarah Pomeroy (Oxford: Oxford Clarendon Press, 1995).

Yang, Lien-Shang, 'Economic Aspects of Public Works in Imperial China', in *Excursions in Sinology* (Cambridge, MA: Harvard University Press, 1969).

Index

CPSIA information can be obtained at www.ICGtesting.com
Printed in the USA
BVOW06s1528220816

459786BV00004B/5/P